D1473581

INTRODUCTION TO GOVERNMENTAL AND NOT-FOR-PROFIT ACCOUNTING

THIRD EDITION

INTRODUCTION TO GOVERNMENTAL AND NOT-FOR-PROFIT ACCOUNTING

Joseph R. Razek

University of New Orleans

Gordon A. Hosch

University of New Orleans

PRENTICE HALL, Englewood Cliffs, NJ 07632

Library of Congress Cataloging-in-Publication Data

Razek, Joseph R.
    Introduction to governmental and not-for-profit accounting / Joseph
R. Razek, Gordon A. Hosch
        p.   cm.

    ISBN 0-13-064296-7
    1. Fund accounting. 2. Finance, Public--Accounting.
3. Corporations, Nonprofit--Accounting.   I. Hosch, Gordon A.
II. Title.
HF5681.F84R39 1995
657'.835--dc20   95-30455
                                                                        CIP

To our families . . .
Cordelia, Erica, Margaret, and Eleanor Razek
Kathy, Paige, Keith, and Kyle Hosch

Material from Uniform CPA examination questions and unofficial answers, copyright © 1954, 1964, 1967, 1968, 1970, 1971, 1972, 1974, 1975, 1976, 1977, 1978, 1979, 1980, 1981, 1982, 1983, 1984, 1985, 1986, 1987, 1988 by the American Institute of Certified Public Accountants, Inc., is reprinted (or adapted) with permission.

Portions of various GASB pronouncements, copyright by Governmental Accounting Standards Board, 401 Merritt 7, P.O. Box 5116, Norwalk, CT 06856-5116, U.S.A., are reprinted with permission. Copies of complete documents are available from the GASB.

Portions of various GASB pronouncements, copyright by Financial Accounting Standards Board, 401 Merritt 7, P.O. Box 5116, Norwalk, CT 06856-5116, U.S.A., are reprinted with permission. Copies of complete documents are available from the FASB.

This book contains material copyright © 1949, 1955, 1970, 1973, 1974, 1978, 1980, 1981, 1985, 1987, 1988 by the American Institute of Certified Public Accountants.

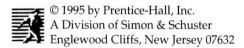 © 1995 by Prentice-Hall, Inc.
A Division of Simon & Schuster
Englewood Cliffs, New Jersey 07632

All rights reserved. No part of this book may be
reproduced, in any form or by any means,
without permission in writing from the publisher.

Printed in the United States of America

10 9 8 7 6 5 4 3 2 1

ISBN 0-13-064296-7

Prentice-Hall International (UK) Limited, *London*
Prentice-Hall of Australia Pty. Limited, *Sydney*
Prentice-Hall Canada Inc., *Toronto*
Prentice-Hall Hispanoamericana, S.A., *Mexico*
Prentice-Hall of India Private Limited, *New Delhi*
Prentice-Hall of Japan, Inc., *Tokyo*
Simon & Schuster Asia Pte. Ltd., *Singapore*
Editora Prentice-Hall do Brasil, Ltda., *Rio de Janeiro*

CONTENTS

Chapter 3   THE BUDGETARY PROCESS   66

Chapter 4   THE GOVERNMENTAL FUND ACCOUNTING CYCLE   125
General and Special Revenue Funds—An Introduction

Chapter 5   THE GOVERNMENTAL FUND ACCOUNTING CYCLE   165
General and Special Revenue Funds—Special Problems

Chapter 6   THE GOVERNMENTAL FUND ACCOUNTING CYCLE   231

Debt Service Funds, Capital Projects Funds, and Account Groups

Chapter 7   THE GOVERNMENTAL FUND ACCOUNTING CYCLE   296

Proprietary-Type Funds and Pension Trust Funds

Chapter 8   **THE GOVERNMENTAL FUND
ACCOUNTING CYCLE** 354
Expendable Trust Funds, Nonexpendable Trust
Funds, Agency Funds, and Special Assessment Accounting

Chapter 9   **THE GOVERNMENTAL FUND
ACCOUNTING CYCLE** 407
Comprehensive Annual Financial Report
and Current Issues

PREFACE

This is a basic-level text on governmental and not-for-profit accounting. While the emphasis is on governmental units, other not-for-profit organizations are covered in some depth.

The text is organized and structured in a manner that permits its use by a number of different types of readers. For example, people interested exclusively in accounting for governmental units can skip the chapters on colleges and universities, hospitals, and other not-for-profit organizations. People interested in accounting for hospitals can skip the chapters on governmental units and other not-for-profit organizations, and so on. We have also included an independent chapter on the fundamentals of bookkeeping for the benefit of those who have had no previous training in the basic accounting cycle.

Consistent with the focus on flexibility, this text can be used by people who want to emphasize the accumulation and reporting of financial information; they can answer the questions and cases and work the exercises and problems at the end of each chapter. Those who are interested in a more conceptual approach (e.g., people in public administration classes) can avoid the presentation of detailed journal entries and financial statements by concentrating on the questions, cases, and conceptual exercises and problems.

To make this text even more flexible we have divided most of the chapters into independent sections, which can be covered as separate units. Thus a section or two may be assigned for a particular class meeting, while an entire chapter may be assigned for another meeting.

This text can be used by the following major groups because of its built-in flexibility:

1. Nonaccounting majors (e.g., students in public administration programs) who desire a basic understanding of the accounting and reporting of governmental units.
2. Accounting majors who wish to learn the fundamentals of governmental not-for-profit accounting in less than a full semester.
3. Accounting majors who desire a full semester or quarter course on governmental and not-for-profit accounting. This text provides an excellent basis for discussion of governmental and not-for-profit topics.
4. Persons employed by governmental and not-for-profit organizations, including the federal government.
5. Persons preparing for civil service examinations.
6. Persons preparing for the Uniform Certified Public Accountant (CPA) Examination.
7. Persons who wish, on their own, to learn about the accounting and reporting practices of governmental and not-for-profit organizations.

In order to facilitate the transition into interfund accounting we have included, in Chapter 2, a conceptual preview of the individual fund financial statements. This preview permits a full discussion, throughout the text, of transactions which affect several funds.

NEW FEATURES OF THIS EDITION

We have increased coverage of several key areas in this edition and have added many new problems and exercises, several of which are taken from past CPA examinations. We have also added thought-provoking cases to provide increased flexibility in how the text is used. Finally, we have added a chapter on auditing governmental units and on federal accounting. In addition, most chapters now contain a vignette, showing how the material covered is applied in a real-world situation, and several minicases, which present the reader with issues requiring judgment and provide a vehicle for class discussion.

The entire text has been rewritten to include developments that have taken place since the previous edition. Throughout, materials on recent GASB and, in some cases, FASB pronouncements have been added. New materials have been added on the environment of governmental and not-for-profit accounting and the hierarchy of generally accepted accounting principles for governmental units.

A comparison of financial statements and financial reporting for governmental and business organizations has been added in addition to several charts identifying and comparing accounting procedures for funds used in governmental accounting. "Real world" financial statements for governmental units have been added to the chapters on governmental accounting, along with a discussion of the relevant activities of each governmental unit presented.

The discussion of the fundamentals of bookkeeping has been moved from Chapter 2 to Chapter 14. This allows a more orderly flow of accounting for governmental units.

Several chapters have been rearranged from the second edition and the discussion of Expendable and Nonexpendable Trust Funds has been combined in the same chapter. The use of Expendable Trust Funds is discussed as a "stand alone" topic and in conjunction with Nonexpendable Trust Funds. In addition, new materials on bonds issued with a discount or premium, issuance of bonds between interest payment dates, and arbitrage have been added. A section on leases has also been added.

The materials on financial reporting have been updated for the reporting entity and the discussion of interim financial reporting has been expanded. In addition, the discussion of *Statement 11* included in the second edition has been updated and expanded.

The materials on budgeting have been expanded to include control reports laws pertaining to budgets. In addition, balanced budgets are discussed and excerpts from the law of one state are included. In this chapter, readers can follow a complete set of illustrations to prepare a budget and a control report for a governmental unit. The problems in this chapter form a case (Bacchus City Levee Board), permitting readers to prepare a complete budget using individual problem materials. These problems have been adapted for a computer project, with additional data and "what-ifs" which, along with a template, are available to adopters.

The chapters on not-for-profit organizations have been updated to show the impact of FASB 116 and FASB 117. Statements prepared under the new format are illustrated. Exercises and problems on the application of these important pronouncements have been added.

As in the second edition, this text includes actual financial statements issued by governmental units. We have, however, changed some of the governmental units illustrated. The use of actual financial statements adds an element of "real world" applications to the text.

ACKNOWLEDGMENTS

We would like to express our most sincere appreciation to the many students, faculty members, and members of the professional community who have reviewed this text and offered suggestions for improvement. We would like to offer special thanks to the following people:

Ms. Millicent Anderson, Jefferson Parish, Louisiana

Ms. Lynne A. Burkart, KPMG Peat Marwick, New Orleans, Louisiana

Mr. Lindsay L. Calub, Duplantier, Hrapmann, Hogan & Maher, LLP, New Orleans, Louisiana

Mr. Hugh J. Dorrian, City of Columbus, Ohio

Dr. C. Willard Elliott, Consultant, Baton Rouge, Louisiana

Dr. Robert J. Freeman, Governmental Accounting Standards Board

Mr. John Hall, Department of Agriculture

Mr. Martin Ives, formerly of the Govermental Accounting Standards Board

Mr. Kenneth J. Kleinschmidt, City of New Orleans, Louisiana

Mr. Anthony P. Lorino, Tulane University, New Orleans, Louisiana

Mr. Paul C. Rivera, Rebowe & Company, Metairie, Louisiana

Ms. Marguerite Russell, Clark County, Nevada

Mr. William G. Stamm, Duplantier, Hrapmann, Hogan & Maher, LLP, New Orleans, Louisiana

Mr. Richard Wascak, Federal Accounting Standards Advisory Board

We would also like to express our gratitude to the people at Prentice Hall, especially our editors, Bill Webber and Maureen Wilson, who contributed greatly to this project. Finally, our thanks go to Mr. Bobby Major of the City of New Orleans and Dr. Jewel Prestage of Southern University in Baton Rouge for their support of the training programs which provided the original impetus for this project.

1

INTRODUCTION TO ACCOUNTING FOR NONBUSINESS ORGANIZATIONS

Accounting and reporting of economic events have evolved from their earliest form, writing on cave walls, to the present state of maintaining complex financial records and preparing sophisticated financial reports. Over this period of time, some changes have been revolutionary. Most, however, can best be described as evolutionary. Until recently there was not much interest in the accounting and reporting procedures used by governmental or other not-for-profit organizations. However, with the financial "crunch" encountered by some major cities in recent years, governmental accounting and reporting have become extremely important. In the not-for-profit field, the emergence of third-party insurers in the health-care field in the 1940s and the rapidly increasing inflation of the 1970s have created a great deal of interest in and attention upon the accounting and reporting problems of these organizations.

Another reason for greater interest in the accounting and reporting problems of governmental and not-for-profit organizations is the growing realization that the financial reports of these organizations are a means by which parties interested in them can evaluate their performance. Financial reports are often an important communication vehicle between these organizations and their constituents.

To simplify the terminology found in this text, we will use the term **nonbusiness organizations** to refer to both governmental units and not-for-profit organizations. This term was first used by the Financial Accounting Standards Board (FASB)[1] and is prevalent in the accounting literature.

Nonbusiness organizations have the following distinguishing characteristics:

1. Receipts of significant amounts of resources from resource providers who do not expect to receive either repayment or economic benefits proportionate to resources provided

[1] The FASB is the accounting rule-setting body of business and not-for-profit organizations.

1

2. Operating purposes other than to provide goods or services at a profit or profit equivalent
3. Absence of defined ownership interests that can be sold, transferred, or redeemed, or that convey entitlement to a share of a residual distribution of resources in the event of liquidation of the organization.[2]

WHAT IS ACCOUNTING?

Accounting has been defined as "the art of recording, classifying, and summarizing, in a significant manner and in terms of money, transactions and events which are, in part at least, of a financial character, and interpreting the results thereof."[3] Note the use of the word *art*. Accounting is an art in that, while it follows a specified set of rules, the final decisions as to what methods and procedures to use and how to present financial information are still up to the accountant. This, of course, is analogous to the artist who, while following specified rules of color and perspective, still dictates the final product.

Another approach to defining accounting is the **trained observer approach.**[4] Under this approach, the accountant is perceived as a trained observer who observes economic events (transactions) and reports on them. The receivers of the reports, the decision makers, then take actions that create new events— which are observed and reported on by the accountant, and so forth.

In short, accounting is a process of communicating financial information. To be effective, the accountant must communicate this information in a manner that is both *useful* and *understandable* to the user.

ENVIRONMENT OF NONBUSINESS ACCOUNTING AND REPORTING

Nonbusiness organizations operate in a different economic, social, legal and political environment than commercial enterprises. As a result, their information needs are different, as are their accounting and reporting practices. Important aspects of the nonbusiness environment are:

Inability to measure efficiency and effectiveness by means of income measures

Commercial enterprises exist to enhance their owners' wealth. When these organizations do engage in social-type activities, it is with the intent of ultimately

---

[2]*Statement of Financial Accounting Concepts No. 4—Objectives of Financial Reporting by Nonbusiness Organizations* (Stamford, CT: Financial Accounting Standards Board, 1980), para. 6.

[3]AICPA, *Accounting Terminology Bulletin No. 2.*

[4]For a more complete discussion of this approach, see Norton M. Bedford and Vahe Baladouni, "A Communication Theory Approach to Accountancy," *Accounting Review* (October 1962), pp. 650–59.

maximizing income. Since income is quantifiable and can be measured in monetary terms, it is a very useful means of evaluating efficiency and effectiveness of commercial organizations.

Nonbusiness organizations exist to provide services to their constituents. The value of these services often cannot be measured in monetary terms. For example, what is the value of a life saved by a team of paramedics? Furthermore, if a nonbusiness organization were to earn a profit, it would be assumed that sufficient services were not being provided or that resource providers were being overcharged or overtaxed. Thus, these organizations must look to other means for evaluating efficiency and effectiveness.

Lack of harmony of purpose

If a commercial organization is to survive, its managers must have one overall goal—to make a profit. Without profits a commercial organization cannot survive. While managers of that organization may disagree on the means of making a profit, they seldom disagree on the importance of the profit itself.

Nonbusiness organizations, on the other hand, have many goals—the relative importance of each varying between both users and producers of services. As a result, the level of resources devoted to each activity is a function of the political process and conflict is often present within an organization's leadership.

Continuity of leadership not very common

When a senior manager of a commercial enterprise leaves that organization, his or her place is usually taken by a hand-picked successor who, at least initially, continues the departing manager's policies. Change tends to be gradual and evolutionary in nature.

When a new administration takes over a nonbusiness organization, especially a governmental unit, a "clean sweep" is usually made by the new administration and new policies are quickly instituted. Furthermore, outgoing officials sometimes engage in practices designed to make their successors appear ineffective and to pave the way for their return to office. This lack of leadership continuity makes managerial accountability difficult to achieve.

Many operational decisions governed by legal compliance

Commercial organizations are free to provide only those goods and services they feel will enhance their profits. They cannot usually be required to provide goods and services against their will and, if they cannot cope with the legal or social environment, they are free to leave the market. Commercial organizations can also borrow money when convenient, subject only to requirements of lenders and investors.

Nonbusiness organizations, especially governmental units, are required by law (charter, constitution, etc.) to provide certain services. For example, most city charters provide for police and fire protection. Managers cannot refuse to provide these services because of cost or because they feel that residents do not deserve such services.

Nonbusiness organizations also are constrained as to when and how much money they can borrow. Most cities and states are subject to borrowing limits. In addition, new bond issues must be approved by the electorate and, in many cases, by a senior legislative body, such as a state legislature.

Because of these factors, accounting for nonbusiness organizations tends to focus on control and legal compliance. It is very conservative, and emphasis is placed on determining if a predetermined amount of resources (the budget) was spent to provide a given level of services. In effect, it measures an organization's ability to perform a prescribed level of services with a given amount of resources, within the constraints of local, state, and federal laws.

USERS OF ACCOUNTING INFORMATION

Generally speaking, users of accounting information of nonbusiness organizations fall into one of two categories: external or internal. **External users** are those persons or organizations who are *not* directly involved in the operations of the reporting entity. Among these users are:

1. The *federal government*—to evaluate the use of the proceeds of grants and to gather statistical information
2. *Bond-rating services*—to evaluate the creditworthiness of organizations issuing debt
3. The *electorate*—to evaluate the performance of elected officials; information is communicated to these persons primarily through the news media
4. *State legislative committees*—to oversee the operations of the various political subdivisions within the state
5. *Potential investors*—to determine the stability of the tax base

Internal users are those persons or groups of persons who are *directly* involved in the operations of the reporting entity. Among these users are:

1. *Program monitors*—to evaluate the activities of the programs
2. The *chief administrative officer*—to evaluate the financial operations and the effectiveness of the operating personnel of the organization
3. *Department heads*—to evaluate the performance of subordinates
4. The *mayor* and the *city council*—to determine the financial condition of the city and the need for additional resources
5. *Internal auditors*—to evaluate the effectiveness of financial and operating controls

GENERALLY ACCEPTED ACCOUNTING PRINCIPLES (GAAP)

The term **generally accepted accounting principles (GAAP)** has been defined as

> . . . the consensus at a particular time as to which economic resources and obligations should be recorded as assets and liabilities by financial accounting, which changes in assets and liabilities should be recorded, when these changes should be recorded, how the assets and liabilities and changes in them should be measured, what information should be disclosed and how it should be disclosed, and which financial statements should be prepared.
>
> Generally accepted accounting principles encompass the conventions, rules, and procedures necessary to define accepted accounting practice at a particular time. The standard of "generally accepted accounting principles" includes not only broad guidelines of general application, but also detailed practices and procedures.[5]

Before embarking on a study of the methods and procedures used by accountants, certain basic underlying concepts should be considered.

THE ENTITY CONCEPT

The reporting unit is a specific, identifiable **entity.** In commercial (business) organizations the reporting unit is *one* entity, no matter how large. For example, General Motors is actually a series of separate, but related, companies (accounting subentities) located throughout the world. For reporting purposes, however, it is one company. The parent company and its subsidiaries are consolidated into one reporting unit.

In nonbusiness organizations the organization as a whole is considered to be the *basic* reporting entity, just as in business enterprises. However, each fund (or fund type) is *separately* identified on the organization's financial statements.[6] The funds are not consolidated into one set of data. Thus, if a nonbusiness organization uses a dozen different funds, it is really a dozen different accounting and reporting subentities.

PLANNING AND CONTROL

Planning is the act of determining the amount of and type of resources to be received and expended by the organization during a given period. Another name for planning is *budgeting.* **Control** is the act of determining whether the resources received and expended are done so in accordance with the budget.

---

[5]*Statement No. 4,* "Basic Concepts and Accounting Principles Underlying Financial Statements of Business Enterprises" (New York: AICPA, 1970), paras. 137 and 138. Copyright © 1993 by American Institute of Certified Public Accountants, Inc. Reprinted with permission.

[6]A **fund,** by definition, is an independent fiscal and accounting entity.

THE MATCHING CONCEPT

The term **matching concept** denotes the fact that revenues are matched or compared with expenses (or expenditures). Business firms match revenues with expenses to determine their income for a period of time. Nonbusiness organizations match revenues with expenditures (or expenses) to determine the changes that take place in their fund balances over a period of time. In addition, they compare their actual revenues and expenditures (or expenses) with their budgetary authorizations to determine compliance with the budget. Governmental accounting generally emphasizes the inflows, outflows, and balances of expendable resources rather than the determination of revenues, expenses, and income.

CONSISTENCY

The term **consistency** denotes the treatment of like transactions in the same manner during consecutive periods so that the financial statements will be comparable. Procedures, once adopted, should be followed from period to period by the reporting entity.

PERIODICITY

The term **periodicity** denotes the practice of preparing financial reports that cover a defined period of time rather than the life of the reporting entity. The period used is generally one year, although quarterly and monthly reports (and sometimes daily and hourly reports) are common in certain instances.

ESTABLISHING GENERALLY ACCEPTED ACCOUNTING PRINCIPLES

As previously mentioned, generally accepted accounting principles are a consensus of acceptable concepts, practices, and so forth, in effect at a certain point in time. Determination of the acceptability of these concepts, practices, and so forth, for governmental-type organizations is made by the Governmental Accounting Standards Board (GASB). The GASB is a five-member board established in 1984 "... to promulgate standards of financial accounting and reporting with respect to activities and transactions of state and local governmental entities. The GASB is the successor organization to the National Council on Governmental Accounting (NCGA)."[7] Members of the GASB are appointed by the Financial Accounting Foundation (FAF). The members of the FAF are appointed by the American Institute of Certified Public Accountants (AICPA) and other accounting-related organizations.

Determination of the acceptability of accounting principles for business organizations is made by the Financial Accounting Standards Board (FASB). The

---

[7]GASB Codification, "Introduction," *Governmental Accounting and Financial Reporting Standards,* p. xi, as of June 15, 1987.

FASB is a seven-member board appointed by the Board of Trustees of the FAF. Both the GASB and the FASB have an advisory council that provides guidance in the standards-setting process. The GASB-FASB structure is shown in Exhibit 1–1.

A jurisdictional agreement was approved by both the GASB and the FASB. This agreement provides for a separation of jurisdiction that makes GASB responsible for all financial accounting and reporting for governmental and government-related organizations. The FASB, on the other hand, is responsible for all other organizations. In summary, this means that if a question arises with respect to an accounting or reporting problem, a governmental organization will first look toward the GASB for a pronouncement. In the absence of such a pronouncement, any relevant FASB pronouncement must be followed.

A not-for-profit organization not related to a governmental unit would follow the same process, but in reverse. Such an organization would first look toward the FASB for a pronouncement on a financial accounting or reporting issue. In the absence of such a pronouncement, any relevant GASB pronouncement would be followed.

If we look closely at the GASB-FASB agreement, a serious "turf" question emerges. What would happen, for example, if the GASB developed a rule for government-owned universities and the FASB developed a different rule, for the same situation, for private universities?

This situation has actually developed. The FASB has recommended depreciation for plant and equipment-type assets, while the GASB has recommended that its constituents not adopt the FASB rule until the question can be studied in more depth. Other potential disagreements exist in the areas of pension accounting. At the time of this writing, efforts are being made to solve this jurisdictional dispute. Hopefully, by the time you read this chapter, an acceptable solution will have been found.

Throughout this text references are made to various industry audit guides. These guides are issued by the AICPA. Although primarily designed for auditors, these publications discuss some of the accounting procedures that are applicable to specific nonbusiness organizations—for example, governmental units, hospitals, colleges and universities, and so forth. The specific sources of GAAP for nonbusiness organizations that are not governmental units will be discussed in the chapters relating to these organizations.

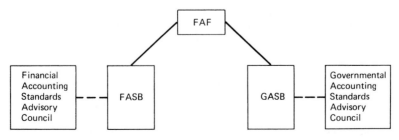

EXHIBIT 1–1   Relationship between the FASB, the GASB, and the FAF

Hierarchy of Government Generally Accepted Accounting Principles

A hierarchy is a ranked order of items. The hierarchy of generally accepted accounting principles (GAAP) for governmental units is established by the American Institute of Certified Public Accountants (AICPA) through its Auditing Standards Division.

The AICPA issued *Statement on Auditing Standards No. 69*, "The Meaning of 'Fairly Presents' in the Auditor's Report" [SAS 69], in January 1992. This statement gives auditors and practitioners guidance in prioritizing accounting pronouncements. It specifies the following order, from most authoritative to least authoritative:

Level I: GASB Statements and Interpretations
AICPA and Financial Accounting Standards Board [FASB] pronouncements that GASB Statements and Interpretations have made applicable to governmental units

Level II: GASB Technical Bulletins
AICPA Industry Audit Guides and AICPA Statements of Position that are made applicable to governmental units by the AICPA and approved by the GASB

Level III: Consensus positions of a GASB Emerging Issues Task Force (not yet established)
AICPA Accounting Standards Executive Committee Practice Bulletins that are made applicable to governmental units by the Committee and approved by the GASB

Level IV: GASB staff Implementation Guides
Current practices widely used by governmental units

Level V: Other accounting literature

Auditors and preparers of financial statements for governmental units must select support for the procedures they follow from the above hierarchy. In other words, if a procedure followed is based on an article in an accounting journal (Level V support), and there is a Level I pronouncement that does not agree with the conclusions of the article, the Level I pronouncement takes precedence.

The purpose of a governmental GAAP hierarchy is to provide order to the practice of accounting and to aid auditors and practitioners in selecting specific accounting procedures.

REVIEW QUESTIONS

Q1–1 How is the term *accounting* defined?

Q1–2 Distinguish between a *commercial* and a *nonbusiness* organization.

Q1–3 Identify and briefly explain four major environmental factors for non-business organizations.

Q1–4 What is the function of the Financial Accounting Standards Board?

Q1–5 List six users of accounting information for nonbusiness organizations and describe the manner in which this information is used by them.

Q1–6 What are *generally accepted accounting principles?*

Q1–7 What is the NCGA? The AICPA? The GASB?

Q1–8 What is the *entity concept?*

Q1–9 What is the *matching concept?*

Q1–10 Distinguish between *planning* and *control.*

Q1–11 What do the terms *consistency* and *periodicity* mean to the accountant?

Q1–12 What is a *hierarchy of generally accepted accounting principles?*

Q1–13 Why is a GAAP hierarchy needed?

Q1–14 Briefly describe the standard-setting relationship between the FASB and the GASB.

CASES

C1–1 James Farnsworth, mayor of Marble City, is desperately trying to reduce the city's budget. He recently came to your office and suggested that the accounting staff could be reduced in half by eliminating some of the accounting reports you now prepare. The source of his suggestion was an article he read in *Mayor's Monthly.* Specifically he wanted to eliminate the cash flow statements for all of the funds that currently prepare them. After careful study, you determine that GASB *Statement No. 9* requires cash flow statements for some of the funds that Marble City uses.
How would you explain your position to Mr. Farnsworth?

C1–2 Discuss the hierarchy of GAAP for governmental units with someone who is familiar with governmental accounting and describe his or her reaction to it. Include in your paper specific examples where the hierarchy has helped and hindered governmental reporting.

EXERCISES

E1–1 (Identifying basic accounting concepts)
Five basic accounting concepts were discussed in this chapter. Which concept is illustrated in each of the following situations?
1. Although its jurisdiction is within the limits of a given city and it performs certain functions that are similar to those of the city (e.g., police patrols on certain streets), the Levee Board of this city main-

tains separate records and prepares an independent set of financial statements.

2. Before the financial statements of an organization are prepared, the revenues of the period are compared with the expenditures of the period to determine if the organization's fund balance has increased or decreased.

3. Before the start of a fiscal year, the city of Jewett prepares a budget. At the end of each month of the fiscal year, a report is prepared for each manager comparing the actual expenditures of his or her department with the budgeted expenditures of the period.

4. Although several different methods of determining the value of its inventories are considered proper, Charity Hospital uses the same method year after year.

5. Although it has been in existence for over two hundred years and will probably be in existence one hundred years from now, Episcopal Academy prepares financial reports every year.

E1–2 (Discussion of the need for a GASB)
Prior to the establishment of the GASB, the FASB wanted to have the authority to establish GAAP for governmental units. Do you think GAAP for governmental units should be established by the same body that is concerned with GAAP for nongovernmental organizations? Why?

E1–3 (Discussion of the GASB's operations with a local governmental official)
The establishment of the Governmental Accounting Standards Board is supposed to solve the major weaknesses of the National Council on Governmental Accounting in the standard-setting area. Contact a local governmental official familiar with the accounting standard-setting process and discuss the GASB's success or lack of success.

E1–4 (Opinion regarding the standard-setting process of the accounting profession)
As an individual with little or no practical accounting experience, what is *your* opinion of the standard-setting process used by the accounting profession?

E1–5 (Comparison of environmental factors for business and nonbusiness organizations)
Compare and contrast the four environmental factors discussed in this chapter for business and nonbusiness organizations.

2

THE USE OF FUNDS IN GOVERNMENTAL ACCOUNTING

LEARNING OBJECTIVES

After completion of this chapter, you should be able to:

1. Identify the major fund categories currently used in governmental accounting
2. Compare and contrast the main features of the cash basis, the accrual basis, and the modified accrual basis of accounting as used by governmental units
3. Identify and describe the function of the funds used in governmental accounting
4. Identify and describe the account groups used in governmental accounting
5. Describe the relationship between the funds and account groups used in a governmental accounting system
6. Describe the financial statements used by each fund and account group in a governmental accounting system

---

The Governmental Accounting Standards Board (GASB) has been very active in establishing accounting and reporting standards for governmental units. The centerpiece of their research is *Concepts Statement No. 1: Objectives of Financial Reporting.* In this statement, the GASB assumes that all "state and local governmental financial reports . . . possess . . . certain basic characteristics: understandability, reliability, relevance, timeliness, consistency, and comparability."[1] Within the context of this background, the GASB has established the following reporting objectives for state and local government units:

   a. Financial reporting should assist in fulfilling government's duty to be publicly accountable and should enable users to assess that accountability by:

      (1) Providing information to determine whether current-year revenues were sufficient to pay for current-year services.

      (2) Demonstrating whether resources were obtained and used in accordance with the entity's legally adopted budget, and demonstrating compliance with other finance-related legal or contractual requirements.

      (3) Providing information to assist users in assessing the service efforts, costs, and accomplishments of the governmental entity.

   b. Financial reporting should assist users in evaluating the operating results of the governmental entity for the year by:

      (1) Providing information about sources and uses of financial resources.

      (2) Providing information about how it financed its activities and met its cash requirements.

      (3) Providing information necessary to determine whether its financial position improved or deteriorated as a result of the year's operations.

   c. Financial reporting should assist users in assessing the level of services that can be provided by the governmental entity and its ability to meet its obligations as they become due by:

      (1) Providing information about its financial position and condition.

      (2) Providing information about its physical and other nonfinancial resources having useful lives that extend beyond the current year, including information that can be used to assess the service potential of those resources.

      (3) Disclosing legal or contractual restrictions on resources and the risk of potential loss of resources.[2]

In summary, governmental units are required to provide information that is *useful* in making decisions about the organization regarding its creditworthiness, its future cash flows, its resources and claims to those resources, and its ability to continue to provide services. These objectives do not differ significantly from the reporting objectives of business organizations. Both types of organizations provide information relating to the acquisition, use, and disposition of their resources.

As we mentioned in Chapter 1, the major difference between business and governmental organizations is that users of commercial accounting data are interested in financial activities that are involved in measuring the profit necessary to ensure the continued existence of the organization. This is generally referred to as the **maintenance of capital** and is a prime directive of all business organizations. The financial literature documents numerous business failures and reorganizations that result from an organization's inability to generate resources to maintain capital.

Governmental organizations, however, are primarily concerned with main-

---

[1]Governmental Accounting Standards Board, *Codification of Governmental Accounting and Financial Reporting Standards* (Norwalk, CT, 1987), Sec. 100.162.

[2]GASB Cod. Sec. 100.177–79.

taining a level of services for their constituents. As discussed in Chapter 1, there is no profit motive in governmental operations. As a result, the financial activities that are of interest to users of governmental accounting deal with the receipt and expenditure of resources. These are generally summarized as **spending activities.** There are, however, some governmental activities that are conducted on a capital maintenance basis. These generally deal with services provided for a fee that is set to cover, at least in part, the cost of the services. Examples of such services include sewer and water services and electrical power services that are financed through user charges and operations of an airport that are financed through landing fees paid by airlines.

In addition, many sources of resources for governmental units are dedicated to a specific function. Examples of such sources are a gasoline tax that is dedicated to highway maintenance and a hotel-motel tax that is dedicated to servicing bonds of a domed stadium.

When the necessity of separately measuring the receipt and use of dedicated resources is combined with the levy of user charges for facilities operated on a capital maintenance basis, the result is a need to maintain records for a series of **separate entities** within the governmental unit. These entities are called funds.

SECTION I—THE FRAMEWORK OF FUND ACCOUNTING

Fund accounting is based on the existence of entities within the organization that have characteristics that distinguish them from one another. The characteristics of these entities are the subject of this section.

The Fund

A **fund** is defined as

> . . . a fiscal and accounting entity with a self-balancing set of accounts recording cash and other financial resources, together with all related liabilities and residual equities or balances, and changes therein, which are segregated for the purpose of carrying on specific activities or attaining certain objectives in accordance with special regulations, restrictions, or limitations.[3]

The term **fiscal entity** refers to the separate *budgetary* nature of a fund that has spendable resources, while the term **accounting entity** refers to the separate financial unit that is treated as an entity for *accounting* purposes. A commercial firm, whether it be General Motors or the corner grocery store, is *one* entity. A small city, however, can be made up of *several* entities, depending on the number of funds used. The exact number of entities (funds) is generally defined in the constitution, charter, or statutes that regulate the governmental unit.

---

[3]GASB Cod. Sec. 1300, Introduction.

Since each fund is a separate accounting entity, each must have a set of **self-balancing accounts.** That is, the total of the assets of a particular fund must equal the total of its liabilities and fund balance (or capital).[4] Thus the accounting records for a particular fund must be designed to identify the resources of that fund and the claims to those resources, as distinguished from all other funds.

Fund Categories

The funds used by a governmental unit are separated into three major categories. The first category includes the funds that focus on **spending activities (governmental-type).** Within this category are the funds that primarily account for the receipt and disbursement of resources. Examples include those funds that account for the general operations of the governmental unit, the use of resources legally earmarked for a particular purpose, and the construction of major assets.

The second category includes the funds that focus on **capital maintenance (proprietary-type).** These funds operate on a basis similar to that of a business in that they are usually self-supporting and involve the measurement of revenues and expenses. Examples include funds that account for the operations of a central motor pool and a government-owned electric utility.

The final category includes funds that involve an agency or trust relationship (**fiduciary-type**). These funds focus on either the spending activities or the capital maintenance of the entity, depending on the nature of the activities involved. An example of a fiduciary-type fund that emphasizes spending activities is the fund used to record the disbursement of income from a trust. An example of a fiduciary-type fund that emphasizes capital maintenance is the fund used to record the operations of an employees' retirement system.

In summary, while a governmental unit may be composed of several different funds, these funds are separated into three major fund categories: governmental, proprietary, and fiduciary. These fund categories are discussed in greater depth later in this chapter and can be summarized as illustrated in Table 2–1.

TABLE 2–1   Fund Categories

GOVERNMENTAL-TYPE FUNDS	PROPRIETARY-TYPE FUNDS	FIDUCIARY-TYPE FUNDS
Spending focus	Capital maintenance focus	Spending focus
		Capital maintenance focus
		Other
General government activities	User fee activities	Dedicated resources that
Legally dedicated resources		cannot be spent
		Dedicated resources that
		can be spent

[4]Fund balance will be defined in detail later in this text. At this point, however, it can be considered to be spendable resources.

Basis of Accounting

The term **basis of accounting** refers to the timing of the recognition (recording) of revenues and expenditures or expenses. Using the **cash basis** of accounting, these items are not recorded until cash changes hands. Receipts are not recognized until cash is received, and disbursements are not recognized until cash is paid out.

Cash basis systems are used primarily by individuals for tax purposes and by small businesses. Although a cash basis system is simple to install and use, it is seldom used to measure revenues and expenses. The reason for this is that management can easily control cash receipts and cash payments to manipulate operating results. In reality, it is simply a measure of cash receipts and disbursements.

The **full accrual basis of accounting** does not require the movement of cash for accounting recognition. Instead, revenues are recognized in the period in which they are earned, and expenses are recognized in the period in which they are incurred in earning the revenue. If cash is not collected by the time the revenue is earned, a receivable is created. This receivable is removed from the accounts when the cash is collected. Expenses that are not paid for by the time they are incurred require recognition of a liability in the accounts. When the liability is paid, it is removed from the accounts.

To illustrate the full accrual basis of accounting, assume that an organization renders a service to Sean Smith on December 20, 19X1, for a fee of $300. Assume also that Mr. Smith agreed to pay for the service in thirty days. The revenue is recorded as follows:

Accounts receivable	300	
Revenue		300
To record revenue for services performed for S. Smith.		

Collection of the receivable in January 19X2 should be recorded as follows:

Cash	300	
Accounts receivable		300
To record collection of the S. Smith account.		

Notice that the $300 is recorded as revenue in the period earned (when the service is performed), *not* the period in which the cash is collected.

Using the cash basis of accounting, the only transaction recorded would be the receipt of cash in January as an **operating receipt.** This would be recorded as follows:

Cash	300	
Operating receipts		300
To record collection of cash for services performed.		

Furthermore, assume that the organization using the full accrual basis of accounting incurred a $150 rent expense on December 20, 19X1, but will not pay for it until January 20, 19X2. The following entry is made on December 20:

Rent expense	150	
Accounts payable		150
To record rent expense.		

Payment of the liability in January would require the following entry:

Accounts payable	150	
Cash		150
To record payment of a liability.		

Notice that the $150 is recorded as an expense in the period incurred (when the benefit is received), *not* the period in which the cash is paid.

Using the cash basis of accounting, the only transaction recorded would be the payment of cash in January as an **operating disbursement.** This would be recorded as follows:

Operating disbursement	150	
Cash		150
To record payment for services received.		

The cash basis and the accrual basis of accounting represent opposite ends of a spectrum. A compromise between these extremes, one used by most governmental units for funds reporting spending activities, is the **modified accrual basis.** When accounting systems use this basis of recognition, revenues are recorded in the period in which they are measurable and available. "Measurable" refers to the ability to state the amount of revenues in terms of dollars. "'Available' means collectible within the current period or soon enough thereafter to be used to pay the liabilities of the current period."[5] In other words, revenues are recognized either when they are received in cash (licenses, fines, and so on) or when collection of the amount can be reasonably estimated to be received in the near future (such as property taxes).

Expenditures in a modified accrual system *generally* are recognized in the period in which goods or services are received or a liability is incurred. This, of course, is similar to the treatment such items would receive using the accrual basis of accounting. (Exceptions to the general rules of revenue and expenditure recognition are discussed in the chapters that follow.)

Notice that in the modified accrual basis of accounting the term *expenditures* is used in place of *expenses.* **Expenditures** include not only certain types of expenses incurred, in the commercial sense of the word, but also retirement of debt and capital outlays. In short, they represent any payment of cash or incurrence of a liability for the purpose of acquiring assets or services or settling losses. Expen-

[5]GASB Cod. Sec. 1600.106.

TABLE 2–2   Cash, Accrual, and Modified Accrual Bases of Accounting

CASH BASIS	ACCRUAL BASIS	MODIFIED ACCRUAL BASIS
Record revenue		
When cash is received	When revenue is earned	When measurable and available
Record expenses (expenditures)		
When cash is paid	When expense is incurred	When expenditure is incurred (exceptions explained later in text)

ditures generally are recorded when goods or services are received or a liability is incurred. The cash, accrual, and modified accrual bases of accounting are summarized in Table 2–2.

As previously discussed, many different funds are used in governmental accounting. Each fund is used to account for a specific type of activity. Table 2–3 presents a summary of the funds used in governmental accounting, together with a brief description of their use. In addition, the two account groups used in governmental accounting are described. The account groups will be discussed later in this chapter.

Table 2–4 is a summary of the accounting procedures applicable to the funds used in governmental accounting. An overview of these funds, together with individual fund financial statements, is presented throughout the remainder of this chapter. Chapter 3 presents a discussion of budgeting for governmental units. Chapters 4 through 9 focus on the activities usually found in each fund, together with the related accounting and reporting principles. Chapter 9 also includes a discussion of financial reporting for governmental units as a whole.

SECTION II—GOVERNMENTAL-TYPE FUNDS AND ACCOUNT GROUPS

In Section I governmental-type funds are defined as those funds in which the accounting emphasis (measurement focus) is placed on spending activities. Within this group are the funds that primarily account for the receipt and disbursement of resources used to provide services. Specifically, the governmental-type funds are the General Fund, Special Revenue Funds, Debt Service Funds, and Capital Projects Funds.

The General Fund

While the specific number and type of funds utilized by a governmental unit are determined by the particular operations of that unit, every governmental body must at least have a **General Fund.** Technically, this fund is a residual fund—it is used to account for all governmental operations not accounted for in some other fund. In reality, however, the General Fund encompasses the overall operations of a governmental unit. Unless there is some legal, contractual, or managerial

TABLE 2–3   Summary of Funds and Account Groups Used in Governmental Accounting

GOVERNMENTAL-TYPE FUNDS	FUNCTION
General Fund	Account for the general operations of the government
	Account for any other activities not accounted for in any other fund
	Examples: Police department, fire department
Special Revenue Funds	Account for resources legally designated for a particular purpose that must be separately reported
	Examples: A dedicated hotel-motel tax, a dedicated motor vehicle tax
Debt Service Funds	Account for resources dedicated to pay principal and interest on general obligation debt
	Examples: Sales tax or a special assessment dedicated to servicing general obligation bonds
Capital Projects Funds	Account for resources dedicated to the acquisition or construction of major capital facilities
	Examples: Construction of a new city hall or bridge

PROPRIETARY-TYPE FUNDS	FUNCTION
Internal Service Funds	Account for resources used to supply goods or services within the governmental unit or to other governmental units
	Examples: A central purchasing function, a central motor pool
Enterprise Funds	Account for resources used to supply goods or services to individuals outside the governmental unit
	Examples: A municipal golf course, a municiapl airport

FIDUCIARY FUNDS	FUNCTION
Pension Trust Funds	Account for resources used for government employees' retirement
	Example: Municipal employees' retirement funds
Nonexpendable Trust Funds	Account for resources not owned by the government, but which the government has a contractual responsibility to invest
	Example: The principal amount of a trust fund
Expendable Trust Funds	Account for resources not owned by the government, but which the government has a contractual responsibility to use within certain limits
	Examples: Income from a nonexpendable trust fund, resources received for a trust that can be spent
Agency Funds	Account for resources held by the government that must be disbursed according to law or contractual agreement
	Examples: Sales taxes collected by the government that are due to specific funds, Social Security collections from employee wages that must be paid to the U.S. government

ACCOUNT GROUPS	FUNCTION
General Fixed Assets Account Group	Account for long-term (fixed) assets acquired by funds using a spending focus
	Examples: Police cars, bridges, city hall, and other public buildings
General Long-Term Debt Account Group	Account for general obligation long-term debt issued by a governmental unit
	Examples: Bonds used to acquire funds to construct a bridge or a public stadium, and some long-term leases

TABLE 2–4 Summary of Fund Accounting Procedure

FUND TYPE	CATEGORY	ACCOUNTING (MEASUREMENT) FOCUS	BASIS OF ACCOUNTING
General Fund	Governmental	Spending	Modified accrual
Special Revenue Funds	Governmental	Spending	Modified accrual
Debt Service Funds	Governmental	Spending	Modified accrual
Capital Projects Funds	Governmental	Spending	Modified accrual
Internal Service Funds	Proprietary	Capital maintenance	Full accrual
Enterprise Funds	Proprietary	Capital maintenance	Full accrual
Pension Trust Funds	Fiduciary	Capital maintenance	Full accrual
Nonexpendable Trust Funds	Fiduciary	Capital maintenance	Full accrual
Expandable Trust Funds	Fiduciary	Spending	Modified accrual
Agency Funds	Fiduciary	N/A*	Modified accrual

*Due to the nature of Agency Funds, there is no concept of measurement of operations.

Source: This table is a compilation of the data included in NCGA *Statement 1* and *Governmental Accounting, Auditing, and Financial Reporting (GAAFR)* (Chicago: Governmental Finance Officers Association of the United States and Canada, 1988).

reason for separately accounting for an activity, it is recorded in the General Fund.

Included in the General Fund records are such activities as the police and fire departments, and the administrative operations of the government. The transactions recorded in the General Fund represent the collection of various sources of revenues and the disbursement of the resources for supplies, services, and so forth.

Assets usually found in the General Fund include cash, investments, receivables (usually property taxes) and receivables from other funds. In governmental accounting terminology, the receivables from other funds are referred to as **due from other funds.** If these receivables are not currently due, they are referred to as **advances to other funds.** Liabilities typically found in the General Fund include claims of various suppliers and payables to other funds. The latter items are referred to as **due to other funds.** As in the case of receivables, if these liabilities are not currently due they are referred to as **advances from other funds.**

Fund balance (equity) represents the excess of assets over liabilities (net resources that are available for spending). In those instances where an asset does not represent a resource available for current use, the fund balance must be restricted.

The accounting equation for governmental-type funds is similar to that used in commercial accounting. The only change is the equity section is referred to as "fund balance" rather than owners' equity. This equation is stated as follows:

Assets = Liabilities + Fund Balance

A simplified balance sheet for the General Fund is presented in Table 2–5. Carefully study this table and notice how the accounting equation is presented in the financial statement. Notice also that the balance sheet of a business organization is included in Table 2–5. A comparison of these two financial statements is the topic of the next section.

Comparison of a balance sheet for a governmental-type fund and a business organization

One of the major differences between accounting for a governmental-type fund and commercial accounting is that the latter uses classified financial statements. That is, elements of the commercial financial statements usually are reported in much smaller groups than elements of governmental-type funds. Notice that the assets, liabilities, and equity sections of the Cool Wheels balance sheet are further divided into subgroups; for example, Current assets, Current liabilities, and the like.

Another major difference between governmental-type fund accounting and commercial accounting lies in the types of assets included in the balance sheet. As previously stated, governmental-type fund assets consist primarily of current assets (spendable resources). Business organizations, on the other hand, report other long-term assets as well, such as property, plant, equipment, and intangibles, on their balance sheets. The reasons for these differences will be explained in detail in a later chapter.

The third major difference between governmental-type fund accounting and commercial accounting lies in the equity section of the balance sheet. In governmental-type funds, equity is reported as "Fund Balance." In business organizations, equity is reported as contributed capital and retained earnings because of limits that most states place on the distribution of dividends.

Balance sheets of both the City of New Example and Cool Wheels are presented with only basic items listed. As we explore the details of fund accounting, many additional differences between governmental accounting and commercial accounting will be identified and explained.

The "income statement" for a governmental-type fund is called a statement of revenues, expenditures, and changes in fund balance. Since governmental units do not usually operate to make a profit, the concept of income is not important. Throughout this text we will use the term *operating statement* to refer to the statement of revenues, expenditures, and changes in fund balance.

Revenues usually available for use by governmental-type funds include taxes, licenses and permits, and fines and forfeitures. Expenditures are generally associated with the services and supplies used in the various operating departments and are reported on the operating statement by function. Examples of these functions include general government, public safety, and recreation and parks.

Operating statements usually include revenues, expenditures, and a reconciliation of fund balance. An example of an operating statement of a governmental unit and the income statement of a business is shown in Table 2–6.

TABLE 2–5   General Fund—Balance Sheet Compared with Corporate Balance Sheet

City of New Example General Fund Balance Sheet December 31, 19X1		Cool Wheels Co., Inc. Balance Sheet December 31, 19X1	
Assets		*Assets*	
Cash and investments	$576,000	Current assets:	
Receivables (net of allowances		Cash and investments	$ 50,000
for uncollectible accounts,		Accounts receivable (net of	
$3,000)	89,000	allowance for uncollectible	
Due from other funds	50,000	accounts, $3,000)	135,000
		Inventory	145,000
Total assets	$715,000	Prepaid expenses	34,000
Liabilities		Total current assets	364,000
Accounts payable	$123,000	Property, plant, and equipment:	
Due to other funds	75,000	Land	100,000
Accrued liabilities	100,000	Buildings (net of accumulated	
		depreciation, $55,000)	150,000
Total liabilities	298,000	Equipment (net of accumulated	
		depreciation, $14,000)	45,000
Fund balance		Total property, plant, and equipment	295,000
Fund balance	417,000	Intangibles:	
Total liabilities and fund balance	$715,000	Patents	30,000
		Total assets	$689,000
		Liabilities	
		Current liabilities:	
		Accounts payable	$35,000
		Accrued expenses payable	55,000
		Dividends payable	10,000
		Total current liabilities:	100,000
		Long-term liabilities:	
		Bonds payable	300,000
		Total liablities	400,000
		Owners' Equity	
		Contributed capital	150,000
		Retained earnings	139,000
		Total owners' equity	289,000
		Total liablities and owners' equity	$689,000

TABLE 2–6   General Fund—Statement of Revenues, Expenditures, and Changes in Fund Balance Compared with Corporate Income Statement

City of New Example General Fund Statement of Revenues, Expenditures, and Changes in Fund Balance For the Year Ended December 31, 19X1			Cool Wheels Co., Inc. Income Statement For the Year Ended December 31, 19X1		

Revenues			*Revenues*		
Income taxes		$990,000	Net sales		$988,000
Property taxes		900,000	Other revenue		10,000
Licenses and permits		550,000			
Fines and forfeits		250,000	Total revenues		998,000
Miscellaneous		92,000			
			Expenses		
Total revenues		$2,782,000			
			Cost of goods sold		450,000
Expenditures			Salaries expense		280,000
			Depreciation expense		175,000
Current:			Interest expense		25,000
General government		550,000	Other expenses		20,000
Public safety		990,000			
Human services		780,000	Total expenses		950,000
Health		300,000			
Recreation and parks		50,000	Net income		$48,000
Capital outlay		100,000			
Total expenditures		2,770,000			
Excess of revenues over expenditures		12,000			
Other Financing Sources (Uses)					
Operating transfers in		50,000			
Operating transfers out		(40,000)			
Total other financing sources		10,000			

Excess of revenues and other financing
  sources over expenditures and other
  financing uses
		22,000			

Fund balance at beginning of year		395,000			
Fund balance at end of year		$417,000			

Notice that the operating statement in Table 2–6 includes Other financing sources (uses). These are increases and decreases in fund balance that are not revenues or expenditures. In governmental-type funds, they consist mainly of operating transfers (transfers of resources between funds). **Operating transfers in** are transfers to a fund from other funds, whereas **operating transfers out** are transfers from a fund to other funds. A discussion of the technical aspects of transfers is included in a later chapter. At this point it is only necessary for the reader to understand that many types of transfers take place in order to move resources from one fund to another.

Comparison of an operating statement
for a governmental-type fund and a business organization

One major difference between governmental units and businesses is that governmental units usually have many more individual sources of revenues than business units. For example, notice that the city of New Example has five revenue sources compared with only two for Cool Wheels.

Another major difference is that commercial operating statements usually are prepared under what is called the "single-step" approach; that is, total revenues less total expenses. The operating statement for governmental units have several different levels of aggregation. They are similar to the multiple step income statements that are no longer in use by business organizations.

A third major difference between the operating statement for the General Fund and a business organization is the presence of depreciation for commercial organizations. Commercial organizations use the full accrual basis of accounting; therefore, total expenses are deducted from total revenues, including depreciation. As you may remember, long-term (fixed) assets are not reported on governmental-type fund balance sheets (see Table 2–5). As a result, depreciation is not an expense for the General Fund.

The lack of depreciation is also based on the focus of the accounting system for governmental-type funds. These funds use a spending focus and depreciation does not involve an expenditure. Instead, all capital assets (fixed assets) acquired by governmental-type funds are treated as expenditures in the year acquired.

Notice the section of the General Fund operating statement labeled "Capital outlay." This represents total fixed assets acquired through the fund during the year. We will explain this point in greater detail in a later chapter.

A fourth major difference between the operating statement of a governmental-type fund and the income statement of a business organization is the presence of operating transfers. While operating transfers are included in the operating results of the governmental-type funds, there is no similar concept in commercial accounting.

Another major difference between business reporting of operations and that of governmental-type funds is the treatment of equity. Traditionally, ending fund balance is reconciled with beginning fund balance on the operating statement of governmental-type funds. While some commercial organizations use this form of reporting, the majority reconcile beginning and ending retained earnings on a separate statement—either a retained earnings statement or a statement of changes in owners' equity.

The operating statement for the City of New Example and the income statement of Cool Wheels are presented with only basic items listed. As we explore the details of fund accounting, many additional differences will be identified and explained.

Other aspects of general fund accounting

Like all governmental-type funds, the accounting records of the General Fund are maintained on the modified accrual basis. This means that revenues are reported when they are measurable and available and expenditures generally are reported as they are incurred.

Unlike the other funds used by a government unit, every governmental unit must have a General Fund, and each governmental unit may have only *one* General Fund.

Special Revenue Funds

Special Revenue Funds are used to account for the proceeds of revenue sources (other than expendable trusts, or those used for major capital projects) that must be spent for a particular purpose. The accounting treatment of these funds is identical to that of the General Fund. The primary difference between the two funds lies in the breadth of activities recorded in each.

Special Revenue Funds should be used only when required by law, charter, or other commitment. The main purpose of separating these types of activities from those of the General Fund is to maintain control over the collection and use of specific sources of revenue. For example, assume that a tax on gasoline is specifically dedicated to highway maintenance. Generally a Special Revenue Fund is required by the law establishing the tax. This makes it easy for a governmental unit to account for the dollars collected from the gasoline tax, as well as the expenditures for highway maintenance. If these funds were commingled with other revenues and expenditures, it would be much more difficult to account for the money collected and its use. Other examples of Special Revenue Funds include special income tax funds, hotel-motel tax funds, street construction and maintenance funds, and community development funds.

A government unit can have several Special Revenue Funds. Usually the law or commitment that requires the use of a Special Revenue Fund also requires that separate records be maintained for the activity. Each of these funds is treated as a separate accounting entity for record-keeping purposes.

The types of assets usually found in Special Revenue Funds include cash, investments, receivables (usually taxes), and amounts due from other funds. Liabilities common to these funds include the claims of various suppliers and payables to other funds. Since the accounting for Special Revenue Funds is identical to that of the General Fund, those comments made regarding the fund balance in our discussion of the General Fund are also relevant here. A balance sheet for a Special Revenue Fund is shown in Table 2–7.

Generally the sources of revenue for Special Revenue Funds are taxes, rents and royalties, and intergovernmental items (grants, shared revenues, and so forth). Expenditures made by these funds are usually for services and supplies specifically identified by the law establishing the particular fund (see Table 2–8). Notice in Table 2–8 that the expenditures for Special Revenue Funds are reported by function like those of the General Fund.

The modified accrual basis of accounting is used for each Special Revenue Fund.

Debt Service Funds

Debt Service Funds account for the accumulation of resources that will be used to make payments of principal and interest on general long-term debt.[6] This type of fund can also be used for payments of long-term liabilities other than bonds, such as installment purchase contracts and lease-purchase agreements. (In some of the latter instances the payments are made directly from general revenues on an annual basis. Therefore, they can be accounted for in the General Fund.) A single Debt Service Fund should be used for all general long-term debt whenever

TABLE 2–7   Special Revenue Fund—Balance Sheet

City of New Example
Special Revenue Fund
Hotel-Motel Tax Fund
Balance Sheet
December 31, 19X1

Assets

Cash and investments	$250,000	
Receivables (net of allowances for uncollectible accounts, $2,000)	50,000	
Due from other funds	10,000	
Total assets		$310,000

Liabilities

Accounts payable	$23,000	
Due to other funds	12,000	
Total liabilities		$35,000

Fund Balance

Fund balance		275,000
Total liabilities and fund balance		$310,000

[6]Debt to be serviced by proprietary fund revenues is not serviced by these funds.

TABLE 2–8   Special Revenue Fund—Statement of Revenues, Expenditures, and Changes in Fund Balance

City of New Example
Special Revenue Fund
Hotel-Motel Tax Fund
Statement of Revenues, Expenditures,
and Changes in Fund Balance
For the Year Ended December 31, 19X1

Revenues

Sales taxes	$530,000	
Investment income	25,000	
Miscellaneous	10,000	
Total revenues		$565,000

Expenditures

Current:		
Public safety	$450,000	
Recreation and parks	100,000	
Total expenditures		550,000
Excess of revenues over expenditures		15,000
Fund balance at beginning of year		260,000
Fund balance at end of year		$275,000

possible. In many instances, however, each debt issue may require the establishment of a separate Debt Service Fund.

The sources of the assets for Debt Service Funds include

1. Transfers from the General Fund (and/or other funds)
2. Income from the investment of resources held by the fund
3. Taxes assessed to service the debt

Expenditures of Debt Service Funds generally involve payment of principal and interest on the debt. A statement of revenues, expenditures, and changes in fund balance for a Debt Service Fund is shown in Table 2–9.

As a result of the above types of transactions, the assets of Debt Service Funds usually consist of cash, investments, and possibly receivables. The liabilities are generally interest and principal *currently due*. The fund balance therefore represents the resources available to *service* (pay principal and interest on) the debt. The liability for the principal not currently due is reported in the General Long-Term Debt Account Group. A balance sheet for a Debt Service Fund is shown in Table 2–10.

Debt Service Funds follow the modified accrual basis of accounting.

TABLE 2-9   Debt Service Fund—Statement of Revenues, Expenditures, and Changes in Fund Balance

City of New Example
Debt Service Fund
General Bond Retirement Fund—Issue A
Statement of Revenues, Expenditures,
and Changes in Fund Balance
For the Year Ended December 31, 19X1

Revenues		
Income taxes	$300,000	
Property taxes	250,000	
Special assessments	250,000	
Investment earnings	100,000	
Total revenues		$900,000
Expenditures		
Debt service:		
Principal retirement	$100,000	
Interest	500,000	
Total expenditures		600,000
Excess of revenues over expenditures		300,000
Other Financing Sources		
Operating transfers in		50,000
Excess of revenues and other financing sources over expenditures		350,000
Fund balance at beginning of year		600,000
Fund balance at end of year		$950,000

Capital Projects Funds

Capital Projects Funds account for receipt and disbursement of resources used to acquire major capital facilities through purchase or construction. A Capital Projects Fund is not used to account for such assets acquired by an Enterprise Fund, an Internal Service Fund, a Trust Fund, or those assets that are purchased directly with current revenues of the General Fund or a Special Revenue Fund. However, it must be used where there is a legal requirement for such accounting or when

TABLE 2–10   Debt Service Fund—Balance Sheet

City of New Example
Debt Service Fund
General Bond Retirement Fund—Issue A
Balance Sheet
December 31, 19X1

Assets		
Cash and investments	$1,075,000	
Receivables (net of allowances for uncollectible accounts, $2,000)	40,000	
Due from other funds	5,000	
Total assets		$1,120,000
Liabilities		
Matured bonds payable	$123,000	
Mature interest payable	47,000	
Total liabilities		$170,000
Fund Balance		
Fund balance		950,000
Total liabilites and fund balance		$1,120,000

the financing of a general governmental project involves the issuance of bonds, intergovernmental revenues, major private donations, or other restricted sources.[7]

Generally a separate Capital Projects Fund is used for each project. When a bond issue is involved in the financing, a separate fund is used for each bond issue. Use of a separate fund provides better control over individual projects or the proceeds from a bond issue.

Projects usually accounted for in these funds include construction of bridges, a new city hall, and acquisition of assets that involve long-term financing. Examples of the types of acquisitions that usually do *not* require the use of a Capital Projects Fund are purchase of automobiles, furniture, and minor equipment.

Assets normally found on the balance sheet of a Capital Projects Fund are shown in Table 2–11. These include cash, investments, receivables, and amounts due from other funds or governments. Liabilities include accounts payable and amounts due to other funds or governments for services and materials associated with the construction projects (or to construction companies if the projects are completed by outside contractors).

A statement of revenues, expenditures, and changes in fund balance for a Capital Projects Fund is shown in Table 2–12. The normal sources of assets for

[7]*Governmental Accounting, Auditing and Financial Reporting (GAAFR)* (Chicago: Government Finance Officers Association of the United States and Canada, 1980), p. 46.

TABLE 2–11   Capital Projects Fund—Balance Sheet

City of New Example
Capital Projects Fund
Green River Bridge Fund
Balance Sheet
December 31, 19X1

Assets		
Cash and investments	$850,00	
Due from other funds	10,000	
Total assets		$860,000
Liabilities		
Accounts payable		$120,000
Fund Balance		
Fund balance		740,000
Total liabilities and fund balance		$860,000

TABLE 2–12   Capital Projects Fund—Statement of Revenues, Expenditures, and Changes in Fund Balance

City of New Example
Capital Projects Fund
Green River Bridge Fund
Statement of Revenues, Expenditures,
and Changes in Fund Balance
For the Year Ended December 31, 19X1

Revenues		
Investment income	$25,000	
Miscellaneous	10,000	
Total revenues		$ 35,000
Expenditures		
Capital outlay		750,000
Excess expenditures over revenues		(715,000)
Fund balance at beginning of year		1,455,000
Fund balance at end of year		$ 740,000

these funds are federal and state grants, earnings on investments, issuance of debt securities, and possible transfers from other funds. Expenditures are usually limited to amounts related to the capital projects and include construction and engineering costs.

Notice the excess of expenditures over revenues in Table 2–12. This is not uncommon for Capital Projects Funds. A careful review of Table 2–12 shows that this fund has a large fund balance of $740,000. This amount was accumulated in previous years when the revenues of the fund (probably government grants) exceeded its expenditures. It is normal for these types of funds to receive most, if not all, of their revenues early in the life of the project and then spend those revenues to complete the project.

Since Capital Projects Funds are governmental-type funds, they follow the modified accrual basis of accounting.

ACCOUNT GROUPS

Certain types of assets and liabilities relate to the operations of the overall governmental unit rather than to those of a particular fund. These assets are not an appropriate resource, and the liabilities are not a current claim against the resources of a specific fund. They are, therefore, not reported on the financial statements of any fund. Instead, these assets and liabilities are recorded in **account groups.** An account group is not a fund because it is not an independent fiscal entity. Instead an account group is simply a self-balancing set of accounts used for *control* purposes. The two types of account groups used in governmental accounting are the General Fixed Assets Account Group and the General Long-Term Debt Account Group.

The General Fixed Assets Account Group (GFAAG)

The General Fixed Assets Account Group (GFAAG) is used to control the property, buildings, furniture, and equipment-type assets used by the governmental unit except for those found in proprietary-type funds and some Trust Funds. In general, the GFAAG is used to keep a record of the assets available for the overall operations of the governmental unit. Remember that the focus of the accounting system for governmental-type funds and Expendable Trust Funds is on the spending of current resources. Since items of property and equipment are not available to be spent, they are not accounted for in those funds. In the balance sheets previously illustrated in this chapter, the assets are generally limited to cash, receivables, investments, and amounts due from other governmental units—spendable resources or resources that will normally be converted into spendable resources.

Every governmental unit has a large amount of money invested in various types of property and equipment, and therefore some form of control is needed. This control is maintained by the accounting procedures followed in the GFAAG. Table 2–13 is a typical example of the financial reporting involved. The assets are

TABLE 2–13   Schedule of General Fixed Assets

City of New Example
General Fixed Assets
Schedule of General Fixed Assets
December 31, 19X1

General Fixed Assets

Land	$ 1,000,000
Buildings and improvements	12,500,000
Equipment	7,600,000
Construction in process	1,000,000
	$22,100,000

Investment in General Fixed Assets From

Capital projects funds:	
General obligation bonds	$ 9,000,000
Federal grants	6,000,000
State grants	5,000,000
General Fund revenues	2,100,000
	$22,100,000

listed first by major category: Land, Buildings, Equipment, and Construction in progress (partially completed assets). The balancing effect is achieved by listing the sources of the resources used to acquire the assets. In Table 2–13, these sources are debt, various types of grants, and resources obtained from specific funds. Note that the totals of the two categories balance. The total assets must *always* equal the total of the sources of the funds used to acquire the assets.

For control over individual assets, detailed subsidiary records must be maintained as to the type and location of each item, and the individual items must be physically identified. This is usually achieved by attaching a tag with a serial number to each asset and by keeping detailed information about each asset by serial number. Although this may be a monumental task, it is necessary to ensure that governmental assets are adequately protected. Such records also provide data needed to acquire adequate insurance coverage and to file claims when losses occur.

A schedule of changes in general fixed assets is shown in Table 2–14. While no activity statement is required for this reporting entity, the schedule of changes is required, either in statement form or in the notes to the financial statements, in order to conform to reporting requirements.

The General Long-Term Debt Account Group (GLTDAG)

Long-term debt is accounted for in the fund that has primary responsibility for generation of the resources that will be used to retire the debt. For example, revenue bonds that will be retired from future revenue generated by an Enterprise Fund are reported as a long-term debt on the balance sheet of that fund.

TABLE 2–14   Schedule of Changes in General Fixed Assets

City of New Example
General Fixed Assets
Schedule of Changes in General Fixed Assets
For the Year Ended December 31, 19X1

	DECEMBER 31, 19X0	ADDITIONS	DEDUCTIONS	DECEMBER 31, 19X1
Land	$ 1,000,000	$ —	$ —	$ 1,000,000
Bildings and improvements	10,100,000	3,000,000	600,000	12,500,000
Equipment	6,000,000	2,000,000	400,000	7,600,000
Construction in progress	500,000	500,000	—	1,000,000
Totals	$17,600,000	$5,500,000	$1,000,000	$22,100,000

By contrast, long-term debt that will be retired through the use of general resources available to the governmental unit is not usually reported on the balance sheet of any particular fund because of the current-spending focus of the accounting system. Instead, such debt (general obligation debt) is reported in the General Long-Term Debt Account Group (GLTDAG) (see Table 2–15).

The format of the statement lists the resources that have been provided in a Debt Service Fund for the retirement of the debt (amount available in Debt Service Funds) and the amount that has yet to be set aside for the retirement of the debt (amount to be provided). These latter amounts will be transferred to a Debt Service Fund in future years. The total of the resources provided and to be provided will be equal to the long-term debt outstanding.

TABLE 2–15   Schedule of Long-Term Debt

City of New Example
General Long-Term Debt Account Group
Schedules of General Long-Term Debt
December 31, 19X1

Amount provided and to be provided for payment of general long-term debt:	
Amount provided in Debt Service Funds	$ 8,000,000
Amount to be provided in Debt Service Funds	17,000,000
Total	$25,000,000
General long-term debt payable:	
Accrued vacation and sick leave	$ 3,000,000
Obligations under installment purchase contracts	4,000,000
Obligations under capitalized leases	3,000,000
Bonds payable	15,000,000
Total	$25,000,000

TABLE 2–16   Schedule of Changes in General Long-Term Debt

City of New Example
General Long-Term Debt Account Group
Schedule of Changes in General Long-Term Debt
For the Year Ended December 31, 19X1

	DECEMBER 31, 19X0	ADDITIONS	DEDUCTIONS	DECEMBER 31, 19X1
Accrued vacation and sick leave	$ 2,700,000	$ 500,00	$200,000	$ 3,000,000
Obligations under installment purchase contracts	4,100,000	200,000	300,000	4,000,000
Obligations under capitalized leases	2,700,000	400,000	100,000	3,000,000
Bonds payable	14,500,000	500,000	—	15,000,000
Totals	$24,000,000	$1,600,000	$600,000	$25,000,000

Notice that all types of long-term debt are contained in the GLTDAG. While bonds have been used as examples in the above discussion, long-term leases, installment purchase contracts, and so forth, are also reported in this account group.

While no activity statement reporting the results of operations is required for an account group, the ending balance in the GLTDAG must be reconciled with the beginning balance. In other words, the changes in the general long-term debt must be reported either in the notes to the financial statements or in a separate statement. Table 2–16 is an example of a typical schedule reporting changes in the GLTDAG.

SECTION III—PROPRIETARY-TYPE FUNDS

Proprietary-type funds are used whenever a governmental unit is involved in activities that are similar to those conducted by business enterprises. Examples of such activities include the operation of electric utilities, airports, golf courses, and central motor pools. These types of activities are usually financed, at least in part, by user charges. As a result, accounting principles followed by these funds are the same as those followed by commercial organizations, that is, a capital maintenance focus. This provides governmental units with accurate measures of revenues and expenses that they can use to develop user charges and/or to help determine any subsidy needed to run an activity. The two types of funds found in this category are Internal Service Funds and Enterprise Funds.

Internal Service Funds

Internal Service Funds are used to account for providing goods or services within the governmental unit, or to other governmental units, on a user charge basis. The main reasons for establishing this type of fund are to reduce the cost of obtaining goods or services and to improve the distribution of goods or services within the governmental unit. Typical Internal Service Funds include those used to account for supplies distribution, motor pool operations, and data processing.

Since Internal Service Funds are classified as proprietary-type funds, the accounting system is designed to accumulate the total cost of the goods or services provided. Therefore, the full accrual basis of accounting is used. The funds receiving the goods or services are billed by the Internal Service Fund and this amount is treated as revenue for the Internal Service Fund and as an expenditure (expense) for the other funds. A separate fund is used for each identifiable unit because the accumulation of costs of goods or services provided must be specifically associated with revenues earned from providing the goods or services.

Full accrual accounting is used for all Internal Service Funds to properly measure revenues and expenses. Here the emphasis shifts from resources available for use (spending activities), as in governmental-type funds, to a capital maintenance approach. The reason for the use of full accrual accounting is to account for the total cost of the goods or services provided. This information is used to develop user charges in a similar fashion to that followed by commercial enterprises, to determine the amount of subsidy needed to support the activities, or some combination of these.

The balance sheet for an Internal Service Fund is essentially the same as that used for a business organization. Several major points regarding this financial statement should be noted. First, the assets include noncurrent assets, such as land and buildings. Second these assets are reported net of accumulated depreciation. Since we are measuring expenses, depreciation is calculated and deducted from revenues. A third difference is found in the fund equity section. Instead of one account called "Fund balance," fund equity is divided into two categories: contributed capital and retained earnings. These two categories represent net assets of the fund that were contributed by some other fund or group and those that were earned.

Assets usually found in these types of funds include cash; amounts due from other funds; inventory (where applicable); and property, plant, and equipment. Liabilities generally include payables arising from operations of the fund and, possibly, advances from the General Fund or other funds. A balance sheet for a typical Internal Service Fund is presented in Table 2–17.

The operating statement (statement of revenues, expenses, and changes in retained earnings) of an Internal Service Fund is prepared in the same way as the income statement of a business. Operating revenues earned by an Internal Service Fund usually result from user charges (see Table 2–18). The operating expenses associated with the operations of the fund depend on the type of operations but usually include the cost of services, supplies used, and depreciation. The excess of operating revenues over operating expenses is called net income (operating income, if other items are reported in the statement). This amount is added to the beginning balance of retained earnings to determine retained earnings at the end of the period. The exact items of revenue and expense depend on the particular types of services performed.

TABLE 2–17   Internal Service Fund—Balance Sheet

City of New Example
Internal Service Fund
Central Motor Pool Fund
Balance Sheet
December 31, 19X1

Assets

Cash	$ 130,000	
Due from other funds	75,000	
Inventory of parts and supplies	105,000	
Property and equipment (net of accumulated depreciation, $1,800,000)	3,200,000	
Total assets		$3,510,000

Liabilities

Accounts payable	$ 24,000	
Accrued liabilities	6,000	
Accrued vacation and sick leave	10,000	
Total liabilities		$ 40,000

Fund Equity

Contributed capital	$2,900,000	
Retained earnings	570,000	
Total fund equity		3,470,000
Total liabilities and fund equity		$3,510,000

Generally accepted accounting principles for Internal Service Funds also require a statement of cash flows, similar to that presented in Table 2–19. Since preparation of this statement is beyond the scope of this text, we have included Table 2–19 for illustrative purposes only.

Enterprise Funds

Enterprise Funds are used to account for products or services continuously provided by a governmental unit where (1) users include the general public and (2) costs of providing the products or services are financed mainly by user charges. These funds are also used when the management of a governmental unit feels that an accounting system similar to that of a commercial business is necessary for operational control over an activity. Operations normally accounted for in Enterprise Funds include municipally owned utilities, airports, swimming pools, and golf courses. Generally a separate fund is established for each type of activity.

Accounting for Enterprise Funds is essentially the same as that used for commercial operations—full accrual accounting. This is the same accounting

TABLE 2-18   Internal Service Fund—Statement of Revenues, Expenses, and Changes in Retained Earnings

City of New Example
Internal Service Fund
Central Motor Pool Fund
Statement of Revenues, Expenses,
and Changes in Retained Earnings
For the Year Ended December 31, 19X1

Operating revenues:		
Charges for vehicle rentals		$1,800,000
Operating expenses:		
Personal services	$720,000	
Contractual services	270,000	
Depreciation	520,000	
Materials and supplies	254,000	
Other	90,500	
Total operating expenses		1,854,500
Operating loss		(54,500)
Other financing sources:		
Operating transfers in		60,000
Net income		5,500
Retained earnings at beginning of year		564,500
Retained earnings at end of year		$ 570,000

focus described in the previous section on Internal Service Funds. As already indicated, the reason for the use of full accrual accounting is to account for the total cost of the goods or services provided. This information is used to develop user charges in a fashion similar to that followed by commercial enterprises, to determine the amount of subsidy needed to support the activities, or some combination of these.

The balance sheet of an Enterprise Fund is shown in Table 2–20. Several major features of this financial statement should be noted. The first is the classified approach. A **classified balance sheet** presents the assets and liabilities grouped by major type. **Current assets** are assets (including cash) that will be used up or collected within one year. **Current liabilities** are debts that will be paid within one year, using current assets. **Long-term liabilities** are debts that will be paid later than one year in the future or will be paid from other than current assets.

The second major point that should be noted is the presence of **restricted assets.** These assets represent resources that have been set aside for some particular use resulting from a legal, contractual, or regulatory restriction and are labeled "Restricted assets" on the balance sheet. Liabilities that will be satisfied

TABLE 2–19 Internal Service Fund—Statement of Cash Flows

City of New Example
Internal Service Fund
Central Motor Pool Fund
Statement of Cash Flows
For the Year Ended December 31, 19X1

Increase (Decrease) in Cash

Cash flows from operating activities:

Cash received from vehicle rentals to departments	$1,700,000
Cash paid to suppliers for goods and services	(610,000)
Cash paid to employees	(720,000)
Net cash provided by operating activities	$370,000

Cash flows from noncapital financing activities:

Operating transfer	60,000

Cash flows from capital and related financing activities:

Purchase of equipment	(500,000)
Net decrease in cash	(70,000)
Cash at beginning of year	200,000
Cash at end of year	$130,000

Reconciliation of operating loss to net cash provided by
operating activities:

Operating loss		($54,500)
Adjustments to reconcile operating loss to net cash provided by operating activities:		
Depreciation	$520,000	
Increase in due from other funds	(33,000)	
Increase in inventory of parts and supplies	(27,500)	
Decrease in accounts payable	(24,000)	
Decrease in accrued liabilities	(8,000)	
Decrease in accrued vacation and sick leave	(3,000)	
Total adjustments		424,500
Net cash provided by operating activities		$370,000

from such resources must also be segregated. These are labeled "Current liabilities payable from restricted assets" in Table 2–20. As a result, there are two sections of current liabilities on the balance sheet.

Other asset categories used on the balance sheet include Advances to other funds; Property, plant, and equipment; and Other assets. The **Advances to other**

TABLE 2–20   Enterprise Fund—Balance Sheet

City of New Example
Enterprise Fund
Sewerage and Water Fund
Balance Sheet
December 31, 19x1

Assets

Current assets:		
Cash	$ 650,000	
Receivables (net of allowance for uncollectibles of $8,000)	547,000	
Due from other funds	75,000	
Inventory of parts and supplies	155,000	
Total current assets		$ 1,427,000
Advances to other funds		300,000
Restricted assets:		
Customer deposits	$ 879,000	
Current debt service account	500,000	
Total restricted assets		1,379,000
Property, plant, and equipment (net accumulated depreciation, $2,400,000)		8,500,000
Total assets		$11,606,000

Liabilities

Current liabilities:		
Accounts payable	$ 235,000	
Due to other funds	100,000	
Accrued liabilities	77,000	
Accrued vacation and sick leave	90,000	
Total current liabilities		$ 502,000
Current liabilities payable from restricted assets:		
Customer deposits	$ 879,000	
Accrued interest	500,000	
Total current liabilities payable from restricted assets		1,379,000
Long-term liabilities:		
Bonds payable		7,890,000

Fund equity

Contributed capital	$1,300,000	
Retained Earnings	535,000	
Total fund equity		1,835,000
Total liabilities and fund equity		$11,606,000

funds section is used to report long-term receivables. The **Property, plant, and equipment** section includes the major assets used to provide the services for which the fund was established. The **Other assets** section is used as a catchall category. Any asset that does not fit into one of the specific categories is reported in the "other" category.

Finally, note that fund equity is divided into (1) capital contributed by the government, customers, and so forth, in the form of permanent contributions; and (2) retained earnings. **Retained earnings** represents the accumulate earnings (income) of the unit.

The balance sheet shown in Table 2–20 is in a form that is typical of commercial business—current assets and liabilities preceding noncurrent. It is not uncommon, however, to find the plant and the long-term debt first on utility balance sheets. This is because of the excessively larger percentage of the total assets or total equities these items represent for utilities, relative to other forms of businesses. The standard commercial form is followed quite often for governmental purposes because of the use of combined statements. (The "combined" aspect of governmental reporting is discussed in Chapter 9.) Unless there are legal restrictions involved, either is acceptable.

The operating revenues earned by an Enterprise Fund usually result from user charges (see Table 2–21). The expenses associated with the operations of the

TABLE 2–21 Enterprise Fund—Statement of Revenues, Expenses, and Changes in Retained Earnings

City of New Example
Enterprise Fund
Sewerage and Water Fund
Statement of Revenues, Expenses,
and Changes in Retained Earnings
For the Year Ended December 31, 19X1

Operating revenues:		
Charges for services		$2,400,000
Operating expenses:		
Personal services	$980,000	
Contractual services	370,000	
Depreciation	620,000	
Materials and supplies	176,000	
Other	101,000	
Total operating expenses		2,247,000
Net income		153,000
Retained earnings at beginning of year		382,000
Retained earnings at end of year		$ 535,000

fund depend on the type of operations but usually include the cost of services, supplies used, utilities, depreciation, and so forth. Notice particularly the charge for depreciation. Since the Enterprise Funds use the full accrual method of accounting, depreciation must be included as an expense.

Notice also that operating expenses are deducted from operating revenues to calculate operating income or loss. The nonoperating items are then added or subtracted to determine the net income for the period. This figure is added, in the case of income, to the beginning balance in Retained earnings (or deducted in the case of a net loss) to determine the ending balance in that account.

Enterprise Funds are part of a governmental unit; therefore, operating transfers are often used to provide operating subsidies for the funds or to move resources from Enterprise Funds or other funds. These transfers should be reported after nonoperating revenues (expenses) and before extraordinary items. Extraordinary items are events that are not typical for such an organization and are incurred infrequently.

Since operations of Enterprise Funds are essentially the same as those of profit-oriented businesses, an additional statement must be prepared. This statement is a **statement of cash flows.** Table 2–22 is an example of a statement of cash flows. The purpose of this statement is to provide information regarding the sources and uses of cash by the fund for operating, investing, and financing activities.

A discussion of the preparation of the cash flow statement is beyond the scope of this text. We have included Table 2–22 for illustrative purposes only.

SECTION IV—FIDUCIARY-TYPE FUNDS

Fiduciary-type funds are used to account for assets held by a government in an agency or trust capacity. In *Statement 1*, the NCGA further classified Trust and Agency Funds as Pension Trust, Nonexpendable Trust, Expendable Trust, and Agency Funds.[8]

The most widely used trust funds are **Pension Trust Funds.** They are used to account for the assets, liabilities, and equity of the public employee retirement systems (PERS) used by governmental units. **Nonexpendable Trust Funds** are those trust funds whose principal must be maintained. In most instances a governmental unit would be permitted to spend the income from the principal in some specified manner—for example to purchase library books. In this instance the principal would constitute a Nonexpendable Trust Fund and the earnings would be spent through an **Expendable Trust Fund.** Expendable Trust Funds are also used to account for those situations where the principal and income can be spent by the governmental unit.

An **Agency Fund** is used when a governmental unit is the *custodian* of resources that belong to some other fund of the government or organization. This type of fund is also used when a single fund is established to perform a central

---

[8]NCGA, *Statement 1*, p. 6 [GASB Cod. Sec. 1300.104].

TABLE 2–22   Enterprise Fund—Statement of Cash Flows

City of New Example
Enterprise Fund
Sewerage and Water Fund
Statement of Cash Flows
For the Year Ended December 31, 19X1

Increase (Decrease) in Cash

Cash flows from operating activities:		
Cash received from vehicle rentals to departments	$2,390,000	
Cash paid to suppliers for goods and services	(560,000)	
Cash paid to employees	(980,000)	
Net cash provided by operating activities		$850,000
Cash flows from capital and related financing activities:		
Purchase of equipment		(720,000)
Net increase in cash		130,000
Cash at beginning of year		520,000
Cash at end of year		$650,000
Reconciliation of operating income to net cash provided by operating activities:		
Operating income		$153,000
Adjustments to reconcile operating loss to net cash provided by operating activities:		
Depreciation	$620,000	
Decrease in accounts receivable	262,000	
Increase in due from other funds	(50,000)	
Increase in inventory of parts and supplies	(40,000)	
Decrease in accounts payable	(50,000)	
Decrease in accrued liabilities	(30,000)	
Decrease in accrued vacation and sick leave	(15,000)	
Total adjustments		697,000
Net cash provided by operating activities		$850,000

collection or distribution function for the resources of other funds of the governmental unit. Since the government does not have an equity interest in the assets, there is no fund balance for this type of fund. Rather, all the resources held are balanced against the liabilities that are to be paid from those resources, including the debt to the legal "owner" of the assets. Resources for which the governmental unit acts as an agent include withheld employees' Social Security and income taxes and taxes collected by a governmental unit for other governmental units (Tax Agency Funds). With respect to employees' Social Security and income tax withholdings, during the period of time in which these amounts are held by the governmental unit, they are properly accounted for in an Agency Fund. However, it is also acceptable to account for withholdings from employees' pay in the fund in which the gross pay is recorded.

It is possible to use one Agency Fund to account for several different agency relationships (assuming there are no legal restrictions). However, due to the legal problems that exist in situations involving trusts, a separate fund is generally used for each individual trust.

When accounting for Expendable Trust Funds, the focus is on the spending of the resources available; whereas Nonexpendable Trust Funds and Pension Trust Funds, by contrast, require a capital maintenance approach. Therefore the accrual basis is used for the latter two funds, while the Expendable Trust Funds follow the modified accrual basis of accounting. Since Agency Funds are strictly custodial in nature, the modified accrual basis of accounting is also used in these funds.

A balance sheet for each fiduciary-type fund is shown in Tables 2–23 through 2–26. Assets usually found in these funds include cash, investments, receivables, and amounts due from other funds. Liabilities include debts incurred in operating each fund and amounts due to other funds. Fund balance of each fund using a spending focus represents spendable resources of the fund. Fund balance of each fund using the capital maintenance focus represents the net assets of the fund.

Tables 2–27 through 2–30 present the operating statements (including an analysis of changes in fund balance) of fiduciary funds. Since Pension Trust Funds and Nonexpendable Trust Funds follow a capital maintenance approach, the operating statements are similar in format to those of proprietary funds, including a measure of net income. The types of revenues and expenses depend on the nature of the funds included. The shift in focus from capital maintenance to spending is highlighted by the fact that the operating statement for Expendable Trust Funds contains revenues and *expenditures* (not expenses) (see Table 2–29). This difference is carried on to the measure of the excess of revenues over expenditures, which is referred to as "excess of revenues over expenditures," *not* net income. For each type of fund, however, the determination of the ending fund balance is the same.

Because of the peculiar relationship that Agency Funds have to the governmental unit, an operating statement is not used. Instead, a statement of changes in assets and liabilities is substituted (see Table 2–30). The purpose of this statement is to relate to the reader changes in the various asset and liability accounts used by the funds. These changes are reflected as "increases" and "decreases" and account for the activity that has taken place within the fund during the reporting period.

We have previously mentioned that those funds which follow commercial-type accounting procedures usually must prepare a statement of cash flows in

TABLE 2–23   Pension Trust Funds—Balance Sheet [9]

City of New Example
Pension Trust Fund
City Employees' Retirement Fund
Balance Sheet
December 31, 19X1

Assets

Cash		$ 5,000
Accrued income		75,000
Investments:		
Bonds at amortized cost (market value $18,600,000)	$18,000,000	
Common stock at cost (market value $6,500,000)	6,000,000	
Total investments		24,000,000
Office equipment and furniture (net of accumulated depreciation, $10,000)		75,000
Total assets		24,155,000

Liabilities

Accounts payable	$ 20,000	
Accrued expenses	34,000	
Total liabilities		55,000
Net assets available for benefits		$24,100,000

Fund Balance

Actuarial present value of projected benefits payable to current retirants and beneficiaries	$ 5,765,000
Actuarial present value of projected benefits payable to terminated vested participants	987,000
Actuarial present value of credited projected benefits for active employees:	
Member contributions	5,783,000
Employer-financed contributions	11,565,000
Total fund balance	$24,100,000

[9]In November 1994, the GASB issued *Statement No. 25*, "Financial Reporting for Defined Benefit Pension Plans and Note Disclosures for Defined Contribution Plans." *Statement No. 25* changes the format for the balance sheet of a defined benefit PERS for fiscal years beginning after June 15, 1996. This statement together with other pronouncements regarding pension accounting and reporting are discussed in Chapter 7.

TABLE 2–24   Nonexpendable Trust Fund—Balance Sheet

City of New Example
Nonexpendable Trust Fund
Theodore M. Paige Library Fund
Balance Sheet
December 31, 19X1

Assets

Cash	$ 12,000	
Investments	1,245,000	
Total assets		$1,257,000

Fund Balance

Fund balance	$1,257,000

TABLE 2–25   Expendable Trust Fund—Balance Sheet

City of New Example
Expendable Trust Fund
Kathy Ledoux Nursing Education Fund
Balance Sheet
December 31, 19X1

Assets

Cash	$ 2,000	
Investments	345,000	
Total assets		$347,000

Fund Balance

Fund balance	$347,000

TABLE 2–26   Agency Fund—Balance Sheet

City of New Example
Agency Fund
Property Tax Fund
Balance Sheet
December 31, 19X1

Assets

Property taxes receivable	$2,400,000

Liabilities

Due to other funds	$2,400,000

TABLE 2–27   Pension Trust Funds—Statement of Revenues, Expenses, and Changes in Fund Balance

City of New Example
Pension Trust Fund
City Employees' Retirement Fund
Statement of Revenues, Expenses,
and Changes in Fund Balance
For the Year Ended December 31, 19X1

Operating revenues	
Member contributions	$2,500,000
Employer contributions	2,500,000
Investment income	1,000,000
Total operating revenues	6,000,000
Operating expenses	
Annuity benefits	2,500,000
Disability benefits	1,000,000
Administrative expenses	200,000
Total operating expenses	3,700,000
Net operating income	2,300,000
Fund balance at beginning of year	21,800,000
Fund balance at end of year	$24,100,000

TABLE 2–28   Nonexpendable Trust Fund—Statement of Revenues, Expenses, and Changes in Fund Balance

City of New Example
Nonexpendable Trust Fund
Theodore M. Paige Library Fund
Statement of Revenues, Expenses,
and Changes in Fund Balance
For the Year Ended December 31, 19X1

Revenues	
Interest and other investment income	$ 65,000
Net income	65,000
Fund balance at beginning of year	1,192,000
Fund balance at end of year	$1,257,000

TABLE 2–29   Expendable Trust Fund—Statement of Revenues, Expenditures,and Changes in Fund Balance

City of New Example
Expendable Trust Fund
Kathy LeDoux Nursing Education Fund
Statement of Revenues, Expenditures,
and Changes in Fund Balance
For the Year Ended December 31, 19X1

Revenues	
Interest and other investment income	$ 17,000
Expenditures	
Nursing services	15,000
Excess of revenues over expenditures	2,000
Fund balance at begining of year	345,000
Fund balance at end of year	$347,000

TABLE 2–30   Agency Fund—Statement of Changes in Assets and Liabilities

City of New Example
Agency Fund
Property Tax Fund
Statement of Changes in Assets and Liabilities
For the Year Ended December 31, 19X1

	Balance December 31, 19X0	Increases	Decreases	Balance December 31, 19X1
Assets				
Property taxes receivable	$2,500,000	$9,000,000	$9,100,000	$2,400,000
Liabilities				
Due to other funds	$2,500,000	$9,000,000	$9,100,000	$2,400,000

addition to a balance sheet and an operating statement. Since the construction of this statement is beyond the scope of this text, we have only illustrated the appropriate statement. A statement of cash flows must be prepared for Nonexpendable Trust Funds (see Table 2–31). It is not required for Pension Trust Funds.

TABLE 2–31   Nonexpendable Trust Fund—Statement of Cash Flows

City of New Example
Nonexpendable Trust Fund
Theodore M. Paige Library Fund
Statement of of Cash Flows
For the Year Ended December 31, 19X1

INCREASE (DECREASE) IN CASH

Cash flows from investing activities:	
Cash received from interest and other in-	
vestment income	$ 65,000
Proceeds from sale of investments	345,000
Purchase of investments	(415,000)
Net cash used in investing activities	(5,000)
Cash at beginning of year	17,000
Cash at end of year	$12,000
Reconciliation of investing income to net cash provided by investing activities:	
Operating income	$ 65,000
Adjustments to reconcile investing income to net cash provided by investing activities:	
Increase in investments	(70,000)
Net cash used by investing activities	$ (5,000)

REVIEW QUESTIONS

Section I

Q2–1   What are the reporting objectives of state and local governmental units as identified by the Governmental Accounting Standards Board?

Q2–2   Define *fund* as the term is used in governmental accounting.

Q2–3   How does the focus of governmental-type funds differ from that of proprietary-type funds?

Q2–4   How do the interests of the users of commercial accounting data differ from the interests of the users of governmental accounting data?

Q2–5   Compare the timing of revenue and expense or expenditure recognition in the full accrual basis with that in the modified accrual basis of accounting.

Q2–6   Why do governmental entities generally use the modified accrual basis of accounting?

Q2–7   Which funds use the modified accrual basis of accounting?

Q2–8   Which funds use the accrual basis of accounting?

Section II

Q2–9   List the governmental-type funds and briefly describe the use of each.

Q2–10 The controller for the city of Walla Walla recently made the following comment: ". . . however, as a minimum, we could run city government with the use of only one fund." Do you agree with this statement? Why or why not?

Q2–11 Special Revenue Funds and the General Fund are identical in accounting treatment. When are Special Revenue Funds used instead of the General Fund, and what purpose do they serve?

Q2–12 Why are some fixed assets recorded in the General Fixed Assets Account Group?

Q2–13 What type of debt is recorded in the General Long-Term Debt Account Group?

Section III

Q2–14 List the proprietary-type funds and briefly describe the use of each.

Q2–15 Why do Enterprise Funds and Internal Service Funds use full accrual accounting?

Q2–16 What are restricted assets?

Q2–17 What is the difference between an Enterprise Fund and an Internal Service Fund?

Section IV

Q2–18 List the fiduciary-type funds and briefly describe the use of each.

Q2–19 Do Agency Funds have a fund balance? Why or why not?

Q2–20 What type of activity statement is prepared for Agency Funds?

CASES

C2–1   Rollin N. Money wishes to establish a fund that will provide children of police and fire personnel killed on the job a college education. Mr. Money contracted you as a government employee and asked you to provide information about how he might achieve his goal. He is very concerned with security over the initial gift and control over the use of any income from the gift. He wants the gift to be a permanent one and the income to be spent for the purpose identified above. A friend of Mr. Money's suggested that he require the establishment of a Special Revenue Fund because the gift and its income would be maintained separate from the other governmental resources.

How would you advise Mr. Money?

C2–2 The newly elected mayor of New Example recently received a copy of the city's annual report. After reviewing the many pages of this report, she feels that the city would be in a better financial position if it privatized its motor pool operations. Privatization would require the city to dispose of the vehicles it now has and hire a private firm to operate the motor pool.

The main objection the mayor has is that the Motor Pool Fund had a loss last year of $54,500. This resulted in the city having to provide a subsidy of $60,000.

Financial statements for the motor pool are contained in Tables 2–17 through 2–19.

How would you advise the mayor of New Example?

C2–3 During a heated campaign for mayor of Megatropolis, an unsuccessful candidate boasted that he would "do away with all the special interests in government. I will abolish all of the Special Revenue Funds and merge that money with the general operating resources of the city." You were the successful candidate in that race and now the local press is pressuring you to respond to the campaign promise of that other candidate.

How would you respond to the press?

EXERCISES

Section I

E2–1 (Compare cash and accrual basis of accounting)

An organization incurred the following transactions:
1. Provided services on credit
2. Incurred cost of materials used to provide the services in part (1)
3. Received payment for services rendered in part (1)
4. Paid for materials used in part (2)

REQUIRED: Compare the different treatment given to each of the transactions above using the cash and the accrual basis of accounting.

E2–2 (Matching—general terminology)

Match the terms on the left with the descriptions on the right by placing the appropriate letter in the space provided (use each letter only once).

_____ 1. Governmental fund type

_____ 2. Fund categories

_____ 3. Definition of a fund

_____ 4. Capital maintenance

_____ 5. Basis of accounting

_____ 6. Recognition of revenue when resources are available and measurable

_____ 7. Available

_____ 8. Expenditure

_____ 9. Spending activities

_____ 10. To evaluate operating results

a. Focus for proprietary-type funds and some fiduciary-type funds

b. Type of fund that accounts for general governmental operations

c. An objective of accounting for governmental units

d. A fiscal and accounting entity with a self-balancing set of accounts

e. Governmental, proprietary, fiduciary

f. Refers to the timing of the recognition of revenues and expenses or expenditures

g. Focus for governmental-type funds and some fiduciary-type funds

h. Modified accrual

i. Collectible within the current period or soon enough thereafter to be used to pay the liabilities of the current period

j. Cash payment for services in a modified accrual accounting system

E2–3 (Explanation of reporting objectives)

The Governmental Accounting Standards Board identified three major reporting objectives for state and local governmental units. Identify each of these objectives and explain how each might be achieved.

E2–4 (Fill-in-the-blanks—general terminology)

1. A _____ is a fiscal and accounting entity with a self-balancing set of accounts.

2. The spending measurement focus is used for _____ funds.

3. The basis of accounting refers to the _____ of the recognition of revenues and expenses (expenditures).

4. In 19X2 Water City collected revenue that was earned in 19X1. The entry to record the collection would include a credit to _____ .

5. In 19X1 Review City recorded an expenditure that was incurred but would not be paid in cash until 19X2. The entry to record the expenditure in 19X1 would include a credit to _____ .

Section II

E2–5 (Fund definitions through examples)

For each of the following situations, indicate which fund and/or account group would be used to report the transaction.

1. Payments made to a contractor on a bridge project that requires separate accounting.
2. The city paid salaries to employees of the Department of Safety.
3. The city collected a special tax that is dedicated to maintaining parks and playgrounds.
4. The Department of Streets purchased materials to be used to repair roads.
5. The General Fund acquired a mainframe computer.
6. The General Fund made its annual contribution to a bond retirement fund.
7. The city acquired land for bridge approaches. This project is part of the project mentioned in part (1).

E2–6 (Use of funds)

The mayor of New West Wall wanted to simplify the accounting system used by the town. He approached you with the following task: reduce the number of funds used in our governmental-type funds. How might you achieve this purpose?

E2–7 (Fill-in-the blanks—general terminology)

1. A _____ is used to identify a portion of a fund balance that is not available for current use.
2. A governmental unit may have _____ (one or more than one) General Fund.
3. Accounting for a _____ is the same as that of the General Fund.
4. _____ Funds are used to account for the receipt and disbursement of resources used to acquire major capital facilities.
5. The _____ is used to control property-type assets used by the general operations of the governmental unit.
6. Payments of principal and interest of general obligation governmental debt are generally recorded in a _____ .

E2–8 (Journal entries and their effect on financial statements)

The controller of the city of Watertite is currently making the final adjusting entries before the financial statements are prepared for the fiscal year ending June 30, 19X2. The balance in the Fund balance account of the General Fund is $507,000. During the year the General Fund advanced $100,000 to the Capital Projects Fund in order to begin the construction of a new city hall. This amount will be repaid in three years when the project has been completed.

REQUIRED:
1. Prepare any necessary entry or entries related to the above facts. Assume that the city had made no entries regarding this event.
2. If you did not make an entry for requirement 1, explain why. If you did make an entry for requirement 1, explain the effect on the financial statements of the General Fund.

Section III

E2–9   (Use of funds)

The city council has asked you to explain why the accounting records for proprietary-type funds use a different basis of accounting than the governmental-type funds. Write the explanation that you would provide to the council.

E2–10   (Fill-in-the-blanks—general terminology)

1.   Three financial statements required for proprietary funds are

_____ , _____ , and

_____ .

2.   The two funds included in the proprietary-type funds are

_____ and _____ .

3.   The basis of accounting used for proprietary-type funds is

_____ .

4.   Assets that are limited in use for a specific purpose are generally referred to as _____ .

5.   The equity section of a proprietary-type fund contains

_____ and _____ .

E2–11   (Matching—use of funds)

Using the following codes, indicate which description best fits the funds listed by placing the code in the space provided.

General Fund	GF
Special Revenue Fund	SRF
Capital Projects Fund	CPF
Debt Service Fund	DSF
Enterprise Fund	EF
Internal Service Fund	ISF

_____   1.   Services are provided to the general public and the costs of providing the services are financed by user charges.

_____   2.   Resources are accumulated to pay principal and interest on general long-term debt.

_____   3.   Accounting for the police department activities.

_____   4.   Goods or services are furnished to other segments of the governmental unit on a user charge basis.

_____   5.   Acquisition and use of resources provided by the U.S. government for a particular purpose.

_____   6.   Expenditures are made by the city's streets department.

_____   7.   A "net income" figure is computed each year.

E2–12   (Fund definitions through examples)

For each of the following situations, indicate which fund and/or account group would be used to report the transaction.

1. A city-owned electric utility sent bills to the city and a separate school board.
2. The General Fund made a periodic payment to a city-owned electric utility as a subsidy of its rates.
3. The city issued property tax bills. These are expected to be collected within the accounting year.
4. The city purchased new police cars.
5. The city paid the principal and interest on a bond issue from resources that were accumulated for the purpose of making the payment.
6. A centralized purchasing facility billed the general city operations for part of the cost of the purchasing operations.
7. The city levied a special hotel tax. This tax is dedicated to paying interest on outstanding debt.

Section IV

E2–13 (Use of funds)

For each of the following independent situations, write a short paragraph describing a specific set of circumstances that would require use of the funds listed.
1. A Nonexpendable Trust Fund *and* an Expendable Trust Fund
2. An Agency Fund
3. A Special Revenue Fund
4. A Capital Projects Fund
5. An Expendable Trust Fund
6. An Enterprise Fund

E2–14 (Fund definitions through examples)

For each of the following situations, indicate which fund and/or account group would be used to report the transaction.
1. A city-owned airport sent bills to various airlines and the mayor's office.
2. The city made an annual payment to the Motor Pool Fund to subsidize its operations.
3. The city issued property tax bills. These are expected to be collected within the accounting year.
4. The city acquired a new computer for its accounting system. Assume the accounting function is included in the General Fund.
5. The city levied a gasoline tax for the purpose of maintaining streets. Assume the tax requires a separate accounting.
6. The city paid the principal and interest on a bond issue from resources that were accumulated for that purpose.

E2–15 (Reporting for fiduciary-type funds)

Listed below are several types of fiduciary funds and several financial statement classifications used in those funds. Match the fund type with the financial statement classifications that would probably be found on the statements for that fund type:

Pension Trust Fund	PTF
Nonexpendable Trust Fund	NTF
Expendable Trust Fund	ETF
Agency Fund	AF

_____ 1. Net assets available for benefits
_____ 2. Amounts owed to contractors in a bid deposits fund
_____ 3. Investments whose principal must be maintained intact
_____ 4. Annuity benefits
_____ 5. Actuarial present value of projected benefits payable to current retirants and beneficiaries
_____ 6. Fund balance
_____ 7. Member contributions

E2–16   (Summary of general reporting)

For each of the following funds and account groups, check the items that would probably be appropriate regarding their financial statements.

FUND/ACCOUNT GROUP	EXPENDITURES	NET INCOME	RESTRICTED ASSETS	REVENUES	STATEMENT OF CHANGES IN ASSETS AND LIABILITIES
General Fund					
Special Revenue Fund					
Debt Service Fund					
Capital Projects Fund					
Enterprise Fund					
Internal Service Fund					
Pension Trust Fund					
Nonexpendable Trust Fund					
Expendable Trust Fund					
Agency Fund					
General Fixed Assets Account Group					
General Long-Term Debt Account Group					

PROBLEMS

Section I

P2–1 (Conceptual section review)
Answer each of the following questions.
1. How does the use of funds in governmental accounting differ from the way business organizations maintain their accounting records?
2. Why is the accrual basis of accounting preferable to the cash basis of accounting?
3. How do expenditures differ from expenses?
4. What is generally required for recognition of revenues under the modified accrual basis of accounting?
5. If you had to develop an accounting system for a governmental unit, would you use the modified accrual basis or the full accrual basis of accounting? Why?

P2–2 (Identification of fund categories)
Identify and differentiate between the three types of fund categories used in governmental accounting. Include in your discussion factors such as use, measurement focus, and basis of accounting.

P2–3 (Differentiation between accrual and cash basis accounting)
Explain what *basis of accounting* means, and identify at least two differences between the accrual basis of accounting and the cash basis of accounting.

P2–4 (Journal entries—cash vs. accrual basis of accounting)

3/4/X1	Performed services for $3,000. This amount was received in cash.
3/7/X1	Incurred expenses totaling $500. This amount was paid in cash.
3/12/X1	Performed services for $2,400. This amount will be collected during the following month.
3/18/X1	Incurred expenses totaling $1,000. This amount will be paid next month.
4/12/X1	Collected the amount due from the 3/12/X1 transaction.
4/18/X1	Paid the amount due from the 3/18/X1 transaction.

REQUIRED: Record the following events assuming (1) the cash basis of accounting and (2) the accrual basis of accounting. If no entry is required, write "none" next to the date.

Section II

P2–5 (Comparison of financial statements)
Review the balance sheet and the operating statement for the General Fund (Tables 2–5 and 2–6) and the balance sheet and the operating statement for the Green River Bridge Fund (Tables 2–11 and 2–12). Identify the major similarities and differences between each type of statement and the types of activities in which each fund is involved.

P2–6   (Conceptual section review)

Answer each of the following questions.

1. What is the relationship between the governmental-type funds and the account groups?

2. Explain how the fund balance of a governmental-type fund represents available spendable resources.

3. Special Revenue Funds, Capital Projects Funds, and Debt Service Funds are similar in nature. Explain this similarity.

4. Why do governmental units use Special Revenue Funds, Capital Projects Funds, and Debt Service Funds?

5. What type of debt is recorded in the General Long-Term Debt Account Group?

P2–7   (Identification of activities recorded in governmental-type funds)

Using *only* the governmental-type funds and account groups, indicate which would be used to record each of the following events.

General Fund	GF
Special Revenue Fund	SRF
Debt Service Fund	DSF
Capital Projects Fund	CPF
General Fixed Assets Account Group	CFAAG
General Long-Term Debt Account Group	GLTDAG

_____   1. Money is transferred from the General Fund to the Debt Service Fund.

_____   2. The city received its share of the state sales tax. The entire amount is legally required to be used to improve the library facilities.

_____   3. General property taxes are levied by the city.

_____   4. The city purchased a fire engine.

_____   5. Property taxes were collected.

_____   6. The city received a grant from the state to build an addition to the city hall.

_____   7. The city issued general obligation bonds to finance the construction of new police stations.

_____   8. The mayor was paid his monthly salary.

_____   9. Expenses for the operation of the police department were recorded.

_____ 10. A new bridge across the Red River was constructed.

_____ 11. Tax monies were collected. These amounts were legally required to be used to maintain the city park system.

_____ 12. General governmental revenues were transferred to the fund that accumulates money to retire general long-term debt.

_____ 13. General governmental revenues were transferred to the City Hall Construction Fund.

_____ 14. A contractor received partial payment for the work done on the new city hall.

_____ 15. The city workers were paid their weekly salaries.

_____ 16. Outstanding bonds were retired, using monies accumulated for that purpose.

_____ 17. A federal grant was received to help pay for the cost of constructing the new city hall.

P2–8   (Statement preparation—General Fund)

Using the following data, prepare a statement of revenues, expenditures, and changes in fund balance for the General Fund of the City of Sertville for the calendar year ended December 31, 19X1.

Miscellaneous revenues	$ 180,000
Licenses and permits revenues	2,000,000
Expenditures for education	3,000,000
Expenditures for corrections	1,400,000
Operating transfers to other funds	1,500,000
Tax revenues	7,000,000
Expenditures for welfare	2,100,000
Federal grants	3,000,000
Expenditures for public safety	750,000
Expenditures for highways	900,000
Operating transfers from other funds	700,000
Fund balance of beginning of year	3,500,000

Section III

P2–9   (Comparison of financial statements)

Review the balance sheet and the operating statement for the General Fund (Tables 2–5 and 2–6) and the balance sheet and the operating statement for the Sewerage and Water Fund (Tables 2–20 and 2–21). Identify the major similarities and differences between each type of statement and the types of activities in which each fund is involved.

P2–10   (Conceptual section review)

Answer each of the following questions.

1. If you were setting up the accounting system for a governmental unit, what type of fund would you use for a municipal clinic? Why?

2. If you were setting up the accounting system for a governmental unit, what type of fund would you use for a centralized computing system? Why?

3. What is a subsidy and how does it enter into the accounting process for an Internal Service Fund? For an Enterprise Fund?

4. Several small governmental units decided to pool their resources and build a regional airport. What type of fund would you recommend for the airport? Why?

5. What sources of capital would you expect to find on the balance sheet of the Electric Utility Fund for the City of Plainville?

P2–11 (Identification of activities recorded in governmental- and proprietary-type funds)

Using the governmental- and proprietary-type funds and the account groups, indicate which would be used to record each of the following events.

General Fund	GF
Special Revenue Fund	SRF
Debt Service Fund	DSF
Capital Projects Fund	CPF
Enterprise Fund	EF
Internal Service Fund	ISF
General Fixed Assets Account Group	GFAAG
General Long-Term Debt Account Group	GLTDAG

_____ 1. Revenue bonds were issued by the Electric Utility Fund to build a new plant.

_____ 2. The Motor Pool Fund loaned $50,000 to the Central Purchasing Fund.

_____ 3. The Electric Utility Fund billed the General Fund for its share of the electricity cost.

_____ 4. The city charter required all hotel taxes to be accounted for in a separate fund. The collections for the period totaled $500,000.

_____ 5. The mayor was paid her salary.

_____ 6. Special assessment–type debt was issued to finance a street lighting project. (The city guaranteed this debt.)

_____ 7. Electric utility revenue bonds were retired.

_____ 8. General obligation city debt was retired, using resources previously accumulated for that purpose.

_____ 9. The city electric utility retired bonds.

_____ 10. Special assessments were levied to service the debt that was incurred to pay for a street-paving project. (The city guaranteed this debt.)

_____ 11. The General Fund made its annual contribution to the fund that pays principal and interest on outstanding debt.

_____ 12. The city acquired land as part of a city hall expansion program. The resources used to acquire the land were provided by a general obligation bond issue.

_____ 13. The Motor Pool Fund billed each department in the city for use of vehicles (assume all departments billed were accounted for in the General Fund).

_____ 14. The police department salaries were paid.

_____ 15. The city sold some of its excess properties (assume the revenue is accounted for in the General Fund).

P2–12   (Correcting a trial balance)

The bookkeeper of Clearview City has recently quit. The clerks working in the records department prepared the trial balance, based on the information in the accounts.

Clearview City
Enterprise Fund
Waldon Swimming Pool Fund
Trial Balance
June 30, 19X1

Cash	$ 210,000	
Prepaid expenses	1,400	
Accounts receivable	303,164	
Supplies inventory	6,000	
Due from other funds	-0-	
Property, plant, and equipment	8,189,655	
Accumulated depreciation		$2,500,000
Accounts payable		681,786
Due to other funds		74,000
Customer advanced for construction		-0-
Revenue bonds payable		396,000
Contributed capital		2,000,000
Retained earnings		3,121,048
Revenue		1,147,705
Operating expenses	748,120	
Administrative expenses	257,400	
Maintenance expenses	204,800	
	$9,920,539	$9,920,539

Your review of the financial records revealed the following:

1. Accounts payable included the following:

    Due to other funds $10,000

2. Accounts receivable includes $100 that is actually a receivable from other governmental funds.
3. Supplies of $300 purchased on credit and received on June 27, 19X1, were not recorded in the accounting records.
4. Depreciation was not recorded for 19X1. The proper amount was $100,000. Assume that the city treats depreciation as an operating expense.
5. The General Fund owes $500 for services rendered in 19X1. The previous bookkeeper recorded revenue from the General Fund only when cash was received; therefore the $500 has not been recorded.

REQUIRED: Prepare an adjusted trial balance for the Waldon Swimming Pool Fund.

Section IV

P2–13 (Comparison of financial statements)

Review the balance sheet and the operating statement for the Theodore M. Paige Library Trust Fund (Tables 2–24 and 2–28) and the balance sheet and the activity statement for the Property Tax Fund (Tables 2–26 and 2–30). Identify the major similarities and differences between each type of statement and the types of activities in which each fund is involved.

P2–14 (Transactions involving all funds and account groups)

Indicate which fund(s) and/or account group(s) would be used to record each of the following events. Use the codes listed below:

General Fund	GF
Special Revenue Fund	SRF
Debt Service Fund	DSF
Capital Projects Fund	CPF
Enterprise Fund	EF
Internal Service Fund	ISF
Pension Trust Fund	PTF
Nonexpendable Trust Fund	NTF
Expendable Trust Fund	ETF
Agency Fund	AF
General Fixed Assets Account Group	GFAAG
General Long-Term Debt Account Group	GLTDAG

_____ 1. The city made a contribution to the employees' retirement fund.

_____ 2. Taxes that are dedicated to street repairs were collected. The ordinance establishing the tax requires a separate accounting for these monies.

_____ 3. The contractors who were building a bridge were paid.

_____ 4. General governmental revenues were transferred to the fund that accumulates money to retire general long-term debt.

_____ 5. The salary of the chief of police was paid.

_____ 6. The central purchasing fund sent out bills for purchases to the police and fire departments and to the city airport.

_____ 7. The city received a gift from a citizen in the form of a trust. The money must be used to provide concerts for local youth groups.

_____ 8. Bonds were issued to finance the construction of a new library.

_____ 9. The police department purchased ten police cars.

_____ 10. Sales taxes were collected.

_____ 11. The city sold some of its excess office equipment. The proceeds from the sale were to be used for general city operations.

_____ 12. General obligation bonds were retired, using monies accumulated in a fund.

_____ 13. The city-owned airport is accounted for as a separate fund. This fund issues bonds to finance airport improvements.

_____ 14. The city uses a separate fund to account for its central purchasing function. Supplies were purchased from this fund.

_____ 15. A wealthy citizen donated securities to the city. The principal amount donated must remain intact and the income must be spent to provide free food to the elderly.

P2–15 (Multiple choice)

1. The liability for special assessment bonds that carry a secondary pledge of a municipality's general credit should be recorded in
   a. An Enterprise Fund
   b. A Special Revenue Fund and the General Long-Term Debt Account Group
   c. A Special Assessment Fund and the General Long-Term Debt Account Group
   d. A Special Assessment Fund and disclosed in a footnote in the Statement of General Long-Term Debt
   e. None of the above

2. The proceeds of a federal grant made to assist in financing the future construction of an adult training center should be recorded in
   a. The General Fund
   b. A Special Revenue Fund
   c. A Capital Projects Fund
   d. A Special Assessment Fund
   e. None of the above

3. The receipts from a special tax levy to retire and pay interest on general obligation bonds issued to finance the construction of a new city hall should be recorded in
   a. A Debt Service Fund
   b. A Capital Projects Fund
   c. A Revolving Interest Fund
   d. A Special Revenue Fund
   e. None of the above

4. Several years ago, a city provided for the establishment of a Debt Service Fund to retire an issue of general obligation bonds. This year the city made a $50,000 contribution to the Debt Service Fund from general revenues and realized $15,000 in revenue from securities in the Debt Service Fund. The bonds due this year were retired. These transactions require accounting recognition in
   a. The General Fund
   b. A Debt Service Fund and the General Long-Term Debt Account Group
   c. A Debt Service Fund, the General Fund, and the General Long-Term Debt Account Group

     d. A Capital Projects Fund, a Debt Service Fund, the General Fund, and the General Long-Term Debt Account Group

     e. None of the above

5. The activities of a central motor pool that provides and services vehicles for the use of municipal employees on official business should be accounted for in

     a. An Agency Fund

     b. The General Fund

     c. An Internal Service Fund

     d. A Special Revenue Fund

     e. None of the above

6. A transaction in which a municipal electric utility paid $150,000 out of its earnings for new equipment requires accounting recognition in

     a. An Enterprise Fund

     b. The General Fund

     c. The General Fund and the General Fixed Assets Account Group

     d. An Enterprise Fund and the General Fixed Assets Account Group

     e. None of the above

7. Which of the following funds of a governmental unit uses the General Fixed Assets Account Group to account for fixed assets?

     a. Internal Service

     b. Nonexpendable Trust

     c. Enterprise

     d. General Fund

8. Which of the following funds of a governmental unit uses the modified accrual basis of accounting?

     a. Internal Service

     b. Enterprise

     c. Nonexpendable Trust

     d. Debt Service

9. Under the modified accrual basis of accounting for a governmental unit, revenues should be recognized in the accounting period in which they

     a. Become available and earned

     b. Become available and measurable

     c. Are earned and become measurable

     d. Are collected

10. Which governmental fund would account for fixed assets in a manner similar to a for-profit organization?

     a. Enterprise

     b. Capital Projects

     c. General Fixed Assets Account Group

     d. General

(AICPA adapted)

P2–16   (Multiple choice)
1.   The fixed assets of a central purchasing and stores department organized to serve all municipal departments should be recorded in
    a.   An Enterprise Fund and the General Fixed Assets Account Group
    b.   An Enterprise Fund
    c.   The General Fixed Assets Account Group
    d.   The General Fund
    e.   None of the above
2.   The monthly remittance to an insurance company of the lump sum of hospital-surgical insurance premiums collected as payroll deductions from employees should be recorded in
    a.   The General Fund
    b.   An Agency Fund
    c.   A Special Revenue Fund
    d.   An Internal Service Fund
    e.   None of the above
3.   The activities of a municipal employee retirement plan that is financed by equal employer and employee contributions should be accounted for in
    a.   An Agency Fund
    b.   An Internal Service Fund
    c.   A Special Assessment Fund
    d.   A Trust Fund
    e.   None of the above
4.   A transaction in which a municipal electric utility issues bonds (to be repaid from its own operations) requires accounting recognition in
    a.   The General Fund
    b.   A Debt Service Fund
    c.   Enterprise and Debt Service Funds
    d.   An Enterprise Fund, a Debt Service Fund, and the General Long-Term Debt Account Group
    e.   None of the above
5.   The operations of a public library receiving most of its support from property taxes levied for that purpose should be accounted for in
    a.   The General Fund
    b.   A Special Revenue Fund
    c.   An Enterprise Fund
    d.   An Internal Service Fund
    e.   None of the above

6. The liability for general obligation bonds issued for the benefit of a municipal electric company and serviced by its earnings should be recorded in
   a. An Enterprise Fund
   b. The General Fund
   c. An Enterprise Fund and the General Long-Term Debt Account Group
   d. An Enterprise Fund and disclosed in a footnote in the Statement of General Long-Term Debt
   e. None of the above

7. To provide for the retirement of general obligation bonds, a city invests a portion of its general revenue receipts in marketable securities. This investment activity should be accounted for in
   a. A Trust Fund
   b. An Enterprise Fund
   c. A Special Assessment Fund
   d. A Special Revenue Fund
   e. None of the above

8. The operations of a municipal swimming pool receiving the majority of its support from charges to users should be accounted for in
   a. A Special Revenue Fund
   b. The General Fund
   c. An Internal Service Fund
   d. An Enterprise Fund
   e. None of the above

9. A city collects property taxes for the benefit of the local sanitary, park, and school districts and periodically remits collections to these units. This activity should be accounted for in
   a. An Agency Fund
   b. The General Fund
   c. An Internal Service Fund
   d. A Special Assessment Fund
   e. None of the above

10. Bay Creek's municipal motor pool maintains all city-owned vehicles and charges the various departments for the cost of rendering those services. In which of the following funds should Bay Creek account for the cost of such maintenance?
    a. A General Fund
    b. An Internal Service Fund
    c. A Special Revenue Fund
    d. A Special Assessment Fund
    e. None of the above

(AICPA adapted)

P2–17   (Financial statements used in governmental accounting)

Indicate which of the following financial statements generally would be used by each of the funds/account groups listed.

Balance sheet	BS
Operating statement	OS
Statement of cash flows	SCF
Schedule of general fixed assets	SGFA
Schedule of general long-term debt	SGLD
Schedule of changes in general fixed assets	SCGFA
Schedule of changes in general long-term debt	SCGLD
Statement of changes in assets and liabilities	SCAL

_____   1. General Fund
_____   2. Special Revenue Funds
_____   3. Debt Service Funds
_____   4. Capital Projects Funds
_____   5. Enterprise Funds
_____   6. Internal Service Funds
_____   7. Pension Trust Funds
_____   8. Nonexpendable Trust Funds
_____   9. Expendable Trust Funds
_____ 10. Agency Funds
_____ 11. General Fixed Assets Account Group
_____ 12. General Long-Term Debt Account Group

3

THE BUDGETARY PROCESS

LEARNING OBJECTIVES

After completion of this chapter, you should be able to:

1. Discuss three types of budgets used by governmental units
2. Explain why budgets of governmental units are legal documents and describe the contents of a typical budget law
3. Contrast four approaches to budgeting
4. List the steps involved in preparing a budget
5. Prepare a revenue forecast
6. Use a trend analysis to project future revenues
7. Prepare an operating budget for a small governmental unit
8. Discuss the contents of a budget document
9. Calculate the millage rate used by a governmental unit
10. Explain how budgets are used to control operations of governmental units

In Chapter 1 we pointed out that commercial organizations are driven by one overriding goal, maximization of profits, while governmental units have many goals, all of which are considered important by their supporters and all of which compete for scarce resources. For example, a governmental unit may support police protection at the expense of street maintenance. Or it may determine that it will use available monies to support public housing, even though it needs to fund a program of economic development.

We also pointed out in Chapter 1 that while commercial organizations are governed by boards of directors and managers who generally hold similar views as to what activities should be conducted and how these activities should be conducted, governmental units are governed by elected bodies representing diverse constituencies. Thus, by their very nature governmental units are faced with competing goals and a high level of politicalization in the allocation of resources. Chaos and/or allocation of resources by means of brute power is prevented by the budgetary process.

A **budget** is a formal estimate of the resources that an organization *plans* to expend for a given purpose of over a given period, and the proposed means of acquiring these resources. It informs the reader of what activities the organization plans to undertake and how the organization expects to finance these activities; and thus it acts as a standard against which efficiency and effectiveness can be measured. It also acts as a representation of public policy in that its adoption implies that certain objectives, as well as the means of accomplishing these objectives, have been determined by the legislative body. In addition to serving as a framework for operations, the budget often acts as a legal document for certain types of organizations, principally governmental units, as it forms the basis for the appropriations made by legislative bodies of these organizations.

Even if not required by law, the use of a budget is strongly recommended. The GASB, for example, expresses the need for budgets in the following principles:

a. An annual budget(s) should be adopted by every governmental unit.
b. The accounting system should provide the basis for appropriate budgetary control.
c. Budgetary comparisons should be included in the appropriate financial statements and schedules for governmental funds for which an annual budget has been adopted.[1]

In this chapter we will discuss some types of budgets and approaches to budgeting, as well as the process of preparing a budget.

BUDGET LAWS

States usually have laws governing budgetary activities of local governmental units located within their borders. These laws deal with types of budgets to be prepared, funds required to have budgets, definition of a "balanced" budget, public input into the budgetary process, and means of putting the budget into effect. Table 3–1 contains excerpts from the budget law of the state of Louisiana.

To encourage fiscal responsibility, the Louisiana Local Government Budget Act, like budget laws of nearly all states, requires a balanced budget. In most

---

[1]GASB Cod. Sec. 1100.109.

TABLE 3–1   Excerpts from Louisiana Local Government Budget Act

§ 1301   SHORT TITLE

This Chapter may be cited as the "Louisiana Local Government Budget Act."

§ 1304   BUDGET PREPARATION

A. Each political subdiivsion shall cause to be prepared a comprehensive budget presenting a complete financial plan for the ensuing fiscal year for the general fund and each special revenue fund.

B. The chief executive or administrative officer of the political subdivision or, in the absence of such positions, the equivalent thereof shall prepare the proposed budget.

C. The budget document setting forth the proposed financial plan for the general fund and each special revenue fund shall include the following:

(1) A budget message signed by the budget preparer which shall include a summary description of the proposed financial plan, policies, and objectives, assumptions, budgetary basis, and a discussion of the most important features.

(2) A consolidated statement for the general fund, each special revenue fund and any other fund, showing estimated fund balances at the beginning of the year; estimates of all receipts and revenues to be received; revenues itemized by source; recommended expenditures itemized by agency, department, function, and character; and the estimated fund balance at the end of the fiscal year. . . .

D. A budget proposed for consideration by the governing authority shall be accompanied by a proposed budget adoption instrument. . . . The budget adoption instrument for any municipality, parish, school board, or special district shall be an appropriate ordinance, adoption resolution, or other legal instrument necessary to adopt and implement the budget document.

E. The total of proposed expenditures shall not exceed the total of estimated funds available for the ensuing fiscal year.

§ 1306   PUBLIC PARTICIPATION

A. Political subdivisions with total proposed expenditures of two hundred fifty thousand dollars or more from the general fund or any special revenue funds shall afford the public an opportunity to participate in the budgetary process prior to adoption of the budget.

B. Upon completion of the proposed budget and, if applicable, its submission to the governing authority, the political subdivision shall cause to be published a notice stating that the proposed budget is available for public inspection. The notice shall state that a public hearing on the proposed budget shall be held with the date, time, and place of the hearing specified in the notice.

§ 1308   ADOPTION

A. All action necessary to adopt and otherwise finalize and implement the budget for an ensuing fiscal year shall be taken in open meeting and completed prior to the end of the fiscal year in progress. . . .

B. The adopted budget shall be balanced with approved expenditures not exceeding the total of estimated funds available.

C. The adopted budget shall contain the same information as that required for the proposed budget. . . .

§ 1310   BUDGETARY AUTHORITY AND CONTROL

A. . . . The chief executive or administrative officer shall advise the governing authority or independently elected official in writing when:

(1) Revenue collection plus projected revenue collections for the remainder of the year, within a fund, are failing to meet estimated annual budgeted revenues by five percent or more.

(2) Actual expenditures plus projected expenditures for the remainder of the year, within a fund, are exceeding estimated budgeted expenditures by five percent or more.

(3) Actual beginning fund balance, within a fund, fails to meet estimated beginning fund balance by five percent or more and fund balance is being used to fund current year expenditures.

Source: Louisiana Local Government Budget Act R.S. 39:1304, as amended.

states a budget is considered to be balanced if proposed expenditures do not exceed estimated monies available the following year. This latter amount is the sum of fund balance at the beginning of the year and estimated revenues. A few states take a more conservative approach to balanced budgets and define them as ones in which estimated revenues equal or exceed proposed expenditures.

TYPES OF BUDGETS

Nonbusiness organizations use many different types of budgets. They use short- and long-term operating budgets, capital budgets, and, in many cases, cash budgets.

Operating Budgets

Operating budgets (also known as current budgets) are general-purpose budgets used by organizations to formalize their activities of a given period, usually a fiscal year. They include estimates of the resources expected to be available during the year and projections of how these resources will be expended.

For many organizations, the use of an operating budget is required by law. Many cities and states also require that by the beginning of each fiscal year, a *balanced* budget (one in which the total of the estimated funds available from the projected revenues and fund balance must be sufficient to meet the anticipated expenditures) be approved by their legislative bodies (e.g., city councils or boards of trustees). Even if not required by law, however, every organization should adopt an annual operating budget to control its expenditures. Preparing the budget in conformity with generally accepted accounting principles (GAAP) will ensure that the accounting records are also prepared in this manner and will make it easier for the organization to prepare monthly and annual budgetary control reports.

Operating budgets are generally prepared for each fund used, as well as for the organization as a whole. Revenues are broken down by source; and expenditures are broken down by type and by department, program, or other operating unit. Actual revenues and expenditures are generally shown for one or two prior years and, if possible, the current year. In addition, the estimated revenues and proposed expenditures of the budget year are shown.

A budget can provide information on the specific purpose of and services performed by each operating unit. It can also provide information on (1) personnel and salaries, (2) proposed bond issues, (3) proposed methods of reducing costs, and (4) the cost of operating specific facilities and providing specific services. Since the budget is often a widely read legal document, great care should go into its preparation. The organization should use it, along with an annual report, as a means of presenting its "story" to the public.

Capital Budgets

Capital budgets (also known as capital programs) are the plans of expenditures, and the means of financing these expenditures, expected to be made for long-lived or "capital" assets, such as land, buildings, and equipment. They usually cover a four- to six-year period. Many organizations maintain a "running" or "continuous" capital budget, adding a future year and dropping the past year when annual revisions are made. Such budgets are very helpful when an organization is attempting to determine when and if it will be necessary to incur debt.

Cash Budgets

Cash budgets are plans of the actual monies expected to be received and expended during a particular period. Since most governmental units use the modified accrual basis of accounting, their operating budgets often do not reflect the actual inflows and outflows of cash. In addition, many governmental units receive a large percentage of their revenues in the latter part of the fiscal year. Since their expenditures are generally spread out evenly over the year, cash shortages often result. Organizations that use cash budgets can anticipate cash shortages and surpluses before they occur. As a result, these organizations are able to obtain more favorable interest rates than organizations that borrow or invest on a "crash" basis. A cash budget is shown in Table 3–2.

APPROACHES TO BUDGETING

Uses of budgets are many and varied. Budgets can serve as contracts (legal documents), control mechanisms, means of communication, planning tools, and bases for the creation of short- and long-term policies. Depending on their intended usage, they can be prepared under one of several approaches: object-of-expenditure, performance, program and planning-programming-budgeting (PPB), or zero-based-budgeting. Budgets prepared under each approach differ as to what type of information is presented and as to how expenditures are aggregated.

The Object-of-Expenditure Approach

The **object-of-expenditure approach** (also known as the traditional or line-item approach) is the most popular approach to budgeting. Under this approach, the budgets that are prepared show, as **line items,** every category of expenditure to be made during the year. For example, the budget of a state-run university might show each faculty and administrative position by salary, by title, and, in many cases, by the name of the person holding that position, as a line item. Supplies used by a particular department, however, would be shown in their entirety, even though several purchases (and expenditures) might be made during the year.

After review and revision by the chief executive officer (CEO) of the organi-

TABLE 3–2   Sample Cash Budget

Tiger City
General Fund
Cash Budget
Second Quarter, 19X1

	APRIL	MAY	JUNE	QUARTER
Beginning cash balance	$ 12,000	$ 10,500	$ 16,350	$ 12,000
Cash receipts:				
Property taxes	$ 83,000	$ 90,000	$ 98,500	$271,500
Sales taxes	95,000	98,000	96,000	289,000
Fixed asset sales	500	—	3,000	3,500
Fines and penalties	15,000	15,000	18,000	48,000
License fees	5,500	3,000	1,600	10,100
Total cash receipts	$199,000	$206,000	$217,100	$622,100
Cash available*	$211,000	$216,500	$233,450	$634,100
Cash disbursements:				
Personal services	$ 56,000	$ 58,000	$ 57,500	$171,500
Travel	2,500	6,000	9,000	17,500
Operating expenses	32,000	36,000	35,500	103,500
Equipment	10,000	40,000	15,000	65,000
Transfers to Capital Projects Funds	200,000	—	12,000	212,000
Transfers to Debt Service Funds	—	50,000	—	50,000
Total disbursements	$300,500	$190,000	$129,000	$619,500
Minimum cash balance	10,000	10,000	10,000	10,000
Total cash required	$310,500	$200,000	$139,000	$629,500
Excess (deficiency) of cash available over cash required	$ (99,500)	$ 16,500	$ 94,450	$ 4,600
Financing:				
Tax anticipation notes	$100,000	—	—	$100,000
Repayment of notes	—	$(10,000)	$(90,000)	(100,000)
Interest	—	(150)	(800)	(950)
Net financing	$100,000	$(10,150)	$(90,800)	$ (950)
Ending cash balance	$ 10,500	$ 16,350	$ 13,650	$ 13,650

*Before financing.

zation, the budget is submitted to the organization's legislative body (e.g., city council, state legislature, board of trustees, and so forth). This body reviews and sometimes revises the budget. After it approves the budget, the legislative body makes line-item appropriations, which are incorporated into the organization's accounts.

Performance or program data may be included with an object-of-expenditure-type budget. Such data, however, are used only to support or supplement the various requests for funding. A portion of an object-of-expenditure budget is shown in Table 3–3.

Among the advantages of the object-of-expenditure approach to budgeting are the following:

1. The budgets are uncomplicated and can easily be prepared.
2. Not only the preparers but also the users can understand the budgets.
3. Information presented in this type of budget can easily be incorporated into the accounting system.
4. Detailed comparisons between budgeted and actual revenues and expenditures can easily be made.

Critics of this approach, however, cite the following points:

1. It provides data useful primarily in the short run. As a result, the long-run goals of the organization may be jeopardized.
2. It is oriented more toward providing a framework for sets of financial records that comply with legal requirements than with providing useful management-type information.
3. It encourages, rather than discourages, spending. Managers are led to believe that an important objective is to spend exactly the amount budgeted and that if this amount is not spent, the following year's appropriation will be cut. As a result, there is little incentive for them to economize.
4. Legislative bodies are given more detail than they can handle. Therefore, they tend to focus on individual items (such as the amount of supplies consumed) rather than on the overall goals and programs of the organization.

In spite of these deficiencies, the object-of-expenditure approach to budgeting is the one most commonly used by nonbusiness organizations. Because of its popularity, it will be discussed in greater detail later in this chapter.

The Performance Approach

Budgets prepared under the **performance approach** emphasize output and efficiency. **Output** is measured in terms of the amount of goods or services produced, the number of cases handled, the number of persons impacted, and so forth. **Efficiency** is usually measured in terms of cost per unit (e.g., persons trained). The main focus of the performance approach to budgeting is the **evaluation of performance.**

The information presented in a performance budget centers on **activities** and **tasks,** rather than on organizational subunits and objects-of-expenditure. Thus, it is possible to include costs incurred by several different departments within one expenditure category and to see the "big picture" at a glance. For example, if several persons from different departments work part time on a particular activity, the portions of their salaries allocable to the activity can be combined and treated as an expenditure of the activity, rather than as expenditures of their individual departments. Under the object-of-expenditure approach, this

TABLE 3–3   Sample Object-of-Expenditure Budget

Orleans Levee Board
FY 19X1 Budget Presentation
Airport Safety

ACCT #	ACCOUNT NAME	PREVIOUS ACTUAL FY 19W9	APPROVED BUDGET FY 19X0	PROPOSED FY 19X1
5410	Office supplies	$ 345	$ 1,572	$ 500
5411	Copier supplies	0	0	0
5412	Computer supplies	0	0	0
5431	Janitorial supplies	130	562	262
5432	Medical supplies	0	750	50
5433	Safety apparel and supplies	5,158	0	5,295
5434	Clothing supplies	8,129	10,875	10,000
5435	Police supplies	1,227	5,050	2,000
5436	Fire fighting supplies	4,507	9,980	6,000
5437	Sodding/herbicides/fertilizer	0	0	0
5440	Improvements—other than buildings	0	0	0
5441	Hardware supplies	210	1,044	300
5442	Mounted patrol	0	0	0
5443	Dive team supplies	0	0	0
5451	Boat/motor/trailer—GOS	0	0	0
5452	Autos/trucks—GOS	8,447	7,706	9,000
5453	Tractors and grass cutters	120	0	0
5461	Buildings	36	0	0
5471	Airfield/runways/taxiway	0	0	0
5472	Bridges/floodgate/floodwall	0	0	0
5473	Grounds	0	0	0
5474	Levees	0	0	0
5475	Emergency supplies	0	0	0
5476	Fountain and pool supplies	0	0	0
5477	Piers, catwalks, bulkheads	0	0	0
5478	Roads, streets, parking lots	0	0	0
5481	Miscellaneous equipment	0	0	0
5482	Autos (parts)	1,809	1,808	1,900
5483	Boats, motors, trailers	49	0	0
5484	Heavy construction equipment	0	0	0
5485	Office equipment—furniture	0	0	0
5486	Police	0	0	0
5487	Radio communications	194	0	0
5488	Recreational	0	0	0
5489	Tractors and grass cutters	0	0	0
5490	Trucks and trailers	0	0	0
5491	Hand tools and minor equipment	273	0	0
	Total material and supplies	$30,634	$39,347	$35,307

Source: A recent budget of the Orleans Levee Board.

grouping is more difficult, since expenditures are recorded by department (or other subunit) and by object-of-expenditure.

Among the advantages of the performance approach to budgeting are the following:

1. Since the budget includes a narrative description of each project, the CEO and the members of the legislative body are well informed as to the goals of and the services provided by the organization.
2. Both input *and* output are measured. The results of each activity are formally monitored, as are the costs incurred in obtaining these results.
3. Emphasis is placed on carrying out the activities of the organization, as well as on controlling costs. As a result, each manager can be evaluated on how well he or she meets certain stated objectives, as well as on how well he or she controls costs.
4. Because of the emphasis on the activities of each subunit and the narrative description of these activities provided in the budget, decision makers can readily see the big picture. That is, they can see how each activity interrelates with other activities can easily spot those activities that duplicate or conflict with other activities.
5. Each subunit of the organization is forced to think through its objectives. The managers of the various subunits are forced to take a close look at each activity and to determine whether it is justified and whether it fits into the overall goals of the organization.

In spite of its many advantages, performance budgeting is not as widely used as object-of-expenditure budgeting. This is because performance budgets are more difficult to prepare and to understand than object-of-expenditure budgets. To use performance budgets effectively requires a staff of accountants and budget analysts. Few nonbusiness organizations can afford such a staff. In addition, many objectives of such organizations are not measurable in quantitative terms (e.g., fire protection). Thus the practical applications of this method of budgeting are somewhat limited.

The Program and Planning-Programming-Budgeting (PPB) Approaches

The **program** approach to budgeting is a *planning-oriented* one which emphasizes programs, activities, and functions rather than evaluation and control. It takes several forms, the best known of which is the *planning-programming-budgeting system* (PPB or PPBS). Under this system, information is presented in the form of budgetary requests and reports on broad programs, rather than in the form of detailed listings of activities and line items.

Before a program budget can be prepared, the fundamental objectives of the organization must be identified. All activities must then be related to these objectives, and the future implications and costs of each activity must be identified. Finally, an analysis of the various alternatives must be performed, and the alternatives that will enable the organization to meet its goals in the most efficient manner, using available resources, must be selected. These alternatives then become the programs that make up the budget.

The PPB approach offers a number of advantages over other approaches to budgeting.

1. It forces users to practice long-range planning on a routine basis and to review and update programs and objectives frequently.
2. It forces various subunits of the organization to coordinate their efforts and resources, since PPB budgets are organized by programs rather than by administrative units.
3. It permits flexibility in the management of the organization, since appropriations are by "lump sum" rather than by line item.
4. It permits an analysis of changes in existing programs, in terms of marginal (additional) costs and benefits. Other approaches to budgeting tend to focus on total or average expenditures.

While PPB has many attractive features, certain realities have limited its acceptance.

1. It is difficult to formulate a set of goals that will be acceptable to all parties involved.
2. Elected officials are often reluctant to commit themselves to policies with long-run payoffs.
3. A great deal of time and money, as well as analytical ability on the part of both preparers *and* users, is required if a sound PPB-type budget is to be prepared and properly used.
4. PPB-type budgets require many long-run estimates of costs and benefits. The use of such estimates makes objective measurement of performance very difficult.

The PPB approach to budgeting was developed by the federal government in the 1950s. It proved unworkable in practice, however, and was discontinued by the Nixon administration. This approach was somewhat more successful when used by certain state and local governmental units, especially after these organizations had modified it to make it more compatible with object-of-expenditure budgeting. Today PPB-type budgets are used by a limited number of organizations to supplement object-of-expenditure-type budgets.

The Zero-Based-Budgeting Approach

The **zero-based-budgeting (ZBB) approach** is one that forces managers to assess the value of and to justify the continuation of each activity under their supervision. Since every activity must be justified each year, the managers, in a sense, start from scratch or "zero"—hence the name "zero-based budgeting."

Zero-based budgeting is a combination of thought and action processes. After a top-to-bottom review, a series of **budget units** is developed. Each unit consists of a description of (1) the project or activity, (2) the expected level of accomplishment, (3) the advantages of retaining the activity, and (4) the consequences of eliminating it, as well as dollar estimates of alternative ways of performing it.

An important aspect of zero-based budgeting is the consideration given to each level of "accomplishment" that is likely to result from an activity. In presenting safety messages, for example, the activity might be the reaching of a television audience. Relevant questions might deal with the demographics of the audience—that is, what type of person is most likely to benefit from the message.

Questions might also be raised as to what effect increasing or decreasing the amount of funding provided to the activity by various increments (e.g., 10 percent, 20 percent, and so on) would have on the level of accomplishment. This step—the dividing of budget units into different levels of accomplishment—results in basic decision units called **decision packages.** A typical decision package is illustrated in Exhibit 3–1.

The final step in the process is to rank the decision packages. Management lists these packages in order of decreasing benefit to the organization, identifies the benefits likely to be derived from various overall levels of spending, and studies the consequences of not approving those decision packages ranked below any given level of spending.

Because of the forced-thought process inherent in ZBB, managers must view their areas of responsibility more completely and more objectively than under other approaches to budgeting. Other benefits of ZBB include:

1. Identification of identical services and activities being performed within a given unit,
2. Emergence of a systematic priority of services, and
3. Matching of costs and benefits at the lowest spending levels.

Benefits, however, do not accrue without costs. Among the disadvantages of ZBB are:

1. The large amount of effort and paperwork required to implement ZBB-type budgets,
2. Resistance on the part of managers and other decision makers to the abandonment of other forms of budgeting, and
3. Inability of many managers to accept the idea of a reduction in the scope of their activities.

Zero-based budgeting is an idea whose time appears to have come and gone. Under the Carter administration, it was instituted in the federal government with much fanfare. It met with a great deal of resistance, however. The idea of curtailing certain governmental activities was unthinkable to many personnel inside and outside of the government. In addition, it was felt that benefits resulting from the use of ZBB did not justify the effort and disruption of routine activities involved in preparing and ranking decision packages. Finally, popular sentiment at this time was moving toward fewer, rather than more, governmental activities. The public was not in the mood for innovations that created more bureaucracy. When the Reagan administration assumed power, ZBB on the federal level became a thing of the past. Its use on the state and local levels also seems to have diminished.

EXHIBIT 3–1   Example of a ZBB Decision Package

ACTIVITY: Television Advertising

PURPOSE OF ACTIVITY: To make television viewers aware of our agency and its services.

EXPECTED LEVEL OF ACCOMPLISHMENT: To reach all TV viewers who might be potential users of our services.

DESCRIPTION OF ACTIVITY:

(1) Design format for commercials.
(2) Select TV stations for presentation.
(3) Decide upon appropriate time period for broadcasting commercials.
(4) Write script.
(5) Present message.
(6) Oversee development of presentation.

ADVANTAGES OF RETAINING ACTIVITY:

(1) Retain complete control over the agency's approach to informing the public.
(2) Cost savings by having in-house function.
(3) Greater flexibility in setting deadlines since only one user (this agency) is seeking the service.

CONSEQUENCES OF ELIMINATING THE ACTIVITY:

(1) Increased costs which might lead to offsetting economies, such as cutting down on TV exposure.
(2) Potential increased creativity through a broader input of ideas from a professional advertising agency.
(3) Consistency of our policies might be threatened.

RESOURCES REQUIRED ($ in thousands):

Sub-activity	FY 19X1	FY 19X2	FY X2/X1
Design format for commrcials	$ 50	$ 52	104%
Select TV stations for presentation	3	4	133%
Select appropriate time periods for commercials	5	6	120%
Write script	50	54	108%
Present messages	80	85	106%
Oversee development of program	36	45	125%
Total	$ 224	$ 246	110%

ALTERNATIVES:

(1) Concentrate on one particular segment of the public (e.g., juvenile) with resulting loss of exposure to other segments. Estimated savings—$30,000.
(2) Hire advertising agency to design format, write script and oversee development of program. A marginal increase in quality and originality should result, along with a loss of control over consistency and adherence to our policies. Estimated cost—$250,000.
(3) Use our employees to present message, with resulting loss of credibility, viewing audience and competitive advantage. Estimated savings—$70,000.

Adapted from Razek, Joseph R. and Daniel Pearl. "Zero-Based Budgeting: An Idea Whose Time Has Come," *Louisiana Business Survey,* 9 (2) Winter 1978): 2–3.

Conclusion

In this section we have discussed the major types of budgets used by nonbusiness organizations—operational, capital, and cash. We have also discussed the four approaches to budgeting most commonly used by these organizations—object-of-expenditure, performance, planning-programming-budgeting (PPB), and zero-based budgeting (ZBB). Table 3–4 compares the four approaches to

TABLE 3–4   Approaches to Budgeting

BUDGETARY PURPOSES	BUDGET FORMAT	FOCUSES MAINLY ON THESE PROGRAM MEASURES
Control *Communication* —tells how many and how much resources will be utilized	Line item/ object-of- expenditure	*Input*
Contract —lets citizens know what products they will receive and the relative efficiency of their government *Management* —provides information that allows managers to assess efficiency of their agency *Communication* —shows basis of estimation —provides information as to what is being produced	Performance	*Efficiency* *Output* —workload —product —program size
Planning —shows the goals and objectives to be achieved *Policy* —allows choice beween different policy goals and between alternative means of reaching these goals *Communication* —shows the purpose of expenditures, the policies and priorities of the government *Contract* —lets citizens see what objectives are achieved	PPB(S) (Program)	*Impact* —measure of effectiveness
Policy —allows choices beween different levels of output associated with each funding level	Zero-based (ZBB)	*Output* —product *Input* —costs Perhaps impact

Source: Blue Wooldridge, "Towards the Development of an Integrated Financial Management System," *Government Accountants' Journal*, 31, no. 3 (1982), 39.

budgeting. Note that each approach is appropriate for a given purpose. Because most nonbusiness organizations are primarily concerned with control and communication, the object-of-expenditure approach is the one most commonly used. We will focus on this approach in the next section.

PREPARING A BUDGET

The preparation of a budget, although difficult at first, becomes easier with practice. After a while it just becomes a matter of "doing it." It can, however, be very time-consuming.

The budgetary process can be broken down into the following steps, the order of which may vary between organizations:

1. Prepare budgetary policy guidelines
2. Prepare a budget calendar
3. Prepare and distribute budget instructions
4. Prepare revenue estimates
5. Prepare departmental (or program) expenditure requests[2]
   a. Personal services work sheet
   b. Travel work sheet
   c. Operating expense work sheet
   d. Equipment work sheet
   e. Capital outlay request summary
6. Prepare nondepartmental expenditure requests
7. Consolidate departmental expenditure requests, nondepartmental expenditure requests, and revenue estimates. Submit to the CEO for review and revision
8. Prepare the budget document.
9. Present the budget document to the legislative body
10. Record the approved budget in the accounts
11. Determine the property tax (millage) rate

Budgetary Policy Guidelines

Before considering the various segments involved in the budgetary process, the CEO, the budget officer, or both should discuss with the members of the legislative body what policies will be followed when preparing the budget. During the these discussions, the fiscal conditions of the current year should be reviewed, along with the prospects for the following year. In addition, the following points should be considered:

1. The level of revenues collected, to date, during the current year, and the level of revenues likely to be collected during the remainder of the year

---

[2]The same procedures are used for both departmental and program expenditure requests. To facilitate this presentation, we will discuss departmental expenditure requests. However, everything said for departmental expenditure requests also applies to expenditure requests prepared for programs.

2. Possible increases or decreases in current taxes and fees, and ideas for new taxes and fees
3. Current and future economic conditions, as well as any possible developments that might affect the revenues or expenditures of the following year (e.g., a plant closing or the loss of federal funds)
4. Items that fall due the following fiscal year and might require an unusually large expenditure, such as the repayment of a bond issue
5. The status of the current year's expenditures and the possibility of a surplus (or deficit)

An analysis of the above issues will provide insight into the financial problems likely to be faced by the organization during the following year. From the discussions of these issues, budgetary policies satisfactory to the legislative body, the CEO, and other affected parties should emerge. These policies should cover, at a minimum

1. Permissible merit salary increases
2. Permissible cost-of-living adjustments
3. Inflationary adjustments to be used
4. Permissible increases or decreases in taxes and fees
5. Changes in capital spending
6. Types of programs and services to be emphasized and deemphasized

The budgetary policies should be disseminated, in the form of **budgetary policy guidelines,** to all persons responsible for preparing and reviewing the various segments of the budget.

Budget Calendar

In order for the budgetary process to proceed in an organized manner, certain deadlines must be met. If each person involved in this process is aware of when his or her part is due and if the time allotted to each task is reasonable, the process should take place smoothly with misunderstandings kept to a minimum. One way to ensure that each person knows when his or her (and everyone else's) part of the budgetary process is due is to prepare a **budget calendar.**

A budget calendar formalizes all key dates in the budgetary process. The calendar itself can be a simple listing of dates or it can be in the form of a complex flow chart. At a minimum, it should list the steps of the budgetary process and the dates on which each of the various steps should be finished. More elaborate calendars often list who is responsible for each step and what data must be provided by whom and to whom. A sample budget calendar is shown in Table 3–5.

TABLE 3–5   Typical Budget Calendar

July 6	Departments receive instructions for the preparation of the budget.
August 15	Departmental expenditure requests are returned to the budget officer.
September 6–21	Departmental hearings are held with the mayor.
October 1–8	Review and preliminary presentation is made to the city council.
October 9–31	Budget is reviewed and finalized by the mayor.
November 5–18	Budget printing and production take place.
November 20	Mayor formally presents the budget to the city council.
November 21–December 15	City council conducts public hearings.
December 18	City council formally votes on the budget.
December 20–30	Budgetary information is entered into the computer.
January 1	New fiscal year begins.

Budget Instructions

To disseminate the budgetary policy guidelines and to assist the various subunits in the preparation of their expenditure requests, a set of **budget instructions** should be prepared and sent to each person responsible for a segment of the budget. These instructions should be distributed early enough to provide these persons sufficient time to prepare their budget requests in a thoughtful, orderly manner.

In addition to copies of the forms and work sheets to be used, the budget instructions should contain

1.   A budget calendar
2.   A copy of the budgetary policy guidelines
3.   A statement summarizing the organization's anticipated fiscal condition for the following year
4.   A statement of specific policies to be followed when preparing expenditure requests
5.   A set of inflationary guidelines to be used in estimating the future costs of equipment, supplies, and so on
6.   Specific instructions on how each form and work sheet should be completed
7.   Instructions on where to seek help and clarification of any ambiguities that might arise

Revenue Estimates

A key part of the budgetary process is determining how much money the organization will have available for spending the next year. This amount consists of (1) the surplus or deficit (fund balance) carried forward into the budget year, and (2) the revenues expected to be collected during the budget year.

The process of determining how much money the organization will have available for spending the next year consists of the following steps:

1.   Determine current-year revenues and probable balance in each fund at the end of current year.

2. Project revenues expected to be collected during budget year:
    a. Determine revenues or revenue bases for several prior years and the current year.
    b. Apply a trend analysis to above data in order to obtain a preliminary estimate of revenues or revenue bases of budget year.
    c. Adjust preliminary estimates of revenues or revenue bases for factors likely to affect them, such as condition of the local economy, special events, changes in tax rates, and changes in level of support from outside sources.
    d. If working with revenue bases, multiply by appropriate tax rates, license fees, and so on.
    e. Determine transfers expected from other funds.
3. Prepare a statement of actual and estimated revenues (and transfers-in), such as the one illustrated in Table 3–6.

Current-year revenues and surpluses (deficits)

A surplus can reduce the amount of revenue that must be raised in order to finance a given level of expenditures. A deficit, however, is likely to increase the amount of revenue that must be raised, since most state and local governmental units and not-for-profit organizations are either reluctant or unable to carry deficits forward from year to year.

To determine the amount of surplus or deficit to be carried forward, a projection must be made of the total revenues and expenditures that will be incurred during the current year. A separate projection should be made for each fund used (e.g., General Fund, Special Revenue Fund, and so on).

Current-year revenues are projected by

1. Comparing collections to date with budgeted and prior-year collections
2. Determining the causes of any significant differences found in step 1
3. Determining any factors that might affect the revenues of the remainder of the year (e.g., the effect that closing a major department store will have on sales tax collections during the year)
4. Projecting the revenue collections for the remainder of the year on the basis of information gathered in the preceding steps (this can be done by means of a combination of trend analysis, economic projections, and intuition)

Projecting current-year revenues becomes easier as the year passes. As a result, many organizations delay this process as long as possible. Such delays, however, increase the difficulty of realistically budgeting the following year's expenditures, since the persons preparing such estimates have no solid information on how much money will be available.

One solution to this problem is the preparation of tentative revenue estimates early in the budgetary process, deliberately erring on the side of conservatism. As better information becomes available, the current-year revenue estimates can be updated. Another approach is to use three levels of estimates—optimistic, probable, and pessimistic—and to ask the subunits to prepare three levels of expenditure requests. This approach, while providing flexibility, requires signifi-

TABLE 3–6 Statement of Actual and Estimated Revenues (and Transfers-in)

Fund: General
Date: September 15, 19X0

Prepared by ___PNW___
Approved by ___LVT___

ACCT. NO.	SOURCE	19W9 ACTUAL	JAN.-AUG. 19X0 ACTUAL	SEPT.-DEC. 19X0 EST. ACT.	TOTAL 19X0 EST. ACT.	19X0 BUDGET	19X1 BUDGET	REMARKS
1110	Property tax	$3,246,575	$1,384,300	$1,940,700	$3,325,000	$3,325,000	$3,550,000	Reassessment of property
1112	Liquor tax	355,240	235,650	124,350	360,000	354,000	480,000	International Exposition
1114	Sales tax	1,864,680	1,252,840	857,160	2,110,000	2,200,000	2,650,000	Same as above
1116	Royalty payments	385,000	245,000	120,000	365,000	375,000	300,000	Decline in gas production
1119	Fines and penalities	84,610	63,450	30,000	93,450	92,000	100,000	International Exposition
1121	Rental charges	8,500	6,500	3,500	10,000	9,500	11,000	Same as above
	Subtotal	$5,944,605	$3,187,740	$3,075,710	$6,263,450	$6,355,500	$7,091,000	
2010	Transfer from Expendable Trust Fund	122,000	—	145,000	145,000	145,000	150,000	Higher interest rates
	Total	$6,066,605	$3,187,740	$3,220,710	$6,408,450	$6,500,500	$7,241,000	

cantly more effort on the part of all concerned and can lead to misunderstand-ings and credibility gaps.

The methods used to project revenues vary from source to source. Property taxes are generally easy to project for the remainder of the year because they have already been levied and are secured by the property being taxed. In addi-tion, most governmental units set up an allowance for uncollectibles early in the year, and patterns of collection usually remain constant from year to year. Unless some major event has taken place (or is expected to), property tax collections can be assumed to follow prior-year patterns of activity.

Collections of other taxes, license fees, fines, and fees for services are more difficult to project. The best approach to predicting these sources of revenue is to apply a trend analysis to the prior-year collections and to temper the result with knowledge of current and future events (such as closing a large factory, a change in tax rates, or an increase in the legal drinking age).

Federal grants and state revenue-sharing monies can usually be predicted for the current year with a degree of certainty, since commitments for these items are made early in the year. Even in this area, however, problems can arise if the organization's fiscal year differs from that of the grantor agency or if the grantor agency cuts back on its outlays due to its own financial problems.

The best way to project total current-year expenditures is to determine, on an item-by-item basis, whether the expenditures incurred to date are above or below the budgeted level and at what rate the various subunits will continue to spend. Since budgets usually show only annual dollar amounts, it is often neces-sary to assume a constant rate of spending and to project the year-to-date expen-ditures forward at this rate. The budget officer should also discuss the current year's spending with the director or manager of each subunit in order to deter-mine the existence of any factors that might increase or decrease the rate of spending for the remainder of the year. This task can be simplified if each sub-unit produces periodic reports comparing budgeted and actual expenditures, such as the ones described at the end of this chapter.

The process of projecting annual expenditures is simplified in organizations that have rules against, or operate in jurisdictions that have laws against, over-spending their budgets. In these organizations, the budget officer can usually as-sume that the amount budgeted is the amount that will be spent.

Once the current year's projected revenues and expenditures have been de-termined, the surplus or deficit to be carried to the next year can be calculated as follows:

Prior-year surplus (deficit)
Plus: Estimated current-year revenues
Less: Estimated current-year expenditures

To illustrate, assume that at the end of the prior year the General Fund of a city had a surplus of $500,000. The budget officer of this city determines that the total revenues of the current year, recorded in this fund, will amount to $8 million and that the total expenditures will amount to $8.2 million. The projected surplus in this fund for the current year is calculated as follows:

	Prior-year surplus	$ 500,000
Plus:	Projected revenues	8,000,000
Less:	Projected expenditures	(8,200,000)
	Projected surplus	$ 300,000

The handling of surpluses varies among organizations. Some organizations feel free to spend their surpluses the following year. Others follow a policy of building them up and saving them for emergencies. The policy to be followed in the treatment of surpluses should be made clear by law and/or by the legislative body of the organization.

Budget-year revenue projections

When projecting the revenues of the budget year, each source should be considered separately. Revenue sources consist of two components:

1. A **revenue base**—The entity on which the revenues are based (e.g., property values, retail sales, number of parking tickets, number of admissions to municipal swimming pool, number of memberships, and so on).
2. A **revenue rate**—The percentage of the value of the revenue base that, by law or prior agreement, is transferred to the organization or the revenue per unit of service (e.g., New Orleans has a 4 percent city sales tax; therefore, an amount equivalent to 4 percent of the retail sales that take place there will eventually be transferred to the city).

The amount of revenue collected is the product of the revenue base and the revenue rate:

Revenues Collected = Revenue Base × Revenue Rate

To illustrate: Assume that the budget officer of a city estimates that the retail sales of the following year will amount to $10 million and that the city taxes retail sales at the rate of 3 percent. The *estimated* revenues from sales taxes will be:

$10,000,000 × .03 = $300,000

This analysis should be performed on all taxes, fees, and other revenues. For some types of revenues, the analysis can be fairly simple. For example, the tax assessor can generally supply information on the assessed value of all real property in the jurisdiction. The estimated property taxes can then be determined by multiplying the valuation provided by the assessor's office by the estimated millage (tax) rate.

Other revenues are more difficult to predict, as they are controlled by such factors as the national economy and/or the fortunes of a local industry. For example, a source of revenue for one tourist-oriented city is a hotel occupancy tax. Many of the people who visit this city are from the Midwest, a region whose economy is heavily dependent on the automotive and steel industries. A downturn in the level of activity of these industries results in fewer people visiting the city, fewer hotel bookings, and lower revenues from the hotel occupancy tax (as well as from the sales and amusement taxes). Thus, when forecasting revenues from "tourist-oriented" sources, the budget officer of this city must consider the condition of the economies of the various regions (and nations) from which visitors are drawn. The following factors must also be considered when projecting revenues:

1. **Local economic conditions** can be influenced by the projected activity of local industries as well as national and, in many cases, worldwide economic conditions. Measures of these conditions are found in the various business and commodity-price indices and in locally generated statistics, such as housing starts, school enrollments, sales tax collections, population trends, and trends in building permits.
2. **Special events** that will take place in a particular year. For example, a city might host an international exhibition. Such an event would attract an unusually large number of tourists—which would significantly increase revenues from various tourist-oriented sources.
3. **Legal factors** such as changes in tax rates, the addition or deletion of fees and taxes, possible reassessments of real property, and changes in taxes and fees mandated by the courts or higher governmental units.
4. **Internal or administrative factors** such as opening a self-financing facility or the receipt of federal funds, the amount of which is based on the level of a particular activity.

When gathering information, outside sources should be used extensively but not exclusively. Groups such as the League of Women Voters and the various chambers of commerce devote a great deal of time and effort to gathering information relevant to the operation of governmental and other not-for-profit organizations. This information can prove very useful. It should be remembered, however, that the preparers of this information are often lobbying organizations. Persons using this information should therefore be alert for possible biases.

Certain types of revenues, such as fines and sales taxes, may be projected by using past trends. A tool commonly used to make such projections is **trend analysis.** Trend analysis can be used to estimate future revenues from any source that increases (or decreases) at a reasonably steady pace. To perform a trend analysis, data for the past five or more years should be assembled, along with an estimate for the current year. The revenue base rather than the level of collections should be measured, since tax rates, the levels of fines, and so forth, tend to rise over a period of time, adding an extra variable. Determining the following year's revenue base and multiplying by the expected rates provides more accurate projections.

Once the data have been assembled, the analysis involves the following steps:

1. Determine year-to-year changes in the revenue base for each of the prior years.
2. Determine the average rate of change over the period.
3. Multiply the average rate of change (plus 100 percent) by the estimated revenue base of the current year, to obtain the *unadjusted* projected revenue base.
4. Adjust the unadjusted projected revenue base for known factors that may cause a deviation from past patterns of behavior, to obtain the *adjusted* projected revenue base.
5. Multiply the adjusted projected revenue base by the appropriate tax rate, license fee, level of average fine, and so on, to obtain the projected revenues.

To illustrate, assume that a city wishes to project revenues from a tax on hotel occupancy. The tax rate for the budget year 1995 is expected to be 5 percent of the price paid for each room. The number of people visiting the city has been growing at a fairly steady rate, as have the room rates. Hotel occupancy rates have averaged around 80 percent. In the budget year, however, the city will host an international exposition. The local chamber of commerce estimates that hotel occupancy rates will average 96 percent that year. Due to the construction of several new hotels, the number of rooms available will rise by 10 percent, all of which will be available at the beginning of the year. Room rates, however, will rise at only about the same rate that they have in the past, due to the increased competition brought about by the new hotels.

Room occupancy revenues reported by the hotels in this city over the past five years have been as follows (in millions of dollars)

1989	$1.2
1990	1.4
1991	1.7
1992	2.1
1993	2.5
1994	3.0 (est.)

To project the revenues from the hotel occupancy tax for the budget year, the following steps are performed:

1. Determine year-to-year changes in the revenue base for each of the prior years:

$$1990/1989 = 1.4/1.2 = 1.167 - 1.000 = \underline{\underline{16.7\%}}$$
$$1991/1990 = 1.7/1.4 = 1.214 - 1.000 = \underline{\underline{21.4\%}}$$
$$1992/1991 = 2.1/1.7 = 1.235 - 1.000 = \underline{\underline{23.5\%}}$$
$$1993/1992 = 2.5/2.1 = 1.190 - 1.000 = \underline{\underline{19.0\%}}$$
$$1994/1993 = 3.0/2.5 = 1.200 - 1.000 = \underline{\underline{20.0\%}}$$

2. Determine the average rate of change over the period. Since we are working with estimates, a simple arithmetic average will suffice:

$$
\begin{array}{r}
16.7\% \\
21.4 \\
23.5 \\
19.0 \\
\underline{20.0} \\
5\ \overline{|\ 100.6\%} \\
\underline{20.1\%} = \text{Average rate of change over period}
\end{array}
$$

3. Multiply the average rate of change (plus 100 percent) by the estimated revenue base of the current year:

$120.1\% \times \$3.0 = \$3,603,000$ (rounded) = unadjusted projected 1995 revenue base

4. Adjust the unadjusted projected revenue base for known factors that may cause a deviation from past patterns of behavior. In this problem, the occupancy rate is expected to rise from 80 to 96 percent during the budget year because of the international exposition. In addition, the number of available hotel rooms is expected to increase by 10 percent, all of which will be available at the beginning of the year:
   a. Percentage increase in occupancy rate = $96\%/80\% = 1.20 - 1.00 = 20\%$
   b. Percentage increase in hotel rooms = 10%

$\$3,603,000 \times 120\% \times 110\% = \underline{\$4,755,960} =$ adjusted projected 1995 revenue base

Do not try to multiply the unadjusted projected 1995 revenue base by 130 percent, as each of the above factors is independent of the other. For example, even if no new rooms were added, the base would rise by 20 percent due to the increase in the occupancy rate. If the occupancy rate were to remain constant, the base would rise by 10 percent because of the new rooms.

5. Multiply the adjusted projected 1995 revenue base by the projected tax rate (5%):

$\$4,755,960 \times 5\% = \underline{\$237,800}$ (rounded) = projected 1995 revenue

Thus the revenue from the hotel occupancy tax for 1995 can be budgeted at $237,800.

When dealing with estimates it is best to use simple, rounded figures in order to avoid falling into the GIGO (garbage in–garbage out) trap. This happens when rough estimates are multiplied by various factors and odd numbers result. Regrettably, many people tend to assume that if a number is carried out to pennies or to several decimal places it must be correct, regardless of its source.

Revenues that must be handled separately are grants, entitlements, and shared revenues. These revenues are usually received from other governmental units and are known collectively as **intergovernmental revenues.** According to the National Council on Governmental Accounting (NCGA), **grants** are contributions or gifts of cash or other assets that must be used or expended for specified purposes, activities, or facilities. **Entitlements** are payments to which state or local governmental units are entitled, pursuant to an allocation formula determined by the organization providing the monies (usually the federal government, but some states also have entitlement programs). **Shared revenues** are revenues that are received by one governmental unit (e.g., a state) and are shared, on a predetermined basis, with another governmental unit or class of governmental units.[3]

The difficulty of projecting intergovernmental revenues varies by type of revenue. Revenues based on formula distributions of state revenues, such as sales taxes, are fairly easy to predict. Revenues from federal grants, however, are more difficult to predict, although the distributing agencies are often able to provide tentative information on the probable distributions from continuing sources, on which grants are likely to be approved, and on the levels of payments likely to be made on existing and approved grants.

Once the projected revenues have been determined, they should be recorded on a **statement of actual and estimated revenues** (also known as a revenue summary). This statement is used to present the estimated revenues of the budget year and to compare these estimated revenues with the actual revenues of prior years and, as far as possible, the current year. It can also be used to present transfers expected to be received from other funds. When preparing a statement of actual and estimated revenues, it is advisable to include an explanation of the assumptions made and the methods used to derive the estimates shown. Such a statement is shown in Table 3–6 (p. 83). This particular summary is a simplified one and is applicable to a small city. The statements of large organizations, however, are similar. They just contain more detailed information.

Departmental Expenditure Requests

Expenditure requests should be prepared by each department, program, or other subunit of the organization. These documents should show the expenditures of the prior year, the total estimated expenditures of the current year, and the proposed level of expenditures of the budget year. They should be accompanied by detailed supporting statements for each major object of expenditure. Such work sheets can be used to answer questions that may be raised by the budget officer, the CEO, or the legislative body. They can also be used to justify both new and continuing expenditures.

Expenditure requests serve a number of purposes. First, they enable the CEO and the legislative body to evaluate the performance of each subunit (this same function, of course, can also be performed by quarterly or monthly budget comparisons, which will be discussed later). They also enable persons making

---

[3]National Council on Governmental Accounting, *Statement 2,* "Grant, Entitlement and Shared Revenue Accounting and Reporting by State and Local Governments" (Chicago: Municipal Finance Officers Association of the United States and Canada, 1980), p. 1.

budgetary decisions to determine the propriety of each request in terms of the goals of the *entire* organization as opposed to the individual subunits; and when resources are limited, they enable these persons to allocate resources to those activities of each subunit that best serve the organization as a *whole.*

Finally, expenditure requests force department heads and other managers, at least once a year, to take a close look at the objectives and the current levels of activity of their subunits and to determine whether more efficient methods can be developed to meet these objectives. If these persons wish to expand the scope of the activities of their subunits, they must be able to justify the additional expenditures necessary and to disclose the impact on the organization, as a whole, of disallowing the additional expenditures.

The following series of steps should be applied to each expenditure when preparing departmental expenditure requests:

1. Determine the level of the expenditure for the past year and project the level of the expenditure for the current year.
2. Apply inflation and cost-of-living factors and other allowances for "uncontrollable" factors to each current-year expenditure. This will result in a "stand-still" expenditure request.
3. Determine what activities should be expanded, contracted, or discontinued. Identify any new activities that, if funded, will commence the following year.
4. Adjust each proposed expenditure for the changes in the type and level of activities determined and identified in step 3.
5. Prepare a justification for each new activity or each increase in the level of an existing activity. Include, in this justification, the effect that *not* adopting or increasing the level of the activity will have on the organization. For this step, a PPB or ZBB type of analysis can be helpful.
6. Prepare a **budgetary work sheet** for each type of expenditure. The formats of the work sheets will vary with the type of expenditure being projected, although each work sheet should show the prior-year, current-year, and projected budget-year level of expenditures for each line item (object-of-expenditure).
7. Summarize the information from each work sheet on the expenditure request.

Departmental or program expenditures are generally broken into three categories: personal services, operating expenses, and equipment.

Personal services

The heart of a personal services budget is the **position classification plan.** This document lists all the position titles and their corresponding salaries. From it, past and current personnel costs can be identified. The positions expected to be occupied during the budget year should be recorded on the budgetary work sheet, along with the past, current, and projected rate or salary attached to each position.

Employee (fringe) benefits should be treated as a separate item, although they can be combined with salaries and wages on the budgetary work sheet. The best approach to handling this item of cost is to determine the total expenditures for the prior year or the current year to date, and to divide this amount by the total payroll, to obtain the **employee benefit cost per payroll dollar.** This ratio can then be used when determining the full cost of new positions or existing positions at new salary levels.

Since employee benefits (Social Security, vacation pay, sick pay, and so on) are generally a function of salaries, the above method usually provides accurate data. However, the cost of certain benefits, such as paid hospitalization, may be fixed. That is, it may be the same for all employees regardless of salary level. Generally speaking, however, the cost of such benefits is a relatively small part of the total employee benefit cost. In addition, it tends to average out, and since the budget is based on estimates, the cost of "fixed" benefits does not usually create any serious problems.

One final note: When budgeting employee benefits, be sure to apply the budget year's rates. Unemployment insurance and FICA (Social Security) rates, in particular, tend to change very frequently.

Other personal service costs that must be considered are overtime, shift differentials, and requests for temporary help. For example, on certain holidays it is sometimes necessary to ask police officers to work overtime in order to handle the crowds of parade watchers. In addition, some cities hire students to perform special tasks, such as street repairs, during the summer. These costs are usually known well in advance and can easily be determined by multiplying projected hours by appropriate pay and fringe benefit rates.

Compensation for members of the legislative body must also be included in the personal services section of the budget request. These people are paid either a fixed salary per year or a certain stipend for each meeting attended. In the latter case, their compensation can be estimated by multiplying the number of meetings expected to be held (a number often set by law) by a fixed rate per meeting.

In many organizations, a **salary-vacancy factor (SVF)** is used to fine-tune the expected cost of personal services. A SVF represents the portion of the budgeted salaries that is not expected to be spent because of a delay in hiring personnel or because vacancies will be filled at lower-than-budgeted salaries. This factor can be estimated by looking at past experience and future hiring policies. If a hiring freeze is expected to be in effect during the budget year, the SVF can be significant.

A personal services (budgetary) work sheet is shown in Table 3–7. Note that it includes prior- and current-year data, as well as adjustments for cost-of-living and changes in fringe benefit rates. Note also that it gives a brief justification for the expansion of the level of service. The total of the personal services expenditures is transferred to the departmental expenditure request shown in Table 3–13 (p. 99). To assist in the preparation of their personal services work sheets, many governmental units prepare a salary work sheet, one of which is shown in Table 3–8.

TABLE 3-7 Personal Services Work Sheet

Fund: General
Function: Public Safety
Department: Police

Prepared by _P E_
Approved by _PRT_
Date: September 15, 19X0

CODE	POSITION TITLE	PRIOR-YEAR ACTUAL			CURRENT-YEAR EST. ACTUAL			BUDGET REQUEST†			REMARKS
		NO.	RATE*	AMOUNT	NO.	RATE*	AMOUNT	NO.	RATE*	AMOUNT	
101	Chief	1	$30,300	$30,300	1	$31,500	$31,500	1	$34,504	$34,504	
102	Captain	2	26,000	52,000	2	27,000	54,000	2	29,737	59,474	
104	Lieutenant	4	22,500	90,000	4	23,500	94,000	4	24,896	99,584	
105	Detective	2	17,200	34,400	2	18,000	36,000	2	19,068	38,136	
106	Sergeant	5	18,000	90,000	5	18,500	92,500	5	19,598	97,990	
180	Police Officer	12	16,000	192,000	12	17,000	204,000	14	18,007	252,098	Two new positions‡
	Total	26		$488,700	26		$512,000	28		$581,786	

*Includes employee benefits, which are budgeted at 13.5% of salaries and wages. This rate is 1% higher than the current rate (12.5%) because of an expected increase in the FICA rate (.6%) and the state unemployment rate (.4%). The prior-year rate is 11.1% of salaries and wages.

†Includes a cost-of-living factor of 5.0% plus an additional merit increase of $1,000 each for the Chief and Captains.

‡*Justification and new positions:* In the latter part of the current year, an area of four square miles was annexed. To provide an adequate level of protection in this area and the original parts of the city, an additional patrol unit is necessary. If this additional unit is denied, the annexed area containing 562 residents will receive inadequate police protection or the entire city will receive a lower level of protection due to the overextending of available personnel and equipment. In either case the level of crime can be expected to rise significantly if the additional unit is not approved.

92

TABLE 3–8   Budget Yearly Salary Work Sheet

Fund: General
Function: Public Safety
Department: Police

Prepared by *PE*
Approved by *PRT*
Date: September 10, 19X0

CODE	POSITION TITLE	19X0 BASE	COST-OF-LIVING ADJ.	MERIT	19X1 BASE	FRINGE BENEFITS	BUDGET REQUEST
101	Chief	$28,000	$1,400	$1,000	$30,400	$4,104	$34,504
102	Captain	24,000	1,200	1,000	26,200	3,537	29,737
104	Lieutenant	20,890	1,045	—	21,935	2,961	24,896
105	Detective	16,000	800	—	16,800	2,268	19,068
106	Sergeant	16,445	822	—	17,267	2,331	19,598
180	Police Officer	15,110	755	—	15,865	2,142	18,007

Cost of living adjustment is 5.0% of 19X0 base. Fringe benefits are expected to average 13.5% of wages and salaries in 19X1.

Operating expenses

Operating expenses are those outlays necessary in carrying out the organization's routine operations. Examples of such expenses are postage, office supplies, utilities, printing, reproduction, professional services, employee travel, fuel, and vehicle maintenance. If the scope of the organization's operations does not change, the level of these expenses can be estimated by using the current year's level plus an inflation factor.

When budgeting operating expenses, each item should be questioned in order to determine whether it is necessary and, if so, whether its usage can be reduced. For example, can fuel be saved by replacing the existing police cruisers with more fuel-efficient models?

In the budgetary work sheet, the prior- and current-year outlays should be listed for each object of expenditure, along with the budget request. As with personal services, the inflation factor used should be shown. In addition, a justification should be made for any new items or any item whose usage is expected to increase significantly.

Travel.   All employee travel should be shown on a separate work sheet that lists the name of the person traveling and the date, destination, purpose, and estimated cost of each trip. Many organizations also show employee travel as a separate item on their departmental expenditure requests. A sample operating expense worksheet is shown in Table 3–9. A sample travel work sheet is shown in Table 3–10.

TABLE 3–9 Operating Expense Work Sheet*

Prepared by *WPE*
Approved by *PRT*
Date September 15, 19X0

Fund: General
Function: Public Safety
Department: Police

CODE	OBJECT	PRIOR-YEAR ACTUAL	CURRENT-YEAR BUDGET	CURRENT-YEAR EST. ACTUAL	BUDGET REQUEST†	REMARKS
	Contractual Services					
301	Advertising	$ 110	$ 100	$ 85	$ 100	
310	Printing	1,500	1,600	1,650	1,800	
320	Vehicle maintenance	7,500	8,000	8,000	8,400	Improved radio system
330	Communication	6,000	5,600	6,000	6,200	
350	Dues and subscriptions	180	200	200	200	
360	Postage	280	300	325	350	
370	Telephone	580	600	750	600	Staff training, medical
380	Professional services	425	400	450	500	
	Subtotal	$16,575	$16,800	$17,460	$18,150	
	Supplies and Materials					
401	Office supplies	$ 1,200	$ 1,100	$ 1,150	$ 1,200	
410	Building maintenance	4,500	4,700	4,800	5,000	
420	Fuel	10,135	10,500	10,250	12,000	Extra patrol unit
430	Ground maintenance	975	1,000	950	1,000	
440	Reproduction'	1,250	1,400	1,420	1,500	
450	Uniform allowances	175	400	250	800	New personnel
460	Security supplies	1,010	1,200	1,235	1,300	New personnel
490	Miscellaneous	450	400	350	500	
	Grand total	$60,500	$61,600	$61,450	$62,350	

*Employee travel is reported separately.
†An inflation factor of 4.5% is used where applicable.

TABLE 3–10 Travel Work Sheet

Fund: General

Function: Public Safety

Department: Police

Prepared by _BRE_

Approved by _PRE_

Date: September 15, 19X0

NAME AND/OR POSITION	DATES OF TRAVEL	DESTINATION	PURPOSE OF TRAVEL	BUDGET REQUEST*
K. Lacho, Chief	3/1–3/3	Biloxi	Supervisory training	$ 500
S. Spade, Detective	4/11–4/12	Las Vegas	Technical training	1,200
B. Miller, Captain	7/22	Local	Sensitivity training	100
R. Harris, Detective	8/15	Local	Report-writing training	50
R. Columbo, Lieutenant	9/18	San Pedro	Technical training	1,100
K. Lacho, Chief	11/15–11/18	Orlando	Professional meetings	800
B. Miller, Captain	11/15–11/18	Orlando	Professional meetings	800
R. Mankin, Lieutenant	11/15–11/18	Orlando	Professional meetings	800
Total requested travel				$5,350

*Includes conference fees or tuition, airfare, lodging, and a per diem allowance at locally authorized rates.

Equipment

The **equipment** category includes items that normally last more than one year and cost more than a predetermined dollar amount (e.g., $50). Items not meeting both criteria should be classified as operating expenses. Typical items of equipment are furniture, typewriters, police cruisers, and lawn mowers.

Many organizations include purchases of equipment in their capital budget. Other organizations use their capital budgets to record only construction of buildings, streets, bridges, and so forth.

The work sheet used when budgeting expenditures for equipment should contain a description of each item of equipment requested and should state whether each item is an addition to or a replacement for an existing item. The work sheet should also indicate the number of items of each type requested and cost per item. Finally, the work sheet should contain a justification for all additional items of equipment requested. An equipment work sheet is shown in Table 3–11.

Capital Outlays

The term **capital outlays** is used to describe the cost of major building and renovation projects undertaken by the organization. These activities include new construction as well as the repair, alteration, and expansion of various facilities, such as buildings, roads, parks, bridges, airports, and levees. Capital projects can be performed by outside contractors or by organizational personnel. In many cases these projects are partially funded by state and federal grants. They can also be funded by the proceeds of bond issues.

Many organizations prepare capital budgets, which are approved separately from their operating budgets. Other organizations include capital projects in their operating budgets, treating their capital outlays in the same manner as other expenditures. In this text we will assume the latter approach and will include capital outlay requests in the operating budget.

A **capital outlay request summary** is shown in Table 3–12. In the illustration, the city has been given a plantation house, which it intends to restore and turn into a museum. In addition, the city is planning to build a new police station, work on a stadium (a three-year project), and rebuild several bridges. The capital outlay request summary contains information describing each project, the dollar amounts requested, and the amount of the cost allocated to the various departments (when more than one department or program benefits from a particular project). Supplementary schedules (not shown) can be used when many like items are requested for one project, such as pieces of antique furniture for the plantation house.

Some organizations prepare narrative explanations of the various projects under construction. Such explanations usually contain detailed descriptions of the projects, as well as discussions of the cost of finishing the projects and maintaining them when they are complete. The narrative explanations can also con-

TABLE 3–11   Equipment Work Sheet

Fund: General
Function: Public Safety
Department: Police

Prepared by _____
Approved by _PRT_
Date: September 15, 19X0

CODE	ITEM	ADDITION OR REPLACEMENT	NUMBER REQUESTED	NET COST PER UNIT*	BUDGET REQUEST	AMOUNT APPROPRIATED	REMARKS
504	Motor scooter	R	1	$ 1,800	$1,800		
505	Police cruiser	R	2	12,000	24,000		Necessary because of the annexation of four square miles of outlying area
505	Police cruiser	A	1	12,500	12,500		Same as above
506	.38-caliber pistol	A	3	150	450		
510	Typewriter	R	2	800	1,600		
515	Desk	R	2	350	700		
518	File cabinet	A	4	100	400		Necessary because of increased number of records that must be maintained due to federal grant
522	Radio transmitter (used)	A	1	7,600	7,600		Necessary to improve communication between police patrol and dispatcher
	Total				$49,050		

*Cost of new item less trade-in or resale value of item being replaced.

TABLE 3–12   Capital Outlay Request Summary

Date: September 15, 19X0   Prepared by **_BER_**

PROJECT DESCRIPTION	BUDGET REQUEST	DEPARTMENT CHARGED	REMARKS
Restore Ellett plantation house	$100,000	Parks	Purchase of furniture
Police station	300,000	Police	Darby and Manoa Roads
Rebuild bridges	800,000	Streets	Marple Canal and Darby Creek
C. S. "Doc" Watson Stadium	300,000	Parks	1/3 of estimated cost
Total requested	$1,500,000		

tain information on sources of financing, completion dates, and justifications for the projects.

Many governmental units supplement their capital outlay request summaries with **long-run capital programs.** A long-run capital program presents information on the capital improvements desired over a long period of time (e.g., five years). It lists the projects planned, the estimated cost of each project, and the proposed source or sources of funding for each project. Generally it is prepared on a "continuous" basis, with a future year added, the past year dropped, and the other years "fine-tuned."

Although some people may regard long-run capital programs as "wish lists" and many projects may never be started, long-run capital programs are good organizing, planning, and communicating tools. They enable users to see at a glance what is needed, what is wanted, and what the organization can afford. Such information is particularly valuable to legislators who must balance the needs of one organization against the needs of others in order to allocate limited resources.

One question that often arises is whether costly items, such as fire engines and road machinery, should be placed in the capital budget or in the operating budget. The authors of this book believe that items of a routine nature, such as police cruisers, should be included in the operating budget regardless of cost, and that the capital budget should be used exclusively for nonroutine items, such as buildings, bridges, and the *initial* paving of streets. This is not, however, a unanimously held view.

Departmental Expenditure Request Document

When the work sheets for personal services, operating expenses, and equipment and the capital outlay request summaries are finished, certain information is transferred from these forms to the **departmental expenditure request document.** This schedule contains, at a minimum, the title of each object-of-expenditure, the level of prior- and current-year expenditures, and the requested level of expenditures for the budget year. It can also contain a column in which the amount actually appropriated by the legislative body is recorded.

Some organizations summarize the requested level of expenditures by activity (e.g., vice squad, juvenile control, traffic control, and so on) and include this summary in a supplementary schedule. Such information can help the CEO and the members of the legislative body to make judgments on the costs and benefits of specific activities. A departmental expenditure request is shown in Table 3–13.

Nondepartmental Expenditure Requests

Nondepartmental expenditures are expenditures that do not relate to any one specific department or activity. Instead, they benefit the organization as a whole. Examples of nondepartmental expenditures include interest on bonds, utilities and maintenance costs of buildings used by different departments or programs (such as a city hall), certain pension costs, and liability insurance premiums for city-owned vehicles. In addition, many organizations set up a reserve, or "slush fund," to cover emergencies or contingencies (such as cleaning up after a flood).

The work sheet used to budget nondepartmental expenditures is similar to the one used to budget departmental operating expenses. However, since nondepartmental operating expenditures are usually of a fixed nature (e.g., interest on a bond issue), and since their planned level is usually determined by the budget officer or the CEO, the work sheet used to budget them is prepared by the budget officer. A nondepartmental expenditure request is shown in Table 3–14.

TABLE 3–13   Departmental Expenditure Request

Fund: General
Function: Public Safety
Department: Police
Prepared by: B FR
Approved by: PRT
Date: September 15, 19X0

CODE	OBJECT	PRIOR-YEAR ACTUAL	CURRENT-YEAR BUDGET	CURRENT-YEAR EST. ACTUAL	BUDGET REQUEST	AMOUNT APPROPRIATED
100	Personal services	$488,700	$515,600	$512,000	$581,786	
200	Travel	4,600	4,800	4,800	5,350	
3–600	Operating expenses	60,500	61,600	61,450	62,350	
700	Equipment	42,470	46,500	45,800	49,050	
800	Capital outlays	236,000	100,000	110,000	300,000	
	Total	$832,270	$728,500	$734,050	$998,536	

Narrative: The police department maintains law and order in the community. Major departmental expenditures are for personnel, operating expenses, and equipment. Because of the increased area of the city, the department must add two police officers and an additional police cruiser. In addition, it must replace three police cruisers that have reached the end of their useful lives. The department also plans to build a substation at Darby and Manoa Roads to service the area that was recently annexed by the city. Finally, the department must upgrade its communication system because of a recently passed law requiring that police departments throughout the state maintain comprehensive networks that are integrated into the state system.

TABLE 3-14 Nondepartmental Expenditure Request

Fund: General
Date: September 15, 19X0

Prepared by __CCW__
Approved by __LYT__

CODE	OBJECT	PRIOR-YEAR ACTUAL	CURRENT-YEAR BUDGET	CURRENT-YEAR EST. ACTUAL	BUDGET REQUEST	AMOUNT APPROPR.	REMARKS
710	Redemption of bonds*	$500,000	$500,000	$500,000	$1,300,000		6.0% debentures of 20X5
725	Interest on bonds*	205,000	180,000	180,000	165,000		Extra costs of redeeming bonds
730	Fiscal agent fees*	1,000	1,000	1,000	1,500		Damage to City Hall from dust
810	Repairs	—	—	3,000	20,000		storm
850	Legal settlements	150,000	120,000	210,000	200,000		Uninsured portion of damage claims
925	Audit fees	12,000	15,000	15,500	18,000		Inflation
930	Legal services	35,000	35,000	40,000	40,000		Inflation
950	Advertising	2,000	2,500	2,450	8,000		Promote international exposition
	Total	$905,000	$853,500	$951,950	$1,752,500		

*Transfer to Debt Service Fund.

Work Programs

Many organizations supplement their budget requests with **work programs,** which are schedules of specific activities to be performed by the organization in carrying out its assigned functions. They may be in narrative or tabular form, although the latter is preferable because it is easier to read. Regardless of their form, work programs should indicate the following:

1. The purpose of the subunit of the organization (e.g., public safety)
2. Each activity to be performed, along with a description of the activity when its nature is not obvious
3. The units used to measure the activity
4. The value of the work performed, expressed in the units described in number 3
5. The cost of each unit of work performed
6. The total cost of each activity

Data should also be provided on the personnel, materials, supplies, and equipment needed to carry out each activity.

A work program should, at a minimum, cover the past year, the current year, and the budget year. It can be enhanced by comparisons between the three years, narrative descriptions of existing and proposed activities, and the reasons for changes in the level or scope of the various activities.

Budgetary Review

The departmental expenditure request documents are submitted to the budget officer, along with the work sheets, work programs (if any), and any other supporting materials. The budget officer, or a member of his or her staff, determines whether each expenditure request document has been properly prepared and whether each requested item is justified and realistic, as well as appropriate. If the budget officer believes that the expenditure request documents have been properly prepared and that each item is justified, realistic, and appropriate, he or she summarizes the information received and transmits it, along with the backup materials and revenue estimates, to the CEO. The CEO reviews the information and prepares recommendations for the legislative body. A budget summary is shown in Table 3–15.

Determining whether the expenditure request documents have been properly prepared is a relatively simple procedure. It consists primarily of ascertaining that all requested information has been provided, that the arithmetic on each form is correct, and that no errors have been made when transferring information from one form to another.

Determining whether each requested item is justified, realistic, and appropriate is more difficult. The budget officer must determine the need for each activity and level of service, the validity of the assumptions underlying each budgetary calculation, and whether each requested item falls within the budgetary

TABLE 3–15   Budget Summary

Fun City
General Fund
Budget Summary
Fiscal Year 19X1

Revenues			
Property tax		$3,550,000	
Liquor tax		480,000	
Sales tax		2,650,000	
Royalty payments		300,000	
Fines and penalties		100,000	
Rental charges		11,000	$7,091,000
Appropriations			
Administration:			
Personal services	$435,000		
Travel	22,400		
Operating expenses	85,800		
Equipment	24,600	$ 567,800	
Fire:			
Personal services	$715,000		
Travel	12,500		
Operating expenses	335,000		
Equipment	146,250	1,208,750	
Parks:			
Personal services	$246,350		
Travel	1,850		
Operating expenses	82,350		
Equipment	72,300		
Capital outlays	400,000	802,850	
Police:			
Personal services	$581,786		
Travel	5,350		
Operating expenses	62,350		
Equipment	49,050		
Capital outlays	300,000	998,536	
Streets:			
Personal services	$364,750		
Travel	1,150		
Operating expenses	103,360		
Equipment	246,000		
Capital outlays	800,000	1,515,260	
Nondepartmental:			
Repairs	$ 20,000		
Legal settlements	200,000		
Audit fees	18,.000		
Legal services	40,000		
Advertising	8,000	286,000	5,379,196
Excess of revenues over appropriations			$1,711,804

(continued)

TABLE 3–15   Budget Summary (*Continued*)

Other Financing Sources (Uses)		
Transfer from Expendible Trust Fund	$ 150,000	
Transfer to Debt Service Fund'	(1,466,500)	(1,316,500)
Excess of revenues and other sources over expenditures and other uses		$395,304
Estimated fund balance—January 1, 19X1		1,000,000
Estimated fund balance—December 31, 19X1		$1,395,304

guidelines. If a requested item exceeds these guidelines, the budget officer must determine why this is so and whether the additional request is justified.

For example, in the personal services work sheet in Table 3–7, two additional police officers are requested, along with additional equipment, because of the annexation of an unincorporated area into the city. If the budgetary guidelines specify no new positions or if the revenue picture is not optimistic, the budget officer must determine whether the same level of services can be delivered with existing resources or whether a lower level of services will suffice.

If the CEO and the legislative body are to make *informed* decisions, supplementary data must be included with the expenditure requests. This information can come from

1. *Performance reports*—work plans, personnel reports, productivity studies, and so on
2. *Independent research*—cost-benefit analyses, program audits, feasibility studies, and so on
3. *Reports and studies from outside sources*—press releases, program status reports prepared for funding agencies, reports prepared by citizens' groups, and so on

At all times, the budget officer should be in close contact with department heads, program directors, and other persons responsible for preparing expenditure requests. A budget officer who feels that a request is questionable should meet with the person who prepared the request to resolve the matter. If the matter cannot be resolved at this level, the person preparing the request should have the right to appeal to the CEO.

The budget officer is also responsible, in most organizations, for ensuring that the total proposed expenditures do not exceed the estimated revenues plus any surplus likely to be on hand at the end of the current year. Since the total expenditure requests of most organizations usually exceed the projected revenues of those organizations, even after the screening process discussed above, and since most organizations are required, by law or charter, to operate within a balanced budget, the budget director is usually forced to decide which requests should be included in the budget document and which requests should be reduced or eliminated.

When balancing the budget, the budget officer should first determine whether a perceived need for more resources can be met by shifting existing resources from another area. For example, the budget officer may agree with the need for an additional police officer position. Upon reviewing the budget of another department, the budget officer might discover that that department employs a security guard. In this case the budget officer might arrange a meeting between the police chief and the head of that department to determine whether the job performed by the security guard can be performed by extending the police patrols to include that department's facility. If the outcome of this meeting is positive, a transfer can be made from the budget of the department employing the security guard to the police department's budget at very little cost to the organization. (The authors realize that not all trade-offs are this easy.)

The budget officer must also determine whether each activity should expand or reduce the level of its objectives and whether the objectives of each activity can be achieved just as effectively with fewer resources. To assist the budget officer in making such decisions (and to defend their subunits from the consequences of such decisions), persons preparing expenditure requests should include sound justifications and detailed backup data with each request.

The final review of the expenditure requests is made by the CEO. The data from the various subunits should be presented to this executive in summary form, with backup information readily available. Both subunit and organization-wide requests should be presented.

The purposes of the final review are (1) to obtain the input of the CEO into the budgetary process, (2) to act as a court of last resort for disputes between the budget officer and the persons preparing the expenditure requests, and (3) to enable the CEO to prepare specific budget recommendations before submitting them to the legislative body.

The best approach to the final review is to have each person responsible for preparing expenditure requests brief the CEO on those requests and provide "ammunition" that the CEO can use when presenting the budget to the legislative body. If the CEO has been involved in the budgetary process from its inception, and if all differences between the budget officer and the persons responsible for preparing the expenditure requests have been resolved, this final review can be a positive experience.

The Budget Document

After the final review has been completed, the budget officer assembles the budget requests, the revenue projections, and the CEO's recommendations into a comprehensive **budget document,** which is presented to the legislative body. The magnitude of a budget document can range from one to several volumes, depending on the organization's size and complexity. At a minimum, a budget document should contain

1. A *budget message*—which, in general terms, discusses
    a. The fiscal experience of the current year
    b. The present financial position of the organization
    c. The major financial issues faced during the past year and the ones that are expected to be faced during the budget year
    d. Major assumptions used when preparing the budget requests (e.g., the expected rate of inflation)
    e. Significant changes from the current year's budget
    f. The CEO's recommendations for action on the budget year's programs and financial policies
    g. Major personnel changes
    h. The future economic outlook of the organization
2. A *budget summary*—which lists the total budgeted revenues by source, and lists the total budgeted expenditures by program or department and for the organization as a whole. This part of the budget document can be enhanced by including comparisons between the budgeted revenues and expenditures and the actual revenues and expenditures of the current and past year. It can also be made more effective by highlighting significant changes in the levels of specific sources of revenue and specific expenditures.
3. *Detailed supporting schedules*—among which should be schedules of
    a. Estimated revenues by source
    b. Departmental and nondepartmental expenditure requests
    c. Budgeted fixed charges such as the repayment of debt
4. A *capital projects schedule*
5. *Detailed justifications of the budgetary recommendations*
6. *Supplementary information*—such as
    a. Departmental budget request work sheets
    b. Departmental work programs
    c. Pro forma balance sheets for each fund, as of the beginning and the end of the budget year
    d. A cash budget
    e. A schedule of interest payments, sinking fund contributions, and bond issues and retirements
7. *Drafts of appropriation and tax levy ordinances or acts*

Legislative Consideration and Adoption of the Budget

The completed budget document is sent to the legislative body, which reviews, modifies, approves, and adopts it. Before approving the budget document, the legislative body usually conducts both formal and informal private hearings, as well as formal public hearings. In some cases the budget document is turned over to a legislative finance or ways-and-means committee for recommendations. Such recommendations, however, are just that—recommendations. They are not binding on the entire legislative body.

Private hearings can be in the form of informal briefings, such as workshop sessions conducted by the CEO, the budget officer, or the persons responsible for preparing budgetary requests. They can also take the form of lists of questions to be answered in writing by officials of the organization, and of meetings between individual legislators and the CEO or budget officer. During these hearings, items of concern to the members of the legislative body can be discussed, as can the impact of programs in which the legislators are particularly interested. As a result, many issues and questions can be resolved by the time the budget is formally presented.

At a designated meeting, the CEO formally presents the budget document to the legislative body. This presentation should include a general overview of the contents of the budget document, a discussion of the assumptions made when preparing the budget document, and a discussion of the major financial difficulties that the organization will face during the budget year. The revenue estimates and budget requests should also be reviewed, as should the justification for each new or nonroutine request.

Many organizations are required by law (or political expediency) to hold public hearings on the budget. Citizen input to budgetary decisions is obtained by allowing interested parties to comment to the legislative body on their own concerns. The process of budgetary approval is expedited if copies of the budget document (or a summary) are disseminated to the members of the legislative body and to the public in advance of public hearings and the formal presentation. If the users of the budget document are allowed a reasonable amount of time to "digest" its contents, issues of concern can more readily be identified and the public hearings and deliberations of the legislative body will proceed more smoothly.

When the budget hearings are finished, the legislative body completes its deliberations, makes any modifications to the budget document it feels are necessary, and enacts a final **appropriation ordinance** or, in the case of a state, **appropriation act.** The purpose of this ordinance or act is to establish a spending ceiling for the budget year and to authorize the organization to make the expenditures listed in the budget.

Once the appropriation ordinance or act has been passed, the budget document is returned to the organization, where the budgeted amounts are entered into the accounts. Most governmental units also publish their approved budget.

Property Tax Levy

Once the budget has been approved, the legislative body must take action to raise revenues necessary to finance the budgeted expenditures. The collection of many types of revenue does not require frequent action on the part of the legislative body. These revenues are usually the result of past actions (e.g., license fees, sales taxes, income from investments, and so on). Other revenue measures, however, require legal action more frequently, the most common example being property taxes.

Two different approaches can be used to determine the taxes to be assessed on each piece of property. Under the first approach the assessed value of the property (less any exemptions) is multiplied by a flat rate, which is "permanently" fixed by law. Under the second, and more common, approach the property taxes are treated as a residual source of revenue.

Before an organization using the second approach can send tax bills to the property owners, it must determine a tax (millage) rate that, when applied to the assessed valuation of the property, will provide the desired amount of revenue. This is usually the amount shown as part of the revenue estimates in the budget. Although simple in concept, the second approach can become complicated because of (1) uncollectible or delinquent taxes and (2) property exempt from taxation (such as land belonging to religious organizations) and exemptions due to the military service, age, physical condition, and economic status of the owner and the use of the property as a homestead. This last exemption can be particularly costly to taxing organizations. In Louisiana, for example, the homestead exemption is applied to the first $75,000 of the current market value of any piece of property used as the principal residence of its owner.

Using the residual approach, the tax (millage) rate is computed as follows:

Amount to be collected	$ 100,000	
Allowance for uncollectible property taxes	4%	
Required tax levy	$ 104,166 ($100,000/.96)	
Total assessed value of property	$10,000,000	
Less: Property not taxable	(2,000,000)	$8,000,000
Less: exemptions:		
Homestead	$ 1,000,000	
Veterans	500,000	
Old age, blindness, etc.	900,000	2,400,000
Net assessed value of property		$5,600,000

$$\text{Tax (Millage) Rate} = \frac{\text{Required Tax Levy}}{\text{Net Assessed Value of Property}}$$

$$= \frac{104,166}{5,600,000} = .0186$$

In this example, the property tax will be levied at the rate of $1.86 per $100 of net assessed valuation. If the tax rate is expressed in mills (thousandths of a dollar), it will be 18.60 mills. Thus the owner of a piece of property with a net (after exemptions) assessed value of $80,000 will be required to pay property taxes of $1,488 ($80,000 × .0186).

USING BUDGETARY INFORMATION

One purpose of budgets is to provide a measure or "standard" against which actual results can be measured. If the actual expenditures are equal to the budget, the activity is *under control.* If the actual expenditures are greater than or less than the budget, the activity is *out of control.* Thus, by comparing actual expenditures with budgeted expenditures, managers, legislators, and other decision makers can judge the organization's performance and can take corrective action when necessary.

Budgetary comparisons can take several forms. For example, the GASB recommends that the operating statements of many funds show the budgeted and actual revenues and expenditures of each period.[4]

Some organizations also produce monthly statements that detail budgeted and actual expenditures, by object, and the amount of remaining budget for each item. This latter piece of information is particularly important to organizations that are subject to **antideficiency laws** (laws that make the overspending of one's budget an act subject to civil and/or criminal penalties), as well as to those managers and program directors whose performance is judged, in some measure, by whether they meet their budgets. In addition, knowledge of this amount is helpful to organizational personnel when they plan the activities of their work unit for the remainder of the fiscal year. If the amount of the remaining budget is lower than originally planned, their unit must curtail its activities or ask for more money from the legislative body. If the amount of remaining budget is higher than originally planned, their unit can expand its activities.

A well-designed **budgetary control report** (budget comparison) is illustrated in Table 3–16. In addition to showing the budget for the current month and the year to date, it shows (1) actual expenditures incurred for these periods; (2) differences between budgeted and actual expenditures (called **variances**), in both absolute numbers and as a percentage of budget; and (3) amounts that can be spent for the remainder of the year without exceeding the budget. If the amount spent is less than the amount budgeted, a *favorable* (F) variance is shown. If the amount spent is more than the amount budgeted, an *unfavorable* (U) variance is shown.

The budgetary control report in Table 3–16 is presented in one of several possible formats and is based on the 19X0 (current-year) budget. For example, some organizations show amounts that have been encumbered, as well as spent. Other organizations include the following month's budget in this report. Regardless of the format used, the report should meet the organization's needs, all the users should be able to understand the report, and the report's use should be strongly encouraged by the upper levels of management and the legislative body of the organization.

GOVERNMENTAL BUDGETING IN PRACTICE— CLARK COUNTY, NEVADA

In addition to serving as a financial plan, the budget can serve as an operations guide and a communications medium. Clark County, Nevada (the region surrounding Las Vegas), includes a mission statement and statements of goals, performance objectives, and major accomplishments of the past year for each operational unit. It also publishes a separate budget fact book, which contains summary budgets, statistical information and graphical presentations of revenue sources and types of expenditures. Shown below are the mission statement and program information of Clark County's public defender and summary budgets and graphical presentations from that county's fact book.

[4]GASB Cod. Sec. 1100.109.

TABLE 3–16 Budgetary Control Report

Fund: General
Function: Public Safety
Department: Police

Prepared by _RAM_
Date: September 30, 19X0

	YEAR TO DATE				CODE	OBJECT OF EXPENDITURE	CURRENT MONTH				AVAILABLE FOR SPENDING
	BUDGET	ACTUAL	VARIANCE	% BUDGET			BUDGET	ACTUAL	VARIANCE	% BUDGET	
						Contractual Services					
	$ 75	$ 60	$ 15 (F)	20	301	Advertising	$ 8	$ 10	$ 2(U)	25	$ 40
	1,200	1,300	100(U)	8	310	Printing	133	120	13 (F)	10	300
	6,000	6,200	200(U)	3	320	Vehicle maintenance	667	645	22 (F)	3	1,800
	4,200	3,900	300 (F)	7	330	Communication	467	378	89 (F)	19	1,700
	150	180	30(U)	20	350	Dues and subscriptions	17	21	4(U)	24	20
	225	200	25 (F)	11	360	Postage	25	30	5(U)	20	100
	450	550	100(U)	22	370	Telephone	50	35	15 (F)	30	50
	300	300	—	—	380	Professional Services	33	0	33 (F)	100	100
	12,600	$ 12,690	$ 90(U)	1		Subtotal	$ 1,400	$ 1,239	$ 161 (F)	12	4,110
						Supplies and Materials					
	$825	$ 850	$ 25(U)	3	401	Office supplies	$ 92	$97	$ 5(U)	5	250
	3,525	3,595	70(U)	2	410	Building maintenance	392	370	22 (F)	6	1,105
	7,875	7,750	125 (F)	2	420	Fuel	875	825	50 (F)	6	2,750
	$546,375	$563,430	$17,055(U)	3		Grand total	$60,708	$63,386	$2,678(U)	4	$165,070

109

PUBLIC DEFENDER

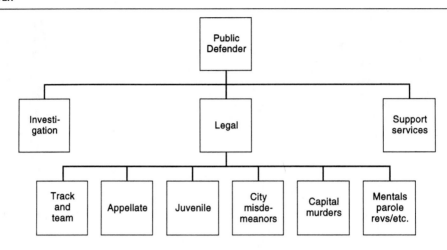

Mission

The Office of the Public Defender protects the rights of all indivdiduals charged with a criminal offense who are not financially able to retain private counsel.

Description

The Office of the Public Defender is responsible for the representation of indigent defendants charged with a criminal offense in Clark County. This includes providing defender representation to juveniles whose parents cannot afford to retain private counsel, and to the City of Las Vegas on a contractual basis for indigents charged with a criminal misdemeanor offense.

Not all defendants are represented with no out-of-pocket expense. The judges, at times, see fit to assess a defendant a certain amount to reimburse the County, at least in part, for costs of representation. This year the Office of the Public Defender was able to collect $22,895 of these assessments which were turned over to Clark County.

Expenditures

	1990–91 ACTUAL	1991–92 ESTIMATE	1992–93 BUDGET
Salaries and wages	$3,229,909	$3,855,159	$4,234,644
Employee benefits	919,902	1,117,856	1,244,946
Services and supplies	274,090	293,054	317,662
Capital Outlay	8,903	12,332	0
Total	$4,432,804	$5,278,401	$5,797,252
Full-time equivalents	69.0	76.5	76.5

Goals

- To ensure that any person this office is appointed to represent receives the highest quality representation guaranteed by law.
- To provide support staff with personal computers to enable them to produce a quality product.
- To increase deputy access to their clients incarcerated at the Clark County Jail.
- To ensure that all circumstances resulting in the charge against the accused are adequately investigated.

Performance objectives (FY 1992–93)

- Assure that sufficient deputy defenders appear at all defense proceedings throughout the year.
- Integrate the computer network upgrades for the word processing, the statistical reporting, the case management, and the departmental accounting systems.
- Implement the incarcerated defendants' communication system at the Clark County Jail.

Major accomplishments/targets (FY 1991–92)

- Established a "Murder Team" whose sole responsibility is representation of individuals charged with a capital offense where the prosecutor seeks the death penalty.
- Became an integral part of the Criminal Justice Information System (CJIS) which resulted in simplifying case access information to staff deputies.
- Acquired computer terminals for clerical employees saving valuable time in locating files to obtain requested information.

Performance indicators

	ACTUAL 1990–91	ESTIMATED 1991–92	PROJECTED 1992–93
Total Cases Handled	31,605	32,500	33,000
Total Court Appearances	64,062	66,000	67,000
Cost Per Case	$140.26	$162.41	$175.67

FUND: *General*
FUNCTION: *Judicial*
TYPE: *N/A*

Source: Adapted from Clark County (Nevada) Final Budget, 1992–1993.

Summary of Revenues
Proprietary Funds

	FY 1991–92 ESTIMATE	FY 1992–93 BUDGET
REVENUES:		
Taxes	$ 19,403	$ 20,147
Licenses and Permits	5,400,000	5,700,000
Charges for Services	365,144,003	426,423,913
Subtotal Operating Revenues	$370,563,406	$432,144,060
Non-Operating Revenue:		
Interest	15,005,298	18,393,570
Miscellaneous	7,718,592	3,253,277
Subtotal Non-Operating Revenue	$ 22,723,890	$ 21,646,847
TOTAL REVENUES	$393,287,296	$453,790,907
EXPENDITURES	$374,517,657	$400,748,143
Revenues over/(under) Expenses	$ 18,769,639	$ 53,042,764

Summary of Expenditures by Major Program
General Fund

	FY 1991–92 ESTIMATE	FY 1992–93 BUDGET
EXPENDITURES:		
General Government	$ 71,539,219	$ 84,755,145
Judicial	60,214,229	67,662,696
Public Safety	38,941,383	40,425,887
Public Works	13,121,996	14,638,499
Health	4,142,510	4,301,755
Welfare	17,331,617	19,007,643
Culture & Recreation	9,248,912	10,533,563
TOTAL EXPENDITURES	$214,539,866	$241,325,188

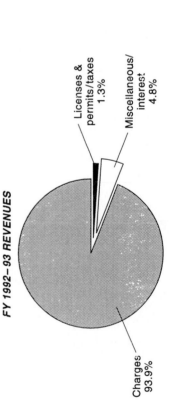

FY 1992–93 EXPENDITURES

Judicial 28.0%
Public works 6.1%
General government 35.1%
Culture & recreation 4.3%
Welfare 7.9%
Public safety 16.7%
Health 1.8%

FY 1992–93 REVENUES

Licenses & permits/taxes 1.3%
Miscellaneous/interest 4.8%
Charges 93.9%

Source: Adapted from Clark County, Nevada, Final Budget Fact Book, Fiscal Year 1992–1993.

REVIEW QUESTIONS

Q3–1   What is a budget? What purpose(s) does it serve?

Q3–2   List the steps involved in preparing a budget.

Q3–3   Why should revenue estimates be prepared before expenditure requests? What steps are taken when preparing revenue estimates?

Q3–4   What information should be contained in a set of budgetary instructions?

Q3–5   What is the purpose of a budget calendar?

Q3–6   How can the current year's surplus or deficit be calculated?

Q3–7   What factors should be considered when projecting (1) sales taxes, (2) property taxes, and (3) hotel occupancy taxes?

Q3–8   What are the three categories of departmental, or program, expenditures?

Q3–9   What are fringe benefits? How should they be handled in the budget?

Q3–10   What is a salary-vacancy factor? How can it be estimated?

Q3–11   What is a capital program? Why should it be prepared for several years beyond the budget year?

Q3–12   Name three sources of supplementary information that should be included with budget requests.

Q3–13   What is the purpose of a budgetary review? By whom should it be performed?

Q3–14   What is a millage rate? How is it determined?

Q3–15   What is the purpose of a cash budget? How can it assist in the smooth functioning of an organization?

Q3–16   Does your state have a budget law? Does it require a balanced budget? How is "balanced budget" defined in your state?

CASES

C3–1   The City of Toth produces monthly budgetary control reports. The amount shown in the budget column is one twelfth of the annual budget. Over lunch, two department heads were discussing this report.

The first manager said, "I like the idea of using one twelfth of my annual budget each month. My costs are constant throughout the year. I can usually find small savings and show favorable variances each month."

The second manager disagreed. "I don't like it. Most of my costs are incurred during Carnival and around Christmas. As a result, I always have unfavorable variances in March and December regardless of what I do. This is especially upsetting since employee performance appraisals are made in April and the council looks especially hard at our March results."

What is the problem with the way these control reports are prepared? What do you think should be done to make the reports more reflective of actual performance of the departments?

C3–2   At a staff meeting of the Parkways Department of the City of Isis, the director, who had been with the city for over thirty years, reminisced about various approaches to budgeting tried by the city during his career. "I was partial to program budgeting. It gave a better picture of our efforts and accomplishments during the year than simply comparing our costs with those budgeted. Everyone else, however, said it was too time-consuming to prepare these budgets and that they didn't provide objective information."

"That was thirty years ago," said a recently hired college graduate. "With today's computers and improved presentation techniques, isn't there some way we can prepare a variant of a performance budget, along with our usual object-of-expenditure budget?"

"Good thinking," said the director. "Why don't you give it a try and show us what you have come up with at the next staff meeting?"

How do you think the recently hired college graduate should proceed? What information should this person provide to tell the department's "story" and future prospects?

C3–3   You have just been elected to your state legislature. One piece of proposed legislation that has crossed your desk is a new law requiring all governmental units in the state to prepare balanced budgets. In this bill, balanced budgets are defined as ones in which expected resources available at the beginning of a fiscal year (beginning fund balance plus estimated revenues) must equal or exceed that year's appropriations. A conservative legislator from a rural county has attached a rider to the bill deleting the above definition of balanced budgets and substituting one in which budgets are balanced only if estimated revenues equal appropriations.

Would you vote for this rider? State your reasons. Why might feelings vary on this issue between legislators from large cities and those from rural counties?

EXERCISES

E3–1   (Discussion of uses of budgeting)

Rex, a budget officer, conducted a class for nonaccounting managers and program directors on the subject of budgets. Rex began the class discussion by asking, "What are some of the uses of a budget?"

One manager replied, "Planning." Another said, "Evaluating performance." Still another suggested, "Coordinating activities." "What about implementing plans?" inquired another. "Or communicating them?" added still another. "Don't forget motivation," one manager warned from the rear of the room. "I'm on the school board," commented another, "and we use it to authorize actions."

Finally, one manager asked, "Can budgets do all that?"

"Yes," Rex responded, "all that *and more.*"

REQUIRED: 1. Define the term *budget*.
2. Select any four of the uses suggested by the managers and explain how a budget might accomplish each of the four uses selected.

(IIA adapted)

E3–2   (Budgeting cash disbursements)
The City of Argus is preparing its cash budget for the month of July. The following information is available with respect to its proposed disbursements:

Items vouchered in July	$650,000
Estimated payments in July for items vouchered in July	50%
Items vouchered in June	$400,000
Estimated payments in July for all items vouchered in June	70%
Estimated payments in July for items vouchered prior to June	$50,000
Items purchased and vouchered in June but returned in July before payment was made	$20,000

REQUIRED: What are the estimated cash disbursements for July?

E3–3   (Budgeting cash receipts)
The City of Comus is preparing a cash budget for the month of May. The following information is available with respect to its sales tax collections:

Sales tax rate	5%
Estimated retail sales in May	$2,000,000
Actual retail sales in April	1,500,000
Estimated payments by merchants to city in May of sales taxes collected in May	20%
Estimated payments by merchants to city in May of sales taxes collected in April	70%
Estimated payments by merchants to city in May of sales taxes collected prior to April	$10,000

REQUIRED: Compute the estimated cash receipts from sales tax collections in May.

E3–4   (Determination of property tax rate)
The legislative body of Pandorra County has just approved the 19X0–19X1 fiscal year budget. Revenues from property taxes are budgeted at $800,000. According to the county assessor, the assessed valuation of all of the property in the county is $50 million. Of this amount, however, property worth $10 million belongs to either the federal government or to religious organizations and, therefore, is not subject to

property taxes. In addition, certificates for the following exemptions have been filed:

Homestead	$2,500,000
Veterans	1,000,000
Old age, blindness, etc.	500,000

In the past, uncollectible property taxes have averaged around 2 percent of the levy. This rate is not expected to change in the foreseeable future.

REQUIRED: 1.   Determine the property tax rate that must be used in order to collect the desired revenue from property taxes.
2.   How much would the levy be on a piece of property that was assessed for $100,000 (after exemptions)?

E3–5   (Estimating the fund balance at the end of the year)
At the end of the preceding year, the General Fund of the Atlas Township School Board had a surplus of $800,000. Revenues and expenditures of the current year are expected to be as follows:

	YEAR-TO-DATE ACTUAL	REMAINDER OF YEAR ESTIMATED
Revenues		
Property taxes	$1,250,000	$500,000
Out-of-township tuition	50,000	20,000
Share of lottery receipts	100,000	50,000
State grants	500,000	—
Expenditures		
Salaries	$875,000	$450,000
Fringe benefits	90,000	40,000
Operating expenses	588,000	240,000
Equipment	110,000	50,000
Transportation	15,000	10,000
Repayment of debt	100,000	100,000

REQUIRED: Determine the projected year-end fund balance for this fund.

E3–6   (Trend analysis)
The City of Endymion levies a tax of 5 percent on all retail sales throughout the City. Retail sales for the current year and the past five years are as follows (rounded and in millions):

1989	$12.1
1990	15.4
1991	17.3
1992	20.8
1993	23.4
1994 (est.)	27.3

In 1995 a new retail complex will be opened that should attract shoppers from nearby cities. As a result, retail sales are expected to be 10 percent higher than they would be if the complex had not been erected.

REQUIRED: Determine how much the city should budget for revenue from sales taxes in 1995.

E3–7 (Multiple choice—budgeting)
1. A key difference between budgets prepared by governmental units and by commercial organizations is
    a. Budgets prepared by commercial organizations must be approved by a governing body, while those prepared by governmental units need no approvals
    b. Budgets prepared by governmental units are legal documents, while those prepared by commercial organizations are not
    c. Operating, capital, and cash budgets are prepared by governmental units, but only operating budgets are prepared by commercial organizations
    d. Budgets prepared by commercial organizations are formally recorded in the organizations' operating accounts, while those prepared by governmental units are not
2. Which of the following expenditures is *not* included in a cash budget?
    a. Personal services
    b. Redemption of bonds
    c. Utilities
    d. Depreciation
3. A nondepartmental expenditures request is prepared by
    a. The department heads as a group
    b. The auditor
    c. The city council
    d. The CEO or the budget director
4. An objection to the object-of-expenditure approach to budgeting is
    a. Budgets prepared under this approach are complicated and difficult to prepare
    b. Information presented in this type of budget is difficult to incorporate into the accounting system
    c. Legislative bodies are given more detail than they can handle; therefore, they tend to focus on individual items rather than on the overall goals and programs of the organization.
    d. Detailed comparisons between budgeted and actual revenues and expenditures are difficult to make
5. A tool commonly used to project certain types of revenues is
    a. Trend analysis
    b. PERT

      c. Queuing theory

      d. Cost-volume-profit analysis

6. Which of the following is *not* a basic rule to follow when using budgets?

    a. The budget must be presented in a positive manner

    b. The budget must have the support of top management

    c. Managers must only be held responsible for revenues and costs over which they have a degree of control

    d. The budget must be prepared by top management

7. A continuous budget

    a. Is used only by commercial organizations

    b. Covers a specific period but is continuously updated

    c. Is also known as a line-item budget

    d. Is valid over a range of activity, rather than just one level

8. The approach to budgeting that forces managers to assess the value and justify the continuation of each activity under their supervision is the

    a. Zero-based budgeting approach

    b. Planning-programming-budgeting approach

    c. Flexible budgeting approach

    d. Object-of-expenditure approach

E3–8 (Behavioral aspects of budgeting)

The operating budget is a very common instrument used by many organizations. While it usually is thought to be an important and necessary tool for management, it has been subject to some criticism from managers and researchers studying organization and human behavior.

REQUIRED: a. Describe and discuss some benefits of budgeting from the behavioral point of view.

                  b. Describe and discuss some criticisms leveled at the budgetary process from the behavioral point of view.

                  c. What solutions do you recommend to overcome the criticisms described in part b?

(CMA adapted)

E3–9 (Budget laws)

Every state has a law or laws regulating its own budgetary practices and those of its local governmental units. Check the law(s) of your state to determine the following:

1. Are budgets legally required by local governmental units, such as cities and counties, in your state?

2. For what funds must budgets be prepared?

3. Must governmental budgets prepared in your state be "balanced"? If so, what does your state law consider to be a "balanced" budget?

4. What legal provisions are made for public input into the budgetary process in your state?

PROBLEMS

P3–1   (Budgeting revenues)
The following information relates to the prior- and current-year revenues of the General Fund of the Bacchus City Levee Board.

	19W9 ACTUAL	JAN.–SEPT. 19X0 ACTUAL	OCT.–DEC. 19X0 EST. ACT.	19X1 BUDGET
Property taxes	$3,436,720	$2,334,000	$1,150,000	$3,504,000
Interest and penalties	38,486	22,800	15,000	38,000
Sales taxes	272,680	154,500	145,000	300,000
Fines and penalties	64,842	39,240	30,000	70,000
Share of lottery receipts	—	54,250	175,750	225,000
License fees	9,650	7,540	2,460	10,000

Additional information:
1.   Because of a reassessment of commercial property, property taxes are expected to increase by $400,000 in 19X1.
2.   Interest and penalties and license fees are expected to remain constant over the next several years.
3.   Because of an increase in the sales tax from 4 to 6 percent and the expectation of several large conventions in 19X1, sales tax revenues are expected to increase by 60 percent.
4.   Because of the conventions, fines and penalties should rise by 10 percent in 19X1.
5.   The lottery has been very successful in its first few months of operation. Levee Board officials expect the board's share of the lottery receipts to double in 19X1.

REQUIRED: Prepare a statement of actual and estimated revenues for 19X1. Assume that you are preparing it on October 15, 19X0, and that the **changes given above are with respect to the 19X0 budget.**

P3–2   (Personal services and travel work sheets)
The director of the Maintenance Department of the Bacchus City Levee Board has prepared the following position classification plan:

CODE	POSITION	19W9 NO.	19W9 RATE	19X0 NO.	19X0 RATE
101	Director	1	$28,000	1	$30,000
102	Assistant director	1	24,000	1	26,000
104	Foreman	4	17,500	4	19,000
110	Equipment operator II	8	14,250	7	16,000
112	Equipment operator I	12	12,100	13	13,880
115	Laborer, utility	30	9,200	26	10,300
120	Secretary	1	9,500	1	10,600

Additional information:

1. Fringe benefits are not included in the above rates. In 19W9, they averaged 12.2 percent of wages and salaries. In 19X0, they are averaging 12.8 percent. In 19X1, they should average 13.6 percent.
2. Permission has been obtained from the legislative body to budget an 8 percent cost-of-living increase for 19X1. In addition, the president of the board has recommended that the director and the assistant director each be given a $1,000 merit increase, in addition to their cost-of-living increases.
3. Due to the building of several miles of new levees in 19X0, the management of the Levee Board believes that an additional maintenance crew, consisting of one foreman, one equipment operator II, and two laborers, should be hired.
4. From March 3 to March 7, the director of the Maintenance Department plans to attend a professional conference in Milwaukee, at a cost of $750. In addition, the director and the assistant director plan to attend a technical workshop in Tampa from April 21 through April 25, at a cost of $500 each. Finally, the five foremen are expected to attend a supervisory workshop, given at a nearby city, on August 18. The cost of this travel for all five foremen is expected to be $100. In 19W9, travel costs amounted to $1,425. In 19X0, they were budgeted at $1,500. A total of $1,600 is expected to be spent this year.
5. Assume that in 19X0 budgeted salaries are the same as actual salaries. Assume also that the Maintenance Department's activities are recorded in the General Fund and that this department's function falls under the heading of Public Safety.

REQUIRED: For fiscal year 19X1 prepare

1. A personal services work sheet and a budget year salary work sheet
2. A travel work sheet

P3–3   (Equipment work sheet)

During 19X1, the Maintenance Department of the Bacchus City Levee Board plans to make the following purchases of equipment. Since these items each cost more than $200, they are budgeted under the category of "Equipment." The items are:

1. Two three-quarter-ton pickup trucks. These will be replacements for existing trucks and will have a net cost (after trade-in) of $9,500 each.
2. One two-ton flatbed truck. This is a new item that will be necessary because of the new work crew expected to be hired and the additional levees to be maintained. Estimated cost of the truck is $22,500.
3. Other new items to be purchased for use of the new work crew are:

a. One chipper $3,750
b. Two 24" lawn mowers 700 each
c. Two lawn vacuum cleaners 650 each
d. One hedge trimmer 240
e. One 5' by 8' trailer 500

4. Other items, which are replacements for existing items, to be purchased are:

a. Three 22" lawn mowers $300 each
b. Two grass trimmers 2,200 each
c. One welding machine (used) 3,000

In 19W9, the Maintenance Department spent $36,450 on equipment. For 19X0, $30,000 has been budgeted, but only $18,360 of this amount has been spent to date. The director of this department estimates that by the end of fiscal year 19X0, another $8,000 will be spent or encumbered for equipment.

REQUIRED: Prepare an equipment work sheet for the Maintenance Department.

P3–4 (Operating expense work sheet)

From the following data, prepared as of August 30, 19X0, prepare an operating expense work sheet to be used in the fiscal year 19X1 budget of the Maintenance Department of the Bacchus City Levee Board.

CODE	OBJECT OF EXPENDITURE	PRIOR-YEAR ACTUAL	CURRENT-YEAR BUDGET	YEAR-TO-DATE ACTUAL	REST OF YEAR EST. ACTUAL
	Contractual Services				
320	Vehicle and equpiment maintenance	$18,450	$20,000	$15,000	$6,000
330	Communication	1,200	1,200	800	400
340	Rentals	648	800	400	200
365	Utilities	1,146	1,200	952	300
370	Telephone	240	240	180	80
380	Professional services	300	500	350	—
	Supplies and Materials				
410	Office supplies	214	200	158	42
415	Auto and truck	286	300	200	100
418	Equipment supplies	1,614	1,500	1,250	400
420	Fuel	3,847	4,000	3,000	1,500
425	Gardening materials	1,206	1,200	860	300
430	Emergency supplies	152	200	50	100
440	Tools	876	1,000	800	200
450	Miscellaneous	136	100	75	—

Additional information:

1. Because of the crew expected to be added in 19X1, the budgeted vehicle and equipment maintenance, equipment supplies, tools, and

gardening materials expenditures are to be increased by 15 percent in 19X1.

2. The budgets for communications, professional services, and miscellaneous supplies and materials should remain at their present levels.

3. An inflation factor of 8 percent should be applied to the fiscal year 19X0 budget for the remaining items.

4. For this department, professional services consist largely of tree surgery and medical expenses for minor injuries of work crews.

P3–5   (Capital outlay requests)

The management of the Bacchus City Levee Board wishes to start or continue the following capital projects in fiscal year 19X1.

1. Raise the height of the lakefront levee from 12 feet to 18 feet. This will decrease the probability of flooding in a hurricane from 25 to 5 percent. The estimated cost of this project is $450,000. The entire cost will be charged to the Facilities Department.

2. Continue construction of the Taos Avenue Bridge. The estimated cost to be incurred in fiscal year 19X1 is $750,000, which is to be charged to the Facilities Department. This cost represents approximately one-half of the total cost of the project.

3. Build a new equipment storage facility. This is necessary because of the additional equipment that is expected to be purchased by the Maintenance Department. The estimated cost of this project is $50,000, all of which will be charged to the Maintenance Department.

4. Build a new office building to house the various administrative functions. The building is expected to cost $800,000. Of this amount 10 percent will be charged to the Maintenance Department. The remaining 90 percent will be charged to the Department of Administration.

REQUIRED: Prepare a capital outlay request summary for the Bacchus City Levee Board.

P3–6   (Departmental expenditure request)

Using the information given in Problems 3–2 through 3–5 and the information below, prepare a departmental expenditure request for the Maintenance Department of the Bacchus City Levee Board.

1. The function of the department is to assist in guarding the public's safety by maintaining the levees around Bacchus City. This consists primarily of caring for the grass and trees on the levees, filling in eroded spots, and maintaining the floodgates and supply of sandbags. Because of the growth of the city, new levees have been built in outlying areas and certain levees have been raised. The care of these new levees has put a severe strain on the existing work crews' ability to maintain all of the levee system adequately.

2. In fiscal year 19W9, no capital expenditures were charged to the Maintenance Department. For fiscal year 19X0, $100,000 has been budgeted. It is expected that the actual capital expenditures charged to this department in fiscal year 19X0 will amount to $95,000.

P3–7 Budgeting Nondepartmental Expenditures

From the following data, prepare a nondepartmental expenditures request for the Bacchus City Levee Board for fiscal year 19X1.

CODE	OBJECT OF EXPENDITURE	PRIOR-YEAR ACTUAL	CURRENT-YEAR BUDGET	JAN.–SEPT. ACTUAL	OCT.–DEC. EST. ACT.
710	Redemption of bonds	$715,000	$890,000	$445,000	$445,000
725	Interest on bonds	52,000	60,000	30,000	30,000
730	Fiscal agent fees	554	600	450	200
810	Liability insurance	15,436	16,000	12,315	4,000
925	Audit fees	5,000	6,000	—	6,200
930	Legal services	10,000	10,000	8,500	2,000

Additional information:

1. In 19X1, bond redemptions should amount to $1 million, and interest on the bonds should be approximately $50,000. Fiscal agent fees for 19X1 should amount to $600.
2. Because of the new levees, the board is increasing the amount of its insurance coverage. The 19X1 premium is expected to amount to $20,000.
3. The cost of legal services and the annual audit are expected to be 10 percent higher than the amount budgeted for 19X0. The 19X1 budget should be adjusted accordingly.
4. Bond redemptions, interest, and fiscal agent fees are paid by the Debt Service Fund. During the year, the amounts budgeted (Codes 710, 725, and 730) will be transferred to that fund.

P3–8 (Budget summary)

Using the information given in P3–1 through P3–7 and the information below, prepare a budget summary for the General Fund of the Bacchus City Levee Board for fiscal year 19X1.

1. The Bacchus City Levee Board has three departments: Maintenance, Facilities, and Administration.
2. Budgeted data pertaining to the Facilities and Administration departments for fiscal year 19X1 are as follows:

Facilities:
Personal services	$115,000
Travel	5,000
Equipment	65,000
Operating expenses	15,000
Capital outlays	?

Administration:

Personal services	$500,000
Travel	10,000
Equipment	40,000
Operating expenses	30,000
Capital outlays	?

P3–9 (Control report)

Refer to P3–4. Prepare a control report, like the one shown in Table 3–16, for *operating expenses* of the Maintenance Department for the month of August 19X0. Assume that August is the eighth month of the fiscal year and that the year-to-date budget is two thirds of the entire 19X0 budget. Assume also that the budget for *August* is one twelfth of the entire 19X0 budget. Year-to-date actual results are given in P3–4. Actual results for the month of August are as follows:

Contractual services:	
Vehicle & equipment maintenance	$1,567
Communication	75
Rentals	89
Utilities	110
Telephone	15
Professional services	50
Supplies and materials:	
Office supplies	$ 15
Auto and truck	30
Equipment supplies	110
Fuel	300
Gardening supplies	120
Emergency supplies	25
Tools	75
Miscellaneous	5

4

THE GOVERNMENTAL FUND ACCOUNTING CYCLE

General and Special Revenue Funds—An Introduction

LEARNING OBJECTIVES

After completion of this chapter, you should be able to:

1. Compare the objectives of fund accounting with those of commercial accounting
2. Contrast the accounting cycle of a governmental unit with that of a commercial organization
3. Explain why separate budgetary entries are used
4. Prepare operating entries for a governmental unit
5. Prepare closing entries for a governmental unit
6. Explain why revenues from property taxes are recorded when these taxes are levied, rather than when they are collected
7. Describe how control and subsidiary accounts are used
8. Explain the use of encumbrances and how they should be recorded in the accounts

---

The most basic funds used by nonbusiness organizations are the General Fund and the Special Revenue Funds. The **General Fund** is used to record the overall operations of the organization and is a catchall for all revenues and expenditures not recorded in other funds. Activities accounted for in this fund include police and fire protection and other day-to-day operations of the governmental unit.

Special Revenue Funds are used to account for the proceeds of revenue sources (other than special assessments, expendable trusts, and those used for major capital projects) that must be spent for particular purposes. Examples of Special Revenue Funds include funds used to account for the activities of libraries and parks and for federal and state grants. From an accounting standpoint, General and Special Revenue Funds are very similar.

Since General Funds are the most commonly used funds and the accounting for most other funds is very similar to that of General and Special Revenue Funds, these funds are discussed first. If you understand the entries used by these funds, you can easily learn those unique to the other funds.

As in commercial accounting, the objective of fund accounting is to convey to the reader of financial statements a picture of what happened in the past. From this information, the reader can make financially related decisions. Fund accounting, however, is also concerned with the future and with certain legal considerations. As a result, the fund accounting cycle is somewhat more complicated than the commercial accounting cycle—even though the end products are essentially the same. The two cycles are contrasted in Table 4–1.

TABLE 4–1   Fund Accounting Versus Commercial Accounting

FUND ACCOUNTING	COMMERCIAL ACCOUNTING
Objectives*	Objectives
• To show the financial condition of the organization	• To show the financial condition of the firm
• To show the results of operations of the organization	• To show the results of operations of the firm
• To show changes in the financial condition of the organization	• To show changes in the financial condition of the firm
• To show compliance with legal restrictions	
Accounting Cycle	Accounting Cycle
• Record the budget in the accounting records	
• Record transactions for the period	• Record transactions for the period
• Prepare closing entries	• Prepare closing entries
• Prepare financial statements	• Prepare financial statements
—Balance sheet	—Balance sheet
—Statement of revenues, expenditures, and changes in fund balance	—Income statement and statement of changes in retained earnings
—Statement of cash flows (only for proprietary funds and similar funds)	—Statement of cash flows
—Statement comparing budgeted and actual revenues and expenditures (of certain governmental-type funds)	

*For a more detailed listing of these objectives, see Chapter 2.

SECTION I—A BASIC FUND ACCOUNTING SYSTEM

The steps in the fund accounting cycle are shown in Table 4–1. Note that the cycle begins with the budget and that, unlike commercial accounting, the budget is formally recorded in the accounts.

The Budget

In fund accounting, the **budget** is usually a legal document. It is an estimate of the expenditures of a fiscal year and the means proposed to finance them. It is also the end product of a series of requests and proposals that originate with department heads and other managers and, after being screened and adjusted by the budget officer, are put into budgetary form. A typical budget is shown in Table 4–2.

The principal items in this budget are Estimated revenues, Appropriations, and Other financing sources and (uses). **Estimated revenues** are resources that have been, or are expected to be, made available to the organization. They include taxes, fines and penalties, and service charges. One such resource, unique to governmental units, is the right to levy taxes on real and personal property. In this budget, Estimated revenues are broken down into those obtained from ad valorem (property) taxes and other sources of income such as royalties, revenue sharing, and interest on investments.

Appropriations are allocations of resources that will be used to carry out the activities of the organization (proposed expenditures). They represent the authority to spend money in accordance with the approved budget. This is not to imply, of course, that the money must be spent. Appropriations are made with the expectation of receiving a certain level of services. If such services should happen to be provided at less cost, the monies saved can be used to increase the fund balance or to provide additional services.

Appropriations are broken down by category or object and, in some cases, by department or function as well (e.g., Police—salaries). In this text, however, we will assume that appropriations are budgeted by object. This simplification makes it appear that each organization has only one department. In reality, of course, most organizations have many departments (or functions), with each department using its own set of operating accounts. Nevertheless, the entries illustrated in this chapter and Chapter 5 are applicable to nearly all nonbusiness organizations, the only difference being the level of detail involved.

Other financing sources are receipts of resources that are not revenues. Examples include the proceeds of an issue of notes and certain types of transfers from other funds, such as those from a trust fund to a Library (Special Revenue) Fund.

Other financing uses are disbursements of resources that are not expenditures. Examples include payments made by the General Fund to a Capital Projects Fund for the General Fund's share of the cost of constructing new facilities, and payments made by Special Revenue Funds to Debt Service Funds for the re-

TABLE 4–2

Orleans Levee Board
General Fund
Estimated Revenues, Appropriations, and Other Sources (Uses)
Fiscal Year July 1, 19X1, to June 30, 19X2

Estimated Revenues		
Ad valorem taxes	$6,720,232	
Royalties	1,000,000	
State revenue sharing	600,000	
New Orleans Lakefront Airport	1,086,361	
Orleans Marina	1,004,000	
Lake Vista Community Center	132,759	
Other locations	330,105	
Lakefront camps	15,450	
Interest on investments	785,000	
Miscellaneous	5,700	
Total estimated revenues		$11,679,607
Appropriations		
Personal services	$6,305,764	
Travel	40,000	
Contractual services	2,670,040	
Materials and supplies	1,061,792	
Professional services	497,905	
Other charges	34,806	
Equipment	609,897	
Total appropriations		11,220,204
Excess of estimated revenues over appropriations		$ 459,403
Other Financing Sources (Uses)		
Transfer from Special Levee Improvement Project Fund	$ 821,640	
Transfer to General Improvement Project Fund	(862,500)	
Transfer to Debt Service Fund	(70,878)	
Orleans Marina transfer to South Shore Harbor	(1,004,000)	
Contingent transfer from South Shore Harbor to Board	384,657	
Designations:		
Contingency—unemployment compensation payments	(9,500)	
Contingency—materials and supplies purchases	(5,000)	
Contingency—equipment purchases	(3,000)	
Contingency—A/C replacements	(25,000)	
Major heavy equpiment replacement	(105,000)	
Amount provided for Capital Projects from prior-year project allocations	425,000	
Total other sources (uses)		(453,581)
Excess of estimated revenues and other financing sources over appropriations and other financing uses		$ 5,822

Source: Adapted from a current *Annual Approved Budget* of the Orleans Levee Board.

tirement of debt. Other financing sources (and uses) are broken down by type of transfer to and from the budgetary unit.

Opening Entries

At the beginning of the fiscal year, the approved budget is recorded in the accounts. Debits are made to estimated revenue accounts and credits are made to appropriation accounts. Any difference between Estimated revenues and Appropriations is debited or credited to Unreserved fund balance.

Fund balance is a residual account whose balance is equal to the difference between the assets and the liabilities of an organization. The account itself is "permanent" in nature—that is, its balance is carried forward into future periods. It is usually called **Unreserved fund balance,** the term *unreserved* indicating that part of the fund balance has not been set aside for any special purpose.

The difference (if any) between Estimated revenues and Appropriations represents the expected change in Unreserved fund balance during the year. If actual revenues recorded during the year equal Estimated revenues and expenditures incurred during the year equal Appropriations, no further adjustments to Unreserved fund balance will be necessary. The dollar amounts shown in the opening entry, which is known as a **budgetary entry,** should correspond to those found in the budget.

To illustrate the fund accounting cycle, assume that the city council of Simple City has just approved the budget shown in Table 4-3. At the beginning of the fiscal year, the following budgetary entry is made:

Estimated revenues	1,000,000	
Appropriations		990,000
Unreserved fund balance		10,000

To record estimated revenues and appropriations for FY 19X1.

After this entry has been posted, the general ledger will appear as follows:

ASSETS	=	LIABILITIES	+	FUND BALANCE
Estimated revenues	=	Appropriations	+	Unreserved fund balance
$1,000,000	=	$990,000	+	$10,000

Estimated revenues and Appropriations are budgetary accounts. **Budgetary accounts,** by definition, are accounts used to enter the formally adopted annual budget into the general ledger. At the end of the period, all budgetary accounts are closed out (their balances are reduced to zero). Many nonbudgetary accounts, by contrast, are "permanent" in nature (e.g., the Unreserved fund balance); their balances are carried forward to the next accounting period.

TABLE 4–3

Simple City
General Fund Budget
Fiscal Year, 19X1

Estimated Revenues		
Property taxes	$900,000	
Fines, licenses, etc.	100,000	$1,000,000
Appropriations		
Salaries	$700,000	
Materials	200,000	
Other	90,000	990,000
Projected Increase in Fund		
Balance		$ 10,000

Recording Revenues and Expenditures

Revenue and expenditure accounting provides information for several purposes:

1. *To determine whether all revenues have been received.* Revenue accounting is the process of recording the amount of taxes, fees, and other revenues that have been received, as well as those still outstanding. Although the organization has the *right* to tax, it does not necessarily follow that the taxes have actually been collected.
2. *To determine whether expenditures were made in accordance with the budget.* Expenditure accounting is the process of recording the *actual* monies spent, on an item-by-item basis. It provides information on the relationship between budgeted and actual expenditures, as to both their nature and their size.
3. *To prepare various financial statements.* Revenue and expenditure accounting provide information for the balance sheet; for the statement of revenues, expenditures, and changes in the fund balance; and for any other financial statements that may be prepared.
4. *To assist in the preparation of future budgets.* Actual revenues collected are often used as a base in determining the size and composition of future tax levies and service charges. Actual expenditures determine the cost of services rendered. Both provide inputs into decisions as to what services should be made available in the future.

Revenue and expenditure accounts, like their commercial counterparts, are *nominal* accounts. They are not permanent in nature, as are assets and liabilities. Instead they are closed out (reduced to zero) at the end of each period.

Entries to record revenues are similar to those found in commercial accounting—debits to Cash or receivable accounts and credits to revenue accounts. To continue with the previous example, if all revenues are collected at once and in cash, the entry is:

Cash	1,000,000	
Revenues		1,000,000
To record collection of FY 19X1 revenues.		

Entries to record expenditures are also similar to those used in commercial accounting: debits to expenditure accounts and credits to Cash or payable accounts. If all monies appropriated for the period are spent (expended), the entry is:

Expenditures	990,000	
Cash		990,000

To record incurrence of FY 19X1 expenditures.

Closing Entries

A **closing** usually takes place at year-end. Its purpose is to *close* (reduce to zero) nominal (revenue and expenditure) and budgetary (estimated revenue and appropriation) accounts and, if necessary, to adjust Unreserved fund balance to its "true" value.

In commercial accounting, revenues and expenses are "matched," and any difference is added to or deducted from capital or retained earnings. In not-for-profit accounting, a slightly different process is followed. Actual revenues are matched against estimated revenues, and expenditures are matched against appropriations. Any differences are added to or deducted from Unreserved fund balance. The net result of these entries is zero balances in the budgetary accounts and the revenue and expenditure accounts and, possibly, a revised end-of-year balance in Unreserved fund balance.

Continuing with our illustration, let us assume that revenues of $1 million are collected and that $990,000 is expended (paid out) during the year. The closing entries are

1.	Revenues	1,000,000	
	Estimated revenues		1,000,000

To close revenue and estimated revenue accounts for FY 19X1.

2.	Appropriations	990,000	
	Expenditures		990,000

To close appropriation and expenditure accounts for FY 19X1.

Each of the four accounts now has a zero balance. Since actual revenues equal estimated revenues and expenditures equal appropriations, there is no need to adjust Unreserved fund balance. Its end-of-year balance ($10,000) will exceed its beginning-of-year balance ($0) by the amount recorded in the opening (budgetary) entry, $10,000.

An alternative approach to closing, preferred by some accountants, is to close budgetary and nonbudgetary accounts separately. Thus, Estimated revenues are closed to Appropriations and Revenues are closed to Expenditures. Any differences between Estimated revenues and Appropriations and between Revenues and Expenditures are debited or credited to Unreserved fund balance.

Under this approach, the closing entries in our illustration would be:

1.	Appropriations	990,000	
	Unreserved fund balance	10,000	
	Estimated revenues		1,000,000
	To close budgetary accounts for FY 19X1.		
2.	Revenues	1,000,000	
	Expenditures		990,000
	Unreserved fund balance		10,000
	To close nonbudgetary accounts for FY 19X1.		

The net effect of these entries is the same as that of the entries previously illustrated—that is, zero balances in the Revenue, Estimated revenue, Expenditure, and Appropriation accounts and a $10,000 increase in the Unreserved fund balance. Although both approaches to closing are sound, we will follow the first approach because it is the one most commonly used.

After the closing entries have been posted, a postclosing trial balance is prepared, followed by financial statements. The postclosing trial balance for Simple City is shown in Table 4–4. The resulting financial statements are shown in Table 4–5.[1]

Table 4–5 is simplified and not very realistic. Nevertheless, all the elements of the fund accounting cycle are present. If you *understand* the example, you will easily master the refinements that are present in "real world" problems.

The example used in this section is summarized in Table 4–6. Before continuing, be certain that you understand *why* each entry was made and *what effect* it has on the accounting equation. The budget from which the opening entries are derived is on page 130. The statements are on page 133.

TABLE 4–4   Postclosing Trial Balance

Simple City
General Fund
Postclosing Trial Balance
December 31, 19X1

	DEBITS	CREDITS
Cash	$10,000	
Unreserved fund balance		$10,000
	$10,000	$10,000

[1]For the sake of brevity, it is assumed that the reader is able to make entries to the ledger. The mechanics of posting are discussed in Chapter 14.

TABLE 4–5   Illustrative Financial Statements

Simple City
General Fund
Balance Sheet
December 31, 19X1

ASSETS		LIABILITIES AND FUND BALANCE	
Cash	$10,000	Unreserved fund balance	$10,000

Simple City
General Fund
Statement of Revenues, Expenditures, and
Changes in Fund Balance
Fiscal Year 19X1

Revenues	$1,000,000
Expenditures	990,000
Increase in fund balance	$ 10,000
Fund balance, 1/1/X1	-0-
Fund balance, 12/31/X1	$ 10,000

TABLE 4–6   Summary of the Accounting Cycle of the General Fund of Simple City for Fiscal Year 19X1

The budgetary, or opening, entry is:

Estimated revenues	1,000,000	
Appropriations		990,000
Unreserved fund balance		10,000

To record estimated revenues and
  appropriations for 19X1.

The operating entries are:

Cash	1,000,000	
Revenues		1,000,000

To record FY 19X1 revenues.

Expenditures	990,000	
Cash		990,000

To record FY 19X1 expenditures.

The closing entries are:

Revenues	1,000,000	
Estimated revenues		1,000, 000

To close revenue and estimated revenue accounts for FY 19X1.

Appropriations	990,000	
Expenditures		990,000

To close appropriations and
  expenditures accounts for FY 19X1.

SECTION II—A MORE-REFINED SYSTEM

The example in the preceding section, although theoretically correct, is oversimplified. Revenues are actually collected in uneven amounts throughout the year and revenues and expenditures seldom equal Estimated revenues and Appropriations. In addition, many different revenue and expenditure accounts are used by most governmental units, and when certain goods or services are ordered monies are set aside (encumbered). In this section, three refinements will be made to the basic system previously illustrated: receivables, subsidiary accounts, and encumbrances.

Receivables

After the approved budget of a governmental unit has been recorded in the accounts, property taxes are levied. The governmental unit now has a claim against each taxpayer for his or her share of the property taxes due. To recognize this **receivable,** a debit is made to Property taxes receivable and a credit to a revenue account. When the taxes are collected, Cash is debited and Property taxes receivable is credited. The legal claim against the taxpayer or taxpayers has now been satisfied.

The above procedure differs from the one discussed in the preceding section in that revenues from property taxes are recorded when they are levied, rather than when they are collected. Under the modified accrual basis of accounting, which is used by governmental-type funds, such a procedure is required. This is because the amounts received from property taxes, unlike those received from other sources, are *available* and *measurable,* with a reasonable degree of accuracy, when the property taxes are levied.

In addition, the collection of revenues from property taxes is, in theory, fairly certain because the organization has a claim against specific tangible property. In the event of nonpayment of taxes, the governmental unit has the legal right to force the sale of the property and to deduct the taxes due from the proceeds.

To illustrate, assume that property taxes are budgeted at $900,000. The entry to recognize (record) the receivable is:

Property taxes receivable	900,000	
Revenues		900,000
To set up receivable for FY 19X1 property taxes.		

When the property taxes are collected, the entry is:

Cash	900,000	
Property taxes receivable		900,000
To record collection of property taxes.		

The above entry assumes, for illustrative purposes, that all taxes are collected at once. In reality, smaller amounts are collected each day. As a result, a *series* of entries, similar to the one shown above, is made, with the collections totaling $900,000.

Receivable accounts are generally used to record the assessment of property taxes. This is because property taxes are levied against a given base (the assessed value of the property within the governmental unit). Once the millage (tax rate) has been determined (usually when the budget is approved), the amount that should be received is known with a reasonable degree of certainty.

Income taxes, fees, fines, and other sources of revenue, however, are influenced by such variables as the level of employment, housing starts, and number of tourists. These revenues cannot be determined with certainty until they have been received. Therefore they are recognized when the cash is collected. This is done by means of a debit to Cash and a credit to a revenue account.

To illustrate, assume that the monies actually collected from "other" sources of revenue are $100,000 and that they all are received at once. The entry to recognize these revenues is:

Cash	100,000	
Revenues		100,000
To record revenues from sources other than property taxes, FY 19X1.		

Closing with a Surplus or Deficit

Up to this point it has been assumed that actual revenues equal estimated revenues and that expenditures equal appropriations. This seldom happens in real life. In a more typical situation, actual revenues will be greater than or less than estimated revenues, and expenditures will not equal appropriations. When this happens, any differences must be added to or deducted from Unreserved fund balance. To illustrate, assume the following:

Estimated revenues from all sources	$1,000,000
Actual revenues from all sources	996,000
Appropriations of all types	990,000
Expenditures of all types	987,000

The entry to close the estimated and actual revenue accounts is:

Revenues—all sources	996,000	
Unreserved fund balance	4,000	
Estimated revenues—all sources		1,000,000
To close estimated and actual revenue accounts.		

The entry to close the appropriation and expenditure accounts is:

Appropriations—all types	990,000	
Expenditures—all types		987,000
Unreserved fund balance		3,000

To close appropriation and expenditure accounts.

These entries have the effect of decreasing the Unreserved fund balance from its planned end-of-the-year-balance (assumed to be $10,000) to its actual end-of-year-balance ($10,000 − $4,000 + $3,000 = $9,000).

Occasionally the Unreserved fund balance account becomes negative and has a debit balance. A negative fund balance is known as a **deficit.** This is a very unhealthy situation.

Control and Subsidiary Accounts

In the preceding examples all revenues were combined into one account, as were all expenditures. This is not realistic or practical. Nonbusiness organizations, like their commercial counterparts, use control and subsidiary accounts. A **control account** is a summary account whose balance is equal to the total of the individual balances of its **subsidiary accounts.** The balances in the control accounts are changed when, and by the same amount that, changes are made in the subsidiary accounts. Examples of control accounts include Property taxes receivable (which are backed up by accounts for each taxpayer), Estimated revenues, Appropriations, and Expenditures (see Table 4–7).

An alternative to subsidiary and control accounts is the use of a large number of specialized accounts, similar in nature but different in detail. Many organizations do this on several levels. For example, appropriation and expenditure accounts are sometimes broken down by function or department (public safety, welfare, and so on) and then by object or category (salaries, supplies, and so on). Thus the account used to record the salaries of police officers would be Expenditures—Police Department—salaries. An account used to record revenues from licenses issued to owners of tour buses would be Revenues—license fees—tour buses.

Except for the following illustration, in which control and subsidiary accounts are used to record the collection of property taxes, a one-step breakdown is used throughout this text and control and subsidiary accounts are combined. This is done in order to keep the illustrative problems to a manageable size. Expanding the illustrations to include a two- or three-level breakdown or to include separate subsidiary and control accounts is fairly simple, requiring little more than time and a great deal of paper.

To illustrate the use of control and subsidiary accounts, as well as a number of different revenue and expenditure accounts, assume that a city has the following budgeted sources of revenue:

TABLE 4–7 Examples of Control and Subsidiary Accounts

CONTROL	SUBSIDIARY	DETAIL
Revenues	Taxes	Property taxes Sales tax Penalties and interest on delinquent taxes
	Licenses and permits	Business licenses and permits Nonbusiness licenses and permits
	Intergovernmental reveues	Federal grants State grants
	Charges for services	General government Public safety Highways and streets Sanitation
	Fines and forfeitures	Fines Forfeitures
Expenditures	General government	Salaries Supplies Capital outlays Other services
	Public safety	Salaries Supplies Capital outlays Other services
	Highways and streets	Salaries Supplies Capital outlays Other services
	Sanitation and health	Salaries Supplies Capital outlays Other services
	Education	Salaries Supplies Capital outlays Other services
Receivables	Property taxes receivable	C. Ives A. Dvorak P. Pratt S. Joplin J. Gilberto

Property taxes	$900,000
License fees	50,000
Fines	40,000
Income taxes	10,000
Total	$1,000,000

Assume also that this city has five property owners, whose property taxes are levied as follows:

J. Brill	$500,000
R. Jewett	300,000
G. Kuhlman	45,000
A. Niles	30,000
P. Thomas	25,000
Total	$900,000

Finally, assume that the city has one department whose appropriations are as follows:

Salaries	$700,000
Supplies	200,000
Other	90,000
Total	$990,000

The budgetary, or opening, entry is:

Estimated revenues—property taxes	900,000	
Estimated revenues—license fees	50,000	
Estimated revenues—fines	40,000	
Estimated revenues—service charges	10,000	
Appropriations—salaries		700,000
Appropriations—supplies		200,000
Appropriations—other		90,000
Unreserved fund balance		10,000

To record estimated revenues and appropriations for FY 19X1.

If subsidiary and control accounts are used for property taxes, the entry to set up the receivable is

Property taxes receivable—control	900,000	
Revenues—property taxes		900,000

To set up receivable for FY19X1 property taxes.

Property Taxes Receivable—Subsidiary Ledger

DEBIT

J. Brill	500,000
R. Jewett	300,000
G. Kuhlman	45,000
A Niles	30,000
P. Thomas	25,000
	900,000

If these taxpayers pay their property tax bills in full during the period, the entry to record the payments is:

Cash	900,000	
Property taxes receivable—control		900,000
To record collection of FY 19X1 property taxes.		

Property Taxes Receivable—Subsidiary Ledger

CREDIT

J. Brill	500,000
R. Jewett	300,000
G. Kuhlman	45,000
A Niles	30,000
P. Thomas	25,000
	900,000

Other revenues are recorded when collected or, in the case of self-assessed taxes like those on income and sales, when available and measurable.[2] The entry to record these revenues (amounts assumed) is:

Cash	96,000	
Revenues—license fees		47,000
Revenues—fines		38,000
Revenues—service charges		11,000
To record receipt of nonproperty tax revenues, FY 19X1.		

Entries to record expenditures and their subsequent payment (amounts assumed) are:

1.	Expenditures—salaries	700,000	
	Expenditures—supplies	195,000	
	Expenditures—other	92,000	
	Vouchers payable		987,000
	To record FY 19X1 expenditures.		
2.	Vouchers payable	987,000	
	Cash		987,000
	To record payment of outstanding FY 19X1 vouchers.		

[2]Self-assessed taxes are discussed in Chapter 5.

Finally, the closing entries are:

1.	Revenues—property taxes	900,000	
	Revenues—license fees	47,000	
	Revenues—fines	38,000	
	Revenues—service charges	11,000	
	Unreserved fund balance	4,000	
	Estimated revenues—property taxes		900,000
	Estimated revenues—license fees		50,000
	Estimated revenues—fines		40,000
	Estimated revenues—service charges		10,000
	To close revenue and estimated revenue accounts for FY 19X1.		
2.	Appropriations—salaries	700,000	
	Appropriations—supplies	200,000	
	Appropriations—other	90,000	
	Expenditures—salaries		700,000
	Expenditures—supplies		195,000
	Expenditures—other		92,000
	Unreserved fund balance		3,000
	To close appropriation and expenditure accounts for FY 19X1.		

Notice that these entries are very similar to those found in earlier illustrations. The only differences are that specific revenues and expenditures are now recorded in the accounts and that estimated revenues and appropriations do not exactly match actual revenues and expenditures.

Vouchers

In the above example, the account Vouchers payable was used. A **voucher** is a written document that provides evidence that a transaction is proper. It also indicates the accounts in which the transaction is recorded.

The term *vouchers payable* is used in fund accounting in the same manner that the term *accounts payable* is used in business accounting—to represent the recording of a liability. The use of a voucher, however, indicates that payment has been approved by the appropriate authority and will definitely be made at a particular time. It also serves as a basis for classifying expenditures (i.e., putting them into various accounts).

Expenditure Control—Encumbrances

Before a nonbusiness organization makes an expenditure for materials or services, a **requisition** (a formal written order or request) is prepared. After this document has been approved, a *purchase order* is sent to the vendor. The organization now has an obligation to have sufficient funds available to pay the vendor within a reasonable length of time after the arrival of the materials or the performance of the services.

To meet this obligation, funds are set aside, or **encumbered.** The obligation itself is called an **encumbrance.** It represents resources that are now committed to a specific use and are no longer available for other expenditures. Since the materials or services have not yet been received, however, the organization has no legal financial obligation to the vendor. No liability (in the accounting sense) has been incurred, assets have not been increased, and the total fund balance has not been changed.

An encumbrance is recorded by means of a budgetary entry. Recording the encumbrance causes a portion of the appropriation to be set aside or "encumbered" until the materials are received or the services are performed. After the materials have been received or the services have been performed, the encumbrance is reversed out and a liability and an expenditure are recorded.

To determine the amount available for spending at any given point in time, both expenditures *and* encumbrances must be deducted from the appropriation or appropriations. To illustrate:

FY 19X1 appropriation	$990,000
Expenditures to date	500,000
Unexpended balance	$490,000
Outstanding encumbrances	200,000
Unencumbered (free) balance (available for spending)	$290,000

The above information tells us that the organization is "obligated" to spend $990,000 during the current fiscal year, of which $500,000 has already been spent and $200,000 is committed to specific purchases. Therefore the unit has $290,000 to spend for the remainder of the fiscal year.

When an encumbrance is recorded, a debit is made to an encumbrance account (e.g., Encumbrances—supplies) and a credit is made to an offsetting account called Reserve for encumbrances.

Reserves are used to set aside monies for specific purposes. They are also used to identify resources committed, but not expended, so that the unencumbered balance will reflect only monies that can still be spent.

The purpose of the Reserve for encumbrances account is to indicate that even though goods and services have not yet been received, an outstanding commitment exists for a given dollar amount. It also provides information on outstanding purchase orders. Like other reserves, the Reserve for encumbrances is a part of the fund balance.

To illustrate, assume that an order is placed for supplies costing, at the time of the order, $200,000. When the order is placed, an encumbrance is set up by means of the following entry:

Encumbrances—supplies	200,000	
Reserve for encumbrances		200,000
To record the encumbering of Purchase Order		
No. 1426		

Upon receipt of the supplies, the encumbrance is removed (reversed out) and an expenditure and a liability or a reduction of cash is recorded.

1.   Reserve for encumbrances   200,000

        Encumbrances—supplies   200,000

     To record receipt of supplies ordered under Purchase Order No. 1426 and removal of the encumbrance.

2.   Expenditures—supplies   200,000

        Cash or Vouchers payable   200,000

     To record expenditure for the supplies purchased under Purchase Order No. 1426.

When an encumbrance is removed, the reversing entry is in the amount of the *purchase order.* The entry to record the expenditure, however, is in the amount of the *invoice,* the "actual" cost of the materials or services received. As long as these two dollar amounts are equal, there is no problem.

In many cases, however, the amount of the invoice differs from the amount of the purchase order. It is not unusual, for example, to have a price change between the time an order is placed and the time the materials or services ordered are received. In such a situation, the amount reversed out is the amount of the purchase order.

For example, if the actual invoice cost in the preceding illustration had been $195,000, the entry removing the encumbrance would still have been for the amount shown in the purchase order, $200,000. The original amount is *always* used, since the purpose of the reversing entry is to remove the purchase order and encumbrance from an outstanding status, not to record the expenditure. The expenditure, of course, would have been for $195,000.

If there is a difference between the amount of the purchase order and the invoice amount, the **unencumbered balance** of the appropriation is automatically adjusted because the outstanding encumbrance is replaced by an expenditure for the actual amount of the purchase.

To illustrate, assume that a city's appropriation for materials is for $100,000 and that a purchase order is issued for materials costing $34,000 (see Table 4–8). The balance of the appropriation, at the time the order is placed, is shown on the left. The effect of three different "actual" invoice amounts is shown on the right. Notice that

1. Regardless of the size of the invoice, the encumbered amount (the amount of the purchase order) is reversed out when the purchased materials arrive or the services ordered are provided.
2. If the amount of the invoice *equals* the amount of the purchase order (Case 1), recording the expenditure does *not* alter the unencumbered balance.
3. If the amount of the invoice is *smaller* than the amount of the purchase order (Case 2), the unencumbered balance is *increased* by the amount of the difference.
4. If the amount of the invoice is *greater* than the amount of the purchase order (Case 3), the unencumbered balance is *decreased* by the amount of the difference.

TABLE 4–8   Effect of Different Invoice Amounts on Unencumbered Balance

	When Purchase Order Is Sent to Vendor	CASE 1 Actual Invoice Is $34,000	CASE 2 Actual Invoice Is $33,000	CASE 3 Actual Invoice Is $35,000
Appropriations—materials	$100,000	$100,000	$100,000	$100,000
Expenditures—materials	-0-	34,000	33,000	35,000
Unexpended balance	$100,000	$ 66,000	$ 67,000	$ 65,000
Amount encumbered for materials	34,000	-0-	-0-	-0-
Unencumbered ("free") balance— available for the purchase of additional material	$ 66,000	$ 66,000	$ 67,000	$ 65,000

Budgetary and actual data are accumulated, for control purposes, in an **appropriation/expenditure ledger.** To illustrate, assume that the legislative body of a city approves the purchase of ten police cruisers for $80,000. On January 8, five cruisers are ordered. The vehicles are expected to cost $37,000. On March 18, the five cruisers arrive, along with an invoice for $36,000. On April 5, five more police cruisers are ordered, at an estimated cost of $43,000. On May 20, these cruisers arrive, along with an invoice for $44,000. Table 4–9 shows how this information would appear in an appropriation/expenditure ledger account.

Notice how both the budgetary information and the actual information in Table 4–9 are used to control expenditures.

1. The original budgetary appropriation is the *absolute* maximum that can legally be spent without further action by the legislative body.
2. The placement of each order reduces the available balance, because of the effect of the encumbrance procedure.
3. The receipt of each order causes the available balance to be increased or decreased. In this illustration, the actual cost of the first order of police cruisers was less than the amount encumbered. Therefore the available balance increased from $43,000 to

TABLE 4–9   Appropriation/Expenditure Ledger (Police Vehicles)

DATE	ITEM	APPROPRIATION CR	ENCUMBRANCES DR	ENCUMBRANCES CR	EXPENDITURES DR	AVAILABLE BALANCE CR
1/1	Budget	$80,000				$80,000
1/8	Order 5 vehicles		$37,000			43,000
3/18	5 vehicles arrive			$37,000		80,000
3/18	Record invoice				$36,000	44,000
4/5	Order 5 vehicles		43,000			1,000
5/20	5 vehicles arrive			43,000		44,000
5/20	Record invoice				44,000	-0-

TABLE 4–10   Revenue Ledger (Parking Meter Receipts)   **FY 19X1**

DATE	ITEM	ESTIMATED REVENUES DR	ACTUAL REVENUES CR	DIFFERENCE DR (CR)
1/1	Budget	$10,000		$10,000
1/31	Jan. collections		$1,000	9,000
2/28	Feb. collections		1,500	7,500

$44,000. As a result, the city was able to order better-equipped vehicles after April 5. If the actual cost of the first order of vehicles had been greater than the amount encumbered, the available balance would have been reduced. As a result, it would have been necessary for the city to order either fewer vehicles or the same number of vehicles with less equipment.

Revenue Control

Revenues are controlled by means of a comparison of budgetary and actual data. This information is accumulated, by type of revenue, in a revenue ledger. An account from a revenue ledger is shown in Table 4–10.

SUMMARY PROBLEM

This problem brings together the illustrations in this chapter. If you have any questions as you review the problem, turn back to the appropriate sections and reread the material.

On December 31, 19X0, the city council of Refined City approved the budget shown in Table 4–11. Refined City has five property owners, whose fiscal year (FY) 19X1 property taxes are as follows:

TABLE 4–11   Annual Budget

Refined City
General Fund Budget
For the Year Ended December 31, 19X1

Estimated Revenues		
Property taxes	$900,000	
License fees	50,000	
Fines	40,000	
Service charges	10,000	$1,000,000
Appropriations		
Salaries	$700,000	
Supplies	200,000	
Other	90,000	990,000
Projected increase in Fund Balance		$ 10,000

J. Brill	$500,000
R. Jewett	300,000
G. Kuhlman	45,000
A. Niles	30,000
P. Thomas	25,000
Total	$900,000

Among the accounting policies of Refined City are the following:

1. All purchases of supplies are encumbered.
2. Other expenditures do not require encumbrances.
3. Separate accounts (as opposed to control and subsidiary accounts) are maintained for each taxpayer.

The opening, or budgetary, entry is:

Estimated revenues—property taxes	900,000	
Estimated revenues—license fees	50,000	
Estimated revenues—fines	40,000	
Estimated revenues—service charges	10,000	
Appropriations—salaries		700,000
Appropriations—supplies		200,000
Appropriations—other		90,000
Unreserved fund balance		10,000

To record estimated revenues and appropriations for FY 19X1.

The operating entries are:

1.

Property taxes receivable—Brill	500,000	
Property taxes receivable—Jewett	300,000	
Property taxes receivable—Kuhlman	45,000	
Property taxes receivable—Niles	30,000	
Property taxes receivable—Thomas	25,000	
Revenues—property taxes		900,000

To set up receivable for FY 19X1 property taxes.

2.

Encumbrances—supplies	200,000	
Reserve for encumbrances		200,000

To record encumbering of Purchase Order No. 1426.

3.

Cash	900,000	
Property taxes receivable—Brill		500,000
Property taxes receivable—Jewett		300,000
Property taxes receivable—Kuhlman		45,000
Property taxes receivable—Niles		30,000
Property taxes receivable—Thomas		25,000

To record collection of FY 19X1 property taxes.

| 4. | Reserve for encumbrances | 200,000 | |
| | Encumbrances—supplies | | 200,000 |

To record receipt of supplies ordered under Purchase Order No. 1426 and removal of encumbrance.

| 5. | Expenditures—supplies | 195,000 | |
| | Vouchers payable | | 195,000 |

To record expenditure for supplies purchased under Purchase Order No. 1426.

6.	Cash	96,000	
	Revenues—license fees		47,000
	Revenues—fines		38,000
	Revenues—service charges		11,000

To record collection of nonproperty tax revenues, FY 19X1.

| 7. | Vouchers payable | 195,000 | |
| | Cash | | 195,000 |

To record payment for supplies purchased under Purchase Order No. 1426.

8.	Expenditures—salaries	700,000	
	Expenditures—other	92,000	
	Vouchers payable		792,000

To record expenditures for salaries and other items during Fy 19X1.

| 9. | Vouchers payable | 792,000 | |
| | Cash | | 792,000 |

To record payment of outstanding FY 19X1 vouchers.

The closing entries are:

1.	Revenues—property taxes	900,000	
	Revenues—license fees	47,000	
	Revenues—fines	38,000	
	Revenues—service charges	11,000	
	Unreserved fund balance	4,000	
	Estimated revenues—property taxes		900,000
	Estimated revenues—license fees		50,000
	Estimated revenues—fines		40,000
	Estimated revenues—service charges		10,000

To close revenue and estimated revenue accounts for FY 19X1.

2.	Appropriations—salaries	700,000	
	Appropriations—supplies	200,000	
	Appropriations—other	90,000	
	Expenditures—salaries		700,000
	Expenditures—supplies		195,000
	Expenditures—other		92,000
	Unreserved fund balance		3,000

To close appropriation and expenditure accounts for FY 19X1.

After closing entries have been posted, the *postclosing trial balance* will appear as shown in Table 4–12.

The resulting financial statements are shown in Table 4–13.

TABLE 4–12   Postclosing Trial Balance

Refined City
General Fund
Postclosing Trial Balance
December 31, 19X1

	DEBITS	CREDITS
Cash	$9,000	
Unreserved fund balance		$9,000
	$9,000	$9,000

TABLE 4–13   Financial Statements

Refined City
General Fund
Balance Sheet
December 31, 19X1

ASSETS		LIABILITIES AND FUND BALANCE	
Cash	$9,000	Unreserved fund balance	$9,000

Refined City
General Fund
Statement of Revenues, Expenditures,
and Changes in Fund Balance
For the Fiscal Year Ended December 31, 19X1

Revenues		
Property taxes	$900,000	
License fees	47,000	
Fines	38,000	
Service charges	11,000	$996,000
Expenditures		
Salaries	$700,000	
Supplies	195,000	
Other	92,000	987,000
Increase in Fund Balance		$ 9,000
Fund balance, 1/1/X1		-0-
Fund balance, 12/31/X1		$ 9,000

REVIEW QUESTIONS

Q4–1　How does the accounting cycle of a governmental unit differ from that of a business firm?

Q4–2　Define the term *budget.* What principal items are contained in a budget of a governmental unit?

Q4–3　Distinguish between *expenditures* and *expenses.*

Q4–4　What is an appropriation? How does it differ from an expenditure?

Q4–5　Why is the budget used by governmental units a "legal" document?

Q4–6　What are "budgetary" entries? When are they made?

Q4–7　Does the fund balance account usually have a debit or a credit balance? What does the amount accumulated in the fund balance account represent?

Q4–8　Why can a governmental unit record property tax revenues in the accounts before these revenues are actually received in cash? Why are other types of revenues, such as income taxes and license fees, recorded in the accounts after cash is received?

Q4–9　What is a *control account? A subsidiary account?*

Q4–10　What is a *voucher?* What purpose does it serve?

Q4–11　What is a *purchase order? A requisition? An invoice?*

Q4–12　How is a levy of property taxes recorded in the accounting records? How is the collection of the taxes recorded?

Q4–13　What is an *encumbrance?* When is it used? Is it used for all expenditures of a governmental unit?

Q4–14　Why are city officials interested in the unencumbered balance of an appropriation?

Q4–15　What is the effect of encumbrances on the amount of an appropriation available for spending?

CASES

C4–1　Because of lax tax collections, the City of Bliss has run out of money on several occasions. Upon reviewing this situation, the new finance director has noticed that most purchases of goods and services are actually for less than amounts encumbered for these purchases. As a result, he has requested that, when removing encumbrances, only the actual amount of the purchase be reversed out, not the entire amount encumbered. Doing this, he reasons, will provide a "cushion" which can be used to make up any shortfall that might arise by the end of the year.

Do you think this is a sound accounting practice?

C4–2　The newly elected mayor of Wherever noticed that in the recently enacted budget of that city's General Fund, revenues exceeded expenditures by $15,000. Later that year, after a hurricane caused a large amount of damage, she ordered the city's finance officer to write a check for $15,000, on the General Fund, to an emergency relief fund. When confronted by the press, she pointed out that the General Fund was only required under the balanced budget laws of the state to "break even" and that she could not, in good conscience, allow the city to retain idle monies when people needed help.

From an *accounting* standpoint, did the mayor do the right thing?

EXERCISES

E4–1　(Budgetary entries)

The city council of Alhambra approved the following budget:

Estimated Revenues		
Property taxes	$150,000	
Fines and fees	25,000	
Service charges	15,000	
Licenses	10,000	$200,000
Appropriations		
Salaries	$100,000	
Materials and supplies	60,000	
Equipment	30,000	190,000
Projected Increase in Fund Balance		$ 10,000

REQUIRED:　1.　Prepare the appropriate budgetary entry.
　　　　　　2.　Why can an increase in fund balance be put into the accounts at the *beginning* of the year?

E4–2　(Budgetary entries)

The budget for the Graham Park Fund is as follows:

Estimated Revenues	
Property taxes	$2,400,000
Greens fees	600,000
Camping fees	400,000
Fines and permits	200,000
Appropriations	
Wage and salaries	$1,600,000
Grass seed	200,000
Animal food	200,000
Operating supplies	400,000
Outside services	600,000
Repave driveways	200,000
Move locomotive	50,000
Construct shelters	300,000

REQUIRED: 1. Prepare the entry to record the approved budget at the beginning of the year.
              2. If this is the park's first year of operation, how much should the fund balance contain at the end of the year if actual revenues and expenditures are as planned?

E4–3   (Closing entries)

The ledger of the General Fund of the city of New Fargo shows the following balances at the end of the fiscal year:

Estimated revenues	$300,000
Appropriations	285,000
Unreserved fund balance	15,000
Revenues	300,000
Expenditures	285,000

REQUIRED: Prepare closing entries.

E4–4   (Closing entries)

At the end of FY 19X1, the following balances were found in the ledger of the City Park Library Fund:

Estimated revenues	$500,000
Appropriations	475,000
Unreserved fund balance	52,000
Revenues	450,000
Expenditures	440,000

REQUIRED: Prepare closing entries. What was the net effect on Unreserved fund balance?

E4–5   (Complete budgetary cycle)

The board of supervisors of Delaware County approved the following budget for FY 19X1:

Estimated Revenues		
Property taxes	$66,000	
Traffic fines	40,000	$106,000
Appropriations		
Salaries	$80,000	
Supplies	12,000	
Other	8,000	100,000
Projected Increase in Fund Balance		$ 6,000

Transactions for the year were as follows:

1. Collected property taxes of $66,000 in cash
2. Purchased supplies for $12,000
3. Paid salaries of $80,000

4. Collected traffic fines of $40,000

5. Purchased a membership in the Kenner Country Club for Sheriff Lee in recognition of his services to the county. The cost of the membership was $8,000

REQUIRED: Prepare journal entries to set up the budgetary accounts, to record the above transactions, and to close the budgetary and nonbudgetary accounts. Do not make entries to record encumbrances.

E4–6 (Compelte budgetary cycle)

The city council of Avalon approved the following budget for FY 19X1:

Estimated Revenues		
Property taxes	$150,000	
Fines and penalties	40,000	
Service charges	10,000	$200,000
Appropriations		
Salaries	$100,000	
Supplies	30,000	
Equipment	65,000	195,000
Projected Increase in Fund Balance		$ 5,000

During the year the following transactions took place:

1. Collected property taxes of $150,000.

2. Purchased equipment for $60,000.

3. Purchased supplies for $34,000.

4. Collected fines and penalties of $38,000 and service charges of $7,000 in cash.

5. Paid salaries of $98,000.

REQUIRED: Prepare journal entries to set up budgetary accounts, to record the above transactions, and to close the budgetary and nonbudgetary accounts. Do not make entries to record encumbrances.

E4–7 (Complete budgetary cycle)

The board of supervisors of Biloxi Township approved the following budget for FY 19X1:

Revenues		
Licenses	$10,000	
Fines	5,000	
Parking	3,000	
Parade permits	2,000	
Gas royalties	20,000	$40,000
Appropriations		
Salaries	$25,000	
Materials	10,000	
Equipment	3,000	38,000
Projected Increase in Fund Balance		$ 2,000

During the year, actual revenues were:

Licenses	$11,000
Fines	7,000
Parking	3,000
Parade permits	2,500
Gay royalties	19,500

Actual expenditures were:

Salaries	$24,000
Materials	8,000
Equipment	5,000

The township does *not* use encumbrances. All expenditures are paid in cash.

REQUIRED: 1.   Prepare budgetary entries.
              2.   Prepare operating entries.
              3.   Prepare closing entries.

E4–8   (Receivables)

The city council of Great Knox has budgeted property tax revenues of $10,000 for fiscal year 19X1. The city has four property owners, whose property tax levies are as follows:

A. Able	$ 4,000
B. Baker	3,000
C. Charles	2,000
D. Delta	1,000
	$10,000

During the year, each of these property owners pays his taxes in full and on time. The city uses a one-step breakdown when recording revenues (e.g., Property taxes receivable—Baker   ).

REQUIRED: Prepare journal entries recording

              1.   The setting up of the receivable for property taxes due.
              2.   The payment of the property taxes.

E4–9   (Encumbrances)

In February 19X1, the City of Golders Green ordered a fire engine, for which the manufacturer quoted a price of $120,000. The machine arrived the following month, along with an invoice for $120,000.

REQUIRED: 1.   Make the appropriate journal entries to record
                   a.   The setting up of the encumbrance.

   b.   The removal of the encumbrance.
   c.   The recording of the expenditure and the liability to the vendor.
2.   Assume that the actual cost of the fire engine was $125,000. Would your entries be the same as above? Why?

E4–10 (Encumbrances)

On January 10, the City of Wynnewood issued a purchase order to its stationery supplier for $50,000. On March 20, the stationery arrived, along with an invoice for $50,000, which was paid on April 15.

REQUIRED: Prepare the journal entries necessary to record

1.   The setting up of the encumbrance.
2.   The arrival of the stationery on March 20.
3.   The payment for the stationery on April 15.

E4–11 (Encumbrances)

On April 25, the City of Alden ordered supplies with a quoted price of $80,000. On May 15, one half of the supplies arrived, along with an invoice for $40,000. On June 6, the other half of the order arrived, accompanied by an invoice for $42,000. Both invoices were paid at the end of the month of arrival.

REQUIRED: 1.   Prepare entries to record
   a.   The setting up of the encumbrance.
   b.   The arrival of the goods in May and June.
   c.   The payment for the goods.
2.   What effect, if any, will the second invoice have on the balance of the appropriation?

E4–12 (Receivables)

The city council of Collegeville budgeted revenues of $100,000 from the following sources:

Property taxes	$ 60,000
Fines and penalties	30,000
Service charges	10,000
	$100,000

The city has three property owners, whose tax bills are as follows:

J. Davis	$30,000
R. Lee	20,000
R. Butler	10,000
	$60,000

During the year, all property owners paid their taxes on time and in full. Collections from other sources of revenue were:

Fines and penalties	$30,000
Service charges	10,000
	$40,000

Assume that appropriations amount to $100,000.

REQUIRED: Using a one-step breakdown (e.g., Revenues—income taxes), prepare the

1. Budgetary entry.
2. Entry to set up receivable accounts for property taxes.
3. Entry or entries to record the collection of revenues.
4. Entry to close out the revenue accounts.

E4–13   (Receivables—subsidiary and control accounts)
The city council of Small Rock estimated that revenues of $95,000 would be collected for the General Fund. The sources and amounts would be as follows:

Property taxes	$80,000
Parking meters	10,000
Fines and penalties	5,000

The city has four taxpayers, whose shares of the tax levy are as follows:

T. Canyon	$40,000
M. Rose	30,000
C. Sark	6,000
S. Vasa	4,000

All of the taxpayers paid their property taxes on time and in full. Other collections throughout the year were as follows:

Parking meters	$6,000
Fines and penalties	8,000

REQUIRED: Prepare journal entries to record

1. The entry of the budgeted revenues into the accounts.
2. The setting up of the receivable, using a subsidiary account for each taxpayer.
3. The collection of the taxes.
4. The collection of the other revenues.

PROBLEMS

P4–1 (Discussion question on governmental accounting)

Governmental accounting gives substantial recognition to budgets, with those budgets being recorded in the accounts of the governmental unit.

REQUIRED: a. What is the purpose of a governmental accounting system and why is the budget recorded in the accounts of a governmental unit? Include in your discussion the purpose and significance of appropriations.

b. Describe when and how a governmental unit records its budget and closes it out.

(AICPA)

4–2 (Complete set of entries and statements)

The following transactions apply to the fiscal year 19X1 operations of the Humid City Levee Board, a recently formed organization:

a. Revenues were estimated at $150,000. Appropriations of $145,000 were made.

b. Property taxes of $120,000 were collected during the year. Fines and penalties amounted to $28,000.

c. Supplies worth $33,000 were purchased during the year. Salaries paid amounted to $100,000, while utilities for the year amounted to $9,000.

REQUIRED: 1. Prepare journal entries to record the transactions.
2. Post the entries made in requirement 1. (Use T-accounts.)
3. Prepare a preclosing trial balance.
4. Prepare closing entries.
5. Post the entries made in requirement 4.
6. Prepare a postclosing trial balance.
7. Prepare, in good form, a balance sheet and a statement of revenues, expenditures, and changes in fund balance of FY 19X1. Assume that the fund balance at the beginning of the year was zero.

P4–3 (Beginning balances; complete set of statements; easy)

The ledger of the General Fund of the City of Bayou Cactus shows the following balances at the beginning of FY 19X1:

Cash	$38,000	Unreserved fund balance	$38,000

The following transactions take place during the year:

a. The city council estimates General Fund revenues from all sources to be $600,000 and has approved a budget authorizing appropriations of $580,000.

b. Service charges amount to $75,000 and fines total $25,000, all collected in cash.

c.   Property owners pay $490,000 in taxes during the year in cash. Peter Smith has promised to pay his bill ($10,000) early in February of the *following* fiscal year, as soon as he receives his dividend check from a local utility. (*Hint:* Assume that this item is treated as a revenue of the current year and set up a receivable.)

d.   Expenditures of $580,000 are incurred and are paid in cash during the year.

REQUIRED: 1.   Prepare appropriate journal entries.
            2.   Post the above entries to the ledger. (Use T-accounts.)
            3.   Prepare a preclosing trial balance.
            4.   Prepare closing entries and post to the ledger.
            5.   Prepare a postclosing trial balance.
            6.   Prepare, in good form, a balance sheet and a statement of revenues, expenditures, and changes in fund balance for FY 19X1.

P4–4   (Beginning balances: complete set of statements)
       The December 31, 19X0, postclosing trial balance of the General Fund of the City of Sunfish was as follows:

	DEBITS	CREDITS
Cash	$500	
Accounts receivable	300	
Vouchers payable		$400
Unreserved fund balance		400
	$800	$800

a.   The city council estimated revenues for FY 19X1 to be $1,500 and expenditures to be $1,450.

b.   The city's outstanding voucher payable, due to a contractor for remodeling city hall, was paid off in March.

c.   Service charges of $800 were collected during the year.

d.   The Logan Bread Company paid the city $300 it owed for repairs to a fire hydrant because of damage done by a runaway delivery truck.

e.   Speeding tickets, which resulted in fines of $500, were issued to tourists en route to Fun City. The fines were paid in cash.

f.   Salaries of $1,000 were paid to the mayor and the city clerk. Supplies costing $125 were purchased for cash.

g.   A used traffic light was purchased from the city of Brownsville for $150, to be paid the following year.

REQUIRED: 1.   Prepare journal entries to record the above transactions in the General Fund.
            2.   Post the above journal entries to the ledger. (Use T-accounts.)

3. Prepare a preclosing trial balance.
4. Prepare closing entries and post to the ledger.
5. Prepare a postclosing trial balance.
6. Prepare, in good form, a balance sheet and a statement of revenues, expenditures, and changes in fund balance.

P4–5 (Multiple choice)

1. Which of the following revenues can be recorded at the beginning of the fiscal year, rather than when actually received?
   a. Fines
   b. Property taxes
   c. Service charges
   d. Licenses and permits

2. The Estimated revenues control account of a governmental unit is debited when
   a. Budgetary accounts are closed at the end of the year
   b. The budget is recorded
   c. Actual revenues are recorded
   d. Actual revenues are collected

3. Which of the following accounts of a governmental unit is debited when a purchase order is approved?
   a. Encumbrances
   b. Reserve for encumbrances
   c. Vouchers payable
   d. Appropriations

4. When a police car is received by a governmental unit, the entry on the books of the General Fund should include a debit to
   a. Appropriations—police cars
   b. Expenditures—police cars
   c. Encumbrances—police cars
   d. Unreserved fund balance

5. Which of the following terms refers to an actual cost, rather than an estimate?
   a. Expenditure
   b. Appropriation
   c. Budget
   d. Encumbrance

6. In approving the budget of the city of Troy, the city council appropriated an amount greater than expected revenues. This action will result in
   a. A cash overdraft during the fiscal year
   b. An increase in outstanding encumbrances by the end of the fiscal year

    c.   A debit to Unreserved fund balance

    d.   A necessity for compensatory offsetting action in the Debt Service Fund

7. If a credit was made to Unreserved fund balance when recording the budget, it can be assumed that

    a.   Estimated expenditures exceed actual revenues

    b.   Actual expenditures exceed estimated expenditures

    c.   Estimated revenues exceed appropriations

    d.   Appropriations exceed estimated revenues

8. Which of the following is a budgetary account?

    a.   Expenditures—supplies

    b.   Appropriations

    c.   Revenues—property taxes

    d.   Vouchers payable

9. If estimated revenues exceed actual revenues at year-end, the closing entry must include

    a.   A debit to Estimated revenues

    b.   A credit to Revenues—control

    c.   A debit to Unreserved fund balance

    d.   A credit to Unreserved fund balance

10. Entries similar to those for the General Fund may also appear on the books of a municipality's

    a.   General Fixed Assets Account Group

    b.   General Long-Term Debt Account Group

    c.   Nonexpendable Trust Fund

    d.   Special Revenue Fund

11. What type of account is used to earmark a portion of the fund balance to liquidate the contingent obligation for goods ordered but not yet received?

    a.   Appropriations

    b.   Encumbrances

    c.   Obligations

    d.   Reserve for encumbrances

12. Authority granted by a legislative body to make expenditures and to incur obligations during a fiscal year is the definition of an

    a.   Appropriation

    b.   Authorization

    c.   Encumbrance

    d.   Expenditure

(AICPA adapted)

P4–6 (Complete set of entries; breakdown of revenue and expenditure accounts)

The city council of Epping approved the following budget for its General Fund on December 31, 19X1:

Revenues	
Property taxes	$ 85,000
Service charges	35,000
Parking meters	15,000
Fines and penalties	10,000
Liquor licenses	5,000
Appropriations	
Salaries	$100,000
Supplies	20,000
Equipment	15,000
Motorcycles	10,000

The city has four property owners, whose tax assessments for fiscal year 19X1 are:

A. Basquez	$30,000
H. Gomez	25,000
F. Franco	20,000
M. Guinane	10,000

Fiscal year 19X1 is the first year of operation for this city. As a result, there are no balances in the accounts as of January 1, 19X1. During 19X1, the following transactions took place:

a. FY 19X1 tax bills were sent to the property owners.

b. Ordered supplies costing $20,000.

c. The supplies arrived, along with an invoice for $21,000; the invoice was paid immediately.

d. Paid salaries for the year—$97,000.

e. Ordered equipment costing $15,000.

f. Collected property taxes for the year, in full, from all property owners. Collections of service charges were $33,000.

g. Four motorcycles were ordered from a local dealer, who had submitted a bid for $10,000.

h. Parking meter revenues for the year were $18,000, while receipts from the issue of liquor licenses amounted to $2,000.

i. Collections from fines and penalties were $9,000.

j. The equipment ordered arrived, along with an invoice for $15,000; the invoice was paid immediately.

k. The motorcycles arrived; because of an increase in their costs, the dealer asked the city to pay an additional $500 over the amount bid.

Because of political considerations, the city agreed to do this and promptly issued a check for $10,500 to the dealer to cover the cost of the motorcycles.

REQUIRED: 1. Prepare appropriate journal entries to record the budget and these transactions.
2. Post the entries and prepare a preclosing trial balance.
3. Make closing entries and prepare a postclosing trial balance.
4. Prepare, in good form, a balance sheet and a statement of revenues, expenditures, and changes in fund balance.

P4–7 (Prior balances, encumbrances, complete cycle)
The city council of Watford approved the following budget for the General Fund for fiscal year 19X1:

Revenues		
Property taxes	$50,000	
License fees	10,000	
Fines and penalties	15,000	
Parking meters	5,000	
Federal grants	20,000	$100,000
Appropriations		
Salaries	$50,000	
Materials	20,000	
Police cars	$24,000	
Interest	1,000	95,000
Projected Increase in Fund Balance		$ 5,000

The postclosing trial balance for the fund, as of December 31, 19X0, was as follows:

	DEBITS	CREDITS
Cash	$ 5,000	
Due from federal government	10,000	
Vouchers payable		$ 8,000
Unreserved fund balance		7,000
	$15,000	$15,000

Transactions for FY 19X1 include the following:
a. FY 19X1 property tax bills were sent to the property owners, $50,000.
b. Ordered two new police cars at an estimate total cost of $24,000.
c. Received a check from the federal government to cover 19X0 and 19X1 federal grants, $30,000.
d. Borrowed $15,000 from the Bank of Watford for six months.
e. Ordered materials costing $20,000.
f. Paid vouchers outstanding at the end of 19X0, $8,000.

   g. License fees for 19X1 were $9,500. Fines and penalties were $16,000.

   h. The police cars arrived, along with an invoice for $23,400.

   i. Parking meter revenues for 19X1 were $6,500.

   j. Repaid loan to bank, along with accrued interest of $1,200.

   k. The materials arrived, accompanied by an invoice for $19,500.

   l. Paid the outstanding voucher for $23,400 to the vendor who supplied the police cars.

   m. Salaries for the year were $50,000.

   n. Property taxes received during the year were $50,000.

REQUIRED:
1. Prepare journal entries to record the budget and the above transactions.
2. Prepare a preclosing balance.
3. Prepare closing entries.
4. Prepare a postclosing trial balance.
5. Prepare a balance sheet and a statement of revenues, expenditures, and changes in fund balance for FY 19X1.

P4–8 (Comprehensive problem on fund accounting cycle)

The general ledger of the Grenox Park Fund shows the following balances as of December 31, 19X0:

	DEBITS	CREDITS
Cash	$10,000	
Accounts receivable—White	500	
Property taxes receivable—	1,500	
Copeland	1,500	
Due from General Fund		
Vouchers payable		$ 4,000
Notes payable		2,000
Due to Debt Service Fund		3,000
Unreserved fund balance		4,500
	$13,500	$13,500

The budget for FY 19X1 is as follows:

Revenues and Transfers	
Property taxes	$10,000
Rentals	4,000
Concession fees	2,000
Transfer from General Fund	4,000
Appropriations	
Salaries	$8,000
Outside services	4,000
Materials	3,000
Equipment	2,000
Interest	1,000

The Grenox Park Fund collects taxes directly from five property owners, whose land adjoins the park. The property owners and their FY 19X1 assessments are:

G. Almstead	$5,000
P. Copeland	2,000
C. Joiner	1,000
P. Mitchell	1,200
E. Priddle	800

The Park Fund follows the policy of encumbering purchases of materials, equipment, and outside services. Since there has never been a problem with collections, no provision is made for uncollectible accounts.

Transactions for FY 19X1 are as follows:

a. Bills for their FY 19X1 taxes were sent to the property owners.

b. G. Almstead and P. Mitchell paid their property taxes upon receipt of their tax bills.

c. E. Priddle paid one half of his FY 19X1 property tax bill.

d. The commission paid the vouchers open (unpaid) as of the end of FY 19X0.

e. The commission issued notes of $10,000 on January 1. These notes bore interest at the rate of a 6 percent per annum. (Note: These notes are recorded only in the Grenox Park Fund.)

f. P. Copeland paid her taxes for FY 19X0, $1,500; and for FY 19X1, $2,000.

g. Materials expected to cost $2,500 were ordered.

h. A contract was awarded to Morganics, Inc., to conduct a series of training programs for park personnel. The contract price was $4,000.

i. A check was received from the General Fund for $5,500 to cover its obligations from FY 19X0 and for FY 19X1. (*Hint:* Make a credit to Operating Transfers from General Fund for $4,000.)

j. A new lawn mower was ordered. The price quoted by the dealer was $2,000.

k. The notes outstanding at the end of FY 19X0 were paid off, along with accrued interest of $100.

l. A check for $300 was received from the parents of Bob White, a local juvenile delinquent, who were paying for damage he did to the park in FY 19X0.

m. Paid $3,000 (in cash) to the Debt Service Fund. This amount represented the final payment on a bond issue and was owed to the Debt Service Fund at the end of FY 19X0.

n. The materials ordered in part g arrived, along with an invoice for $3,200, which the park commissioners agreed to eventually pay.

o. Received a check for $1,800 from the operator of the park's concessions to cover her fee for the year.

p. Received a check for $1,000 from C. Joiner for payment of his property taxes.

q. The lawn mower arrived in December, along with an invoice for $1,800.

r. Paid the vendor for the materials, $3,200.

s. Repaid the notes recorded in part e, $10,000 *plus* accrued interest of $500.

t. Received rentals of $4,800 from people who camped in the park.

u. Morganics, Inc., finished conducting the training programs and submitted a bill for $4,000, which was approved by the finance officer.

v. Paid salaries in cash, $7,500.

w. Paid voucher for payment to Morganics, Inc., $4,000.

REQUIRED:
1. Prepare appropriate budgetary and operating entries.
2. Prepare a preclosing trial balance.
3. Prepare closing entries.
4. Prepare a postclosing trial balance.
5. Prepare appropriate financial statements.

P4–9 (Relationship between encumbrances and free balance; appropriation/ expenditure ledger)

The city council made an appropriation to the police department of $100,000 for the purchase of supplies, equipment, and vehicles.

1. The department placed an order for ten police cars, estimated to cost $5,000 each.

2. The department placed an order with Owen Supply Company for crime prevention supplies; the estimated cost of the order was $30,000.

3. The police cars arrived in good condition, along with an invoice for $50,000.

4. An order was placed for radio equipment; estimated cost was $10,000.

5. The supplies ordered in number 2 arrived, along with an invoice for $32,000.

6. The radio equipment was received in acceptable condition; actual cost was $9,000.

7. The department purchased a new firearm for $75 cash, on an "emergency" basis, directly from a local dealer; no order had been placed.

REQUIRED: 1. Prepare an appropriation/expenditure ledger. Use columns for Appropriations, Encumbrances (Dr. and Cr.), Expenditures, and Available balance.
             2. What was the free balance at the end of the period?

5

THE GOVERNMENTAL FUND ACCOUNTING CYCLE

> General and Special Revenue Funds—Special Problems

LEARNING OBJECTIVES

After completion of this chapter, you should be able to:

1. Identify two methods of handling uncollectible property taxes
2. Explain the purpose of liens and how to account for them
3. Demonstrate how to handle encumbrances when partial orders are received
4. Explain two approaches to the handling of open encumbrances and the appropriate journal entries for each method
5. Explain how accounting for grants differs from accounting for other inflows of resources
6. Explain the use of and accounting for allotments
7. Identify and account for five types of interfund transactions
8. Show how a budget revision is handled
9. Explain the accounting for fixed assets and prepaid expenses
10. Demonstrate two methods of accounting for inventories
11. Prepare the closing entries necessary when a surplus or deficit occurs
12. Prepare financial statements for the General Fund and for Special Revenue Funds

Up to this point we have assumed that almost everything falls right into place. For example, all property taxes assessed have been collected and all encumbrances have been removed by the end of the fiscal year.

Such assumptions, of course, are unrealistic. Taxpayers are sometimes unable or unwilling to pay their taxes or, if they do pay them, it is too late to treat them as revenues of the year in which they are assessed. In addition, certain encumbrances are removed on a piecemeal basis while others are still outstanding at the end of the fiscal year. Finally, many transactions take place between various funds of governmental units. The treatment of these and certain other problems will be discussed in this chapter.

UNCOLLECTIBLE RECEIVABLES

As was noted in Chapter 4, revenues from property taxes are recorded when these taxes are levied rather than when they are collected. This is because property taxes meet the "measurable" and "available" criteria at this point in time. While governmental units can, and sometimes do, jail people or seize their property for the nonpayment of taxes, such actions are not always expedient, especially in periods of high unemployment. Therefore, it is necessary to make some provision for uncollectible receivables.

There are two approaches to this problem: the direct write-off method and the allowance method.

Direct Write-Off Method

Under the **direct write-off method**, uncollectible accounts are treated as reductions of revenue. When a debt is determined to be uncollectible, a revenue account is debited and a receivable account is credited.

To illustrate, assume that in March property taxes of $800 are levied against R. Grimm. In July, it is determined that Mr. Grimm will be unable to pay his tax bill and that it is not expedient to seize his property. As a result, city officials decide to write off the Grimm account as a total loss.

The appropriate entries are:

March 5	Property taxes receivable—all taxpayers	10,000	
	Revenues—property taxes		10,000
	To record property tax revenues for FY 19X1, including the Grimm account.		
July 15	Revenues—property taxes	800	
	Property taxes receivable—Grimm		800
	To write off the Grimm account as uncollectible.		

If, at a later date (either in the current or in some later period), Mr. Grimm should pay his tax obligations, his payment will be treated as a revenue:

December 12	Cash	800	
	Revenues—property taxes		800

To record payment in full of the Grimm account, which was written off as uncollectible on July 15.

It should be noted that the direct write-off method is *not* consistent with generally accepted accounting principles (GAAP). Therefore, its use is normally limited to those cases in which uncollectible accounts are few in number and relatively small.

Allowance Method

The second, and more commonly used, method of handling uncollectible accounts is the **allowance method**. This procedure contains a built-in assumption that a certain portion of the taxes levied will not be collected. Using past experience and predictions of future economic conditions, finance officials can estimate what percentage of the *total* taxes will be uncollectible. This can be done even though, at the time of the levy, it is not known which or whose particular taxes will not be collected.

When the taxes are levied, an **Allowance for uncollectibles** is recorded. This account has a credit balance and is a *contra asset*. Recording the Allowance has the effect of reducing the revenues of the period in which taxes are levied, rather than the period in which they are determined to be uncollectible, and provides a better measurement of revenues for each period. When it becomes known that a specific taxpayer's account is uncollectible, the Allowance for uncollectibles is debited (reduced) and the receivable in question is credited (also reduced).

To illustrate, assume that the property taxes levied in a given year amount to $1 million and that past experience has shown that 4 percent of the taxes levied are usually not collected. Therefore, an allowance of $40,000 is necessary. The entry to set up this allowance is:

Property taxes receivable—Morgan	525,000	
Property taxes receivable—Lohmann	350,000	
Property taxes receivable—Parker	35,000	
Property taxes receivable—Davis	50,000	
Property taxes receivable—Gales	40,000	
Allowance for uncollectible property taxes		40,000
Revenues—property taxes		960,000

To set up receivable for FY 19X1 property taxes, including an estimated 4 percent that is expected to remain uncollectible.

Assume further that in June it becomes apparent that Parker will be unable to pay his property taxes and it is not expedient to force a sale of his property. Thus, the account must be written off. The entry to do this is:

Allowance for uncollectible property taxes	35,000	
Property taxes receivable—Parker		35,000
To write off the Parker account for FY 19X1.		

The entry to record the collection of the remaining property taxes is the same as the one previously illustrated:

Cash	965,000	
Property taxes receivable—Morgan		525,000
Property taxes receivable—Lohmann		350,000
Property taxes receivable—Davis		50,000
Property taxes receivable—Gales		40,000
To record the collection of property taxes in FY 19X1.		

Notice that when the allowance method is used, writing off a bad debt does not affect revenues. The effect on revenues occurs when the Allowance is set up (i.e., when taxes are levied). Notice also that a bad debts expense account is *not* used, as in commercial accounting. This is because under the flow of financial resources concept used in governmental accounting noncash items, like depreciation and bad debts, do not represent an outflow of resources and, as a result, are not reported. Since the focus of accounting by governmental-type funds is on spending, rather than on capital maintenance, there is (theoretically) no distortion of operating results.

Adjustments to the Allowance for Uncollectibles

Sometimes the estimate of uncollectible property taxes is either too high or too low. When this happens an adjustment is made, either during or at the end of the year. If, for example, the allowance is too low and it has been decided to make an upward adjustment, the allowance account is credited (increased) and the revenue account is debited (decreased).

To illustrate, assume that in July city officials conclude that uncollectible property taxes will be $5,000 *higher* than anticipated. The adjusting entry is:

Revenues—property taxes	5,000	
Allowance for uncollectible property taxes		5,000
To adjust the revenue and allowance for uncollectible property tax accounts to reflect an increase in the estimate of uncollectible property taxes.		

If, on the other hand, city officials conclude that uncollectible property taxes will be $5,000 *lower* than anticipated, the reverse of the above entry is made:

Allowance for uncollectible property taxes	5,000	
Revenues—property taxes		5,000

To adjust the revenue and allowance for uncollectible property tax accounts to reflect a
decrease in the estimate of uncollectible
property taxes.

At the end of the year, the balance in the Allowance for uncollectible property taxes account may not agree with taxes still outstanding. For example, the account may have a credit balance after all taxes have been collected or written off (the actual collections were higher than anticipated). In this case the remaining allowance must be reversed out. That is, the allowance must be reduced to zero and property tax revenues must be increased. This entry is necessary because when the original entry to record the tax levy was made, the amount that would prove uncollectible was overestimated and the revenues were underestimated.

To continue with the illustration on page 167 assume that the original allowance is $40,000 and uncollectible accounts for the year amount to $35,000, leaving a credit balance of $5,000 in the Allowance for uncollectible property taxes account. The adjusting entry is:

Allowance for uncollectible property taxes	5,000	
Revenues—property taxes		5,000

To decrease the FY 19X1 allowance for uncollectible property taxes to reflect actual collections.

If, on the other hand, the allowance turns out to be inadequate and no adjustment has been made during the year (the Allowance for uncollectible property taxes account has a debit balance), an adjusting entry must be made to bring the balance in this account back to zero or to the remaining amount not expected to be collected. This is done by crediting the allowance account for the shortfall and debiting (reducing) Property tax revenues for the same amount. To illustrate, assume that the original Allowance for uncollectible property taxes for 19X1 is $40,000, that FY 19X1 taxes of $35,000 have been written off so far, and that another $15,000 of taxes is not likely to be collected, resulting in a total of $50,000 of uncollectible, or potentially uncollectible, property taxes. The adjusting entry is:

Revenues—property taxes	10,000	
Allowance for uncollectible property taxes		10,000

To increase the FY 19X1 allowance for uncollectible property taxes to reflect actual collections.

DELINQUENT TAXES

Often a governmental unit will not write off a property tax receivable until officials are certain that the tax is uncollectible. Sometimes this is several years after the tax has been levied. Prudent management, however, necessitates keeping past due or delinquent taxes separate from those levied in the current year. To accomplish this, receivables are classified as *current* and *delinquent*. At some point in time (often the day they are due), outstanding current receivables are reclassified as delinquent. To illustrate, assume that on September 30, the due, or delinquent, date, taxpayers Davis and Gales owe $50,000 and $40,000, respectively, some of which the city reasonably expects to collect in the future. The adjusting entry is:

Property taxes receivable—delinquent— Davis	50,000	
Property taxes receivable—delinquent— Gales	40,000	
Property taxes receivable—current— Davis		50,000
Property taxes receivable—current— Gales		40,000

To reclassify FY 19X1 property taxes not collected by due date as delinquent.

In addition, the related Allowance for uncollectible property taxes must also be adjusted. Assume that this Allowance is equal to $15,000, which is the amount of the FY 19X1 property tax levy that city officials feel is unlikely to be collected. The entry to make this adjustment is:

Allowance for uncollectible property taxes— current	15,000	
Allowance for uncollectible property taxes— delinquent		15,000

To adjust the allowance for uncollectible property taxes—current for FY 19X1 property taxes that are no longer current.

Sometimes interest is charged on the delinquent taxes, or penalties are assessed against the taxpayer. When this happens, a debit is made to a receivable account in order to recognize this additional claim against the taxpayer. An offsetting credit to a revenue account is also made.

If penalties totaling $900 are assessed against Davis and Gales, the entry is:

Interest and penalties receivable—Davis	500	
Interest and penalties receivable—Gales	400	
Revenues—interest and penalties		900

To record the assessment of late-payment penalties.

If the receivables are eventually determined to be uncollectible, the previous entry will be reversed.

Sometimes an Allowance for uncollectible interest and penalties account is used. In most cases, however, the balance in the Interest and penalties receivable account is not large enough to warrant the extra effort involved in setting up an offsetting allowance.

When back taxes are owed, a governmental unit will sometimes place a lien against a piece of property. A **lien** is the legal right of hold or sell a piece of property in order to satisfy a claim against its owner. Such property cannot be sold or transferred by its owner until the lien is removed.

In extreme cases a governmental unit will exercise its right to seize the property and sell it to the highest bidder. After the taxes, penalties, and expenses of the sale have been deducted, the proceeds will be remitted to the former owner or owners of the property.

When a lien is placed against a piece of property, existing receivable accounts are replaced by a new account called **Tax liens receivable**. To illustrate, assume that a lien is placed against the Davis property. When this happens, delinquent taxes, interest, and penalties are reclassified to reflect their new status:

Tax liens receivable—Davis	50,500	
Property taxes receivable—delinquent—		
Davis		50,000
Interest and penalties receivable—Davis		500
To reclassify property taxes, interest, and penalties receivable to reflect the lien on the Davis property.		

If it costs $300 to process and advertise the lien, this cost will be added to the new receivable:

Tax lines receivable—Davis	300	
Cash		300
To record the cost of processing and advertising the tax lien against the Davis property.		

If the Davis property is sold for $120,000 and expenses related to the sale amount to $1,500, the following entries are used to record the sale and the amounts due to the auctioneer and to R. Davis:

Cash	120,000	
Tax liens receivable—Davis		50,800
Vouchers payable		69,200
To record the sale of the Davis property, removal of the lien, and expenses related to the sale ($1,500).		
Vouchers payable	69,200	
Cash		69,200
To record the payment of the expenses of the sale of the Davis property and the amount due to R. Davis.		

DEFERRED PROPERTY TAXES

Under the modified accrual basis of accounting, revenues are not "available" unless they are received during a period or close enough to the end of the period to pay its liabilities. The GASB has specified that, unless a governmental unit justifies a longer period in the notes to its financial statements, the period should not be more than sixty days.[1] Revenues expected to be collected after this period should be reclassified and reported as deferred revenues.

To illustrate, assume that at the end of 19X1 a governmental unit determines that property tax revenues amounting to $250,000 will not be collected until the middle of the following year. Since the expected time of collection is more than sixty days past year-end, it must make the following entry:

Revenues—property taxes	250,000	
Deferred revenues—property taxes		250,000
To record deferral of property taxes expected to be collected in 19X2.		

At the beginning of 19X2, the above entry would be reversed and the monies collected would be treated as a revenue of that year, rather than 19X1.

TAX DISCOUNTS

Sometimes governmental units allow cash discounts to encourage early payment of property taxes. Revenue losses from this practice are usually offset by reduced borrowings and a lessened need to carry over a sizable cash balance from the preceding year. If allowable, discounts should be treated as a reduction of revenue—in the same manner as uncollectible accounts. To illustrate, assume that a governmental unit levies property taxes of $600,000. To speed up tax collections, it offers a 2 percent discount for prompt payment. For purposes of this illustration assume that all taxpayers take the discount and that all taxes are received in a timely manner. When taxes are levied, the entry is

Property taxes receivable—current	600,000	
Estimated discounts on property taxes		12,000
Revenues—property taxes		588,000
To set up receivable for property taxes, together with an allowance for a 2 percent discount for prompt payment.		

When the taxes are collected, the entry is:

Cash	588,000	
Estimated discounts on property taxes	12,000	
Property taxes receivable—current		600,000
To record collection of property taxes.		

[1]GASB Cod. Sec. P70.103

If the governmental unit records estimated revenues of $600,000 in its budget, it is not possible for actual revenues to equal estimated revenues. To get around this problem, the governmental unit should budget the amount it actually expects to receive ($588,000), or treat the discounts as expenditures. If the latter approach is followed, the entries will be:

Property taxes receivable—current	600,000	
Revenues—property taxes		600,000
To set up receivable for property taxes.		
Cash	588,000	
Expenditures—discounts on property taxes	12,000	
Property taxes receivable—current		600,000
To record receipt of property taxes and discount allowed for prompt payment.		

PAYMENTS IN LIEU OF TAXES

Governmental units sometimes receive payments from other governmental units, or from certain not-for-profit organizations, to reimburse them for revenues lost because these organizations are not required to pay taxes. Amounts received are usually based on amounts the governmental units would have received if the paying organizations had been required to pay taxes.

Examples of payments in lieu of taxes include impact payments made by the federal government to school districts near military installations and amounts contributed by certain religious organizations owning large amounts of real estate. Payments in lieu of property taxes are treated in the same manner as tax revenues.

ESCHEATS

In most states, net assets of persons who die intestate (without a valid will) and who have no known relatives revert to the state, as do inactive bank accounts (after a certain period of time, often seven years). Such reversions are known as **escheats**. When escheats are in the form of cash or securities, they are recorded as revenues by the state. When escheats are in the form of fixed assets, they are recorded in the state's General Fixed Assets Account Group at fair market value as of the time they are received.

TAXPAYER-ASSESSED TAX REVENUES

Certain taxes are assessed by individual taxpayers, following legal guidelines set out by the governmental unit. Examples include sales taxes and income taxes. Sales taxes are paid by merchants and represent a fixed percentage of the merchants' sales. Income taxes represent taxpayers' income, less certain deductions and credits. In both cases, the amount of taxes that must be paid is determined by the taxpayers, rather than the governmental unit.

In the past, revenues from taxpayer-assessed taxes were not recognized (recorded) by governmental units until actually received. Current practice, however, requires that revenues from these taxes be recognized in the accounting period in which they become "susceptible to accrual." That is, when they become measurable *and* available to finance expenditures of the period. As a result, an adjusting entry must now be prepared at the end of each fiscal year to recognize revenue from self- assessed taxes which will be collected early in the following year. Fortunately, tax collections tend to be predictable over time, and it is generally possible to make reasonable estimates of the amount of each tax that will be collected by a given date.

To illustrate, assume that at the end of FY 19X1 it is estimated that income taxes amounting to $500,000 will be collected during the first month of the following year and, as a result, are "susceptible to accrual." The adjusting entry to record these revenues is:

Income taxes receivable	500,000	
Revenues—income taxes		500,000
To record income taxes which are susceptible to accrual at the end of FY 19X1.		

OTHER ADJUSTMENTS

Even the best of systems is prone to error. Those used by governmental units are no exception. One source of error lies in the assessing of taxes. Taxpayers will often appeal their assessments, and as a result their tax bills will be adjusted. This, of course, increases or, more commonly, decreases the revenues of the governmental unit.

To adjust for an **overassessment**, the revenue account is debited (decreased) and the receivable account is credited (also decreased). If the taxpayer has already paid his or her entire tax bill, a cash refund is issued.

To illustrate, assume that the taxes originally levied on W. M. Lohmann's property are $350,000 and that when Mr. Lohmann appeals to his assessor, the taxes are lowered to $300,000. If Mr. Lohmann's tax reduction takes place *before* he pays his tax bill, the adjusting entry will be:

Revenues—property taxes	50,000	
Property taxes receivable—current—		
Lohmann		50,000
To adjust for an error on the FY 19X1 tax assessment of W. M. Lohmann.		

If, however, Mr. Lohmann pays the $350,000 when due and successfully appeals the assessment at a later date, the entry will be:

| Revenues—property taxes | 50,000 | |
| Vouchers payable | | 50,000 |

To adjust for an error on the FY 19X1 tax assessment of W. M. Lohmann and to set up a liability for a refund

In the case of **underassessments**, the receivable (and revenue) accounts are increased to cover the additional assessments. Assume, for example, that Mr. Lohmann not only loses his appeal but is assessed an additional $75,000. The adjusting entry is:

| Property taxes receivable—current— Lohmann | 75,000 | |
| Revenues—property taxes | | 75,000 |

To adjust for an error on the FY 19X1 tax assessment of W. M. Lohmann.

WARRANTS

Before a check can be "cut" (prepared) and payment made, a warrant is usually prepared. A **warrant** is an order, drawn by the appropriate authority, requesting the treasurer (or someone designated by that person) to pay a specified sum of money to a particular person or organization. Its purpose is to assist in the prevention of unauthorized payments. No journal entries are necessary when warrants are prepared.

PARTIAL ORDERS

In our previous discussion of encumbrances we emphasized that when an encumbrance is removed, the amount reversed out is the amount of the encumbrance. This is true even if the actual purchase cost is different. The amount shown as an expenditure, of course, always equals the amount *actually* paid.

The example used to illustrate the above points assumed that the *entire* order was received at one time. In many cases, however, orders of goods and services are received piecemeal throughout the year. A governmental unit will often place a **blanket order** for a quantity of goods or services, to be received gradually over a period of time (e.g., one sixth of the order each month for six months). Payment for these goods or services is usually made shortly after the receipt of each shipment rather than at the end of the period covered by the order.

When this happens, a problem is created as to when the encumbrance should be removed. Although some accountants advocate waiting until the last item is received, most realize that this approach causes a loss of control over expenditures and defeats the purpose of the encumbrance. In addition, before all goods or services are received, the order may be canceled by operating personnel without informing the accounting department. This causes monies that could be used elsewhere to be tied up until year-end because accounting personnel are unaware that the funds will not be spent. As a result, they inadvertently turn down spending requests even though monies are actually available.

The alternative used by most organizations requires more paperwork but results in tighter control over expenditures. Under this approach, a portion of the encumbrance *equivalent to the portion of the goods or services that have been received* is removed when the voucher for payment is prepared. Thus, when one fourth of an order arrives, one fourth of the encumbrance is removed.

To illustrate, assume that one fourth of the $200,000 of supplies ordered in the example in the previous chapter has been received, along with an invoice for $45,000. One fourth of the encumbrance, $50,000, is removed while a voucher for the *actual* invoice amount is prepared:

Reserve for encumbrances	50,000	
Encumbrances—supplies		50,000
To record receipt of one fourth of supplies ordered under P.O. No. 1426.		
Expenditures—supplies	45,000	
Vouchers payable		45,000
To record liability for payment of one fourth of goods received under P.O. No. 1426.		

The first entry removes one fourth of the original encumbrance. This reflects the fact that one fourth of the goods were received. The second entry records the *actual* expenditure and liability.

This method gives managers a fairly accurate idea of how much of the order has arrived. It also prevents the tying up of large amounts of money until year-end, by which time the appropriation may have expired, and allows managers, if they desire, to adjust the encumbrances to correspond with actual prices at the end of the period.

OPEN ENCUMBRANCES

Until now it has been assumed that all materials and services ordered during a given period are received in that period. In reality, however, this is seldom the case. Deliveries are sometimes made after year-end. Materials that are ordered near the end of one year often arrive the following year. Finally, certain items have long lead times between order and delivery dates (e.g., fire engines). Since encumbrances are not removed until materials or services are received, a problem is created as to what to do with them at year-end. There are two approaches to the handling of this problem: (1) allow the encumbrances to lapse, or (2) keep the encumbrances "open" and remove them when the goods or services are received.

Encumbrances Lapse

The first approach is the one commonly used in practice (and is often the one legally required). When it is followed, all unexpended appropriations (encumbered and unencumbered) lapse at the end of the year, even if the governmental unit is committed to eventually accepting the goods and services. The expenditures relating to the items ordered, but not yet received, must be charged against the appropriations of the following year. To indicate that commitments are still outstanding, the balance in the Reserve for encumbrances is left intact.

To illustrate, assume that in fiscal year 19X1, the first year of operation of a governmental unit, appropriations of $750,000 are approved by the legislative body, all of which are encumbered. During the year goods and services, expected to cost $700,000, are received, along with invoices for $695,000. The purchase orders outstanding at the end of the year will be honored in fiscal year 19X2, even though the associated encumbrances have lapsed. The entry to set up the encumbrances for FY 19X1 is:

Encumbrances	750,000	
Reserve for encumbrances		750,000
To record the encumbering of FY 19X1 purchase orders.		

The entries to record the receipt of goods and services are:

1.	Reserve for encumbrances	700,000	
	Encumbrances		700,000
	To record the receipt of goods and services in FY 19X1 and the removal of outstanding encumbrances.		
2.	Expenditures	695,000	
	Vouchers payable		695,000
	To record the expenditures for goods and services received in FY 19X1.		

At the end of the year, the appropriation and expenditure accounts are closed out.

Appropriations	750,000	
Expenditures		695,000
Unreserved fund balance		55,000
To close the appropriation and expenditure accounts for FY 19X1.		

The remaining encumbrances are also closed out. However, in order to keep the balance in Reserve for encumbrances intact, these encumbrances are closed to Unreserved fund balance.

| Unreserved fund balance | 50,000 | |
| Encumbrances | | 50,000 |

To close the outstanding encumbrances for FY
19X1.

At the beginning of the following year, the above entry is reversed. This reversal has the effect of returning the Encumbrances and the Reserve for encumbrances accounts to their usual offsetting relationship. It also increases the Unreserved fund balance by a like amount, as it is no longer necessary to set aside this reserve for prior-year commitments.

| Encumbrances | 50,000 | |
| Unreserved fund balance | | 50,000 |

To reestablish the encumbrances for goods
and services ordered, but not received, in FY
19X1.

In 19X2, the legislative body should appropriate $50,000 to cover the expenditures for goods and services not received in 19X1, as well as an amount sufficient to cover the cost of goods and services expected to be purchased that year.

Some governmental units do not bother to keep their Reserve for encumbrances intact. They close their Encumbrances *and* their Reserve for encumbrances accounts at the end of the year. If they intend to honor prior-year commitments the following year, they set up appropriations, encumbrances, and a new Reserve for encumbrances for these purchase orders in the new year. Such commitments should be described in the notes to the financial statements.

Encumbrances Remain Open

Under the second approach encumbrances and their corresponding appropriations are kept "open" at year-end and are removed when goods and services are actually received. The journal entries used are similar to those used in the first approach. However, since Encumbrances and Appropriations are budgetary accounts, which are related only to the current period, they are closed at year-end. At the beginning of the following year, they are reopened and added to the "new" encumbrances and appropriations.

To illustrate, assume that at the end of 19X0 encumbrances amounting to $50,000 are still outstanding, and the governmental unit follows a policy of not allowing encumbrances to lapse. At the end of the year, the spent appropriations and the expenditure accounts are closed out.

Appropriations	700,000	
Expenditures		695,000
Unreserved fund balance		5,000

To close the spent appropriation and the expenditure accounts for FY 19X0.

The entry to close the remaining encumbrances and appropriations is:

Appropriations	50,000	
Encumbrances		50,000

To close the outstanding encumbrances and their corresponding appropriations for FY 19X0.

As with the previous approach, the Reserve for encumbrances remains intact, in order to indicate to readers of the financial statements that the governmental unit plans to honor those purchase orders still outstanding at the end of the year.

At the beginning of the next year, the following entry is made:

Encumbrances	50,000	
Appropriations—prior year		50,000

To restore the outstanding encumbrances and their corresponding appropriations.

This entry restores the outstanding encumbrances and their corresponding appropriations. It also indicates that these encumbrances represent prior-year commitments. The Reserve for encumbrances, of course, remains intact because it was never closed. A summary of the two methods of handling encumbrances is found in Exhibit 5–1. Notice that under both methods, encumbrances of $50,000

EXHIBIT 5–1   Summary of Methods of Treating Encumbrances at Year-End

Estimated Revenues	XXX	
Appropriations		750,000
Unreserved fund balance		XXX
Encumbrances	750,000	
Reserve for encumbrances		750,000
Reserve for encumbrances	700,000	
Encumbrances		700,000
Expenditures	695,000	
Vouchers payable		695,000

ENCUMBRANCES LAPSE			ENCUMBRANCES REMAIN OPEN		
			End of Year		
Appropriations	750,000		Appropriations	700,000	
Expenditures		695,000	Expenditures		695,000
Unreserved fund balance		55,000	Unreserved fund balance		5,000
Unreserved fund balance	50,000		Appropriations	50,000	
Encumbrances		50,000	Encumbrances		50,000
			Beginning of Following Year		
Encumbrances	50,000		Encumbrances	50,000	
Unreserved fund balance		50,000	Appropriations— prior year		50,000

are still outstanding. Since these encumbrances will be honored the following year, the Reserve for encumbrances remains on the books and appears on the balance sheet (see Table 5–5 on page 205 and Table 5–8 on page 208).

ACCOUNTING FOR GRANTS

Grants received by governmental units are frequently restricted for specific activities. To maximize control over these resources, restricted grants should be accounted for in Special Revenue Funds. The GASB requires that revenue from restricted grants not be recognized until agreed-upon expenditures have taken place. This is because grant revenue has not been "earned" until the terms of the grant have been met through agreed-upon expenditures. Cash or a receivable account is debited when a grant is received. An offsetting credit to Deferred revenue, a liability account, is also made to indicate that no revenue has been earned. When agreed-upon expenditures take place, revenues are recognized in the amount of the expenditures.

To illustrate, assume that a city receives a grant for $500,000, to be used to supplement salaries of police officers. When the grant is received, the following entry is made:

Cash	500,000	
Deferred revenues—grants		500,000
To record receipt of grant.		

During the year, $300,000 is spent in accordance with the terms of the grant. The entries to record the expenditures and to recognize revenue from the grant are:

Expenditures—salaries	300,000	
Vouchers payable		300,000
To record payment of supplemental pay to police officers.		
Deferred revenues—grants	300,000	
Revenues—grants		300,000
To record revenue from grant.		

The remainder of revenue from the grant will be recognized the following year.

ALLOTMENTS

To maintain closer control over its own expenditures, as well as organizations to which they award grants, governmental units sometimes divide their appropriations into **allotments**. These segments of the appropriations may be encumbered (obligated) or expended during the **allotment period**, which can be a month, a quarter year, or a half year.

When allotments are used, **Unalloted appropriations** replaces Appropriations. The budgetary entry is (amounts assumed):

Estimated revenues—various sources	1,000,000	
Unallotted appropriations		990,000
Unreserved fund balance		10,000
To record estimated revenues and unallotted		
appropriations for FY 19X1.		

At the time formal allotments are made, Unalloted appropriations is reduced (debited) and an allotment account is set up by means of a credit to Allotments. If, in the above illustration, the first period's allotment is $495,000, the following entry is appropriate:

Unallotted appropriations	495,000	
Allotments		495,000
To record allotment for first half of 19X1.		

If $485,000 is actually expended during the allotment period, the following entry is appropriate:

Expenditures (various)	485,000	
Vouchers payable		485,000
To record expenditures incurred during first		
half of 19X1.		

Under the more commonly used procedure, allotments are controlled by means of a three-column subsidiary ledger, which provides a running total of the balance available for spending. A subsidiary ledger is shown in Table 5–1.

TABLE 5–1   Subsidiary Ledger for Allotments

DATE	ALLOTMENT	EXPENDITURES	REMAINING BALANCE
1/1	$495,000		$495,000
1/8		$ 75,000	420,000
3/15		200,000	220,000
5/17		150,000	70,000
6/25		60,000	10,000
7/1	495,000		505,000
7/15		200,000	305,000
9/26		75,000	230,000
11/15		100,000	130,000
12/18		30,000	100,000
12/29		88,000	12,000
	$990,000	$978,000	$ 12,000

(continued)

TABLE 5–1   Subsidiary Ledger for Allotments (*Continued*)

January 1	Estimated revenues—various sources	1,000,000	
	Unallotted appropriations		990,000
	Unreserved fund balance		10,000
	To record estimated revenues, unallotted appropriations, and projected increase in fund balance for FY 19X1.		
January 1	Unallotted appropriations	495,000	
	Allotments		495,000
	To set up allotment for first half of 19X1.		
January 1– *June 30*	Cash	500,000	
	Revenues—various sources		500,000
	To record revenues for first half of FY 19X1.		
	Expenditures—various	485,000	
	Vouchers—payable		485,000
	To record expenditures for first half of FY 19X1.		
July 1	Unallotted appropriations	495,000	
	Allotments		495,000
	To set up allotment for second half of FY 19X1.		
July 1– *December 31*	Cash	500,000	
	Revenues—various sources		500,000
	To record revenues for second half of FY 19X1.		
	Expenditures—various	493,000	
	Vouchers payable		493,000
	To record expenditures for second half of FY 19X1.		
December 31	Revenues—various sources	1,000,000	
	Estimated revenues—various sources		1,000,000
	To close out revenue and estimated revenue accounts for FY 19X1.		
	Allotments	990,000	
	Expenditures—various		978,000
	Unreserved fund balance		12,000
	To close out allotment and expenditure accounts for FY 19X1.		

At year-end Estimated revenues is closed out to Revenues, with any difference between these account balances being added to or deducted from Unreserved fund balance. Allotments is closed out to Expenditures, any difference between these account balances also being added to or deducted from Unreserved fund balance.

To illustrate, assume that in fiscal year 19X1, of the $990,000 allocated to an organization, $950,000 is actually spent. Assume also that this organization receives its funding in semiannual allotments of $495,000 and that the subsidiary ledger illustrated in Table 5–1 is maintained by this organization.

INTERFUND TRANSACTIONS

Transactions between the individual funds of a governmental unit are called **interfund transactions**. Interfund transactions include (1) interfund loans or advances, (2) quasi-external transactions, (3) reimbursements, (4) residual equity transfers, and (5) operating transfers. Each of these is discussed below.

Interfund Loans or Advances

Interfund loans or advances arise when one fund lends money to another fund. The recipient fund recognizes a liability to the paying fund, and the paying fund recognizes a receivable from the recipient fund. When recording *short-term* receivables and payables (those due within one year), the terms *due from* and *due to* are used. When recording *long-term* receivables and payables (those due after one year), the terms *advances to* and *advances from* are used. The amounts shown on the financial statements as *due to* and *due from* and *advances to* and *advances from*, for the governmental unit as a *whole*, should be equal at all times.

To inform readers of the financial statements that certain current financial resources are not available for spending, advances to other funds are generally reported as reservations of fund balance. The entries to record interfund loans or advances are (amounts assumed):

Entry in the books of the lending fund	Due from (advance to[2]) XX Fund 　　Cash To record loan to XX Fund.	5,000	5,000
Entry in the books of the borrowing fund	Cash 　　Due to (advance from) YY Fund To record loan from YY Fund.	5,000	5,000

Quasi-external Transactions

Quasi-external transactions are interfund transactions that result in the recognition of revenues and expenditures (or expenses) to the funds involved. These transactions are unique in that they are the only ones, not involving parties external to the governmental unit, in which revenues and expenditures (or expenses) are recognized.

Quasi-external transactions occur when one fund performs services for another, one fund makes a payment to another in lieu of property taxes, and so forth. For example, a fund recognizes revenue when it provides services to an

[2]This transaction requires a reservation of fund balance.

outside party. If, instead, it provides those same services to another fund, it is still appropriate for the fund to recognize revenue.

To continue with the analogy, if the fund receiving the services mentioned above contracts with an outside party for the same services, it will have an expenditure (or expense). The fact that the supplier of the services is another governmental unit will not change the recognition of the expenditure (or expense).

For example, assume that an Enterprise Fund (Water Utility Fund) provides water and sewerage services to the governmental unit. The billing from the Water Utility Fund to the General Fund will be recorded as follows (amounts assumed):

Entry in the books of the Enterprise Fund	Due from General Fund	123,000	
	Sale of water and sewerage services		123,000
	To record billing to General Fund.		
Entry in the books of the General Fund	Expenditures—water and sewerage services	123,000	
	Due to Water Utility Fund		123,000
	To record billing from Water Utility Fund.		

Since these transactions involve the recognition of revenues and expenditures (or expenses), they are reported on the statement of revenues, expenditures (or expenses), and changes in fund balance (or retained earnings).

Reimbursements

In some instances expediency may require that an expenditure (or expense) be paid by a fund other than the one properly chargeable for the transaction. For example, assume that the General Fund makes an expenditure of $25,000 for consulting services that benefit several different funds. If the General Fund initially pays the bill, with the allocation of the charges to be made at a later date, and if it is determined that the amount of the charge allocable to the Auditorium Fund, a Capital Projects Fund, is $5,000, the following entries will be made:

Entry in the books of the General Fund	Expenditures—consulting services	25,000	
	Cash		25,000
	To record payment for consulting services that benefit several funds.		
Entry in the books of the Auditorium Fund	Expenditures—consulting services	5,000	
	Cash		5,000
	To record payment for consulting services.		
Entry in the books of the General Fund	Cash	5,000	
	Expenditures—consulting services		5,000
	To record reimbursement by Auditorium Fund for consulting services paid for by General Fund.		

The above entries "transfer" the expenditure from the books of the General Fund to the books of the Auditorium Fund. This ensures that the expenditure will not be recorded more than once and that the fund receiving the benefit will recognize the expenditure.

Residual Equity Transfers

Transfers in general are defined as "all interfund transactions except loans or advances, quasi-external transactions, and reimbursements. . . . "[3] **Residual equity transfers** are further defined as "nonrecurring or nonroutine transfers of equity between funds. . . . "[4] Thus a contribution made by the General Fund to supply capital to an Electric Utility Fund (Enterprise Fund) is treated as a residual equity transfer. Likewise, the return of all or part of this contribution in a later period is treated as a residual equity transfer—assuming the return was not originally planned.

Other types of transactions that represent residual equity transfers include the transferring of the ending balance of a Capital Projects Fund to a Debt Service Fund and the transferring of any remaining fund balance of a Debt Service Fund to the General Fund, after the principal and interest have been paid.

A residual equity transfer of the remaining balance of a Debt Service Fund to the General Fund is recorded as follows (amounts assumed):

Entry in the books of the Debt Service Fund	Residual equity transfer to General Fund	32,000	
	Cash		32,000
	To record equity transfer of remaining fund balance to General Fund.		
Entry in the books of the General Fund	Cash	32,000	
	Residual equity transfer from Debt Service Fund		32,000
	To record equity transfer of remaining fund balance from Debt Service Fund.		

Residual equity transfers should not be treated as revenues or expenditures (or expenses). Instead they should be treated as increases or decreases in the fund balances of governmental-type funds or as increases or decreases in the contributed capital of proprietary-type funds. In some instances these transfers should be treated as direct reductions of the retained earnings of proprietary-type funds.

Operating Transfers

All transfers that are not residual equity transfers are **operating transfers**. Thus the annual debt service payment made by the General Fund to a Debt Service Fund is classified as an operating transfer. Other examples of this type of shifting

[3]GASB Cod. Sec. 1800.106.
[4]Ibid.

of resources include (1) an operating subsidy from the General Fund to an Electric Utility Fund (Enterprise Fund) and (2) a payment made by the General Fund for its share of the cost of constructing a civic auditorium.

Operating transfers should *not* be treated as revenues or expenditures (or expenses) by either fund involved in the transaction. Instead they should be reported as "Other Financing Sources (Uses)" for governmental-type funds and other funds that use a spending measurement focus in the statement of revenues, expenditures, and changes in fund balance. Proprietary-type funds and other funds that use the capital maintenance focus should report these transactions in the "Operating Transfers" section of the statement of revenues, expenses, and changes in retained earnings. The reporting of these transfers is illustrated in Chapter 2 and 9.

A typical operating transfer is a transfer from the General Fund to a Capital Projects Fund. The following entries are used to record this transfer (amounts assumed):

Entry in the books of the General Fund	Operating transfer to Capital Projects Fund Cash To record transfer to Capital Projects Fund	8,000	8,000
Entry in the books of the Capital Projects Fund	Cash Operating transfer from General Fund To record transfer from General Fund.	8,000	8,000

OTHER PROBLEMS

Other problems faced by governmental units include the borrowing of money for short periods of time, budget revisions, the acquisition of assets with lives of more than one year, depreciation on long-lived assets, inventories, prepaid items, and reserves.

Borrowings

Governmental organizations sometimes make short-term (less than one year) borrowings. These are generally in the form of **notes**, which are often issued to banks and other financial institutions. A note is a written promise to pay a given amount of money at a particular point(s) in time. It can be secured by *collateral*, as in the case of a note signed by the purchaser of an automobile, or it can be *unsecured*. The latter type is more common in governmental units, as loans to these organizations are generally not very risky because these organizations (theoretically) have the power to raise taxes in the event of a need for more revenues.

Among the more commonly used types of notes are **tax anticipation notes**. These are used by governmental units to cover current financing obligations until the taxes are collected, which is often late in the year. The taxes collected are then used to retire the debt. Notes are also issued in anticipation of receiving funds from a bond issue. When the bonds are sold (issued), the proceeds are used to repay the notes.

The entries used to account for the issuance and repayment of notes are similar to those used by commercial enterprises. To illustrate, assume that a city borrows $100,000 from a bank, to be repaid (during the same fiscal year) from future tax revenues. The entry to record this transaction is:

Cash	100,000	
Tax anticipation notes payable		100,000
To record issuance of tax anticipation notes.		

When the notes are repaid, the above entry will be reversed. This will result in a reduction of Cash and a reduction of the outstanding liability.

Budget Revisions

Sometimes budgets are revised during the year. Conditions such as disasters or severe unemployment can cause serious shortages of actual revenues. If this happens and a balanced budget is to be maintained, the appropriations must be reduced (many city charters and state constitutions require a balanced budget). Such adjustments are recorded by debiting *Appropriation* accounts, crediting *Estimated revenue* accounts, and reflecting any differences in **Unreserved fund balance**.

Assume, for example, that a city begins fiscal year 19X1 with the following budget:

Estimated revenues	$1,000,000
Appropriations	990,000
Increase in fund balance	$ 10,000

Several months after the beginning of the year, the city council concludes that revenues for the year will be about 10 percent less than projected and votes to reduce the budget by the same percentage. The appropriate adjusting entry is:

Appropriations	99,000	
Unreserved fund balance	1,000	
Estimated revenues		100,000
To reflect revisions to FY 19X1 budget.		

The governmental unit must now operate within the new budgetary constraints.

Assets with a Life of More Than One Year

Generally speaking, the purchase of assets with a life of more than one year is treated as an expenditure. That is, if a governmental unit acquires real estate or equipment, the *entire* outlay is charged against an appropriation of the year of *purchase.* This is different from commercial accounting, where a building or a piece of equipment expected to last for more than one year is recorded as an asset and "written off," as an expense, over its *useful life.*

For the purpose of control, most fixed assets of governmental units are listed in the General Fixed Assets Account Group, where debits are made to asset accounts (e.g., Equipment) and credits are made to accounts listing the sources of funding for the assets. The assets are *not* shown on the balance sheets of governmental-type funds. They are, however, shown as separate items on these organizations' schedules of general fixed assets. To illustrate, assume that equipment costing $975,000 is purchased by a governmental unit:

Entry in the books of the General Fund	Expenditures—capital equipment	975,000	
	Vouchers payable		975,000
	To record purchase of equipment in General Fund and to recognize liability to vendor.		
Entry in the books of the General Fixed Assets Account Group	Equipment	975,000	
	Investments in general fixed assets from General Fund revenues		975,000
	To record purchase of equipment in General Fixed Assets Account Group.		

Sometimes it is necessary to dispose of property or equipment. This is done either because the asset is no longer needed by the governmental unit (surplus property) or because it has become obsolete or damaged. Such a transaction requires entries in the General Fund (or the fund that financed the purchase of the asset) and the General Fixed Assets Account Group. In the General Fund, Cash is debited and either an other financing source or a revenue account is credited. (While the first approach is more correct from a theoretical standpoint, the second approach is the one commonly used by governmental units and, as a result, will be followed throughout this text.) In the General Fixed Assets Account Group, the entry recording the purchase of the fixed asset is reversed. To illustrate, assume that a governmental unit disposes of a fire engine, which originally cost $75,000, for $15,000.

Entry in the books of the General Fund	Cash	15,000	
	Revenues (or proceeds)—sale of general fixed assets		15,000
	To record sale of one fire engine.		
Entry in the books of the General Fixed Assets Account Group	Investment in general fixed assets from General Fund revenues	75,000	
	Equipment		75,000
	To record sale of one fire engine.		

This topic will be covered in greater depth in Chapter 6.

Depreciation

Except for the Internal Service, Enterprise, and certain Nonexpendable Trust Funds, no formal entries are made for depreciation. This means, of course, that only the original cost of most assets is shown in the accounting records.

Depreciation is not recorded in most funds for three reasons:

1. Governmental units are concerned with matching actual revenues and expenditures with *estimated revenues* and *appropriations* rather than determining net income. Since depreciation is a "noncash" expense, it does not require an appropriation; and since there is no appropriation for depreciation, there is no need to recognize an expenditure. When an asset is replaced, an appropriation is made for the entire cost of the new asset.
2. Governmental units do not pay income taxes. Thus, there is no reason to account for the tax deduction that can be taken for depreciation.
3. No need exists for information on "return on investment," since governmental units are not expected to make a profit. Hence this measure of performance is superfluous.

Inventories

Governmental units normally record purchases of materials and supplies as expenditures when those purchases take place, even though the items purchased might be inventoried and not used until a later fiscal year. Under this procedure, called the **purchases method**, inventories are treated in the same manner as fixed assets. That is, they are "expensed" when purchased. However, since they are not recorded in the General Fixed Assets Account Group, there is no record of their existence on the date of the balance sheet.

When the purchases method is used, *spending* is defined as "the *acquisition* of assets." To meet the principle of full disclosure and to indicate that they are not "available spendable resources," the existence of these inventories is reported on the balance sheet by means of inventory accounts and a reserve account. To illustrate, assume that supplies costing $10,000 are still on hand at the end of a fiscal year and that this fact should be disclosed to readers of the financial statements. The appropriate entry is:

Supplies on hand	10,000	
Reserve for supplies on hand		10,000
To record amount of supplies on hand at the end of FY 19X1.		

At the end of the following year, the inventory accounts and the reserve account should be adjusted to reflect the balance on hand at that point in time. For example, if the cost of the supplies on hand at the end of the second year is $14,000, the balance in the inventory and in the reserve account should be adjusted to this amount, as follows:

Supplies on hand	4,000	
Reserve for supplies on hand		4,000

To adjust supplies and reserve accounts so
that they reflect the amount of supplies on
hand at the end of FY 19X2.

If the amount of supplies on hand had decreased rather than increased, the supplies account would have been credited and the reserve account would have been debited by the amount necessary to bring their balances down to the new level. Notice that only the *reserve* changes, not the Unreserved fund balance. This is because no change in available *spendable* resources has taken place.

Many governmental units, especially those with a large number of proprietary-type funds, follow the same practice as commercial organizations when recording inventoriable items. They record these items as assets when purchased, and as expenditures when "consumed." This method is known as the **consumption method**.

The logic behind the consumption method is that "spending" occurs when an asset is used. Therefore, the acquisition of an inventoriable item merely represents the exchange of one asset for another. To illustrate, assume that during the year purchases of supplies amount to $8,000 and that supplies costing $6,500 are used. The entry to record the purchases of supplies is:

Supplies on hand	8,000	
Vouchers payable		8,000

To record purchase of supplies in FY 19X1.

The entry to record the usage of supplies is:

Expenditures—supplies	6,500	
Supplies on hand		6,500

To record usage of supplies in FY 19X1.

Because inventories are *spendable* assets, reserves are required only in those instances when a certain minimum amount of inventory must be kept on hand and, therefore, is not considered to be a spendable asset.

Prepaid Items

Prepaid items (e.g., prepaid rent, prepaid insurance, etc.) are charged to expenditure accounts when the *payment* is made. Such items are not usually reported on the balance sheet, as they are in commercial accounting. If the governmental unit does decide to report prepaid items on the balance sheet, the purchases method is generally used.

Reserves and Designations

According to governmental GAAP, " . . . the use of the term 'reserve' should be limited to indicating that a portion of the Fund Balance [a] is not appropriable for expenditure or [b] is legally segregated for a specified future use."[5] An example of the first use of reserves (to indicate to the reader of the financial statements that a portion of the fund balance is not appropriable for future expenditures) is the Reserve for inventories, which is discussed above. An example of the second use of reserves (to indicate to the reader of the financial statements that a portion of the fund balance is legally segregated for a specific future use) is the Reserve for encumbrances. This reserve reflects the purchase orders that are outstanding as of the end of the fiscal year.

Sometimes a governmental unit will set aside or *designate* a portion of its fund balance in order to inform the readers of its financial statements of *tentative* or "informal" plans for the future use of financial resources, such as extra police protection for a special event or equipment replacement. These designations reflect *managerial* plans and have no formal legal basis. As a result, they should be clearly distinguished from formal reserves of fund balance. Unlike fund balance reserves, they are subject to change at the discretion of the management, rather than the legislative body, of the governmental unit. For example, the mayor of a city might decide that resources designated for extra police protection during Mardi Gras parades should be used to provide security for the Superbowl. Such a decision does not usually require the approval of the city council.

Year-end Financial Statements

Financial statements prepared at year-end for the General Fund and each Special Revenue Fund include the balance sheet; the statement of revenues, expenditures and changes in fund balance, and the statement of revenues, expenditures and changes in fund balance—budget and actual. Examples of these statements are found in Tables 5–5, 5–6, and 5–7 on pages 205, 206, and 207, respectively.

When preparing a statement of revenues, expenditures, and changes in fund balance—budget and actual, a problem arises if the budget is recorded on one basis and actual data are recorded on another (e.g., the budget is recorded on the cash basis and actual data are recorded on the modified accrual basis). To make budget and actual comparisons meaningful, it is necessary to present actual data on the same basis as budgetary data. As a result, if the budget is prepared on a basis other than that provided by generally accepted accounting principles (GAAP), actual data must be converted so that they follow the measurement rules used to develop the budget (e.g., from the modified accrual basis to the cash basis). This practice will often result in inconsistencies between this statement and the statement of revenues, expenditures and changes in fund balance.

Even when the budget is prepared on the modified accrual basis (as in the

---

[5]GASB Cod. Sec. 1800.122.

illustrative problem), differences may appear between the statement of revenues, expenditures, and changes in fund balance and the statement of revenues, expenditures, and changes in fund balance—budget and actual. For example, in Table 5–6, expenditures for supplies are shown as $154,500, the amount actually spent. In Table 5–7, they are shown as $204,500. This difference is due to an outstanding encumbrance of $50,000, which has been charged against departmental budgets but which has not been spent by year-end. A reconciliation of differences between the two statements should be provided, either on the statement of revenues, expenditures, and changes in fund balance—budget and actual or in the notes to the financial statements.

SUMMARY PROBLEM

The city council of Realistic City approved the budget shown in Table 5–2 for that municipality's General Fund on December 31, 19X0.

Realistic City *currently* has five property owners, whose fiscal 19X1 property taxes are as follows:

H. R. Morgan	$525,000
W. M. Lohmann	350,000
G. R. Parker	35,000
J. R. Davis	50,000
R. R. Gales	40,000
	$1,000,000

Table 5–2   Budget of Realistic City

REALISTIC CITY
GENERAL FUND
BUDGET
FOR THE YEAR ENDED DECEMBER 31, 19X1

Estimated Revenues and Proceeds		
of Issue of General Obligation Bonds		
Property taxes	$960,000	
License fees	45,000	
Interest and penalties	40,000	
Income taxes	55,000	
Proceeds from issue of bonds	800,000	$1,900,000
Appropriations		
Salaries	$585,000	
Supplies	220,000	
Capital equipment	950,000	
Transfer to Frazer Park Fund	20,000	
Transfer to Debt Service Fund	100,000	1,875,000
Projected Increase in Fund Balance		$25,000

One former property owner, L. J. Ahrens, still owes $500 of FY 19X0 property taxes. Past experience has shown that 4 percent of the property taxes levied are usually not collected.

Among the city's accounting principles are the following:

1. All purchases of supplies and capital equipment are encumbered.
2. Expenditures for salaries, interest, and transfers to other funds do not require encumbrances.
3. Encumbrances lapse at the end of the fiscal year; however, the Reserve for encumbrances is shown on the year-end balance sheet.
4. Separate accounts are maintained for each taxpayer.

The *postclosing* trial balance of the General Fund of Realistic City, as of December 31, 19X0, is as follows:

	DEBITS	CREDITS
Cash	$51,850	
Property taxes receivable—delinquent—Ahrens	500	
Allowance for uncollectible property taxes—delinquent		$ 400
Interest and penalties receivable—Ahrens	50	
Vouchers payable		8,000
Due to Frazer Park Fund		9,000
Reserve for encumbrances		20,000
Unreserved fund balance		15,000
	$52,400	$52,400

During fiscal year 19X1, the following transactions take place:

1. Purchase orders outstanding at the beginning of the year are encumbered. They are for supplies and amount to $20,000.
2. Individual accounts for Property taxes receivable are set up, along with an Allowance for uncollectible property taxes equal to 4 percent of the amount levied.
3. Property taxes are collected on time and in full from H. R. Morgan.
4. L. J. Ahrens is unable to pay her FY 19X0 property taxes in full. She pays the $50 penalty and $100 of these taxes. The remainder of her account is written off.
5. The city council decides, in late August, that the Allowance for uncollectible property taxes is too low and orders the city controller to increase it by $10,000.
6. The amount due to the Frazer Park Fund and the vouchers that were outstanding at the end of FY 19X0 are paid.
7. G. R. Parker is unable to pay his FY 19X1 property taxes. The city decides to write off the account without foreclosing on his property.
8. J. R. Davis and R. R. Gales fail to pay their property taxes by the

due date (September 30). The taxes are reclassified as delinquent, along with the current balance in the Allowance for uncollectible property taxes, $15,000.

9. Penalties of $500 and $400, respectively, are levied against Davis and Gales.

10. A tax lien is placed against the Davis property.

11. Costs of processing and advertising the lien amount to $300. They are paid immediately.

12. In November, the Davis property is sold for $120,000. The auctioneer submits a bill for $1,500. Mr. Davis and the auctioneer are paid in full.

13. Mrs. W. M. Lohmann protests W. M. Lohmann's tax bill. As a result, it is lowered to $325,000. Mr. and Mrs. Lohmann then pay the tax bill in full.

14. Supplies and equipment ordered the previous year arrive. Actual cost is $19,500. Payment is made the following week.

15. A cash payment of $13,000, representing part of the FY 19X1 contribution, is made to the Frazer Park Fund. Because of a shortfall in property tax collections, the General Fund will be unable to contribute the budgeted amount. A liability for the amount it expects to contribute by the end of the fiscal year or shortly thereafter, $5,000, is set up.

16. Supplies costing $200,000 are ordered on Purchase Order No. 1426.

17. New fire engines, expected to cost $950,000, are ordered on Purchase Order No. 1427.

18. One fourth of the supplies ordered arrive, along with an invoice for $45,000. The invoice is paid the following week.

19. One half of the supplies arrive, along with an invoice for $90,000. Payment will not be made until the following year.

20. Salaries for the year amount to $580,000. They are paid in cash.

21. General obligation bonds are issued in March. Proceeds from these bonds, $810,000, will be used by the General Fund to help pay for the fire engines ordered in number 17.

22. In December, a transfer of $100,000 to the Debt Service Fund is recorded. Actual payment will be made the following year.

23. At the end of the year, it is determined that the balance in the Allowance for uncollectible property taxes account is too low. The allowance is raised by $5,000.

24. The city disposes of an old fire engine for $10,000 (original cost was $50,000).

25. The new fire engines arrive, along with an invoice for $975,000. The invoice is paid immediately.

26. Revenues from other sources, which have been collected but not yet recorded, are:

License fees	$50,000	
Interest and penalties	$38,000	
Income taxes	$47,000	

Income taxes are considered to be self-assessed taxes. The city's finance officer estimates that, in addition to the amount shown above, another $5,000 of income taxes will be collected in the first month of the following year and, therefore, are "susceptible to accrual."

27. Supplies costing $10,000 are still on hand at the end of the year. It is felt that this fact should be disclosed in the financial statements.

REQUIRED: For FY 19X1:

1. Prepare appropriate budgetary and operating entries in the General Fund.
2. Prepare a preclosing trial balance.
3. Prepare closing entries.
4. Prepare a postclosing trial balance.
5. Prepare appropriate financial statements.

The **budgetary**, or opening, entry is:

B-1.	Estimated revenues—property taxes	960,000	
	Estimated revenues—license fees	45,000	
	Estimated revenues—interest and penalties	40,000	
	Estimated revenues—income taxes	55,000	
	Estimated proceeds from issue of bonds	800,000	
	Appropriations—salaries		585,000
	Appropriations—supplies		220,000
	Appropriations—capital equipment		950,000
	Appropriations—transfer to Frazer Park Fund		20,000
	Appropriations—transfer to Debt Service Fund		100,000
	Unreserved fund balance		25,000

To record estimated revenues, estimated proceeds from issue of bonds, appropriations, and projected increase in fund balance for FY 19X1.

The **operating** entries are:

1.	Encumbrances—supplies	20,000	
	Unreserved fund balance		20,000

To reestablish encumbrances for supplies ordered, but not received, in FY 19X0.

2. Property taxes receivable—current—Morgan 525,000

   Property taxes receivable—current—
   Lohmann 350,000

   Property taxes receivable—current—
   Parker 35,000

   Property taxes receivable—current—
   Davis 50,000

   Property taxes receivable—current—
   Gales 40,000

       Allowance for uncollectible property
       taxes—current 40,000

       Revenues—property taxes 960,000

   To set up receivable for FY 19X1 property
   taxes, along with an allowance for uncollectible property taxes of 4 percent.

3. Cash 525,000

       Property taxes receivable—current—
       Morgan 525,000

   To record payment of property taxes by H. R.
   Morgan.

4. Cash 150

   Allowance for uncollectible property
   taxes—delinquent 400

       Interest and penalties receivable
       —Ahrens 50

       Property taxes receivable—
       delinquent—Ahrens 500

   To record collection of penalties and part
   of FY 19X0 property taxes levied on L. J.
   Ahrens and to write off remainder of
   account.

5. Revenues—property taxes 10,000

       Allowance for uncollectible property
       taxes—current 10,000

   To increase FY 19X1 allowance for uncollectible property taxes to reflect actual collections.

6. Due to Frazer Park Fund 9,000

   Vouchers payable 8,000

       Cash 17,000

   To record payment of liabilities outstanding at
   end of 19X0.

7. Allowance for uncollectible property
   taxes—current 35,000

       Property taxes receivable—current—
       Parker 35,000

   To write off Parker account for FY 19X1.

8a.	Property taxes receivable—delinquent— Davis	50,000	
	Property taxes—receivable—delinquent— Gales	40,000	
	Property taxes receivable— current—Davis		50,000
	Property taxes receivable— current—Gales		40,000
	To reclassify FY 19X1 property taxes not collected by due date as delinquent.		
8b.	Allowance for uncollectible property taxes—current	15,000	
	Allowance for uncollectible property taxes—delinquent		15,000
	To adjust allowance for uncollectible property taxes—current for FY 19X1 property taxes that are no longer current.		
9.	Interest and penalties receivable—Davis	500	
	Interest and penalties receivable— Gales	400	
	Revenues—interest and penalties		900
	To record assessment of late payment penalties.		
10.	Tax liens receivable—Davis	50,500	
	Property taxes receivable— delinquent—Davis		50,000
	Interest and penalties receivable— Davis		500
	To reclassify property taxes, interest, and penalties receivable to reflect lien on Davis property.		
11.	Tax liens receivable—Davis	300	
	Cash		300
	To record cost of processing and advertising tax lien against Davis property.		
12a.	Cash	120,000	
	Tax liens receivable—Davis		50,800
	Vouchers payable		69,200
	To record sale of Davis property, removal of lien, and expenses related to sale ($1,500).		
12b.	Vouchers payable	69,200	
	Cash		69,200
	To record payment to J. R. Davis and of expenses related to sale of Davis property ($1,500).		

13a.	Revenues—property taxes	25,000	
	Property taxes receivable— current—Lohmann		25,000
	To adjust for error in FY 19X1 tax assessment of W. M. Lohmann.		
13b.	Cash	325,000	
	Property taxes receivable— current—Lohmann		325,000
	To record payment of W. M. Lohmann's FY 19X1 property taxes.		
14a.	Reserve for encumbrances	20,000	
	Encumbrances—supplies		20,000
	To record receipt of supplies ordered in FY 19X0.		
14b.	Expenditures—supplies	19,500	
	Vouchers payable		19,500
	To record liability for payment of supplies ordered in FY 19X0.		
14c.	Vouchers payable	19,500	
	Cash		19,500
	To record payment of voucher.		
15.	Operating transfer to Frazer Park Fund	18,000	
	Due to Frazer Park Fund		5,000
	Cash		13,000
	To record FY 19X1 contribution to Frazer Park Fund.		
16.	Encumbrances—supplies	200,000	
	Reserve for encumbrances		200,000
	To record placement of order for FY 19X1 supplies, Purchase Order No. 1426.		
17.	Encumbrances—capital equipment	950,000	
	Reserve for encumbrances		950,000
	To record placement of order for new fire engines, Purchase Order No. 1427.		
18a.	Reserve for encumbrances	50,000	
	Encumbrances—supplies		50,000
	To record receipt of one-fourth of supplies ordered under Purchase Order No. 1426.		
18b.	Expenditures—supplies	45,000	
	Vouchers payable		45,000
	To record liability for one fourth of supplies received under Purchase Order No. 1426.		

18c.	Vouchers payable	45,000	
	Cash		45,000
	To record payment of voucher.		
19a.	Reserve for encumbrances	100,000	
	Encumbrances—supplies		100,000
	To record receipt of one-half of supplies ordered under Purchase Order No. 1426.		
19b.	Expenditures—supplies	90,000	
	Vouchers payable		90,000
	To record liability for payment of one-half of supplies received under Purchase Order No. 1426.		
20.	Expenditures—salaries	580,000	
	Cash		580,000
	To record salaries paid during FY 19X1.		
21.	Cash	810,000	
	Proceeds from issue of bonds		810,000
	To record issue of general obligation bonds.		
22.	Operating transfer to Debt Service Fund	100,000	
	Due to Debt Service Fund		100,000
	To record liability for FY 19X1 contribution toward service of bond issue.		
23.	Revenues—property taxes	5,000	
	Allowance for uncollectible property taxes—delinquent		5,000
	To adjust property tax revenues for expected uncollectible amounts in excess of adjusted FY 19X1 allowance. (Note: Since FY 19X1 property taxes outstanding are past due at this point, the "delinquent" allowance is increased.)		
24.	Cash	10,000	
	Revenues—sale of general fixed assets		10,000
	To record sale of one surplus fire engine.		
25a.	Reserve for encumbrances	950,000	
	Encumbrances—capital equipment		950,000
	To record receipt of fire engines ordered under Purchase Order No. 1427.		
25b.	Expenditures—capital equipment	975,000	
	Vouchers payable		975,000
	To record purchase of fire engines ordered under Purchase Order No. 1427 and to recognize liability to vendor.		

25c.	Vouchers payable	975,000	
	Cash		975,000
	To record payment of voucher.		
26.	Cash	135,000	
	Income taxes receivable	5,000	
	Revenues—license fees		50,000
	Revenues—interest and penalties		38,000
	Revenues—income taxes		52,000
	To record FY 19X1 revenues from various sources.		
27.	Supplies on hand	10,000	
	Reserve for supplies on hand		10,000
	To record amount of supplies on hand at end of FY 19X1.		

The **closing** entries are:

C-1.	Revenues—property taxes	920,000	
	Revenues—license fees	50,000	
	Revenues—interest and penalties	38,900	
	Revenues—income taxes	52,000	
	Revenues—sale of general fixed assets	10,000	
	Proceeds from issue of bonds	810,000	
	Unreserved fund balance	19,100	
	Estimated revenues—property taxes		960,000
	Estimated revenues—license fees		45,000
	Estimated revenues—interest and penalties		40,000
	Estimated revenues—income taxes		55,000
	Estimated proceeds from issue of bonds		800,000
	To close revenue and estimated revenue accounts for FY 19X1.		
C-2.	Appropriations—salaries	585,000	
	Appropriations—supplies	220,000	
	Appropriations—capital equipment	950,000	
	Appropriations—transfer to Frazer Park Fund	20,000	
	Appropriations—transfer to Debt Service Fund	100,000	
	Expenditures—salaries		580,000
	Expenditures—supplies		154,500
	Expenditures—capital equipment		975,000
	Operating transfer to Frazer Park Fund		18,000
	Operating transfer to Debt Service Fund		100,000
	Unreserved fund balance		47,500
	To close appropriation and expenditure accounts for FY 19X1.		
C-3.	Unreserved fund balance	50,000	
	Encumbrances—supplies		50,000
	To close encumbrances still outstanding at end of FY 19X1.		

Realistic City
General Fund
General Ledger
Year Ended December 31, 19X1

Cash

Beg.	51,850	17,000	(6)
(3)	525,000	300	(11)
(4)	150	69,200	(12b)
(12a)	120,000	19,500	(14c)
(13b)	325,000	13,000	(15)
(21)	810,000	45,000	(18c)
(24)	10,000	580,000	(20)
(26)	135,000	975,000	(25c)
	1,977,000	1,719,000	
	258,000		

Income Taxes Receivable

(26)	5,000		

Vouchers Payable

(6)	8,000	8,000	Beg.
(12b)	69,200	69,200	(12a)
(14c)	19,500	19,500	(14b)
(18c)	45,000	45,000	(18b)
(25c)	975,000	90,000	(19b)
		975,000	(25b)
	1,116,700	1,206,700	
		90,000	

Property Taxes Receivable—Delinquent—Ahrens

Beg.	500	500	(4)

Allowance for Uncollectible Property Taxes—Delinquent

(4)	400	400	Beg.
		15,000	(8b)
		5,000	(23)
	400	20,400	
		20,000	

Property Taxes Receivable—Current—Morgan

(2)	525,000	525,000	(3)

Property Taxes Receivable—Current—Parker

(2)	35,000	35,000	(7)

Property Taxes Receivable—Current—Gales

(2)	40,000	40,000	(8a)

Interest and Penalties Receivable—Ahrens

Beg.	50	50	(4)

Allowance for Uncollectible Property Taxes—Current

(7)	35,000	40,000	(2)
(8b)	15,000	10,000	(5)
	50,000	50,000	

Supplies on Hand

(27)	10,000		

Property Taxes Receivable—Current—Lohmann

(2)	350,000	25,000	(13a)
		325,000	(13b)
	350,000	350,000	

Property Taxes Receivable—Current—Davis

(2)	50,000	50,000	(8a)

Property Taxes Receivable—Delinquent—Gales

(8a)	40,000		

Realistic City
General Fund
General Ledger
Year Ended December 31, 19X1

Reserve for Encumbrances			
(14a)	20,000	20,000	Beg.
(18a)	50,000	200,000	(16)
(19a)	100,000	950,000	(17)
(25a)	950,000		
	1,120,000	1,170,000	
		50,000	

Unresrved Fund Balance			
		15,000	Beg.
		25,000	(B-1)
		20,000	(1)
		60,000	
(C-1)	19,100	47,500	(C-2)
(C-3)	50,000		
	69,100	107,500	
		38,400	

Estimated Revenues— Property Taxes			
(B-1)	960,000	960,000	(C-1)

Property Taxes Receivable— Delinquent—Davis			
(8a)	50,000	50,000	(10)

Interest and Penalties Receivable—Davis			
(9)	500	500	(10)

Due to Frazer Park Fund			
(6)	9,000	9,000	Beg.
		5,000	(15)
	9,000	14,000	
		5,000	

Encumbrances—Supplies			
(1)	20,000	20,000	(14a)
(16)	200,000	50,000	(18a)
		100,000	(19a)
	220,000	170,000	
	50,000	50,000	(C-3)

Estimated Revenues— License Fees			
(B-1)	45,000	45,000	(C-1)

Tax Liens Receivable—Davis			
(10)	50,500	50,800	(12a)
(11)	300		
	50,800	50,800	

Interest and Penalties Receivable—Gales		
(9)	400	

Due to Debt Service Fund		
		100,000	(22)

Encumbrances— Capital Equipment			
(17)	950,000	950,000	(25a)

Reserve for Supplies on Hand		
		10,000	(27)

Estimated Revenues— Interest and Penalties			
(B-1)	40,000	40,000	(C-1)

Realistic City
General Fund
General Ledger
Year Ended December 31, 19X1

Estimated Revenues—Income Taxes			
B-1	55,000	55,000	C-1

Appropriations—Supplies			
C-2	220,000	220,000	B-1

Appropriations—Transfer to Debt Service Fund			
C-2	100,000	100,000	B-1

Revenues—Interest and Penalties

		900	9
		38,000	26
C-1	38,900	38,900	

Prceeds from Issue of Bonds

C-1	810,000	810,000	21

Expenditures—Supplies

14b	19,500		
18b	45,000		
19b	90,000		
	154,500	154,500	C-2

Estimated Proceeds from Issue of Bonds

B-1	800,000	800,000	C-1

Appropriations—Capital Equipment

C-2	950,000	950,000	B-1

Revenues—Property Taxes

5	10,000	960,000	2
13a	25,000		
23	5,000		
	40,000	960,000	
C-1	920,000	920,000	

Expenditures—Salaries

20	580,000	580,000	C-2

Operating Transfer to Frazer Park Fund

15	18,000	18,000	C-2

Appropriations—Salaries

C-2	585,000	585,000	B-1

Appropriations—Transfer to Frazer Park Fund

C-2	20,000	20,000	B-1

Revenues—License Fees

C-1	50,000	50,000	26

Revenues—Income Taxes

C-1	52,000	52,000	26

Revenues—Sale of General Fixed Assets

C-1	10,000	10,000	24

Expenditures—Capital Equipment

25b	975,000	975,000	C-2

Operating Transfer to Debt Service Fund

22	100,000	100,000	C-2

TABLE 5–3   Realistic City—Preclosing Trial Balance

Realistic City
General Fund
Preclosing Trial Balance
December 31, 19X1

	DEBITS	CREDITS
Cash	$ 258,000	
Property taxes receivable—delinquent—Gales	40,000	
Allowance for uncollectible property taxes—delinquent		$ 20,000
Interest and penalties receivable—Gales	400	
Income taxes receivable	5,000	
Supplies on hand	10,000	
Vouchers payable		90,000
Due to Frazer Park Fund		5,000
Due to Debt Service Fund		100,000
Encumbrances—supplies	50,000	
Reserve for supplies on hand		10,000
Reserve for encumbrances		50,000
Unreserved fund balance		60,000
Estimated revenues—property taxes	960,000	
Estimated revenues—license fees	45,000	
Estimated revenues—interest and penalties	40,000	
Estimated revenues—income taxes	55,000	
Estimated proceeds from issue of bonds	800,000	
Appropriations—salaries		585,000
Appropriations—supplies		220,000
Appropriations—capital equipment		950,000
Appropriations—transfer to Frazer Park Fund		20,000
Appropriations—transfer to Debt Service Fund		100,000
Revenues—property taxes		920,000
Revenues—license fees		50,000
Revenues—interest and penalties		38,900
Revenues—income taxes		52,000
Revenues—sale of general fixed assets		10,000
Proceeds from issue of bonds		810,000
Expenditures—salaries	580,000	
Expenditures—supplies	154,500	
Expenditures—capital equipment	975,000	
Operating transfer to Frazer Park Fund	18,000	
Operating transfer to Debt Service Fund	100,000	
	$4,090,900	$4,090,900

TABLE 5–4 Realistic City—Postclosing Trial Balance

Realistic City
General Fund
Postclosing Trial Balance
December 31, 19X1

	DEBITS	CREDITS
Cash	$258,000	
Property taxes received—delinquent—Gales	40,000	
Allowance for uncollectible property taxes—delinquent		$ 20,000
Interest and penalties receivable—Gales	400	
Income taxes receivable	5,000	
Supplies on hand	10,000	
Vouchers payable		90,000
Due to Frazer Park Fund		5,000
Due to Debt Service Fund		100,000
Reserve for supplies on hand		10,000
Reserve for encumbrances		50,000
Unreserved fund balance		38,400
	$313,400	$313,400

TABLE 5–5 Realistic City—Balance Sheet

Realistic City
General Fund
Balance Sheet
December 31, 19X1

Assets		
Cash		$258,000
Property taxes receivable—delinquent	$40,000	
Less: Allowance for uncollectible property taxes	(20,000)	20,000
Interest and penalties receivable		400
Income taxes receivable		5,000
Supplies on hand		10,000
		$293,400
Liabilities and Fund Balance		
Vouchers payable		$ 90,000
Due to Frazer Park Fund		5,000
Due to Debt Service Fund		100,000
Reserve for supplies on hand		10,000
Reserve for encumbrances		50,000
Unreserved fund balance		38,400
		$293,400

TABLE 5–6   Realistic City—Statement of Revenues, Expenditures and Changes in Fund Balance

Realistic City
General Fund
Statement of Revenues, Expenditures,
and Changes in Fund Balance
Year Ended December 31, 19X1

Revenues		
Property taxes	$920,000	
License fees	50,000	
Interest and penalties	38,900	
Income taxes	52,000	
Sale of general fixed assets	10,000	$1,070,900
Expenditures		
Salaries	$580,000	
Supplies	154,500	
Capital equipment	975,000	1,709,500
Excess (Deficiency) of Revenues over Expenditures		$ (638,600)
Other Financing Sources (Uses)		
Proceeds from issue of bonds	$810,000	
Operating transfer to Frazer Park Fund	(18,000)	
Operating transfer to Debt Service Fund	(100,000)	692,000
Excess (Deficiency) of Revenues and Other Sources over Expenditures and Other Uses		$ 53,400
Reserves and (Unreserved) Fund Balance at Beginning of Year		35,000
		$ 88,400
Increase in Reserve for Supplies on Hand		10,000
Reserves and (Unreserved) Fund Balance at End of Year		$ 98,400

GOVERNMENTAL ACCOUNTING IN PRACTICE—
JEFFERSON PARISH, LOUISIANA

Jefferson Parish (1992 population, 456,389) is a residential suburb of New Orleans. (In Lousiana, a parish is the equivalent of a county.) Jefferson Parish consists of two cities and a large, unincorporated but heavily populated area. It also has large areas of wetlands noted for their variety of wildlife. Industries include shipbuilding, petrochemicals, and financial services.

The financial statements of the General Fund of Jefferson Parish follow, along with selected notes to the financial statements (Table 5–11). Included are a balance sheet (Table 5–8); a combined statement of revenues, expenditures, and changes in fund balances—all governmental fund types (Table 5–9); and a statement of revenues, expenditures, and changes in fund balance—actual and budget (Table 5–10). Notice that a reconciliation of results prepared on the GAAP

TABLE 5–7   Realistic City—Statement of Revenues, Expenditures and Charges in Fund Balance–
Budget and Actual

Realistic City
General Fund
Statement of Revenues, Expenditures, and
Changes in Fund Balance—Budget and Actual
Year Ended December 31, 19X1

	BUDGET	ACTUAL	VARIANCE— FAVORABLE (UNFAVORABLE)
Revenues			
Property taxes	$ 960,000	$ 920,000	$(40,000)
License fees	45,000	50,000	5,000
Interest and penalties	40,000	38,900	(1,100)
Income taxes	55,000	52,000	(3,000)
Sales of general fixed assets	—	10,000	10,000
Total revenues	$1,100,000	$1,070,900	$(29,100)
Expenditures			
Salaries	$ 585,000	$ 580,000	$ 5,000
Supplies*	220,000	204,500	15,500
Capital equipment	950,000	975,000	(25,000)
Total expenditures	$1,755,000	1,759,500	$ (4,500)
Excess (Deficiency) of Revenues over Expenditures	$ (655,000)	$ (688,600)	$(33,600)
Other Financing Sources (Uses)			
Proceeds from issue of bonds	$ 800,000	$ 810,000	$ 10,000
Operating transfer to Frazer Park Fund	(20,000)	(18,000)	2,000
Operating transfer to Debt Service Fund	(100,000)	(100,000)	—
Total other financing sources (uses)	$ 680,000	$ 692,000	$ 12,000
Excess (Deficiency) of Revenues and Other Sources over Expenditures and Other Uses	$ 25,000	$ 3,400	$(21,600)
Reserves and Unreserved Fund Balance at Beginning of Year	35,000	35,000	—
	$ 60,000	$ 38,400	$(21,600)
Increase in Reserve for Supplies on Hand	—	10,000	10,000
Reserves and Unreserved Fund Balance at End of Year	$ 60,000	$ 48,400	$(11,600)

*Expenditures shown for supplies include the amount actually spent in FY 19X1 ($154,500) plus out-standing encumbrances of $50,000, which will be honored the following year but are charged against the FY 19X1 budget.

and the budgetary basis is presented on the latter statement. The principal adjustment to revenue results from the practice of budgeting only interest actually expected to be received during the year, even though accrued interest is considered measurable and available and is recorded on the GAAP basis. The primary adjustment to expenditures is due to the parish's policy of recording encumbrances as expenditures under the budgetary basis.

TABLE 5–8   Jefferson Parish, Louisiana—Balance Sheet

Jefferson Parish, Louisiana
General Fund
Balance Sheet
December 31, 19X1

Assets	
Cash and certificates of deposit	$2,984,560
Share of pooled assets	4,292,123
Receivables	
Ad valorem tax	2,443,380
Accounts	507,487
Intergovernmental	4,241,606
Advance to other funds	300,000
Deposits and other assets	1,202,894
Total assets	$15,972,050
Liabilities and Fund Balance	
Liabilities:	
Accounts payable	$1,123,210
Intergovernmental payable	1,501,569
Due to other funds	244,223
Deposits	144,594
Other payables and accruals	3,557,887
Deferred revenue	3,490,025
Total liabilities	10,061,508
Fund Balance:	
Reserved for encumbrances	174,097
Reserved for judges' annuities	1,069,430
Reserved for community service programs	358,229
Reserved for advances	300,000
Unreserved	
Designated for subsequent year's expenditures	1,825,172
Designated for debt service	2,000,000
Undesignated	183,614
Total fund balance	5,910,542
Total Liabilities and Fund Balance	$15,972,050

Source: A recent Jefferson Parish, Louisiana, annual report.

TABLE 5-9

Jefferson Parish, Louisiana
Combined Statement of Revenues, Expenditures, and Changes in Fund Balances
All Governmental Fund Types
Year Ended December 31, 19X1
(in thousands of dollars)

	GENERAL	SPECIAL REVENUE	DEBT SERVICE	CAPITAL PROJECTS	TOTAL (MEMORANDUM ONLY)
Revenues:					
Taxes	$18,984	$83,998	$46,425	$ 5,479	$ 154,886
Licenses and permits	7,031	—	—	—	7,031
Intergovernmental	562	26,404	—	8,748	35,714
Charges for services	4,350	9,314	—	—	13,664
Fines and forfeits	2,058	170	—	—	2,228
Special assessments	—	—	209	—	209
Interest income	547	2,434	2,428	8,625	14,034
Miscellaneous	4,820	5,407	1,030	1,259	12,516
Total revenues	38,352	127,727	50,092	24,111	240,282
Other financing sources:					
Bond proceeds	—	400	—	—	400
Donation of property	3,762	—	—	—	3,762
Operating transfers in	1,028	8,936	1,824	16,572	28,360
Total revenues and other financing sources	43,142	137,063	51,916	40,683	272,804
Expenditures:					
Current					
General government	31,263	—	—	—	31,263
Public safety	8,631	26,204	—	—	34,835
Public works	988	50,388	—	—	51,376
Transit	—	6,007	—	—	6,007
Health and welfare	1,359	18,383	—	—	19,742
Culture and recreation	588	18,507	—	—	19,095
Economic development	—	1,981	—	—	1,981
Urban redevelopment and housing	—	3,530	—	—	3,530
Capital outlay	—	—	—	40,674	40,674
Debt service					
Principal retirement	—	13	20,860	—	20,873
Interest and fiscal charges	—	2	28,648	—	28,650
Other	—	—	72	—	72
Total expenditures	42,829	125,015	49,580	40,674	258,098
Other financing uses:					
Payment to refunded bond escrow agent	—	—	803	—	803
Operating transfers out	3,431	11,272	6,951	6,685	28,339
Total expenditures and other financing uses	46,260	136,287	57,334	47,359	287,240
Excess (deficiency) of revenues and other sources over expenditures and other uses	(3,118)	776	(5,418)	(6,676)	(14,436)
Fund balances:					
Beginning of year, as restated	9,029	22,009	41,280	170,405	242,723
Residual equity transfers	—	154	(317)	—	(163)
End of year	$ 5,911	$22,939	$35,545	$163,729	$228,124

The accompanying notes are an integral part of this statement.

Source: A recent Jefferson Parish, Louisiana, annual report.

TABLE 5-8   Jefferson Parish, Louisiana—Statement of Revenues, Expenditures and Changes in Fund Balances—Actual and Budget

Jefferson Parish, Louisiana
General Fund
Statement of Revenues, Expenditures, and Changes in Fund Balances
Actual and Budget (Budgetary Basis)
Year Ended December 31, 19X1

	ACTUAL GAAP BASIS	ADJUSTMENT TO BUDGETARY BASIS	ACTUAL ON BUDGETARY BASIS	BUDGET	VARIANCE— FAVORABLE (UNFAVORABLE)
Revenues:					
Taxes	$18,983,841	$0	$18,983,841	$19,280,864	$ (297,023)
Licenses and permits	7,030,636	(18)	7,030,618	6,908,076	122,542
Intergovernmental	562,565	0	562,565	448,368	114,197
Charges for services	4,349,593	(75)	4,349,518	4,242,336	107,182
Fines and forfeits	2,057,899	0	2,057,899	2,004,850	53,049
Interest income	546,950	(69,393)	477,557	469,784	7,773
Miscellaneous	4,819,631	(559)	4,819,072	4,624,217	194,855
Total revenues	38,351,115	(70,045)	38,281,070	37,978,495	302,575
Other financing sources:					
Operating transfers in	1,028,334	0	1,028,334	1,326,389	(298,055)
Donation of property	3,762,236	0	3,762,236	0	3,762,236
Total other financing sources	4,790,570	0	4,790,570	1,326,389	3,464,181
Total revenues and other financing sources	43,141,685	(70,045)	43,071,640	39,304,884	3,766,756
Expenditures:					
Current					
General government	31,263,278	200,364	31,463,642	28,224,403	(3,239,239)
Public safety	8,630,431	39,474	8,669,905	8,932,294	262,389
Public works	988,002	2,021	990,023	1,291,454	301,431
Health and welfare	1,359,162	(1,520)	1,357,642	1,435,331	77,689
Culture and recreation	587,905	16,322	604,227	767,725	163,498
Total expenditures	42,828,778	256,661	43,085,439	40,651,207	(2,434,232)
Other financing uses:					
Operating transfers out	3,431,341	0	3,431,341	2,982,810	(448,531)
Total expenditures and other financing uses	46,260,119	256,661	46,516,780	43,634,017	(2,882,763)
Excess (deficiency) of revenues and other sources over expenditures and other uses	(3,118,434)	(326,706)	(3,445,140)	(4,329,133)	883,993
Fund balance:					
Beginning of year	9,028,976	(823,493)	8,205,483	7,065,112	1,140,371
End of year	$ 5,910,542	(1,150,199)	4,760,343	2,735,979	2,024,364

Source: A recent Jefferson Parish, Louisiana, annual report.

TABLE 5–11   Jefferson Parish, Louisiana—Notes to Financial Statements

Jefferson Parish, Louisiana
Notes to Financial Statements (Continued)
December 31, 19X1

NOTE A—SUMMARY OF SIGNIFICANT ACCOUNTING POLICIES (Continued)

3. BASIS OF ACCOUNTING

The accounting and financial reporting treatment applied to a fund is determined by its measurement focus. All governmental funds are accounted for using a current financial resources measurement focus. With this measurement focus, only current assets and current liabilities generally are included on the balance sheet. Operating statements of these funds present increases (i.e., revenues and other financing sources) and decreases (i.e., expenditures and other financing uses) in net current assets.

All proprietary funds and pension trust funds are accounted for on a flow of economic resources measuement focus. With this measurement focus, all assets and all liabilities associated with the operation of these funds are included on the balance sheet. Fund equity (i.e., net total assets) is segregated into contributed capital and retained earnings components. Proprietary fund–type operating statements present increases (e.g., revenues) and decreases (e.g., expenses) in net total assets.

The modified accrual basis of accounting is used by all governmental fund types and agency funds. Under the modified accrual basis of accounting, revenues are recognized when susceptible to accrual (i.e., when they become both measurable and available). "Measurable" means the amount of the transaction can be determined and "available" means collectible within the current period or soon enough thereafter to be used to pay liabilities of the current period. The Parish considers ad valorem (property) taxes revenue in the year for which they are levied. Expenditures are recorded when the related fund liability is incurred. Principal and interest on general long-term debt are recorded as fund liabilities when due.

Those revenues susceptible to accrual are chain store taxes, franchise taxes, special assessments, licenses, interest revenue and charges for services. Sales taxes collected and held by intermediary collecting governments at year end on behalf of the Parish government also are recognized as revenue. Fines and permits are not susceptible to accrual because generally they are not measurable until received in cash.

The accrual basis of accounting is utilized by proprietary fund types and pension trust funds. Under this method, revenues are recorded when earned and expenses are recorded at the time liabilities are incurred. East Jefferson General Hospital and West Jefferson Medical Center provide care to patients that meet certain criteria without charge or at amounts less than its established rates, and are not reported as revenue. Net patient service revenues are reported at the estimated net realizable amounts from patients, third-party payors, and others for services rendered.

The Parish reports deferred revenue on its combined balance sheet. Deferred revenues arise when a potential revenue does not meet both the "measurable" and "available" criteria for recognition in the current period. Deferred revenues also arise when resources are received by the Parish before it has a legal claim to them, as when grant monies are received prior to the incurrence of qualifying expenditures. In subsequent periods, when both revenue recognition criteria are met, or when the Parish has a legal claim to the resources, the liability for deferred revenue is removed from the combined balance sheet and revenue is recognized.

(continued)

TABLE 5–11 (*Continued*)

NOTE A—SUMMARY OF SIGNIFICANT ACCOUNTING POLICIES (Continued)

4. BUDGETARY ACCOUNTING

Formal budgetary accounting is employed as a management control device during the year for the General Fund, Special Revenue Funds (except for Federal and State grants), and proprietary funds (except for East Jefferson General Hospital and West Jefferson Medical Center and Subsidiary Enterprise Funds). Budgetary data for the Federal and State Grant Special Revenue Funds and the Capital Project Funds are not presented since these funds are budgeted over the life of the respective project or grant and not on an annual basis. Formal budgetary accounting is not employed for Debt Service Funds because effective control is alternatively achieved through the indenture provisions of the bonds and certificates.

Expenditures may not exceed budgeted appropriations at the fund/department level. Appropriations whch are not expended nor encumbered lapse at year end.

Budgets for the General, Special Revenue (except Federal and State grants), and proprietary funds (except for East Jefferson General Hospital and West Jefferson Medical Center and Subsidiary Enterprise Funds) are adopted on a basis consistent with generally accepted accounting principles (GAAP), except that (1) shared revenues received from other governments are recognized when received in cash, (2) expenditures represented by unpaid invoices which are received after the year-end budgetary cut-off which have not been encumbered are recognized when paid, (3) losses resulting from claims and litigation are recorded when paid instead of when the liability arises, and (4) encumbrances are recorded as expenditures.

5. ENCUMBRANCES

Encumbrance accounting, under which purchase orders, contracts, and other commitments for the expenditure of monies are recorded in order to reserve that portion of the applicable appropriation, is employed as an extension of formal budgetary accounting in the General Fund, Special Revenue Funds, and Capital Projects Funds. Encumbrances outstanding at year end are reported as reservations of fund balances because they do not constitute expenditures nor liabilities.

Source: A recent Jefferson Parish, Louisiana, annual report.

REVIEW QUESTIONS

Q5–1 What are the two methods of handling open encumbrances at year-end? What are the advantages and disadvantages of each method?

Q5–2 What is an allotment? Describe two methods of accounting for allotments. Describe the advantages of each.

Q5–3 Why is depreciation not always recorded by governmental units?

Q5–4 What are the two methods of handling uncollectible receivables? What are the advantages of each method?

Q5–5 Why aren't inventories of governmental units treated in the same manner as those of commercial enterprises? When it is necessary to record a change in the level of inventories at year-end, what entry is appropriate?

Q5–6 Why is a portion of an encumbrance removed from the accounting records when an order is only partially filled?

Q5–7   How are transfers between funds of the same organization recorded?

Q5–8   In the balance sheet of a commercial entity, assets are classified as short-term or long-term. Is this classification necessary for a governmental-type fund? Explain.

Q5–9   What does the term *lapse* mean when referring to encumbrances?

Q5–10 What events take place when a receivable becomes a lien and the property is subsequently seized and sold at auction? What are the appropriate entries?

Q5–11 What entries are appropriate to describe short-term borrowing by the General Fund? How does this differ from the treatment of long-term borrowing?

Q5–12 An Allowance for uncollectible taxes account is often set up when uncollectible taxes are *not* expected to be few in number and/or relatively small in amount. What advantage does this method offer over the direct write-off method?

Q5–13 What are interfund transactions?

Q5–14 Which type or types of interfund transactions result in the recognition of revenues and expenditures (expenses)?

Q5–15 Name two types of taxpayer-assessed revenues. When are these revenues recognized? Is a year-end adjusting entry necessary in order to recognize some of these revenues?

CASES

C5–1   When reviewing the financial statements of Crescent City, Councilwoman Peggy Doubleton noticed that the city uses an Allowance for uncollectible property taxes. This seemed odd to her since the city had recently sold several acres of land that had been seized for nonpayment of property taxes. At the next council meeting, Councilwoman Doubleton made a motion that the city no longer use an Allowance for uncollectible property taxes. She argued that the city had the right to seize property for nonpayment of taxes. As a result it could eventually recover any lost revenue and did not need to provide for uncollectible property taxes. Furthermore, by eliminating this allowance, revenues would be raised by a substantial amount and additional services could be provided without incurring a deficit.

Would you vote for Councilwoman Doubleton's motion if you were a member of the city council?

C5–2   The City of Khatt recently received a $500,000 grant from the federal government to operate a day-care center for two years. Feeling pressure to maximize revenues, the city's accountant credited a revenue account for the entire $500,000 when the check arrived. He explained to you that since the entire amount was in the city's possession, it was "measurable and available" and, therefore, should be treated as revenue.

Do you agree? Why?

C5–3 Joe Babitt, a former executive of T-Mart, has just started his term as mayor of Saulk Center. For the past several days he has been looking for a way to keep his campaign promise to increase services without raising taxes or service charges. While lunching at the local country club with the treasurer of T-Mart, the subject of a recent sale and leaseback of one of T-Mart's stores came up. Following a common practice in retailing, T-Mart had just erected a building and sold it to an investor. It then assigned a long-term lease on the building.

Bingo!! That's it, thought Mayor Babitt. We can sell several of the city's buildings, as well as police cars, fire engines, and other vehicles, to investors and lease them back. That will give us the revenues we desperately need. In addition, we won't need to worry about depreciation or future capital outlays. Now I can concentrate on fighting crime.

Do you agree with Mayor Babitt. If not, what are the flaws in his reasoning?

EXERCISES

E5–1 (Uncollectible accounts—allowance method)

The City of Golder's Green levied property taxes of $150,000 in FY 19X1. Prior experience has shown that 10 percent of these taxes will not be collected.

REQUIRED: a. What is the appropriate entry to set up the receivable for FY 19X1 property taxes if the allowance method is used?

b. Taxpayer Holmes, whose tax levy is $2,000, is unable to pay her property taxes. The city decides to write off her account. Make the entry necessary to record this event.

c. If the Holmes account is not written off until FY 19X2, what effect will this have on the FY 19X2 revenues? Why?

E5–2 (Uncollectible accounts—direct write-off method)

The City of Erica uses the direct write-off method of treating uncollectible accounts. If Henry Tudor is unable to pay his tax levy of $200, what is the appropriate entry to write off his account?

E5–3 (Prior-year encumbrances that remain open)

The City of Eleanor follows a policy of allowing encumbrances to remain in force until the goods are delivered or the purchase orders are canceled. At the end of FY 19X1, supplies costing $10,000 have not been delivered. In March 19X2, the supplies arrive, accompanied by an invoice for $12,000.

REQUIRED: 1.   What entry or entries should be made at the end of FY 19X1?
              2.   What entry or entries should be made at the beginning of FY 19X2?
              3.   What entry or entries should be made when the supplies arrive?

   E5–4   (Prior-year encumbrances that lapse)
          The City of Margaret follows a policy of allowing encumbrances to lapse
          at the end of the year if the goods are not received, the services are not
          performed, or the purchase orders are not canceled. At the end of FY
          19X1, supplies expected to cost $50,000 have not been delivered.

REQUIRED: a.   What entry or entries should be made at year-end, assuming the pur-
                   chase orders will be honored in FY 19X2?
              b.   What entry or entries should be made at the beginning of FY 19X2?
              c.   The supplies arrive in FY 19X2, accompanied by an invoice for
                   $49,500. What entry or entries should be made at this time?

   E5–5   (Interfund transactions)
          Identify the types of interfund transactions and briefly explain the pur-
          pose of each type.

   E5–6   (Treatment of inventories—purchases method)
          At the end of FY 19X1, the City of Kensington has a balance of $6,000 in
          its Reserve for supplies account. An inventory, taken at the end of 19X2,
          reveals that supplies valued at $7,000 are on hand. Kensington uses the
          purchases method to account for supplies.

REQUIRED: a.   What entry should be made at the end of 19X2 to disclose this change
                   in the amount of supplies on hand?
              b.   Suppose the inventory shows that supplies valued at $4,000 are on
                   hand. What entry should be made to disclose this fact?

   E5–7   Multiple choice—General and Special Revenue Funds
          1.   The budget of Laxey County shows estimated revenues in excess of
               appropriations. When preparing budgetary entries at the beginning
               of the fiscal year, an increase will be recorded in which of the fol-
               lowing accounts?
               a.   Encumbrances
               b.   Due from other funds
               c.   Unreserved fund balance
               d.   Reserve for encumbrances
          2.   Reversions of property of persons not leaving a will, and with no
               known relatives, to a state are known as
               a.   Reversions
               b.   Entitlements
               c.   Escheats
               d.   Contributions
          3.   A routine transfer from the General Fund to a Debt Service Fund,

to provide resources to pay interest and principal on a bond issue, is an example of
   a.   A residual equity transfer
   b.   An operating transfer
   c.   A reimbursement
   d.   A quasi-external transaction

4.   At the end of FY 19X1, Bond City has outstanding encumbrances amounting to $15,000. Although the city follows a policy of allowing outstanding encumbrances to lapse, it plans to honor the related purchase orders in FY 19X2. The management of the city wants the users of its financial statements to be aware of these outstanding purchase orders. Therefore, at year-end, the city's accountant should
   a.   Debit Reserve for encumbrances
   b.   Credit Appropriations
   c.   Debit Unreserved fund balance
   d.   Debit an expenditure account

5.   Which of the following revenues of the General Fund are usually recorded before they are actually received?
   a.   Sales taxes
   b.   Property taxes
   c.   Fines and penalties
   d.   Parking meter receipts

6.   If the City of Castletown sells an ambulance, which had been purchased by the General Fund several years earlier, to a local rock group, the entry to record this sale on the books of the General Fund should include
   a.   A credit to Revenues—sale of general fixed assets
   b.   A debit to Unreserved fund balance
   c.   A debit to Encumbrances—capital equipment
   d.   A credit to a fixed asset account

7.   The town council of Bayou Brilleaux adopted a budget for FY 19X1 that indicated revenues of $750,000 and appropriations of $800,000. The entry to record this budget into the accounts is

	DR	CR
a. Estimated revenues	750,000	
Reserve for deficits	50,000	
Appropriations		800,000
b. Appropriations	800,000	
Unreserved fund balance		50,000
Estimated revenues		750,000
c. Estimated revenues	750,000	
Unreserved fund balance	50,000	
Appropriations		800,000
d. Only a memorandum entry is necessary		

8. Which of the following will increase the fund balance of a governmental unit at the end of a fiscal year?
   a. Appropriations are less than expenditures and reserve for encumbrances
   b. Appropriations are less than expenditures and encumbrances
   c. Appropriations are more than expenditures and encumbrances
   d. Appropriations are more than estimated revenues

9. The Reserve for encumbrances—prior-year account represents amounts recorded by a governmental unit for
   a. Anticipated expenditures in the next year
   b. Expenditures for which purchase orders were made in the prior year but disbursement will be in the current year
   c. Excess expenditures in the prior year that will be offset against the current-year budgeted amounts
   d. Unanticipated expenditures of the prior year that become evident in the current year

10. The budget of the General Fund of the City of Dhoon Glen shows an appropriation for capital equipment of $150,000. So far a fire engine, costing $50,000, has been received and paid for. Another fire engine, expected to cost $60,000, has been ordered and an encumbrance for this amount is outstanding. How much can the city legally spend for a third fire engine this year?
    a. $100,000
    b. $90,000
    c. $40,000
    d. $0

11. Which of the following accounts of a governmental unit is (are) closed out at the end of the fiscal year?

	Estimated Revenues	Fund Balance
a.	No	No
b.	No	Yes
c.	Yes	Yes
d.	Yes	No

12. Which of the following is an appropriate basis of accounting for the General Fund of a governmental unit?

	Cash Basis	Modified Accrual Basis
a.	Yes	No
b.	Yes	Yes
c.	No	Yes
d.	No	No

(AICPA adapted)

13. Which of the following is *not* included among the financial statements of the General Fund of a city?
    a. Balance sheet
    b. Statement of revenues, expenditures, and changes in fund balance
    c. Statement of revenues, expenditures, and changes in fund balance—budget and actual
    d. Statement of cash flows

14. In 19X1, Manx City received a capital grant from the federal government to purchase a fleet of streetcars for its Promenade line. It also received a grant from the state to cover certain operating costs of this line. Because of the difficulty of finding manufacturers of horse-drawn streetcars, only 60 percent of the capital grant was spent by the end of 19X1 and the city does not expect to spend the remainder until mid-19X2. Because of an unexpected increase in the price of hay; however, the entire operating grant was spent by the end of the first half of 19X1. With respect to these grants, what should Manx City record as revenue from grants on its FY 19X1 financial statements?

	100% of Capital Grant	60% of Capital Grant	Operating Grant
a.	Yes	No	Yes
b.	No	Yes	Yes
c.	Yes	No	No
d.	No	Yes	No

E5–8 (Tax discounts and deferred property taxes)

The city of Snape allows taxpayers who pay their property taxes by the end of the fiscal year to take a 3 percent discount for prompt payment. The city budgets, as Estimated revenues, the amount it actually expects to receive. During FY 19X1, the city sent bills to property owners totaling $150,000 (gross amount). Two thirds of the amount billed (less discounts) was received by the end of the year. The remainder, $50,000, will not be collected until the middle of the following year.

REQUIRED: 1. Prepare an entry recording the collection of property taxes in FY 19X1.
           2. Prepare a year-end adjusting entry recording FY 19X1 property taxes expected to be collected in FY 19X2.

PROBLEMS

P5–1 (Theory problem on the basis of accounting)

The accounting system of the municipality of Kemp is organized and operated on a fund basis. Among the types of funds used are a General Fund, a Special Revenue Fund, and an Enterprise Fund.

REQUIRED: a. Explain the basic differences in revenue recognition between the accrual basis of accounting and the modified accrual basis of accounting as it relates to governmental accounting.

           b. What basis of accounting should be used for each of the following funds?

- General Fund
- Special Revenue Fund
- Enterprise Fund

Why?

           c. How should fixed assets and long-term liabilities related to the General Fund be accounted for?

(AICPA adapted)

P5–2 (Entries when actual and budgeted revenues and expenditures differ) The commissioners of the Regents Park Commission have approved the budget shown below. Assume that the Unreserved fund balance at the beginning of the year was $10,000 and that no encumbrances were outstanding and no supplies were on hand at the beginning or the end of the year.

Estimated Revenues		
Property taxes	$300,000	
Concession rentals	100,000	
User charges	200,000	$600,000
Appropriations		
Wages and salaries	$200,000	
Capital equipment	300,000	
Supplies	50,000	550,000
Projected Increase in Fund Balance		$ 50,000

During the year, actual revenues were:

Property taxes	$300,000
Concession rentals	120,000
User charges	185,000

Actual expenditures were:

Wages and salaries	$205,000
Capital equipment	290,000
Supplies	40,000

REQUIRED: a. Prepare a statement of revenues, expenditures, and changes in fund balance.

           b. Prepare a statement of revenues, expenditures, and changes in fund balance—budget and actual.

P5–3   (Allowance for uncollectible property taxes— allowance method)

The City of Aldwich uses the allowance method of handling uncollectible property taxes. In FY 19X1, the following transactions took place:

1.   At the end of FY 19X0, property taxes receivable were $10,000. The allowance for uncollectible property taxes was $3,000.

2.   In FY 19X1, collections of FY 19X0 property taxes were as follows:

J. Bond	$5,000
J. Steed	3,000

J. Tebbe, who owed $2,000, was unable to pay his property taxes. The account was written off.

3.   During FY 19X1, property taxes of $50,000 were levied. An Allowance for uncollectible property taxes of 6 percent was established for this particular tax levy. The property taxes were levied as follows:

J. Bond	$10,000
J. Steed	20,000
T. King	10,000
E. Peel	5,000
S. Templar	5,000
	$50,000

4.   Bond and Steed paid their FY 19X1 property taxes in full and on time.

5.   King refused to pay his FY 19X1 property taxes. As a result, a lien was placed against his property. Costs of processing the lien amounted to $200. Shortly thereafter, his property was seized and sold for $30,000. Costs of the sale were $2,000. After the appropriate deductions had been made, a check for the balance of the sale price of the property was sent to King.

6.   E. Peel was unable to pay her taxes. Since her property was not salable, the account was written off without further legal action.

7.   At the end of FY 19X1, S. Templar had not paid his property taxes. The Templar account was reclassified as delinquent.

8.   In FY 19X2, the city established an allowance for uncollectible property taxes of $15,000. The FY 19X2 property taxes were levied as follows:

J. Bond	$10,000
J. Steed	25,000
E. Peel	10,000
S. Templar	5,000
J. Bergerac	10,000
	$60,000

9.   J. Steed appealed his tax assessment and his levy was lowered to $20,000.

10. During the year, S. Templar paid his FY 19X1 property taxes. He was, however, unable to pay his FY 19X2 property taxes. Therefore, the account was written off.
11. Other collections during FY 19X2 were:

J. Bond	$10,000
J. Steed	20,000
E. Peel	10,000

12. J. Bergerac was unable to pay his property taxes. The account was written off because of Bergerac's adverse situation.

The city identifies receivables by year and by taxpayer (e.g., Property taxes receivable—FY 19X1—Bond, $10,000); and it identifies the allowance for uncollectible property taxes by year (e.g., Allowance for uncollectible property taxes— FY 19X1).

REQUIRED: Prepare entries to record (in chronological order):

1. The setting up of the FY 19X1 and the FY 19X2 receivable (and allowance for uncollectible property taxes)
2. The collection of property taxes in each year
3. The writing-off of uncollectible accounts
4. The treatment of the prior-year allowance for uncollectible property taxes in FY 19X1 and FY 19X2
5. The lien against, seizure, and sale of King property

P5–4 (Allotments)

The City of Picadilly divides its appropriations into allotments, which are expended during the allotment period. In this city, allotments are made at the beginning of each quarter. In FY 19X1, estimated revenues are $500,000 and unallotted appropriations are $480,000. A $20,000 increase is projected for the fund balance. Actual revenues are $500,000. The allotments for the year are as follows:

1st quarter	$150,000
2nd quarter	100,000
3rd quarter	130,000
4th quarter	100,000

Expenditures for the year are as follows:

1/8	$20,000	7/28	$30,000
2/2	80,000	8/16	40,000
3/15	40,000	9/14	19,000
4/18	35,000	10/15	10,000
5/20	45,000	11/18	30,000
6/15	20,000	12/22	35,000
7/12	50,000	12/30	5,000

REQUIRED: 1.   Prepare journal entries to record the allotments, expenditures, and unallotted appropriations for each period, including the year-end closing entries.
             2.   Prepare a subsidiary ledger for the allotments, using the following format:

Date   Allotments   Expenditures   Remaining Balance

P5–5   (Complete accounting cycle)

The Sherwood Park Commissioners have approved the following budget for fiscal year 19X1 for that governmental unit's General Fund:

Estimated Revenues		
Property taxes	$85,000	
License fees	25,000	
Fines and penalties	35,000	
Sales taxes	25,000	
Federal grant	30,000	$200,000
Appropriations and Transfers		
Salaries	$80,000	
Supplies	40,000	
Capital equipment	40,000	
Transfers to other funds	20,000	180,000
Projected increase in Fund Balance		$20,000

The park uses the allowance method of handling past-due accounts. An allowance equal to 15 percent of property taxes billed is recorded when the bills are sent. The park's accounting policies include the following:

1.   All purchases of supplies and capital equipment are encumbered.
2.   Expenditures for salaries and transfers to other funds do not require encumbrances.
3.   Outstanding encumbrances lapse at the end of each fiscal year. Outstanding purchase orders that will be honored the following year, however, are reported on its financial statements.
4.   Separate accounts are maintained for each taxpayer.
5.   At the end of each fiscal year, all outstanding property tax receivables are reclassified as delinquent.
6.   The park uses the purchases method to record the purchase and use of supplies.

An inventory taken at the end of FY 19X0 revealed that supplies costing $5,000 were still on hand. At the beginning of FY 19X0, there were no supplies on hand.

The park has four property owners, whose taxes for FY 19X1 are:

R. Hood	$ 40,000
F. Tuck	10,000
M. Marian	20,000
A. Adale	30,000
	$100,000

The preclosing trial balance of the General Fund of Sherwood Park, as of December 31, 19X0, was:

	DEBITS	CREDITS
Cash	$ 20,000	
Property taxes receivable—L. John	3,000	
Property taxes receivable—A. Adale	8,000	
Allowance for uncollectible property taxes—current		$ 3,000
Encumbrances—capital equipment	10,000	
Vouchers payable		8,000
Reserve for encumbrances		10,000
Unreserved fund balance		40,000
Estimated revenues—property taxes	80,000	
Estimated revenues—license fees	20,000	
Estimated revenues—fines and penalties	30,000	
Estimated revenues—sales taxes	20,000	
Appropriations—salaries		70,000
Appropriations—supplies		30,000
Appropriations—capital equipment		40,000
Revenues—property taxes		80,000
Revenues—license fees		10,000
Revenues—fines and penalties		30,000
Revenues—sales taxes		25,000
Expenditures—salaries	85,000	
Expenditures—supplies	40,000	
Expenditures—capital equipment	30,000	
	$346,000	$346,000

During FY 19X1, the following transactions occurred:

1. The FY 19X0 encumbrance for capital equipment was restored.
2. Tax bills amounting to $100,000 were sent to the FY 19X1 property taxpayers. Of the amount billed, $15,000 is not expected to be collected.
3. L. John left town suddenly. When he departed, his account was written off.
4. A. Adale paid his FY 19X0 property taxes in full, along with a late-payment penalty of $100.
5. R. Hood and M. Marian paid their property taxes on time and in full.
6. The capital equipment ordered in Fy 19X0 arrived, along with an invoice for $10,000. The invoice was paid immediately.

7. Supplies expected to cost $40,000 were ordered.
8. An operating transfer of $18,000 was made to the Hyde Park Fund. Of this amount, $10,000 was paid in cash. The remainder will be paid in the future.
9. All outstanding FY 19X0 vouchers were paid.
10. The federal grant, $30,000, was received.
11. Salaries for the year were $80,000.
12. Five motorcycles, costing $8,000 each, were ordered.
13. One half of the supplies arrived in August, along with an invoice for $25,000. The invoice was paid in October.
14. Three of the motorcycles arrived. The actual cost of $28,000 was paid immediately.
15. F. Tuck was unable to pay his property taxes. The account was written off.
16. A. Adale paid $25,000 of the FY 19X1 property taxes. He hopes to pay the remainder next year.
17. Other FY 19X1 revenues were:

License fees	$25,000
Fines and penalties	40,000

Sales taxes amounting to $25,000 were collected during the year. The park's accountant estimates that another $5,000 will be collected in January 19X2 and, therefore, are "susceptible to accrual."
18. One fourth of the supplies arrived, along with an invoice for $9,000.
19. By the end of 19X1, only $20,000 of the federal grant had been spent. The remainder will be spent in the middle of 19X2. (*Hint:* Use a Deferred revenues account.)

REQUIRED:
1. Prepare adjusting and closing entries and a post-closing trial balance for FY 19X0.
2. Prepare budgetary, operating, and closing entries for FY 19X1. Assume that outstanding purchase orders will be honored the following year and that supplies on hand at the end of FY 19X1 amount to $8,000.
3. Prepare preclosing and postclosing trial balances for FY 19X1.
4. Prepare a balance sheet and a statement of revenues, expenditures, and changes in fund balance for FY 19X1.
5. Prepare a statement of revenues, expenditures, and changes in fund balance—budget and actual—for FY 19X1.

P5–6 (Journal entries and financial statement presentation— interfund transactions).

Following are several transactions for the City of Cricklewood:
1. The Water Purification Fund billed its customers for $124,000. Included in this amount was $12,000 to the General Fund (not encumbered by the General Fund) and $5,000 to the Electric Utility

Fund. Both the Water Purification Fund and the Electric Utility Fund are Enterprise Funds.

2. A Special Revenue Fund lent a Capital Projects Fund $25,000, to be repaid in nine months.

3. The General Fund made a permanent contribution of capital to the Civic Swimming Pool Fund, an Enterprise Fund. The amount of the contribution was $50,000.

4. The General Fund made its annual payment of $200,000 to a Debt Service Fund. Assume that $150,000 of the payment was for interest.

5. The General Fund paid $34,000 for consulting services. At the time the transaction was incurred, a debit for the entire amount was made to Expenditures—consulting services. Later a Capital Projects Fund paid the General Fund $9,000 for its share of the consulting costs.

REQUIRED: Prepare the journal entries necessary to record the above transactions and to identify the fund or funds used.

P5–7   (Errors in recording interfund transfers)

Recently, the General Fund of the City of Cats received the monies from the following sources:

1. $10,000 from a Debt Service Fund when that fund was closed out after a bond issue was repaid.

2. $25,000 from the Library Fund, representing that fund's share of the annual audit.

3. $5,000 from the Royal Park Fund, to be used for general operations of the city. Every year the Royal Park Fund makes such a contribution to the General Fund.

4. $15,000 from the Regional Transit Authority (an Enterprise Fund) to be used to pay salaries of police riding on its buses in high-crime areas.

5. $50,000 from the federal government as a grant to fund a program for homeless accountants. The city has already spent $35,000 of this money and will spend the remainder in the latter part of the following year.

Each of these receipts has been recorded in the General Fund as a current revenue. Do you agree? If not, how should they have been recorded?

P5–8   (Preparing financial statements from a trial balance)

Shown below is the preclosing trial balance of Olympic City at the end of FY 19X1. Assume that at the beginning of the year no encumbrances were outstanding, that the Reserve for supplies on hand amounted to $4,000, and that the Unreserved fund balance was $21,000.

Olympic City
General Fund
Preclosing Trial Balance
December 31, 19X1

	DEBITS	CREDITS
Cash	$ 22,450	
Marketable securities	50,000	
Property taxes receivable	35,525	
Allowance for uncollectible property taxes		$18,000
Sales taxes receivable	8,500	
Due from state government	16,000	
Supplies on hand	7,000	
Vouchers payable		12,275
Due to other funds		13,400
Advances from other funds		35,000
Encumbrances—contractual services	10,000	
Reserve for supplies on hand		7,000
Reserve for encumbrances		10,000
Unreserved fund balance		42,500
Estimated revenues—property taxes	125,000	
Estimated revenues—sales taxes	73,000	
Estimated revenues—charges for services	14,000	
Estimated revenues—fines and forfeits	8,500	
Estimated revenues—federal grants	10,000	
Estimated residual equity transfer from Enterprise Fund	30,000	
Appropriations—salaries		107,000
Appropriations—contractual services		27,000
Appropriations—materials and supplies		15,000
Appropriations—capital equipment		70,000
Appropriations—transfer to Debt Service Fund		20,000
Revenues—property taxes		117,500
Revenues—sales taxes		73,600
Revenues—charges for services		12,400
Revenues—fines and forfeits		8,900
Revenues—federal grants		10,000
Residual equity transfer from Enterprise Fund		35,000
Expenditures—salaries	105,200	
Expenditures—contractual services	15,000	
Expenditures—materials and supplies	15,300	
Expenditures—capital equipment	69,100	
Operating transfer to Debt Service Fund	20,000	
	$634,575	$634,575

REQUIRED: a. Prepare closing entries for FY 19X1.
           b. Prepare a postclosing trial balance for FY 19X1.
           c. Prepare a balance sheet for FY 19X1.
           d. Prepare a statement of revenues, expenditures, and changes in fund balance for FY 19X1.
           e. Prepare a statement of revenues, expenditures, and changes in fund balance—budget and actual—for FY 19X1. Show outstanding encumbrances as expenditures, in order to provide a more meaningful comparison, and prepare a note to this effect on the statement (see Table 5–7).

P5–9   (CPA Examination question on activities of a General Fund)
The General Fund trial balance of the city of Solna at December 31, 19X0,
was as follows:

	DEBITS	CREDITS
Cash	$ 62,000	
Taxes receivable—delinquent	46,000	
Estimated uncollectible taxes—delinquent		$ 8,000
Stores inventory—program operations	18,000	
Vouchers payable		28,000
Fund balance reserved for stores inventory		18,000
Fund balance reserved for encumbrances		12,000
Unreserved, undesignated fund balance		60,000
	$126,000	$126,000

Collectible delinquent taxes are expected to be collected within 60 days
after the end of the year. Solna uses the purchases method to account for
stores inventory. The following data pertain to 19X1 General Fund operations:

1. Budget adopted:

Revenues and Other Financing Sources

Taxes	$220,000
Fines, forfeits, and penalties	80,000
Miscellaneous revenues	100,000
Share of bond issues proceeds	200,000
	$600,000

Expenditures and Other Financing Uses

Program operations	$300,000
General administration	120,000
Stores—program operations	60,000
Capital outlay	80,000
Periodic transfer to special assessment fund	20,000
	$580,000

2. Taxes were assessed at an amount that would result in revenues of
    $220,800, after deduction of 4 percent of the tax levy as uncol-
    lectible.

3. Orders placed but not received:

Program operations	$176,000
General administration	80,000
Capital outlay	60,000
	$316,000

4. The city council designated $20,000 of the unreserved, undesig-
    nated fund balance for possible future appropriation for capital
    outlays.

5. Cash collections and transfer:

Delinquent taxes	$ 38,000
Current taxes	226,000
Refund of overpayment of invoice for purchase of	
equipment	4,000
Fines, forfeits, and penalties	88,000
Miscellaneous revenues	90,000
Share of bond issue proceeds	200,000
Transfer of remaining fund balance of a	
discontinued fund	18,000
	$664,000

6. Canceled encumbrances:

	ESTIMATED	ACTUAL
Program operations	$156,000	$166,000
General administration	84,000	80,000
Capital outlay	62,000	62,000
	$302,000	$308,000

7. Additional vouchers:

Program operations	$188,000
General administration	38,000
Capital outlay	18,000
Transfer to special assessment fund	20,000
	$264,000

8. Albert, a taxpayer, overpaid his 19X1 taxes by $2,000. He applied for a $2,000 credit against 19X2 taxes. The city council granted his request.

9. Vouchers paid amounted to $580,000.

10. Stores inventory on December 31, 19X1, amounted to $12,000.

REQUIRED: Prepare journal entries to record the effects of the foregoing data as well as closing entries. Omit explanations.

(AICPA adapted)

P5–10 (Adjusting and closing entries for a General Fund)
You have been engaged by the town of Rego to examine its June 30, 19X1, balance sheet. You are the first CPA to be engaged by the town and find that acceptable methods of municipal accounting have not been employed. The town clerk stated that the books had not been closed and presented the following preclosing trial balance of the General Fund, as of June 30, 19X1:

	DEBITS	CREDITS
Cash	$150,000	
Taxes receivable—current year	59,200	
Estimated losses—current year taxes receivable		$ 18,000
Taxes receivable—prior year	8,000	
Estimated losses—prior year taxes receivable		10,200
Estimated revenues	310,000	
Appropriations		348,000
Donated land	27,000	
Expenditures—building addition constructed	50,000	
Expenditures—serial bonds paid	16,000	
Other expenditures	280,000	
Special assessment bonds payable		100,000
Revenues		354,000
Accounts payable		26,000
Unreserved fund balance		44,000
	$900,200	$900,200

Additional information

1. The estimated losses of $18,000 for current year taxes receivable were determined to be a reasonable estimate.

2. Included in the Revenues account is a credit of $27,000, representing the value of land donated by the state as a grant-in-aid for the construction of a municipal park.

3. The Expenditures—building addition constructed account balance is the cost of an addition to the town hall. This addition was constructed and completed in June 19X1. The General Fund recorded the payment as authorized.

4. The Serial bonds paid account reflects the annual retirement of general obligation bonds issued to finance the construction of the town hall. Interest payments of $7,000 for this bond issue are included in Expenditures—serial bonds paid account.

5. Operating supplies ordered in the prior fiscal year and chargeable to that year were received, recorded, and consumed in July 19X0. The outstanding purchase orders for these supplies—which were not recorded in the accounts at June 30, 19X0—amounted to $8,800. The vendors' invoices for these supplies totaled $9,400. Appropriations lapse one year after the end of the fiscal year for which they are made.

6. Outstanding purchase orders at June 30, 19X1, for operating supplies, totaled $2,100. These purchase orders were not recorded on the books.

7. The special assessments bonds were sold in June 19X1 to finance a street-paving project. No contracts have been signed for this project and no expenditures have been made.

8. The balance in the Revenues account includes credits for $20,000 for a note issued to a bank to obtain cash in anticipation of tax collections and for $1,000 for the sale of scrap iron from the town's water plant. The note was still outstanding at June 30, 19X1. The operations of the water plant are accounted for in the Water Fund.

REQUIRED: Prepare the formal adjusting and closing journal entries for the General Fund for the fiscal year ended June 30, 19X1.

(AICPA adapted)

6

THE GOVERNMENTAL FUND ACCOUNTING CYCLE

Debt Service Funds, Capital Projects Funds, and Account Groups

---

LEARNING OBJECTIVES

After completion of this chapter, you should be able to:

1. Explain why and how Debt Service Funds are used in governmental accounting
2. Prepare the journal entries normally used in Debt Service Funds
3. Prepare financial statements for Debt Service Funds
4. Explain why and how Capital Projects Funds are used in governmental accounting
5. Prepare the journal entries normally used in Capital Projects Funds
6. Prepare financial statements for Capital Projects Funds
7. Explain why and how the General Fixed Assets Account Group and the General Long-Term Debt Account Group are used in governmental accounting
8. Prepare the journal entries normally used in the account groups
9. Explain the relationship between the account groups and the governmental-type funds
10. Prepare financial statements for the account groups

In Chapters 4 and 5 we discussed the accounting procedures used in the General Fund and Special Revenue Funds. In this chapter we discuss the accounting procedures used to account for issuances of general obligation long-term debt, acquisition and construction of long-lived assets, and the related account groups.

We begin with an overview of what is measured in the accounting records (measurement focus) and when the items are recorded (basis of accounting).

MEASUREMENT FOCUS AND BASIS OF ACCOUNTING

The accounting procedures used for the General Fund and Special Revenue Funds concentrate on the spending activities of a governmental unit. The accounting system used for these funds is designed to measure the dollars "received" and "spent" in accordance with legal or contractual restrictions. It does this by reporting the revenues and expenditures of each fund. Such a system provides the user of the financial statements with information about the number of dollars received from the various forms of financing used by the governmental unit and the number of dollars spent for each functional activity. Thus the **measurement focus** (what is being measured) of both the General and the Special Revenue Funds is *resources that are available for spending.* Generally accepted accounting principles require that all governmental-type funds (General, Special Revenue, Capital Projects, and Debt Service) follow this approach.

Emphasis on resources that are available for spending requires measurement of the movement of dollars into and out of each fund. As a result, governmental-type funds generally do not include assets that cannot be "spent" in the coming period. Emphasis on resources that are available for spending also means that these types of funds generally do not include debt that will become due in periods beyond one year. Exceptions to these rules will be discussed in the present chapter and in Chapters 7, 8, and 9.

The timing of the recognition of the resources that are available for spending is referred to as the **basis of accounting.** This concept determines *when* individual revenues and expenditures will be recorded (recognized). All governmental-type funds use the **modified accrual basis of accounting.** Using this approach, revenues are recorded when they are measurable and available. *Measurable* means that the accountant can place a monetary value on the amount of revenues. *Available* means that the revenues can be collected in time to pay the debts of the current period. For property taxes, this has been interpreted to mean due or past due and collectible during the current period or within sixty days after the end of the current period.[1] In general, application of the modified accrual basis of accounting results in the use of accrual accounting procedures for revenues, such as property taxes, where the amount and collectibility can reasonably be determined at the time the tax is levied.[2] Other items of revenue such as fines, forfeits, sales taxes, fees, parking meter receipts, and income taxes generally are recognized on the *cash* basis because they usually are not both measurable and available until received.

---

[1] Additional discussion of the "available" criteria can be found in NCGA *Statement 1*, pp. 11–12; and NCGA *Interpretation No. 3*, pp. 1–3. (GASB Cod. Sec. P70.101–108)

[2] If you are not familiar with accrual accounting concepts, you should review Chapter 14.

Using the modified accrual basis of accounting, expenditures generally are recognized on the accrual basis.[3] This means that the expenditures are recorded when the *liability* is incurred. The major exceptions to this general rule are:

1. *Inventories of materials and supplies.* These may be recorded as expenditures as they are being acquired (purchase method) or used (consumption method). Due to the popularity and simplicity of the purchases method, we will use it in all the illustrations in this text.
2. *Prepaid expense items (such as insurance).* These can be recognized as expenditures when incurred.
3. *Interest on long-term debt.* This is generally recognized when it becomes legally payable during the period rather than as it accrues.
4. *Pensions, claims, and judgments.* The amount of these items recorded as an expenditure of the current period is that which would normally be liquidated with expendable available financial resources.

In summary, revenues are recorded in governmental-type funds when they are measurable and available and expenditures are recorded under the accrual basis of accounting, with limited exceptions.

SECTION I—DEBT SERVICE FUNDS

Definition of Fund

Almost every government issues **general obligation debt.** This debt is in the form of liabilities, usually bonds, that are secured by the "full faith and credit" of the governmental unit. The payment of principal and interest on a debt is called **servicing the debt.** Thus **Debt Service Funds** are used to accumulate resources that will be used to pay principal and interest on general obligation long-term debt. General obligation debt does not include debt that will be serviced from resources accumulated in Enterprise Funds or similar funds.[4]

In many instances debt that becomes due in installments—e.g., **serial bonds**—can be serviced directly by the General Fund on an annual basis. However, if there is a legal requirement for a separate Debt Service Fund, such a fund must be established. In addition, a separate Debt Service Fund must be established if the governmental unit is accumulating resources now for the future servicing of bonds. Although this section will concentrate on bonds, it is important to remember that any form of long-term obligation, such as installment purchases or notes, may require the establishment of a Debt Service Fund.

---

[3]See Chapter 14.

[4]While it is possible to have general obligation debt that will be serviced by an Enterprise Fund, a discussion of such debt instruments is beyond the scope of this section.

Summary of Fund Activities

While the exact events recorded in Debt Service Funds will vary according to the specific requirements of the bond indenture or the ordinance authorizing the bond issue, the following general summary of activity reflects the types of events normally incurred in Debt Service Fund operations. First, the resources are received by the fund. These are recorded as revenues or transfers from other funds—usually the General Fund. If the time period between receipt of the resources and payment of principal and interest permits, the governmental unit will invest the assets. These investments are made in order to accumulate additional resources that can be used to service the debt, thus reducing the direct drain on existing assets. The investing activities are recorded in the Debt Service Fund. Finally, as the principal and interest come due, they are paid from the Debt Service Fund assets.

Control of Fund Activities

The operations of Debt Service Funds generally are controlled through the provisions of bond indentures and budgetary authorizations. Many governmental units do not actually record a budget for these funds. For purposes of uniformity, however, we will assume that a budget is recorded and used for control purposes. Even though the budget is recorded in the accounts, a governmental unit need not report comparisons of budget and actual data for Debt Service Funds unless there is a legally adopted annual budget.

Encumbrance accounting is seldom found in Debt Service Funds because of the lack of purchase orders, contracts, and so forth. The expenditures of these funds primarily consist of payments of principal and interest. Since these types of expenditures are made according to the terms prescribed in the bond indenture, the addition of encumbrance accounting would not improve control over the use of resources.

As with all governmental-type funds, the measurement focus of Debt Service Funds is available spendable resources. This means that the accounting system centers on the accumulation of resources and the expenditure of those resources. As a result, long-lived (fixed) assets are not found in Debt Service Funds, nor is there any long-term debt in the accounts. The "available spendable" criterion focuses on assets currently available and the claims currently against those assets.

The timing of the recognition of revenues and expenditures is the same for Debt Service Funds as for all other governmental-type funds—modified accrual. Therefore the rules for recognition discussed at the beginning of this chapter are applicable to Debt Service Funds. In general, revenues are recorded when they are measurable and available, and expenditures are recorded when a liability is incurred.

When accounting for the operations of Debt Service Funds, it is important to remember that as few individual funds as possible should be used. In other words, individual Debt Service Funds should be combined into a single Debt Service Fund whenever such a combination is not prohibited by law or the individual debt instruments.

Accounting for Fund Activities

Operating entries

For illustrative purposes, assume that the city of New Example issues $10 million of serial bonds on January 1, 19X1, for the construction of a sports complex. The bond indenture provides for semiannual interest payments of 5 percent (the annual interest rate is 10 percent), with $1 million of principal to be repaid on January 1, 19X3, and every year thereafter until the bonds mature on January 1, 19Y3 (ten years later). These bonds pay interest on January 1 and July 1 of each year. Further assume that the city desires to spread the burden of servicing the debt on the taxpayers evenly throughout the life of the bonds. To do this, a special addition to the local property tax for servicing the bonds is approved by the voters. This tax should provide $1.25 million of revenue in 19X1. In addition, it is agreed that the General Fund will transfer $250,000 to the Debt Service Fund on July 1, 19X1. (Entries involved in the actual issuance of the bonds are illustrated in Section II of this chapter.)

The entry to record the legally adopted budget for the fund is as follows (amounts assumed):

Estimated revenues	1,250,000	
Estimated other financing sources	250,000	
Appropriations		505,000
Unreserved fund balance		995,000
To record the legally adopted budget.		

The account **Estimated other financing sources** is the budgetary account used to record the anticipated transfers from the General Fund.

Appropriations for the year include one interest payment that will be made on July 1, 19X1, $500,000, and a fee of $5,000 that will be paid to the fiscal agent, who will keep records of the sale of the bonds and will make semiannual interest payments and payments of principal when the bonds mature. Usually a fiscal agent is a local bank or other financial institution. Notice that only one interest payment will be made in 19X1; therefore, only that amount is included in the current year's annual budget.

Recording the tax accrual requires the following entry:

Taxes receivable—current	1,256,000	
Estimated uncollectible current taxes		6,000
Revenues—taxes		1,250,000
To record the tax levy.		

The above entry assumes that $6,000 of the taxes will be uncollectible. Therefore, the governmental unit will have to assess $1,256,000 in order to collect the needed $1,250,000.

Collection of $1,150,000 of the taxes results in the same entries as those illustrated for the General Fund and the Special Revenue Funds:

Cash	1,150,000	
Taxes receivable—current		1,150,000
To record collection of current taxes.		

If $2,500 of uncollectible taxes are written off, the following entry is made:

Estimated uncollectible current taxes	2,500	
Taxes receivable—current		2,500
To write off uncollectible accounts.		

To generate assets in addition to those contributed by the taxpayers and the General Fund, the tax receipts are invested in marketable securities. If $1 million is invested, the following entry is made:

Investments	1,000,000	
Cash		1,000,000
To record the investment of excess cash.		

When some of the investments mature, the following entry is made:

Cash	500,000	
Investments		450,000
Revenues—investments		50,000
To record investments liquidated and related income.		

The interest due to the city's bondholders on July 1, 19X1, is recorded as follows:

Expenditures—interest	500,000	
Matured interest payable		500,000
To record mature interest.		

When cash is transferred to the fiscal agent for the July 1 interest payment, the following entry is made:

Cash with fiscal agent	500,000	
Cash		500,000
To record the payment of cash to the fiscal agent.		

Periodically the fiscal agent will report to the city regarding the amount of principal and interest paid. The entry to record this is (amount assumed):

Matured interest payable	450,000	
Cash with fiscal agent		450,000
To record payment of interest made by fiscal agent.		

The transfer of $250,000 from the General Fund is classified as an *operating transfer* and recorded as follows:

Entry in the books of the General Fund

Operating transfer to Debt Service Fund	250,000	
Cash		250,000
To record transfer to Debt Service Fund.		

Entry in the books of the Debt Service Fund

Cash	250,000	
Operating transfer from General Fund		250,000
To record transfer from General Fund.		

Notice the difference between the accounting recognition given to the taxes, which are classified as revenues, and the accounting recognition given to operating transfers received by the Debt Service Fund.

When the fiscal agent submits a bill for $5,000 to the fund for servicing the debt, the following entry is made:

Expenditures—fiscal agent fees	5,000	
Cash		5,000
To record fiscal agent fees.		

The treatment of taxes receivable from the current stage through the delinquent and, finally, the lien stage in the Debt Service Fund is the same as in the General Fund. If you do not remember the sequence of entries, you should review Chapters 4 and 5.

One of the exceptions to the use of full accrual accounting, for expenditures in a modified accrual system, is interest on long-term debt. The general rule is that such interest is recorded as an expenditure in the period in which it becomes *legally due (matures)*. The reason for this rule is that most governmental units provide only enough resources to service principal and interest due each period. If interest payments are accrued or principal payments are recorded before due, it is possible that a debit balance (a *deficit*) will result in fund balance. This will give the reader of the financial statements an incorrect picture of the financial status of the fund. Rather than not being able to meet current debt interest or principal, the government has simply not yet provided the resources for the payments because they are not yet due. Even with extensive use of notes to the financial statements, it is difficult to explain a deficit in fund balance.

In those instances where resources are available for Debt Service Fund payments, governmental units have the option, under generally accepted accounting principles, of recording the liability and the associated expenditure at the end of the year before the payments are due. The appropriate entry is the same as that used when the interest matures except that an additional liability is established for the bond principal payable and the account titles do not include the word *mature.*

In contrast, an end-of-the-year entry is needed in order to record the interest earned but not received on the investments:

Interest receivable on investments	25,000	
Revenues—investments		25,000
To record the interest earned on investments.		

A trial balance for the city at the end of the year is shown in Table 6–1.

Closing entries

At the end of the accounting period, December 31, 19X1, in our example, the following entries will be necessary to close the books:

TABLE 6–1   Trial Balance—Debt Service Fund

City of New Example
Debt Service Fund
Sports Complex Bond Fund
Trial Balance
December 31, 19X1

	DEBITS	CREDITS
Cash	$ 395,000	
Cash with fiscal agent	50,000	
Taxes receivable—current	103,500	
Estimated uncollectible taxes receivable—current		$ 3,500
Investments	550,000	
Interest receivable on investments	25,000	
Mature interest payable		50,000
Revenues—taxes		1,250,000
Revenues—investments		75,000
Operating transfer from General Fund		250,000
Expenditures—interest	500,000	
Expenditures—fiscal agent fees	5,000	
Estimated revenues	1,250,000	
Estimated other financing sources	250,000	
Appropriations		505,000
Unreserved fund balance		995,000
	$3,128,500	$3,128,500

Revenues—taxes	1,250,000	
Revenues—investments	75,000	
Estimated revenues		1,250,000
Unreserved fund balance		75,000
To close the revenue and estimated revenue accounts for 19X1.		
Appropriations	505,000	
Expenditures—interest		500,000
Expenditures—fiscal agent fees		5,000
To close the appropriations and expenditures for 19X1.		
Operating transfer from General Fund	250,000	
Estimated other financing sources		250,000
To close the Operating transfer and Estimated other financing sources accounts for 19X1.		

The balance in the Unreserved fund balance account at the end of the year is $1,070,000. Since the interest for 19X2 will be paid before the retirement of principal, it is assumed that $1,000,000 will be applicable to interest and $70,000 to principal. Therefore, an entry in the books of the General Long-Term Debt Account Group is necessary:

Entry in the books of the General Long-Term Debt Account Group

Amount provided in Debt Service Fund	70,000	
Amount to be provided in Debt Service Fund		70,000
To record the increase in the resources available in Debt Service Fund.		

Since there are sufficient resources in the Sports Complex Bond Fund to make the January 1, 19X2, interest payment, the city of New Example has the option of accruing the interest. This is not done by most cities; therefore, we have omitted it from this illustration.

Selected entries for payment of principal

The entries in the General Long-Term Debt Account Group and the Debt Service Fund associated with the issuance of the sports complex bonds and the accumulation of resources to retire the principal are as follows:

Entry in the books of the General Long-Term Debt Account Group

Amount to be provided in Debt Service Fund	10,000,000	
Serial bonds payable		10,000,000
To record issuance of general obligation serial bonds.		

Accumulation of resources to retire principal is recorded as follows (this is the same amount recorded in the Debt Service Fund in 19X1):

Entry in the books of the General Long-Term Debt Account Group	Amount provided in Debt Service Fund	70,000	
	Amount to be provided in Debt Service Fund		70,000
	To record accumulation of resources.		

When all or a portion of the principal of the bond issue is paid, the liability must be "moved" from the General Long-Term Debt Account Group to the Debt Service Fund. The following entries are made for this purpose (assume we are recording the first principal payment in 19X3):

Entry in the books of the General Long-Term Debt Account Group	Serial bonds payable	1,000,000	
	Amount provided in Debt Service Fund		1,000,000
	To record the maturity of part of serial bond issue and the transfer of the liability to the Debt Service Fund.		
Entries in the books of the Debt Service Fund	Expenditures—bond principal	1,000,000	
	Matured serial bonds payable		1,000,000
	To record matured bond principal.		
	Matured serial bonds payable	1,000,000	
	Cash with fiscal agent		1,000,000
	To record payment of matured principal.		

Financial statements—illustration

The individual financial statements for the Debt Service Funds are a balance sheet and an operating statement. These are illustrated for 19X1 in Tables 6–2 and 6–3. In addition, you should review the section on Debt Service Funds in Chapter 2 and compare those financial statements (Tables 2–9 and 2–10) with the statements presented. A budget-actual comparison will be required if the budget for the fund is a legally adopted annual budget. The overall reporting process is discussed in Chapter 9.

GOVERNMENTAL ACCOUNTING IN PRACTICE— THE CITY OF NEW ORLEANS

The city of New Orleans maintains three Debt Service Funds. One is for all general obligation debt outstanding. As mentioned earlier in this chapter, this is an acceptable alternative to a separate fund for each bond issue if it does not violate any provisions of the bond indentures. The other two funds are for the Audubon Park Commission Limited Tax Bonds. One issue is for improvements to the park

TABLE 6–2   Statement of Revenues, Expenditures, and Changes in Fund Balance—Debt Service Fund

City of New Example
Debt Service Fund
Sports Complex Bond Fund
Statement of Revenues, Expenditures,
and Changes in Fund Balance
For Year Ended December 31, 19X1

Revenues		
Taxes	$1,250,000	
Investments	75,000	
Total revenues		$1,325,000
Expenditures		
Interest	$ 500, 000	
Fiscal agent fees	5,000	
Total expenditures		505,000
Excess of revenues over expenditures		820,000
Other Financing Sources		
Operating transfer in		250,000
Excess of revenues and other financing sources over expenditures		1,070,000
Fund balance at beginning of year		-0-
Fund balance at end of year		$1,070,000

TABLE 6–3   Balance Sheet—Debt Service Fund

City of New Example
Debt Service Fund
Sports Complex Bond Fund
Balance Sheet
December 31, 19X1

Assets	
Cash	$ 395,000
Cash with fiscal agent	50,000
Taxes receivable—current (net of allowance for uncollectible taxes, $3,500)	100,000
Interest receivable on investments	25,000
Investments	550,000
Total assets	$1,120,000
Liabilities and Fund Balance	
Matured interest payable	$ 50,000
Fund balance	1,070,000
Total liabilities and fund balance	$1,120,000

and the other is for bonds issued to finance the construction of the Aquarium of the Americas. The balance sheet and the statement of revenues, expenditures, and changes in fund balances (operating statement) are reported in the city's annual report as illustrated in Tables 6–4 and 6–5.

Notice that Tables 6–4 and 6–5 include all of the city's Debt Service Bonds on one statement labeled a "combining" statement. Individual fund statements usually are not separately included in the annual financial report of a governmental unit. Instead, they are aggregated on the "combining" statements for each fund type. This process is described fully in Chapter 9.

Since no resources have been provided for the payment of principal and interest on the aquarium bonds, there are no balance sheet entries for these securities. As monies are provided, they will be reported on the balance sheet. Notice that on the operating statement, resources to service the aquarium bonds were provided by an operating transfer to the fund.

TABLE 6–4   Combining Balance Sheets—City of New Orleans

City of New Orleans, Louisiana
Debt Service Funds
Combining Balance Sheet
December 31, 19X1
With Comparative Totals for December 31, 19X0

		Audubon Park Commission Limited Tax Bonds		Totals	
	GENERAL OBLIGATION BONDS	IMPROVEMENT BONDS	AQUARIUM BONDS	19X1	19X0
Assets					
Cash	$ —	$ 9,407	—	$ 9,407	$ 3,351,522
Time certificates of deposit	20,864,273	307,088	—	21,171,361	32,645,899
Investments	10,400,677	—	—	10,400,677	—
Total assets	$31,264,950	$316,495	—	$31,581,445	$35,997,421
Liabilities and Fund Balances					
Liabilities:					
Cash overdraft	$ 184,504	—	—	$ 184,504	$ —
Due to other funds	8,000,000	—	—	8,000,000	—
Matured bonds and interest payable:					
General obligation	522,814	—	—	522,814	3,911,373
Limited tax	—	9,407	—	9,407	37,395
Total liabilities	8,707,318	9,407	—	8,716,725	3,948,768
Fund balances—reserved for debt service	22,557,632	307,088	—	22,864,720	32,048,653
Total liabilities and fund balances	$31,264,950	$316,495	—	$31,581,445	$35,997,421

See accompanying auditors' report.
Source: Adapted from a recent annual financial report of the City of New Orleans.

TABLE 6–5   Combining Statement of Revenues, Expenditures, and Changes in Fund Balances—City of New Orleans

City of New Orleans, Louisiana
Debt Service Funds
Combining Statement of Revenues, Expenditures, and Changes in Fund Balances
Year Ended December 31, 19X1
With Comparative Totals for the Year Ended December 31, 19X0

| | | Audubon Park Commission Limited Tax Bonds | | Totals | |
	GENERAL OBLIGATION BONDS	IMPROVEMENT BONDS	AQUARIUM BONDS	19X1	19X0
Revenues					
Property taxes	$45,888,091	$ —	$—	$45,888,091	$48,841,937
Interest income	3,724,142	23,808	—	3,747,950	4,560,696
Total revenues	49,612,233	23,808	—	49,636,041	53,402,633
Expenditures					
General government					
Personal services	245,316	—	—	245,316	235,688
Contractual services	65,586	—	—	65,586	71,183
Office and legal expense	49,964	—	—	49,964	16,955
	360,866	—	—	360,866	323,826
Debt Service					
Principal retirement	8,628,000	95,000	750,000	9,473,000	21,998,000
Interest and fiscal charges	14,807,300	195,948	1,855,660	16,858,908	29,567,707
Total expenditures	23,796,166	290,948	2,605,660	26,692,774	51,889,533
Excess (deficiency) of revenues over expenditures	25,816,067	(267,140)	(2,605,660)	22,943,267	1,513,100
Other Financing Sources (uses)					
Proceeds from bond issuance	179,880,829	—	—	179,880,829	—
Payment to refunded bond escrow account	(165,811,491)	—	—	(165,811,491)	—
Other bond issuance costs, net	(14,069,338)	—	—	(14,069,338)	—
Operating transfers in	—	290,948	2,605,660	2,896,608	2,143,663
Operating transfers out	(35,000,000)	(23,808)	—	(35,023,808)	(953,067)
Total other financing sources (uses)	(35,000,000)	267,140	2,605,660	(32,127,200)	1,190,596
Excess (deficiency) of revenues and other sources over expenditures and other uses	(9,183,933)	—	—	(9,183,933)	2,703,696
Fund balances at beginning of year	31,741,565	307,088	—	32,048,653	29,344,957
Fund balances at end of year	$22,557,632	$307,088	—	$22,864,720	$32,048,653

See accompanying auditors' report.
Source: Adapted from a recent annual financial report of the City of New Orleans.

The City of New Orleans uses a "Board of Liquidation" for oversight purposes with respect to issuances of debt. This board holds all resources that will be used to service general obligation, long-term debt. It must approve the sale of all general obligation bonds and special or limited tax bonds or revenue bonds of the Sewerage and Water Board, the Downtown Development District, or the Audubon Park Commission. The French Market Corporation, Municipal Yacht Harbor, and the New Orleans Aviation Board can issue bonds without the approval of the Board of Liquidation.

All property taxes levied by the city and dedicated to the payment of outstanding general obligation and limited tax bonds are collected by the city and, as required by law, paid to the Board of Liquidation. This board also determines the annual property tax millage required to service all general obligation bonds of the city. The city council formally levies the millage suggested by the board. Millages for various limited tax bonds issued by the city were established when the bonds were approved by the voters.

SECTION II—CAPITAL PROJECTS FUNDS

Definition of Fund

The acquisition or construction of major capital facilities, other than those financed by proprietary and trust funds, is accounted for in **Capital Projects Funds.** Capital Projects Funds must be used where they are legally required or where the projects are at least partially financed with restricted resources. Such projects generally include the construction of a new city hall, a new civic auditorium, or a bridge. The resources used to finance Capital Projects Funds usually come from general obligation debt, transfers from other funds, intergovernmental revenues, or private donations.

The acquisition of a capital asset of a relatively minor nature, such as a piece of furniture or an automobile, usually is financed through the General Fund or a Special Revenue Fund. For example, the purchase of a new police car or a desk for the mayor's office is recorded as an expenditure in the fund that made the acquisition (see Chapter 5).

Since generally accepted accounting principles require that the number of funds used be held to a minimum, related projects should be combined into a single Capital Projects Fund whenever possible. However, careful attention must be paid to any bond indenture provisions or restrictions placed on the use of certain types of resources. In many instances such restrictions will prevent the combination of different projects into the same fund.

Summary of Fund Activities

The nature and order of events involving capital projects vary according to local ordinances and procedures, the relative size of the project, and the type of financing involved. However, these projects usually begin in the capital budget of the governmental unit. After approval, financing arrangements are made and contracts are let, if applicable. Although a Capital Projects Fund can be used to record the acquisition of assets, such funds are generally used for large construction projects.

To obtain financing for projects, governmental units usually issue general obligation bonds, solicit federal or state grants, and so forth. These funds are not always spent immediately upon receipt. In such cases the Capital Projects Fund will contain some investment activity.

As the construction work progresses, investments are liquidated and payments are made to the contractor until the project is completed and finally accepted. At this time, any assets remaining in the fund are transferred to another fund or returned to the donors.

Control of Fund Activities

The operations of a Capital Projects Fund are generally controlled through provisions of bond indentures, restrictive provisions of grant agreements, and so forth. Therefore, formal budgetary integration into the accounts, as used in the General and Special Revenue Funds, is not always necessary. For purposes of uniformity, however, we will assume that a budget is recorded and used for control purposes. Such accounting procedures are especially helpful if a single fund is being used to account for more than one project. Since the Capital Projects Funds are classified as governmental-type funds, reporting of budget and actual data is only required in those instances where there is a legally adopted annual budget.

Encumbrance accounting is ordinarily used for these funds because of the extent of involvement with contracts and purchase orders and because of the need to control the related expenditures. Thus, in our example of a construction project, a regular encumbrance entry is made upon signing the contract. Expenditures on the contract are treated in the manner previously illustrated for encumbered purchase orders.

As with all governmental-type funds, the measurement focus of Capital Projects Funds is available spendable resources. Thus the accounting system is designed to provide information regarding the receipt and disbursement of resources. As a result, long-lived assets are not found in these types of funds, nor is there any long-term debt in the accounts. The "available spendable" criterion focuses on assets currently available and the current claims against those assets.

The modified accrual basis of accounting is used for Capital Projects Funds. Thus the timing of the recognition of revenues and expenditures is the same as that followed by the other governmental-type funds.

Accounting for Fund Activities

Operating entries

For illustrative purposes, assume that the City of New Example decides to build a sports complex and includes the project in its 19X1 capital budget. This is the same project described in Section I of this chapter. Financing for the project consists of a general obligation bond issue for $10 million and an $8 million grant from the state. Since the state grant is considered as revenue to the Capital Projects Fund and the proceeds from the bond issue are considered to be an "other financing source," the following entry is made to record the budget:

Estimated revenues	8,000,000	
Estimated other financing sources	10,000,000	
Appropriations		18,000,000
To record the budget.		

If the bonds are sold at par (face) value, the following entry is made:

Cash	10,000,000	
Proceeds from bond issue		10,000,000
To record the issuance of bonds.		

There are three reasons why the principal of the bonds is not recorded as a liability of the Capital Projects Fund: (1) Capital Projects Funds follow a spending measurement focus; therefore, they are used primarily to account for current items; (2) Capital Projects Funds are used to account only for acquisition or construction activities; and (3) Debt Service Funds are used to account for debt service activities (payment of principal and interest). Since the principal of the bonds is not recorded in a fund, control over general obligation long-term debt is maintained in the General Long-Term Debt Account Group. The entry to record the principal of the debt is:

Entry in the General Long-Term Debt Account Group

Amount to be provided in Debt Service Fund	10,000,000	
Serial bonds payable		10,000,000
To record issuance of general obligation serial bonds.		

In the Debt Service Fund, the issuance of bonds may be accompanied by the recording of the budget. The entry to record the budget is (see Section I of this chapter):

Entry in the Debt Service Fund

Estimated revenues	1,250,000	
Estimated other financing sources	250,000	
Appropriations		505,000
Unreserved fund balance		995,000
To record the budget.		

Thus the issuance of the bonds to finance the sports complex requires entries in two funds and an account group: a Capital Projects Fund, a Debt Service Fund, and the General Long-Term Debt Account Group. The issuance of the bonds should be recorded in the Capital Projects Fund and the General Long-Term Debt Account Group when the bonds are sold. However, the entry to record the budget of the Debt Service Fund and the Capital Projects Fund should be made at the beginning of the year.

A grant is determined to be measurable and available, based upon its terms. We will assume that the terms of all grants mentioned in our illustrations and problems make them measurable and available in the period they are received. As a result, the appropriate entry in the Capital Projects Fund is as follows:

Due from state government	8,000,000	
Revenues—state grant		8,000,000
To record state grant.		

After the financing has been completed, the government will place the project in the hands of an architect, who has agreed to work on it for $400,000. Since this person is the "city architect," no public bids are necessary. At this time the contract with the architect is encumbered as follows:

Encumbrances	400,000	
Reserve for encumbrances		400,000
To record encumbrance of architect's fee.		

(For purposes of simplicity, a single encumbrance control account will be used in the remainder of this text.)

The contract with the architect requires the city to pay 90 percent of the fee when the plans are completed. Since the architect agreed to act as the adviser to the city for the project, the remainder of the fee will be paid upon completion of the sports complex. The following entries must be made when the plans for the sports complex are accepted:

Reserve for encumbrances	360,000	
Encumbrances		360,000
To remove the part of the encumbrance earned by the architect.		
Expenditures—architect's fees	360,000	
Vouchers payable		360,000
To record the liability for architect's fees.		
Vouchers payable	360,000	
Cash		360,000
To record payment of vouchers payable.		

After soliciting bids on the project, the city accepts the low bid of PPK Construction Company of $17.6 million. Upon signing the contract, the following entry is made:

Encumbrances	17,600,000	
Reserve for encumbrances		17,600,000
To record encumbrance of construction contract.		

Since the funds on hand are not needed immediately, the city invests $9 million in short-term securities:

Investments	9,000,000	
Cash		9,000,000
To record investment of idle cash.		

Several months later the contractor sends a progress billing report to the city requesting payment of $5.5 million on the project. The payment is approved, less the standard 10 percent **retained percentage.** The retained percentage will not be paid to the contractor until the project has been accepted and it has been determined that there are no outstanding liens relative to the contract. The following entries are made for the billing:

Reserve for encumbrances	5,500,000	
Encumbrances		5,500,000
To record removal of part of the encumbrance for the construction contract.		
Expenditures—construction costs	5,500,000	
Construction contracts payable		5,500,000
To record progress billing by contractor.		

Receipt of grant money from the state is recorded as follows:

Cash	8,000,000	
Due from state government		8,000,000
To record collection of state grant.		

This money is then used to pay the contractor as follows:

Construction contracts payable	5,500,000	
Retained percentage on construction contracts		550,000
Vouchers payable		4,950,000
To record voucher for payment to contractor.		

Note the use of the Retained percentage on construction contracts account. Retaining a certain amount from each payment to a contractor enables the city to accumulate enough resources to "guarantee" that the contractor will complete the job satisfactorily or provide the monies to pay another contractor to complete the project. Since this amount is "owed" to the contractor, it is reported as a liability on the balance sheet of the appropriate fund—in this instance the Capital Projects Fund.

Vouchers payable	4,950,000	
Cash		4,950,000
To record payment of the voucher.		

Interest earned on the investments is $300,000. This amount is not received in cash but is accrued. Assume that the local laws permit Capital Projects Funds to use any interest earned through the investment of idle funds. The entry to record this interest is:

Interest receivable on investments	300,000	
Revenues—investments		300,000
To record interest earned on investments.		

Notice that during the year, all costs incurred in the construction of the sports complex are charged (debited) to expenditures. At the end of the year, the Expenditures—construction costs account will be closed into the fund balance. As a result, there will be no permanent record of the asset acquired on the books of the Capital Projects Fund. This approach is consistent with the spending measurement focus used for governmental-type funds. To maintain a permanent record of the assets acquired through this fund, the following entry is made in the books of the General Fixed Assets Account Group:

Entry in the books of the General Fixed Assets Account Group

Construction in progress	5,860,000	
Investment in general fixed assets from state government grants		5,500,000
Investment in general fixed assets from bond proceeds		360,000
To record the construction costs incurred during the year on the sports complex.		

In this illustration, some of the cash provided by the bond issue was used for payment of architect's fees ($360,000) while most of the remainder was invested. Therefore, the state grant was the main source of payment to the contractor. The debit to Construction in progress is the total of the amounts charged to expenditure during the period $360,000 (architect's fees) + $5,500,000 (construction costs). In many cases, however, such identification during the project is impossible. When this happens, an arbitrary decision is made on an interim basis. When the project is completed, a final breakdown is determined. In addition, the Construction in progress account is closed and a building account is opened.

Although commercial accounting has specific rules regarding the inclusion of interest expense as part of the cost of assets constructed (capitalization of interest), the question is unanswered for governmental-type funds. In the governmental accounting literature, the only mention of interest capitalization is that "the accounting policy with respect to capitalization of interest costs incurred during construction should be disclosed and consistently applied."[5] Since application of this concept is beyond the scope of this text, we have *not* included interest as part of the cost of assets constructed.

At this time there is in excess of $3 million in the Cash account. Prudent

---

[5]NCGA *Statement 1*, p. 10 (GASB Cod. Sec. 1400.111).

management requires that at least $3 million be invested. The entry to record the investment is:

Investments	3,000,000	
Cash		3,000,000

To record investment of excess cash.

Since all entries for the year have been recorded, a trial balance can be prepared (see Table 6–6).

Closing entries—19X1

At the end of the accounting period, December 31, 19X1, the following entries are necessary to close the books:

Revenues—state grant	8,000,000	
Revenues—investments	300,000	
Estimated revenues		8,000,000
Unreserved fund balance		300,000

To close the revenues and estimated revenues for 19X1.

Proceeds from bond issue	10,000,000	
Estimated other financing sources		10,000,000

To close the estimated other financing sources and the proceeds from bond issue for 19X1.

Appropriations	18,000,000	
Expenditures—architect's fees		360,000
Expenditures—construction costs		5,500,000
Encumbrances		12,140,000

To close the appropriations and expenditures for 19X1.

One entry was used in the above example to close the Appropriations and Expenditures accounts. In Chapter 5, two entries were used to close these accounts. The one-entry approach is used here and in Chapters 7 and 8 for purposes of simplicity. Both approaches accomplish the desired results: close the nominal accounts and transfer any balance to the Fund balance account.

Continuation of the project—the following year

Although most governmental units use the fiscal year as their accounting period, the authorization and control of capital projects relate to the projects' entire lives. In our illustration, therefore, it is necessary to record the remainder of the original budget, $12,140,000. This is the amount originally approved ($18,000,000) less the expenditures in 19X1 ($5,860,000). In addition, we must

TABLE 6-6   Trial Balance—Capital Projects Fund

City of New Example
Capital Projects Fund
Sports Complex Fund
Trial Balance
December 31, 19X1

	DEBITS	CREDITS
Cash	$ 690,000	
Investments	12,000,000	
Interest receivable	300,000	
Retained percentage on construction contracts		$ 550,000
Revenues—state grant		8,000,000
Revenues—investments		300,000
Proceeds from bond issue		10,000,000
Expenditures—architect's fees	360,000	
Expenditures—construction costs	5,500,000	
Estimated revenues	8,000,000	
Estimated other financing sources	10,000,000	
Appropriations		18,000,000
Encumbrances	12,140,000	
Reserve for encumbrances		12,140,000
	$48,990,000	$48,990,000

record the budgeted revenues from investments in 19X2 of $720,000 and reestablish the budgetary accounts for encumbrances ($12,140,000) at the beginning of 19X2. The entries to record these are:

Estimated revenues	720,000	
Unreserved fund balance	11,420,000	
Appropriations		12,140,000

To record the remaining budget for the sports complex project for 19X2.

Encumbrances	12,140,000	
Unreserved fund balance		12,140,000

To reestablish encumbrances at the beginning of the second year of the construction of the sports complex.

When the project is completed, the contractor will submit a final bill for the amount due, $12,100,000 (assume that only one billing is made in 19X2), and the architect will submit a final bill for $40,000. Since the project has not yet been examined and accepted, the city will withhold the 10 percent retained percentage from the payment to the contractor. The entries to record these events will be:

| Reserve for encumbrances | 12,140,000 | |
| Encumbrances | | 12,140,000 |

To remove the encumbrances for the remaining cost of the contract.

| Expenditures—architect's fees | 40,000 | |
| Vouchers payable | | 40,000 |

To record the amount owed the architect.

| Expenditures—construction costs | 12,100,000 | |
| Construction contracts payable | | 12,100,000 |

To record the final progress billing submitted by the contractor.

Construction contracts payable	12,100,000	
Retained percentage on construction contracts		1,210,000
Vouchers payable		10,890,000

To record the amount owed to the contractor.

In order to be able to pay the above amounts, the city will need to liquidate all the investments held by the Capital Projects Fund and record the related income. The entry to do this, assuming $13,000,000 has been received, is:

Cash	13,000,000	
Interest receivable on investments		300,000
Revenues—investments		700,000
Investments		12,000,000

To record the liquidation of investments and related revenues.

Upon receipt of the proceeds of the sale of the investments, the contractors and the architect will be paid the amounts due:

| Vouchers payable | 10,930,000 | |
| Cash | | 10,930,000 |

To record payment of vouchers to contractors and architect ($10,890,000 + $40,000).

At this time, the Retained percentage on construction contracts account will have a $1,760,000 balance. Assume that upon final inspection, the project manager finds several defects that need to be repaired before the project can be accepted. Since the construction company has already removed its equipment and employees, its owner authorizes the city to have the repairs made by another contractor. If this is done at a cost of $450,000, the following entry will be made:

| Retained percentage on construction contracts | 450,000 | |
| Cash | | 450,000 |

To record payments to contractors to repair building defects.

After the building has been accepted, the contractor will be paid the remaining amount under the contract, $1,310,000 ($1,760,000 − $450,000). This payment will be recorded as follows:

Retained percentage on construction contracts	1,310,000	
Cash		1,310,000
To record the final payment to the contractor on the sports complex.		

Closing entries—19X2

Upon completion and acceptance of the project, the Sports Complex Fund must be closed. To do this, the following entries will be made:

Revenues—investments	700,000	
Unreserved fund balance	20,000	
Estimated revenues		720,000
To close revenue and estimated revenue for 19X2.		
Appropriations	12,140,000	
Expenditures—architect's fees		40,000
Expenditures—construction costs		12,100,000
To close the appropriations and expenditures for 19X2.		

When the above entries are made, the general fixed assets records will be updated to reflect the expenditures recorded in the current period as follows:

Entry in the books of the General Fixed Assets Account Group

Buildings	18,000,000	
Construction in progress		5,860,000
Investment in general fixed assets from state grants		2,500,000
Investment in general fixed assets from bond proceeds		9,640,000
To record the construction costs incurred during the year and to establish the total cost of the sports complex.		

Notice that the above entry only records the construction costs incurred in the second year. The costs incurred in the first year were previously recorded as Construction in progress. In addition, this entry closes the Construction in progress account and establishes the total cost of the sports complex in the Buildings account. A reconciliation of the sources for construction follows:

SOURCE	RECORDED IN 19X1	RECORDED IN 19X2	TOTAL
State grant	$5,500,000	$2,500,000	$ 8,000,000
Bond issue	360,000	9,640,000	10,000,000
Total cost			$18,000,000

After completion of the project, the Capital Projects Fund for the sports complex has two account balances: Cash, $1 million, and Unreserved fund balance, $1 million. These monies are equal to the earnings of the investments ($300,000 + $700,000). Use of these resources will depend on the provisions of the state grant and the bond issue. For illustrative purposes, assume these amounts must be used to retire the bonds. This will require the following entries:

Entry in the books of the Capital Projects Fund	Residual equity transfer to Debt Service Fund	1,000,000	
	Cash		1,000,000
	To record the residual equity transfer to the Debt Service Fund.		
Entry in the books of the Capital Projects Fund	Unreserved fund balance	1,000,000	
	Residual equity transfer to Debt Service Fund		1,000,000
	To close the residual equity transfer account.		
Entry in the books of the Debt Service Fund	Cash	1,000,000	
	Residual equity transfer from Capital Projects Fund		1,000,000
	To record the residual equity transfer from the Capital Projects Fund.		
Entry in the books of the General Long-Term Debt Account Group	Amount provided in Debt Service Fund	1,000,000	
	Amount to be provided in Debt Service Fund		1,000,000
	To record the increase in the resources available to pay principal in the Debt Service Fund.		

The General Fixed Assets Account Group and the General Long-Term Debt Account Group are discussed in the next section; the Debt Service Fund is discussed in Section I of this chapter.

Financial statements—illustration

Individual financial statements used by Capital Projects Funds are an operating statement and a balance sheet. These are illustrated for the Sports Complex Fund in Tables 6–7 and 6–8 for the first year of the fund. A budget-actual comparison is required if the budget for the fund is a legally adopted annual budget. The overall reporting process is discussed in Chapter 9.

TABLE 6–7   Statement of Revenues, Expenditures, and Changes in Fund Balance—Capital Projects Fund

City of New Example
Capital Projects Fund
Sports Complex Fund
Statement of Revenues, Expenditures, and
Changes in Fund Balance
For the Year Ended December 31, 19X1

Revenues		
State grant	$8,000,000	
Investments	300,000	
Total revenues		$ 8,300,000
Expenditures		
Construction costs	$5,500,000	
Architect's fees	360,000	
Total expenditures		5,860,000
Excess of revenues over expenditures		2,440,000
Other Financing Sources		
Proceeds from bond issue		10,000,000
Excess of revenues and other financing sources over expenditures		12,440,000
Fund balance at beginning of year		-0-
Fund balance at end of year		$12,440,000

TABLE 6–8   Balance Sheet—Capital Projects Fund

City of New Example
Capital Projects Fund
Sports Complex Fund
Balance Sheet
For the Year Ended December 31, 19X1

Assets		
Cash		$ 690,000
Investments		12,000,000
Interest receivable		300,000
Total assets		$12,990,000
Liabilities		
Retained percentage on construction contracts		$ 550,000
Fund Balance		
Reserved for encumbrances	$12,140,000	
Unreserved fund balance	300,000	12,440,000
Total liabilities and fund balance		$12,990,000

Issuance of Bonds at a Premium or Discount

The bonds issued for the construction of the sports complex were sold at face value. Often government bonds are sold at a price above or below face value because of the prevailing interest rates. When this happens, the entries made in the fund that receives the bond proceeds must properly account for the issue price.

As an example, assume that the bonds issued by the city of New Example were sold for $11 million. Since the face value of these bonds is $10 million, the city has to deal with an extra million dollars. The treatment of a premium is dependent on the bond indenture. In some instances, a premium may be used for the purpose for which the bonds were issued. In other instances, a premium must be used to retire the debt. If we assume that this premium may be used for construction of the sports complex, the following entry is made in the Capital Projects Fund when the bonds are issued:

Cash	11,000,000	
Proceeds from bond issue		11,000,000
To record the issuance of bonds.		

The entry in the General Long-Term Debt Account Group is the same as if the bonds were issued at face value. This is because only the face (maturity) value is recorded in the account group.

If the premium must be used to retire the bonds, the following entries are made:

Entries in the books of the Capital Projects Fund

Cash	11,000,000	
Proceeds from bond issue		11,000,000
To record the issuance of bonds.		
Operating transfer to Debt Service Fund	1,000,000	
Cash		1,000,000
To record transfer of bond premium to Debt Service Fund.		

Entry in the books of the Debt Service Fund

Cash	1,000,000	
Operating transfer from Capital Projects Fund		1,000,000
To record transfer of bond premium from Capital Projects Fund.		

While other methods of recording a premium are possible, this approach maintains the total proceeds upon issuance in the fund that received the monies and clearly develops an audit trail for the transfer.

If bonds are issued for less than face value, the total proceeds are recorded in the Capital Projects Fund, as indicated above. This, however, may cause a problem if the bonds do not provide enough resources to complete the project. At this point, the project manager must either scale down the project or seek additional funds.

Issuance of Bonds between Interest Payment Dates

If bonds are issued between interest payment dates, the interest accrued to the date of sale must be paid by the buyer to the city. Since this amount will be used to pay interest on the next interest date, it is recorded directly in the Debt Service Fund. It is not recorded in the Capital Projects Fund.

Arbitrage

The Internal Revenue Code (the Code) provides strict provisions regarding tax-exempt interest paid by a governmental unit and investment interest earned. These rules provide that interest earned on investment of tax-exempt debt proceeds cannot be greater than interest paid. If the interest earned is higher, then the governmental unit is subject to the **arbitrage** provisions of the Code. Excess interest earned by a governmental unit must be paid to the federal government or it will be subject to either a 50 percent penalty or revocation of the tax-exempt status of its debt. Revocation of the tax-exempt status of its debt would not harm the governmental unit immediately, but it would play an important role in the cost of future debt issues.

The arbitrage provisions of the Code are very difficult to interpret and a complete discussion is beyond the scope of this text. Because of complex laws regulating the types of securities in which a governmental unit may invest and the arbitrage regulations, governmental units usually seek the aid of their accountants and attorneys whenever tax-exempt debt proceeds are invested.

GOVERNMENTAL ACCOUNTING IN PRACTICE—
THE CITY OF NEW ORLEANS

The City of New Orleans maintains four Capital Projects Funds. One is used to account for the capital projects of all city departments. As mentioned earlier in this chapter, this is an acceptable alternative to a separate fund for each bond issue, if it does not violate any provisions of restricted monies used to finance the projects. The other three funds relate to the Audubon Park Commission (Aquarium and Riverfront Park Fund, Audubon Species Survival Center, and Audubon Zoo Fund). The purpose of each is to account for resources received and used for construction and development of the particular activities. The balance sheet and the statement of revenues, expenditures, and changes in fund balances are reported in the city's annual report, as illustrated in Tables 6–9 and 6–10.

Notice that Tables 6–9 and 6–10 include all of the city's Capital Projects Funds on one statement labeled a "combining" statement. This type of statement is described in Section I of this chapter and in Chapter 9.

The particular assets, liabilities, and fund balance accounts appearing in Table 6–9 are similar to those discussed in this section and in Chapter 2. In addition, revenues, expenditures, and other financing sources are also similar to those discussed in this section and in Chapter 2. Notice the excess of expenditures over

TABLE 6–9   Balance Sheet—Capital Projects Funds—City of New Orleans

City of New Orleans, Louisiana
Capital Projects Funds
Combining Balance Sheet
December 31, 19X1
With Comparative Totals for December 31, 19X0

| | | Audubon Park Commission | | | Totals | |
	CAPITAL	AQUARIUM AND RIVER-FRONT PARK	AUDUBON SPECIES SURVIVAL CENTER	AUDUBON ZOO	19X1	19X0
Assets						
Cash	$ 1,292,013	$ 500	$ —	$ 4,246	$ 1,296,759	$ 1,330,942
Time certificates of deposit	93,814,709	—	—	—	93,814,709	122,356,305
Investments, at cost or amortized cost	8,728,626	—	—	—	8,728,626	22,821,416
Accounts receivable	269,791	454,285	1,616,203	106,495	2,446,774	3,074,945
Due from other funds	2,087,970	—	—	153,820	2,241,790	492,124
Due from other governments	727,408	—	—	—	727,408	4,737,105
Total assets	$106,920,517	$454,785	$1,616,203	$264,561	$109,256,066	$154,812,837
Liabilities and Fund Balances						
Liabilities:						
Accounts payable	$ 4,616,739	$139,140	$ 230,708	$ —	$ 4,986,587	$ 8,817,132
Due to other funds	4,588	315,645	—	—	320,233	330,994
Advances from other funds	33,708,970	—	—	—	33,708,970	50,986,833
Total liabilities	38,330,297	454,785	230,708	—	39,015,790	60,134,959
Fund balances:						
Reserved for encumbrances	19,986,780	—	—	—	19,986,780	21,624,797
Unreserved:						
Designated for subsequent years' expenditures	46,951,715	—	1,385,495	264,561	48,601,771	71,835,120
Undesignated	1,651,725	—	—	—	1,651,725	1,217,961
Total fund balances	68,590,220	—	1,385,495	264,561	70,240,276	94,677,878
Total liabilities and fund balances	$106,920,517	$454,785	$1,616,203	$264,561	$109,256,066	$154,812,837

See accompanying auditors' report.
Source: Adapted from a recent annual financial report of the City of New Orleans.

TABLE 6–10   Statement of Revenues, Expenditures, and Changes in Fund Balance—Capital Projects Funds—City of New Orleans

City of New Orleans, Louisiana
Capital Projects Funds
Combining Statement of Revenues, Expenditures and
Changes in Fund Balances
Year Ended December 31, 19X1
With Comparative Totals for the Year Ended December 31, 19X0

		Audubon Park Commission			Totals	
	CAPITAL	AQUARIUM AND RIVER-FRONT PARK	AUDUBON SPECIES SURVIVAL CENTER	AUDUBON ZOO	19X1	19X0
Revenues						
Intergovernmental	$ 6,579,023	$ —	$ —	$ —	$ 6,579,023	$11,702,567
Interest income	119,585	—	57,084	—	176,669	109,670
Miscellaneous	5,402,848	489,966	1,086,637	—	6,979,451	15,840,024
Total revenues	12,101,456	489,966	1,143,721	—	13,735,143	27,652,261
Expenditures—capital projects	37,286,766	1,570,616	649,331	—	39,506,713	72,977,904
Excess (deficiency) of revenues over expenditures	(25,185,310)	(1,080,650)	494,390	—	(25,771,570)	(45,325,643)
Other Financing Sources						
Operating transfers in	53,318	1,080,650	—	—	1,133,968	4,488,000
Excess (deficiency) of revenues and other sources over expenditures and other uses	(25,131,992)	—	494,390	—	(24,637,602)	(40,837,643)
Fund balances at beginning of year	93,522,212	—	891,105	264,561	94,677,878	135,515,521
Residual equity transfers	200,000	—	—	—	200,000	—
Fund balances at end of year	$68,590,220	$ —	$1,385,495	$264,561	$70,240,276	$94,677,878

See accompanying auditors' report.
Source: Adapted from a recent annual financial report of the City of New Orleans.

revenues and other sources in the operating statement of the Capital Projects Fund for 19X1. This is not uncommon for Capital Projects Funds. In many instances, revenues and other financing sources are received early in the projects' lives and expenditures of these resources are made in later years. As long as the fund balance is positive, and it is ($68,590,220), the fund is usually in strong financial shape.

Notice that there is no fund balance for the Aquarium and Riverfront Park project. In this instance, assets are equal to liabilities as of the end of the year. This fund had an operating transfer in (see the operating statement) that brought assets up to liabilities. Notice also that the Audubon Zoo Fund had no operations for the current year. This is because no major construction took place during 19X1. The fund was not closed out because more additions to the zoo are planned in the near future.

SECTION III—ACCOUNT GROUPS: GENERAL FIXED ASSETS ACCOUNT GROUP

Definition of Account Group

In Chapters 4 and 5 and Section II of this chapter, the acquisition of a fixed asset (land, buildings, equipment, and so on) is recorded as an expenditure. In other words, the assets are "written off" at the time they are acquired. This procedure results from the spending measurement focus that emphasizes assets which are spendable in nature. Under this approach, we concentrate on accounting for current assets and current liabilities. Since fixed assets cannot be spent, they have no place in the accounting records of governmental-type funds and some fiduciary-type funds. For effective control and management use, however, adequate records of such assets must be maintained. In addition, these records must serve as a basis for determining which assets are to be insured.

In Chapter 8 we will find that proprietary-type funds and those trust funds that use fixed assets to generate income are accounted for like businesses. Thus the land, equipment, and so forth, used by these funds are recorded as assets of the particular fund. The **General Fixed Assets Account Group** is used to account for the fixed assets that are acquired by the General Fund, Special Revenue Funds, Capital Projects Funds, and certain trust funds. It is not used to account for those fixed assets acquired by the proprietary-type funds and those trust funds that use such assets to generate income.

Certain fixed assets such as streets, lighting, and drainage are referred to as **infrastructure,** or **public domain, assets.** Since these have value only to the governmental unit, it is not considered mandatory to record them. However, it is important to maintain adequate control records for managerial purposes. The **summary of significant accounting policies** must fully disclose the procedures followed in accounting for these assets. The summary of significant accounting policies is generally the first note that follows the financial statements included in the annual report of a governmental unit and is discussed in greater detail in Chapter 9.

Summary of Activities

The fixed assets acquired by the funds using a spending measurement focus are maintained on the books of the account group until they are sold, traded in, or discarded. While it is permissible to record depreciation on these assets, most governmental units do not. If depreciation is recorded, it must *not* be included in the statement of revenues, expenditures, and changes in fund balance for the

General Fund or any other governmental or similar fund. Thus the entry will be made only in the General Fixed Assets Account Group accounts.

Control of Activities

The General Fixed Assets Account Group does not have an operating budget. Instead, acquisition and disposal of these assets are controlled through the operating budgets and capital budgets of the funds that use a spending measurement focus. The purpose of the General Fixed Assets Account Group is to provide accounting control over the physical assets themselves. Since it is not a fund, there is no concept of measurement focus or basis of accounting. Instead, recording of these assets is determined by the accounting rules for the funds that acquire and use them.

Accounting for Activities

Operating entries

The accounting procedures followed in the General Fixed Assets Account Group can be summarized as follows:

1. The acquisition of general fixed assets is recorded by debiting an appropriately entitled asset account and crediting an account called Investment in general fixed assets, followed by an identification of the source of the funds used.
2. When disposal of an asset takes place, the preceding entry is reversed. Note that the resources received from the sale or other disposition of the asset are recorded in the fund legally prescribed to receive them. If no such laws exist, the General Fund usually receives the resources.

Fixed assets are recorded at their cost. **Cost** is defined in governmental accounting as it is in commercial accounting: "the cash or cash equivalent price of the asset." In those instances where an asset has been donated to the governmental unit, the estimated fair market value should be used for recording purposes.

To illustrate, assume that the City of New Example acquires a new fire engine at a cost of $250,000. This transaction is recorded as follows:

Entry in the books of the General Fund	Expenditures—capital equipment	250,000	
	Vouchers payable		250,000
	To record purchase of fire engine.		
Entry in the books of the General Fixed Assets Account Group	Equipment	250,000	
	Investment in general fixed assets from General Fund revenues		250,000
	To record purchase of fire engine.		

Disposal of the fire engine for $10,000 after it is no longer useful to the city is recorded as follows:

Entry in the books of the General Fund

Cash	10,000	
Revenue—sale of general fixed assets		10,000
To record sale of fire engine.		

Entry in the books of the General Fixed Assets Account Group

Investment in general fixed assets from		
General Fund revenues	250,000	
Equipment		250,000
To record sale of fire engine.		

In the above entries, notice that the acquisition of the fire engine is recorded as an expenditure in the fund making the purchase and as revenue in that same fund when the asset is sold. The proceeds from disposition of the asset can also be recorded as an other financing source. If there are no restrictions on the use of proceeds from the disposition of assets, they may be recorded in the General Fund without consideration for the fund used to make the original purchase. Notice also that the original cost of the asset is removed from the accounts when it is sold. Most governmental units do not record depreciation on general fixed assets; therefore, the balance in the account is the original cost of the asset.

In the Capital Projects Fund section, we discussed the acquisition of assets through construction. If an outside contractor is used to build assets, the cost of the project will be determined by the contract price plus any incidental costs. If the governmental unit uses its own employees, materials, and so forth to construct the asset, the recorded cost will be the total of the materials, labor, and overhead costs incurred.

The acquisition of the sports complex discussed earlier involved costs incurred over a two-year period for the construction of the asset. These costs were recorded in the Capital Projects Fund and the General Fixed Assets Account Group. The entries in the records of the Capital Projects Fund in 19X1 were in the following form:

Entries in the books of the Capital Projects Fund

Expenditures—architect's fees	360,000	
Vouchers payable		360,000
To record the liability for architect's fees.		
Expenditures—construction costs	5,500,000	
Construction contracts payable		5,500,000
To record progress billing by contractor.		

The entry during each period to record the expenditure was made only once, although there could have been several progress payments. Costs were debited to Expenditures during the first year totaling $5,860,000. Therefore, the entry to record the asset in the books of the General Fixed Assets Account Group was:

Entry in the books of the General Fixed Assets Account Group	Construction in progress	5,860,000	
	Investment in general fixed assets from state government grants		5,500,000
	Investment in general fixed assets from bond proceeds		360,000
	To record the construction costs incurred during the year on the sports complex.		

The identification of the source of the funds is discussed in detail in the Capital Projects Fund section of this chapter.

During the second and final year of the project, an additional $12,140,000 of costs were incurred. The entry to record the completion of the project was:

Entry in the books of the General Fixed Assets Account Group	Buildings	18,000,000	
	Construction in progress		5,860,000
	Investment in general fixed assets from state grants		2,500,000
	Investment in general fixed assets from bond proceeds		9,640,000
	To record the construction costs incurred during the year and to establish the total cost of the sports complex.		

Although many other examples of the recording of general fixed assets could be given, those discussed above are representative and should enable you to understand the use of the General Fixed Assets Account Group.

Closing entries

Due to the continuous nature of the General Fixed Assets Account Group, there are no closing entries.

Leased assets

Governmental units often lease assets rather than purchasing them. Since governmental-type funds report only spendable resources, a lease presents problems beyond those found in commercial accounting. The illustration presented in this section is not intended to be all-inclusive with respect to leased assets. Complications like residual values and bargain purchase options are omitted in favor of a straightforward general lease model.

As in commercial accounting, governmental units enter into operating leases and capital leases in their everyday operations. A lease is classified as an **operating lease** if the lessee does not acquire any property rights through the contract. These leases are generally short-term and are recorded by a debit to an expenditure account and a credit to cash when the rental payments are made.

A lease is classified as a **capital lease** for the lessee if the lessee acquires property rights through the contract, the lease is noncancelable, and it meets at least one of the following tests:

1. The lessee owns the property at the conclusion of the lease, through either a transfer of title or a bargain purchase option.
2. The life of the lease is 75 percent or more of the expected economic life of the asset.
3. The present value of the minimum lease payments is 90 percent or more of the fair market value of the leased asset.

Items 2 and 3 are not considered if the lease term is in the last 25 percent of the economic life of the asset.

For a capital lease, the lessee must record the leased asset and the related liability. To illustrate, assume the City of New Example leases a new computer from JCN, Inc., which has a fair market value of $862,426 and an economic life of five years. Assume further that the relevant interest rate is 8 percent. Based on this information, the government (lessee) must record the present value of the minimum lease payments as an asset and a liability. If these payments are $200,000 per year, payable on January 1 of each year, the present value of the rental payments is $862,426 ($200,000 × 4.31213). If the computer is to be used by a department in the General Fund, the following entry is required:

Entry in the books of the General Fund

Expenditures—capital lease principal	862,426	
Other financing sources—capital leases		862,426
To record a capital lease.		

Notice that the initial recording of the lease has no effect on the fund balance of the General Fund. The expenditure is offset by the other financing source.

Since the computer and the associated long-term liability are not recorded in the General Fund, the following entries must also be made:

Entry in the books of the General Fixed Assets Account Group

Leased equipment—computer	862,426	
Investment in general fixed assets from leases		862,426
To record leased asset.		

Entry in the books of the General Long-Term Debt Account Group

Amount to be provided in General Fund for capital lease obligation	862,426	
Capital lease obligation payable		862,426
To record liability under a capital lease.		

Since the first lease payment is due at the time the lease is signed, the following entries would also be made:

Entry in the books of the General Fund	Expenditures—capital lease	200,000	
	Vouchers payable		200,000
	To record lease payment due.		

Entry in the books of the General Long-Term Debt Account Group	Capital lease obligation payable	200,000	
	Amount to be provided in General Fund for capital lease obligation		200,000
	To record reduction in lease obligation.		

There are two additional points regarding the two transactions above. First, there is no interest because the payment is made as soon as the lease is signed. Second, the obligation is financed through the General Fund. Often leases are financed without the use of a Debt Service Fund. It is possible, however, that a Debt Service Fund could be used.

The second payment on the lease obligation occurs one period after the lease is signed. As a result, interest has accrued and is due. Since the interest payment is not usually appropriated until the period in which it is due, no entry to accrue the interest is made. Instead, the following entries are made at the beginning of the second year of the lease:

Entry in the books of the General Fund	Expenditures—capital lease principal	147,006	
	Expenditures—interest on capital leases	52,994	
	Vouchers payable		200,000
	To record a capital lease.		

Interest calculation:	
Initial debt	$862,426
First payment	200,000
Book value of obligation during first year	662,426
Interest rate	$\times .08$
Interest	$52,994

Entry in the books of the General Long-Term Debt Account Group	Capital lease obligation payable	147,006	
	Amount to be provided in General Fund for capital lease obligation		147,006
	To record reduction in lease obligation.		

Governmental leases usually contain a fiscal funding clause. A **fiscal funding clause** is a provision in the lease that permits the government to cancel the lease if resources are not appropriated to make lease payments. If the possibility of actual cancelation is remote, a fiscal funding clause does not affect the noncancelable test. In other words, the lease is still capitalized.

Financial statements—illustration

The financial statements previously illustrated for governmental-type funds are not used for the General Fixed Assets Account Group. A schedule of general fixed assets is presented instead. This schedule contains a listing of the general fixed assets and the source of the resources that were used to acquire them. In addition to the schedule of general fixed assets, a schedule of changes in general fixed assets must also be presented, either as a separate statement or as a note to the financial statements. This schedule is a reconciliation of the beginning and ending balances of the general fixed assets, together with the total increases and decreases that took place during the period. This schedule takes the place of the operating statement used by the governmental-type funds. In addition, most governmental units prepare a schedule of general fixed assets by function and activity. Actual schedules used by the City of New Orleans are discussed in the next section.

GOVERNMENTAL ACCOUNTING IN PRACTICE— THE CITY OF NEW ORLEANS

The City of New Orleans uses three schedules to report its general fixed assets: (1) general fixed assets classified by the source of the resources used to acquire them, (2) general fixed assets classified by function and activity, and (3) changes in general fixed assets by function and activity. These are illustrated in Tables 6–11 through 6–13.

TABLE 6–11   Schedule of General Fixed Assets by Source—City of New Orleans

City of New Orleans, Louisiana
Schedule of General Fixed Assets—by Source
December 31, 19X1

General fixed assets:	
Land	$ 29,662,918
Buildings and improvements	204,639,663
Equipment	48,917,720
Construction in progress	112,935,492
Total general fixed assets	$396,155,793
Investment in general fixed assets from:	
Special Revenue Funds	$ 60,354,342
Capital Projects Funds:	
General obligation bonds	107,366,777
Federal grants	33,469,042
State grants	4,140,672
Miscellaneous capital funds	7,433,337
Gifts	3,833,881
Miscellaneous revenues	14,994,855
General Fund revenues	44,347,275
Unidentified sources*	120,215,612
Total investment in general fixed assets	$396,155,793

*Purchases prior to January 1, 19W3, for which a funding source could not be identified.
Source: Adapted from a recent annual financial report of the City of New Orleans.

TABLE 6–12   Schedule of General Fixed Assets by Function and Activity—City of New Orleans

City of New Orleans
City of New Orleans, Louisiana
Schedule of General Fixed Assets—by Function and Activity
December 31, 19X1

FUNCTION AND ACTIVITY	TOTAL	LAND	BUILDINGS AND IMPROVEMENTS	EQUIPMENT
General government:				
The Council	$ 290,881	$ —	$ —	$ 290,881
The Mayor	4,387,531	—	—	4,387,531
Department of Law	87,960	—	—	87,960
Judicial and Parochial	1,036,330	—	—	1,036,330
Department of Finance	1,834,198	—	—	1,834,198
Unattached boards and commissions	54,306,081	—	52,622,376	1,683,705
Department of Civil Service	104,565	—	—	104,565
General services	74,226	—	—	74,226
General government	78,910,464	14,153,545	64,756,919	—
Total general government	141,032,236	14,153,545	117,379,295	9,499,396
Public safety:				
Department of Police	23,269,466	1,742,723	5,664,785	15,861,958
Department of Fire	13,100,722	538,850	4,264,680	8,297,192
Department of Safety and Permits	1,829,540	—	1,660,626	168,914
Total public safety	38,199,728	2,281,573	11,590,091	24,328,064
Public works:				
Department of Streets	5,745,768	—	338,712	5,407,056
Department of Sanitation	8,981,938	16,980	6,463,564	2,501,394
Department of Property Management	2,372,434	—	1,662,352	710,082
Department of Utilities	52,345	—	—	52,345
Total public works	17,152,485	16,980	8,464,628	8,670,877
Health and welfare:				
Department of Health	6,168,932	48,708	4,954,831	1,165,393
Department of Welfare	3,626,779	160,000	3,162,342	304,437
Total health and welfare	9,795,711	208,708	8,117,173	1,469,830
Culture and recreation:				
Public Library	5,672,910	478,335	4,569,317	625,258
Cultural Commission	4,779,256	—	4,531,699	247,557
Department of Recreation	65,697,627	12,523,777	49,987,460	3,186,390
Total culture and recreation	76,149,793	13,002,112	59,088,476	4,059,205
Urban development and housing	828,196	—	—	828,196
Economic development and assistance	62,152	—	—	62,152
Total general fixed assets allocated to functions	283,220,301	$29,662,918	$204,639,663	$48,917,720
Construction in progress	112,935,492			
Total general fixed assets	$396,155,793			

See accompanying auditors' report.
Source: Adapted from a recent annual financial report of the City of New Orleans.

TABLE 6-13   Schedule of Changes in General Fixed Assets by Function and Activity—City of New Orleans

City of New Orleans
City of New Orleans, Louisiana
Schedule of General Fixed Assets—by Function and Activity
December 31, 19X1

FUNCTION AND ACTIVITY	GENERAL FIXED ASSETS JANUARY 1, 19X1	ADDITIONS	DEDUCTIONS	GENERAL FIXED ASSETS DECEMBER 31, 19X1
General government:				
The Council	$ 290,355	$ 526	$ —	$ 290,881
The Mayor	4,071,824	330,621	14,914	4,387,531
Department of Law	87,960	—	—	87,960
Judicial and Parochial	1,095,538	12,791	71,999	1,036,330
Department of Finance	1,810,618	23,580	—	1,834,198
Unattached boards and commissions	1,591,651	53,164,599	450,169	54,306,081
Department of Civil Service	104,565	—	—	104,565
General services	74,226	—	—	74,226
General government	77,691,192	1,219,272	—	78,910,464
Total general government	86,817,929	54,751,389	537,082	141,032,236
Public safety:				
Department of Police	22,853,335	416,131	—	23,269,466
Department of Fire	13,095,672	5,050	—	13,100,722
Department of Safety and Permits	1,827,671	1,869	—	1,829,540
Total public safety	37,776,678	423,050	—	38,199,728
Public works:				
Department of Streets	5,692,722	53,046	—	5,745,768
Department of Sanitation	8,978,635	3,303	—	8,981,938
Department of Property Management	1,824,861	547,573	—	2,372,434
Department of Utilities	51,434	911	—	52,345
Total public works	16,547,652	604,833	—	17,152,485
Health and welfare:				
Department of Health	6,140,467	28,465	—	6,168,932
Department of Welfare	3,626,779	—	—	3,626,779
Total health and welfare	9,767,246	28,465	—	9,795,711
Culture and recreation:				
Public Library	5,664,434	120,797	112,321	5,672,910
Cultural Commission	4,789,003	2,362	12,109	4,779,256
Department of Recreation	63,797,742	1,899,885	—	65,697,627
Total culture and recreation	74,251,179	2,023,044	124,430	76,149,793
Urban development and housing	862,257	17,348	51,409	828,196
Economic development and assistance	62,152	—	—	62,152
Construction in progress	129,529,738	43,279,591	59,873,837	112,935,492
Total general fixed assets	$355,614,831	$101,127,720	$60,586,758	$396,155,793

See accompanying auditors' report
Source: Adapted from a recent annual financial report of the City of New Orleans.

Notice that in Table 6–11, the city could not locate a specific funding source for assets acquired before January 1, 19W3. Until recently, general fixed assets were not of particular interest to government officials and detailed records often were not maintained. Recent emphasis on audited financial statements, however, has made the General Fixed Assets Account Group an important part of a government's annual report.

SECTION III—ACCOUNT GROUPS: GENERAL LONG-TERM DEBT ACCOUNT GROUP

Definition of Account Group

Governmental-type funds do not report long-term debt on their balance sheets. Instead, the proceeds for the issuance of such debt are reported as an "other financing source" on the statement of revenues, expenditures, and changes in fund balance. This practice results from the emphasis placed on the spending activities of the fund and the focus on current assets and liabilities.

The difficulty with this procedure is that it results in no accounting for general long-term debt—that is, debt secured by the "full faith and credit" of the governmental unit. To solve this problem, governmental units use a **General Long-Term Debt Account Group** to fill this important void. This account group is used to record all the long-term debt that will be repaid from general governmental resources and the means by which such debt will be repaid.

Previous discussions have limited general long-term debt to bonds. However, any general obligation debt that will be paid in the future may be reported in the General Long-Term Debt Account Group. This includes debt arising from installment purchases, notes, pension contracts, and so forth. The key requirement for inclusion in this account group is that *general governmental resources* must be used to retire the debt. As a result, debt that will be retired with funds accumulated by proprietary-type funds or some trust funds is not included in this group.

It is also possible that general obligation debt will be serviced from the resources of an Enterprise Fund (a proprietary-type fund). In that case the debt should be reported on the balance sheet of that fund. Again, the *source* of the resources that will be used to retire the debt is the key for classification purposes.

The General Long-Term Debt Account Group is used to report only the *principal* amount of debt. Interest is not recorded in these accounts. Matured interest that has not been paid is included as a liability of the fund that is servicing the debt. In most instances a Debt Service Fund is used to account for the payment of principal and interest on general long-term debt.

Summary of Activities

General long-term debt is recorded when the debt is incurred—when the bonds are issued, when an installment purchase is made, and so forth. The debt remains in the account group until it becomes a liability that is payable by a specific fund.

At that time, the fund servicing the debt will record an expenditure, and the related liability and the debt will be removed from the books of the General Long-Term Debt Account Group.

Control of Activities

The General Long-Term Debt Account Group is used to record the principal of the general obligation debt that is outstanding. It does not have operations as such. Instead, this account group is used to account for the outstanding general obligation debt. The issuance of new general obligation debt and the retirement of outstanding general obligation debt is controlled through the capital budgets of the governmental-type funds. Since the General Long-Term Debt Account Group is not a fund, there is no concept of measurement focus or basis of accounting. Instead, the recording of these obligations is determined by the accounting rules for the funds that issue, service, and retire them.

Accounting for Activities

Operating entries

Accounting for general obligation debt is a three-step process:

1. When the debt is incurred, a liability is recorded in the General Long-Term Debt Account Group. The offsetting debit is to an account entitled Amount to be provided in Debt Service Fund (or whatever fund will be used to service the debt.)
2. As amounts are accumulated to retire the debt, the amount to be provided is reduced (credited) and an account entitled Amount provided in Debt Service Fund (or whatever fund will be used to service the debt) is debited.
3. When the debt is recorded as a liability of the servicing fund, it is removed from the records of the General Long-Term Account Group.

To illustrate, let us review the sports complex project discussed in Sections I and II. The entries to record the issuance of the bonds were:

Entry in the books of the Capital Projects Fund	Cash	10,000,000	
	Proceeds from bond issue		10,000,000
	To record the issuance of bonds.		
Entry in the books of the General Long-Term Debt Account Group	Amount to be provided in Debt Service Fund	10,000,000	
	Serial bonds payable		10,000,000
	To record the issuance of general obligation serial bonds.		

At the end of the year, if the $1,070,000 of resources accumulated in the Debt Service Fund is applied to the principal of the debt, the following entry would be made:

Entry in the books of the General Long-Term Debt Account Group

Amount provided in Debt Service Fund	1,070,000	
Amount to be provided in Debt Service Fund		1,070,000
To record the increase in resources available in Debt Service Fund.		

When debt is retired, the principal must be removed from the General Long-Term Debt Account Group. The entry to retire $1 million of debt is as follows:

Entry in the books of the General Long-Term Debt Account Group

Bonds payable	1,000,000	
Amount provided in Debt Service Fund		1,000,000
To record mature bond principal.		

Several observations can be made regarding the above entries:

1. Only the amount of the principal is recorded in the General Long-Term Debt Account Group.
2. When the liability is paid, it must be removed from the books of the General Long-Term Debt Account Group.
3. Usually the type of debt is identified in the accounts of the General Long-Term Debt Account Group (e.g., serial bonds, term bonds, and so on).

Many other examples of transactions recorded in the General Long-Term Debt Account Group could be presented. However, those discussed above illustrate the types of events that affect these accounts and should be sufficient to enable you to understand the use of this account group.

Closing entries

Due to the continuous nature of the General Long-Term Debt Account Group, there are no annual closing entries.

Financial statements—illustration

The financial statements previously illustrated for the governmental-type funds are not used for the General Long-Term Debt Account Group. A schedule of general long-term debt is presented instead. This schedule contains a listing of the outstanding long-term obligations and the resources accumulated, and to be accumulated, that will be used to retire the debt. In addition to a schedule of general long-term debt, a schedule of changes in general long-term debt must also be presented either as a separate statement or as a note to the financial statements. This schedule presents a reconciliation of the beginning and ending balances of the general long-term debt together with the total increases and decreases that took place during the period. It takes the place of the operating statement used by the governmental-type funds. In addition, other schedules detailing interest and principal payments, due dates, and so forth are required to be presented in the annual financial report. Actual schedules of long-term debt used by the City of New Orleans are discussed in the next section.

GOVERNMENTAL ACCOUNTING IN PRACTICE—THE CITY OF NEW ORLEANS

The City of New Orleans uses several schedules to report its general long-term debt, all of which appear in the notes to the financial statements. The major schedules are (1) a summary of bond transactions, (2) a complete listing and description of each bond issue outstanding, (3) the cash flow requirements to retire the principal and interest outstanding for the next ten years, and (4) a schedule of other general long-term debt. In addition, the notes to the financial statements for general long-term debt cover eight pages in the city's annual financial report. The disclosures mentioned above are illustrated in Tables 6–14 through 6–17.

The City of New Orleans does not use the typical schedule of long-term debt, illustrated in Chapter 2. You should review that schedule at this time (Table 2–15, p. 32).

TABLE 6–14   Summary of Bond Transactions—City of New Orleans

Long-Term Debt

(A) Bond Transactions

The following is a summary of bond transactions of the city for the year ended December 31, 19X1 (in thousands of dollars):

	GENERAL OBLIGATION	LIMITED TAX	REVENUE	REFUNDING	SPECIAL ASSESSMENT	TOTAL
Bonds payable at January 1, 19X1	$390,523	$111,060	$214,695	$ —	$112	$716,390
Bonds issued	—	—	12,920	16,375	—	29,295
Bonds retired	21,913	4,545	24,460	—	56	50,974
Bonds payable at December 31, 19X1	$368,610	$106,515	$203,155	$16,375	$ 56	$694,711

Source: Adapted from a recent annual financial report of the City of New Orleans.

TABLE 6–15   Listing and Description of Bond Issues (Partial)—City of New Orleans

Bonds payable at December 31, 19X1 are comprised of the following (all bonds are serial bonds):

DESCRIPTION	ORIGINAL ISSUE (IN THOUSANDS OF DOLLARS)	RANGE OF AVERAGE INTEREST RATES	AMOUNT OUTSTANDING (IN THOUSANDS OF DOLLARS)
General obligation bond:			
19T6 Civic Center Bonds, Series C, due in annual installments of $260,000 to $282,000 through July 19X5	$ 7,000	2.69%	$ 1,083
19T2–T3 Grade Separation Bonds, Series E–F, final payment of $188,000 due November 19X2	7,000	2.23%–2.58%	188
19T7 Incinerator Bonds, due in annual installments of $26,000 to $28,000 through September 19X6	750	2.69%	135
19T7 Library Bonds, due in annual installments of $95,000 to $106,000 through September 19X6	2,650	2.65%	504
19U7–W9 Public Improvement Bonds, due in annual installments of $12,570,000 to $22,685,000 through October 19Y4	475,965	3.86%–11.70%	240,225
19T6–T7 Sewerage, Water and Drainage Bonds, Series G–H, due in annual installments of $1,000 to $84,000 through September 19X6	2,200	2.62%–2.69%	295
19W7 General Obligation Bonds, due in annual installments of $1,900,000 to $15,320,000 through December 19Y5	135,515	7.24%	126,180
Total general obligation bonds			$368,610
Limited tax bonds:			
19U8 Drainage System Bonds, Series 19U8 (3-mills), due in annual installments of $910,000 to $945,000 through September 19X3	$ 15,000	4.27%	$ 1,855
19V9 Drainage System Bonds, Series A (6-mills), due in annual installments of $670,000 to $1,355,000 through November 19Y4	18,000	6.04%	12,695
19W3 Drainage System Bonds, Issue of 19W3 (9-mills), due in annual installments of $1,450,000 through October 19X3 when final payment of $13,600,000 is due	22,000	10.50%	15,050
19W4 Drainage System Bonds, Issue (9-mills), due in annual installments of $1,840,000 to $2,025,000 through December 19X4 when final payment of $17,180,000 is due	30,000	9.71%	21,045
19W7 Drainage System Bonds, Series 19W7A, due in installments of $2,085,000 to $2,960,000 commencing December 19X4 through December 19X8	12,525	6.96%	12,525

Source: Adapted from a recent annual financial report of the City of New Orleans.

TABLE 6-16   Cash Flow Requirements—Principal and Interest—City of New Orleans

The requirement to amortize all bonds outstanding as of December 31, 19X1, including interest payments of $515,032,892, are as follows (in thousands of dollars):

YEAR ENDING DECEMBER 31	GENERAL OBLIGATION	LIMITED TAX	REVENUE	REFUNDING	SPECIAL ASSESSMENT	TOTAL
19X2	$ 49,381	$ 14,126	$ 25,107	$ 1,204	$59	$ 89,877
19X3	49,389	26,136	23,321	1,204	—	100,050
19X4	49,379	27,201	23,238	1,204	—	101,022
19X5	49,367	11,142	25,644	1,204	—	87,357
19X6	49,426	11,219	20,978	1,204	—	82,827
19X7–19Y1	194,392	39,528	96,814	8,519	—	339,253
19Y2–19Y6	118,368	18,761	83,201	8,271	—	228,601
19Y7–19Y11	—	7,751	81,191	8,787	—	97,729
19Y12–19Y16	—	—	63,788	1,836	—	65,624
19Y17–19Y21	—	—	17,404	—	—	17,404
	$559,702	$155,864	$460,686	$33,433	$59	$1,209,744

Source: Adapted from a recent annual financial report of the City of New Orleans.

TABLE 6-17   Other Long-Term Debt—City of New Orleans

(E) OTHER GENERAL LONG-TERM DEBT

The following is a summary of other payables and accruals recorded in the General Long-Term Debt Account Group for the year ended December 31, 19X1 (in thousands of dollars):

	BALANCE JANUARY 1, 19X1	ADDITIONS	DELETIONS	BALANCE DECEMBER 31, 19X1
Claims and judgments (note 14(b) and (d))	$ 77,000	$ 2,666	$ 1,466	$ 78,200
Landfill closing costs (note 14(e))	5,997	—	146	5,851
Accrued annual and sick leave (note 1(o))	39,461	9,762	6,204	43,019
State of Louisiana World Expositions loans (see below)	12,746	—	499	12,247
Due to Municipal and State Police Employees' Retirement System (MSPRS) (see below)	92,478	—	1,141	91,337
HUD 108 loan (Pic 'N' Save) (see below)	5,200	—	—	5,200
Certificates of participation (see below)	3,125	—	1,300	1,825
Total	$236,007	$12,428	$10,756	$237,679

Source: Adapted from a recent annual financial report of the City of New Orleans.

REVIEW QUESTIONS

Section I

Q6–1   How are the activities of Debt Service Funds controlled?

Q6–2   Are budgets usually used for Debt Service Funds?

Q6–3   When is interest recorded as an expenditure in Debt Service Funds?

Q6–4   When is the principal of general long-term debt recorded in Debt Service Funds?

Q6–5   What information can a city oversight body obtain from a Debt Service Fund?

Q6–6   What function does the Board of Liquidation serve for the City of New Orleans?

Section II

Q6–7   When are Capital Projects Funds used?

Q6–8   How are Capital Projects Funds controlled?

Q6–9   Why is encumbrance accounting generally used for Capital Projects Funds?

Q6–10   Are closing entries necessary in the accounting records for a capital project that is not completed in the first year?

Q6–11   Are fixed assets recorded in Capital Projects Funds? Why or why not?

Q6–12   Bonds that finance capital projects are sometimes issued at a premium or a discount. What is the effect on the accounting records of the premium or discount?

Section III

Q6–13   Are the account groups *funds* as the term is used in governmental accounting? Why or why not?

Q6–14   What is the purpose of the General Fixed Assets Account Group?

Q6–15   What is "Construction in progress" and how is it reported?

Q6–16   When general obligation long-term debt is issued by a government, where is the principal of the obligation reported?

Q6–17   Would you recommend that a governmental unit use account groups? Why or why not?

Q6–18   Explain the relationship among the Debt Service Funds, the Capital Projects Funds, and the account groups.

CASES

C6–1 Gail Dumas, manager of Sun View City, has come to your office to discuss the terms of a bond issue the city plans to sell. Since a new bridge over Muddy Creek will be financed with a $25-million bond issue, Ms. Dumas feels that as chief finance officer, you should have some input into the terms included in the bond indenture. The bonds will be redeemed in a lump sum at the end of twenty years, and Ms. Dumas is concerned that Sun View might not be able to make principal and interest payments as they come due. What recommendations do you have for Ms. Dumas?

C6–2 David Hemtoks, president of the city council of New City, is reviewing his financial reporting system. He is attempting to write a note to the financial statements for "Other General Long-Term Debt." Mr. Hemtoks wants to use note (e) from the City of New Orleans annual financial report as a guide; however, he does not understand how some of the items in that note relate to the general long-term debt of the city. He thought general long-term debt was limited to bonds.

Review Table 6–17 and write an explanation of how each item is logically a long-term debt item and why general long-term debt is or is not limited to only long-term bonds. Do you agree that general long-term debt should be limited to bonds? Explain.

C6–3 Denise DuPepe, chief finance officer for the City of Moonview, is preparing the city's first annual report. Ms. DuPepe cannot decide how to best present the changes in general fixed assets and the general long-term debt in the report.

Recently Ms. DuPepe read an article in a governmental accounting magazine that mentioned a choice of how these items are reported, but the article did not go into detail on how to do it. Ms. DuPepe is concerned that the reporting choices will lead to confusion on the part of the readers of the annual report.

Assume you are hired as a consultant to the city and your first task is to explain the reporting options for general fixed assets and general long-term debt to Ms. DuPepe. Also express your preference and explain why you prefer one approach over the other. Finally comment on Ms. DuPepe's concern over reader confusion.

C6–4 Jim Lin, mayor of Muddville, is trying to locate available resources in the governmental-type funds to help "bail out" the General Fund. The General Fund is currently $9 million in the "red" and there are still two months remaining in the fiscal year. Mr. Lin feels there must be some unused resources in a Capital Projects Fund and/or a Debt Service Fund that could be transferred to the General Fund to alleviate the impending budget deficit. Each of these funds has a fund balance of at least $100 million.

If Mr. Lin cannot locate the needed resources, he will have to borrow money using tax anticipation notes based on an emergency tax levy. This is a major problem for him because the current year is an election year.

Do you think Mr. Lin can find the resources he needs to balance the budget? Explain.

EXERCISES

Section I

E6–1 (Fill-in-the-blanks—general terminology)
1. Payment of principal and interest on debt is referred to as _____.
2. A periodic transfer of resources from the General Fund to a Debt Service Fund is reported as a(n) _____ on the operating statement of both funds.
3. Payment of principal is reported as a(n) _____ on the _____ of a Debt Service Fund.
4. A financial institution that makes principal and interest payments in the name of a governmental unit is called a _____ .
5. A debit balance in Fund balance is called a(n) _____ .

E6–2 (Use of a Debt Service Fund)
The City of Crestview has only one Debt Service Fund for all of its bond issues. Is the city in compliance with GAAP for governmental units? Explain.

E6–3 (Multiple choice)
1. Several years ago a city provided for the establishment of a sinking fund to retire an issue of general obligation bonds. This year the city made a $50,000 contribution to the sinking fund from general revenues and realized $15,000 in revenue from securities in the sinking fund. The bonds due this year were retired. These transactions require accounting recognition in
   a. The General Fund
   b. A Debt Service Fund and the General Long-Term Debt Account Group
   c. A Debt Service Fund, the General Fund, and the General Long-Term Debt Account Group
   d. A Capital Projects Fund, a Debt Service Fund, the General Fund, and the General Long-Term Debt Account Group
   e. None of the above

   (AICPA adapted)

2. To provide for the retirement of general obligation bonds, a city invests a portion of its general revenue receipts in marketable securities. This investment activity should be accounted for in

a. A Trust Fund
b. An Enterprise Fund
c. A Special Assessment Fund
d. A Special Revenue Fund
e. None of the above

(AICPA adapted)

3. In preparing the General Fund budget of Brockton City for the forthcoming fiscal year, the city council appropriated a sum greater than expected revenues. This action of the council will result in
   a. A cash overdraft during the fiscal year
   b. An increase in encumbrances by the end of the fiscal year
   c. A debit to Fund balance
   d. A necessity for compensatory offsetting action
   e. None of the above

(AICPA adapted)

4. The operations of a public library receiving the majority of its support from property taxes levied for that purpose should be accounted for in
   a. The General Fund
   b. A Special Revenue Fund
   c. An Enterprise Fund
   d. An Internal Service Fund
   e. None of the above

(AICPA adapted)

5. A special tax was levied by Downtown City to retire and pay interest on general obligation bonds that were issued to finance the construction of a new city hall. The receipts from the tax should be recorded in
   a. A Capital Projects Fund
   b. A Special Revenue Fund
   c. A Debt Service Fund
   d. The General Fund
   e. None of the above

6. Which of the following funds uses modified accrual accounting?
   a. All governmental-type funds
   b. The General Fund and Special Revenue Funds only
   c. Only the General Fund
   d. Only Debt Service Funds
   e. None of the above

7. The term *spending measurement focus* refers to
   a. The use of the modified accrual basis of accounting
   b. The measurement of resources available for spending
   c. The use of the full accrual basis of accounting
   d. The timing of the recognition of revenues and expenditures
   e. None of the above

8. In general, the modified accrual basis of accounting is similar to the accrual basis of accounting with respect to recognition of expenditures. Which of the following is an exception to this general rule?
   a. Inventories
   b. Prepaid expenses
   c. Interest on long-term debt
   d. All of the above
   e. None of the above

E6–4 (Explanation of the financial reporting effects of the issuance and servicing of general obligation long-term debt)

When a city issues general obligation long-term debt, the accounting procedures are quite different from those found in profit-oriented organizations. Explain the financial reporting effects of the issuance and servicing of a general obligation long-term debt issue.

E6–5 (Journal entries for long-term debt)

Structure City issued $10 million of general obligation bonds to finance the construction of a new city hall. During the year, the Debt Service Fund levied $2,500,000 of taxes to service the bonds and collected $2,000,000 by year-end. Principal of $900,000 and interest of $500,000 matured and was paid during the year by Debt Service Fund.

REQUIRED: Prepare the journal entries to record the events described above and identify the fund(s) and/or account group(s) used.

Section II

E6–6 (Fill-in-the-blanks—general terminology)
   1. Encumbrance accounting usually (is or is not) _____ used in Capital Projects Funds.
   2. The entry to record the budget of a Capital Projects Fund would include a (debit or credit) _____ to Appropriations.
   3. A contractor recently completed a bridge for the City of Paige. After the contractor removed his men and equipment, several deficiencies were noticed. Another contractor was hired to repair these deficiencies. The cost of the repairs should be charged to _____ .
   4. A Capital Projects Fund must be used when fixed assets are _____ or _____ using restricted resources.
   5. Long-term bonds issued by a Capital Projects Fund (are or are not) _____ reported as a liability of that fund.
   6. During the year, a city acquired new furniture for the mayor's office, land for a parking garage, and a new fire truck. The furniture was financed from general city revenues; the land and part of the cost of the parking garage were financed primarily from bond proceeds; and the fire truck was financed from general tax revenues.

Which of these projects would require the use of a Capital Projects Fund? _____ .

E6–7   (Use of Capital Projects Funds)

The City of New Falls is planning to acquire furniture and fixtures for the mayor's office and the council chambers. One of the council members has sent you a memo asking if a Capital Projects Fund is needed to record the acquisition of the furniture. Write a memo in response to Council member Dunn.

E6–8   (Multiple choice)

1. The resources that may be used to finance Capital Projects Funds come from
   a. Private donations
   b. General obligation debt
   c. Intergovernmental revenues
   d. Transfers from other funds
   e. All of the above

2. The issuance of bonds to provide resources to construct a new courthouse should be recorded in a Capital Projects Fund by crediting
   a. Bonds payable
   b. Revenues—bonds
   c. Fund balance
   d. Proceeds from bond issue

3. When a construction project continues beyond the end of an accounting period, a special entry must be made at the beginning of the new period when encumbrance accounting is used. This entry includes
   a. A credit to Revenues
   b. A debit to Cash
   c. A debit to Expenditures
   d. A debit to Encumbrances

4. Resources that remain in a Capital Projects Fund after the project is completed should be
   a. Transferred to the General Fixed Assets Account Group
   b. Transferred to the General Long-Term Debt Account Group
   c. Disbursed according to any restrictions in the agreement between the provider of the resources and the government
   d. Transferred to the General Fund

5. The journal entry that is made in the Capital Projects Fund when a contract is signed and encumbrance accounting is used is

   a. Encumbrances   xxxx
          Reserve for encumbrances   xxxx
   b. Vouchers payable   xxxx
          Reserve for encumbrances   xxxx
   c. Expenditures—construction costs   xxxx
          Vouchers payable   xxxx

       d. Reserve for encumbrances   xxxx
           Fund balance   xxxx

6. The principal amount of bonds issued to finance the cost of a new city hall would be recorded as a liability in
   a. The General Long-Term Debt Account Group
   b. The General Fixed Assets Account Group
   c. A Capital Projects Fund
   d. A Debt Service Fund
7. Encumbrance accounting is usually used in Capital Projects Funds because
   a. Long-term debt is not recorded in these funds
   b. The budget must be recorded in these funds
   c. It helps the government to control the expenditures
   d. The modified accrual basis of accounting is used
8. The City of New Easton had a bridge constructed across the Lincoln Bayou. After completion of the project, the bridge should be recorded as an asset in
   a. The General Fund
   b. A Capital Projects Fund
   c. The General Fixed Assets Account Group
   d. both b and c

E6–9 (Treatment of fixed assets in Capital Projects Funds)

The City of False Creek started its first construction project, a new city hall. The city's accountant is not sure of how to record the payments made to the contractor. He knows that the city hall will be eventually recorded in the General Fixed Assets Account Group, but he is not sure how it will "get there." Explain the process to him.

E6–10 (Closing journal entries)

The following are selected accounts from the trial balance of the Walker Tunnel Fund, a Capital Projects Fund, as of June 30, 19X1 (the end of the fiscal year):

Appropriations	$3,711,000
Fund balance	78,000
Cash	245,000
Encumbrances	1,345,000
Revenues—grants	2,000,000
Estimated revenues	2,020,000
Expenditures—construction costs	2,356,000
Investments	75,000
Revenue—investments	19,000

REQUIRED:
1. Prepare the closing entry for 19X1.
2. Assuming no revenues are budgeted for fiscal 19X2, prepare the opening entries necessary for July 1, 19X1.

Section III

E6–11   (Fill-in-the-blanks—general terminology)
1. Assets such as land, buildings, and equipment used by a city, in general, are recorded in the _____.
2. Assets such as lighting, drainage, and streets are called _____.
3. The cost of a fixed asset is defined as _____.
4. The General Long-Term Debt Account Group is used to account for the _____ amount of the outstanding debt.
5. The total of the Amount to be provided in the Debt Service Fund plus the Amount provided in the Debt Service Fund is equal to _____.
6. The General Long-Term Debt Account Group (is or is not) _____ used to accumulate assets to retire general obligation debt.

E6–12   (Use of account groups)
The city manager for Newfound Island has asked you to explain the use of account groups to the city's management board. After reviewing the financial statements, members of the board, who are all business owners, do not understand why long-term "fixed" assets and long-term debt are separated from governmental-type funds. Explain the use of account groups to the management board.

E6–13   (Journal entries for account groups)
Identify which of the following situations would result in a journal entry in one of the account groups and identify the account group affected. Explain your answer in each case.
1. The city received a federal government grant and issued twenty-year general obligation bonds to purchase land and develop the land into a park.
2. The city issued six-month tax anticipation notes to obtain working capital until tax receipts are collected.
3. Revenue bonds were issued to finance the construction of an electric generating plant. The bonds will be serviced from the sale of electricity.
4. The current year's payment of principal and interest was made on general long-term debt.
5. The city paved several miles of streets.

E6–14   (Journal entries)
Prepare the journal entries for each of the following transactions that would be recorded in an account group. In addition, identify the account group used.
1. A $5 million bond issue matured and was paid using resources previously accumulated for that purpose.
2. The chief of police acquired $3,000 of office furniture, using part of his general appropriation for the year.

3. The city sold the furniture used in the old Civil Court Building. The furniture originally cost $245,000. The proceeds from the sale totaled $10,000. There are no restrictions on the use of this money.

4. Interest of $234,000 on general obligation long-term debt matured and was paid.

5. A new computer was acquired at a cost of $1,000,000, using general tax revenues. The old computer was scrapped—it had no value; the original cost was $500,000.

E6–15 (Description of financial statements)

Using the transactions presented in E6–14, describe how each transaction will affect the balance sheet of the funds and account groups involved.

E6–16 (Leases)

Dodge City leased equipment with a fair market value of $905,863. The life of the noncancelable lease is ten years and the economic life of the property is ten years. Using an 8 percent interest rate, the present value of the minimum lease payments is $905,863. The first payment of $125,000 is due January 1 of the current year. Each additional payment is due on the first of January in the next nine years. What is the amount of the asset to be recorded on Dodge City's books? If no asset will be recorded, explain why.

PROBLEMS

Section I

P6–1 (Journal entries and trial balance for a Debt Service Fund)

The following are a trial balance and several transactions that relate to New Basin City's City Hall Bond Fund:

New Basin City
Debt Service Fund
City Hall Bond Fund
Trial Balance
July 1, 19X1

Cash	$30,000	
Investments	20,000	
Fund balance		$50,000
	$50,000	$50,000

7/1/X1–6/30/X2

1. The city council of New Basin City legally adopted the budget for the City Hall Bond Fund for the fiscal year. The estimated revenues totaled $100,000, the estimated other financing sources totaled $50,000, and the appropriations totaled $125,000.

2. The General Fund transferred $50,000 to the fund.
3. To provide additional resources to service the bond issue, a tax was levied upon the citizens. The total levy was $95,000, of which $93,000 was expected to be collected. Assume the allowance method is used.
4. Taxes of $60,000 were collected.
5. Income received in cash from the investments totaled $1,000.
6. Taxes of $30,000 were collected.
7. The liability of $37,500 for interest was recorded, and that amount of cash was transferred to the fiscal agent.
8. The fiscal agent reported that all the interest had been paid.
9. A fee of $500 was paid to the fiscal agent.
10. Investment income totaling $1,000 was received.
11. The liabilities for interest in the amount of $37,500 and principal in the amount of $50,000 were recorded and the total was transferred to the fiscal agent.
12. The fiscal agent reported that $45,000 of principal and $35,000 of interest were paid.
13. Investment revenue of $500 was accrued.

REQUIRED:
1. Prepare all the journal entries necessary to record the above transactions on the books of the City Hall Bond Fund.
2. Prepare a trial balance for the City Hall Bond Fund as of June 30, 19X2.
3. Prepare a statement of revenues, expenditures, and changes in fund balance and a balance sheet for the City Hall Bond Fund.
4. Prepare closing entries for the City Hall Bond Fund.

P6–2 (Journal entries, trial balance, and financial statements for a Debt Service Fund)

Following is a trial balance for the City of Dolby and the transactions that relate to the Debt Service Fund:

City of Dolby
Debt Service Fund
Bridge Bonds Fund
Trial Balance
December 31, 19X0

	DEBIT	CREDIT
Cash	$60,000	
Investments	30,000	
Fund balance		$90,000
	$90,000	$90,000

1. The city council of Dolby legally adopted the budget for the Debt Service Fund for 19X1. The estimated revenues totaled $1 million; the estimated other financing sources totaled $500,000; and the appropriations totaled $202,000.
2. The receivable from the General Fund for $500,000 was recorded.
3. To provide additional resources to service the bond issue, a tax was levied upon the citizens. The total levy was $1 million, of which $975,000 was expected to be collected. (Assume the allowance method is used.)
4. Taxes of $780,000 were collected.
5. Receivables of $5,000 were written off.
6. Income received in cash from investments totaled $5,000.
7. Taxes of $150,000 were collected.
8. The liability of $50,000 for interest was recorded, and that amount of cash was transferred to the fiscal agent.
9. The fiscal agent reported that $45,000 of interest had been paid.
10. The fiscal agent was paid a fee of $1,000.
11. Investment income of $3,000 was received in cash.
12. The liabilities for interest in the amount of $50,000 and principal in the amount of $100,000 were recorded and the total was transferred to the fiscal agent.
13. The fiscal agent reported that interest of $51,000 and principal of $95,000 had been paid.
14. Investment revenue of $1,000 was accrued.
15. Collected the amount due from the General Fund.
16. Purchased $1 million of investments.

REQUIRED:
1. Prepare all the journal entries necessary to record the above transactions on the books of the Debt Service Fund.
2. Prepare a trial balance for the Debt Service Fund as of December 31, 19X1.
3. Prepare a statement of revenues, expenditures, and changes in fund balance for 19X1 and a balance sheet as of December 31, 19X1, for the Debt Service Fund.
4. Prepare closing entries for the Debt Service Fund.

P6–3 (Journal entries for several funds)

Following are several transactions that relate to Sunshine City for the fiscal year 19X1 (assume a voucher system is not used):
1. The general operating budget was approved. It included Estimated revenues of $1 million, Estimated other financing sources of $300,000, Appropriations of $1,150,000, and Estimated other financing uses of $100,000.
2. The police department paid its salaries of $30,000.
3. The General Fund made its contribution to a Debt Service Fund of $100,000.

4. The city acquired new office furniture for $45,000. Old furniture that cost $23,000 was sold for $500. The proceeds could be used in any manner by the city.
5. The fire chief ordered $500 of supplies.
6. General obligation long-term debt principal matured and the final interest payment became due. These amounts were $75,000 and $7,500, respectively. (Assume a Debt Service Fund and a fiscal agent are used.)
7. The appropriate amount of cash was sent to the fiscal agent to process the debt service payments described in number 6.
8. The supplies ordered in number 5 arrived. The actual cost was $490. A check was sent to the supplier.
9. The fiscal agent for the bonds notified the government that $70,000 of principal and $7,000 of interest had been paid.
10. The property tax for the year was levied by the General Fund. The total amount of the tax was $500,000. City officials estimated that 99 percent would be collected.
11. Collections of property taxes during the year totaled $490,000.
12. The remaining property taxes should be classified as delinquent after $2,000 were written off as uncollectible.
13. The General Fund received a $1,000 operating transfer from an Enterprise Fund (record only the General Fund portion).

REQUIRED: Prepare all the journal entries necessary to record the above transactions and identify the fund(s) and account group(s) used.

P6–4 (Journal entries and trial balances for several funds)

Following are several transactions that relate to the City of New Ion in 19X1:

1. The general operating budget was approved. It included estimated revenues of $500,000, appropriations of $400,000, and estimated other financing uses of $90,000.
2. Encumbrances of $100,000 were recorded in the General Fund.
3. The budget for the Parks Special Revenue Fund was approved. It included estimated revenues of $60,000 and appropriations of $59,000.
4. The General Fund made its annual contribution of $90,000 to the Debt Service Fund.
5. The Debt Service Fund recorded the liability for principal and interest, $20,000 and $40,000, respectively.
6. The fiscal agent invested $10,000 of Debt Service Fund cash in securities.
7. The salaries of the general governmental administrative staff were paid, $10,000. Assume that salaries were not encumbered.

8. The fiscal agent who manages the investment activities of the Debt Service Fund was paid a fee of $1,000.
9. The tax used to partially service the bond issue was levied. The total levy was $30,000, of which $29,000 is expected to be collected.
10. A cash expenditure for office supplies for the mayor's office was made, $1,000. The encumbered amount was $900.
11. Debt Service Fund cash of $60,000 was paid to the fiscal agent to pay interest and principal.
12. The principal and interest previously recorded were paid by the fiscal agent.

REQUIRED:
1. Prepare all the journal entries necessary to record the above transactions. In addition, identify the fund or account group in which each entry is recorded.
2. Prepare a trial balance for the Debt Service Fund as of December 31, 19X1.

P6–5 (Journal entries)

Prepare journal entries for each of the following transactions. In addition, identify the fund in which each entry would be recorded.

1. The General Fund made its annual contribution of $1,500,000 to the fund, which will pay $1 million principal and $500,000 interest on outstanding general obligation debt.
2. The city paid $1 million of principal and $500,000 of interest on outstanding general obligation bonds from resources previously accumulated.
3. A Debt Service Fund previously paid the total principal and interest on an outstanding bond issue. Currently there is $300,000 in the fund. These resources can be spent by the General Fund in any way the city manager feels is appropriate.
4. The police chief paid $300,000 for equipment. This equipment was ordered three months prior to delivery at an estimated cost of $295,000 (assume a voucher system is used and the excess expenditure is approved).
5. The fiscal agent for the city was paid her annual $10,000 fee from resources accumulated in the only Debt Service Fund used by the city.

Section II

P6–6 (Journal entries and financial statements—Capital Projects Fund)

19X1
1. The City of Towerville approved the construction of an enclosed concert arena for a total cost of $75 million in order to attract professional events. On the same day, a contract was signed with

Shady Construction Company for the arena. The arena will be financed by a general obligation bond issue. Investment revenue of $4 million was also included in the budget. (Assume that the budget is recorded in the accounts and encumbrance accounting is used.)

2. The bonds were issued for $76 million (the principal was $75 million). The amount received over $75 million was immediately transferred to the Debt Service Fund.
3. The city invested $74.9 million in marketable securities.
4. The contract signed with Shady stipulated that the contract price included the architect fees. On this date, the architects were paid their fee of $25,000 by Towerville. (Assume that a vouchers payable account was not used.)
5. The contractor submitted a progress billing of $5 million.
6. Investments that cost $5 million were redeemed for $5 million plus $50,000 interest.
7. Shady was paid the amount billed less a 5 percent retained percentage.
8. Income totaling $3.7 million was received on the investments.
9. Shady submitted another progress billing. This time the amount was $8 million.
10. Additional investments were redeemed in order to make the payment to Shady. The investments originally cost $7.8 million. The proceeds of $8.1 million included investment income of $300,000.
11. The contractor was paid, less the 5 percent retainage.
12. Investment income of $60,000 was accrued.

REQUIRED:
1. Prepare the journal entries necessary to record the above transactions in the Capital Projects Fund. Assume that the city operates on a calendar year.
2. Prepare a trial balance for the Capital Projects Fund at December 31, 19X1, before closing.
3. Prepare any necessary closing entries at December 31, 19X1.
4. Prepare a statement of revenues, expenditures, and changes in fund balance for 19X1 and a balance sheet as of December 31, 19X1.
5. Prepare the journal entries necessary to record the remainder of the budget and to reestablish the budgetary accounts for encumbrances at January 1, 19X2.

P6–7 (Journal entries and financial statements—Capital Projects Fund)

7/1/X1–6/30/X2
1. The City of New Rouge approved the construction of a city hall complex for a total cost of $120 million. A few days later, a contract was signed with the Walker Construction Company for the complex. The buildings will be financed by a federal grant of $25 million and a general obligation bond issue of $100 million. During the current year, investment revenue of $4 million is budgeted. (As-

sume the budget is recorded in the accounts and encumbrance accounting is used.)

2. The bonds were issued for $90 million (the principal was $100 million). The difference between the actual cost and the bonds and the grant was expected to be generated by investing the excess cash during the construction period.
3. The city collected the grant from the government.
4. The city invested $90 million in certificates of deposit.
5. The contract signed with Walker stipulated that the contract price included architect fees. On this date, the architects were paid their fee of $45,000 by New Rouge. (Assume a vouchers payable account is used.)
6. Walker submitted a progress billing for $25 million.
7. Investments that cost $5 million were redeemed for a total of $5,020,000.
8. Investment income totaling $3,500,000 was received in cash.
9. The contractor was paid the amount billed in number 6, less a 5 percent retainage.
10. The contractor submitted another progress billing for $25 million.
11. Investments totaling $14,600,000 were redeemed, together with additional investment income of $1,400,000.
12. The contractor was paid the amount billed in number 10, less a 5 percent retainage.
13. Investment income of $250,000 was accrued.
14. Bond interest totaling $10 million was paid.

REQUIRED:

1. Prepare the journal entries necessary to record the above transactions in a Capital Projects Fund for the City of New Rouge. Assume the city operates on a fiscal year: July 1 to June 30.
2. Prepare a trial balance for the fund at June 30, 19X2, before closing.
3. Prepare any necessary closing entries at June 30, 19X2.
4. Prepare a statement of revenues, expenditures, and changes in fund balance for the year ended June 30, 19X2 and a balance sheet as of June 30, 19X2.
5. Prepare the journal entry (entries) necessary to record the remainder of the budget and to reestablish the budgetary accounts for encumbrances as of July 1, 19X2. Assume investment revenues of $2 million are expected in the 19X2 fiscal year.

P6–8 (Journal entries regarding a bond issue and an explanation of how a premium should be accounted for)

The City of Straights authorized a bond issue for a parking garage. The estimated cost was $4 million. The garage would be financed through a $3 million bond issue and a $1 million contribution from the General Fund. The General Fund made its contribution and the bonds were sold for $3,200,000.

REQUIRED: 1.   Prepare journal entries to record the budget for the parking garage, the payment and receipt of the General Fund's contribution, and the issuance of the bonds, assuming the premium remained in the Capital Projects Fund. Identify the fund(s) and account group(s) used to record the transactions.

2.   Discuss alternate methods of dealing with the bond premium.

P6–9   (Journal entries for several funds)

Following is a trial balance for the Old York Marina Capital Projects Fund and the transactions that relate to the 19X1–X2 fiscal year:

Old York
Capital Projects Fund
Boat Marina Fund
Trial Balance
July 1, 19X1

Cash	$ 30,000	
Investments	500,000	
Retained percentage on construction contracts		$ 10,000
Reserve for encumbrances		500,000
Unreserved fund balance		20,000
	$530,000	$530,000

19X1–X2   1.   The budget for the marina project provided for a remaining appropriation of $500,000. Record the budget and reestablish the budgetary accounts for encumbrances. Assume $30,000 of investment income is budgeted.

2.   The contractor, Sir Fixit, Inc., submitted a progress billing on the marina for $300,000.

3.   Investments were redeemed for $320,000. This amount included $20,000 of investment income.

4.   Sir Fixit was paid the amount billed, less a 10-percent retained percentage.

5.   Investment income of $15,000 was received in cash.

6.   The final billing was received from Sir Fixit for $200,000.

7.   All remaining investments were redeemed for $205,000. This amount included $5,000 of investment income.

8.   Sir Fixit was paid the amount billed, less a 10 percent retained percentage.

9.   Before the project was formally approved, one of the piers fell into the lake. Since Sir Fixit had already removed its men and equipment, the city was authorized to have the repairs made by a local contractor at a cost not to exceed $40,000. The actual cost of the repairs totaled $32,000. The remainder of the retainage was sent to Sir Fixit.

After the repairs, the project was formally approved and the accounting records were closed. The remaining cash should be transferred to the Debt Service Fund. The funds for this project came from a general obligation bond issue.

REQUIRED:

1. Prepare all the journal entries necessary to record the above transactions and close the Capital Projects Fund. In addition, identify the fund(s) and/or account group(s) used. A vouchers payable account is not used.

2. Prepare a statement of revenues, expenditures, and changes in fund balance for the Marina Capital Projects Fund for the 19X1–X2 fiscal year.

P6–10 (Prepare a budget for a capital project and the related bond issue)

The Town of Gateway plans to build an auditorium. The plans were drawn by an architect for $100,000. The city accepted a bid from Cracks R Us contractors for $8 million for the entire project. The project should take two years to build. Since it will not be started until October 1, 19X1, the completion date is September 30, 19X3.

The town manager of Gateway, Phyllis Main, plans to establish a Debt Service Fund for the bonds that will be issued to finance the project. These bonds will be serviced from tax revenues. During 19X1, $100,000 of revenue is expected to be available. The bonds will pay interest on April 1 and October 1 of each year.

REQUIRED:

1. Prepare the journal entries necessary to record the above information in the appropriate funds.

2. Explain which account groups will be used for the project.

Section III

P6–11 (Journal entries for several funds and account groups)

The following transactions were incurred by Lake Ponchatrain Township:

1. The township paid cash for four new police cruisers. Each car cost $18,000. They were originally ordered at $19,000 each.

2. The township issued bonds for the purpose of constructing a levee along the south shore of the lake. The bonds had a face value of $20 million and were sold for $19,500,000.

3. Mr. JoJo Smith, the mayor of the township, signed a contract with the Dumas Office Furniture Company to buy new furniture for his office. The total cost of the furniture was $8,900. The furniture will be delivered next month.

4. Two additional policemen were hired to help patrol the west and east shores of the lake.

5. The fire department sold several pieces of old equipment. They originally cost the township $20,000. The fire chief, Emma Peeler, negotiated a selling price of $3,000 for the used equipment.

6. The township made its annual payment of principal and interest on its outstanding debt. A total of $4 million was paid—$1 million of principal and $3 million of interest.

7. The township levied a property tax to service the outstanding debt. The total amount of the tax was $4 million, of which $3,900,000 was expected to be collected.

8. The city hall construction project was completed this year. Due to construction delays, it took three years to build the new office building. This year $2,600,000 of costs were incurred. In previous years a total of $7,500,000 were incurred. Financing for the project came from a bond issue that was sold at the time the project was started.

9. The township's board of managers approved a budget amendment for the General Fund. An extra $240,000 appropriation was included in the budget for the current year.

10. The township made payments on outstanding leases totaling $300,000. This amount included $175,000 for interest. The leases are accounted for in the General Fund.

REQUIRED: Record the above transactions in journal form. Also indicate the fund or account group in which each transaction is recorded.

P6–12 (Leased assets)

On January 1, 19X1, the chief operating officer of New Innport signed a noncancelable lease for street equipment. The lease was for ten years, the economic life of the property. The fair market value of the equipment (and present value of the minimum rentals) is $72,469. The township's incremental borrowing rate is eight percent; however, the rate implicit in the lease is not known. The $10,000 annual rentals are due on the first day of the year.

REQUIRED: Prepare all journal entries necessary to record the lease for 19X1 and the payment made in 19X2.

P6–13 (Journal entries for several funds and account groups)

19X2
1. The city sold some of its street repair equipment. The equipment originally cost $50,000, but it was sold for $500.

2. A $2 million bond issue was sold at par. The bonds were general obligation debt issued to finance the cost of an addition to the local court system building.

3. Property taxes totaling $100,000 were collected.

4. The construction of a bridge across the High Water River was com-

pleted at a total cost of $8 million. The bridge had been under construction since 19X0. Costs incurred in previous years totaled $7 million. With respect to the Capital Projects Fund, prepare only the closing entry for the expenditure. The cost of construction was entirely financed by a federal grant.

5. A Debt Service Fund paid the interest on outstanding debt, $800,000.

6. A Debt Service Fund retired bonds with a face value of $3 million.

7. The General Fund made its annual payment of $5 million to a Debt Service Fund. Of this amount, $4 million was for retirement of principal.

8. Old office equipment was discarded. The original cost of the equipment was $900.

9. A contract was signed with Legal, Inc., to construct an addition to the court building. The amount of the contract was $5 million.

10. The construction costs paid during the year on the court addition were $500,000. With respect to the Capital Projects Fund, record only the closing entry for the expenditure. Bonds were used to finance the project.

11. The fire department acquired a new fire engine. The vehicle was ordered earlier in the year. The order was encumbered for $140,000. The actual cost was $138,000.

REQUIRED: Record the above transactions in journal form. Also indicate the fund or account group in which each transaction is recorded.

P6–14   (Leased assets)
The police department of the Tooman Township signed a noncancelable lease for computer equipment. The lease was for five years, the economic life of the property. The fair market value of the equipment (and present value of the minimum rentals) is $18,954. The Township's incremental borrowing rate is 10 percent. The annual rentals are $5,000 and are due on the first day of the year, beginning January 1, 19X1.

REQUIRED: Prepare all journal entries necessary to record the lease for 19X1 and the payment made in 19X2.

P6–15   (Journal entries and correcting entries for several funds and account groups)
The Township of Briner recently hired an inexperienced bookkeeper. Accounting records prior to January 1, 19X1, were maintained by the same individual who designed the accounting system and were audited each year. On January 2, 19X2, the bookkeeper accepted a job in another state and a new bookkeeper was hired. Below is a selection of transactions

that occurred during 19X1 and a description of how each transaction was recorded.

1. The township adopted a budget for the General Fund for 19X1 that included Estimated revenues of $900,000, Estimated other financing sources of $200,000, Appropriations of $800,000, and Estimated other financing uses of $150,000. The budget was not recorded in the books.

2. The township purchased a fire truck in February. The bookkeeper made the following entry in the General Fund:

Fire truck	100,000	
Vouchers payable		100,000

   Payment of the voucher was not recorded.

3. A property tax levy was made in March. The total levy was $400,000. Approximately 3 percent was expected to be uncollectible. By the end of the year $390,000 had been collected and the remainder was delinquent. The only entries made during the year were for the collections as a debit to Cash and credit to Revenues—property taxes.

4. Bonds were retired in June. The township had accumulated $505,000 in a Debt Service Fund by the end of 19X0. Part of these resources ($500,000) were used to retire the bonds. The remainder were available to be used by the township in any way it desired. The only entries recorded during the year were as follows (these entries were recorded in the General Fund, using Debt Service Fund resources):

Bonds payable	500,000	
Vouchers payable		500,000
Vouchers payable	500,000	
Cash		500,000

5. Some surplus equipment was sold in September for $20,000 (there were no restrictions on the use of these resources). The equipment was originally purchased for $245,000 several years ago. The following entry was made in the General Fixed Assets Account Group:

Cash	20,000	
Loss on sale of equipment	225,000	
Equipment		245,000

6. The General Fund made its annual contribution to a Debt Service Fund. These resources will be used to pay interest. The only entry made was in the General Fund:

Bonds payable	50,000	
Cash		50,000

7. The interest paid during 19X1 on the debt mentioned in number 6 was recorded in the General Fund as follows:

Interest expense	50,000	
Cash		50,000

REQUIRED: Record the adjusting or correcting entries that are required by the above events. Also identify the fund(s) or account group(s) involved. Closing entries are not required. If no entry is required, write "None" next to the description number on your paper. The books for the current year have not been closed.

7

THE GOVERNMENTAL FUND ACCOUNTING CYCLE

> Proprietary-Type Funds
> and Pension Trust Funds

LEARNING OBJECTIVES

After completion of this chapter, you should be able to:

1. Explain why and how Internal Service funds are used in governmental accounting
2. Prepare the journal entries normally used in Internal Service Funds
3. Prepare financial statements for Internal Service Funds
4. Explain why and how Enterprise Funds are used in governmental accounting
5. Prepare the journal entries normally used in Enterprise Funds
6. Prepare financial statements for Enterprise Funds
7. Explain why and how Pension Trust Funds are used in governmental accounting
8. Prepare the journal entries normally used in Pension Trust Funds
9. Prepare financial statements for Pension Trust Funds

SECTION I—PROPRIETARY-TYPE FUNDS: INTERNAL SERVICE FUNDS

Definition of Fund

A governmental unit will often find that certain goods or services can be supplied by a department or agency to other departments or agencies at a lower cost than if the same function were to be supplied by an outside organization. It is also possible that an internal department or agency can supply these goods or services more conveniently or dependably than a private contractor. Thus the government will establish an **Internal Service Fund** to account for business-type activities of supplying goods or services to departments or agencies within the governmental unit or to other governmental units.

The result is that the government establishes a business operation. The accounting and management procedures followed should be similar to those followed by business organizations outside the governmental unit. Thus the users of these goods or services should be charged on a cost-reimbursed basis. The amount of the charge generally should be at least enough to recover the costs incurred. Therefore, it is necessary to measure the full cost of the goods or services.

Internal Service Funds are usually established to account for such activities as central data-processing services, central motor pools, and central inventory and supply functions. Since the purpose of this type of fund is to provide information for a businesslike evaluation of the operations, it is essential that each activity be accounted for by a separate fund.

Use of an Internal Service Fund is especially important in those instances where the governmental unit provides an operating subsidy for an activity. By computing the activity's full cost of operations, and comparing these costs with the revenues earned, the extent of the subsidy needed can easily be determined.

Summary of Fund Activities

Many different types of activities require the use of an Internal Service Fund. In this chapter we will limit our discussion to a central motor pool. The operations of this type of service are typical for governmental units and are illustrative of the general operations of Internal Service Funds.

The first step is to acquire capital from the General Fund or some other fund. This money is used to acquire automobiles, trucks, and so forth. As the vehicles are being used, each department is billed based on the miles driven. The revenue from the billings is used to pay the operating costs of the vehicles and, possibly, for their replacement.

Control of Fund Activities

The operations of Internal Service Funds are controlled indirectly by the operating budgets of the funds using the goods or services and directly by means of flexible budgets. Since other funds must pay for the goods or services supplied, the approval of their budgets acts as an indirect control device for the Internal Service Fund.

A **flexible budget** is a budget in which the level of budgeted expenses is related to the level of operations. Thus, in our example of a central motor pool, the allowable gasoline and oil costs will vary directly with the number of miles the vehicles are used. Governmental-type funds, by contrast, operate under a **fixed budget.** Thus, if a department head is given $4,000 for supplies for the year, that amount cannot be exceeded—regardless of the level of operations. In effect, the use of a fixed budget actually sets the limit on the level of operations of the governmental unit.

The difference in budgeting practices between governmental-type funds and Internal Service Funds results from the fact that the revenue generated by the latter will increase as the level of operations increases. Since there is this cause-and-effect relationship between the level of operations and the revenues earned and the expenses incurred, a flexible budget will allow higher levels of expenses at higher levels of operating activity. As previously explained, no such relationship usually exists between revenues and expenditures of governmental-type funds.

Because flexible operating budgets are used, we usually do not find the budget recorded in the accounts of Internal Service Funds, nor do we usually find the use of encumbrance accounting for these funds. Since there is no absolute spending limit, the use of encumbrance accounting would not serve any purpose. However, some state or local laws do require the use of encumbrances for Internal Service Funds. Since this is not the general case, we will assume that encumbrance accounting is not used.

The operations of an Internal Service Fund are similar to those of a private business. The users of goods or services are charged a fee based on what is provided. Therefore, it is necessary to measure the full costs incurred in providing goods or services. This results in a **capital maintenance measurement focus.** The extent of the charges will depend on the management philosophy employed. It is possible to set the charges to simply cover the actual cash costs incurred. It is also possible to set the charges to permit replacement of any fixed assets involved, or to allow for future expansion of the fund activities.

Use of the capital maintenance approach results in recording *all* of the costs incurred in providing the goods or services. These costs include depreciation on fixed assets, an item not found in the governmental-type funds or in the other funds that follow a spending measurement focus. In addition, fixed assets are included on the balance sheet of an Internal Service Fund. Thus the balance sheet and the income statement of an Internal Service Fund will be similar to those of a private business providing the same goods or services.

The **full accrual** basis of accounting is used for Internal Service Funds. Revenues are recognized when they are earned and expenses are recorded when they are incurred in earning the revenues. Use of the capital maintenance measurement focus, together with the full accrual basis of accounting, makes accounting for Internal Service Funds very similar to that used for commercial enterprises.

GASB *Statement No. 20,* "Accounting and Financial Reporting for Proprietary Funds and Other Governmental Entities That Use Proprietary Fund Accounting," defines the applicability of business-type pronouncements for governmental entities. In general, these funds must follow applicable FASB Statements and Interpretations, APB Opinions, and Committee on Accounting Procedure (CAP) Accounting Research Bulletins issued on or before November 30, 1989, unless there is a conflict with a GASB pronouncement. These funds *may* follow *all* FASB Statements and Interpretations issued after November 30, 1989, that do not conflict with a GASB pronouncement.

Accounting for Fund Activities

Operating entries

For illustrative purposes, let us continue with the example of a central motor pool. Assume that to start up the fund, the General Fund makes an equity transfer of $500,000 to the Motor Pool Fund. The entries to record this transfer are:

Entry in the books of the General Fund	Residual equity transfer to Motor Pool Fund	500,000	
	Cash		500,000
	To record transfer to Internal Service Fund for start-up purposes.		
Entry in the books of the Internal Service Fund	Cash	500,000	
	Contributed capital from General Fund		500,000
	To record equity transfer from General Fund.		

Notice that the transfer of resources from the General Fund to the Internal Service Fund is a residual equity transfer. Also notice that the receipt of the resources is also a residual equity transfer in the Internal Service Fund, but it is called "Contributed capital from General Fund." Remember, the equity section of an Internal Service Fund includes contributed capital and retained earnings.

If the Internal Service Fund acquires a fleet of vehicles for $400,000, the following entry is made:

Automobiles	300,000	
Trucks	100,000	
Cash		400,000
To record the acquisition of vehicles.		

Billings of $57,000 to the various departments for use of the vehicles are recorded as follows:

Entry in the books of the Internal Service Fund	Due from departments	57,000	
	Revenues—vehicle charges		57,000
	To record charges to departments for use of vehicles		
Entry in the books of a governmental-type fund using the vehicles	Expenditures—vehicle usage	8,000	
	Due to Motor Pool Fund		8,000
	To record the use of vehicles during the period.		

Payments of $45,000 from the departments are recorded as follows:

Entry in the books of the Internal Service Fund

Cash	45,000	
Due from departments		45,000
To record payments received from departments using vehicles.		

Entry in the books of a governmental-type fund using the vehicles

Due to Motor Pool Fund	8,000	
Cash		8,000
To record payment to Motor Pool Fund.		

The above illustration is used to show how billings to the departments and collections are recorded. Notice that the entries regarding the departmental usage are limited, for illustrative purposes, to a single department and that the "due to" and "due from" account titles are still used for intergovernmental receivables and payables.

During the year, gasoline, oil, and maintenance expenses totaling $14,000 are incurred. These are recorded in the Internal Service Fund as follows:

Gasoline and oil expense	9,500	
Maintenance expense	4,500	
Cash		10,000
Accounts payable		4,000
To record the gasoline and oil and maintenance expense for the period.		

Payment of salaries of $10,000, ignoring withholdings and so forth, is recorded as follows:

Salaries expense	10,000	
Cash		10,000
To record salaries expense.		

If the motor pool rents warehouse space from the government for $2,000 per year, the entry to record the rental will be:

Rent expense	2,000	
Cash		2,000
To record the rent for the year.		

The General Fund will record the receipt of the rent as follows:

Entry in the books of the General Fund

Cash	2,000	
Revenues—rental of warehouse space		2,000
To record the receipt of the rent from the motor pool.		

TABLE 7-1   Trial Balance—Internal Service Fund

City of New Example
Internal Service Fund
Motor Pool Fund
Trial Balance
December 31, 19X1

	DEBITS	CREDITS
Cash	$123,000	
Due from departments	12,000	
Automobiles	300,000	
Accumulated depreciation—automobiles		$ 20,000
Trucks	100,000	
Accumulated depreciation—trucks		10,000
Accounts payable		4,000
Contributed capital from General Fund		500,000
Revenues—vehicle charges		57,000
Gasoline and oil expense	9,500	
Maintenance expense	4,500	
Salaries expense	10,000	
Rent expense	2,000	
Depreciation expense—automobiles	20,000	
Depreciation expense—trucks	10,000	
	$591,000	$591,000

As previously indicated, depreciation is an expense that is recognized in Internal Service Funds. Assuming the amounts given, the entry to record this for the year is:

Depreciation expense—automobiles	20,000	
Depreciation expense—trucks	10,000	
Accumulated depreciation— automobiles		20,000
Accumulated depreciation—trucks		10,000
To record depreciation for the year.		

Although additional entries can be made, the above summary journal entries are sufficient to reflect the type of activities engaged in by Internal Service Funds and the recording of the related revenues and expenses.

A trial balance for the Motor Pool Fund at the end of the year is shown in Table 7-1.

Closing entry

The closing process for Internal Service Funds is similar to the one used for commercial enterprises. That is, each of the revenue, expense, and other temporary accounts is closed; and the net operating figure is recorded in Retained earnings. The entry on the following page relates to our illustration.

Revenues—vehicle charges	57,000	
Gasoline and oil expense		9,500
Maintenance expense		4,500
Salaries expense		10,000
Rent expense		2,000
Depreciation expense—automobiles		20,000
Depreciation expense—trucks		10,000
Retained earnings		1,000

To close the revenue and expense accounts
for the period.

Financial statements—illustration

The individual financial statements for Internal Service Funds are a statement of revenues, expenses, and changes in retained earnings; a balance sheet; and a statement of cash flows. These are illustrated for 19X1 in Tables 7–2, 7–3, and 7–4. In addition, you should review the section on Internal Service Funds in Chapter 2. The overall reporting process is discussed in Chapter 9.

Often fixed assets are acquired by using contributed capital. It is permissible (not required) to deduct depreciation on these assets directly from contributed capital instead of treating it as an expense and deducting it from retained earnings. If this is done, net income is usually reported in the manner described above and the depreciation to be charged against contributed capital is added to net income. This clearly reflects the effect of depreciation on net income and lets the reader know that it is being deducted from contributed capital.

TABLE 7–2   Statement of Revenues, Expenses, and Changes in Retained Earnings—Internal Service Fund

City of New Example
Internal Service Fund
Motor Pool Fund
Statement of Revenues, Expenses, and Changes in Retained Earnings
For the Year Ended December 31, 19X1

Revenues		
Vehicle charges		$57,000
Expenses		
Gas and oil expense	$ 9,500	
Maintenance expense	4,500	
Salaries expense	10,000	
Rent expense	2,000	
Depreciation expense—autos	20,000	
Depreciation expense—trucks	10,000	
Total expenses		56,000
Net income		1,000
Retained earnings at beginning of year		-0-
Retained earnings at end of year		$ 1,000

TABLE 7–3   Balance Sheet—Internal Service Fund

City of New Example
Internal Service Fund
Motor Pool Fund
Balance Sheet
December 31, 19X1

Assets		
Cash		$123,000
Due from departments		12,000
Automobiles	$300,000	
Less accumulated depreciation	20,000	280,000
Trucks	$100,000	
Less accumulated depreciation	10,000	90,000
Total assets		$505,000
Liabilities and Fund Equity		
Liabilities:		
Accounts payable		$ 4,000
Fund Equity		
Capital contributed from General Fund	$500,000	
Retained earnings	1,000	
Total fund eqity		501,000
Total liabilities and fund equity		$505,000

TABLE 7–4   Cash Flow Statement—Internal Service Fund

City of New Example
Internal Service Fund
Motor Pool Fund
Cash Flow Statement
For the Year Ended December 31, 19X1

Cash flows from operating activities:		
Net income	$ 1,000	
Adjustments to reconcile operating income to		
net cash provided by operating activities:		
Increase in Due from departments	(12,000)	
Increase in Accounts payable	4,000	
Depreciation	30,000	
Net cash provided by operating acitivities		$ 23,000
Cash flows from capital and related financing activities:		
Capital contributed by municipality	500,000	
Acquisition of automobiles and trucks	(400,000)	
Net cash provided by capital and related financing activities		100,000
Increase in cash during year		123,000
Cash at beginning of year		-0-
Cash at end of year		$123,000

Some governmental units use a classified balance sheet for their proprietary funds. If this is done, assets and liabilities are grouped into classifications similar to those used on a commercial balance sheet. This is not done in Table 7–3 because the classified approach is not used in reporting the overall balance sheet for a governmental unit, and we prefer to have the individual fund statements appear as close to the overall reporting format as possible.

GOVERNMENTAL ACCOUNTING IN PRACTICE— THE CITY OF COLUMBUS, OHIO

The City of Columbus, Ohio, uses Internal Service Funds to account for a central purchasing function, construction inspection, land acquisition, information services, and fleet management. We will use the Purchasing Stores Fund and the Construction Inspection Fund as examples. These funds report the activities of a central purchasing function and a department that inspects new construction to

TABLE 7–5   Statement of Revenues, Expenses, and Changes in Retained Earnings—Internal Service Fund—City of Columbus, Ohio

City of Columbus, Ohio
Combining Statement of Revenues, Expenses and
Changes in Retained Earnings
All Internal Service Funds
Year Ended December 31, 19X1

	PURCHASING STORES	CONSTRUCTION INSPECTION
Operating revenues:		
Charges for services	$508,475	$5,357,841
Other	—	28,081
Total operating revenues	508,475	5,385,922
Operating expenses:		
Personal services	—	4,398,601
Materials and supplies	288,409	39,770
Contractual services	131,418	649,837
Depreciation	—	83,982
Other	—	—
Total operating expenses	419,827	5,172,190
Operating income (loss)	88,648	213,732
Nonoperating expenses:		
Interest expense	—	—
Net income (loss)	88,648	213,732
Retained earnings at beginning of year	421,894	1,242,841
Retained earnings at end of year	$510,542	$1,456,573

Source: Adapted from a recent annual financial report of the City of Columbus, Ohio.

TABLE 7–6 Balance Sheet—Internal Service Fund—City of Columbus, Ohio

City of Columbus, Ohio
Combining Balance Sheet
All Internal Service Funds
December 31, 19X1

	PURCHASING STORES	CONSTRUCTION INSPECTION
Assets		
Cash and cash equivalents:		
Cash and investments with treasurer	$451,684	$1,605,393
Receivables	1,647	24,273
Due from other:		
Governments	—	565
Funds	36,981	1,796,232
Inventory	28,832	—
Property, plant and equipment:		
At cost	—	933,209
Less accumulated depreciation	—	(528,463)
Net property, plant and equipment	—	404,746
Total assets	519,144	3,831,209
Liabilities		
Accounts payable	8,305	18,258
Customer deposits	—	1,619,965
Due to other funds	297	1,907
Accrued wages and benefits	—	161,692
Accrued vacation and sick leave	—	572,814
Notes payable	—	—
Total liabilities	8,602	2,374,636
Fund Equity		
Contributed capital	—	—
Unreserved retained earnings	510,542	1,456,573
Total fund equity	510,542	1,456,573
Total liabilities and fund equity	$519,144	$3,831,209

Source: Adapted from a recent annual financial report of the City of Columbus, Ohio.

make sure that all "code" provisions are followed. The operating statement, balance sheet, and cash flow statement of these funds are presented in Tables 7–5 through 7–7.

Notice that two funds are included in the Columbus reports. These exhibits are part of the combining financial statements included in that city's annual financial report. The process of combining financial statements is explained in Chapter 9.

TABLE 7–7   Cash Flow Statement—Internal Service Fund—City of Columbus, Ohio

City of Columbus, Ohio
Combining Statement of Cash Flows
All Internal Service Funds
Year Ended December 31, 19X1

	PURCHASING STORES	CONSTRUCTION INSPECTION
Operating activities:		
Cash received from customers	$510,452	$5,395,821
Cash paid to employees	—	(4,343,301)
Cash paid to suppliers	(430,901)	(695,621)
Other receipts (expenses)	—	4,583
Net cash provided by (used in) operating activities	79,551	361,482
Capital and related financing activities:		
Purchases of property, plant and equipment	—	(150,068)
Principal payments on notes	—	—
Interest paid on notes	—	—
Net cash used in capital and related financing activities	—	(150,068)
Increase (decrease) in cash and cash equivalents	79,551	211,414
Cash and cash equivalents at beginning of year	372,133	1,393,979
Cash and cash equivalents at end of year	$451,684	$1,605,393
Operating income (loss)	88,648	213,732
Adjustments to reconcile operating income (loss) to net cash privided by (used in) operating activities:		
Depreciation	—	83,982
Loss on disposal of fixed assets	—	—
Increase (decrease) in operating assets and liabilities		
Receivables	1,125	23,907
Due from other governments	—	(565)
Due from other funds	852	12,687
Inventory	1,508	—
Accounts payable—net of items affecting property, plant and equipment	(12,879)	(1,842)
Customer deposits	—	(23,498)
Due to other funds	297	(1,723)
Accrued wages and benefits	—	39,237
Accrued vacation and sick leave	—	15,565
Net cash provided by (used in) operating activities	$ 79,551	$ 361,482

Source: Adapted from a recent annual financial report of the City of Columbus, Ohio

SECTION II—PROPRIETARY-TYPE FUNDS: ENTERPRISE FUNDS

Definition of Fund

An **Enterprise Fund** is used when a governmental unit provides goods or services to consumers who are not part of a government. Although it is possible that other governmental departments, agencies, or other units will use these goods or services, the factor that separates use of Enterprise Funds from use of Internal Service Funds is the presence of consumers outside a governmental unit.

While these goods or services are usually financed through user charges, such charges are not mandatory. Enterprise Fund accounting can be used in any instance where the government feels that the calculation of net income can provide information for control of the activities.

The types of operations that normally require use of an Enterprise Fund(s) are those that perform services like those rendered by public utilities. However, Enterprise Funds are also used for the operations of ports, airports, public swimming pools, golf courses, and so forth. In other words, an Enterprise Fund should be used anytime a governmental unit supplies goods or services to outsiders, and the determination of the cost of the operations is relevant for the purpose of pricing or management.

Use of an Enterprise Fund is especially important in those instances where the governmental unit provides an operating subsidy for an activity. By computing the activity's full cost of operations, and comparing these costs with the revenues earned, the extent of the subsidy needed can easily be determined.

Summary of Fund Activities

The operating cycle of an Enterprise Fund is similar to that of a business organization. That is, goods or services are provided to consumers, who must pay for them. During the operating period, the fund acquires assets such as supplies, property, and equipment. The cost of using these assets is recorded along with other operating expenses. Revenues from user charges must also be recorded. Thus we have the cause-and-effect relationship mentioned earlier—that is, the expenses are incurred in order to earn the revenues.

Control of Fund Activities

The operations of an Enterprise Fund are controlled by many different means. Since the functions of this type of activity are to supply goods or services to a general market, there is some control exercised by the consumer. The purchase or nonpurchase of a particular good or service is true "marketplace control." However, since many Enterprise Funds are public utilities, they have **monopoly operating rights.** In many cases, therefore, no competitive goods or services are available. Control must be achieved through the governing boards that determine the rates the utility can charge. These boards use outside consultants and operating data extensively to determine reasonable service charges. In these cases, accounting data are invaluable for measuring the results of operations.

Flexible budgets are used for the measurement and control of operations in Enterprise Funds in the same manner that they are used in Internal Service Funds. Thus we have an additional element of control. Since the use of flexible budgets precludes recording the budget in the accounts, the direct spending control we found in the General Fund is not present in Enterprise Funds. In addition, because of the lack of absolute spending control, encumbrance accounting is not generally used for Enterprise Funds.

Still another method of control lies in the budgets of those funds that use the goods or services provided by the fund. While this is an indirect method of control, it is still effective, especially for those funds that follow a spending measurement focus.

The *capital maintenance* measurement focus is used in Enterprise Fund accounting because of the need to determine the full cost of operations. Thus, as with Internal Service Funds, we have abandoned the spending measurement focus for a much more comprehensive approach. The provisions of GASB *Statement No. 20,* as discussed in the section on Internal Service Funds, also apply to accounting for Enterprise Funds. The capital maintenance focus is combined with the computation of expenses (including depreciation) and revenues, that are recorded under the *accrual* basis of accounting. Therefore, we will record revenues when earned and expenses when incurred in the earning of the revenues. Because of the use of these procedures, the financial statements for Enterprise Funds include all the assets used in the operations of the funds: liquid assets (cash, receivables, inventory, and so on) and fixed assets (property, plant, and equipment). In addition, both current and long-term liabilities are carried on the balance sheet.

Accounting for Fund Activities

Operating entries

For illustrative purposes, assume the City of New Example owns and operates the French Market Corporation. This governmental unit was established to operate a local tourist attraction—a large open market like those used by the early colonists. Individuals and businesses can rent space in the market to sell anything from fresh fruits and vegetables to clothing and jewelry. A trial balance for the fund is presented in Table 7–8.

If billings to the retailers during 19X1 totaled $500,000, and $5,000 of that amount is for space provided to the city, the following entry should be made:

Accounts receivable	495,000	
Due from General Fund	5,000	
Revenue from rentals		500,000
To record rental revenue for the year.		

Collections during the year total $490,000, of which $5,000 is from the General Fund. They are recorded as follows:

Cash	490,000	
Accounts receivable		485,000
Due from General Fund		5,000
To record collections from customers.		

TABLE 7–8   Trial Balance—Enterprise Fund

City of New Example
Enterprise Fund
French Market Corporation Fund
Trial Balance
December 31, 19X0

	DEBITS	CREDITS
Cash	$ 25,000	
Accounts receivable	15,000	
Supplies	2,000	
Restricted assets	150,000	
Land	500,000	
Equipment	200,000	
Accumulated depreciation—equipment		$ 90,000
Buildings	1,500,000	
Accumulated depreciation—buildings		600,000
Accounts payable		20,000
Revenue bonds payable		1,000,000
Contributions from municipality		400,000
Retained earnings reserved for restricted assets		150,000
Unreserved retained earnings		132,000
	$2,392,000	$2,392,000

The appropriate entries in the books of the General Fund for these two events are:

Entries in the books of the General Fund

Expenditures—rentals	5,000	
Due to French Market Corporation Fund		5,000
To record cost of rentals of 19X1.		
Due to French Market Corporation Fund	5,000	
Cash		5,000
To record payment made to French Market Corporation Fund.		

Operating expenses (exclusive of depreciation) total $400,000. Of this amount, $50,000 is paid in cash and the remainder is on credit. The entry to record this information is:

General operating expenses	400,000	
Cash		50,000
Accounts payable		350,000
To record operating expenses for 19X1.		

The above expenses do not include depreciation. Since we are accumulating the full cost of operating the market, depreciation must be recorded. Assuming the appropriate amounts are as indicated in the entry, the following is recorded:

Depreciation expense—equipment	15,000	
Depreciation expense—buildings	50,000	
Accumulated depreciation— equipment		15,000
Accumulated depreciation— buildings		50,000

To record depreciation for 19X1.

Payments to creditors total $350,000 during the year. These payments are recorded as follows:

| Accounts payable | 350,000 | |
| Cash | | 350,000 |

To record payments on accounts payable.

The account generally used to record the long-term debt is called **Revenue bonds payable.** Revenue bonds are debt securities that are serviced by the revenues generated by the fund. The entry to record interest of $40,000 for the current year on the long-term debt is:

| Interest expense | 40,000 | |
| Cash | | 40,000 |

To record bond interest for the year.

Here it is assumed the bond interest is all paid in cash—that is, $20,000 is payable on June 30 and December 31 of each year. If the interest is not due at the end of the year, a proportionate amount is still recorded as an expense. When this happens, however, Interest payable is credited. For simplicity we have assumed the interest payments on the revenue bonds do not require the use of restricted assets.

Notice the treatment of the accrued interest under the accrual basis as opposed to that followed by the modified accrual basis used in the Debt Service Funds. In most governmental-type funds, interest is not recorded until it legally matures and becomes payable.

Assume that during the year the French Market management begins a policy of requiring a $50 deposit from each customer. This policy is designed to reduce the losses suffered in prior years due to customers not paying their bills. Since these assets are owned by the customers, they must be recorded in a restricted asset account. The offsetting liability is Customers' deposits. If $20,000 is collected, the actual entry appears as follows:

| Restricted assets | 20,000 | |
| Customers' deposits | | 20,000 |

To record amounts received for customers' deposits.

Also assume that in addition to requiring deposits, management establishes a provision for uncollectible accounts. The proper amount for 19X1 is $5,000. This is recorded as follows:

Uncollectible accounts expense	5,000	
Estimated uncollectible accounts		5,000
To record the estimated uncollectible accounts at December 31, 19X1.		

The Estimated uncollectible accounts account is reported as a deduction from Accounts receivable on the balance sheet. The Uncollectible accounts expense is reported on the operating statement. Notice the treatment afforded uncollectible accounts for proprietary-type funds as opposed to that used for governmental-type funds. Remember that in governmental-type funds, the provision for uncollectible accounts is treated as a direct reduction from revenue rather than as an expenditure.

The Restricted assets account represents the amounts the corporation is required to set aside each year according to the bond indenture, customer deposit agreements, and so forth. Although these amounts should be identified in more detail, we will use one account for simplicity. In addition, with the exception of customers' deposits, we will assume that no special liabilities exist at the balance sheet date that will require the use of restricted assets.

Refer to the trial balance in Table 7–8. Notice that the total of the Restricted assets ($150,000) less the liabilities payable with restricted assets ($-0-) is equal to the Retained earnings reserved for restricted assets ($150,000). This equality should be maintained. At the end of each period, therefore, the reserve should be adjusted to the difference between any restricted assets and the liabilities payable from the restricted assets.

In this illustration we have assumed that the only restricted assets or related liabilities to change were the customers' deposits. Since that amount is offset by the liability account, there is no need to change the reserve amount.

In summary, Retained earnings generally is reserved to reflect the restricted use of the assets. In each case, simplifying assumptions are made to keep the illustration at an elementary level. This type of use of reserve accounts is not required by GAAP.

During the year the fund used $1,000 of supplies. The entry to record this is:

Supplies expense	1,000	
Supplies		1,000
To record supplies used during 19X1.		

Although additional entries can be made, the above summary journal entries reflect the type of activities and the recording of revenues and expenses normally incurred by Enterprise Funds.

A trial balance for the French Market Corporation Fund at December 31, 19X1, is presented in Table 7–9.

TABLE 7–9   Trial Balance—Enterprise Fund

City of New Example
Enterprise Fund
French Market Corporation Fund
Trial Balance
December 31, 19X1

	DEBITS	CREDITS
Cash	$ 75,000	
Accounts receivable	25,000	
Estimated uncollectible accounts		$ 5,000
Supplies	1,000	
Restricted assets	170,000	
Land	500,000	
Equipment	200,000	
Accumulated depreciation—equipment		105,000
Buildings	1,500,000	
Accumulated depreciation—buildings		650,000
Accounts payable		20,000
Customers' deposits		20,000
Revenue bonds payable		1,000,000
Contributions from municipality		400,000
Retained earnings reserved for restricted assets		150,000
Unreserved retained earnings		132,000
Revenues from rentals		500,000
General operating expenses	400,000	
Depreciation expense—equipment	15,000	
Depreciation expense—building	50,000	
Interest expense	40,000	
Uncollectible accounts expense	5,000	
Supplies expense	1,000	
	$2,982,000	$2,982,000

Closing entry

The closing process for Enterprise Funds involves transferring the balances of the revenues, expenses, and other temporary accounts to Unreserved retained earnings. The appropriate entry, using the data given in the example, is:

Revenues from rentals	500,000	
Unreserved retained earnings	11,000	
General operating expenses		400,000
Depreciation expense—equipment		15,000
Depreciation expense—building		50,000
Interest expense		40,000
Uncollectible accounts expense		5,000
Supplies expense		1,000

To close the revenue and expense accounts for the period.

Financial statements—illustration

Individual financial statements for Enterprise Funds are an operating statement, a balance sheet, and a cash flow statement. These are illustrated for 19X1 in Table 7–10, 7–11, and 7–12. The overall reporting process is discussed in Chapter 9.

GOVERNMENT ACCOUNTING IN PRACTICE—
THE CITY OF COLUMBUS, OHIO

The city of Columbus, Ohio, uses three Enterprise Funds: Water, Sewer, and Electricity. These are illustrated in Tables 7–13, 7–14, and 7–15. The use of these funds is explained by their titles. In Table 7–13, four items are of particular interest. The first item is the Electricity Fund, which had an operating loss of over $17 million. This was partially offset by an operating transfer from various funds of over $6 million. The city plans to continue to fund the Electricity Enterprise Fund's obligations in the future. The second item is that the Sewer Fund and the Electricity Fund each had an extraordinary item. The extraordinary item was an accounting loss on the advanced refunding of debt. A recent statement issued by the Governmental Accounting Standards Board (*Statement No. 23*) has changed the accounting procedures for gains and losses on debt retired before maturity by proprietary-type funds. Since this topic is beyond the scope of this text, we will not explore this issue further. The third item is the depreciation adjustment in the

TABLE 7–10   Statement of Revenues, Expenses, and Changes in Retained Earnings—Enterprise Fund

City of New Example
Enterprise Fund
French Market Corporation Fund
Statement of Revenues, Expenses, and Changes in Retained Earnings
For the Year Ended December 31, 19X1

Revenues		
Rentals		$500,000
Expenses		
General operating expenses	$400,000	
Depreciation expense—equipment	15,000	
Depreciation expense—building	50,000	
Interest expense	40,000	
Uncollectible accounts expense	5,000	
Supplies expense	1,000	
Total expenses		511,000
Net loss		(11,000)
Unreserved retained earnings at beginning of year		132,000
Unreserved retained earnings at end of year		$121,000

TABLE 7–11   Balance Sheet—Enterprise Fund

City of New Example
Enterprise Fund
French Market Corporation Fund
Balance Sheet
December 31, 19X1

Assets

Current assets:		
Cash	$ 75,000	
Accounts receivable (net of estimated uncollectible		
accounts of $5,000)	20,000	
Supplies	1,000	
Total current assets		$ 96,000
Restricted assets		170,000
Fixed assets:		
Land	$500,000	
Equipment (net of accumulated depreciation of $105,000)	95,000	
Buildings (net of accumulated depreciation of $650,000)	850,000	
Total fixed assets		1,445,000
Total assets		$1,711,000

Liabilities and Fund Equity

Liabilities:		
Current liabilities:		
Accounts payable		$ 20,000
Liabilities payable from restricted assets		20,000
Long-term liabilities:		
Revenue bonds payable		1,000,000
Total liabilities		1,040,000
Fund equity:		
Contributed capital:		
Contributions from municipality	$400,000	
Retained earnings:		
Reserve for restricted assets	150,000	
Unreserved retained earnings	121,000	
Total fund equity		671,000
Total liabilities and fund equity		$1,711,000

Sewer Fund. As previously discussed, governmental units have the option of adding depreciation on fixed assets funded by capital grants back to income. This was done in the case of the Sewer Fund. The fourth item is the deficit balance in Retained earnings in the Electricity Fund. This means that the fund is not billing its customers for an amount large enough to cover its operating expenses. City management does not expect this condition to continue because of the transfer of a solid waste recovery plant.

TABLE 7–12 Cash Flow Statement—Enterprise Fund

City of New Example
Enterprise Fund
French Market Corporation Fund
Cash Flow Statement
For the Year Ended December 31, 19X1

Cash flows from operating activities:		
Operating loss	$(11,000)	
Adjustments to reconcile operating loss to net cash provided by operating activities:		
Increase in accounts receivable (net)	(5,000)	
Decrease in supplies	1,000	
Depreciation—equipment and buildings	65,000	
Cash received from customers' deposits	20,000	
Net cash provided by operating activities		70,000
Net increase in cash		70,000
Unrestricted and restricted cash at beginning of year		25,000
Unrestricted and restricted cash at end of year		$95,000
Cash summary at end of year:		
Unrestricted cash	$75,000	
Cash in restricted assets	20,000[1]	
Total cash	$95,000	

[1]Customers' deposits

Balance sheets for the Enterprise Funds of the City of Columbus are presented in Table 7–14. Notice the detail included for restricted assets. This is the traditional method of financial statement presentation. We have used one account for restricted assets in order to simplify our illustrations. The total restricted assets in Table 7–14 for the Water Fund, $51,820,352, less the liabilities payable from restricted assets, $2,070,653, is $49,749,699. This situation differs from that explained earlier in that we assume there was a legal or contractual requirement for the establishment of the reserve. In those situations encountered by Columbus there is no such requirement; therefore, the city chose not to reserve retained earnings. Also notice how similar all of the accounts are for each of the Enterprise Funds in Table 7–14.

Table 7–15 contains cash flow statements for the Enterprise Funds of the City of Columbus. Cash receipts and disbursements are classified in the categories found in the table. There are four items of particular interest on these statements. The first is the format of the cash flows from operating activities. The method used by Columbus is called the **direct method.** In the text table, we use the **indirect method.** Using the indirect method, operating income (loss) is adjusted to identify the total cash flow from operating activities. Both methods are acceptable for financial statement purposes. If the direct method is used, a reconciliation schedule like the format for the indirect method must accompany the

TABLE 7-13 Statement of Revenues, Expenses, and Changes in Retained Earnings—Enterprise Fund—City of Columbus, Ohio

City of Columbus, Ohio
Combining Statement of Revenues, Expenses, and Changes in
Retained Earnings—All Enterprise Funds
Year Ended December 31, 19X1

	WATER	SEWER	ELECTRICITY	TOTAL
Operating revenues:				
Charges for service	$58,444,036	$89,055,804	$46,405,173	$193,905,013
Other	81,968	282,664	486,043	850,675
Total operating revenues	58,526,004	89,338,468	46,891,216	194,755,688
Operating expenses:				
Personal services	19,457,858	22,168,025	17,161,179	58,787,062
Materials and supplies	6,217,118	4,209,442	4,222,195	14,648,755
Contractual services	14,036,333	18,817,407	10,074,188	42,927,928
Purchased power	—	—	9,088,391	9,088,391
Coal	—	—	1,161,546	1,161,546
Depreciation	9,748,896	12,025,953	10,796,370	32,571,219
Other	321,492	707,583	711,746	1,740,821
Total operating expenses	49,781,697	57,928,410	53,215,615	160,925,722
Operating income (loss)	8,744,307	31,410,058	(6,324,399)	33,829,966
Nonoperating revenues (expenses):				
Interest income	2,052,219	4,236,171	472,045	6,760,435
Interest expense	(14,747,307)	(24,988,390)	(12,132,594)	(51,868,291)
Total nonoperating revenues (expenses)	(12,695,088)	(20,752,219)	(11,660,549)	(45,107,856)
Income (loss) before operating transfers	(3,950,781)	10,657,839	(17,984,948)	(11,277,890)
Operating transfers in—Notes H and Q	—	—	6,583,265	6,583,265
Income (loss) before extraordinary item	(3,950,781)	10,657,839	(11,401,683)	(4,694,625)
Extraordinary item:				
Accounting loss on advance refunding—Note G	—	(12,982,000)	(6,002,008)	(18,984,008)
Net income (loss)	(3,950,781)	(2,324,161)	(17,403,691)	(23,678,633)
Add depreciation on fixed assets acquired by capital grants	—	3,471,871	—	3,471,871
Increase (decrease) in retained earnings	(3,950,781)	1,147,710	(17,403,691)	(20,206,762)
Retained earnings (deficit) at beginning of year	77,648,920	118,643,780	(21,206,048)	175,086,652
Retained earnings (deficit) at end of year	$73,698,139	$119,791,490	$(38,609,739)	$154,879,890

See accompanying notes to the general purpose financial statements.

Source: Adapted from a recent annual financial report of the City of Columbus, Ohio.

TABLE 7-14 Balance Sheet—Enterprise Fund—City of Columbus, Ohio

City of Columbus, Ohio
Combining Balance Sheet—All Enterprise Funds
December 31, 19X1

	WATER	SEWER	ELECTRICITY	TOTAL
Assets				
Cash and cash equivalents—				
Cash and investments with treasurer—Note C	$ 19,753,465	$43,950,919	$836,880	$64,541,264
Receivables (net of allowances for uncollectibles)—				
Note D	7,001,797	10,961,357	4,572,558	22,535,712
Due from other:				
Governments	—	9,426,327	—	9,426,327
Funds—Note E	2,335,223	377,585	468,982	3,181,790
Inventory	4,820,437	2,490,841	5,330,526	12,641,804
Deferred charges and other	611,492	458,761	666,005	1,736,258
Restricted assets:				
Cash and cash equivalents:				
Cash and investments with treasurer—Notes C				
and G	51,081,555	43,393,125	6,146,369	100,621,049
Cash and cash equivalents with trustees—Note C				
and G	738,621	13,616,011	724,440	15,079,072
Investments with trustees—Notes C and G	—	11,049,833	6,976,294	18,026,127
Accrued interest receivable—Note D	176	80,506	28,925	109,607
Property, plant and equipment—Note F:				
At cost	398,172,125	790,216,333	276,377,636	1,464,766,094
Less accumulated depreciation	(144,731,152)	(154,308,855)	(100,798,289)	(399,838,296)
Net property, plant and equipment	253,440,973	635,907,478	175,579,347	1,064,927,798
Total assets	$339,783,739	$771,712,743	$201,330,326	$1,312,826,808
Liabilities				
Accounts payable	$ 2,162,426	$ 3,756,396	$ 1,747,313	$ 7,666,135
Customer deposits	548,166	—	459,554	1,007,720
Due to other funds—Note E	674,028	1,922,841	468,413	3,065,282
Payable from restricted assets:				
Accounts payable	1,066,948	4,603,932	68,291	5,739,171
Due to other funds—Note E	266,716	38,223	6,563	311,502
Accrued interest payable—Note G	736,989	918,051	166,428	1,821,468
Deferred revenue	—	2,418,643	85,993	2,504,636
Accrued interest payable	2,957,996	6,390,492	5,215,421	14,563,909
Accrued wages and benefits	766,453	798,281	695,377	2,260,111
Accrued vacation and sick leave	2,117,256	1,827,422	1,366,716	5,311,394
Bonds and loans payable—Note G	255,363,000	499,454,398	210,827,290	965,644,688
Less unamortized bond discount	(1,176,727)	(2,379,096)	—	(3,555,823)
Net bonds and loans payable	254,186,273	497,075,302	210,827,290	962,088,865
Total liabilities	265,483,251	519,749,583	221,107,359	1,006,340,193
Fund Equity				
Contributed capital—Note S	602,349	132,171,670	18,832,706	151,606,725
Unreserved retained earnings (deficit)—Note O	73,698,139	119,791,490	(38,609,739)	154,879,890
Total fund equity (deficit)	74,300,488	251,963,160	(19,777,033)	306,486,615
Commitments and contingencies—Notes B, F, G and T	—	—	—	—
Total liabilities and fund equity	$339,783,739	$771,712,743	$201,330,326	$1,312,826,808

See accompanying notes to the general purpose financial statements.

Source: Adapted from a recent annual financial report of the City of Columbus, Ohio.

TABLE 7–15   Cash Flow Statement—Enterprise Fund—City of Columbus, Ohio

City of Columbus, Ohio
Combining Statement of Cash Flows—All Enterprise Funds
Year Ended December 31, 19X1

	WATER	SEWER	ELECTRICITY	TOTAL
Operating activities:				
Cash received from customers	$61,229,609	$ 81,828,955	$46,955,003	$190,013,567
Quasi external operating receipts	—	7,407,077	—	7,407,077
Cash paid to employees	(19,260,883)	(21,914,101)	(17,043,976)	(58,218,960)
Cash paid to suppliers	(20,858,024)	(23,868,940)	(25,786,735)	(70,513,699)
Other receipts (expenses)	955,414	428,975	(79,488)	1,304,901
Net cash provided by operating activities	22,066,116	43,881,966	4,044,804	69,992,886
Noncapital financing activities:				
Operating transfers in	—	—	6,583,265	6,583,265
Net cash provided by noncapital financing activities	—	—	6,583,265	6,583,265
Capital and related financing activities:				
Purchases of property, plant and equipment	(26,183,849)	(57,044,588)	(4,204,533)	(87,432,970)
Contributed Capital	—	9,206,877	—	9,206,877
Proceeds from issuance of bonds and loans	45,830,000	149,898,000	95,554,000	291,282,000
Bond discounts and bond issuance costs	—	(2,422,947)	(685,032)	(3,107,979)
Principal payment on notes	—	(822,108)	—	(822,108)
Principal payments on bonds and loans	(7,952,000)	(140,234,000)	(101,082,936)	(249,268,936)
Interest paid on bonds, loans and notes	(15,283,559)	(31,430,495)	(5,694,597)	(52,408,651)
Net cash used in capital and related financing activities	(3,589,408)	(72,849,261)	(16,113,098)	(92,551,767)
Investing activities:				
Purchase of investment securities	—	(27,369,762)	(19,036,370)	(46,406,132)
Proceeds from sale or maturity of investment securities	—	26,691,047	15,424,395	42,115,442
Interest received on investments	2,123,490	5,014,753	526,175	7,664,418
Net cash provided by (used in) investing activities	2,123,490	4,336,038	(3,085,800)	3,373,728
Increase (decrease) in cash and cash equivalents	20,600,198	(24,631,257)	(8,570,829)	(12,601,888)
Cash and cash equivalents at beginning of year (including $107,713,998 in total restricted accounts)	50,973,443	125,591,312	16,278,518	192,843,273
Cash and cash equivalents at end of year (including $115,700,121 in total restricted accounts)	$71,573,641	$100,960,055	$ 7,707,689	$180,241,385
Operating income (loss)	$ 8,744,307	$ 31,410,058	$(6,324,399)	$ 33,829,966
Adjustments to reconcile operating income (loss) to net cash provided by operating activities:				
Depreciation and amortization	9,853,637	12,127,007	10,815,397	32,796,041
Loss on disposal of fixed assets	201,169	242,636	116,653	560,458

TABLE 7-15   Cash Flow Statement—Enterprise Fund—City of Columbus, Ohio (Continued)

	WATER	SEWER	ELECTRICITY	TOTAL
Increase (decrease) in operating assets and liabilities:				
Receivables	2,845,663	198,683	601,982	3,646,328
Due from other governments	—	(1,282,746)	—	(1,282,746)
Due from other funds	900,493	232,982	(17,887)	1,115,588
Inventory	(604,623)	(175,426)	(314,979)	(1,095,028)
Accounts payable—net of items affecting property, plant and equipment	(530,784)	802,968	(1,106,031)	(833,847)
Customer deposits	(60,965)	—	17,587	(43,378)
Due to other funds	517,069	(1,190,678)	180,589	(493,020)
Deferred revenue	—	1,261,252	(42,575)	1,218,677
Accrued wages and benefits	184,382	200,530	148,266	533,178
Accrued vacation and sick leave	15,768	54,700	(29,799)	40,669
Net cash provided by operating activities	$22,066,116	$43,881,966	$4,044,804	$69,992,886
Supplemental Information				
Noncash activities:				
Accounting loss on advance refunding	$ —	$12,982,000	$6,002,008	$18,984,008
Interest financed through refunded debt	$ —	$ —	3,497,992	3,497,992

See accompanying notes to the general purpose financial statements.
Source: Adapted from a recent annual financial report of the City of Columbus, Ohio.

statement. This schedule is presented after the main statement by the City of Columbus.

The second item of importance is that of Noncapital financing activities, in this case, Operating transfers in. These were not included in the text illustration.

The third item is that cash and cash equivalent items are combined in the definition of cash used for this statement. While a complete discussion of this topic is beyond the scope of this text, it is sufficient to mention that some short-term investments should be combined with cash when preparing this statement.

The fourth item is the noncash activities listed after the income reconciliation. These are important financing activities that did not involve cash. Since these items are self-explanatory, we will not discuss them further.

Use of Special Assessments for Services

Special assessments are a means of financing services or capital improvements that benefit one group of citizens more than the general public. Taxpayers who receive the benefits of these activities are assessed for their share of the cost. Examples of special assessment activities include projects such as special police protection, paving streets, and building parking structures. Prior to the issuance of GASB *Statement No. 6*, "Accounting and Financial Reporting for Special Assessments," these activities were accounted for and reported in a separate governmental fund: Special Assessments Funds. GASB *Statement No. 6*, requires that Special Assessments Funds be discontinued as a reporting entity and that these activities be reported as any other service or capital improvement-type project.

If a governmental unit wishes to charge a full-cost price for the services to determine the "true" cost of the services, or the "true" subsidy provided to the citizens, an Enterprise Fund should be used to account for the service. This is because the accrual basis of accounting is used, including a calculation of a charge for depreciation.

Use of an Enterprise Fund for service activities that are financed with special assessments results in entries similar to those previously presented in this chapter. The only major change is that the term *special assessment* is generally used to describe the receivable for the charge. Special assessment–type projects are discussed further in Chapter 8.

SECTION III—FIDUCIARY-TYPE FUNDS: PENSION TRUST FUNDS

Definition of Fund

Public Employee Retirement Systems (PERS) operated by governmental units are accounted for in **Pension Trust Funds.** These systems provide retirement benefits for governmental employees. The employee groups can be defined as narrowly as the employees of a particular department of a governmental unit, or as broadly as the employee of an entire state. The expenditures (or expenses) associated with the contributions to the pension plans are recorded in the particular funds from which the employees are paid.

Summary of Fund Activities

The normal activities of a PERS include the accumulation of direct contributions made by the governmental units or withholdings from the salaries of their employees or both. In addition, investment of assets to generate a return in the form of interest or dividends is accounted for in these funds. One unique activity to PERS is the periodic payments made to those employees who have retired from the system. In summary, Pension Trust Funds are used to account for resources accumulated in the PERS and the payment of retirement benefits.

Control of Fund Activities

Pension fund activities are controlled by a pension agreement, and local, state, and federal laws. These laws cover operations of retirement systems in general and PERS in particular. They vary in scope, ranging from laws that limit the types of investments that can be made with fund assets to laws that require specified periods of service before employees can qualify for pension benefits.

As a result of the extensive legal involvement with Pension Trust Funds, their accounting systems and financial reports must be designed to provide information necessary to satisfy generally accepted accounting principles and to comply with the various legal requirements. In addition, the accounting system must be designed to measure the capital maintenance aspects of the operations of the fund based on the full accrual basis of accounting. Encumbrance accounting generally is not used. The provisions of GASB *Statement No. 20,* as discussed in the section on Internal Service Funds, also apply to accounting for Pension Trust Funds.

Types of Pension Funds

Local governmental units have their own pension plans or participate in state-sponsored plans. These plans can be grouped in two major categories: defined benefit plans and defined contribution plans. **Defined benefit plans** are retirement plans that guarantee specific benefits when employees retire. These benefits are usually determined by a formula. A relatively common formula is one that gives employees 2 percent credit for each year they work. The total percentage is then applied to some base salary. A common base salary is the average salary for the employee's highest three consecutive years. For example, assume an employee works for twenty-five years and her highest three consecutive years' salaries are $35,000, $37,000, and $39,000. Using the formula, she would be entitled to retirement benefits of $18,500 ($37,000 × .50) per year.

   Defined contribution plans are retirement plans that do not guarantee specific benefits. Instead, the employee's retirement benefits are determined when he or she retires, based on the amount accumulated in the plan. In most instances, the government and the employees contribute to both types of plans, but any combination of relative contributions is possible.

   Since benefits are not guaranteed under a defined contribution plan, the only obligations the governmental unit has are to make its contribution to the plan and to forward contributions of employees. Contributions made by the government are expenses of the period and, if the amount required is paid to the plan, the governmental unit has no further obligation.

   Defined benefit plans specifically identify the amount the employee is to receive upon retirement. As a result, the calculations are quite complex because they must take into consideration expected salary increases, mortality rates, plan funding, investment gains and losses, administrative costs, and other related items. Due to the popularity of defined benefit plans, we have assumed that type of plan is used by the City of New Example in the illustrations in this text.

Accounting for Fund Activities

Operating entries

   The operating entries illustrated in this chapter are based on NCGA *Statement No. 6,* "Pension Accounting and Financial Reporting: Public Employee Retirement Systems and State and Local Government Employers." In November 1994, the GASB issued three statements regarding pension and postretirement benefits: *Statement No. 25,* "Financial Reporting for Defined Benefit Pension Plans and Note Disclosures for Defined Contribution Plans," *Statement No. 26,* "Financial Reporting for Postemployment Healthcare Plans Administered by Defined Benefit Pension Plans," and *Statement No. 27,* "Accounting for Pensions by State and Local Governmental Employers." The accounting procedures required to provide the information necessary to prepare an operating statement and a balance sheet as illustrated in this section for a PERS are consistent with the reporting requirements of the new GASB statements when combined with additional information. In the "Concluding Comment" at the end of this section, we present illustrations of a statement of changes in plan net assets and a statement of plan net assets that follow the requirements of *Statement No. 25. Statements 26* and *27* are not discussed in detail because they are beyond the scope of this section.

For illustrative purposes, assume that the City of New Example has had a PERS in operation for several years. The PERS trial balance as of December 31, 19X0, is presented in Table 7–16.

Note that Table 7–16 contains five new accounts. These accounts are used to accumulate data regarding the financial status of the fund, based upon the assets

TABLE 7–16   Trial Balance—Pension Trust Fund

City of New Example
Pension Trust Fund
Public Employees Retirement System
Trial Balance
December 31, 19X0

	DEBITS	CREDITS
Cash	$ 15,000	
Interest receivable	55,000	
Investments	5,617,000	
Accounts payable		$ 75,000
Actuarial present value of projected benefits payable to current retirants and beneficiaries		987,000
Actuarial present value of projected benefits payable to terminated vested participants		269,000
Actuarial present value of credited projected benefits for active employees—member contributions		2,328,000
Actuarial present value of credit projected benefits for active employees—employer-financed portion		2,328,000
Unfunded actuarial present value of credited projected benefits	300,000	
	$5,987,000	$5,987,000

valued at cost (or amortized cost), and the liabilities that existed at a particular date. The first of these accounts, **Actuarial present value of projected benefits payable to current retirants and beneficiaries,** represents the present value of amounts payable in the future to individuals who have retired and their beneficiaries, based upon mortality tables and other actuarial and retirement plan assumptions. The second of these accounts, **Actuarial present value of projected benefits payable to terminated vested participants,** represents the present value of amounts payable in the future to individuals who are no longer in the employ of the governmental unit, but have earned pension benefits that are guaranteed to them.

The third and fourth of these accounts, **Actuarial present value of credited projected benefits for active employees** . . . , represents the present value of amounts payable in the future to individuals who are currently working for the government and earning additional pension benefits. Notice that this amount is presented in two parts: the amount financed through member (employee) contributions, and the amount financed through contributions of the governmental unit (employer-financed portion).

The final account in the fund equity section, **Unfunded actuarial present value of credited projected benefits,** represents the lack of sufficient net assets (assets – liabilities) in the plan, based upon the benefits prescribed in the plan that have been earned by the employees. If the net assets in the plan exceeded the actuarial present value calculations, the excess (a credit) would be **Net assets available for future benefit credits.**

Some additional key definitions that are important to an understanding of pension accounting are:

> **Actuarial present value.** The value, as of a specified date, of an amount or series of amounts payable or receivable thereafter, with each amount adjusted to reflect (a) the time value of money (through discounts for interest) and (b) the probability of payment (by means of decrements for events such as death, disability, withdrawal, or retirement) between the specified date and the expected date of payment.
>
> **Pension benefit obligation.** The actuarial present value of credited projected benefits, prorated on service, and discounted at a rate equal to the expected return on present and future plan assets.
>
> **Pension obligation.** . . . [The] benefits attributable to (a) retirees, beneficiaries, and terminated employees entitled to benefits and (b) current covered employees, as a result of their credited service to date.
>
> **Projected benefit obligation.** . . . [T]he actuarial present values as of a date of all benefits attributed by the pension benefit formula to employee service rendered prior to that date.
>
> **Vested benefits.** Benefit rights are vested when employees may retain them, even if they withdraw from active service before normal retirement age.[1]

The definitions above clearly indicate that the computations of the contribution requirements and the balance in the actuarial present value accounts are very

---

[1]GASB Cod. Sec. Pe6.530.

complex. They involve estimation of future benefits to be paid to retired employees, based upon salary increases, expected mortality rates, and so on. These amounts are then discounted by the expected earnings rate to determine their present value. Since the exact determination of these amounts is beyond the scope of this text, we will provide these figures in the illustrations and problems without further discussion. In addition, it is important to understand that the coverage of pension accounting and reporting presented in this section is merely an overview, at an introductory level. Coverage in more depth is beyond the scope of this textbook.

The PERS plan illustrated requires equal contributions by the employees and the governmental unit. When the amount of each contribution is determined, $200,000 in this case, the following entry is made:

Due from General Fund	400,000	
Revenues—pension contributions— members		200,000
Revenues—pension contributions— employer		200,000
To record amount due from the General Fund for pension contributions.		

Note that the receivable is specifically identified as being from the General Fund. For simplicity, we will assume that the General Fund is the only fund that has employees who participate in the PERS. If any other funds become involved, a separate receivable will be established for each.

Collections from the General Fund of $400,000 are recorded as follows:

Cash	400,000	
Due from General Fund		400,000
To record payment received from the General Fund.		

The entries in the books of the General Fund are (amounts assumed):

Entries in the books of the General Fund

Expenditures—payroll	997,000	
Due to U.S. government		120,000
Due to PERS		200,000
Cash		677,000
To record payroll.		
Expenditures—retirement benefits	200,000	
Due to PERS		200,000
To record retirement contributions.		
Due to PERS	400,000	
Cash		400,000
To record payment to PERS.		

Assume that investment income of $500,000 is received in cash. This amount includes income accrued at the beginning of the year, $55,000. In addition, sales of investments result in a gain of $10,000. The amount collected from these sales is $50,000. These items of investment income are recorded as follows:

Cash	500,000	
Interest receivable		55,000
Revenues—Investments		445,000
To record the receipt of income from investments.		
Cash	50,000	
Investments		40,000
Revenues—gain on sale of investments		10,000
To record the sale of investments.		

When employees retire, an entry is made to transfer the appropriate present value amount from the active employees' accounts to the retired employees' account. The amount of the transfer is computed in accordance with the pension plan regulations and should be the present value of the future benefits earned by the newly retired employees. Assuming the amount is $57,500, the entry to record this is:

Actuarial present value of credited projected benefits for active employees— member contributions	57,500	
Actuarial present value of credited projected benefits for active employees— employer-financed portion	57,500	
Actuarial present value of projected benefits payable to current retirants and beneficiaries		115,000
To record the retirement of employees.		

When the payment of retirement annuities is made to the retired employees, an expense and a liability are recorded. Since both the expense and the liability are recorded on the accrual basis, the timing of the actual cash payment may differ. If they are the same, $230,000, the accounting recognition of these events results in the following entries:

Expenses—retirement annuities	230,000	
Retirement annuities payable		230,000
To record the retirement annuities.		
Retirement annuities payable	230,000	
Cash		230,000
To record the payment of retirement annuities.		

In some instances the operating costs of PERS are borne by the General Fund and no operating costs appear on the financial statements of the Pension Trust Fund. In our illustration, however, we will assume that the PERS must pay for its share of the accounting and investment management costs. If these costs amount of $20,000, the following entry is made:

Expenses—operating costs	20,000	
Due to General Fund		20,000
To record operating costs for the current year.		

This information would be recorded in the General Fund as follows:

Entry in the books of the General Fund

Due from PERS	20,000	
Expenditures—operating costs		20,000
To record reimbursement of operating costs from PERS.		

Since we are using full accrual accounting, investment income of $50,000 that has been earned but not received at the end of the year will be recorded as follows:

Interest receivable	50,000	
Revenues—investments		50,000
To record investment income earned but not received.		

During the year, the Accounts payable balance was paid and operating costs of $15,000 were incurred and will be paid in 19X2. These activities result in the following journal entries:

Accounts payable	75,000	
Cash		75,000
To record payments of liabilities.		
Expenses—operating costs	15,000	
Accrued expenses		15,000
To record operating costs.		

Excess cash was invested. The total cost of the investments was $600,000. The entry to record this is:

Investments	600,000	
Cash		600,000
To record investments made during the year.		

While additional journal entries can be made, the above summary entries are sufficient to reflect the type of activities and the recording of the revenues and expenses normally incurred by the typical PERS.

A trial balance for the fund at the end of the year is shown in Table 7–17.

TABLE 7–17   Trial Balance—Pension Trust Fund

City of New Example
Pension Trust Fund
Public Employees Retirement System
Trial Balance
December 31, 19X1

	DEBITS	CREDITS
Cash	$ 60,000	
Interest receivable	50,000	
Investments	6,177,000	
Due to General Fund		$ 20,000
Accrued expenses		15,000
Actuarial present value of projected benefits payable to current retirants and beneficiaries		1,102,000
Actuarial present value of projected benefits payable to terminated vested participants		269,000
Actuarial present value of credited projected benefits for active employees—member contributions		2,270,500
Actuarial present value of credited projected benefits for active employees—employer-financed portion		2,270,500
Unfunded actuarial present value of credited projected benefits	300,000	
Revenues—pension contributions—members		200,000
Revenues—pension contributions—employer		200,000
Revenues—investments		495,000
Revenues—gain on sale of investments		10,000
Expenses—retirement annuities	230,000	
Expenses—operating costs	35,000	
	$6,852,000	$6,852,000

Closing entries

At the end of the accounting period, several closing/adjusting entries must be made in order to complete the recording of the activities of a Pension Trust Fund. The first entry closes the contributions received during the period into the appropriate projected benefit obligation account:

Revenues—pension contributions—members	200,000	
Revenues—pension contributions—employer	200,000	
Actuarial present value of credited projected benefits for active employees—member contributions		200,000
Actuarial present value of credited projected benefits for active employees—employer-financed portion		200,000
To close the contribution accounts into the appropriate projected benefit obligation accounts.		

The second entry reduces the pension obligation account by the benefits paid during the year:

Actuarial present value of projected benefits payable to current retirants and beneficiaries	230,000	
Expenses—retirement annuities		230,000
To reduce the pension obligation account by the benefits paid during the year.		

The third and fourth entries adjust the present value of the pension fund balance accounts (the pension benefit obligation accounts) by the amount of the earnings for the current year included in the present value calculations. The account that reflects the relationship between the net assets of the fund and the present value of the benefits is also adjusted by the difference between the actual earnings of the fund and the amounts assumed in the present value calculations. Since the pension fund balance accounts represent the present value of the pension benefits, each must be updated to reflect the increase or decrease during the period. As explained earlier, this involves many complex calculations. For our purposes, the appropriate amounts are presented in the journal entries:

Revenues—investments	495,000	
Revenues—gain on sale of investments	10,000	
Expenses—operating costs		35,000
Excess of investment revenues over operating costs		470,000
To close the investing and operating accounts.		
Excess of investment revenues over operating costs	470,000	
Actuarial present value of projected benefits payable to current retirants and beneficiaries		83,481
Actuarial present value of credited projected benefits payable to terminated vested participants		14,481
Actuarial present value of credited projected benefits for active employees—member contributions		178,889
Actuarial present value of credited projected benefits for active employees—employer-financed portion		178,889
Unfunded actuarial present value of credited projected benefits		14,260
To record the distribution of the net investment earnings over the pension fund balance accounts.		

In the above entry, notice that the investment earnings for the year were in excess of the amount needed to update the pension fund balance accounts for their theoretical growth. As a result, the portion of the fund balance that has not yet been funded had decreased from $300,000 to $285,740 ($300,000 – $14,260).

Financial statements—illustration

The individual financial statements for Pension Trust Funds are a statement of revenues, expenses, and changes in fund balance, and a balance sheet. These are illustrated for 19X1 in Tables 7–18 and 7–19. In addition, you should review

TABLE 7–18   Statement of Revenues, Expenses, and Changes in Fund Balance—Pension Trust Fund

City of New Example
Pension Trust Fund
Public Employees Retirement System
Statement of Revenues, Expenses, and Changes in Fund Balance
For the Year Ended December 31, 19X1

Operating Revenues		
Member contributions	$200,000	
Employer contributions	200,000	
Investment revenue	495,000	
Gain on sale of investments	10,000	
Total operating revenues		$ 905,000
Operating Expenses		
Retirement annuities	$230,000	
Operating costs	35,000	
Total operating expenses		265,000
Net income		640,000
Fund balance at beginning of year*		5,612,000
Fund balance at end of year*		$6,252,000

*The composition of the beginning and ending fund balance is as follows:

	ENDING FUND BALANCE	BEGINNING FUND BALANCE
Actuarial present value of projected benefits payable to current retirants and beneficiaries	$ 955,481	$ 987,000
Actuarial present value of projected benefits payable to terminated vested participants	283,481	269,000
Actuarial present value of credited projected benefits for active employees—member contributions	2,649,389	2,328,000
Actuarial present value of credited projected benefits for active employees—employer-financed portion	2,649,389	2,328,000
Unfunded actuarial present value of credited projected benefits	(285,740)	(300,000)
Total fund balance	$6,252,000	$5,612,000

Information on GASB *Statement No. 25* is included in the "Concluding Comment" at the end of this section.

TABLE 7–19   Balance Sheet—Pension Trust Fund

City of New Example
Pension Trust Fund
Public Employees Retirement System
Balance Sheet
December 31, 19X1

Assets		
Cash	$ 60,000	
Interest receivable	50,000	
Investments	6,177,000	
Total assets		$6,287,000
Liabilities		
Due to General Fund	$ 20,000	
Accrued expenses	15,000	
Total liabilities		(35,000)
Net assets available for benefits		$6,252,000
Fund Balance		
Actuarial present value of projected benefits payable to current retirants and beneficiaries	$ 955,481	
Actuarial present value of projected benefits payable to terminated vested participants	283,481	
Actuarial present value of credited projected benefits for active employees:		
Member contributions	2,649,389	
Employer-financed portion	2,649,389	
Total actuarial present value of credited projected benefits		$6,537,740
Unfunded actuarial present value of credited projected benefits		(285,740)
Total fund balance		$6,252,000

Information on GASB *Statement No. 25* is included in the "Concluding Comment" at the end of this section.

the section on Pension Trust Funds in Chapter 2. The overall reporting process is discussed in Chapter 9.

Concluding Comment

The actuarial information in Table 7–18 is required for the individual fund statements of Pension Trust Funds. When these funds are combined with the other funds in the annual report of a governmental unit, a single fund balance account entitled Fund balance reserved for employees' retirement system is used. This makes reporting of the fund balance consistent among the funds. When this is done, the actuarial information is presented in the notes to the financial statements. This process is described in greater detail in Chapter 9.

The above discussion of pension plan accounting is, by design, an overview. We have described the basic concepts involved in the area of accounting and financial reporting for Pension Trust Funds. Because of the complexities involved in pension plan accounting, the users of the financial statements must be supplied with extensive notes that fully disclose the provisions of the plan together with is actuarial status. These notes should include such information as a description of the plan, actuarial cost method and assumptions, and funding schedules. In addition, schedules are prepared to report such information as the net assets of the plan for the past ten years and the actuarial present value of credited projected benefits for the past ten years.

As mentioned earlier in this section, the GASB recently issued three statements regarding accounting and reporting for pensions and postemployment healthcare plans administered by defined benefit pension plans. Since the materials presented in this section do not encompass detailed coverage of the calculation of pension expense and postemployment benefits, *Statements 26* and *27* are not discussed further. *Statement No. 25,* however, deals with financial reporting for defined benefit pension plans. This statement does not become effective until fiscal years beginning after June 15, 1996. As a result, the main discussion in this chapter is presented to correspond to NCGA *Statement 6.*

In place of the operating statement illustrated in Table 7–18, GASB will require a statement of changes in plan net assets (see Table 7–19a) and in place of the balance sheet illustrated in Table 7–19, GASB will require a statement of plan net assets (see Table 7–19b). While the information contained in the discussion of operating entries for a PERS was originally intended to provide the financial statements required by NCGA *Statement 6,* the authors feel they will also provide the information needed and note disclosures required under GASB *Statement No. 25,* when combined with additional information. They realize that some of the information provided by the entries in this section is not needed for reporting and note disclosures required by the GASB, but they feel it is needed for a proper evaluation of the financial status of a pension plan.

One of the more significant differences in the *Statement No. 25* format is that only plan net assets are reported (see Table 7–19b). If one compares this financial statement to that prescribed by NCGA *Statement 6,* the lack of a fund balance and an over- or underfunded account is obvious. While funding information is included in the notes, the financial statement itself does not report this important comparison. This is a serious deficiency. Another significant difference between the two statements is that NCGA *Statement 6* requires that investments be reported at cost (or amortized cost), whereas GASB *Statement No. 25* requires that investments be reported at fair market value.

When solving end of chapter materials, use NCGA *Statement No. 6* procedures, unless otherwise instructed.

TABLE 7-19a   Statement of Changes in Plan Net Assets

Columbine Retirement System
Statements of Changes in Plan Net Assets
As of June 30, 19X2 and 19X1
(Dollar Amounts in Thousands)

	STATE EMPLOYEES	SCHOOL DISTRICTS	MUNICIPAL EMPLOYEES	19X2 TOTAL	19X1 TOTAL
Additions					
Contributions:					
Employer	$ 137,916	$ 157,783	$ 19,199	$314,898	$ 284,568
Employer—long-term		102		102	102
Plan member	90,971	117,852	16,828	225,651	216,106
Total contributions	228,887	275,737	36,027	540,651	500,776
Investment income:					
Net appreciation (depreciation) in fair value of investments	(241,408)	(344,429)	(35,280)	(621,117)	788,913
Interest	157,371	225,446	23,098	405,915	422,644
Dividends	123,953	177,654	18,191	319,798	560,848
Real estate operating income, net	10,733	15,383	1,575	27,691	25,296
	50,649	74,054	7,584	132,287	1,797,701
Less investment expense	54,081	61,872	7,529	123,482	500,674
Net investment income	(3,432)	12,182	55	8,805	1,297,027
Total additions	225,455	287,919	36,082	549,456	1,797,803
Deductions					
Benefits	170,434	172,787	18,073	361,294	325,881
Refunds of contributions	15,750	13,200	3,671	32,621	38,406
Administrative expense	4,984	5,703	694	11,381	12,681
Total deductions	191,168	191,690	22,438	405,296	376,968
Net increase	34,287	96,229	13,644	144,160	1,420,835
Net assets available for benefits:					
Beginning of year	3,649,858	5,105,636	606,504	9,361,998	7,941,163
End of year	$3,684,145	$5,201,865	$620,148	$9,506,158	$9,361,998

Source: GASB *Statement No. 25,* "Financial Reporting Fax Defined Benefit Pension Plans and Note Disclosure for Defined Contribution Plans," pp. 102–103.

GOVERNMENT ACCOUNTING IN PRACTICE—THE LOUISIANA STATE EMPLOYEES' RETIREMENT SYSTEM

The Louisiana State Employees' Retirement System (the System) follows the provisions of NCGA *Statement 6* for reporting purposes Tables 7–20 and 7–21 are the balance sheet and operating statement for the System. Notice the diverse investments listed in the balance sheet in Table 7–20. The System has many different forms of investments that range from common stocks to real estate pools. The lia-

TABLE 7–19b   Statement of Plan Net Assets

Columbine Retirement System
Statements of Plan Net Assets
As of June 30, 19X2 and 19X1
(Dollar Amounts in Thousands)

	STATE EMPLOYEES	SCHOOL DISTRICTS	MUNICIPAL EMPLOYEES	19X2 TOTAL	19X1 TOTAL
Assets					
Cash and short-term investments	$ 66,129	$ 116,988	$ 27,014	$ 210,131	$ 440,146
Receivables:					
Employer	16,451	18,501	2,958	37,910	45,770
Employer—long-term		986		986	1,088
Interest and dividends	33,495	48,299	4,951	86,745	81,183
Total receivables	49,946	67,786	7,909	125,641	128,041
Investments, at fair value:					
U.S. government obligations	541,289	780,541	80,001	1,401,831	1,571,404
Municipal bonds	33,585	48,416	4,969	86,970	86,417
Domestic corporate bonds	892,295	1,217,251	191,801	2,301,347	1,961,288
Domestic stocks	1,276,533	1,784,054	183,893	3,244,480	3,230,446
International stocks	461,350	665,269	68,187	1,194,806	1,187,703
Mortgages	149,100	209,099	24,453	382,652	319,745
Real estate	184,984	266,748	27,350	479,082	420,806
Venture capital	26,795	38,638	3,960	69,393	37,120
Total investments	3,565,931	5,010,016	584,614	9,160,561	8,814,929
Properties, at cost, net of accumulated depreciation of $5,164 and $4,430, respectively	6,351	8,924	1,040	16,315	16,093
Total assets	3,688,357	5,203,714	620,577	9,512,648	9,399,209
Liabilities					
Refunds payable and other	4,212	1,849	429	6,490	37,211
Net assets held in trust for pension benefits (A schedule of funding progress for each plan is presented on page ——.)	$3,684,145	$5,201,865	$620,148	$9,506,158	$9,361,998

Source: GASB *Statement No. 25,* "Financial Reporting for Defined Benefit Pension Plans and Note Disclosures for Defined Contribution Plans," pp. 100–101.

bility DROP deposits due retirees is a payable arising from a special retirement program called the DROP Program. Notice also that the Unfunded actuarial present value of credited projected benefits is in excess of $2 billion. This amount is almost equal to the net assets of the fund. Recently the citizens of Louisiana approved a constitutional amendment to fully fund all state pension plans. While

TABLE 7–20   Balance Sheet—Pension Trust Fund—Louisiana State Employees' Retirement System

Louisiana State Employees' Retirement System
Balance Sheet
June 30, 19X1

Assets	
Cash	$ 587,476
Investments:	
Bonds and U.S. Treasury notes	1,499,587,321
Common stocks	490,793,975
Repurchase agreements	258,718,293
Real estate investment pools	80,578,170
Real estate debt securities	11,408,597
Commercial paper and short term investments	42,895,391
Convertible preferred stock	6,390,043
Receivables:	
Unsettled investment sales	41,142,501
Accrued interest and dividends	26,573,690
Employer contributions	11,831,626
Member contributions	8,456,524
Other	140,660
Land, building and equipment, net of accumulated depreciation	5,436,954
Total assets	2,484,541,221
Accounts payable and other accrued liabilities	1,107,272
DROP deposits due retirees	2,412,337
Net assets available for benefits	$2,481,021,612
Fund Balance	
Pension benefit obligation:	
Actuarial present value of projected benefits payable to current retirants and beneficiaries	$2,155,577,301
Actuarial present value of projected benefits payable to terminated vested participants	17,883,293
Actuarial present value of credited projected benefits for active employees:	
Member contributions	674,210,732
Employer-financed portion	1,651,641,004
Total actuarial present value of credited projected benefits	4,499,312,330
Unfunded actuarial present value of credited projected benefits	2,018,290,718
Total fund balance	$2,481,021,612

The accompanying notes are an integral part of the financial statements.

Source: Adapted from a recent Comprehensive Annual Financial Report of the Louisiana State Employees' Retirement System.

this is a long-term process, it does show concern over the unfunded status of the plans.

The operating statement of the System plan follows the same general format illustrated in the text. Notice that revenues are categorized as contributions, investment income, and other. In addition, notice that operations of the fund increased fund balance by over $200,000,000.

TABLE 7–21   **Statement of Revenues, Expenses, and Changes in Fund Balance—Pension Trust Fund—Louisiana State Employees' Retirement System**

Louisiana State Employees' Retirement System
Statement of Revenues, Expenses, and Changes in Fund Balance
For the Year Ended June 30, 19X1

Operating Revenues	
Contributions:	
Employer	$ 142,951,649
Member	102,446,164
Investment income:	
Interest	134,509,465
Dividends	23,063,501
Gain on sale of investments, net	69,307,045
Other operating revenues:	
Judges supplemental benefits	1,512,027
Legislative appropriations	3,426,547
Transfers from other systems	579,699
Purchase of service and repayment of refunds	1,907,130
Interest on prior service, delinquent contributions, and other	1,056,639
Total operating revenues	480,759,866
Operating Expenses	
Benefits paid to members and beneficiaries	240,622,226
Refunds to members and transfers of service to other systems	22,955,119
Administrative expenses	4,279,820
Other expenses	478,160
Total operating expenses	268,335,325
Net revenue in excess of expenses	212,424,541
Fund balance, beginning of year	2,268,597,071
Fund balance, end of year	$2,481,021,612

The accompanying notes are an integral part of the financial statements.

Source: Adapted from a recent Comprehensive Annual Financial Report of the Louisiana State Employees' Retirement System.

REVIEW QUESTIONS

Section I

Q7–1   What is the cause-and-effect relationship between the revenues and expenses of a proprietary fund?

Q7–2   Why are the revenues and expenditures of governmental-type funds "independent" of each other?

Q7–3   When should an Internal Service Fund be used?

Q7–4   What is a *flexible budget?*

Q7–5   How does the *fund equity* section of a balance sheet of an Internal Service Fund differ from that of a governmental-type fund?

Q7–6   Why is depreciation recorded as an expense in Internal Service Funds, but not as an expenditure in governmental-type funds?

Section II

Q7–7   What is the difference between an *Enterprise Fund* and an *Internal Service Fund?*

Q7–8   Is there a cause-and-effect relationship between the revenues and expenses of an Enterprise Fund? Explain your answer.

Q7–9   Why is depreciation considered to be an expense for Enterprise Funds?

Q7–10   What are revenue bonds?

Section III

Q7–11   What is a PERS?

Q7–12   How are the operations of PERS controlled?

Q7–13   Explain the difference, if any, between the following actuarial present value computations:
   1. Projected benefits payable to current retirants and beneficiaries
   2. Projected benefits payable to terminated vested participants
   3. Credited projected benefits for active employees
   4. Unfunded actuarial present value of credited projected benefits

Q7–14   What types of financial reporting are usually done for PERS?

Q7–15   What are two major differences in reporting for Pension Trust Funds under NCGA *Statement 6* and GASB *Statement No. 25*?

CASES

C7–1   The City of Iota recently incorporated and, therefore, became a separate legal entity in Bower County. You have been hired as the first chief administrative officer. Your task is to determine how to account for the various activities in which the government is involved.

The first activity is a hotel-motel tax that is dedicated to building a new sports arena. The mayor, Phinius T. Bower, feels that these activities should be accounted for in a Capital Projects Fund. He said that he remembered from his college days at Old War-Horse U. that Capital Projects Funds are used for construction of major fixed assets. After examining the situation, you find that the city has arranged temporary financing from the Only National Bank in Cut-Off. Permanent financing will be achieved through a bond issue when the project is completed.

The second is a printing office. This office has extensive up-to-date facilities and prepares documents for the city. In addition, to help finance the cost of the equipment and operating costs, the city also does private printing and copying for various companies and citizens. Mayor Bower suggests that you use a Special Revenue Fund for these activities because the revenues from the outside will be used for a specific purpose.

The third is a central purchasing function. In order to insure that the city obtains the best possible price for its supplies and equipment, all purchases must be made through the Purchasing Department. Mayor Bower also stated that he felt the city could use its Purchasing Department for control purposes. He said that when he attended a meeting of mayors in Gulfberg last year, one of the speakers discussed controlling purchases through a centralized purchasing function.

Write a report to the mayor on your suggestions for the above items.

C7–2   You have recently been asked by your undergraduate university to make a presentation to an accounting class. After a lengthy thought process, you decide to discuss governmental financial reporting. Carefully review the financial statements for the Internal Service Funds (Tables 7–5 through 7–7), and contrast them with the statements prepared for the Capital Projects Funds (Tables 6–9 and 6–10). Identify similarities and differences. You should write a paper to present to the students.

C7–3   Ms. Mary Ann LaPlace, the president of the city council of West Sunview, has asked that you assist the council in setting the pricing policy for its only Internal Service Fund. The fund is the Motor Pool Fund, and its operations are similar to those described in the illustration in this chapter.

Write a report to Ms. LaPlace and outline the options the city has with respect to pricing the use of the vehicles in the Motor Pool Fund. After you complete your report, write a recommendation of one of your choices and justify it.

C7–4   Laserville has decided to change its accounting records and prepare all of its financial statements according to governmental generally accepted accounting principles. Your first task as a consultant is to advise them regarding the options available for their pension plan. The city manager, Mr. Tim Flower, has been discussing this matter with the city managers of several cities in his state. As far as he can determine, there are several methods available; however, he does not understand how there can be more than one acceptable way to account for something. Explain the current situation in pension accounting and then summarize the procedures as suggested by NCGA *Statement 6* and GASB *Statement No. 25*.

EXERCISES

Section I

E7-1 (Interpreting the operating statement for an Internal Service Fund)
The City of New Example has an operating policy that its Internal Service Funds will operate on a break-even basis—that is, revenues will equal expenses. Did the Motor Pool Fund illustrated in this chapter operate at a break-even level during 19X1? Explain.

E7-2 The following transactions were incurred in establishing a central purchasing fund (an Internal Service Fund):
1. The General Fund made a permanent transfer of $100,000 to establish the fund.
2. The Purchasing Fund billed revenues of $200,000.
3. The Purchasing Fund incurred expenses of $300,000. *Hint:* Credit Cash for $250,000 and Accumulated depreciation for $50,000.
4. The General Fund subsidized the operations of the Purchasing Fund by transferring an additional $100,000.

Record the above entries and identify the fund(s) and account group(s) used.

E7-3 (Explanation of the relationship of a fixed asset to depreciation)
Since the Motor Pool Fund illustrated in this chapter records the acquisition of an automobile by debiting an asset account, does the cost of that automobile ever enter into the determination of income? Explain.

E7-4 (Fill-in-the-blanks)
1. An Internal Service Fund is used when goods and/or services are furnished to _____ .
2. A budget that is based on the level of activity attained in a fund is called a _____ .
3. The _____ basis of accounting is used in Internal Service Funds.
4. A permanent transfer of equity to an Internal Service Fund is credited to _____ in the Internal Service Fund.
5. When an Internal Service Fund acquires a truck, the account that is debited is _____ .

E7-5 (True or false)
Indicate whether the following statements are true or false. If any are false, indicate why each is false.
1. There is a direct cause-and-effect relationship between the revenues and expenses of an Internal Service Fund.
2. Internal Service Funds are used to account for activities that involve providing services and/or products to the general public.

3.   Internal Service Funds use the modified accrual basis of accounting.
4.   All capital received by an Internal Service Fund is credited to the Fund balance account.
5.   A flexible budget is used to control Internal Service Funds.
6.   The budget is not usually recorded for an Internal Service Fund.
7.   Fixed assets used in an Internal Service Fund are reported in the General Fixed Assets Account Group.
8.   Depreciation expense is recorded in an Internal Service Fund that uses fixed assets.
9.   A net income figure is calculated for Internal Service Funds.
10. Contributed capital for an Internal Service Fund includes the accumulated earnings since the date of establishment of the fund.

Section II

E7–6   (True or false)
Indicate whether the following statements are true or false. If any are false, indicate why each is false.
1.   Enterprise Funds are used to account for the construction of major highways.
2.   User charges must be assessed if an Enterprise Fund is to be used for accounting purposes.
3.   Flexible budgets are used to control Enterprise Fund operations.
4.   Depreciation is not recorded in an Enterprise Fund.
5.   Estimated bad debts are charged to an expense account in an Enterprise Fund.
6.   Restricted assets are not separately reported on an Enterprise Fund balance sheet.
7.   The difference between restricted assets and liabilities payable from restricted assets must be reported in a reserve account on an Enterprise Fund balance sheet.
8.   Permanent transfers of capital to an Enterprise Fund are reported in a Fund balance account.

E7–7   (Billings and collections between an Enterprise Fund and the General Fund)
A city used an Enterprise Fund to provide services to the General Fund. A total of $10,000 was billed and collected thirty days later.
Prepare the journal entries necessary to record the above information and label the fund(s) and account group(s) used.

E7–8   (Closing entries for an Enterprise Fund)
The Municipal Park Fund for the Directory Township had the following preclosing trial balance:

Directory Township
Enterprise Fund
Municipal Park Fund
Preclosing Trial Balance
June 30, 19X1

Cash	$ 500	
Membership dues receivable	200	
Land	10,000	
Equipment	2,000	
Accumulated depreciation—equipment		$ 400
Accounts payable		200
Contribution from municipality		10,000
Retained earnings		800
Revenues from fees		5,000
Salaries expense	3,000	
Depreciation expense—equipment	100	
Utilities expense	400	
Miscellaneous expense	200	
	$16,400	$16,400

REQUIRED: 1. Prepare the closing entry or entries necessary at June 30, 19X1.
           2. Did the fund earn a profit during 19X1? How can you tell?

E7–9 (Fill-in-the-blanks)
   1. A _____ is used to account for goods and/or services provided only to other governmental units.
   2. The activities of a government-owned utility are usually accounted for in a(n) _____ .
   3. Enterprise Fund accounting follows a _____ measurement focus.
   4. Bonds that are serviced from specific revenues are called _____ .
   5. Customers' deposits are usually classified as _____ .
   6. Reserves are reported in the _____ section of an Enterprise Fund balance sheet.

E7–10 (Comparison of accounting for long-term debt and acquisition of fixed assets, using governmental-type funds and proprietary-type funds.)
   The Village of d'East acquired a computer for $300,000. The computer was financed through a bond issue.
   Prepare the journal entries necessary to record the above events assuming the computer was acquired using (1) the General Fund and (2) an Enterprise Fund. Also label the fund(s) and account group(s) used.

Section III

E7–11   (Description of net assets and fund balance)

Refer to the trial balance in Table 7–16. Calculate the fund balance and the net assets for the Public Employees Retirement System. Are the two amounts equal? Why or why not?

E7–12   (Explanation of balance sheet items)

Explain the difference, if any, between the balance sheet categories Unfunded actuarial present value of credited projected benefits and Net assets available for future benefit credits. How does this relate to the fund balance of a PERS?

E7–13   (True or false)

Indicate whether the following statements are true or false. If any are false, indicate why each is false.

1.   NCGA *Statement 6* is the only way to account for pension funds.
2.   If GASB *Statement No. 25* is used to account for a pension fund, there is no actual "fund balance" account.
3.   The major pension fund balance accounts under NCGA *Statement 6* are based on present value calculations.
4.   Vested benefits are benefits not earned by employees.
5.   Net assets available for future benefit credits represents an excess of the fund balance accounts over the net assets of the fund.
6.   Contributions from members of a PERS are recorded as revenues.
7.   Retirement annuity payments increase the assets of a Pension Trust Fund.
8.   Retirement annuity payments decrease the Actuarial present value of projected benefits payable to current retirants and beneficiaries.

E7–14   (Definition of terms)

Define the following terms as they relate to Pension Trust Funds:

1.   Actuarial present value of projected benefits payable to current retirants and beneficiaries.
2.   Actuarial present value of projected benefits payable to terminated vested participants.
3.   Actuarial present value of credited projected benefits for active employees.
4.   Unfunded actuarial present value of credited projected benefits.
5.   Net assets available for future benefit credits.

E7–15   (Financial reporting for a PERS)

Obtain a copy of a set of financial statements for a PERS and a governmental unit that reports the PERS as part of its Comprehensive Annual Financial Report (CAFR). Compare the reporting with that described in the text.

PROBLEMS

Section I

P7–1   Journal entries and financial statements for an Internal Service Fund
The following entries and financial statements relate to Thomasville. (Assume a voucher system is used.)

19X1   1. The General Fund made a permanent contribution of capital to the Data Processing Fund (an Internal Service Fund). This fund will provide data processing services to all governmental units for a fee. The initial contribution was $2 million.
2. The fund paid $1.9 million for a Z109 computer.
3. Supplies costing $1,500 were purchased on credit.
4. Bills totaling $650,000 were sent to the various city departments.
5. Repairs to the computer were made at a coast of $400. A voucher was prepared for that amount.
6. Collections from the departments for services were $629,000.
7. Salaries of $180,000 were paid to the employees.
8. Vouchers totaling $1,900 were paid.
9. As of the end of the period, $300 of supplies had not been used.
10. Depreciation on the computer was $250,000.
11. The city charged the computer center $2,000 for the rental of office space and $500 for the rental of office equipment for the year. This amount was not paid at the end of the year.
12. Miscellaneous expenses not paid by the end of the year totaled $700. These amounts were owed to businesses outside the governmental unit.

REQUIRED: 1. Prepare the journal entries necessary to record the above information in the Data Processing Fund.
2. Prepare a statement of revenues, expenses, and changes in retained earnings for the Data Processing Fund for 19X1 and a balance sheet as of December 31, 19X1.

P7–2   (Journal entries for several funds and account groups)
The following transactions were incurred by the City of Cut-Off Ridge. Record the journal entry (entries) necessary for each and identify the fund(s) and account group(s) used. If no entry is required, write "None" next to the transaction number.
1. The mayor hired a new chief financial officer for the city.
2. The police department ordered ten new cruisers at a cost of $14,000 each.
3. The Central Computer Fund billed the General Fund for $2,000 of services.
4. The Central Computer Fund acquired a new computer at a cost of $450,000. The old computer was sold for $50,000; it originally cost $245,000 and had a book value of $45,000 at the time of the sale.

5. The fund used to account for the construction of a new bridge over the Miss River received a progress billing from the contractor for $500,000. The bill, less an 8 percent retainage, was paid.
6. Interest of $100,000 and principal of $1,000,000 was paid on general obligation bonds. The bond indenture required a separate accounting for these types of transactions.
7. The police cruisers ordered in number 2 above arrived. The total invoice cost was $139,000. This amount was paid to the dealer.
8. The city collected $200,000 of gasoline taxes. These taxes must be used to repair city streets. A separate accounting is required.
9. The mayor was paid his salary of $5,000.
10. The General Fund budget was amended. The appropriation for supplies was increased $45,000.

P7–3 (Preparing a budget for an Internal Service Fund)

The City of Adolphusville established a Central Computer Service Fund (an Internal Service Fund) during 19X0. The trial balance for the fund after all nominal accounts were closed and a statement of revenues, expenses, and changes in retained earnings are presented below:

City of Adolphusville
Internal Service Fund
Central Computer Service Fund
Trial Balance
June 30, 19X1

	DEBITS	CREDITS
Cash	$ 7,000	
Due from other funds	38,000	
Supplies	23,000	
Office equipment	75,000	
Accumulated depreciation—office equipment		$ 7,500
Computer	1,385,500	
Accumulated depreciation—computer		76,000
Accounts payable		9,000
Accrued expenses		4,000
Due to Special Revenue Fund		32,000
Advance from Special Revenue Fund		400,000
Contributed capital from municipality		1,000,000
	$1,528,500	$1,528,500

Note: 1. The advance is due in five annual payments of $80,000, beginning on December 31, 19X1. Simple interest of 8 percent is calculated and due on December 31 of each year. Payment was held up because of a cash shortage. The advance was made on July 1, 19X0. The fund must make both interest payments by June 30, 19X2. In addition, the principal payment due on December 31, 19X1, may be delayed until June 30, 19X2. The extension of terms was agreed to by the city management to allow the fund to get its operations started.

City of Adolphusville
Internal Service Fund
Central Computer Service Fund
Statement of Revenues, Expenses, and Changes
in Retained Earnings
For the Year Ended June 30, 19X1

Operating revenues:		
Billings to departments	$592,300	
Miscellaneous	3,000	
Total revenues		$595,300
Operating expenses:		
Salaries	$350,000	
Supplies	78,000	
Utilities	65,000	
Interest	32,000	
Depreciation—office equipment	7,500	
Depreciation—computer	76,000	
Total expenses		608,500
Operating loss		($ 13,200)
Operating transfers:		
From General Fund		13,200
Net income		$ -0-
Fund balance at beginning of year		-0-
Fund balance at end of year		$ -0-

Additional information:

1. Management of the computer fund expects to bill the departments for 10,000 hours of operating time in fiscal year 19X1–X2.
2. Supplies and utilities will vary directly with the number of hours the computer is used (billed). The computer was used 8,000 hours in fiscal year 19X0–X1.
3. Salaries and depreciation are fixed—that is, they will not change in fiscal 19X1–X2.
4. Miscellaneous revenues of $5,000 (all cash) are expected in fiscal 19X1–X2.
5. All receivables and payables as of June 30, 19X1, will be collected or paid during the year.
6. Ninety-five percent of the billings during fiscal 19X1 will be collected during that year.
7. The supplies inventory will remain the same dollar amount.
8. Accounts payable and accrued expenses at June 30, 19X2, will be $4,000 and $6,000, respectively.
9. Cash should be $11,000 at June 30, 19X2.

REQUIRED: 1.   Prepare a cash budget for the computer fund for fiscal 19X1–X2. Assume the General Fund will not provide any additional transfers, and all payments on the advance and the interest will be delayed until June 30, 19X2. (Round out all calculations to whole dollars.)

                2.   What billing rate should the management of the computer fund charge for fiscal 19X1–X2 (Round your answer to cents.)

P7–4   (Journal entries for several funds and statements for an Internal Service Fund)

The following transactions relate to Pleasant Village for the fiscal year ended June 30, 19X2:

1. The city established a Central Supplies Fund for the purpose of handling the acquisition and disbursement of supplies. The General Fund made a capital contribution of $60,000 to form the initial capital for the fund.

2. The General Fund ordered equipment for the police department. The total cost was $34,000.

3. The Central Supplies Fund purchased supplies for $25,000. This amount will be paid later.

4. The Debt Service Fund paid $120,000 of interest that had not previously been recorded.

5. Central Supplies Fund billings to departments totaled $30,000. These supplies cost $22,000. Record the cost of the supplies as an expense.

6. A Capital Projects Fund paid a contractor $100,000. The contractor had previously submitted a progress billing for $110,000. The difference between the billing and the amount paid is the retained percentage. The billing was properly recorded when received by the fund.

7. The Central Supplies Fund acquired office equipment for $2,000. A 90-day note was signed for that amount.

8. Collections from the departments by the Central Supplies Fund totaled $28,000.

9. Collections of current special assessments for debt service totaled $50,000.

10. Salaries paid to Central Supplies Fund employees were $20,000.

11. The police department equipment ordered in number 2 was delivered at a cost of $35,000. The invoice price will be paid later. Assume the excess was approved.

12. Depreciation on the office equipment of the Central Supplies Fund was $400.

13. Old office furniture used by the governmental unit was scrapped, with no cash received. The furniture originally cost $2,800.

14. The Central Supplies Fund paid $25,000 to various creditors outside the governmental unit.
15. Interest of $50 is accrued by the Central Supplies Fund.

REQUIRED: 1. Prepare all the journal entries necessary to record the above transactions and identify the fund(s) and account group(s) used.
2. Prepare a statement of revenues, expenses, and changes in retained earnings for the Central Supplies Fund for fiscal 19X1–X2 and a balance sheet as of June 30, 19X2.

Section II

P7–5 (Journal entries and financial statements for an Enterprise Fund)

The following transactions relate to New Louie City's Municipal Airport Fund for the fiscal year ended June 30, 19X1:

1. The General Fund made a permanent contribution of $3 million for working capital to start a municipal airport. The city used part of that money, together with the proceeds from a $25 million revenue bond issue, to purchase an airport from a private company. The fair market value of the assets and liabilities were as follows:

Accounts receivable	$ 8,000
Land	21,000,000
Buildings	5,000,000
Equipment	1,800,000
Accounts payable	12,000

The city purchased the airport for the fair market value of its net assets.

2. Airlines were billed $3,700,000 for rental rights to use ticket counters and landing and maintenance space. Of this amount, $3,690,000 is expected to be collectible.
3. Supplies totaling $1,500 were purchased on credit.
4. Collections from airlines totaled $3,680,000.
5. Salaries of $200,000 were paid to airport personnel.
6. Utility bills totaling $100,000 were paid.
7. A notice was received from the Last District Bankruptcy Court. Air Lussa was declared bankrupt. The airport collected only $1,000 on its bill of $5,000.
8. The airport collected $3 million of permanent contributions from the city to help finance the improvements at the airport.
9. Interest of $2,125,000 was paid to the bondholders.
10. Supplies used during the year totaled $1,200.
11. The General Fund made an advance to the airport of $2 million.

This amount must be repaid within five years. Currently, airport management plans to begin repaying the advance in 19X4.

12. A contract was signed with The Construction Company for the new facilities for a total price of $5 million.
13. Airport management invested $2 million in certificates of deposit.
14. Airport management received $315,000 upon redeeming $300,000 of the certificates of deposit mentioned in number 13.
15. The airport purchased additional equipment for $300,000 cash.
16. Interest expense of $500,000 was accrued at the end of the year.
17. Other accrued expenses totaled $50,000.
18. Depreciation was recorded as follows:

Buildings	$500,000
Equipment	180,000

19. Paid $13,000 of Accounts payable.
20. Received $150,000 of interest revenue.
21. Excess cash of $4.3 million was invested in certificates of deposit.

REQUIRED:
1. Prepare the journal entries necessary to record the above transactions in the Municipal Airport Fund.
2. Prepare a trial balance at June 30, 19X1.
3. Prepare a statement of revenues, expenses, and changes in retained earnings for the 19X0–X1 fiscal year and a balance sheet as of June 30, 19X1.

P7–6 (Journal entries for several funds and account groups)
1. The city council of Gateway City approved its General Fund budget for the year July 1, 19X1–June 30, 19X2. The budget contained the following: revenues, $3,500,000; transfers from other funds of $200,000; transfers to other funds, $500,000; and expenditures, $4,000,000. The city has a fund balance of $2,300,000 at the beginning of the year.
2. During the year, interest of $400,000 and principal of $2,000,000 were paid from resources accumulated for that purpose.
3. The REBAR COMPANY submitted a progress billing for work done on the new city hall. The bill was for $800,000. This was for work done to the end of the year. Bonds were used to finance this project.
4. The Airport Board Fund submitted a bill to the city and to Mid-West Airlines for $200,000 each. The bill was for landing fees for aircraft owned by the two entities.
5. The city sold surplus equipment. The equipment originally cost $45,000. Only $500 was received from the sale. There are no restrictions placed on the use of the $500.

6. Gateway paid the bill received from REBAR less a 10 percent retainage.
7. Gateway paid the bill received from the Airport Board Fund.
8. Books R Us won a suit against the city. Gateway attempted to revoke its store's license so that it could sell the land used by Books to a local theater group. The court gave Books an award of $400,000. This amount will be paid from general tax revenues. An encumbrance was not set up.
9. A bridge over the East River was completed at a total cost of $5,000,000. In previous years, costs of $4,500,000 were recorded. The bridge was paid for from bond proceeds. After paying all bills, $200,000 remained in the construction fund. The bond indenture requires that this amount be transferred into the fund that will service the bonds.
10. The Electric Utility Fund paid $1,200,000 to contractors for various construction jobs currently in process. This amount was not previously recorded. Assume encumbrance accounting is not used.

REQUIRED: Prepare the journal entries to record the above information. Identify each fund and account group used.

P7–7 (Journal entries for several funds and a statement of revenues, expenses, and changes in retained earnings for an Enterprise Fund)

Following are several transactions for Green Valley Village:

19X1
1. The Electric Fund, an Enterprise Fund that supplies electricity to the city, returned part of the original contribution made by the General Fund. The amount returned was $100,000. The General Fund transferred $500,000 to the Electric Fund ten years ago. At that time, the transfer was treated as a permanent contribution by both funds. No other such payments are planned in the future.
2. Police department salaries of $50,000 were paid.
3. A Special Revenue Fund collected $64,000 of taxes previously levied against property holders in the city.
4. The Electric Fund mailed bills of $400,000 to the residents.
5. Two years ago, the city began to construct several housing units. Currently the Iberville Street units are under construction. The contractor submitted a progress billing for $300,000. The total contract price was $3 million. Encumbrance accounting is used. Record the progress billing. Bonds were used to finance this project.
6. Salaries paid to Electric Fund employees totaled $130,000.
7. Collections of electric bills were $385,000.
8. The Electric Fund issued $1 million of two-year notes.
9. To finance the paving of some of the city's streets, $3 million of spe-

cial assessment bonds were issued. Assume the city is liable for these bonds.

10. To provide funds for the construction of new housing units on Fifth Street, $4.5 million of general obligation bonds were issued.
11. Other operating expenses of the Electric Fund were $150,000. Of this amount, $130,000 was paid in cash.
12. The city was billed for $12,000 for electric service.
13. Depreciation on plant and equipment for the Electric Fund was $50,000.
14. Supplies previously ordered by the General Fund were received. The actual cost was $14,000. The order was encumbered for $15,000.

REQUIRED: 1. Prepare all the journal entries necessary to record the above transactions; identify the fund(s) and account group(s) involved.

              2. Prepare a statement of revenues, expenses, and changes in retained earnings for the Electric Fund for 19X1. (Assume that the beginning balance in Retained earnings was $31,400.)

P7–8 (Explanation of basis of accounting and fixed assets for different funds)

The accounting system of the municipality of Kemp is organized and operated on a fund basis. Among the types of funds used are a General Fund, a Special Revenue Fund, and an Enterprise Fund.

a. Explain the basic differences in revenue recognition between the accrual basis of accounting and the modified accrual basis of accounting, as it relates to governmental accounting.
b. What basis of accounting should be used for each of the following funds?

- General Fund
- Special Revenue Funds
- Enterprise Funds

Why?

c. How should fixed assets and long-term liabilities related to the General Fund and to the Enterprise Fund be accounted for?

(AICPA adapted)

Section III

P7–9 (Journal entries and statements for a Pension Trust Fund using NCGA *Statement 6* and GASB *Statement No. 25*)

The City of Saintsville has had an employee pension fund for several years. The following is a trial balance for the fund at December 31, 19X0, and several transactions that occurred during 19X1:

City of Saintsville
Pension Trust Fund
Employees Retirement Fund
Trial Balance
December 31, 19X0

	DEBITS	CREDITS
Cash	$ 52,500	
Investment income receivable	210,000	
Investments	50,575,000	
Accrued Expenses		$ 12,000
Actuarial present value of projected benefits payable to current retirants and beneficiaries		20,000,600
Actuarial present value of projected benefits payable to terminated vested participants		8,600,000
Actuarial present value of credited projected benefits for active employees—member contributions		7,850,000
Actuarial present value of credited projected benefits for active employees—employer-financed portion		14,896,600
Unfunded actuarial present value of credited projected benefits	521,700	
	$51,359,200	$51,359,200

19X1

1. Contributions from the General Fund totaled $750,000; included in this amount was $258,750 from the employees and $491,250 from the city.
2. Investments costing $500,000 were purchased.
3. Income earned from investments was $4,800,000. Of this amount, $4,500,000 was in cash. This included the investment income that was accrued at the end of 19X0.
4. Employee retirement benefits of $3,500,000 were paid.
5. Additional investments of $1,100,000 were acquired.
6. Several employees retired during 19X1. The amount that should be transferred to the current accounts—members and employer are $2,088,975 and $3,966,025, respectively.
7. Costs of operating the pension plan were $175,000; of this amount $150,000 was paid in cash and the remainder was accrued expenses. The accrued expenses at the beginning of the year were also paid.
8. Close the contribution revenue accounts to the appropriate fund balance accounts.
9. Close the retirement benefits expense to the appropriate fund balance account.

10. Close the other revenue and expense accounts to the "Excess of investment revenues over operating costs" account.
11. Close the Excess account established in number 10 to the fund balance accounts in the following percentages:

. . . current retirants and beneficiaries	38%
. . . vested participants	17
. . . member contributions	15
. . . employer-financed portion	29

Hint: Remember to watch for an adjustment in the "unfunded" account.

REQUIRED:
1. Prepare the journal entries necessary to record the above transactions in the pension fund, using NCGA *Statement 6* as a guide.
2. Prepare a statement of revenues, expenses, and changes in fund balance and a balance sheet for the fund for 19X1.
3. Is this fund in good shape financially? Explain.
4. Assume the market value of the investments on December 31, 19X1, is $53 million and the cost of the investments was equal to their market value at December 31, 19X0. Prepare a statement of changes in plan net assets and a statement of plan net assets in accordance with the provisions of GASB *Statement No. 25.*

P7–10 (Journal entries for several funds and account groups)

Following are several transactions for the Village of Sol:

19X1
1. Supplies of $15,000 were ordered by the General Fund.
2. Property taxes of $325,000 were assessed through a Special Revenue Fund. Of this amount, $290,000 is expected to be collected.
3. Contributions to the PERS from the General Fund were $150,000. An equal amount was deducted from the salaries of the city workers. Assume that the entire payroll was $1 million and that $200,000 was withheld and recorded as "Due to U.S. Government." The entire amount due was paid to the pension fund.
4. Collections of water bills by the Water Utility Fund were $1,300,000. Of this amount, $100,000 was from the General Fund. Assume that any revenue/expenditure had previously been recorded.
5. The General Fund made its annual payment to a Debt Service Fund, $250,000 of which $200,000 was for principal. Assume that this amount was not encumbered.
6. Interest of $100,000 and principal of $100,000 were paid by a Debt Service Fund. Assume that no previous entries were made for these amounts.
7. Interest of $50,000 was paid by the Electric Utility Fund on outstanding bank loans.
8. New furniture was received for the mayor's office. The actual cost

was $30,000. An encumbrance was set up for $30,000 when the order was placed.

9. Benefits paid to retired employees were $50,000.
10. Property tax receivables totaling $500 were written off as uncollectible in the Special Revenue Fund.

REQUIRED: Prepare all the journal entries necessary to record the above transactions and identify the fund(s) and account group(s) used.

P7–11   (Preparation of a balance sheet for a Pension Trust Fund)
The following information is available for the City of Cod:

Cash	$180,000
Accrued expenses	56,000
Accounts payable	33,000
Actuarial present value of credited projected benefits for active employees—member contributions	4,350,000
Member contributions	340,000
Interest revenue	250,000
Actuarial present value of credited projected benefits for active employees—employer-financed portion	4,360,000
Loss on sale of investment securities	30,000
Interest receivable	20,000
Due to other funds	54,000
Actuarial present value of projected benefits payable to current retirants and beneficiaries	1,234,000
Investments	9,765,000
Operating costs	42,000
Retirement annuities	987,000
Actuarial present value of projected benefits payable to terminated vested participants	743,000

REQUIRED: 1. Prepare a balance sheet for the City of Cod Pension Trust Fund as of June 30, 19X2. Use the format in NCGA *Statement 6* as a guide.
2. Assuming the fair market value of the investments is $10 million, prepare a statement of plan net assets. Use the format in GASB *Statement No. 25* as a guide.

P7–12   (Adjusting and correcting entries for several funds)
With the exception of the following events, the City of Lizabethville's books were maintained according to GAAP. Prepare any necessary adjusting or correcting entries based upon the information given and identify the fund(s) and account group(s) used. The current year is 19X1.

1. Interest of $149,000 had been earned by general obligation bondholders. This amount, together with $21,000 more, would be paid in February 19X2. No entries were made for these amounts.
2. The General Fund paid $200,000 in cash to the PERS for the govern-

mental employees. The city contributed $165,000 of the total. The entry in the PERS to record the receipt was:

Cash	200,000	
Revenues—pension contribution		200,000

3. A general obligation bond issue was sold by a Capital Projects Fund for $3,050,000. The face value of the bonds is $3 million. Local laws permit the fund to use the premium for construction costs. The only entry made for the sale of the bonds was recorded in the Capital Projects Fund as follows:

Cash	3,050,000	
Bonds payable		3,000,000
Premium on bonds payable		50,000

4. The city purchased ten police cars for a total of $200,000. The only entry made for the purchase was recorded in the General Fund as follows:

Automobiles	200,000	
Cash		200,000

5. Revenue bonds with a face value of $8,000,000 were issued by the Municipal Electric Fund, an Enterprise Fund. The entries made for the issuance were recorded as follows:

EF	Cash	8,000,000	
	Proceeds from bond issue		8,000,000
GF	Bonds in Municipal Electric Fund	8,000,000	
	Bonds payable		8,000,000

8

THE GOVERNMENTAL FUND ACCOUNTING CYCLE

> Expendable Trust Funds,
> Nonexpendable Trust Funds,
> Agency Funds, and Special
> Assessment Accounting

LEARNING OBJECTIVES

After completion of this chapter, you should be able to:

1. Explain why and how Expendable Trust Funds are used in governmental accounting
2. Prepare the journal entries normally used in Expendable Trust Funds
3. Prepare financial statements for Expendable Trust Funds
4. Explain why and how Nonexpendable Trust Funds are used in governmental accounting
5. Prepare the journal entries normally used in Nonexpendable Trust Funds
6. Prepare financial statements for Nonexpendable Trust Funds
7. Explain why and how Agency Funds are used in governmental accounting
8. Prepare the journal entries normally used in Agency Funds
9. Prepare financial statements for Agency Funds
10. Define special assessments
11. Explain current accounting and reporting practices with respect to special assessments

In this chapter we will discuss accounting for Expendable Trust Funds, Nonexpendable Trust Funds, Agency Funds, and special assessments. Expendable Trust Funds follow a spending measurement focus and use the modified accrual basis of accounting. Under the modified accrual basis of accounting:

1. Revenues are recognized when they are measurable and available.
2. Expenditures are generally recognized when the associated liability has been incurred (with noted exceptions).
3. Transfers are recognized when the interfund receivable and payable arise.

Nonexpendable Trust Funds follow the capital maintenance measurement focus and use the full accrual basis of accounting. Under the full accrual basis of accounting:

1. Revenues are recognized when they are earned.
2. Expenses are recognized when the related liability is incurred or an asset is used.
3. Transfers are recognized when the interfund receivable and payable arise.

Agency Funds do not report revenues and expenditures (expenses) and do not follow a measurement focus. They do, however, follow the modified accrual basis of accounting.

SECTION I—FIDUCIARY-TYPE FUNDS: EXPENDABLE TRUST FUNDS

In Chapter 2, fiduciary-type are subdivided into Pension Trust, Expendable Trust, Nonexpendable Trust, and Agency Funds. Pension Trust Funds were discussed in Chapter 7. Expendable Trust, Nonexpendable Trust, and Agency Funds are discussed in this chapter.

Definition of Fund

Expendable Trust Funds are generally used to account for resources a governmental unit can spend within the limits of a trust agreement. Sources of these resources are usually (1) a trust that permits the governmental unit to spend both the principal and any income generated by the principal and/or (2) the income generated by a trust whose principal must be maintained intact. As the title indicates, activities of these funds are governed by state and local trust laws. Since the assets of a trust can be used only in accordance with the trust agreement, a separate fund must be established for each individual trust.

Expendable Trust Funds should be established only when a legal trust agreement exists or when required by law. When legal or contractual agreements requiring the use of trusts are not present, the General Fund or a Special Revenue Fund should be used.

Summary of Fund Activities

The operations of Expendable Trust Funds are basically simple. Assets of the fund are recorded in the books when received from the **donor** (the individual establishing the trust) or from a Nonexpendable Trust Fund. These resources are then used within the guidelines established by the trust agreement. Often the most complex aspect of the operation of a trust fund is the determination of what activities can be funded through the assets accumulated. For this reason, a thorough understanding of the trust agreement is important.

Control of Fund Activities

The operations of all trust funds are controlled through the applicable state laws and the provisions of the individual trust agreements. Therefore, the accounting system must be designed to provide the information and reports that permit a review of this stewardship role. Unless legally stipulated, formal integration of the budget into the accounting system is not usually required. In some instances, however, adequate control can be maintained only through the use of the budgetary procedures described for the General Fund. Likewise, the use of encumbrance accounting depends on applicable laws and the need for extensive spending control.

Recognition of revenues and expenditures is determined by the rules established for the governmental-type funds—spending measurement focus, which is consistent with the spendable nature of the assets. Like the governmental-type funds, Expendable Trust Funds also use the modified accrual basis of accounting for determining the timing of the recognition of the revenues and expenditures.

Accounting for Fund Activities

Operating entries

Expendable Trust Funds can be "stand-alone" or linked to a Nonexpendable Trust Fund. In this section we will illustrate a stand-alone Expendable Trust Fund. We will illustrate one linked with a Nonexpendable Trust Fund in Section II. For illustrative purposes, assume that a prominent citizen established an educational trust fund for governmental employees. The trust agreement provides for an initial contribution of $2 million. This amount must be invested, and the principal and any income generated by the investments must be spent on annual scholarships for governmental officials.

In 19X1, receipt of the gift, the original investment, and income from the investments are recorded as follows (amounts assumed):

Cash	2,000,000	
Revenues—donations		2,000,000
To record receipt of gift for scholarships		
Investments	1,500,000	
Cash		1,500,000
To record investment of fund assets.		
Cash	60,000	
Revenues—investments		60,000
To record income from investments.		

If payments for tuition total $300,000, the following entry is made:

Expenditures—scholarships	300,000	
Cash		300,000

To record payment of tuition for students.

Assuming the trust agreement permits reimbursement of any operating expenses, a payment to the General Fund of $300 is recorded as follows:

Entry in the books of the Expendable Trust Fund

Expenditures—operating costs	300	
Cash		300

To record payment of operating costs to General Fund.

Entry in the books of the General Fund

Cash	300	
Expenditures—salaries		300

To record receipt of reimbursement from Expendable Trust Fund.

Accrual of income earned by investments of the Expendable Trust Fund at the end of the year is as follows:

Investment income receivable	10,000	
Revenues—investments		10,000

To accrue revenues earned by investments.

A trial balance for the fund at the end of the year is presented in Table 8–1. In this illustration, we do not use budgetary entries nor did we use encumbrance accounting. Since Expendable Trust Funds are accounted for like governmental-type funds, budgetary entries and encumbrance accounting could be used. However, the activities of this fund are so simple, they are not needed for control purposes.

TABLE 8–1   Trial Balance—Expendable Trust Fund

City of New Example
Expendable Trust Fund
Employees Scholarship Fund
Trial Balance
December 31, 19X1

	DEBITS	CREDITS
Cash	$ 259,700	
Investments	1,500,000	
Investment income receivable	10,000	
Revenues—donations		$2,000,000
Revenues—investments		70,000
Expenditures—scholarships	300,000	
Expenditures—operating costs	300	
	$2,070,000	$2,070,000

Closing entry

At the end of the accounting period, December 31, 19X1, the following entry is necessary to close the books:

Revenues—donations	2,000,000	
Revenues—investments	70,000	
Expenditures—scholarshiops		300,000
Expenditures—operating costs		300
Fund balance		1,769,700

To close revenue and expenditure accounts to
fund balance.

Note: A single closing entry is used in this illustration because a budget was not recorded and there were only a few accounts involved. In more complex situations, the closing process illustrated for the General Fund would be followed.

Financial statements—illustration

The financial statements for Expendable Trust Funds are a statement of revenues, expenditures, and changes in fund balance (operating statement) and a balance sheet. These are illustrated in Tables 8–2 and 8–3. In addition, you should review the section on Expendable Trust Funds in Chapter 2. The overall reporting process is discussed in Chapter 9.

In this illustration, we did not use budgetary entries for the Expendable

TABLE 8–2   Statement of Revenues, Expenditures, and Changes in Fund Balance—Expendable Trust Fund

City of New Example
Expendable Trust Fund
Employees Scholarship Fund
Statement of Revenues, Expenditurres, and Changes in Fund Balance
For the Year Ended December 31, 19X1

Revenues		
Donations	$2,000,000	
Investment revenue	70,000	
Total revenues		$2,070,000
Expenditures		
Scholarships	$ 300,000	
Operating costs	300	
Total expenditures		300,300
Excess of revenues over expenditures		1,769,700
Fund balance at beginning of year		-0-
Fund balance at end of year		$1,769,700

TABLE 8–3   Balance Sheet—Expendable Trust Fund

City of New Example
Expendable Trust Fund
Employees Scholarship Fund
Balance Sheet
December 31, 19X1

Assets	
Cash	$ 259,700
Investments	1,500,000
Investment income receivable	10,000
Total assets	$1,769,700
Fund Balance	
Fund balance	$1,769,700

Trust Fund. Since Expendable Trust Funds are accounted for like governmental-type funds, budgets are sometimes used to control their operations. In this illustration, however, the budget was omitted because of the simplicity of the fund activities. In a more complex situation, a budget would have been recorded and used for control purposes.

GOVERNMENT ACCOUNTING IN PRACTICE— THE CITY OF COLUMBUS, OHIO

The City of Columbus, Ohio, uses Expendable Trust Funds to account for donations or bequests to the city for a specific purpose. The City has eleven such funds, including Prepaid Legal Services, Hare Charity, Columbus Jubilee, Heartmobile Maintenance, and Dysart Paramedic Education. In general, the names of the funds are descriptive of the specific uses of the resources. Generally investment earnings constitute the major portion of revenues. Notice, however, that miscellaneous sources provided about 99 percent of the revenues of the Prepaid Legal Services Fund. All of the funds included in Table 8–4 have an excess of revenues over expenditures, except the Hare Charity Fund. Notice also how simple these statements are when compared with previously illustrated operating statements. This is generally the case for Expendable Trust Funds. Their operations are so narrow in scope that there are very few revenues and expenditures.

The balance sheets for the Expendable Trust Funds listed above are illustrated in Table 8–5. Notice how simple these statements are when compared with previously illustrated balance sheets. This is generally the case for Expendable Trust Funds. Their operations are so narrow in scope that there are very few assets and liabilities. Most of the assets of these funds consist of investments with a few receivables and payables.

TABLE 8–4   Statement of Revenues, Expenditures, and Changes in Fund Balance—Expendable Trust Fund—City of Columbus, Ohio

City of Columbus, Ohio
Combining Statement of Revenues, Expenditures
and Changes in Fund Balances
Fiduciary Fund Type
All Expendable Trust Funds
Year Ended December 31, 19X1

	PREPAID LEGAL SERVICES	HARE CHARITY	COLUMBUS JUBILEE	HEARTMOBILE MAINTENANCE	DYSART PARAMEDIC EDUCATION
Revenues					
Investment earnings	$ 8,714	$ 47,993	$ 28	$ —	$ 5,628
Miscellaneous	1,161,580	19,930	—	205	—
Total revenues	1,170,294	67,923	28	205	5,628
Expenditures					
Current					
General government	1,092,563	578,650	—	—	—
Recreation and parks	—	—	—	—	—
Total expenditures	1,092,563	578,650	—	—	—
Excess (deficiency) of revenues over expenditures	77,731	(510,727)	28	205	5,628
Fund balances at beginning of year	138,483	510,819	655	5,821	153,349
Fund balances at end of year	$ 216,214	$ 92	$683	$6,026	$158,977

Source: Adapted from a recent Comprehensive Annual Financial Report of the City of Columbus, Ohio.

SECTION II—FIDUCIARY-TYPE FUNDS: NONEXPENDABLE TRUST FUNDS

Definition of Fund

A **Nonexpendable Trust Fund** is used to account for the portions of the resources held by a governmental unit, in a trustee capacity, that must be maintained intact—that is, cannot be spent. This is usually the principal amount of a trust. In Section I we discussed the use of an Expendable Trust Fund to account for the portion of the trust principal and income that can be spent by a governmental unit. We will now concentrate on the portion that is *not* spendable.

The same laws that govern the expendable portion of a trust have provi-

TABLE 8–5   Balance Sheet—Expendable Trust Fund—City of Columbus, Ohio

City of Columbus, Ohio
Combining Balance Sheet
Fiduciary Fund Type
All Expendable Trust and Agency Funds
December 31, 19X1

	PREPAID LEGAL SERVICES	HARE CHARITY	COLUMBUS JUBILEE	HEARTMOBILE MAINTENANCE	DYSART PARAMEDIC EDUCATION
Assets					
Cash and cash equivalents					
Cash and investments with treasurer	$286,180	$—	$680	$6,026	$158,337
Cash and investments with fiscal and escrow agents	—	92	—	—	—
Investments, at cost	—	—	—	—	—
Receivables	1,217	—	3	—	640
Due from other funds	—	—	—	—	—
Total assets	287,397	92	683	6,026	158,977
Liabilities					
Accounts payable	71,183	—	—	—	—
Due to other					
Governments	—	—	—	—	—
Funds	—	—	—	—	—
Others	—	—	—	—	—
Total liabilities	71,183	—	—	—	—
Fund Balances					
Fund balances					
Unreserved, undesignated	216,214	92	683	6,026	158,977
Total fund balances	216,214	92	683	6,026	158,977
Total liabilities and fund balances	$287,397	$ 92	$683	$6,026	$158,977

Source: Adapted from a recent Comprehensive Annual Financial Report of the City of Columbus, Ohio.

sions for the nonexpendable portion. Therefore, we must look to the particular trust agreement, and to the applicable state and local laws, for guidance as to the definition of income and principal, permissive investment activity, and so forth.

Summary of Fund Activities

The receipt of the principal from the donor provides resources (cash or investments) to the governmental unit. If not already in investment form, these amounts are invested according to the provisions of the *trust agreement*. As income is received, it is recorded in the Nonexpendable Trust Fund. If the government has the authority to spend it, the income is transferred to an Expendable Trust Fund. The other type of activity usually found in a Nonexpendable Trust Fund is buying and selling investments in order to earn an additional return on the principal.

In some instances a nonexpendable trust will receive rental or business property as a donation. The operations of such a business will be accounted for in the same manner as a commercial-type operation. In this section we will limit our discussion to those instances where the income earned is from investments.

Control of Fund Activities

The operations of all trust funds are controlled through applicable state laws and the provisions of individual trust agreements. Thus the accounting system must be designed to provide information and reports that permit a review of this stewardship role from an accounting and a legal perspective. Unless legally required, the budget is not formally integrated into the accounting system.

The capital maintenance measurement focus is used for Nonexpendable Trust Funds. In addition, the full accrual basis of accounting is followed. Thus the basic accounting principles of Nonexpendable Trust Funds are similar to those of proprietary-type funds. The provisions of GASB *Statement No. 20,* as discussed in the section on Internal Service Funds, also apply to accounting for Nonexpendable Trust Funds.

General Accounting Procedures

Operating entries

To illustrate the activities of a Nonexpendable Trust Fund (Educational Principal Trust Fund) and its associated Expendable Trust Fund (Educational Income Trust Fund), assume a prominent citizen establishes an educational trust fund for governmental employees. The trust agreement provides for an initial contribution of $5 million. This amount will be invested and the income will be used to grant low-interest loans to employees. Contrast this agreement with that illustrated above for an Expendable Trust Fund, in which the entire amount of principal and any income earned are available for spending.

Also assume that the trust agreement provides that if an individual receives a college degree, one half of the loan principal will be canceled. In this situation, the income is transferred to an Expendable Trust Fund. Both the Nonexpendable Trust Fund and the Expendable Trust Fund are included in this illustration.

In 19X1, the original receipt of $5 million and subsequent investment of the entire amount are recorded as follows:

*Entries in the books of the **Nonexpendable** Trust Fund*	Cash	5,000,000	
	Fund balance		5,000,000
	To record receipt of cash to establish an Educational Principal Trust Fund.		
	Investments	5,000,000	
	Cash		5,000,000
	To record investment of fund resources.		

The entry to record $250,000 of investment earnings, of which $200,000 is received in cash during the first six months of the year, is as follows:

*Entry in the books of the **Nonexpendable** Trust Fund*	Cash	200,000	
	Investment income receivable	50,000	
	Revenues—investments		250,000
	To record income earned during the first six months of the year.		

Since the income earned will be transferred to the Expendable Trust Fund, the following entries are required:

*Entries in the books of the **Nonexpendable** Trust Fund*	Operating transfer to Educational Income Trust Fund	250,000	
	Due to Educational Income Trust Fund		250,000
	To record amount owed to the operating fund.		
	Due to Educational Income Trust Fund	200,000	
	Cash		200,000
	To record payment of part of the amount owed to the operating fund.		

*Entries in the books of the **Expendable** Trust Fund*	Due from Educational Principal Trust Fund	250,000	
	Operating transfer from Education Principal Trust Fund		250,000
	To record receivable from Educational Principal Trust Fund for the first six months' income.		
	Cash	200,000	
	Due from Educational Principal Trust Fund		200,000
	To record receipt of cash from Educational Principal Trust Fund.		

Assume that investments that cost $140,000 are sold at a gain of $15,000. The entry to record this sale is as follows:

*Entry in the books of the **Nonexpendable** Trust Fund*	Cash	155,000	
	Investments		140,000
	Fund balance—gain on sale of investments		15,000
	To record sale of investments.		

Notice how the sale is recorded. The total of the receipts is debited to Cash; the cost of the investments is credited to Investments. The difference, a credit, is recorded as Fund balance—gain on sale of investments.

The treatment of gains (or losses) may vary under some circumstances. Whether they are treated as part of trust income or part of trust principal depends on the trust agreement. If no mention is made of how income is defined, applicable local and state laws should be followed. In the above example, we assume that all gains become part of principal, since this is the usual case. If the amount of the gain is *not* part of principal, the gain should be recorded in a revenue account and an operating transfer to the operating fund should be established, like that illustrated above for investment income. In addition, in the operating fund, an operating transfer should also be recorded like that illustrated above.

If educational loans totaling $190,000 are made during 19X1, the following entry is made:

Entry in the books of the **Expendable** *Trust Fund*

Loans receivable	190,000	
Cash		190,000
To record loans made.		

Assume that the total cash collected from investment earnings in the last half of the year is $250,000, of which $50,000 is earnings previously recorded but not received (see entry above). The entry to record this is as follows:

Entry in the books of the **Nonexpendable** *Trust Fund*

Cash	250,000	
Investment income receivable		50,000
Revenues—investments		200,000
To record investment income.		

Additional investment earnings of $40,000 are accrued at the end of the year. The entry to record this is:

Entry in books of the **Nonexpendable** *Trust Fund*

Investment income receivable	40,000	
Revenues—investments		40,000
To record investment earned but not received by year-end.		

The entries necessary to record the amounts owed to the operating fund and the actual transfer of $245,000 are as follows:

Entries in the books of the **Nonexpendable** *Trust Fund*

Operating transfer to Educational Income Trust Fund	240,000	
Due to Educational Income Trust Fund		240,000
To record amount owed to the operating fund.		

Due to Educational Income Trust Fund	245,000	
Cash		245,000

To record payment of part of the amount
owed to the operating fund.

*Entries in
the books of
the **Expend-
able** Trust
Fund*

Due from Educational Principal Trust Fund	240,000	
Operating transfer from Education Principal Trust Fund		240,000

To record receivable from Educational Principal Trust Fund for the last six months' income.

Cash	245,000	
Due from Educational Principal Trust Fund		245,000

To record receipt of cash from Educational
Principal Trust Fund.

Loan repayments during the year amount to $5,000 and interest of $10,000 is earned, of which $5,000 is received in cash. In addition, loan principal of $15,000 is reduced because some students graduated. These events are recorded in the following entry:

*Entry in the
books of the
Expendable
Trust Fund*

Cash	10,000	
Loan interest receivable	5,000	
Loans receivable		5,000
Revenues—loan interest		10,000

To record repayments of loans and interest
earned during 19X1 on the loans outstanding.

*Entry in the
books of the
Expendable
Trust Fund*

Expenditures—loan reductions	15,000	
Loans receivable		15,000

To record reduction in loan principal resulting
from graduation of individuals.

Trial balances for the two funds are presented in Tables 8–6 and 8–7. Notice that there are no operating expenses for the Principal Trust Fund. It is assumed that the terms of the trust agreement specified that the General Fund should absorb all costs of operating the loan trust. Contrast this with the illustration presented in Section I.

Closing entries

At the end of the accounting period, December 31, 19X1, the following entries are made to close the books of the loan funds:

*Entry in the
books of the
**Nonex-
pendable**
Trust Fund*

Revenues—investments	490,000	
Fund balance—gain on sale of investments	15,000	
Operating transfers to Educational Income Trust Fund		490,000
Fund balance		15,000

To close the revenue, gain, and transfer accounts to fund balance.

TABLE 8–6   Trial Balance—Nonexpendable Trust Fund

City of New Example
Nonexpendable Trust Fund
Educational Principal Trust Fund
Trial Balance
December 31, 19X1

	DEBITS	CREDITS
Cash	$ 160,000	
Investments	4,860,000	
Investment income receivable	40,000	
Due to Educational Income Trust Fund		$ 45,000
Fund balance		5,000,000
Revenues—investments		490,000
Fund balance—gain on sale of investments		15,000
Operating transfers to Educational Income Trust Fund	490,000	
	$5,550,000	$5,550.000

TABLE 8–7   Trial Balance—Expendable Trust Fund

City of New Example
Expendable Trust Fund
Educational Income Trust Fund
Trial Balance
December 31, 19X1

	DEBITS	CREDITS
Cash	$265,000	
Due from Educational Principal Trust Fund	45,000	
Loans receivable	170,000	
Loan interest receivable	5,000	
Revenues—loan interest		$ 10,000
Expenditures—loan reductions	15,000	
Operating transfer from Educational Principal Trust Fund		490,000
	$500,000	$500,000

Entries in the books of the Expendable Trust Fund

Operating transfer from Educational Principal Trust Fund	490,000	
Revenues—loan interest	10,000	
Expenditures—loan reductions		15,000
Fund balance		485,000

To close the revenue, expenditure, and transfer accounts to fund balance.

Note: A single closing entry is used for each fund in this illustration because a budget was not recorded in either, and there were only a few accounts involved.

In more complex situations, the closing process illustrated for the General Fund would be followed.

Financial statements—illustration

The financial statements for a Nonexpendable Trust Fund are an operating statement, a balance sheet, and a statement of cash flows. These are illustrated in Tables 8–8, 8–9, and 8–10. The financial statements for an Expendable Trust Fund are an operating statement and a balance sheet. These are illustrated in Tables 8–11 and 8–12. In addition to reviewing these statements, you should review the

TABLE 8–8   Statement of Revenues, Expenses, and Changes in Fund Balance—Nonexpendable Trust Fund

City of New Example
Nonexpendable Trust Fund
Educational Principal Trust Fund
Statement of Revenues, Expenses, and Changes in Fund Balance
For the Year Ended December 31, 19X1

Revenues:	
Investment revenue	$ 490,000
Operating income	490,000
Operating transfer to Educational Income Trust Fund	(490,000)
Net income	-0-
Fund balance at beginning of year	-0-
Principal of gift received during year	5,000,000
Gain on sale of investments	15,000
Fund balance at end of year	$5,015,000

TABLE 8–9   Balance Sheet—Nonexpendable Trust Fund

City of New Example
Nonexpendable Trust Fund
Educational Principal Trust Fund
Balance Sheet
December 31, 19X1

Assets	
Cash	$ 160,000
Investment income receivable	40,000
Investments	4,860,000
Total assets	$5,060,000
Liabilities and Fund Balance	
Liabilities:	
Due to Educational Income Trust Fund	$ 45,000
Fund balance:	
Fund balance	5,015,000
Total liabilities and fund balance	$5,060,000

TABLE 8–10   Cash Flow Statement—Nonexpendable Trust Fund

City of New Example
Nonexpendable Trust Fund
Educational Principal Trust Fund
Statement of Cash Flows
For the Year Ended December 31, 19X1

Cash flows from operating activities:		
Operating income	$ 490,000	
Adjustments to reconcile operating income to net cash provided by operating activities:		
Increase in Investment income receivable	(40,000)	
Increase in Due to Educational Income Trust Fund	45,000	
Cash provided by operating activities		$ 495,000
Cash flows from noncapital financing activities:		
Gift received during the year	5,000,000	
Operating transfer to Educational Income Trust Fund	(490,000)	
Cash provided by noncapital financing activities		4,510,000
Cash flows from investing activities:		
Purchase of investments	(5,000,000)	
Sale of investments	155,000	
Cash used by investing activities		(4,845,000)
Net increase in cash		160,000
Cash at beginning of year		-0-
Cash at end of year		$ 160,000

TABLE 8–11   Statement of Revenues, Expenditures, and Changes in Fund Balance—Expendable Trust Fund

City of New Example
Expendable Trust Fund
Educational Income Trust Fund
Statement of Revenues, Expenditures, and Changes in Fund Balance
For the Year Ended December 31, 19X1

Revenues	
Interest on loans	$ 10,000
Expenditures	
Loan reductions	15,000
Excess of expenditures over revenues	(5,000)
Other Financing Sources	
Operating transfer from Educational Principal Trust Fund	490,000
Excess of revenues and other financing sources over expenditures	485,000
Fund balance at beginning of year	-0-
Fund balance at end of year	$485,000

TABLE 8-12   Balance Sheet—Expendable Trust Fund

City of New Example
Expendable Trust Fund
Educational Income Trust Fund
Balance Sheet
December 31, 19X1

Assets	
Cash	$265,000
Due from Educational Principal Trust Fund	45,000
Loan interest receivable	5,000
Loans receivable	170,000
Total assets	$485,000
Fund Balance	$485,000

materials in Chapter 2 on Nonexpendable Trust Funds and Expendable Trust Funds. The overall reporting process is discussed in Chapter 9.

GOVERNMENT ACCOUNTING IN PRACTICE—
THE CITY OF BALTIMORE, MARYLAND

The City of Baltimore uses two Nonexpendable Trust Funds: the Enoch Pratt Free Library Fund and the Memorials Fund. The balance sheet for the Enoch Pratt Free Library Fund is presented in Table 8–13. Notice that the City of Baltimore presents its financial statements rounded to thousands of dollars. This is common in financial reporting. Notice also that the assets consist primarily of in-

TABLE 8-13   Balance Sheet—Nonexpendable Trust Fund—City of Baltimore, Maryland

City of Baltimore
Nonexpendable Trust Fund
Enoch Pratt Free Library Fund
Balance Sheet
June 30,19X1
(Expressed in Thousands)

Assets	
Cash and cash equivalents	$ 4
Investments	2,065
Other assets, primarily accrued interest receivable	33
Total assets	$2,102
Fund Balance	
Reserved for library services	$2,102

Source: Adapted from a recent Comprehensive Annual Financial Report of the City of Baltimore, Maryland.

TABLE 8–14   Statement of Revenues, Expenses, and Changes in Fund Balance—Nonexpendable Trust Fund—City of Baltimore, Maryland

City of Baltimore
Nonexpendable Trust Fund
Enoch Pratt Free Library Fund
Statement of Revenues, Expenses, and Changes in Fund Balance
For the Year Ended June 30, 19X1
(Expressed in Thousands)

Revenues	
Interest and other investment income	$ 204
Expenses	
Total expenses—claims, awards, and benefits	184
Net income	20
Fund balance, July 1, 19X0	2,082
Fund balance, June 30, 19X1	$2,102

Source: Adapted from a recent Comprehensive Annual Financial Report for the City of Baltimore, Maryland.

vestments and the related accrued interest. Since the fund does not have any liabilities, fund balance equals assets. In the case of the Enoch Pratt Free Library Fund, the fund balance is reserved for library services.

The operating statement for the Enoch Pratt Free Library Fund contains investment income and a category labeled "Total expenses—claims, awards and benefits." Since the individual expenses of the fund are not material, they are not identified in the Comprehensive Annual Financial Report. See Table 8–14.

The cash flow statement for the Enoch Pratt Free Library Fund is a very simple statement. Income provided by operations is the same as cash flow from operations; therefore, no adjustments are necessary. The only cash use identified is the purchase of investments. See Table 8–15.

SECTION III—FIDUCIARY-TYPE FUNDS: AGENCY FUNDS

Definition of Fund

An **Agency Fund** is used when a governmental unit is the *custodian* of resources that belong to some other organization. This type of fund is also used when a single fund is established to perform a central collection or distribution function for the resources of other funds of the governmental unit. Since the Agency Fund does not have title to nor control over these resources, there is no fund balance for this type of fund. Instead, all the resources held are balanced against the liabilities that are to be paid from those resources, including the debt to the legal "owner" of the assets.

TABLE 8–15   Cash Flow Statement—Nonexpendable Trust Fund—City of Baltimore, Maryland

City of Baltimore
Nonexpendable Trust Fund
Enoch Pratt Free Library Fund
Statement of Cash Flows
For the Year Ended June 30, 19X1
(Expressed in Thousands)

Cash flows from operating activities:	
Net operating income	$ 20
Adjustments to reconcile net operating income to net cash provided by operating activities	-0-
Net cash provided by operating activities	20
Cash flows from investing activities:	
Purchase of investments	(100)
Net cash used for investing activities	(100)
Net decrease in cash and cash equivalents	(80)
Cash and equivalents, July 1, 19X0	84
Cash and cash equivalents, June 30, 19X1	$ 4

Source: Adapted from a recent Comprehensive Annual Financial Report for the City of Baltimore, Maryland.

A typical Agency Fund is one used to record the collection of property taxes. After the taxes have been collected at a central location, they are disbursed to the legally authorized recipients. It is also possible to use an Agency Fund to record FICA and other payroll deductions before these amounts are sent to the appropriate recipients. Agency Funds are also used for resources held in escrow, deposits from contractors doing business with the government, and unclaimed monies held by the government. A key factor in determining if an Agency Fund should be used is whether the government unit disburses the assets according to a previously agreed-upon formula, legal requirement, or instruction by the "owner." In other words, the government does not have discretionary use of the resources in these funds, and there is no trust agreement.

Summary of Fund Activities

If the City of New Example establishes a Property Tax Collection Fund and the fund is used to account for the taxes collected, an Agency Fund would be created. (The actual levy would still be recorded in the General Fund, Special Revenue Fund, and so on.) In addition, this fund is used to record the distribution of the taxes to the legal recipients—for example, school boards, levee districts, and so forth.

It should be noted that these activities are not unique to this particular fund; rather they are conducted by all Agency Funds—that is, the collection and disbursement of resources.

If the resources received by an Agency Fund are not disbursed immediately, the governmental unit should invest them in marketable securities. Any income or expenses produced by these investments is usually distributed to the beneficiaries of the Agency Fund.

Control of Fund Activities

The primary element of control over an Agency Fund is the agreement between the governmental unit and the legal "owner" of the funds. As a result, there is usually no legally adopted budget, nor is there any need for encumbrance accounting. Since the governmental unit will disburse the assets of the fund only for the purposes indicated by the "owner" and only based on the request of the "owner," these controls are not needed.

While the modified accrual basis of accounting is used to determine the timing of the transactions recorded, there are no operations from the point of view of the governmental unit. Therefore, there is no concept of measurement focus applicable to Agency Funds.

Depending on the legal or contractual problems involved, a separate Agency Fund may have to be established for each unique relationship. However, related situations can often be combined into a single fund.

Accounting for Fund Activities

Operating entries

For illustrative purposes, let us continue with the example of the Property Tax Collection Fund mentioned above. Assume that the city collects property taxes and distributes one third of the collections to the local school board, a levee district, and the General Fund of the city, respectively. The levy of the tax is recorded by each governmental unit. To keep the example manageable, however, we will illustrate only the General Fund and the Agency Fund for the City of New Example. Entries similar to those for the General Fund are made by the other governmental units. The applicable entries are, assuming the amounts as given:

Entry in the books of the General Fund	Property taxes receivable—current	5,000,000	
	Estimated uncollectible property taxes—current		1,000
	Revenues—property taxes		4,999,000
	To record levy of 19X1 property tax.		

Entry in the	Property taxes receivable for the city and		
books of the	other governmental units—current	15,000,000	
Agency	Due to the city and other		
Fund	governmental units		15,000,000
	To record levy of 19X1 property tax.		

Because of the services provided, the city charges the school board and the levee district a 2 percent fee. This amount is deducted from the amount owed to them when the taxes are collected. Any amounts earned by an Agency Fund are usually recorded as revenues of the General Fund.

If $9 million is collected, the school board and the levee district will each receive $2,940,000 ($3,000,000 × .98), and the General Fund will receive $3,120,000 ($3,000,000 + $60,000 + $60,000). The entries in the Agency Fund necessary to record the collection and the distribution are as follows:

Cash	9,000,000	
Property taxes receivable for the city		
and other governmental units—current		9,000,000
To record the collection of part of the 19X1		
property tax		
Due to the city and other governmental		
units	9,000,000	
Due to General Fund		3,120,000
Due to School Board		2,940,000
Due to Levee District		2,940,000
To record allocation of taxes collected.		
Due to General Fund	3,120,000	
Due to School Board	2,940,000	
Due to Levee District	2,940,000	
Cash		9,000,000
To record distribution of the collection of part		
of the 19X1 property taxes net of collection		
fees.		

The entry in the books of the General Fund to record the receipt of its share of the property taxes and the collection fee is:

Entry in the	Cash	3,120,000	
books of the	Property taxes receivable—current		3,000,000
General	Revenues—miscellaneous		120,000
Fund	To record receipt of part of the 19X1 property		
	tax plus a collection fee.		

The other governmental units will recognize the difference between the debit to Cash and the credit to Property tax receivable—current as a debit to an expenditure or an expense, as appropriate. To illustrate, the entry that would be recorded on the books of the Levee District (a Special Revenue Fund) is:

Cash	2,940,000	
Expenditure—fee for collection of property taxes	60,000	
Property taxes receivable—current		3,000,000

To record receipt of part of the 19X1 property tax and a collection fee owed to the General Fund.

When the uncollectible accounts are written off, the appropriate entry in the books of the Agency Fund is:

Due to the city and other government units	300	
Property taxes receivable for the city and other governmental units— current (delinquent or lien)		300

To record the write-off of uncollectible property taxes.

In addition, the appropriate entry or entries, as discussed in Chapter 5, are made in the books of the General Fund and any other appropriate fund. Notice that the activities described do not result in either a revenue or an expenditure to the Agency Fund.

A trial balance for the fund at the end of the year is presented in Table 8–16.

Closing entries

Since only balance sheet accounts are involved in the activities of an Agency Fund, no closing entries are needed.

TABLE 8–16

City of New Example
Agency Fund
Tax Agency Fund
Trial Balance
December 31, 19X

	DEBITS	CREDITS
Property taxes receivable for the city and other governmental units—current	$5,999,700	
Due to the city and other governmental units		$5,999,700
	$5,999,700	$5,999,700

Financial statements—illustration

The financial statements of Agency Funds are a statement of changes in assets and liabilities and a balance sheet. These are illustrated for 19X1 in Tables 8–17 and 8–18. In addition, you should review the section on Agency Funds in Chapter 2 and compare those financial statements with the statements presented. The fact that there is no fund balance for Agency Funds cannot be overempha-

TABLE 8–17   Statement of Changes in Assets and Liabilities—Agency Fund

City of New Example
Agency Fund
Tax Agency Fund
Statement of Changes in Assets and Liabilities
For the Year Ended December 31, 19X1

	BALANCE DECEMBER 31, 19X0	ADDITIONS	DEDUCTIONS	BALANCE DECEMBER 31, 19X1
Assets				
Cash	-0-	$ 9,000,000	$ 9,000,000	-0-
Property taxes receivable	-0-	15,000,000	9,000,300	$5,999,700
	-0-	$24,000,000	$18,000,300	$5,999,700
Liabilities				
Due to the city and other governmental units	-0-	$15,000,000	$ 9,000,300	$5,999,700
Due to General Fund	-0-	3,120,000	3,120,000	-0-
Due to School Board	-0-	2,940,000	2,940,000	-0-
Due to Levee District	-0-	2,940,000	2,940,000	-0-
	-0-	$24,000,000	$18,000,300	$5,999,700

TABLE 8–18   Balance Sheet—Agency Fund

City of New Example
Agency Fund
Tax Agency Fund
Balance Sheet
December 31, 19X1

Assets	
Property taxes receivable for the city and other governmental units—current	$5,999,700
	$5,999,700
Liabilities	
Due to the city and other governmental units	$5,999,700
	$5,999,700

sized. These funds do not have title to, nor do they control, any of their assets. A review of the Tax Agency Fund described in this chapter clearly illustrates this point. The overall reporting process is discussed in Chapter 9.

GOVERNMENTAL ACCOUNTING IN PRACTICE— THE CITY OF NEW ORLEANS

The City of New Orleans uses fourteen Agency Funds, which are grouped as "Clearing Funds." In addition, the city uses three other groups of Agency Funds—Deposit Funds, Escrow Funds, and a Property Tax Fund. A partial balance sheet for the Clearing Funds is included in Table 8–19. This balance sheet includes a Parking Bond Refund Account, RTA (Regional Transit Authority) Sales Tax Fund, and an Occupancy Privilege Tax Fund. As is true for all Agency Funds, notice that there is no fund balance; instead, the assets equal the liabilities. Notice that the total column does not equal the sum of the three funds listed. This is because eleven other funds are included in the previous part of the balance sheet.

TABLE 8–19   Balance Sheet—Agency Funds—City of New Orleans

City of New Orleans, Louisiana
Agency Funds—Clearing Funds
Combining Balance Sheet—Continued
December 31, 19X1
With Comparative Totals for December 31, 19X0

	PARKING BOND REFUND ACCOUNT	RTA SALES TAX	OCCUPANCY PRIVILEGE TAX	Totals 19X1	Totals 19X0
Assets					
Cash	$25,961	$ 432,026	$351,334	$11,187,952	$ 9,800,761
Time certificates of deposit	—	—	—	1,159,000	—
Investments	—	—	—	—	1,100,839
Accounts receivable	—	—	41,538	3,757,156	3,374,409
Due from other funds	—	2,120,441	—	9,789,130	7,903,394
Due from other governments	—	—	—	657,508	725,888
Total assets	$25,961	$2,552,467	$392,872	$26,550,746	$22,905,291
Liabilities					
Accounts payable	$ —	$ —	$ —	$ 38,801	$ 175,797
Other payables and accruals	5,961	—	392,872	6,212,081	5,266,743
Due to other funds	20,000	62,264	—	13,275,373	10,146,473
Due to other governments	—	2,490,203	—	7,024,491	7,316,278
Total liabilities	$25,961	$2,552,467	$392,872	$26,550,746	$22,905,291

Source: Adapted from a recent Comprehensive Annual Financial Report of the City of New Orleans.

The schedule of changes in assets and liabilities for all Clearing Funds is illustrated in Table 8–20. For reporting purposes, the city combines individual Clearing Funds into a single group. Notice also that Deposit Funds are included in the schedule in Table 8–20. As noted above, the city also uses Escrow Funds and a Property Tax Fund. These are illustrated in Table 8–21. The schedule of changes is separated into two illustrations to highlight the format used by the City of New Orleans and the method the city uses to report the totals for all Agency Funds.

TABLE 8–20   Schedule of Changes in Assets and Liabilities—Agency Funds—City of New Orleans

City of New Orleans, Louisiana
Agency Funds
Combining Schedule of Changes in Assets and Liabilities
Year Ended December 31, 19X1

	BALANCE JANUARY 1, 19X1	ADDITIONS	DEDUCTIONS	BALANCE DECEMBER 31, 19X1
Clearing Funds				
Assets:				
Cash	$ 9,800,761	$530,487,876	$529,100,685	$11,187,952
Time certificates of deposit	—	1,159,000	—	1,159,000
Investments	1,100,839	1,159,225	2,260,064	—
Accounts receivable	3,374,409	3,633,594	3,250,847	3,757,156
Due from other funds	7,903,394	50,161,907	48,276,170	9,789,131
Due from other governments	725,888	347,020	415,400	657,508
	$22,905,291	$586,948,622	$583,303,166	$26,550,747
Liabilities:				
Accounts payable	$ 175,797	$ 38,801	$ 175,797	$ 38,801
Other payables and accruals	5,266,743	215,914,707	214,969,369	6,212,081
Due to other funds	10,146,473	180,153,831	177,024,931	13,275,373
Due to other governments	7,316,278	142,581,009	142,872,796	7,024,491
	$22,905,291	$538,688,348	$535,042,893	$26,550,746
Deposit Funds				
Assets:				
Cash	$ 657,741	$ 5,200,195	$ 5,523,682	$ 334,254
Time certificates of deposit	1,720,000	2,320,000	1,720,000	2,320,000
Accounts receivable	28,350	158	28,350	158
Due from other funds	44,475	—	1,000	43,475
	$ 2,450,566	$ 7,520,353	$ 7,273,032	$ 2,697,887
Liabilities:				
Accounts payable	$ 71,145	$ 40,500	$ 71,145	$ 40,500
Other payables and accruals	2,092,582	3,662,716	3,260,855	2,494,443
Due to other funds	286,839	162,944	286,839	162,944
	$ 2,450,566	$ 3,866,160	$ 3,618,839	$ 2,697,887

Source: Adapted from a recent Comprehensive Annual Financial Report of the City of New Orleans.

TABLE 8-21   Schedule of Changes in Assets and Liabilities—Agency Funds—City of New Orleans

City of New Orleans, Louisiana
Agency Funds
Combining Schedule of Changes in Assets and Liabilities
Year Ended December 31, 19X1

	BALANCE JANUARY 1, 19X1	ADDITIONS	DEDUCTIONS	BALANCE DECEMBER 31, 19X1
Escrow Funds				
Assets:				
Cash	$ 3,570,039	$ 171,446,075	$170,878,631	$ 4,137,483
Time certificates of deposit	4,500,000	23,093,973	4,500,000	23,093,973
Investments	17,423,283	142,559,021	149,981,890	10,000,414
Accounts receivable	448,397	1,049	448,397	1,049
Due from other funds	500,000	4,588	500,000	4,588
	$26,441,719	$ 337,104,706	$326,308,918	$37,237,507
Liabilities:				
Accounts payable	$ 619,583	$ 4,835,213	$ 1,401,567	$ 4,053,229
Other payables and accruals	24,649,912	38,430,588	36,019,387	27,061,113
Due to other funds	1,172,224	6,123,165	1,172,224	6,123,165
	$26,441,719	$ 49,388,966	$ 38,593,178	$37,237,507
Property Tax Fund				
Assets:				
Property taxes receivable	$20,270,996	$ 78,957,993	$ 75,516,824	$23,712,165
Liabilities:				
Due to other governments	$20,270,996	78,957,993	$ 75,516,824	$23,712,165
Total All Agency Funds				
Assets:				
Cash	$14,028,541	$ 707,134,146	$705,502,998	$15,659,689
Time certificates of deposit	6,220,000	26,572,973	6,220,000	26,572,973
Investments	18,524,122	143,718,246	152,241,954	10,000,414
Receivables:				
Property taxes	20,270,996	78,957,993	75,516,824	23,712,165
Accounts	3,851,156	3,634,801	3,727,594	3,758,363
Due from other funds	8,447,869	50,166,495	48,777,170	9,837,194
Due from other governments	725,888	347,020	415,400	657,508
	$72,068,572	$1,010,531,674	$992,401,940	$90,198,306
Liabilities:				
Accounts payable	$ 866,525	$ 4,914,515	$ 1,648,509	$ 4,132,531
Other payables and accruals	32,009,237	258,008,011	254,249,611	35,767,637
Due to other funds	11,605,536	186,439,940	178,483,994	19,561,482
Due to other governments	27,587,274	221,539,002	218,389,620	30,736,656
	$72,068,572	$ 670,901,468	$652,771,734	$90,198,306

Source: Adapted from a recent Comprehensive Annual Financial Report of the City of New Orleans.

SECTION IV—SPECIAL ASSESSMENT PROJECTS

Description of Project Activities

Special assessments are a means of financing services or capital improvements that benefit one group of citizens more than the general public. Taxpayers who receive the benefits of these activities are assessed for their share of the cost. Examples of these activities include projects such as special police protection, paving of city streets, and building parking structures. Prior to the issuance of GASB *Statement No. 6*, "Accounting and Financial Reporting for Special Assessments," these activities were accounted for and reported in separate governmental-type funds: Special Assessments Funds. GASB *Statement No. 6* requires that Special Assessments Funds be discontinued as a reporting entity and that these activities be reported as any other service or capital improvement-type project.

Control of and Accounting for Project Activities

Service assessments

Service assessments generally include activities such as special police protection, storm sewer cleaning, and snow plowing. If these activities are financed by user charges in the form of special assessments, the reporting should be done in the General Fund, a Special Revenue Fund, or an Enterprise Fund—whichever best reflects the nature of the transactions.

Control over these activities is accomplished in the same manner as any other activity included in the particular fund type. In the governmental-type funds, control is accomplished through state and local laws and budgetary authorizations for the activities. When these funds are used, immediate control is achieved through a comparison of budget and actual data for revenues, expenditures, and other financing sources. This comparison must be presented in the annual report when an annual budget has been legally adopted. Use of encumbrance accounting is generally found in those instances where the General Fund or a Special Revenue Fund is used.

In those instances in which an Enterprise Fund is used, a flexible budget is the central control feature. In general, a flexible budget is prepared based upon the level of activity of the fund, and this is compared with the actual results of the period.

The revenues and expenditures (expenses) are recognized according to the basis of accounting rules that are applicable to the particular fund type being used. Examples of this type of accounting and reporting can be found in Chapters 4 and 5 for the General Fund and Special Revenue Funds and Chapter 7 for Enterprise Funds.

To illustrate the use of the General Fund to account for service assessment activities, assume that the City of New Example levies a special assessment on the property holders in the Central Business District (CBD) to provide for special police protection. Assume further that these activities will be accounted for in the police department budget within the General Fund. The entries to levy the assessment and collect part of the receivables are as follows (amounts assumed):

Entries in the books of the General Fund

Special assessment receivables—current	200,000	
Revenues—special assessments		200,000
To record levy of assessments for special police protection in the CBD.		
Cash	190,000	
Special assessment receivables—current		190,000
To record collection of assessments for special police protection in the CBD.		

If any of the receivables are not expected to be collected, a provision for uncollectible receivables should be established. If these receivables are not collected within a specific time period, they usually become delinquent and eventually are classified as a lien against the property in question. In these instances, the accounting would be the same as that illustrated in Chapter 5 for property taxes.

Any expenditures associated with these activities are recorded in the fund involved. Unless the ordinance establishing the assessment requires a separate accounting, these activities should not be segregated from the other activities of the police department.

Capital improvements assessments

Capital improvements assessments generally include construction projects such as street improvements and sidewalks. If these activities are financed by a special assessment, and the governmental unit is "obligated in some manner," the reporting is done in two funds and two account groups. The construction phase of the project is accounted for in a Capital Projects Fund, the debt service phase of the project is accounted for in a Debt Service Fund, the resulting asset is usually accounted for in the General Fixed Assets Account Group, and the debt is accounted for in the General Long-Term Debt Account Group. A governmental unit is "obligated in some manner" for the special assessment debt ". . . if (a) it is legally obligated to assume all or part of the debt in the event of default or (b) the government *may* take certain action to assume secondary liability for all or part of the debt—*and* the government takes, or has given indication that it will take, those actions."[1]

Accounting for capital improvements assessments in which the government is "obligated in some manner" is exactly like that previously illustrated in Chapter 6 for capital projects. If you are not familiar with those procedures, review that material before continuing.

[1]GASB Cod. Sec. S40.116.

In those instances in which the governmental unit is *not* obligated in any manner, the construction phase is still accounted for in a Capital Projects Fund and the fixed asset is accounted for in the General Fixed Assets Account Group (or an Enterprise Fund, as appropriate). The only significant difference is that the debt service phase of the project is reported in an Agency Fund " . . . to reflect the fact that the government's duties are limited to acting as an agent for the assessed property owners and the bondholders."[2] In addition, the proceeds from the issuance of the special assessment bonds is reported as "contribution from property owners" rather than "bond proceeds" in the Capital Projects Fund.

When special assessments are collected over a period of years, a problem arises as to the amount of revenue that should be recognized. Here we assume that applying the measurable and available concept results in recognition of revenue when the special assessments installments become current assets. Thus, if an assessment of $1 million is levied, of which $100,000 is current, the following entries are appropriate in the Debt Service Fund:

Entry in the books of the Debt Service Fund	Special assessment receivables—current	100,000	
	Special assessment receivables—deferred	900,000	
	Revenues—special assessments		100,000
	Deferred revenues		900,000
	To record the levy of special assessments.		

Collections of the assessments are recorded in the normal manner for receivables.

When the second payment becomes a current asset, a proportionate amount of revenue is recognized (amounts assumed):

Entries in the books of the Debt Service Fund	Special assessment receivables—current	100,000	
	Special assessments receivables—deferred		100,000
	To record the current status of the second installment of the receivable.		
	Deferred revenues	100,000	
	Revenues—special assessments		100,000
	To record the revenue from current special assessments.		

Financial statements

As mentioned above, reporting for special assessment activities can take one of several forms. Now that the GASB has aligned special assessment accounting with that of other types of funds, these activities are reported in the manner described in this and previous chapters, depending on the type of activity involved and the extent to which the governmental unit is obligated for any

---

[2]GASB Cod. Sec. S40.119.

debt. As a result, you should review the accounting and reporting requirements for the General Fund, Special Revenue Funds, Debt Service Funds, Capital Projects Funds, and the General Long-Term Debt Account Group and the General Fixed Assets Account Group at this time.

Special concluding remarks

Local laws sometimes require that special assessment projects be accounted for and reported as separate entities. Since these types of situations are not consistent with current GAAP, additional supplemental information must be disclosed by the governmental unit.

In many situations, the above accounting procedures can be followed and special assessment data can be gleaned from the accounts if it is needed for supplemental reporting. It is also possible to follow the "old" accounting procedures and reclassify the data to comply with current GAAP.

REVIEW QUESTIONS

Section I

Q8–1 When is an Expendable Trust Fund used?

Q8–2 How are the operations of an Expendable Trust Fund controlled?

Q8–3 Jessie Razemink donated $500,000 to a city to provide for concerts for elderly citizens. Explain how you would account for this donation and its expenditure.

Q8–4 Does an Expendable Trust Fund have a fund balance? Why or why not?

Section II

Q8–5 How does a nonexpendable trust differ from an expendable trust?

Q8–6 How are gains and losses on the sale of investments recorded in a Nonexpendable Trust Fund?

Q8–7 Comment on the following statement: "Nonexpendable Trust Funds can only be used by a governmental unit when someone contributes investment securities, and the principal must be maintained intact."

Section III

Q8–8 Assume a freshman approached you and asked you to define an agency relationship. How would you respond?

Q8–9 Is an operating statement prepared for an Agency Fund? Why or why not?

Q8–10 Does an Agency Fund have a fund balance? Why or why not?

Q8–11 If the activities of an Agency Fund produce revenues, where are these revenues usually accounted for?

Section IV

Q8–12 The bookkeeper of the City of New Sherman recently made the following statement: "A Capital Projects Fund should be used for all special assessment projects." Do you agree or disagree? Why?

Q8–13 Lakefront Township recently assessed property holders for the cost of removing snow from the streets in each subdivision. What type of accounting would you recommend for this activity?

Q8–14 Has the GASB eliminated the Special Assessment Fund as an accounting entity?

Q8–15 Explain how the financing of projects with special assessments differs from the use of general obligation bonds.

CASES

C8–1 Ms. J. S. Moneybaggs wants to include a provision in her will that will assure her that her life's work of caring for small children will continue after her death. She currently donates her time to the Recreation Department of the City of Metropolis. She is concerned that any resources given to the city might be used up or used for some other purpose. Ms. Moneybaggs has hired you as her financial consultant. How would you advise her?

C8–2 The city council of Largeville is facing a growing crime problem in its Central Shopping District (CSD). The council wants to increase the presence of police in the CSD, but there is not enough money in the current year's budget to provide for the extra protection. One alternative would be to levy a special tax on the merchants in the CSD but, based on the Largeville City Charter, a tax would require a vote of the merchants and that would take time and additional resources. Mr. Joe del Puerto, the city manager for Largeville, has asked you to help find a solution to their problem. Do you have any suggestions?

C8–3 A new employee of the City of Kashime was working with the accounting records of several of its funds. This employee, John Fergie, recorded income earned by investments in a Nonexpendable Trust Fund as income of the General Fund. John felt that income earned by this fund should not be included in with the principal of the fund. The Nonexpendable Trust Fund was established to provide a continued source of income to permit the public library to acquire new books. Since the principal of the fund must be maintained intact, John felt the income could be spent through the General Fund. Comment on John's logic.

C8–4 The City of Macroville has hired you as a consultant to help establish a procedure to simplify its property tax collection processing and make the process more efficient. Currently the city and six special districts receive money from a property tax. Each district and the city has its own billing, recording, and collection functions. In addition, the taxpayers are upset because they have to pay seven different tax bills. At a recent town hall–type meeting, several citizens spoke and demanded that the city do something to simplify the process. As a consultant, how would you advise the city?

EXERCISES

Section I

E8–1 (True or false)

Indicate whether the following statements are true or false. If any are false, indicate why each is false.

1. Expendable Trust Funds are classified as governmental-type funds.
2. Expendable Trust Funds follow accrual accounting procedures.
3. Expendable Trust Funds are controlled by state laws and the provisions of the individual trust agreement.
4. Funds classified as Expendable Trust Funds follow a spending measurement focus.
5. Resources received by an Expendable Trust Fund from a Nonexpendable Trust Fund are recorded as an operating transfer.
6. Expendable Trust Funds do not have revenues and expenditures.
7. A statement of revenues, expenses, and changes in fund balance is prepared for each Expendable Trust Fund.
8. Expendable Trust Funds do not have a fund balance.
9. If a governmental unit uses an Expendable Trust Fund, it must also use a Nonexpendable Trust Fund for that activity.
10. Budgets are never used to control Expendable Trust Funds.

E8–2 (Journal entries)

Record the following journal entries in the Library Book Fund, an Expendable Trust Fund:

1. A wealthy citizen donated $250,000 to New Hope, a city in the northeastern United States. This money was to be used to acquire children's books for the local library.
2. The city invested $200,000 in certificates of deposit.
3. Books costing $45,000 were acquired.

    4. Income of $20,000 was received in cash from the investments.

    5. The books were closed for the year.

E8–3 (Multiple choice)

    1. Which of the following types of funds use the modified accrual basis of accounting?

      a. Capital Projects Funds

      b. Expendable Trust Funds

      c. The General Fund

      d. Special Revenue Funds

      e. All of the above

    2. Which of the following funds can be used to account for the spendable income from a trust whose principal is nonexpendable?

      a. An Agency Fund

      b. The General Fund

      c. A Capital Projects Fund

      d. An Expendable Trust Fund

      e. None of the above

    3. Which of the following funds does not follow the spending measurement focus?

      a. Expendable Trust Funds

      b. The General Fund

      c. Special Revenue Funds

      d. Capital Projects Funds

      e. All of the above funds follow the spending measurement focus

    4. The use of assets accumulated in a trust fund must conform with the provisions of

      a. State and local laws

      b. The trust agreement

      c. Both a and b

      d. The modified accrual basis of accounting

      e. None of the above

    5. A citizen donated $450,000 to a city upon her death. Her will provided that these resources be maintained in a trust and spent to provide free tickets to local concerts for schoolchildren. Accounting for these activities should be done in

      a. The General Fund

      b. A Special Revenue Fund

      c. An Expendable Trust Fund

      d. A Nonexpendable Trust Fund

      e. Both c and d

E8–4 (Fill-in-the-blanks)

    1. Expendable Trust Funds are controlled through _____ and _____ .

2. Expendable Trust Funds follow a _____ measurement focus and a _____ basis of accounting.
3. Amounts originally contributed to an Expendable Trust Fund are recorded as _____ .
4. The following financial statements are prepared for an Expendable Trust Fund: _____ and _____ .
5. The operations of an Expendable Trust Fund are usually (more or less) _____ complex than those of the General Fund.
6. The most important document with respect to an Expendable Trust Fund is the _____ .

Section II

E8–5 (Compare and contrast the accounting of an Expendable Trust Fund with that of a Nonexpendable Trust Fund)

Identify the major similarities and differences between accounting followed by Expendable Trust Funds and Nonexpendable Trust Funds.

E8–6 (True or false)

Indicate whether the following statements are true or false. If any are false, indicate why each is false.

1. Nonexpendable Trust Funds use a capital maintenance measurement focus for recording events.
2. Nonexpendable Trust Funds use an accrual basis of accounting for recording events.
3. The transfer of income from a Nonexpendable Trust Fund to an Expendable Trust Fund is recorded as a residual equity transfer.
4. Nonexpendable Trust Funds have two fund equity accounts: Contributed capital and Retained earnings.
5. The receipt of a gift by a Nonexpendable Trust Fund is recorded as a direct entry into a contributed capital account.
6. A fixed budget is used to control a Nonexpendable Trust Fund.
7. The gain resulting from a sale of assets held in a Nonexpendable Trust Fund can be considered revenue or a part of fund balance.
8. A statement of cash flows is prepared for a Nonexpendable Trust Fund.
9. A net income figure is calculated for a Nonexpendable Trust Fund.
10. The activities of a Nonexpendable Trust Fund may encompass the operation of a business.

E8–7 (Discussion of Alternatives for use of trusts)

You have recently been approached by a wealthy individual who would like to set up a trust for the education of children of deceased police officers. That person has asked you to explain the types of trusts available and make a recommendation. Prepare a written statement regarding your response.

E8–8   (Multiple choice)
1.   The principal amount of a gift in trust that cannot be spent should be accounted for in
   a.   The General Fund
   b.   A Special Revenue Fund
   c.   A Capital Projects Fund
   d.   A Nonexpendable Trust Fund
2.   Since the principal of a Nonexpendable Trust Fund cannot be spent,
   a.   It cannot be invested in corporate stocks
   b.   It must be invested only in corporate stocks
   c.   It may be invested in corporate stocks, certificates of deposit, and other legally acceptable forms of investment
   d.   The income from the principal cannot be spent
3.   Records maintained for a Nonexpendable Trust Fund use which of the following?
   a.   Full accrual basis of accounting
   b.   Spending measurement focus
   c.   Modified accrual basis of accounting
   d.   Both a and b
4.   Initial contributions of capital to a Nonexpendable Trust Fund are usually credited to
   a.   A revenue account.
   b.   An expenditure account.
   c.   A fund balance account.
   d.   An expense account.
5.   Transfers of income from a Nonexpendable Trust Fund to an Expendable Trust Fund are classified as
   a.   Residual equity transfers
   b.   Operating transfers
   c.   Expenses
   d.   Expenditures
6.   Gains on sales of investments in a Nonexpendable Trust Fund
   a.   May be credited to fund balance
   b.   May not be credited to fund balance
   c.   Must be credited to fund balance
   d.   May be debited to fund balance
7.   Records for an Expendable Trust Fund and a Nonexpendable Trust Fund
   a.   Are not reported in governmental financial statements
   b.   Must be reported in governmental financial statements
   c.   Are included in the General Fund for financial reporting purposes
   d.   Are included in the Special Revenue Fund for financial reporting purposes

Section III

E8–9 (Fill-in-the-blanks)
1.   Agency Funds are classified as _____ type funds.
2.   An Agency Fund is used when the governmental unit is the _____ of resources that belong to some other organization.
3.   Agency Funds (do or do not) _____ have title to the resources in the fund.
4.   The financial statements for an Agency Fund are _____ and _____ .
5.   Revenues generated by an Agency Fund are usually recorded in _____ Fund.
6.   Agency Funds (are or are not) _____ used only as tax collection funds.

E8–10 (Multiple choice)
1.   The fee for the collection of property taxes by an Agency Fund will result in revenue to
     a.   The General Fund and the Agency Fund
     b.   The Agency Fund
     c.   A Capital Projects Fund
     d.   A Special Revenue Fund and the Agency Fund
     e.   None of the above
2.   Blaken Township established an Agency Fund to account for the collection and distribution of a general sales tax. The tax is collected for the General Fund, an independent school district, and several independent drainage districts. The school district and the drainage districts are entities that are separate from the city. During the year, $500,000 was collected in sales tax. Entries to record the collection and distribution of the resources for the city should be made in
     a.   The General Fund
     b.   The Agency Fund
     c.   The General Fund and the Agency Fund
     d.   A Special Revenue Fund and the Agency Fund
     e.   None of the above
3.   Collection of resources that must be distributed to other funds should be recorded in an Agency Fund as a debit to Cash and a credit to
     a.   Revenues
     b.   Expenditures
     c.   Other financing sources
     d.   Other financing uses
     e.   None of the above

4. Which of the following funds does not have a fund balance account?
    a. The General Fund
    b. A Special Revenue Fund
    c. A Capital Projects Fund
    d. An Expendable Trust Fund
    e. An Agency Fund
5. An Agency Fund is used to account for
    a. Revenue generated from a property tax levy
    b. Expenditures of the General Fund
    c. Debt service for Enterprise Fund debt.
    d. Debt service of general obligation bonds used to finance an addition to city hall
    e. None of the above
6. According to GAAP for Expendable Trust Funds, which of the following is true?
    a. Revenues must be transferred to a Nonexpendable Trust Fund
    b. Payments of resources are recorded as expenditures
    c. There is no fund balance
    d. All disbursements must be made to the General Fund
    e. None of the above

E8–11 (Journal entries)

Prepare the following journal entries in the Bid Deposits Fund, an Agency Fund. This fund is used to record all deposits made by contractors doing work for the city. Any earnings of these resources are required to be paid to the depositing companies.
1. Deposits totaling $750,000 were received.
2. The amount received in number 1 was invested in local banks.
3. Income from the investments totaling $70,000 was received.
4. Deposits of $93,750 were returned to contractors upon successful completion of the projects on which they were working. In addition, these contractors received $8,750 of earnings on their deposits (their share of the earnings of the fund for the year). (*Hint:* Don't forget to liquidate some of the investments.)
5. The books were closed for the year.

E8–12 (True or false)

Indicate whether the following statements are true or false. If any are false, indicate why each is false.
1. The resources in an Agency Fund belong to the governmental unit.
2. A separate Agency Fund must be established for each agency relationship.
3. Revenues earned through an Agency Fund are usually recorded as revenue in the General Fund.

4. Uncollectible property taxes will result in an expense in a Property Tax Agency Fund.
5. Closing entries are not required in an Agency Fund.
6. Financial statements are not prepared for an Agency Fund.
7. Agency Funds are used to disburse earnings from a Nonexpendable Trust Fund.
8. An Agency Fund can be used in any situation in which a Special Revenue Fund can be used.

Section IV

E8–13 (Fill-in-the-blanks—general terminology)

1. When special assessment bonds are issued to finance the cost of paving streets, the principal usually is recorded as a liability in _____ .

2. The project described in number 1 is called a _____ by the GASB.

3. If a city used a special assessment to finance the cost of storm sewer cleaning, the project would be called a _____ by the GASB.

4. The accounting procedures used to record the activities involved in installing street lighting in a neighborhood are the same as those used in a _____ .

5. The activities involved in a "service assessment" should be accounted for in _____ , _____ , or _____ as appropriate.

6. If a governmental unit is not "obligated in some manner" for the debt resulting from a special assessment construction project, the debt service activities should be accounted for in a (an) _____ .

7. In the situation described in number 6, the construction activities would be accounted for in a (an) _____ .

E8–14 (Discussion of "obligated in some manner")

Explain the term *obligated in some manner* as it is used by the GASB, and indicate how it affects special assessment accounting.

E8–15 (Multiple choice)

1. The construction of a new criminal court building, using a federal grant for three quarters of the cost, would be accounted for in
   a. The General Fund
   b. A Special Assessment Fund
   c. A Capital Projects Fund
   d. The General Fixed Assets Account Group
   e. Any of the above

2. The City of Milta financed the construction of a new street-lighting system through special assessments. The resulting asset (street lights) should be recorded in

   a. The General Fund
   b. The Street Light Fund (a Special Assessment Fund)
   c. The Street Light Fund (a Capital Projects Fund)
   d. The General Fixed Assets Account Group
   e. None of the above

3. A comparison of budgetary and actual data must be reported for Capital Projects Funds
   a. When the actual amounts exceed the budgeted
   b. When the budgeted amounts exceed the actual
   c. Whenever a Capital Projects Fund is used
   d. When there is a legally adopted annual budget for a Capital Projects Fund
   e. None of the above

4. A deficit in a fund
   a. Results when the revenues in the early years of the project exceed the expenditures
   b. May arise in the early years of a project because the expenditures are usually initially financed with the proceeds of a bond issue
   c. Always indicates that the fund is in serious financial difficulty
   d. Reflects poor management by the government
   e. None of the above

5. The Special assessments receivable—deferred account is used
   a. To record the amount of revenue recognized from special assessments in a particular period
   b. To offset any deficit arising from a special assessment project
   c. As a budgetary account
   d. To record the amount of assessments that will be collected in future periods
   e. None of the above

6. The Encumbrances account is reported
   a. On the balance sheet
   b. On the statement of revenues, expenditures, and changes in fund balance
   c. On either a or b
   d. On the statement comparing the budgeted and actual revenues for a Special Revenue Fund
   e. None of the above

7. The activities of the police department of the City of Brent are recorded in
   a. The General Fund
   b. A Capital Projects Fund
   c. A Special Assessments Fund
   d. A combination of b and c
   e. None of the above

8. The minimum number of funds a city may use for accounting purposes is
   a. One
   b. Two
   c. Three
   d. Four
   e. Eight

9. A city service financed through a special assessment should be accounted for in
   a. A Special Revenue Fund
   b. The General Fund
   c. An Enterprise Fund
   d. Either a, b, or c, as appropriate
   e. None of the above

PROBLEMS

Section I

P8–1 (Journal entries for an Expendable Trust Fund)

Landslot City received a gift from Ms. J. R. Landslot. Ms. Landslot wished to provide operating resources for an annual parade in her husband's honor. The gift was $2 million. To guarantee proper use of the money, Ms. Landslot made the donation in the form of a trust—an Expendable Trust. The following events took place during 19X1:

1. Ms. Landslot gave Landslot City $2 million with the stipulations mentioned above.
2. The city paid $500,000 to a local advertising agency to publicize the parade.
3. The city sponsored a float in the parade. The total cost of building the float was $200,000. Based on the trust agreement, this is an acceptable expenditure from the gift.
4. The police department spent $100,000 for extra police to control the traffic and crowds at the parade. The trust reimbursed the department for these costs.
5. The sanitation department incurred $75,000 of costs in cleaning up after the parade. The trust reimbursed the department for these costs.
6. The city paid $300,000 to various school bands and marching groups to participate in the parade.
7. A "kick-off dinner" was held two months before the parade to start the parade season. The cost of the dinner was $123,000.
8. An office was established to oversee the parade preparations. The total cost of running the office was $35,000, of which $25,000 was paid in cash.

    9.   The cost of permits and other legal obligations totaled $500.
  10.   The remaining cash, except for $10,000, was invested in marketable securities. According to the trust agreement, this money would be invested and used to provide for the 19X2 parade.

REQUIRED: 1.   Record the above entries in the Landslot Parade Fund—an Expendable Trust Fund.
                   2.   Prepare a statement of revenues, expenditures, and changes in fund balance for 19X1 and a balance sheet as of December 31, 19X1, for the fund.

P8–2   (Journal entries for an Expendable Trust Fund)

    1.   The City of Newfonia received a gift of $2 million from the First Tire Company. The company required the city to maintain the principal of the gift and use any income to beautify the town square. A formal trust agreement was prepared and the appropriate legal acts were passed.
    2.   The city invested the entire gift in certificates of deposit.
    3.   Investment income of $100,000 was received in cash and $90,000 was transferred to the fund that will use these resources.
    4.   Since plans to beautify the town square were incomplete, the $90,000 was invested in short-term securities.
    5.   After beautification plans were completed, the city "cashed in" one half of the $90,000 investments and received $54,000; the excess over principal was investment income.
    6.   The city purchased trees and shrubs from a local nursery for $35,000. In addition, the nursery charged the city $8,000 to prepare the ground and plant the trees and shrubs.
    7.   As part of a continuing campaign, the city received a $300,000 gift from the Second Tire Company. The same restrictions, as indicated in number 1, applied to this gift. In an attempt to make the accounting easier, both companies agreed that the income from the gifts could be combined as long as the principal of each gift was separately maintained. The proceeds of the Second Tire Company gift were immediately invested in short-term securities.
    8.   The First Tire Fund received $100,000 in income.
    9.   The Second Tire Fund received $12,000 in income.
  10.   Each of the principal funds transferred the amounts received in numbers 8 and 9 to the income fund.
  11.   Additional beautification projects costing $97,000 were paid for.

REQUIRED: 1.   Prepare the journal entries necessary to record the above events on the books of the fund that will spend the resources to beautify the town square.
                   2.   Prepare a statement of revenues, expenditures, and changes in fund balance and a balance sheet for the fund that will spend the resources

to beautify the town square. The accounting period ended December 31, 19X1.

3. Prepare the closing entry (entries) for the fund.
    (*Note:* Problem 8–5 is a continuation of this problem.)

P8–3   (Journal entries for several funds)

Listed below are several transactions occurring during 19X1 that relate to Canal Vista, a city in the southwestern United States:

1. The general operating budget was approved. It included estimated revenues of $2,000,000 and appropriations of $1,900,000.
2. A general obligation bond issue of $10 million was sold to finance the construction of a new parking garage. The bonds were sold for $10,400,000. The premium was transferred to the fund that will pay the principal and interest on the debt.
3. The city uses a Property Tax Fund (an Agency Fund) to collect property taxes. The tax levy was a total of $20 million. Of this amount, $10 million was for the General Fund, $5 million was for a Special Revenue Fund, and $5 million was for a Debt Service Fund. Each fund expected to collect 99 percent of the taxes.
4. A contract for the parking garage was signed with University Construction, Inc., for $9,500,000.
5. Property taxes were collected totaling $12 million, and amounts proportionate to the original levy were distributed to each participating fund. The Special Revenue Fund and the Debt Service Fund each paid .001 (one tenth of one percent) of the proceeds to have collections made for them.
6. University Construction submitted a progress billing of $1 million.
7. Interest of $200,000 was paid from a Debt Service Fund.
8. University Construction was paid the amount owed after deducting a 5 percent retainage.
9. The salaries of the mayor and the other general governmental employees were paid. These totaled $145,000. Assume salaries are not encumbered.
10. Supplies costing $8,000 were ordered by the mayor's office.
11. Equipment costing $5,000 was acquired for cash by a department in the General Fund.
12. The supplies ordered in number 10 arrived and $8,200 was billed to the city. Assume the invoice was paid after the additional amount was approved.

REQUIRED: Prepare all the journal entries necessary to record the above transactions. In addition, identify the fund(s) and account group(s) in which each entry is recorded.

P8–4   (Financial statements and closing entries for an Expendable Trust Fund)

The City of New Baton received a gift from a wealthy citizen several years past. The gift established a trust of $1 million that must be maintained intact. The income from the trust must be used to maintain an old section of the city called the Vieux Carre. Since the citizen was an accountant, she insisted that an annual budget be prepared and that the fund use budgetary accounting, including the use of encumbrances. After several years of operation, the Expendable Trust Fund had the following account balances at the end of the fiscal year:

City of New Baton
Expendable Trust Fund
Kathy Paige Income Fund
Trial Balance
June 30, 19X1

	DEBITS	CREDITS
Cash	$ 2,000	
Investments	25,000	
Due from Kathy Paige Principal Fund	12,000	
Accounts payable		$ 4,000
Unreserved fund balance		39,000
Reserve for encumbrances		2,000
Encumbrances	2,000	
Estimated revenues	4,100	
Estimated other financing sources	45,000	
Revenues—investments		4,000
Operating transfer from Kathy Paige Principal Fund		40,000
Appropriations		49,100
Expenditures—capital outlay	14,000	
Expenditures—maintenance	34,000	
	$138,100	$138,100

REQUIRED: 1. Prepare a statement of revenues, expenditures, and changes in fund balance and a balance sheet for the Kathy Paige Income Fund.
         2. Prepare any closing entries necessary at June 30, 19X1.

Section II

P8–5 (Journal entries for an Expendable Trust Fund and a Nonexpendable Trust Fund)
(Note: This problem is continuation of P8–2.)

REQUIRED 1. Refer to the transactions presented in P8–2 for the City of Newfonia. Prepare the journal entries necessary to record all of the transactions. Identify each individual fund used.
        2. Prepare a statement of revenues, expenses, and changes in fund balance and a balance sheet for the First Tire Company Principal Trust Fund.

P8–6   (Financial statements for a Nonexpendable Trust Fund)

The following information is available for the City of Id for the fiscal year July 1, 19X1–June 30, 19X2:

City of Id
Nonexpendable Trust Fund
Crystal Scanne Memorial Fund
Trial Balance
June 30, 19X2

	DEBITS	CREDITS
Cash	$ 45,000	
Investments	2,400,000	
Due from other departments	8,000	
Income receivable on investments	20,000	
Due to Crystal Scanne Operating Fund		$ 8,000
Accounts payable		12,000
Fund balance		2,352,000
Fund balance—loss on sale of investments	10,000	
Fund balance—gain on sale of investments		5,000
Revenues—investments		125,000
Rent expense	3,000	
Salaries expense	15,000	
Utilities expense	1,000	
	$2,502,000	$2,502,000

REQUIRED: Prepare a statement of revenues, expenses, and changes in fund balance for the year ending June 30, 19X2, and a balance sheet as of June 30, 19X2.

P8–7   (Journal entries and financial statements for a Nonexpendable Trust Fund and an Expendable Trust Fund)

Following are several transactions incurred by Uno City for the George Ferret Memorial funds—a Nonexpendable Trust Fund for the principal of the gift and an Expendable Trust Fund to spend the income from the fund.

19X1   1.   Mr. George Ferret gave the city ownership of a small service business that had assets of: Cash, $2,000; Accounts receivable, $5,000; and Furniture and fixtures, $15,000. All liabilities were paid before the gift was made. According to the trust document, the income from the business must be used to provide meals and medical care for the elderly and those without homes.

2.   The business billed customers for $236,000.

3.   Customer accounts totaling $232,000 were collected.

4.   Salaries of business employees totaling $79,000 were paid.

5.   Cash of $20,000 was given to the Expendable Trust Fund to provide meals during the Christmas season.

6.   Utilities for the business were paid, $2,500.

7. The income fund paid $3,700 for holiday meals.
8. Medical bills were paid for those citizens who could not afford them, $7,500.
9. Materials used in the operation of the business were acquired and paid for, $4,500. These were used as they were acquired.
10. Depreciation on business assets was $3,000.
11. The books for the business were closed, and the amount due the income fund was paid.
12. The Expendable Trust Fund purchased $100,000 of investments.

REQUIRED:
1. Prepare the journal entries necessary to record the above information and identify the fund(s) and account group(s) used.
2. Prepare a statement of revenues, expenses, and changes in fund balance and a balance sheet for the Nonexpendable Trust Fund.
3. Prepare a statement of revenues, expenditures, and changes in fund balance and a balance sheet for the Expendable Trust Fund.

P8–8 (Journal entries for several funds)

Following are several transactions for the Village of Roux for 19X1:
1. A contract was signed with Signet Construction Company to build a bridge across the Green River. The amount of the contract was $10 million. The financing of the project was through a $5 million general obligation bond issue and a $5 million federal grant. Assume that the bonds were issued at face value and the grant was received. The laws of Roux require that the budget be recorded in the accounts.
2. A citizen of Roux donated $1 million of marketable securities to the city to be used as the principal of a nonexpendable trust—the Concert Principal Trust Fund. This fund would be used to generate income that would be spent through the Concert Operating Fund for free concerts for the youth of the city.
3. The Electric Utility Fund sent bills to its customers for $130,000. In addition, the General Fund was billed for $10,000 for the electricity used by the village.
4. Income of $50,000 was received in cash by the Concert Principal Trust Fund. This amount was transferred to the Concert Operating Fund.
5. The Concert Operating Fund spent $10,000 for a concert.
6. The bridge contractor submitted a progress billing of $200,000.
7. The contractor in number 6 was paid the amount billed, less a 10 percent retainage.
8. Investments held by the Concert Principal Trust Fund that cost $50,000 were sold for $60,000. (Assume that all gains become part of principal.)
9. Additional investments were purchased by the Concert Principal Trust Fund for $50,000.

10. The General Fund levied a property tax of $2,000,000. Of this amount, $1,900,000 is expected to be collected.
11. Current special assessments of $150,000 were collected. These assessments were used to service debt.
12. Salaries of $500,000 were paid to the general governmental employees. Omit withholdings and so on, and assume that all were employed by the General Fund. (Salaries are not encumbered.)
13. The electric utility paid its employees $100,000. Omit withholdings and so on.
14. A fire engine ordered earlier in the year was delivered at a total cost of $120,000. When the order was placed, $118,000 was encumbered. Assume the extra amount was approved.

REQUIRED: Prepare all the journal entries necessary to record the above transactions and identify the fund(s) and account group(s) used.

Section III

P8–9   (Journal entries and financial statements for an Agency Fund)

The City of New Tuckett recently hosted a state fair. The city levied a special 1 percent sales tax on all sales made at the fair, the proceeds of which were used to help retire outstanding debt and finance improvements to the area after the fair closed. The improvements were accounted for in a Special Revenue Fund. Money was used by the Special Revenue Fund as needed, and any excess was paid to a Debt Service Fund. The city used an Agency Fund to account for the collection of all tax monies. The dates of the fair spanned two fiscal periods. The following trial balance is available at the end of 19X1:

City of New Tuckett
Agency Fund
State Fair Sales Tax Fund
Trial Balance
December 31, 19X4

	DEBITS	CREDITS
Cash	$ 3,500	
Time certificates of deposit	46,600	
Due to other governmental funds		50,100
	$50,100	$50,100

The following transactions took place during 19X2:
1. Investments costing $15,000 were redeemed for a total of $18,000; the difference was investment revenue.

2. Contractors were paid $1,000 by the Special Revenue Fund after receiving the money from the Agency Fund. All payments made by the Special Revenue Fund were funded individually from the Agency Fund.
3. The fund collected $800 in interest on investments.
4. Workers were paid $1,000 to begin dismantling the exhibits. City employees were used to begin the cleanup process.
5. The fair paid the fund the total amount due as a result of 19X2 sales, $134,000.
6. A contractor was hired at a cost of $125,000 to finish the cleanup.
7. The contractor was paid $35,000 on the contract.
8. The remaining investments were redeemed for $36,000.
9. The amount due the cleanup contractor was paid to the Special Revenue Fund.

REQUIRED:
1. Prepare the entries necessary to record the above entries on the books of the Agency Fund.
2. Prepare the financial statements for the Agency Fund for 19X2.

P8–10 (Journal entries for an Agency Fund and other funds and account groups)

The City of Kcool maintains an Agency Fund for its employees' insurance withholdings—the Employees' Insurance Deposits Fund. The following are selected transactions incurred during 19X1 by Kcool:

1. A contractor submitted a progress billing of $750,000 on a new sports arena being built for Kcool.
2. The city recorded its monthly payroll. Salaries totaled $350,000. The withholdings were as follows: $70,000 for employees' income taxes, $8,000 for employees' insurance, $15,000 for employees' pension contributions, and $25,000 for miscellaneous deductions. The General Fund paid the Employees' Insurance Deposit Fund.
3. The mayor purchased new office equipment at a cost of $5,000. The purchase was encumbered for $5,500.
4. The contractor mentioned in number 1 received a payment of $700,000. The amount withheld was the retained percentage.
5. Property taxes collected by a Special Revenue Fund totaled $123,000. In addition, accounts of $500 were written off.
6. The city sold old equipment for $500. The equipment originally cost $23,000. There are no restrictions on the use of the proceeds.
7. Supplies totaling $800 were ordered for general government use.
8. The Employees' Insurance Deposits Fund made a payment of $25,000 to the various insurance companies providing insurance coverage to the employees.
9. The city recorded its monthly payroll. Salaries totaled $375,000. The withholdings were as follows: $75,000 for employees' income taxes,

$8,500 for employees' insurance, $18,000 for employees' pension contributions, and $26,000 for miscellaneous deductions. The General Fund paid the Employees' Insurance Deposit Fund.

REQUIRED: Prepare the journal entries necessary to record the above events and identify the fund or account group used.

P8–11 (Correcting entries for several funds)

1. The city acquired land for an expansion of the main library. The entire project was financed through a bond issue. The following entry was made in the General Fund:

Expenditures—capital outlay	123,000	
Cash		123,000

The bond proceeds were used to acquire the land.

2. Interest on outstanding debt was paid from resources previously accumulated for that purpose. The only entry that was made was the following in a Debt Service Fund:

Expenditures—mature interest	50,000	
Cash		50,000

3. Bond principal was retired from resources previously accumulated for that purpose. The only entry that was made was the following in a Debt Service Fund:

Expenditures—mature bond principal	200,000	
Cash		200,000

4. Miscellaneous office equipment that originally cost $5,000 was sold for $800. The proceeds were recorded in a Special Revenue Fund because of the restrictions placed upon the use of the money by the original grant that was used to buy the equipment. No other entries were made.

5. The city acquired several fire engines at a total cost of $500,000. The resources that were used were part of a federal grant to acquire various fire-fighting equipment and build two fire stations. The following entry was recorded in the General Fund:

Equipment	500,000	
Cash		500,000

6. The city entered into a contract with Crackel, Inc., a construction company, to build a bridge across the Bouga Bayou. The contract cost was $1,750,000. The contract was signed on August 1, 19X0, and the appropriate entries were made during that year. An inex-

perienced bookkeeper did not make any entries for 19X1, the current year. After accumulating the appropriate papers, you have been able to determine the following information:
   a. The costs incurred in 19X0 totaled $900,000.
   b. The project was completed on June 15, 19X1, at a total cost of $1,750,000. The job was accepted on June 30, 19X1.
   c. All entries for 19X0 were made correctly.
   d. A progress payment of $400,000 was made on April 1, 19X1.
   e. Instead of retaining some of each progress payment, the last payment to the contractor was not made until the project was completed and accepted.
   f. The project was financed with a bond issue.
   (*Hint:* Don't forget to make budgetary entries.)
7. An Agency Fund is used to collect property taxes. The taxes are then disbursed to various city departments and the local school board (not part of the city). The following entries were made to record the collection and disbursement of the taxes in the Agency Fund (no entries were made in the General Fund):

Cash	1,234,000	
Revenues—property taxes		1,234,000
Expenditures—property taxes—General Fund	234,000	
Expenditures—property taxes—school board	1,000,000	
Cash		1,234,000
Cash	10,000	
Revenues—property tax collection fee from school board		10,0000

REQUIRED: Prepare any correcting entries that are necessary as a result of the above information. Identify any fund(s) and account group(s) used.

P8–12 (Journal entries for several funds)

Following are several transactions that relate to the city of Pagedan.
   1. The general operating budget was approved. It included estimated revenues of $790,000 and appropriations of $800,000
   2. A general obligation bond issue of $6 million was sold to finance the construction of a new bridge. The bonds were sold at their face amount.
   3. The city uses a Property Tax Fund (an Agency Fund) to collect property taxes. The tax levy was a total of $7 million. Of this amount, $4 million was for the General Fund, $2 million for a Special Revenue Fund, and $1 million for a Debt Service Fund.
   4. A contract for the bridge was signed with Wilt Construction Company for $6 million.

5. Property taxes totaling $6.3 million were collected and the appropriate amounts were distributed to each participating fund.
6. Interest of $200,000 was paid from the Debt Service Fund.
7. The bridge contractor submitted a progress billing of $1 million.
8. The bridge contractor was paid the amount of the billing, less a 10 percent retainage.
9. The city has a Housing Trust Fund (a Nonexpendable Trust Fund) established by gifts from several citizens. The income earned by the investments of this fund is spent through the Housing Authority Fund (an Expendable Trust). During the year, the Housing Authority Fund received $25,000 from the Housing Trust Fund. (Omit the entries for the Housing Trust Fund.)
10. The salaries of the mayor and the other general governmental employees were paid. Cash was distributed in the amount of $500,000. (Assume that salaries are not encumbered.)
11. Expenditures of $10,000 were made from Housing Authority funds for repairs to apartments.
12. The General Fund made its annual payment of $200,000 to the Debt Service Fund. Of this amount, $175,000 was for interest.

REQUIRED: Prepare all the journal entries necessary to record the above transactions and identify the fund in which each entry is recorded.

Section IV

P8–13   (Journal entries and financial statements for a street-lighting project that was financed with a special assessment)

19X1–X2   1.   The managing board of Vera Township approved the capital budget for the fiscal year July 1, 19X1–June 30, 19X2. Included in this budget was a drainage project that was to be funded through special assessments and a contribution from the township. Intermediate financing was furnished by a bond issue that would be repaid with collections of the special assessments. The managing board also approved the budget for the project. Included in the budget were estimated revenues of $200,000 for the current year and appropriations of $1,600,000 for the project. The township's share of the cost for this project was $40,000. Assume the township guaranteed payment of the special assessment bonds used to finance the project.
2.   A construction contract with Jorge Construction Company was approved for $1,400,000.
3.   Special assessments totaling $1,360,000 were levied against the property holders that would benefit from the project. Of this amount, $100,000 was considered to be current and recognized as revenue. This same amount will become current next year.

4. Collection from property holders totaled $90,000.
5. Special assessment bonds totaling $1,360,000 were issued for $1,360,000.
6. A progress billing was received from the contractor for $500,000.
7. The contractor was paid the amount of the billing, less a 10 percent retainage. (Assume the city does not use a voucher system.)
8. Short-term securities were purchased for $900,000, using Capital Projects Fund resources.
9. An additional billing was received from the contractor for $600,000.
10. Investments that cost $600,000 were redeemed for $620,000. The difference was investment revenue.
11. The contractor was paid, less the agreed-upon retainage.
12. Investments that cost $300,000 were redeemed for $330,000. The difference was investment revenue.
13. The contractor completed the project and submitted a final bill for $300,000. After an examination of the work, it was accepted by the city and the full amount of the billing plus all previously retained amounts were paid.
14. Interest of $140,000 was paid on the special assessment bonds.
15. The township's share of the project was paid to the fund where the construction was recorded.

REQUIRED:
1. Prepare the journal entries necessary to record the above events and indicate the fund(s) and account group(s) used. (Assume there is no interest on the assessments for 19X1.)
2. Prepare a trial balance for the fund where the construction accounting was recorded.
3. Prepare all necessary year-end entries and closing entries in the Capital Projects Fund. After the project has been completed, any fund balance should be transferred to the Debt Service Fund. Assume the township records all fixed assets. (*Hint:* Don't forget the status of the receivables in the Debt Service Fund at year-end.) Omit year-end entries in the General Long-Term Debt Account Group.
4. Prepare a statement of revenues, expenditures, and changes in fund balance and a balance sheet for the fund where the construction was recorded.

P8–14 (Journal entries for several funds and account groups)

19X1
1. A street-lighting project was approved by the city managers of Wakefield City; the total cost was $750,000. Revenues of the Capital Projects Fund for the current year are estimated to be $50,000 and special assessment bonds will be used to finance the remainder. Interest on outstanding bonds payable is estimated to be $75,000 for the year. (Assume a budget is not recorded in the Debt Service Fund; however, a budget is recorded in the Capital Projects Fund.)
2. General governmental resources were used to acquire new equipment for the mayor's office. The total cost of the equipment was $3,000. This expenditure previously had been encumbered for $3,200.

3. A contract was signed for the construction of an addition to the city hall. The total cost was $900,000.
4. Special assessment bonds were issued for the street-lighting project. The bonds were issued for their face value of $700,000.
5. A contract was let with Old Iron Construction Company for the street-lighting project at a total cost of $750,000.
6. Interest of $95,000 was recorded and paid from a Debt Service Fund.
7. A special assessment of $750,000 was levied to pay for the cost of the street-lighting project. The current portion of the installment was $50,000. Revenue of $50,000 was recorded at that time.
8. Old Iron submitted a progress billing for $200,000.
9. Old Iron was paid $190,000; the remainder was retained until the completion of the project.
10. Construction cash from the street-lighting project totaling $500,000 was invested in marketable securities.
11. Bonds with a face value of $800,000 were issued for that amount. The proceeds were used to begin construction of an addition to the city office building complex. (*Hint:* Don't forget to record the bond liability.)
12. The General Fund transferred $75,000 to a Debt Service Fund to be used to retire outstanding bonds.
13. The Debt Service Fund mentioned above (number 12) retired $100,000 of outstanding bonds. Assume that all interest had previously been paid.
14. Special assessments totaling $50,000 were collected.
15. Interest of $75,000 was paid on the special assessment bonds outstanding.
16. The next installment of the special assessment was $50,000.

REQUIRED: Prepare all the journal entries necessary to record the above transactions. In addition, identify the fund(s) and account group(s) in which each entry is recorded. Where multiple types of the same fund are used, label them as 1, 2, and so on (e.g., CPF-1, CPF-2). The street-lighting project should be CPF-1 and DSF-1; the city office complex addition should be CPF-2; the Debt Service Fund in number 6 should be DSF-3 and the Debt Service Fund in number 12 should be DSF-2.

P8–15 (Multiple choice)
1. When a city acquires equipment that will be used to accomplish the purpose of a Nonexpendable Trust Fund, the equipment should be recorded in
    a. The General Fund
    b. The Fixed Assets Account Group
    c. The Nonexpendable Trust Fund
    d. An Enterprise Fund

2. Which of the following funds does not have a fund balance?
   a. The General Fund
   b. A Nonexpendable Trust Fund
   c. An Agency Fund
   d. An Expendable Trust Fund
3. Which of the following funds would be used to account for a PERS?
   a. A Pension Trust Fund
   b. A Nonexpendable Trust Fund
   c. An Expendable Trust Fund
   d. An Agency Fund
4. When the initial gift is received for a nonexpendable trust, which of the following is credited?
   a. An operating transfer in
   b. A residual transfer in
   c. An operating transfer out
   d. The fund balance
5. Payments made by an expendable trust for the purpose for which the trust was established are debited to
   a. An expense account
   b. An expenditure account
   c. The fund balance
   d. An operating transfer out account
6. The City of Way accumulates its employees' withholdings for income taxes in a separate fund. Which of the following should be used?
   a. The General Fund
   b. An Expendable Trust Fund
   c. A Nonexpendable Trust Fund
   d. An Agency Fund
7. A Debt Service Fund temporarily borrowed $10,000 from a Nonexpendable Trust Fund to meet a current interest payment. Assuming this is a legal transaction, the Debt Service Fund should credit which of the following?
   a. Fund balance
   b. Due to other funds
   c. Revenue
   d. Operating transfer in
8. Revenues earned by an Agency Fund are generally reported as revenue in
   a. The Agency Fund
   b. The General Fund
   c. A Nonexpendable Trust Fund
   d. None of the above

9. A separate trust fund should be established
    a. For each separate trust agreement
    b. For only those funds that involve a nonexpendable principal
    c. To properly measure revenues for the General Fund
    d. Only for pension trusts

10. A payment made by an Agency Fund for the purpose for which it was established is debited to
    a. The fund balance
    b. An asset account
    c. A liability account
    d. An expenditure account

9

THE GOVERNMENTAL FUND ACCOUNTING CYCLE

> Comprehensive Annual Financial
> Report and Current Issues

LEARNING OBJECTIVES

After completion of this chapter, you should be able to:

1. Identify the basic components of a Comprehensive Annual Financial Report (CAFR)
2. List the combined financial statements included in the CAFR
3. Explain how a "combined" financial statement is constructed
4. Explain the relationships presented in the Financial Reporting Pyramid
5. Explain how notes are used for financial statement reporting
6. Explain the relationship between individual fund financial statements and combining and combined financial statements
7. Identify the statistical tables that are required in a CAFR
8. Explain how accountants define the "reporting entity"
9. Explain the importance of interim financial reporting
10. Explain the purpose of the Certificate of Achievement for Excellence in Financial Reporting

---

In previous chapters we have discussed the process of accumulating financial information for governmental units. This information is communicated to individuals and institutions outside the government, and to some extent inside, through the **Comprehensive Annual Financial Report (CAFR).** The purpose of the CAFR has been summarized as follows:

The CAFR is the governmental unit's official annual report and should contain introductory information, schedules necessary to demonstrate compliance with finance-related legal and contractual provisions, and statistical data.[1]

MAJOR COMPONENTS OF THE CAFR

In outline form, the CAFR contains the following major components:

I.   Introductory Section
II. Financial Section
    A.   Auditor's Report
    B.   General Purpose Financial Statements (Combined Statements—Overview)
    C.   Combining and Individual Fund and Account Group Statements and Schedules
III. Statistical Tables

The CAFR begins with an introductory section that includes a table of contents, letters of transmittal, and any other data that the management of the governmental unit feels is important to the reader. The second section of the CAFR is the financial section—the auditor's report, the General Purpose Financial Statements (GPFS), and the combining and individual fund and account group statements and schedules.

The General Purpose Financial Statements consist of the following:

1.   Combined balance sheet—all fund types and account groups
2.   Combined statement of revenues, expenditures, and changes in fund balances—all governmental fund types
3.   Combined statement of revenues, expenditures, and changes in fund balances—budget and actual—general and special revenue fund types (other funds may also be included)
4.   Combined statement of revenues, expenses, and changes in retained earnings (or equity)—all proprietary fund types
5.   Combined statement of cash flows—all proprietary fund types
6.   Notes to the financial statements

(*Note:* The treatment of trust funds is discussed later in this chapter.)

The preparation of the CAFR is basically an aggregation process, as shown in Exhibit 9–1. The transactions form the basis of the system and then, as the "pyramid" indicates, this information is aggregated into the individual fund financial statements. The individual statements are then aggregated into the combining statements, and those data are aggregated again into the combined financial statements. Since the combined financial statements form the main focus of attention in the CAFR, we will discuss the financial report beginning with these statements.

[1]NCGA, *Statement 1*, p. 19 (GASB Cod. Sec. 1900.109).

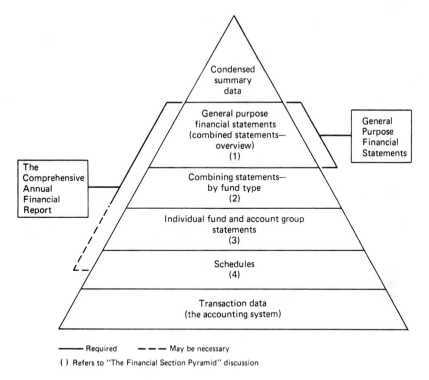

EXHIBIT 9–1   The Financial Reporting "Pyramid"
Source: NCGA, *Statement 1*, p. 20 (GASB Cod. Sec. 1900.114).

Many of the previous exhibits in this text were of financial statements that were prepared for the *individual* funds. The issuance of NCGA *Statement 1* in 1979 changed the emphasis of financial reporting from individual fund statements to **combined financial statements.** A CAFR must treat these combined financial statements as the main focus of the report. A combined financial statement, by definition, is a single financial statement, such as a balance sheet, that has a separate column for each fund included.

Combined financial statements represent an aggregation of the information presented in individual fund financial statements like those used in the illustrations in previous chapters. In the Governmental Accounting in Practice sections of many chapters, combining financial statements were used. The relationship between the individual fund, combining, and combined financial statements is illustrated in Exhibit 9–2.

The first step in the aggregation process is preparation of financial statements for each individual fund. For simplicity, we will study balance sheets of Special Revenue Funds. The first step is to prepare a balance sheet for each individual Special Revenue Fund. On Exhibit 9–2 this is the lowest level. The second step is to prepare a combining balance sheet for all Special Revenue Funds. On this statement, the middle level of aggregation in Exhibit 9–2, each Special Rev-

Combined financial statements—balance sheet

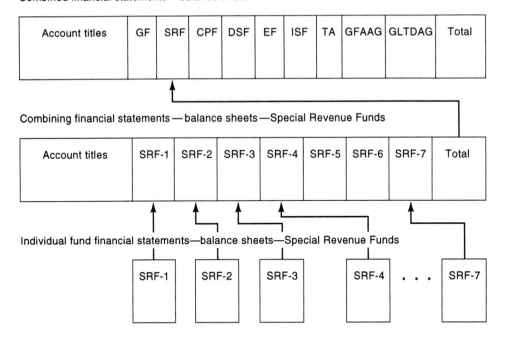

EXHIBIT 9–2   Relationship between Individual, Combining, and Combined Financial Statements

enue Fund is represented by a separate column and a total column is also added. This total column is the summation of all similar account balances for the Special Revenue Funds. For example, the cash for each of the seven funds illustrated is added together to determine the total cash held in Special Revenue Funds. The third step is preparation of a combined balance sheet. On this statement, the top level of aggregation in Exhibit 9–2, the total of all Special Revenue Fund accounts is reported in a single column. As we discuss the statements in the remainder of this chapter, this process should become very clear.

Combined Balance Sheet—All Fund Types and Account Groups

The *combined balance sheet—all fund types and account groups* for the city of Columbus is a typical combined balance sheet.[2] This statement provides an *overview* of the balance sheet accounts of the governmental unit. Notice that only one column is used for each fund type (see Table 9–1).

Notice also that the total columns are labeled "Memorandum Only." These columns are optional, but, if included, they must be labeled "Memorandum Only." They represent totals for each of the balance sheet items of each type of fund listed. Since many restrictions are placed on the use of the asset and fund balance accounts, these totals do not represent a true total for the governmental unit. For example, the total of Cash and cash equivalents is $220,400,674. Only $24,678,333 is General Fund cash. The remaining $195,722,341 is cash and cash equivalents whose use is limited to construction, debt service, fulfilling trust agreements, and so forth. As a result, the reader must be aware of the limitations of the totals.

Some governmental units may choose to eliminate interfund transactions before preparing their financial statements. If any interfund transactions are eliminated, this fact must be clearly disclosed. The process of elimination of interfund transactions is beyond the scope of this text.

Notice also the two columns before the total columns. These are labeled *primary government* and *component unit.* These terms will be explained in more detail later in this chapter. For the present, assume a primary government is the main governmental unit and a component unit is a separate organization for which the primary government is financially accountable. In previous illustrations, the City of New Orleans and the City of Columbus are primary governmental units. Later in this chapter, we will explore the topic of primary governments and component units in more depth.

Combined Statement of Revenues, Expenditures, and Changes in Fund Balances—All Governmental Fund Types

The second combined statement included in the CAFR is the *combined statement of revenues, expenditures, and changes in fund balances—all governmental fund types* (see Table 9–2). Notice that a separate column is used for each fund that uses a spending measurement focus and the modified accrual basis of accounting. This form of reporting is a continuation of the general format illustrated in Exhibit 9–2.

---

[2]The statement titles used in this chapter are those suggested by the NCGA in *Statement 1.* A careful reading of some of the statements issued by the City of Columbus will disclose slight wording differences from those used in the text. The reader should be aware that there are acceptable alternatives to the wording used in *Statement 1.*

TABLE 9–1   Combined Balance Sheet—All Fund Types and Account Groups

City of Columbus, Ohio
Combined Balance Sheet—All Fund Types, Account Groups, and Discretely
Presented Component Unit
December 31, 19X1

	Governmental Fund Types				Proprietary Fund Types	
	GENERAL	SPECIAL REVENUE	DEBT SERVICE	CAPITAL PROJECTS	ENTERPRISE— NOTE S	INTERNAL SERVICE
Assets						
Cash and cash equivalents:						
Cash and investments with treasurer—Note C	$24,678,333	$22,394,981	$39,844,532	$37,358,041	$ 64,541,264	$ 4,622,322
Cash and investments with fiscal and escrow agents and other—Notes C, J and L	—	—	38,493	—	—	—
Investments, at cost—Note C	—	—	4,237,240	—	—	—
Receivables (net of allowances for uncollectibles)—Note D	14,119,105	47,383,366	4,708,456	12,839	22,535,712	264,956
Due from other:						
Governments	99,100	2,229,062	—	2,200,317	9,426,327	21,200
Funds—Note E	1,985,369	1,959,020	191,000	5,330,066	3,181,790	2,548,114
Due from component unit, net— Note E	430,749	—	—	—	—	—
Inventory	—	—	—	—	12,641,804	779,954
Deferred charges and other—Note G	—	—	—	—	1,736,258	—
Restricted assets:						
Cash and cash equivalents:						
Cash and investments with treasurer and other—Notes C and G	—	—	—	—	100,621,049	—
Cash and cash equivalents with trustees—Notes C and G	—	—	—	—	15,079,072	—
Investments with trustees—Notes C and G	—	—	—	—	18,026,127	—
Accrued interest receivable— Note D	—	—	—	—	109,607	—
Due from other funds—Note E	—	—	—	—	—	—
Net investments in direct financing leases	—	—	—	—	—	—
Property, plant and equipment— Note F:						
At cost	—	—	—	—	1,464,766,094	15,338,845
Less accumulated depreciation, where applicable	—	—	—	—	(399,838,296)	(10,154,439)
Net property, plant and equipment	—	—	—	—	1,064,927,798	5,184,406
Amount available in debt service fund	—	—	—	—	—	—
Amount to be provided for retirement of general long-term obligations	—	—	—	—	—	—
Total assets	$41,312,656	$73,966,429	$49,019,721	$44,901,263	$1,312,826,808	$13,420,952

Fiduciary Fund Types	Account Groups		Totals (Memorandum Only)		Totals (Memorandum Only)	
EXPENDABLE TRUST AND AGENCY	GENERAL FIXED ASSETS	GENERAL LONG-TERM OBLIGATIONS	PRIMARY GOVERNMENT	COMPONENT UNIT CMAA	REPORTING ENTITY 19X1	19X0
$26,961,201	$ —	$ —	$ 220,400,674	$ —	$ 220,400,674	$ 228,905,370
69,156,338	—	—	69,194,831	1,083,064	70,277,895	61,123,267
211,658	—	—	4,448,898	—	4,448,898	4,759,367
6,980	—	—	89,031,414	3,220,607	92,252,021	95,527,890
—	—	—	13,976,006	2,807,710	16,783,716	17,384,243
359,670	—	—	15,555,029	—	15,555,029	13,782,464
—	—	—	430,749	—	430,749	4,000,000
—	—	—	13,421,758	—	13,421,758	12,388,635
—	—	—	1,736,258	408,302	2,144,560	1,054,141
—	—	—	100,621,049	11,664,108	112,285,157	93,228,338
—	—	—	15,079,072	—	15,079,072	19,038,106
—	—	—	18,026,127	—	18,026,127	13,735,437
—	—	—	109,607	—	109,607	563,147
—	—	—	—	—	—	201,565
—	—	—	—	1,257,995	1,257,995	—
—	431,205,002	—	1,911,309,941	176,402,808	2,087,712,749	1,967,192,341
—	—	—	(409,992,735)	(50,122,434)	(460,115,169)	(427,196,173)
—	431,205,002	—	1,501,317,206	126,280,374	1,627,597,580	1,539,996,168
—	—	46,084,291	46,084,291	—	46,084,291	38,361,884
—	—	334,611,684	334,611,684	—	334,611,684	332,789,721
$96,695,847	$431,205,002	$380,695,975	$2,444,044,653	$146,722,160	$2,590,766,813	$2,476,839,743

(Continued)

TABLE 9–1   (continued)

	GENERAL	Governmental Fund Types SPECIAL REVENUE	DEBT SERVICE	CAPITAL PROJECTS	Proprietary Fund Types ENTERPRISE— NOTE S	INTERNAL SERVICE
Liabilities						
Accounts payable	$ 1,494,346	$12,915,325	$ 159,270	$ 2,052,033	$ 7,666,135	$ 756,169
Customer deposits	—	—	—	—	1,007,720	1,619,965
Due to other:						
Governments	—	33,000,357	—	—	—	—
Funds—Note E	939,650	1,925,243	1,146,655	5,173,292	3,065,282	190,044
Other	—	—	—	—	—	—
Due to primary government—Note E	—	—	—	—	—	—
Payable from restricted assets:						
Accounts payable	—	—	—	—	5,739,171	—
Due to other funds—Note E	—	—	—	—	311,502	—
Accrued interest payable	—	—	—	—	1,821,468	—
Deferred revenue	—	3,802,446	376,862	737,742	2,504,636	—
Matured bonds payable	—	—	742,000	—	—	—
Matured interest payable	—	—	510,643	—	—	—
Accrued interest payable	—	—	—	—	14,563,909	—
Accrued wages and benefits—Note G	13,442,114	2,092,318	—	—	2,260,111	479,368
Accrued vacation and sick leave—Note G	—	—	—	—	5,311,394	1,426,271
Notes payable—Note G	—	—	—	1,335,000	—	2,590,861
Bonds and loans payable—Note G	—	—	—	—	965,644,688	—
Less unamortized bond discount	—	—	—	—	(3,555,823)	—
Net bonds and loans payable	—	—	—	—	962,088,865	—
Obligation under capitalized lease—Notes G and J	—	—	—	—	—	—
Total liabilities	15,876,110	53,735,689	2,935,430	9,298,067	1,006,340,193	7,062,678
Fund Equity and Other Credits						
Investment in general fixed assets	—	—	—	—	—	—
Contributed capital—Note S	—	—	—	—	151,606,725	1,739,306
Unreserved retained earnings	—	—	—	—	154,879,890	4,618,968
Fund balances (deficit):						
Reserved for encumbrances	5,358,041	21,294,687	3,183,625	35,863,788	—	—
Unreserved:						
Designated for future years' expenditures	7,500,000	—	6,000,000	—	—	—
Undesignated	12,578,505	(1,063,947)	36,900,666	(260,592)	—	—
Total fund balance/retained earnings	25,436,546	20,230,740	46,084,291	35,603,196	154,879,890	4,618,968
Total fund equity and other credits—Note O	25,436,546	20,230,740	46,084,291	35,603,196	306,486,615	6,358,274
Commitments and contingencies—Notes B, F, G, J and T	—	—	—	—	—	—
Total liabilities, fund equity and other credits	$41,312,656	$73,966,429	$49,019,721	$44,901,263	$1,312,826,808	$13,420,952

Source: Adapted from a recent Comprehensive Annual Financial Report of the City of Columbus, Ohio.

Fiduciary Fund Types	Account Groups		Totals (Memorandum Only)		Totals (Memorandum Only)	
EXPENDABLE TRUST AND AGENCY	GENERAL FIXED ASSETS	GENERAL LONG-TERM OBLIGATIONS	PRIMARY GOVERNMENT	COMPONENT UNIT CMAA	REPORTING ENTITY 19X1	19X0
$ 71,183	$ —	$ —	$ 25,114,461	$ 247,385	$ 25,361,846	$ 22,466,541
—	—	—	2,627,685	60,971	2,688,656	2,725,199
11,568,979	—	—	44,569,336	—	44,569,336	46,998,388
2,803,361	—	—	15,243,527	—	15,243,527	13,733,222
81,760,794	—	—	81,760,794	358,883	82,119,677	66,792,389
—	—	—	—	4,430,749	4,430,749	4,123,600
—	—	—	5,739,171	418,926	6,158,097	6,863,582
—	—	—	311,502	—	311,502	250,807
—	—	—	1,821,468	—	1,821,468	1,741,001
—	—	—	7,421,686	—	7,421,686	6,277,674
—	—	—	742,000	—	742,000	4,438,000
—	—	—	510,643	—	510,643	478,742
—	—	—	14,563,909	1,384,006	15,947,915	14,788,756
—	—	42,167,601	60,441,512	3,495,609	63,937,121	60,069,739
—	—	34,889,657	41,627,322	—	41,627,322	40,434,470
—	—	2,000,000	5,925,861	—	5,925,861	7,642,332
—	—	290,438,717	1,256,083,405	68,009,000	1,324,092,405	1,254,147,127
—	—	—	(3,555,823)	—	(3,555,823)	(1,519,349)
—	—	290,438,717	1,252,527,582	68,009,000	1,320,536,582	1,252,627,778
—	—	11,200,000	11,200,000	—	11,200,000	12,060,000
96,204,317	—	380,695,975	1,572,148,459	78,405,529	1,650,553,988	1,564,512,220
—	431,205,002	—	431,205,002	—	431,205,002	406,036,506
—	—	—	153,346,031	55,631,622	208,977,653	198,307,513
—	—	—	159,498,858	12,685,009	172,183,867	180,172,092
—	—	—	65,700,141	—	65,700,141	68,983,666
—	—	—	13,500,000	—	13,500,000	7,500,000
491,530	—	—	48,646,162	—	48,646,162	51,327,746
491,530	—	—	287,345,161	12,685,009	300,030,170	307,983,504
491,530	431,205,002	—	871,896,194	68,316,631	940,212,825	912,327,523
—	—	—	—	—	—	—
$96,695,847	$431,205,002	$380,695,975	$2,444,044,653	$146,722,160	$2,590,766,813	$2,476,839,743

TABLE 9–2 Combined Statement of Revenues, Expenditures, and Changes in Fund Balances—All Governmental Fund Types

City of Columbus, Ohio

Combined Statement of Revenues, Expenditures and Changes in Fund Balances—
All Governmental Fund Types and Expendable Trust Funds
Year Ended December 31, 19X1

| | Governmental Fund Types | | | | Fiduciary Fund Type | Totals (Memorandum Only) | |
	GENERAL	SPECIAL REVENUE	DEBT SERVICE	CAPITAL PROJECTS	EXPENDABLE TRUST	19X1	19X0
Revenues							
Income taxes—Note M	$196,189,023	$ —	$65,396,309	$ —	$ —	$261,585,332	$243,196,869
Property taxes—Note N	26,477,776	—	—	—	—	26,477,776	26,060,725
Grants and subsidies	25,000	27,898,427	—	4,813,796	—	32,737,223	35,691,644
Investment earnings—Note C	7,961,027	84,199	250,506	3,022	63,980	8,362,734	11,417,641
Special assessments	—	—	69,549	—	—	69,549	86,074
Licenses and permits	4,203,407	2,646,722	—	—	—	6,850,129	6,341,270
Shared revenues	32,195,119	18,212,891	—	—	—	50,408,010	49,026,563
Charges for services	19,386,711	24,595,673	667,814	—	—	44,650,198	37,866,526
Fines and forfeits	10,849,291	544,188	—	—	—	11,393,479	10,647,351
Miscellaneous—Note P	5,437,417	14,472,326	1,682,181	1,812,149	1,225,319	24,629,392	16,191,510
Total revenues	302,724,771	88,454,426	68,066,359	6,628,967	1,289,299	467,163,822	436,526,173
Expenditures							
Current:							
General government	45,411,200	16,530,332	4,444,003	—	1,671,213	68,056,748	50,127,937
Public service	22,274,094	24,723,291	2,915,685	—	—	49,913,070	45,638,058
Public safety	186,862,913	603,791	356,225	—	—	187,822,929	173,518,145
Human services	6,152,775	4,045,463	—	—	—	10,198,238	12,714,081
Development	8,702,532	3,938,796	—	—	—	12,641,328	10,280,154
Health	—	23,738,009	—	—	—	23,738,009	22,160,485
Recreation and parks	—	38,264,848	—	—	45,349	38,310,197	34,993,126
Public utilities	—	6,932,020	—	—	—	6,932,020	3,038,985
Capital outlay	2,872,020	2,846,727	538	42,236,225	—	47,955,510	71,291,492

Debt service:					
Principal retirement and payment of obligation under capitalized lease—Note G	—	—	25,134,678	—	25,134,678	18,760,933
Interest and fiscal charges	—	—	23,343,939	—	23,343,939	17,571,357
Total expenditures	272,275,534	121,623,277	56,195,068	42,236,225	494,046,666	460,094,753
Excess (deficiency) of revenue over expenditures	30,449,237	(33,168,851)	11,871,291	(35,607,258)	(26,882,844)	(23,568,580)
Other Financing Sources (Uses)						
Operating transfers in—Note Q	3,445,848	33,674,598	4,320,582	11,558,516	52,999,544	50,633,526
Operating transfers out—Note Q	(33,680,170)	(7,371,893)	(9,150,466)	(9,380,280)	(59,582,809)	(70,994,181)
Proceeds from general obligation bonds—Note G	—	—	681,000	32,820,000	33,501,000	106,440,841
Total other financing sources (uses)	(30,234,322)	26,302,705	(4,148,884)	34,998,236	26,917,735	86,080,186
Excess (deficiency) of revenues and other financing sources over expenditures and other uses	214,915	(6,866,146)	7,722,407	(609,022)	34,891	62,511,606
Fund balances (deficit) at beginning of year	25,221,631	27,096,886	38,361,884	36,212,218	127,811,412	65,299,806
Fund balances at end of year	$25,436,546	$20,230,740	$46,084,291	$35,603,196	$127,846,303	$127,811,412

See accompanying notes to the general purpose financial statements.

Source: Adapted from a recent Comprehensive Annual Financial Report of the City of Columbus, Ohio.

417

Although the City of Columbus combines its Expendable Trust Funds with its governmental-type funds for purposes of this statement, it is possible to report trust activities on a separate combined statement.

The combined statements follow the same general reporting format as that used by the individual fund illustrations in this text. Notice that some of the fund types had an excess of revenues and other financing sources over expenditures and other financing uses, but that all had positive fund balances at the end of the year.

Combined Statement of Revenues, Expenditures, and Changes in Fund Balances—Budget and Actual—Budgetary General and Special Revenue Fund Types

The third combined statement included in the CAFR is the *combined statement of revenues, expenditures, and changes in fund balances—budget and actual—budgetary general and special revenue fund types.* This statement compares the legally adopted annual budget with the actual data for the General Fund, Special Revenue Fund(s), and any other governmental-type funds that have a legally adopted annual budget. See Table 9–3 on pp. 420–21.

Notice that total revenues for the General Fund in this statement ($299,148,000) are not the same as total revenues previously reported on the operating statement (Table 9–2: $302,724,771). This is because the budget is prepared on a basis other than the modified accrual basis of accounting that is used for the statement of revenues, expenditures, and changes in fund balances—all governmental fund types and expendable trust funds. To make the budget and actual comparisons meaningful, it is necessary to prepare this statement using the same measurement rules that were used to prepare the budget. Thus when the budget is prepared on a basis other than that provided by GAAP, the numbers will not be the same on both statements. The same observation is true with respect to the expenditures and other financing sources (uses). One of the causes of the difference between the expenditures on Tables 9–2 and 9–3 is that encumbrances are reported as if they were expenditures on the budget and actual statement (Table 9–3 and Chapter 5). This procedure is not permitted for the regular operating statement (Table 9–2). However, inclusion of encumbrances on the budget and actual statement provides a better comparison of these two sets of data.

When the budgetary basis differs from GAAP, it is necessary to disclose this fact in the report and to reconcile GAAP and budget data. The City of Columbus does this in a note to the financial statements (see Table 9–4 on p. 422). Notice that there are many items in addition to the encumbrances mentioned above that must be included/excluded to reconcile the budgetary and GAAP basis of accounting.

Combined Statement of Revenues, Expenses, and Changes in Retained Earnings (Equity)— All Proprietary Funds

The fourth combined statement included in the CAFR is the *combined statement of revenues, expenses, and changes in retained earnings (equity)—all proprietary funds.* This combined operating statement is for those funds using the accrual basis of accounting. As we noted on the statements previously discussed, a separate column is used for each type of fund—for example, Enterprise and Internal Service (see Table 9–5). The City of Columbus does not include Nonexpendable Trust Funds and Pension Trust Funds on this statement because it does not use these types of funds. Notice that the proprietary-type funds are operated at a loss for the year. This means that the charges for the goods or services were not enough to cover their cost.

The operating transfers in on the Enterprise Funds' books were from various Debt Service Funds and had nothing to do with subsidizing the operations of the funds. The main reason for the operating loss in the Enterprise Funds was a loss in the Electricity Fund. This is not expected to continue because the solid waste recovery plant was transferred to a separate operation.

Combined Statement of Cash Flows

The fifth and final combined statement included in the CAFR is the *combined statement of cash flows—all proprietary fund types.* Whenever the full accrual basis of accounting is used, GAAP require a statement of cash flows. This statement is also prepared for Nonexpendable Trust Funds. As mentioned in Chapter 2, this statement provides information on the operating, financing, and investing activities of the funds. Since preparation of this statement is beyond the scope of this text, we will only mention that it is one of the required statements in the Comprehensive Annual Financial Report (see Table 9–6).

Notes to Financial Statements

At the bottom of each of the financial statements is a notation "See accompanying notes to the general purpose financial statements." The purpose of this notation is to remind the reader that important financial information is included in the notes to the statements. Exhibit 9–3 is a reproduction of three pages of the notes from the CAFR of the City of Columbus. The entire Notes section covers thirty-eight pages.

Exhibit 9–3 presents descriptive materials and additional financial information. Note A, "Summary of Significant Accounting Policies," contains a definition of the reporting entity, a description of each of the funds used by the city in its financial report, a definition of modified accrual accounting, and other items (only the first two pages of the note are reproduced). In general, this note describes the

TABLE 9–3 Combined Statement of Revenues, Expenditures, and Changes in Fund Balances—Budget and Actual—Budgetary General and Special Revenue Fund Types

City of Columbus, Ohio

Combined Statement of Revenues, Expenditures, and Changes in Fund Balances—
Budget and Actual—General, Budgeted Special Revenue, Debt Service and
Capital Projects Funds—Budget Basis—Note R
Year Ended December 31, 19X1

	General Fund			Budgeted Special Revenue Funds		
	REVISED BUDGET	ACTUAL	VARIANCE—FAVORABLE (UNFAVORABLE)	REVISED BUDGET	ACTUAL	VARIANCE—FAVORABLE (UNFAVORABLE)
Revenues						
Income taxes	$193,350,000	$193,007,951	$ (342,049)	$ —	$ —	$ —
Property taxes	26,366,000	26,534,400	168,400	—	—	—
Grants and subsidies	25,000	25,000	—	28,498,691	28,498,691	—
Investment earnings	8,333,000	8,404,680	71,680	90,154	90,154	—
Special assessments	—	—	—	—	—	—
Licenses and permits	4,120,000	4,203,452	83,452	2,646,722	2,646,722	—
Shared revenues	32,420,000	32,477,639	57,639	18,212,891	18,212,891	—
Charges for services	18,565,000	18,878,146	313,146	24,708,010	24,708,010	—
Fines and forfeits	10,780,000	10,861,074	81,074	544,188	544,188	—
Miscellaneous	5,189,000	5,496,535	307,535	18,391,426	18,391,426	—
Total revenues	299,148,000	299,888,877	740,877	93,092,082	93,092,082	—
Expenditures						
Current:						
General government	45,620,121	44,924,830	695,291	10,568,205	10,333,585	234,620
Public service	22,279,940	21,874,827	405,113	28,026,887	26,802,939	1,223,948
Public safety	186,673,166	186,554,553	118,613	1,403,700	1,194,349	209,351
Human services	6,291,358	6,280,414	10,944	4,708,429	4,259,487	448,942
Development	8,684,861	8,656,687	28,174	14,714,742	13,836,358	878,384
Health	—	—	—	28,710,106	23,996,057	4,714,049
Recreation and parks	—	—	—	43,377,120	39,585,698	3,791,422
Public utilities	—	—	—	9,020,000	6,928,750	2,091,250
Expenditures paid through county auditor	1,140,000	1,107,918	32,082	—	—	—
Debt service:						
Principal retirement and payment of obligation under capitalized lease	—	—	—	—	—	—
Interest and fiscal charges	—	—	—	—	—	—
Total expenditures	270,689,446	269,399,229	1,290,217	140,529,189	126,937,223	13,591,966
Excess (deficiency) of revenues over expenditures	28,458,554	30,489,648	2,031,094	(47,437,107)	(33,845,141)	13,591,966
Other Financing Sources (Uses)						
Operating transfers in	3,000,000	3,059,049	59,049	33,710,540	33,710,540	190,020
Operating transfers out	(33,566,480)	(33,510,280)	56,200	(6,170,920)	(5,980,900)	
Proceeds from general bonds obligation	—	—	—	—	—	
Total other financing sources (uses)	(30,566,480)	(30,451,231)	115,249	27,539,620	27,729,640	190,020
Excess (deficiency) of revenues and other financing sources over expenditures and other uses	(2,107,926)	38,417	2,146,343	(19,897,487)	(6,115,501)	13,781,986
Fund balances (deficit) at beginning of year	13,873,222	13,873,222	—	(14,824,961)	(14,824,961)	—
Lapsed encumbrances	618,778	680,434	61,656	8,306,676	8,306,676	—
Fund balances (deficit) at end of year	$ 12,384,074	$ 14,592,073	$2,207,999	$(26,415,772)	$(12,633,786)	$13,781,986

TABLE 9–5 Combined Statement of Revenues, Expenses, and Changes in Retained Earnings (Equity)—All Proprietary Fund Types

City of Columbus, Ohio

Combined Statement of Revenues, Expenses, and Changes in Retained Earnings—
All Proprietary Fund Types and Discretely Presented Component Unit
Year Ended December 31, 19X1

	ENTERPRISE	INTERNAL SERVICE	Totals (Memorandum Only) PRIMARY GOVERNMENT	COMPONENT UNIT CMAA	Totals (Memorandum Only) Reporting Entity 19X1	Totals (Memorandum Only) Reporting Entity 19X0
Operating Revenues						
Charges for services	$193,905,013	$26,958,286	$220,863,299	$28,528,904	$249,392,203	$229,133,817
Other	850,675	199,424	1,050,099	202,258	1,252,357	1,817,443
Total operating revenues	194,755,688	27,157,710	221,913,398	28,731,162	250,644,560	230,951,260
Operating Expenses						
Personal services	58,787,062	12,956,256	71,743,318	5,215,998	76,959,316	73,041,681
Materials and supplies	14,648,755	7,333,647	21,982,402	648,525	22,630,927	21,038,660
Contractual services	42,927,928	4,864,453	47,792,381	5,852,980	53,645,361	52,403,583
Purchased power	9,088,391	—	9,088,391	—	9,088,391	9,585,621
Coal	1,161,546	—	1,161,546	—	1,161,546	914,007
Depreciation	32,571,219	1,819,285	34,390,504	2,452,603	36,843,107	37,855,091
Other	1,740,821	75,523	1,816,344	527,340	2,343,684	1,554,398
Total operating expenses	160,925,722	27,049,164	187,974,886	14,697,446	202,672,332	196,393,041
Operating income	33,829,966	108,546	33,938,512	14,033,716	47,972,228	34,558,219
Nonoperating Revenues (Expenses)						
Interest income	6,760,435	—	6,760,435	422,733	7,183,168	12,905,999
Interest expense	(51,868,291)	(256,139)	(52,124,430)	(4,834,766)	(56,959,196)	(63,321,726)
Other, net	—	—	—	352,644	352,644	—
Total nonoperating revenues (expenses)	(45,107,856)	(256,139)	(45,363,995)	(4,059,389)	(49,423,384)	(50,415,727)
Income (loss) before operating transfers	(11,277,890)	(147,593)	(11,425,483)	9,974,327	(1,451,156)	(15,857,508)
Operating transfers in—Notes H and Q	6,583,265	—	6,583,265	—	6,583,265	20,360,655
Income (loss) before extraordinary item	(4,694,625)	(147,593)	(4,842,218)	9,974,327	5,132,109	4,503,147
Extraordinary item—						
Accounting loss on advance refunding—Note G	(18,984,008)	—	(18,984,008)	—	(18,984,008)	(1,755,000)
Net income (loss)	(23,678,633)	(147,593)	(23,826,226)	9,974,327	(13,851,899)	2,748,147
Add depreciation on fixed assets acquired by capital grants	3,471,871	—	3,471,871	2,391,803	5,863,674	4,450,940
Increase (decrease) in retained earnings	(20,206,762)	(147,593)	(20,354,355)	12,366,130	(7,988,225)	7,199,087
Retained earnings at beginning of year, as restated	175,086,652	4,766,561	179,853,213	318,879	180,172,092	172,973,005
Retained earnings at end of year	$154,879,890	$4,618,968	$159,498,858	$12,685,009	$172,183,867	$180,172,092

See accompanying notes to the general purpose financial statements.

Source: Adapted from a recent Comprehensive Annual Financial Report of the City of Columbus, Ohio.

TABLE 9-6 Combined Statement of Cash Flows—All Proprietary Fund Types

City of Columbus, Ohio
Combined Statement of Cash Flows—
All Proprietary Fund Types and Discretely Presented Component Unit
Year Ended December 31, 19X1

	ENTERPRISE	INTERNAL SERVICE	Totals (Memorandum Only) PRIMARY GOVERNMENT	COMPONENT UNIT CMAA	Totals (Memorandum Only) Reporting Entity 19X1	19X0
Operating activities:						
Cash received from customers	$190,013,567	$ 26,871,152	$216,884,719	$27,998,315	$244,883,034	$222,631,710
Quasi external operating receipts	7,407,077	—	7,407,077	—	7,407,077	6,596,751
Cash paid to employees	(58,218,960)	(12,813,149)	(71,032,109)	(4,502,471)	(75,534,580)	(72,479,439)
Cash paid to suppliers	(70,513,699)	(12,196,171)	(82,709,870)	(5,937,711)	(88,647,581)	(81,361,349)
Other receipts (expenses)	1,304,901	175,800	1,480,701	(527,340)	953,361	972,368
Net cash provided by operating activities	69,992,886	2,037,632	72,030,518	17,030,793	89,061,311	76,360,041
Noncapital financing activities—						
Operating transfers in	6,583,265	—	6,583,265	—	6,583,265	20,360,655
Net cash provided by noncapital financing activities	6,583,265	—	6,583,265	—	6,583,265	20,360,655
Capital financing activities:						
Purchases of property, plant and equipment	(87,432,970)	(333,289)	(87,766,259)	(8,683,182)	(96,449,441)	(92,715,955)
Contributed capital	9,206,877	—	9,206,877	5,556,576	14,763,453	27,352,478
Proceeds from issuance of bonds	291,282,000	—	291,282,000	—	291,282,000	282,208,271
Bond discounts and issuance costs	(3,107,979)	—	(3,107,979)	—	(3,107,979)	(2,408,924)
Proceeds from issuance of notes	—	—	—	—	—	23,000,000
Principal payments on notes	(822,108)	(1,051,471)	(1,873,579)	—	(1,873,579)	(65,871,053)
Principal payments on bonds and loans	(249,268,936)	—	(249,268,936)	(4,954,000)	(254,222,936)	(172,753,327)
Interest paid on bonds, notes, and loans	(52,408,651)	(256,139)	(52,664,790)	(5,039,261)	(57,704,051)	(64,412,539)
Net cash used in capital and related financing activities	(92,551,767)	(1,640,899)	(94,192,666)	(13,119,867)	(107,312,533)	(65,601,049)
Investing activities:						
Purchase of investment securities	(46,406,132)	—	(46,406,132)	—	(46,406,132)	(18,067,036)
Proceeds from sale or maturity of investment securities	42,115,442	—	42,115,442	—	42,115,442	32,479,859
Interest received on investments	7,664,418	—	7,664,418	422,733	8,087,151	13,215,945
Principal payments from direct financing leases	—	—	—	322,412	322,412	—
Other, net	—	—	—	97,967	97,967	—
Net cash provided by investing activities	3,373,728	—	3,373,728	843,112	4,216,840	27,628,768
Increase (decrease) in cash and cash equivalents	(12,601,888)	396,733	(12,205,155)	4,754,038	(7,451,117)	58,748,415

EXHIBIT 9–3   Notes to Financial Statements (*Continued*)

NOTE A—SUMMARY OF SIGNIFICANT ACCOUNTING POLICIES (CONTINUED)

(a)   Basis of presentation—fund accounting

The accounts of the City are organized on the basis of funds or account groups, each of which is considered a separate accounting entity. The operations of each fund are accounted for with a separate set of self-balancing accounts that comprise its assets, liabilities, fund equity, revenues and expenditures (expenses). The various funds are summarized by type in the general purpose financial statements. The following fund types and account groups are used by the City.

GOVERNMENTAL FUNDS

General Fund—The General Fund is the general operating fund of the City. It is used to account for all financial resources except those required to be accounted for in another fund.

Special Revenue Funds—Special Revenue Funds are used to account for revenues derived from specific taxes, grants or other restricted revenue sources. The uses and limitations of each special revenue fund are specified by City ordinances or federal and state statutes.

Debt Service Funds—Debt Service Funds are used to account for the accumulation of resurces for, and the payment of, general long-term debt principal, interest and related costs.

Capital Projects Funds—Capital Projects Funds are used to account for financial resources used for the acquisition or construction of major capital facilities (other than those financed by proprietary or trust funds).

PROPRIETARY FUNDS

Enterprise Funds—Enterprise Funds are used to account for operations that are financed and operated in a manner similar to private business enterprises—where the intent of the governing body is that the costs of providing goods or services to the general public on a continuing basis be financed or recovered primarily through user charges. The City has separate enterprise funds for its water, sanitary sewer and electricity services. In addition, airport services are provided by CMAA.

Internal Service Funds—Internal Service Funds are used to account for the financing of goods or services provided by one department or agency to other departments or agencies of the City generally on a cost-reimbursement basis.

FIDUCIARY FUNDS

Trust and Agency Funds—Trust and Agency Funds are used to account for assets held by the City in a trustee capacity or as an agent for individuals, private organizations, other governments and/or other funds. Assets held for other funds or governments include payroll taxes and other employee withholdings (which are combined into one agency fund for ease of payment) and income taxes and utility charges collected by the City on behalf of other governments. Expendable trust funds are accounted for and reported similar to governmental funds. Agency funds are custodial in nature (assets equal liabilities) and do not involve measurement of results of operations.

EXHIBIT 9–3　Notes to Financial Statements (*Continued*)

NOTE O—DEFICIT FUND EQUITIES

Fund equity balances at December 31, 19X1 include the following individual fund deficits:

	FUND/ ACCUMULATED (DEFICIT)	CONTRIBUTED CAPITAL	TOTAL FUND EQUITY (DEFICIT)
		(in thousands)	
Special Revenue—Golf	$　(47)	$　—	$　(47)
Debt Service—Recreation Debt Service	(94)	—	(94)
Capital Projects—North Market Note	(1,200)	—	(1,200)
Enterprise—Electricity Fund	(38,610)	18,833	(19,777)

The Electricity Fund deficit resulted from expenses in excess of revenues charged and operating transfers in. Electricity Fund losses are not expected to continue due to the transfer of the solid waste recovery plant (See Note T).

Fund balance deficits also exist on the City's budgetary basis of accounting for certain Special Revenue, Debt Service and Capital Projects Funds. These fund balance deficits exist since encumbrances are allowed to be recorded against accounts receivables which are not recognized as revenue on the budget basis of accounting. Deficits in Special Revenue and Debt Service Funds will be eliminated by future increases in charges for services. The deficit in the Capital Projects Fund has been eliminated through repayment of the $1.2 million capital improvement note in February 19X2.

NOTE P—MISCELLANEOUS REVENUES

For the year ended December 31, 19X1, miscellaneous revenues consisted of the following:

	GENERAL	SPECIAL REVENUE	DEBT SERVICE	CAPITAL PROJECTS	EXPENDABLE TRUST
			(in thousands)		
Capital South—income	$　—	$3,059	$　—	$　—	$　—
Hotel/motel taxes	2,292	4,666	—	—	—
Refunds and reimbursements	2,628	147	—	—	—
Rent	33	48	221	52	—
Capital contribution	—	63	—	846	—
Payments in lieu of property taxes	—	—	1,419	—	—
Donations	10	652	—	58	—
CDA and UDAG loan interest	—	1,559	—	—	—
City auto license tax	—	3,408	—	—	—
Sale of assets	—	—	—	77	—
Contributions	—	—	—	—	1,162
Other	474	870	42	779	63
	$5,437	$14,472	$1,682	$1,812	$1,225

Source: Adapted from a recent Comprehensive Annual Financial Report of the City of Columbus, Ohio.

methods and procedures used in the financial accounting system. The other page contains Notes O and P. These notes provide additional descriptive and financial materials.

Other notes provide detailed information on items such as fixed assets, long-term obligations, leases, and retirement plans. While some of this information could be reported on the face of the financial statements, it would require so much detail that the major relationships between important items would be obscured.

In summary, notes to the financial statements provide additional information that should be used in analyzing financial data. The fact that such information is not included on the financial statements themselves does not mean that it is not useful. These data are an integral part of the financial reporting package.

Other Information in the CAFR

Up to this point we have discussed six components of the financial section of the CAFR. These components plus the auditor's report form the General Purpose Financial Statements (GPFS). The GPFS are designed to permit the governmental unit to supply a complete set of financial statements that have been prepared in conformity with GAAP, without having to provide the user with a complete CAFR. In many instances this "summarized disclosure" is sufficient for certain types of users. Thus use of the GPFS enables the governmental unit to supply financial data that are prepared in compliance with GAAP without having to go to the expense of providing a complete annual report.

Combining Financial Statements

The "Combining and Individual Fund and Account Groups Statements and Schedules" section of the CAFR includes the **combining financial statements** and, if necessary, the **individual fund financial statements.** These individual fund statements are the basic support for the combined statements previously discussed (see Exhibit 9–2). A typical combining balance sheet is shown in several illustrations in previous chapters and in Table 9–7.

Notice that this is a combining balance sheet for Special Revenue Funds. This ties Table 9–7 directly to Exhibit 9–2. Notice also that Table 9–7 is only a part of the entire statement. Since the City of Columbus has twenty-six Special Revenue Funds, the actual statement covers four pages in the CAFR. On the combining statements, each individual type of fund is shown in a separate column. To fully understand the relationship between the combined and the combining financial statements, you should trace the amounts included in the total column from this statement to the respective amounts on the combined balance sheet in Table 9–1. For example, the total balance of the Cash and cash equivalents accounts of all Special Revenue Funds is $22,394,981 in Table 9–7. Trace this figure to Table 9–1.

A combining statement for each type of financial statement identified in the GPFS must be presented in the CAFR. By doing this, the reader will be able to identify the specific assets, liabilities, revenues, expenditures (or expenses), and so forth for each fund used by the governmental unit. To provide additional

TABLE 9–7   Combining Balance Sheet

City of Columbus, Ohio
Combining Balance Sheet
All Special Revenue Funds
December 31, 19X1

	LAW ENFORCEMENT	AREA COMMISSIONS	BOXING & WRESTLING	SPECIAL PURPOSE	TOTAL
Assets					
Cash and cash equivalents:					
Cash and investments with treasurer	$1,269,231	$24,008	$3,564	$569,631	$22,394,981
Receivables	1,328	—	—	—	47,383,366
Due from other:					
Governments	—	—	—	—	2,229,062
Funds	—	—	—	—	1,959,020
Total assets	1,270,559	24,008	3,564	569,631	73,966,429
Liabilities					
Accounts payable	8,935	198	—	34,822	12,915,325
Due to other:					
Governments	—	—	—	—	33,000,357
Funds	—	—	—	5	1,925,243
Deferred revenue	—	—	—	—	3,802,446
Accrued wages and bene-fits	—	—	—	—	2,092,318
Total liabilities	8,935	198	—	34,827	53,735,689
Fund Balances					
Fund balances (deficit):					
Reserved for encum-brances	199,054	7,932	—	119,150	21,294,687
Unreserved, undesig-nated	1,062,570	15,878	3,564	415,654	(1,063,947)
Total fund balances (deficit)	1,261,624	23,810	3,564	534,804	20,230,740
Total liabilities and fund balances	$1,270,559	$24,008	$3,564	$569,631	$73,966,429

Source: Adapted from a recent Comprehensive Annual Financial Report of the City of Columbus, Ohio.

information regarding the detailed operations of each type of fund, combining statements usually are presented in more detail than the combined statements.

Individual Fund Financial Statements

In those instances where it is deemed necessary for fair presentation of financial data for the governmental unit, individual fund statements are used. These are similar to the statements in Chapter 2 of this text. When presented in the CAFR, these statements usually are presented in more detail than either the combined or the combining financial statements. This is consistent with the concept of expanding the detail of information disclosed as we descend the Financial Reporting Pyramid (see Exhibit 9–1).

There is a definite trend away from presenting individual fund financial statements in annual reports by governmental units. This approach is based on the emphasis GAAP place on reporting combined financial statements to provide an "overview" of the financial operations and financial condition of governmental units.

The extent to which a governmental unit reports detailed information for each fund—that is, the extent to which it descends the reporting pyramid into the area marked with the broken line (see Exhibit 9–1)—will depend on the interpretation of **adequate disclosure** by the management of the governmental unit. The overall guideline is that each governmental unit must present enough financial information to reflect (1) the financial position and results of operations of each fund and account group, (2) compliance with legal and contractual requirements of a financial nature, and (3) sufficient disclosure of the financial activities of each fund.[3]

The final section of the Comprehensive Annual Financial Report consists of the **statistical tables.** Fifteen individual tables are recommended:

a. General Governmental Expenditures by Function—Last Ten Fiscal Years
b. General Revenues by Source—Last Ten Fiscal Years
c. Property Tax Levies and Collections—Last Ten Fiscal Years
d. Assessed and Estimated Actual Value of Taxable Property—Last Ten Fiscal Years
e. Property Tax Rates—All Overlapping Governments—Last Ten Fiscal Years
f. Special Assessment Billings and Collections—Last Ten Fiscal Years (if the government is obligated in some manner for related special assessment debt)
g. Ratio of Net General Bonded Debt to Assessed Value and Net Bonded Debt per Capita—Last Ten Fiscal Years
h. Computation of Legal Debt Margin, if not presented in the General Purpose Financial Statements (GPFS)
i. Computation of Overlapping Debt (if not presented in the GPFS)
j. Ratio of Annual Debt Service for General Bonded Debt to Total General Expenditures—Last Ten Fiscal Years
k. Revenue Bond Coverage—Last Ten Fiscal Years
l. Demographic Statistics
m. Property Value, Construction, and Bank Deposits—Last Ten Fiscal Years
n. Principal Taxpayers
o. Miscellaneous Statistics[4]

Table 9–8 is an example of General Governmental Expenditures by Function—Last Ten Fiscal Years, and Table 9–9 is an example of General Revenues by Source—Last Ten Fiscal Years reported by the City of Columbus. The purpose of the statistical section of the report is to provide the reader with additional finan-

---

[3]GASB Cod. Sec. 1900.109.
[4]GASB Cod. Sec. 2800.103.

TABLE 9–8 Statistical Tables—General Governmental Expenditures by Function—Last Ten Fiscal Years

City of Columbus, Ohio

General Governmental Expenditures by Function[1]

Last Ten Fiscal Years

FISCAL YEAR	GENERAL GOVERNMENT	PUBLIC SERVICE	PUBLIC SAFETY	HUMAN SERVICES	DEVELOPMENT	HEALTH	RECREATION AND PARKS	PUBLIC UTILITIES	DEBT SERVICE[2]	CAPITAL OUTLAY	TOTAL
19W2	$31,590,284 13.19%	$32,524,519 13.58%	$94,060,294 39.28%	$10,569,040 4.42%	$16,664,277 6.96%	$11,638,727 4.86%	$17,692,734 7.39%	$ — —	$19,555,542 8.17%	$5,147,597 2.15%	$239,443,014 100.00%
19W3	34,228,627 13.80	36,432,064 14.69	96,514,246 38.91	7,379,003 2.97	12,177,467 4.91	13,844,219 5.58	18,591,714 7.49	— —	24,120,634 9.72	4,784,498 1.93	248,072,472 100.00%
19W4	38,588,668 14.07	40,913,504 14.92	106,580,409 38.86	10,526,206 3.84	8,932,388 3.26	14,912,821 5.44	21,592,888 7.87	— —	24,394,400 8.90	7,791,872 2.84	274,233,156 100.00%
19W5	41,333,498 14.35	39,447,132 13.70	112,000,285 38.90	12,500,714 4.34	6,715,960 2.33	15,940,925 5.54	21,955,390 7.62	— —	29,229,092 10.15	8,827,524 3.07	287,950,520 100.00%
19W6	42,425,648 13.95	41,237,139 13.56	120,780,921 39.73	11,600,380 3.82	8,624,522 2.84	16,484,483 5.42	22,545,229 7.42	— —	31,004,379 10.20	9,303,069 3.06	304,005,770 100.00%
19W7	48,946,854 14.34	44,951,132 13.16	137,692,170 40.33	12,844,214 3.76	9,538,981 2.79	18,420,094 5.39	25,934,676 7.60	— —	32,871,020 9.63	10,247,331 3.00	341,446,472 100.00%
19W8	45,698,647 12.85	46,570,713 13.09	146,523,802 41.19	12,751,225 3.58	10,211,538 2.87	20,093,719 5.65	28,704,034 8.07	— —	33,491,034 9.41	11,723,807 3.29	355,768,519 100.00%
19W9	48,376,704 12.56	46,707,742 12.13	162,759,376 42.25	12,897,673 3.35	11,354,848 2.95	22,012,548 5.72	33,018,726 8.57	3,557,766 .92	34,364,300 8.92	10,138,038 2.63	385,187,721 100.00%
19X0	49,107,143 12.46	45,638,058 11.58	173,518,145 44.04	12,714,081 3.23	10,280,154 2.61	22,160,485 5.62	34,942,824 8.87	3,038,985 .77	34,210,175 8.68	8,416,770 2.14	394,026,820 100.00%
19X1	66,385,535 14.75	49,913,070 11.09	187,822,929 41.73	10,198,238 2.27	12,641,328 2.81	23,738,009 5.27	38,264,848 8.50	6,932,020 1.54	48,478,617 10.77	5,719,285 1.27	450,093,879 100.00%

[1]Includes General, Special Revenue, and Debt Service Funds.

[2]Includes all general obligation debt service other than enterprise.

Source: Adapted from a recent Comprehensive Annual Financial Report of the City of Columbus, Ohio.

TABLE 9-9 Statistical Tables—General Governmental Revenues by Source—Last Ten Fiscal Years

City of Columbus, Ohio
General Governmental Revenues by Source[1]
Last Ten Fiscal Years

FISCAL YEAR	INCOME TAXES	PROPERTY TAXES	GRANTS AND SUBSIDIES	INVESTMENT EARNINGS	SPECIAL ASSESSMENTS	LICENSES AND PERMITS	SHARED REVENUES	CHARGES FOR SERVICES	FINES AND FORFEITS	MISCELLANEOUS	TOTAL
19W2	$120,303,375	$14,435,536	$36,202,362	$ 9,500,941	$400,866	$2,817,120	$24,677,573	$11,677,797	$ 7,251,374	$14,855,314	$242,122,258
	49.69%	5.96%	14.95%	3.92%	.17%	1.16%	10.19	4.82%	3.00%	6.14%	100.00%
19W3	150,606,421	15,443,550	28,097,100	13,627,409	415,412	3,122,097	26,961,924	12,430,146	7,369,341	14,948,243	273,021,643
	55.16	5.66	10.29	4.99	.15	1.14	9.88	4.55	2.70	5.48	100.00%
19W4	165,590,910	16,281,132	28,228,303	9,288,445	357,239	3,509,220	28,685,535	12,835,441	7,643,162	21,020,688	293,440,075
	56.43	5.55	9.62	3.17	.12	1.20	9.78	4.37	2.60	7.16	100.00%
19W5	179,212,346	17,268,490	19,831,060	13,018,362	283,804	4,797,572	30,470,274	21,806,426	8,260,685	19,389,912	314,338,931
	57.01	5.49	6.31	4.14	.09	1.53	9.69	6.94	2.63	6.17	100.00%
19W6	195,824,895	17,882,378	22,255,382	5,621,135	487,449	5,165,993	32,620,752	22,172,887	9,371,668	14,372,506	325,775,045
	60.11	5.49	6.83	1.73	.15	1.59	10.01	6.81	2.87	4.41	100.00%
19W7	210,008,309	21,526,805	30,865,650	11,461,992	102,497	5,526,347	37,048,454	25,761,722	10,426,261	17,487,471	370,215,508
	56.72	5.81	8.34	3.10	.03	1.49	10.01	6.96	2.82	4.72	100.00%
19W8	221,177,367	22,289,854	24,422,849	13,598,100	133,235	5,746,532	42,497,977	26,900,693	10,437,113	17,263,769	384,467,489
	57.53	5.80	6.35	3.54	.04	1.49	11.05	7.00	2.71	4.49	100.00%
19W9	232,301,648	23,421,399	26,001,791	13,811,735	100,280	5,901,542	46,450,571	31,943,471	10,704,358	14,952,268	405,589,063
	57.28	5.77	6.41	3.41	.03	1.46	11.45	7.86	2.64	3.69	100.00%
19X0	243,196,869	26,060,725	26,968,050	11,375,073	81,253	6,341,270	49,026,563	37,866,526	10,647,351	13,906,723	425,470,403
	57.16	6.13	6.34	2.67	.02	1.49	11.52	8.90	2.50	3.27	100.00%
19X1	261,585,332	26,477,776	27,923,427	8,295,732	69,549	6,850,129	50,408,010	44,650,198	11,393,479	21,591,924	459,245,556
	56.96	5.77	6.08	1.81	.01	1.49	10.98	9.72	2.48	4.70	100.00%

[1]Includes General, Special Revenue, and Debt Service Funds.
Source: Adapted from a recent Comprehensive Annual Financial Report of the City of Columbus, Ohio.

cial, economic, and social information on the governmental unit. While specific tables are recommended, the governmental unit can, where applicable, add any information its management feels will be useful to the reader.

THE REPORTING ENTITY

Definition of the Reporting Entity

The reporting entity is the basic element used for financial reporting. It identifies governmental units that will be included in the financial statements. The main governmental unit is called the **primary government.** Any other governmental units that are included in the financial statements are called component units. Examples of a primary government are a city, a county (parish), or a state. The primary government is the main government for which the financial statements are prepared. In the examples of combined financial statements presented in this chapter, the City of Columbus, Ohio, is the primary government. The primary government is one that is elected by the citizens. A primary government may also be a special purpose governmental unit like a local school board or hospital district if:

1. The governing body is separately elected,
2. It has a separate legal identity, and
3. It is financially independent.

All subdivisions of a primary government (e.g., agencies and departments) are considered to be part of the primary government. These units of a local government generally consist of activities such as public service, public safety, human services, health services, recreation and parks, and public utilities. The financial data of all such units is combined and reported with the financial data of the primary government.

    Component units are organizations that are financially accountable to the primary government or that are so integrated with the primary government that exclusion of their financial information would make the statements incomplete or misleading. Examples of component units may include housing authorities, school boards, sewer systems, airport authorities, and other activities. In the examples of combined financial statements presented in this chapter, CMAA (Columbus Municipal Airport Authority) is a component unit.

    The **financial reporting entity** consists of:

1. The primary government,
2. Organizations for which the primary government is financially accountable, and
3. Other organizations for which the nature and significance of their relationship with the primary government are such that exclusion would cause the reporting entity's financial statements to be misleading.[5]

[5]GASB, *Statement No. 14,* "The Financial Reporting Entity." June 1991, Summary.

The key element in identifying a component unit is **financial accountability.** An organization is financially accountable to the primary government if

1. The primary government can appoint a majority of the governing board of the organization and
2. The primary government can impose its will on the organization, or
3. The organization can provide potential benefit to the primary government or be a financial burden to the primary government.

If a governmental unit meets number 1 above and number 2 or 3, it is reported as a component unit of the primary government. With respect to the first characteristic, appointments made by the primary government must be substantive. The government must be able to select and appoint candidates. Appointments made from lists of nominees or appointments that are merely a confirmation may not qualify as a substantive appointment. In all instances, "true control" of the process by the primary government is an important factor.

The ability to impose the will of the primary government is determined by its ability to affect the day-to-day operations of an organization. Day-to-day operations of an organization include its programs, projects, activities, and its level of services. Examples of such types of activities include the ability to modify or approve budgets, rate charges, and contracts.

Financial benefit or burden is measured by the ability of the primary government to use the resources of an organization, or be responsible for deficits or other debts of an organization. Transactions in which one unit buys and another sells goods or services do not qualify as a financial benefit or burden. Benefit or burden can also be indirect to the primary government. An indirect benefit or burden is one in which a component unit of the primary government can receive resources from an organization, or is responsible for it. Notice the use of the word *ability* in describing the financial relationship between the primary government and a component unit. The primary government needs only to *have* the ability, *not necessarily to use* it. Examples of financial benefit may include off-track betting and lotteries. Examples of financial burdens may include expressed or implied debt guarantees and operating subsidies.

In the above discussion, we mentioned that a special purpose governmental unit may qualify as a component unit. If such a unit has a separately elected board, but the primary government is financially accountable for that unit, then the separate unit is a component unit of the primary government. Such a situation might exist when a school board has its governing body elected by the public, but its budget must be approved by the primary government.

A separate unit can only be reported as a component unit by one primary government. Problems may arise if two governmental units qualify under the above tests. In such an instance, judgment must be applied as to which government is the primary government. Fiscal dependency is usually the guiding factor.

The above definition of a component unit also includes organizations that, if omitted, would cause the financial statements of the primary government to be misleading. These may include organizations such as hospitals, colleges, and some agencies.

Reporting Component Units in the Body of the Financial Statements

Once all of the organizations included in the reporting entity are identified, the next decision is how these organizations should be included in the financial statements. Two options exist. A component unit can be blended in with the primary government's financial data, or it can be discretely presented in the financial statements. **Blending** is the process of including the financial data of a component unit with the financial data of the primary government. This involves treating the funds used by the component unit as if they were funds of the primary government. It is used in those situations in which the governing body of the component unit is essentially the same as that of the primary government, or the goods or services provided by the component unit are mainly for the primary government.

When the funds of a component unit are blended with those of the primary government, they are included in one or more columns on the combining financial statements of the same fund type. For example, two Special Revenue Funds of a component unit would be treated as two separate columns on the combining financial statements of Special Revenue Funds of the primary government. The exception to this rule is the General Fund of the component unit. Since a reporting entity can have only one General Fund, the General Fund of the primary government is that General Fund. A General Fund used by a component unit is reported as a Special Revenue Fund for the reporting entity.

Discrete presentation of a component unit involves reporting financial data of the component unit's funds in one or more separate columns on the combined financial statements. An example of this type of report is contained in the combined financial statements in Tables 9–1, 9–5, and 9–6. The component unit for the City of Columbus is the CMAA (Columbus Municipal Airport Authority). Examine these financial statements and notice how the CMAA is presented. Also notice how Columbus presents totals for the primary government, the component unit, and overall totals. Remember, reporting these total columns is voluntary. A single column may be used even though the component unit uses governmental or proprietary accounting. If a single column is used, fund equity may be aggregated into one amount or it may be reported as separate amounts for funds using fund balance or retained earnings.

Component unit amounts included in the financial statements should be appropriately labeled. The primary government may choose to use only one column for the operating statements of all component units, whether they follow the governmental or proprietary method of accounting. In this instance, whether a governmental or proprietary fund statement is used should depend on the principal activities of the component unit. It is also possible to report operations of all governmental-type component units on the governmental-type operating statement and all proprietary-type component units on the proprietary-type operating statement. Detailed information on a fund-by-fund basis for a component unit is necessary only in those instances in which that information is not separately reported by the component unit.

Discrete presentation is appropriate in those situations in which a component unit does not meet the requirements for blending. That is, the component unit does not have essentially the same governing body as the primary government or the goods or services provided by the component unit are not mainly for the primary government.

Reporting Notes to the Financial Statements

Notes to the reporting entity's financial statements should identify the component units, the criteria for including the component units in the financial statements, and how the component units are reported. Notice in Exhibit 9–4 that the City of Columbus also identifies governmental units that would seem by their names to be included in the statements but are not component units.

Some units are not component units, but are related organizations. A **related organization** is an organization for which the primary government appoints a voting majority of its members but for which the primary government is not financially accountable, as defined above. Related organizations must be disclosed in the notes to the financial statements. The primary government must also disclose its accountability for those organizations and any information required under the "related party transactions" rules.

EXHIBIT 9–4   Notes to Financial Statements—Component Units

City of Columbus, Ohio

The reporting entity:

The accompanying general purpose financial statements comply with the provisions of Governmental Accounting Standards Board (GASB) Statement No. 14, *The Financial Reporting Entity,* in that the financial statements include all the organizations, activities, functions and component unit for which the City (the reporting entity) is financially accountable. Financial accountability is defined as the appointment of a voting majority of the component unit's board, and either (1) the City's ability to impose its will over the component unit, or (2) the possibility that the component unit will provide a financial benefit to or impose a financial burden on the City. On this basis, the reporting entity of the City includes the following services as authorized by its charter: public service, public safety, human services, development, health, recreation and parks, and public utilities. In addition, the City owns and operates three major enterprise activities: a water system, a sanitary sewer system and an electricity plant and distribution system.

(continued)

EXHIBIT 9–4   Notes to Financial Statements—Component Units (*Continued*)

In August 19W9, the City's Council created the Columbus Municipal Airport Authority (CMAA), a component unit of the City, as permitted by State law to manage the City's two airports. All of the CMAA board members are appointed by the Mayor subject to the approval of Council. Although CMAA is a separate legal entity, the City includes the financial statements of CMAA as a part of the City's reporting entity. CMAA's financial statements are discretely presented in this report. Complete financial statements of CMAA may be obtained from CMAA's administration offices at 4600 International Gateway, Columbus, Ohio 43219.

Certain organizations, although sharing some degree of name similarity with the City, are separate and distinct entities, not only from the City but also from each other. The City is not financially accountable for these entities. Because of their independent nature, none of these organizations' financial statements are included in this report. These organizations are as follows:

- The Columbus City School District (the District), a separate and distinct governmental entity, is independent of the City in governing bodies, financial resources, and management. Their geographic boundaries are also unrelated. While the District lies primarily within the City's incorporated boundaries, portions extend beyond. There are 15 other school districts, all independent of the City and independent of each other, that also partially lie within the City's boundaries. The State of Ohio has 612 school districts.

- The Columbus Metropolitan Housing Authority (CMHA) is organized under the laws of Ohio for purposes of administering a low-rent housing program. The United States Department of Housing and Urban Development (HUD) has the responsibility for administering this program. CMHA is completely separate and distinct from the City in governing bodies, financial resources, and management.

- Columbus Metropolitan Area Community Action Organization (CMACAO) was formed in 19T3 as a non-profit corporation under Ohio laws to provide various community action programs, which were intended to prevent and alleviate poverty and its causes in Columbus and in the Franklin County metropolitan area.

- Columbus Metropolitan Library, formerly The Public Library of Columbus and Franklin County, is also a separate and distinct entity from the City.

- The Central Ohio Transit Authority (COTA) is a related organization of the City, as the Mayor of the City, with the approval of City Council, appoints a voting majority of COTA's Board. However, the financial statements of COTA are not included within the City's "Reporting Entity," as the City cannot impose its will over COTA and there is no financial benefit or financial burden relationship between the City and COTA.

Source: Adapted from a recent Comprehensive Annual Financial Report of the City of Columbus, Ohio.

Overview of the Financial Reporting Entity

A flow chart of the decision process for determining the components of a financial reporting entity is contained in Exhibit 9–5. This represents a summary of the steps needed to determine if a governmental unit is part of a financial reporting entity.

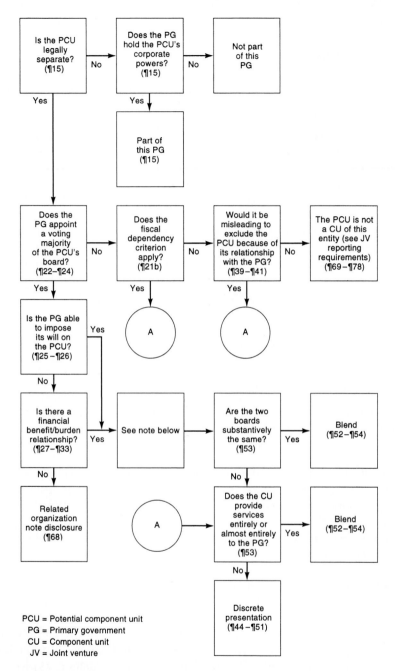

EXHIBIT 9–5 Flow Chart for Evaluating Potential Component Units

Note: A potential component unit for which a primary government is financially accountable may be fiscally dependent on another government. An organization should be included as a component unit of only one reporting entity. Professional judgment should be used to determine the most appropriate reporting entity (¶21b and ¶34–¶38). A primary government that appoints a voting majority of the governing board of a component unit of another government should make the disclosures required by ¶68 for related organizations.

Source: GASB *Statement No. 14*, "The Financial Reporting Entity," GASB, para. 132.

INTERIM FINANCIAL REPORTING

To function properly, a governmental unit needs more information than that which is provided by the annual financial reports. The operations are so complex and dynamic that data for evaluation and control purposes must be available on a more frequent basis—usually monthly, but in some instances daily reports on items such as cash balances are necessary. These reports are generally prepared for internal use and are usually prepared on the budgetary basis. Often they contain year-to-date information in addition to the current data.

Interim reports prepared by some governmental units are as simple as a listing of the accounts under the control of a manager, together with the budgeted and actual balances. Other governmental units use the account format, but include a beginning balance, transactions that occurred during the period, and an ending balance. Some even include a complete set of financial state-ments.

GAAP for interim reporting is very broad and undefined. It can best be summed up with the following statement:

> The key criteria by which internal interim reports are evaluated are their relevance and usefulness for purposes of management control, which include planning future operations as well as evaluating current financial status and results to date. Continual efforts should be made to assure that accounting and related interim information properly serve management control needs. Because managerial styles and perceived information needs vary widely, however, appropriate internal interim reporting is largely a matter of professional judgment . . . [6]

One form of interim balance sheet used by some governmental units presents the assets and liabilities as of the interim date, and it includes the estimated effects of the budgetary accounts. This format is illustrated in Table 9–10.

Notice that the interim balance sheet illustrated below differs from the ending balance sheet in two major respects: (1) estimated revenues (net of revenues) are treated as assets; and (2) appropriations (net of expenditures) are treated as liabilities.

An interim operating statement usually presents budget and actual figures using the budgetary basis of accounting. Remember from our previous discussion of budget-actual combined statements (Table 9–3) that many governmental units do not budget on a GAAP basis. Therefore, a budget-actual interim statement will probably not report the same revenues and expenditures as the statement of revenues, expenditures, and changes in fund balance. Typical budget-actual interim operating statements are presented in Tables 9–11 and 9–12. There are no specific standards for reporting interim financial information; therefore, no two governmental units will use exactly the same format.

[6]GASB Cod. Sec. 2900.103.

TABLE 9–10   Interim Balance Sheet

City of Metairie
General Fund
Balance Sheet
For the Six Months Ended June 30, 19X1

Assets and Estimated Revenues			
Assets:			
Cash			$10,000
Supplies			2,000
Property taxes receivable		$200,000	
Less: Allowance for uncollectible property taxes		10,000	190,000
Due from other funds			12,000
Estimated revenues:			
Estimated revenues		$800,000	
Less: Revenues		350,000	450,000
Total assets and estimated revenues			$664,000
Liabilities, Appropropriations, and Fund Balance			
Liabilities:			
Vouchers payable		$ 6,000	
Due to other funds		4,000	
Total liabilities			$10,000
Appropriations:			
Appropriations		$790,000	
Less: Expenditures and encumbrances		360,000	430,000
Fund balance:			
Reserved for encumbrances			
Unreserved fund balance		$28,000	
Total fund balance		196,000	224,000
Total liabilities, appropriations, and fund balance			$664,000

TABLE 9–11   Interim Statement of Actual and Budgeted Revenues

City of Metairie
General Fund
Statement of Actual and Budgeted Revenues
For the Six Months Ended June 30, 19X1

REVENUE TYPE	BUDGETED	ACTUAL	EXCESS OF BUDGETED REVENUES (EXCESS OF ACTUAL REVENUES)
Taxes:			
Sales taxes	$500,000	$200,000	$300,000
Property taxes	100,000	50,000	50,000
Interest and penalties	1,000	-0-	1,000
Total taxes	601,000	250,000	351,000
Licenses and permits	100,000	90,000	10,000
Fines and forfeits	75,000	5,000	70,000
Miscellaneous	24,000	5,000	19,000
Total revenues	$800,000	$350,000	$450,000

TABLE 9-12 Interim Statement of Actual and Budgeted Expenditures (Including Encumbrances)

City of Metairie
General Fund
Statement of Actual (Including Encumbrances) and Budgeted Expenditures
For the Six Months Ended June 30, 19X1

FUNCTION	BUDGETED EXPENDITURES	EXPENDITURES AND ENCUMBRANCES	UNEXPENDED UNENCUMBERED BALANCE
General government	$200,000	$ 90,000	$110,000
Public safety	350,000	200,000	150,000
Health and welfare	200,000	65,000	135,000
Miscellaneous	40,000	5,000	35,000
Totals	$790,000	$360,000	$430,000

CONCLUDING COMMENT ON FINANCIAL REPORTING

Notice how the fund balance of Pension Trust Funds is reported by the City of Baltimore (see Table 9–13). As indicated in Chapter 7, this format of one fund balance account on the combined balance sheet is different from that used for the individual Pension Trust Funds balance sheets. Compare the reporting format for these funds in Table 7–19 with that followed in Table 9–13. Remember that the actuarial present value information included in Table 7–19 should be reported in the notes to the GPFS.

Whether a PERS is considered to be part of the governmental reporting unit or a separate reporting entity, extensive note disclosure is required. In those instances where the PERS is considered to be part of the governmental unit, the financial statement disclosure is described above. The note disclosure includes (1) an identification of the plan and a description of its terms, (2) a description of the actuarial cost method used, (3) a brief summary of the accounting policies followed, (4) funding schedules, and (5) statistical data.[7]

If a PERS is considered to be a separate reporting entity, a separate set of GPFS and a CAFR must be prepared for it. In such instances, extensive note disclosure is also required.

THE CERTIFICATE OF EXCELLENCE IN FINANCIAL REPORTING

By now it should be apparent that the financial reporting process for governmental units, although very complex, is essential for the dissemination of information on the financial activities of these organizations. In 1945, the Municipal Finance Officers Association, now the Government Finance Officers Association (GFOA), acknowledged the need to recognize those governmental units that produce a

[7]An extended description of the note disclosures can be found in GASB Cod. Sec. Pe5 and Pe6, and GASB *Statement No. 25* (see Chapter 7).

TABLE 9–13 Reporting of Fund Balance for a PERS on a Combined Balance Sheet

City of Baltimore
Combined Balance Sheet
All Fund Types and Account Groups
June 30, 19X1
(Expressed in Thousands)

	Governmental Fund Types				Proprietary Fund Types		Fiduciary Fund Types	Account Groups		TOTAL (MEMORANDUM ONLY)
	GENERAL	SPECIAL REVENUE	DEBT SERVICE	CAPITAL PROJECTS	ENTERPRISE	INTERNAL SERVICE	TRUST AND AGENCY	GENERAL FIXED ASSETS	GENERAL LONG-TERM OBLIGATIONS	
Assets										
Cash and cash equivalents	$ 2,907	$ 445	$23,046	$ 2,851	$ 100,907	$51,051	$ 5,066			$ 186,273
Investments	74,478		5,978	54,286	4,697	9,132	1,763,475			1,912,046
Property taxes receivable	17,661									17,661
Other accounts receivable, net	15,726	479		12,559	50,405	834	5,069			85,072
Due from other governments	23,938	51,077								75,015
Due from other funds	4,527			28,198						32,725
Inventories, at cost	5,930	1,018			3,084	290				10,322
Notes and mortgages receivable, net	37,087	6,324	15,349		118,135					176,895
Other assets	4,003	122			12,691	244				17,060
Restricted assets:										
Cash and cash equivalents					56,272	57				56,329
Investments					32,592					32,592
Accounts receivable, net					47,368					47,368
Property, plant and equipment, net					881,699	27,479		$1,714,968		2,624,146
Amount available in debt service fund for retirement of general long-term debt									$ 28,787	28,787
Resources to be provided in future years									704,005	704,005
Total assets	$186,257	$59,465	$44,373	$97,894	$1,307,850	$89,087	$1,773,610	$1,714,968	$732,792	$6,006,296

See notes to financial statements.

TABLE 9–13 Reporting of Fund Balance for a PERS on a Combined Balance Sheet (Continued)

	Governmental Fund Types				Proprietary Fund Types		Fiduciary Fund Types	Account Groups		
	GENERAL	SPECIAL REVENUE	DEBT SERVICE	CAPITAL PROJECTS	ENTERPRISE	INTERNAL SERVICE	TRUST AND AGENCY	GENERAL FIXED ASSETS	GENERAL LONG-TERM OBLIGATIONS	TOTAL (MEMORANDUM ONLY)
Liabilities and Fund Equity										
Liabilities										
Accounts payable and accrued liabilities	$ 68,419	$24,616		$ 8,819	$ 23,592	$ 5,075	$ 5,857			$ 136,378
Retainages payable				6,898						6,898
Property taxes payable—State	311									311
Due to other governments					10,942					10,942
Due to other funds		4,527			28,198					32,725
Deposits subject to refund	4,703				10					4,713
Estimated liability for claims in progress						38,515				38,515
Other liabilities					35,879	2,572	1,632			40,083
Accounts payable from restricted assets					11,698					11,698
Deferred revenue	67,084	20,997	$15,349		3,714	210				107,354
Vested compensated absences									$82,918	82,918
Notes payable					502					502
Revenue bonds payable					354,481					354,481
Matured bonds—principal and interest payable			237							237
Accrued retirement costs									71,967	71,967
Deferred compensation benefits							86,627			86,627
General long-term debt payable					23,016				468,097	491,113
Capital lease obligations									109,810	109,810
Total liabilities	140,517	50,140	15,586	15,717	492,032	46,372	94,116		732,792	1,587,272

Commitments and contingencies										
Fund equity:										
Contributed capital					776,133	29,920				806,053
Investment in general fixed assets								1,714,968		1,714,968
Retained earnings:										
Reserved for:										
Revenue bond retirements					66,941					66,941
Self-insurance claims						7,453				7,453
Capital improvements						57				57
Unreserved (deficit)					(27,256)	5,285				(21,971)
Fund balance:										
Reserved for:										
Encumbrances	22,335	4,487		53,407						80,229
Inventories	5,930	1,018								6,948
Other assets	1,305	122								1,427
Pension benefits							1,672,311			1,672,311
Library services							2,102			2,102
Scholarships and memorials							5,081			5,081
Unreserved:										
Desigated for:										
Debt service			28,787							28,787
Subsequent years' expenditures	13,720	89								13,809
Undesignated	2,450	3,609		28,770						34,829
Total equity and other credits	45,740	9,325	28,787	82,177	815,818	42,715	1,679,494	1,714,968	—	4,419,024
Total liabilities and fund equity	$186,257	$59,465	$44,373	$97,894	$1,307,850	$89,087	$1,773,610	$1,714,968	$732,792	$6,006,296

See notes to financial statements.

Source: Adapted from a recent Comprehensive Annual Financial Report of the City of Baltimore, Maryland.

445

good annual report. To reward the organizations that meet the high standards of reporting set by the GFOA, the Certificate of Conformance Program was established. When an annual report—now referred to as a Comprehensive Annual Financial Report (CAFR)—is deemed to meet the requirements of the GFOA, a **Certificate of Conformance**—now referred to as a **Certificate of Excellence in Financial Reporting**—is awarded to the organization issuing the report. Exhibit 9–6 contains a copy of the Certificate of Excellence earned by the City of Columbus for its 19X1 CAFR.

> To earn a Certificate of Conformance (Excellence), a CAFR must tell its financial story clearly, thoroughly and understandably. Certificates of Conformance (Excellence) reports are efficiently organized, employ certain standardized terminology and formatting conventions, minimize ambiguities and potentials for misleading inference, enhance understanding of current GAAP theory, and generally demonstrate a constructive "spirit of full disclosure."[8]

Participation by Other Organizations

A major bond-rating agency, Standard & Poor's Corporation, has taken an active role in governmental financial reporting by insisting that governmental units follow GAAP.[9] Standard & Poor's (S&P) has indicated that any problems that arise in the reporting format, timing of the issuance of the report, and so forth, will be taken into consideration when the government's bonds are rated. Since the effect of such ratings is felt immediately in the "pocketbook" of a governmental unit (bonds with low ratings must be issued with higher yields or rates of interest than those with high ratings), it is possible that the actions of S&P may have had a greater impact on governmental financial reporting than the Certificate of Excellence Program.

Other financial institutions are also penalizing governmental units for substandard financial reporting. In a survey, many underwriters, bankers, and managers of other institutions providing financial services to governmental organizations indicated that they often require higher interest rates from those governmental units whose financial reports are not prepared in accordance with GAAP. In addition, they indicated that if poor financial reporting practices persist, future penalties may make it difficult for governmental units to issue debt securities of any kind.[10]

CURRENT ISSUES

Measurement Focus/Basis of Accounting Project

The most far-reaching modification in accounting principles passed by the Governmental Accounting Standards Board is the change in the measurement focus and basis of accounting used by governmental-type funds, as well as Expendable Trust Funds, and general long-term debt. The measurement focus, you will re-

---

[8]"Certificate of Conformance," Supplement to MFOA *Newsletter,* January 16, 1983, p. 1.
[9]For example, see *Standard & Poor's Perspective,* "Who's Watching the Books?" (1980), p. 6.
[10]Ibid., pp. 2–3.

Certificate of Achievement for Excellence in Financial Reporting

Presented to

City of Columbus, Ohio

For its Comprehensive Annual
Financial Report
for the Fiscal Year Ended
December 31, 19X1

A Certificate of Achievement for Excellence in Financial
Reporting is presented by the Government Finance Officers
Association of the United States and Canada to
government units and public employee retirement
systems whose comprehensive annual financial
reports (CAFRs) achieve the highest
standards in government accounting
and financial reporting.

President

Executive Director

Exhibit 9–6   Certificate of Excellence in Financial Reporting
Source: Adapted from a recent Comprehensive Annual Financial Report of the City of Columbus, Ohio.

call, refers to *what* is being measured. The basis of accounting refers to *when* transactions or events should be recorded. The new measurement focus/basis of accounting is described in GASB *Statement 11: Measurement Focus and Basis of Accounting—Governmental Fund Operating Statements.*

The basic premise of *Statement 11* is that the measurement focus used by the affected funds is the **flow of financial resources.** Under this measurement focus, operating results report the extent to which financial resources obtained during a period were sufficient to cover claims incurred in that period. The statement of financial position (balance sheet) under this method reports the net financial resources available for future periods.

The flow of financial resources measurement focus is accomplished by measuring increases or decreases in fund balance and the claims against financial resources by means of what amounts to, for all practical purposes, the *accrual* basis of accounting (see Exhibit 9–7).

The justification for these changes is the perception of many professionals of a need to carefully match revenues and expenditures. While this is done to a certain extent through the budgetary process, *Statement 11* brings the matching process one step closer to reality. The general feeling of those advocating this change is that although specific revenues and specific services of governmental-type activities bear no direct relationship to one another, they both can be related directly to specific time periods and, in the aggregate, can be related to each other. Therefore, a measurement focus that measures the relationship between aggregate revenues and aggregate services within a comparable time period is appropriate for measuring **interperiod equity** (the measure of whether current-year revenues are sufficient to pay for current-year services). The relationship of revenues and services to a specific time period can best be expressed by using the accrual basis of accounting because this basis recognizes effects of transactions or events on the fund balance of an entity when they take place (a specific time period), regardless of when cash is received or paid.

A summary of the major provisions of *Statement 11* is presented in Exhibit 9–7. Notice that revenues are categorized as those from **taxes, other nonexchange transactions,** and **exchange transactions.** In general, (1) revenue from taxes and other nonexchange transactions are recognized when the transactions take place, regardless of when cash is received, and (2) revenue from exchange transactions are recognized when they are earned, regardless of when cash is received. Expenditures are generally recognized when transactions take place or assets are consumed. Notice also that general long-term debt has two components: capital-related debt and noncapital-related (operating) debt.

Statement 11 was originally issued in May 1990 with an effective date of fiscal periods beginning after June 15, 1994 (early application was not permitted). In 1993, however, the GASB realized that the entire project, including related projects on pensions and claims and judgments, could not be completed by the original due date. As a result, after considerable deliberation the Board decided to indefinitely defer implementation of *Statement 11* until all related projects are completed. At the time of this writing, *Statement 11* does not have a specific implementation date because the related projects are not completed.

EXHIBIT 9–7   Summary of Measurement Focus/Basis of Accounting GASB *Statement 11* (as of May 1990)

Taxes: Payments a government requires from its taxpayers to obtain resources to provide services.

Other nonexchange transactions: Payments a government requires for fines, licenses, and other similar activities.

Exchange transactions: Payments received by a government for goods or services provided.

	Recognize	
	STATEMENT 11	CURRENT
REVENUES		
Taxes		
Property taxes	When levied, if demanded	When measurable and available
Income taxes	When earned, if due within two months	When measurable and available
Sales taxes	When sale takes place, if due within two months after end of period	When measurable and available
Other Nonexchange Transactions		
Fines	When enforceable claim is established	When cash is received
Licenses and permits	When enforceable claim is established	When cash is received
Donations	When enforceable claim is established	When resources are received
Exchange Transactions		
Charges for goods and services	When earned	When services are performed, if measurable and available
Other exchange revenues	When earned	When earned, if measurable and available
EXPENDITURES		
Operating (e.g., salaries)	When transaction takes place	When transaction takes place
Inventories (e.g., supplies)	When consumed	When purchased or consumed
Prepaid items (e.g., insurance)	When consumed	When purchased or consumed
Depreciation	Not recognized	Not recognized
Compensated absences and other similar items	When liability is incurred	When accrued during the year and will be liquidated with available spendable resources
Capital	When incurred	When incurred
Debt issue costs	Operating debt—when accrued using the effective interest method / Capital debt—not mentioned	When legally due
General Long-Term Debt		
Debt issued for capital purposes	When issued in General Long-Term Debt Account Group[1]	When issued in General Long-term Debt Account Group. (1)
Noncapital debt	Reporting of principal not covered.[2]	When issued in General Long-term Debt Account Group. (1)

[1]Proceeds are reported on the operating statement.

[2]Proceeds are not reported on the operating statement.

As was mentioned earlier, the GASB is also working on balance sheet reporting for general obligation long-term debt. The current thinking of the Board is to separate this debt into capital-related and noncapital-related elements. **Capital-related debt** is debt issued for capital purposes, such as construction of a new city hall. **Noncapital-related debt (operating debt)** is long-term debt issued for other than capital purposes. *Statement 11* provides that capital-related debt should be reported like general obligation long-term debt is currently reported—the proceeds are another financing source in the governmental-type fund receiving the cash and the principal is reported in the General Long-Term Debt Account Group.

On the other hand, *Statement 11* only indicates that noncapital-related debt should not be recorded as another financing source. In addition, it specifically prevents operating debt from being reported on the operating statement of the fund receiving the cash. Presumably the Board intends this type of debt to be classified as a fund liability, with the liability reported in the fund and not in the General Long-Term Debt Account Group. It must be pointed out, however, that *Statement 11* leaves the question of balance sheet reporting of operating debt unanswered; that is, there is no specific guidance on how to report it. The Board feels that this is the subject of one of the related projects mentioned above.

Current GASB Projects

At the time of this writing, the Governmental Accounting Standards Board is studying topics such as:

1. Measurement focus/basis of accounting (see previous discussion)
2. Capital reporting
3. Other postemployment benefits
4. Fixed assets
5. Fund structure

We have included these brief comments on issues that are on the GASB's agenda to indicate that financial accounting and reporting for governmental units is in a constantly evolving state. As a result, many changes may have taken place by the time you read this text. The role of the governmental accountant is partially devoted to maintaining a current knowledge of the field and an ability to interpret the pronouncements of rule-making bodies.

REVIEW QUESTIONS

Q9–1   What is a CAFR?

Q9–2   What are combined financial statements?

Q9–3   What are notes to the financial statements?

Q9–4   What is a combining financial statement?

Q9–5   What types of funds are included on the combined statement of cash flows?

Q9–6   Define the term *reporting entity.*

Q9–7   What is a component unit?

Q9–8   Compare and contrast blending and discrete presentations with respect to financial reporting for a governmental unit.

Q9–9   What are interim financial statements?

Q9–10   Are PERS reported on a combined balance sheet?

Q9–11   What is the Certificate of Excellence?

Q9–12   How have financial institutions tried to enforce good financial reporting of governmental units?

Q9–13   What are the effects of a lower bond rating when bonds are issued?

Q9–14   What is the overall effect of GASB *Statement 11* with respect to revenues and expenditures?

Q9–15   How does GASB *Statement 11* apply to general long-term debt?

CASES

C9–1   The Building Authority was created by the city and organized as a separate legal entity. The authority is governed by a five-person board appointed for six-year terms by the mayor, subject to city council approval. The authority uses the proceeds of its tax-exempt bonds to finance the construction or acquisition of general capital assets for the city only. The bonds are secured by the lease agreement with the city and will be retired through lease payments from the city.

How should the city report the financial activities of the Building Authority?

(GASB *Statement 14*, para. 134)

C9–2   The Municipal Electric Utility (MEU) was created as a separate legal entity in accordance with state law to own, manage, and operate an electric utilities system in the city. The MEU's governing body consists of five members. It is a self-perpetuating board composed of four citizens (customers) and the mayor of the city serving ex officio. The four citizen board members provide representation from each of the MEU's main service areas. When a board vacancy occurs, the remaining board members must nominate the successor. The MEU board chooses the nominee from a list of candidates proposed by an independent citizens' committee. The MEU's board may reject these candidates for any reason and request additional candidates. The MEU's nomination is then subject to confirmation by the city council. The council's confirmation procedure is essentially a formality. After confirmation, the council cannot remove a member for any reason.

The MEU uses various services provided by departments of the city, including insurance, legal, motor pool, and computer services. The MEU is billed for these services on a proportionate cost basis with other user departments and agencies. The MEU provides customer service and related functions to the city's water department. The estimated cost of providing these services is paid by the water department. The MEU also provides electric service to the city and its agencies and bills the city for those services using established rate schedules. The MEU selects and employs its executives, controls the hiring of its employees, and is responsible for rate setting and its overall fiscal management. The city is not legally or morally obligated for the MEU's debt. The MEU receives no appropriations from the city. In compliance with its charter, the MEU is required to make a payment in lieu of taxes annually to the General Fund, calculated according to a formula based on kilowatt-hour sales for the preceding twelve-month period.

How should the city report the financial activities of the MEU?

(GASB *Statement 14*, para. 141)

C9–3 The State Turnpike Commission (STC) was established by the state to construct, operate, and maintain the state turnpike system. The STC was created as an instrumentality of the state as a separate legal entity with powers to issue revenue bonds payable from tolls and other revenues. The governing body of the STC consists of eight members appointed by the governor for fixed ten-year terms and three state officials serving ex officio—the elected state treasurer, the elected state controller, and the appointed superintendent of highways.

The STC is financially self-sufficient, and the state cannot access its assets or surpluses and is not obligated to subsidize deficits of the STC. The STC sets its own rates and approves its own budget. The bond agreement states that the debt of the STC is not an obligation of the state. However, state statutes authorize the state's budget director to include in the budget submitted to the legislature an amount sufficient to make the principal and interest payments on the STC bonds in the event STC revenues are insufficient to meet debt service requirements.

How should the state report the financial activities of the STC?

(GASB *Statement 14*, para. 142)

C9–4 The Board of Education (BOE) is a separately elected body that administers the public school system in the city. The BOE is not organized as a separate legal entity and does not have the power to levy taxes or issue bonds. Its budget is subject to approval by the city council to the extent that, under state law, the BOE has the discretionary authority to expend the amount appropriated to it by the city. The BOE requests a single amount to fund its operations; the city council can reject the BOE's requested budget.

How should the city report the financial activities of the BOE?

(GASB *Statement 14*, para. 144)

EXERCISES

E9–1   (Organization of the CAFR)

Assume that you have been asked to explain the organization of the Comprehensive Annual Financial Report, as specified in NCGA *Statement 1*, to a group of city controllers. Outline your talk.

E9–2   (Certificate of Excellence)

Obtain a copy of a CAFR from a governmental unit. Determine whether it has received a Certificate of Excellence. How can you determine this? Explain what the "certificate" means.

E9–3   (Analysis of a CAFR)

Obtain a CAFR from a governmental unit and examine the notes section. Write a brief report summarizing three of the notes. In addition, compare the CAFR you have to the statements illustrated in this chapter. Explain any significant differences.

E9–4   (Description of the Financial Reporting Pyramid)

Describe the Financial Reporting Pyramid as set forth in NCGA *Statement 1*. Be sure to explain the relationship between the various levels of the pyramid and the amount of detail that must be included in the CAFR.

E9–5   (Multiple choice)

1.   In governmental financial reporting, blending is
   a.   A method of preparing the notes to the CAFR
   b.   The process of including financial data of a component unit with the financial data of the primary government
   c.   The process of reporting the financial data for a component unit as a separate column in a combining financial statement
   d.   The process of combining city, state, and federal financial data into one report

2.   In governmental financial reporting, a related organization is
   a.   An organization in which the primary government appoints a voting majority of its members, but for which the primary government is not financially accountable
   b.   An organization that has the name of the city (or state) included in its title
   c.   An organization over which the primary government has control and responsibility for its operations
   d.   Any organization that operates in the incorporated area of a city

3. Interim financial statements for a governmental unit may contain
    a. A balance sheet
    b. A statement of actual and budgeted revenues
    c. A statement of actual and budgeted expenditures
    d. All of the above
4. In an interim comparison of budgeted and actual expenditures
    a. Encumbrances cannot be included in the actual data
    b. Encumbrances must be included in the actual data
    c. Encumbrances may be included in the actual data
    d. None of the above
5. The "Certificate of Excellence in Financial Reporting" is issued by the
    a. GASB
    b. FASB
    c. GFOA
    d. AICPA

E9–6 (Fill-in-the-blanks)
1. The GPFS that has separate columns for each type of a given fund is called a _____ .
2. The annual financial report of a governmental unit is called a _____ .
3. The GPFS consist of _____ and _____ .
4. A combined balance sheet includes (all or some) _____ funds and account groups.
5. _____ is the basis of the combined budget and actual financial statement.

E9–7 (Analysis of a CAFR)
Obtain a CAFR of a governmental unit. What statistical tables are included? What is the purpose of the statistical tables?

E9–8 (Analysis of a CAFR)
Examine Table 9–8, General Governmental Expenditures by Function—Last Ten Fiscal Years for the City of Columbus. How much did its expenditures change by function over the period presented?

PROBLEMS

P9–1 (Review of an actual CAFR)
Obtain a CAFR from a governmental unit, and write a report identifying the statements included and your impression of the strengths and weaknesses of the reporting format used.

P9–2 (Multiple choice)

1. The Comprehensive Annual Financial Report (CAFR) of a governmental unit should contain a combined statement of cash flows for

	GOVERNMENTAL FUND	ACCOUNT GROUPS
a.	Yes	No
b.	Yes	Yes
c.	No	Yes
d.	No	No

(AICPA adapted)

2. The Amount available in Debt Service Fund is an account of a governmental unit that would be included in the
    a. Liability section of the Debt Service Fund
    b. Liability section of the General Long-Term Debt Account Group
    c. Asset section of the Debt Service Fund
    d. Asset section of the General Long-Term Debt Account Group

(AICPA)

3. The Comprehensive Annual Financial Report (CAFR) of a governmental unit should contain a combined statement of revenues, expenditures, and changes in fund balances for

	GOVERNMENTAL FUNDS	ACCOUNT GROUPS
a.	Yes	Yes
b.	Yes	No
c.	No	No
d.	No	Yes

(AICPA)

4. Fixed assets should be accounted for in the General Fixed Assets Account Group for the

	CAPITAL PROJECTS FUNDS	INTERNAL SERVICE FUNDS
a.	Yes	Yes
b.	Yes	No
c.	No	No
d.	No	Yes

(AICPA)

5. The Comprehensive Annual Financial Report (CAFR) of a governmental unit should contain a combined balance sheet for

	GOVERNMENTAL FUNDS	PROPRIETARY FUNDS	ACCOUNT GROUPS
a.	Yes	Yes	No
b.	Yes	Yes	Yes
c.	Yes	No	Yes
d.	No	Yes	No

(AICPA)

6. The Comprehensive Annual Financial Report (CAFR) of a government unit should contain a combined statement of revenues, expenses, and changes in retained earnings for

	GOVERNMENTAL FUNDS	PROPRIETARY FUNDS
a.	No	Yes
b.	No	No
c.	Yes	No
d.	Yes	Yes

(AICPA)

7. Which of the following is an appropriate basis of accounting for a proprietary fund of a governmental unit?

	CASH BASIS	MODIFIED ACCRUAL BASIS
a.	Yes	Yes
b.	Yes	No
c.	No	No
d.	No	Yes

(AICPA)

8. Fixed assets used by a governmental unit should be accounted for in a (the)

	CAPITAL PROJECTS FUND	GENERAL FUND
a.	No	Yes
b.	No	No
c.	Yes	No
d.	Yes	Yes

(AICPA)

9. Fixed assets of an Enterprise Fund should be accounted for in the
   a. General Fixed Assets Account Group, but no depreciation on the fixed assets should be recorded
   b. General Fixed Assets Account Group, and depreciation on the fixed assets should be recorded
   c. Enterprise Fund, but no depreciation on the fixed assets should be recorded
   d. Enterprise Fund, and depreciation on the fixed assets should be recorded

(AICPA adapted)

10. Which of the following funds of a governmental unit would include contributed capital in its balance sheet?
    a. An Expendable Trust Fund
    b. A Special Revenue Fund
    c. A Capital Projects Fund
    d. An Internal Service Fund

(AICPA adapted)

P9–3 (Preparation of a partial combined balance sheet)

The following information is available for the City of Ceder's Special Revenue Funds:

ACCOUNT	MOTOR VEHICLE	COMUNITY DEVELOPMENT BLOCK GRANTS	GRANTS REVENUE
Cash	$10,000	$ 5,000	$3,000
Receivables	3,000	2,000	1,000
Due from other governments	12,000	8,000	5,000
Inventories of supplies	2,000	1,000	4,000
Notes and other mortgages receivable, net of $1,000 estimated uncollectibles		11,000	
Other assets	500	800	100
Accounts payable	3,000	2,000	1,000
Due to other funds	1,000	500	800
Encumbrances	4,000	15,000	5,000
Unreserved fund balance	19,500	10,300	6,300

REQUIRED: Prepare the Special Revenue Fund column of a combined balance sheet for the City of Ceder.

P9–4 (Multiple choice)
1. The combined statement of revenues, expenditures, and changes in fund balances—budget and actual—general and special revenue fund types is prepared using
   a. A GAAP basis
   b. The budgetary basis
   c. A cash receipts and disbursements basis
   d. The modified accrual basis
   e. None of the above
2. Which of the following is not a required financial statement in the CAFR?
   a. Combined statement of revenues, expenditures, and changes in fund balance—all governmental-type funds
   b. Combining statement of proprietary fund revenues, expenses, and changes in retained earnings (or equity) by fund type
   c. Combined statement of revenues, expenses, and changes in retained earnings (or equity)—all proprietary fund types
   d. Combined balance sheet—all fund types and account groups
   e. None of the above—that is, all of the above are required statements in the CAFR
3. The term *CAFR* refers to the
   a. Capital Assessments Fund Report
   b. Cumulative Annual Fund Review
   c. City Annual Fund Review
   d. Comprehensive Annual Financial Report
   e. None of the above
4. The revenues and expenditures (expenses) of governmental-type and proprietary-type funds are

457

a. Reported on different statements
b. Reported on the same statements
c. Not both reported for the same governmental unit
d. Not required in the CAFR
e. None of the above

5. The Summary of Significant Accounting Policies
a. Is not required in the CAFR
b. Describes the methods used in the financial accounting system
c. Is a summary of the financial results of the operations of the governmental unit
d. Is usually the last note found in the CAFR
e. Items b and d are correct

6. Individual fund financial statements are
a. Never required in the CAFR
b. Always required in the CAFR
c. Required in the CAFR if necessary to present the financial information fairly
d. The major components of the CAFR
e. None of the above

7. The Financial Reporting Pyramid
a. Is the CAFR for the City of Pyramid
b. Depicts the relationship between the various elements of the financial accounting system
c. Is a listing of the individual parts of a CAFR
d. Is a listing of the various statistical tables required in the CAFR
e. None of the above

8. The financial reporting emphasis in NCGA *Statement 1* is
a. The financial statements of the individual funds
b. The combined financial statements
c. The monthly financial reports issued for internal governmental use
d. Detailed written discussions of the results of operating the government over the past year
e. None of the above

9. A combined financial statement
a. Includes assets, liabilities, revenues, and expenses
b. Must be prepared using the full accrual basis of accounting
c. Has a separate column for each fund type
d. Contains individual fund financial statements
e. None of the above

10. Which of the following is not a major component of the CAFR?
a. Statistical tables
b. Introductory data
c. Financial statements and related data
d. All of the above
e. None of the above—that is, all of the above are major components of the CAFR

P9–5 (Preparation of a budget-actual statement)

The following is information for the General Fund of New Park City:

ITEM	BUDGETED AMOUNT	ACTUAL REVENUE	EXPENDITURES	ENCUMBRANCES
Property taxes	$500,000	$500,000		
Sales taxes	300,000	310,000		
Licenses and permits	55,000	60,000		
Federal and state grants	170,000	170,000		
Miscellaneous	10,000	15,000		
General government	350,000		$345,000	$10,000
Public safety	450,000		395,000	20,000
Education	300,000		304,000	12,000
Highways	23,000		25,000	3,000
Miscellaneous	3,000		1,000	1,000

Assume all excess expenditures and/or encumbrances have been approved. The actual fund balance at the beginning of the year (7/1/X1) was $564,000. The budget basis for New Park City includes encumbrances.

REQUIRED: Prepare a budget-actual statement of revenues and expenditures.

SUMMARY PROBLEMS FOR CHAPTERS 4–9

I. (Adjusting and correcting journal entries for several funds and a General Fund balance sheet)

You have been engaged to examine the financial statements of the City of Rego for the year ended December 31, 19X1. Your examination disclosed that, due to the inexperience of the town's new bookkeeper, all transactions for the year 19X1 were recorded in the General Fund. The following General Fund trial balance, as of December 31, 19X1, was furnished to you.

City of Rego
General Fund
Trial Balance
December 31, 19X1

	DEBITS	CREDITS
Cash	$ 20,800	
Short-term investments	180,000	
Accounts receivable	11,500	
Taxes receivable—current	30,000	
Tax anticipation notes payable		$ 58,000
Appropriations		927,000
Expenditures	795,200	
Estimated revenues	927,000	
Revenues		750,000
General city property	98,500	
General obligation bonds payable	52,000	
Unreserved fund balance		380,000
	$2,115,000	$2,115,000

Note: 1. Single control accounts were used for items such as Appropriations and Expenditures.

2. The budget is only recorded for the General Fund.

Your audit disclosed the following additional information:

1. During the year, equipment with a book value of $9,000 was re-moved from service and sold for $6,400. In addition, new equipment costing $104,900 was purchased. These transactions were recorded in the General city property account. No other amounts were recorded relative to these events.

2. During the year, one hundred acres of land were donated to the town for use as an industrial park. The land had a value of $125,000. No recording of this donation had been made.

3. To service other municipal departments, the town, at the beginning of the year, authorized the establishment of a central supplies warehouse (an Internal Service Fund). During the year, supplies totaling $90,000 were purchased and charged to Expenditures in the General Fund. A physical inventory of supplies on hand at December 31, 19X1, was taken; and this count disclosed that supplies totaling $84,000 had been used. Other records indicate that departments using the supplies were billed $92,400. No entries were made for the billings. The General Fund acquired and used all the supplies mentioned above.

4. Outstanding purchase orders at December 31, 19X1, not recorded in the accounts, amounted to $22,000. While encumbrance accounting is required by city charter, it was not used during the year.

5. On December 31, 19X1, the State Revenue Department informed the town that its share of a state-collected, locally shared tax would be $58,500. No entry was made for this information.

6. The Accounts receivable of $11,500 includes $2,000 due from Rego's electric utility for the sale of old equipment on behalf of the town. Accounts for the municipal electric utility operated by the town are maintained in a separate fund. The scrap was sold to K.R., Inc., which will pay for it in July. The old equipment originally cost $15,000. The entry made on the books of the General Fund to record the sale was:

Accounts receivable	2,000	
Revenues		2,000

No entries were made on the books of the utility for this transaction.

7. The balance in Taxes receivable—current is now considered delinquent, and the town estimates that $4,000 will be uncollectible.

8. On December 31, 19X1, the town retired, at face value, 6 percent general obligation serial bonds totaling $40,000. The bonds were issued on January 1, 19X0, at a face value of $200,000. Interest of $12,000 was paid during 19X1 and debited to General obligation bonds payable. A Debt Service Fund was established in 19X0.

REQUIRED: 1.   Prepare all the entries necessary to correct the town's records. Identify the funds and account groups used.
2.   Prepare a revised trial balance for the General Fund.
3.   Prepare the closing entries for the General Fund after the corrections have been made.
     Hint: If an item is recorded in an incorrect fund, it will require an entry to remove it from that fund and a separate entry to record it in the proper fund.

(AICPA adapted)

II.   (Journal entries for several funds and a balance sheet for a Capital Projects Fund)

The City of Westgate's fiscal year ends on June 30. During the fiscal year ended June 30, 19X2, the city authorized the construction of a new library and sale of general obligation term bonds to finance the construction of the library. The authorization imposed the following restrictions: Construction cost was not to exceed $5,000,000; annual interest rate was not to exceed 8 1/2 percent.

The city records project authorizations, and other budgetary accounts are also maintained in the General Fund and Capital Projects Funds. The following transactions relating to the financing and constructing of the library and other events occurred during the fiscal year ended June 30, 19X2:

1.   On July 1, 19X1, the city issued $5 million of 30-year, 8 percent general obligation bonds for $5,100,000. The semiannual interest dates are December 31 and June 30. The premium of $100,000 was transferred to the Library Debt Service Fund.

2.   On July 3, 19X1, the Library Capital Projects Fund invested $4,900,000 in short-term commercial paper. These purchases were at face value with no accrued interest. Interest on cash invested by the Library Capital Projects Fund must be transferred to the Library Debt Service Fund during the fiscal year; estimated interest to be earned is $140,000.

3.   On July 5, 19X1, the city signed a contract with F & A Construction Company to build the library for $4,980,000.

4.   The General Fund made one half of its annual payment to the Library Debt Service Fund, $200,000. The other half will be made later in the year.

5.   The Library Debt Service Fund made a semiannual interest payment.

6.   On January 15, 19X2, the Library Capital Projects Fund received $3,040,000 from the maturity of short-term notes purchased on July 3. The cost of these notes was $3,000,000. The interest of $40,000 was transferred to the Library Debt Service Fund.

7.   On January 20, 19X2, F & A Construction Company properly billed the city $3,000,000 for work performed on the new library. The con-

tract calls for a 10 percent retention until final inspection and acceptance of the building. The Library Capital Projects Fund paid F & A the appropriate amount.

8. The General Fund made another debt service payment to the Library Debt Service Fund.
9. On June 30, 19X2, the Library Debt Service Fund made the appropriate interest payment.
10. On June 30, 19X2, the Library Capital Projects Fund made the proper adjusting entries (including accrued interest receivable of $103,000) and closing entries. Closing entries are not required for any other fund.

REQUIRED: 1. Prepare in good form journal entries to record the above information and identify each fund(s) or account group(s) used. (Except for the issuance of bonds, assume the General Fixed Assets Account Group and the General Long-Term Debt Account Group are updated for changes during the period in which closing entries are prepared.)
2. Prepare in good form a balance sheet for the City of Westgate—Library Capital Projects Fund as of June 30, 19X2.

(AICPA adapted)

III. (Journal entries for several funds)
Following are several transactions that relate to Weaverstown for 19X1:
1. The general operating budget was approved as follows:

Appropriations	$5,200,000
Estimated revenues	5,000,000
Estimated other financing sources	300,000

2. Plans for a new criminal courts building were approved. General obligation bonds with a face value of $7 million were issued for $7,200,000. Local laws stipulate that any premium must be transferred to the appropriate Debt Service Fund. In addition, a federal grant of $8 million was received.
3. The fire department ordered new equipment to replace outdated equipment. The new equipment cost $35,000. The old equipment cost $23,000 but was sold for $750.
4. The city received $400,000 from the state. This amount represents the city's share of the state gasoline tax. This money can only be spent to repair streets, and a separate accounting is required by the state.
5. General obligation bonds of $5 million were retired by a Debt Service Fund. At this time, interest of $150,000 was also paid to the bondholders.
6. The 19X1 property tax was levied by the city. The total amount was $3,000,000, of which $2,990,000 was expected to be collected.
7. Salaries of governmental employees were paid, totaling $800,000.

Of this amount, $65,000 was withheld and included in an account called "Due to federal government" as income tax payments. In addition, the city paid its share of retirement benefits, $100,000, and the employees' share, $50,000, to the city's PERS. Assume that all employees were paid through the General Fund. (Salaries and related costs are not encumbered.)

8. The Central Supplies Fund, an Internal Service Fund, billed the General Fund $15,000 and the Gas Service Fund, an Enterprise Fund, $8,000 for supplies. Assume that the General Fund previously encumbered $15,500 for supplies.

9. The Gas Service Fund billed the General Fund for $2,500, the Central Supplies Fund for $1,000, and the remainder of its customers for $2,500,000. The General Fund had encumbered $2,600 for this expenditure.

10. The General Fund made its annual contribution of $200,000 to the Debt Service Fund. Assume that $150,000 was for interest.

11. The contract for the new court building was signed with Excell Construction Company for $14,500,000.

12. The fire equipment ordered in number 3 arrived. The total cost was $36,000. The city paid the bill upon delivery. (Assume the excess expenditure was approved.)

13. Excell Construction Company sent a progress billing for $1,500,000.

14. Property taxes of $2,800,000 were collected and $5,000 was written off as uncollectible. The remainder became delinquent.

15. Suzanne Night gave the city $500,000 of marketable securities. The securities were to be used as the principal of a trust that must be maintained intact. The income earned from these investments can only be used for purchasing library books.

16. A property tax bill from 19X0 for $200 was written off as uncollectible. At this time the receivable was in a delinquent state.

17. Special assessment bonds with a face value of $345,000 were issued for a drainage project. The total assessment was $345,000. Of this amount, $30,000 was considered to be current and to be revenue of 19X1. (Assume the city guaranteed the bonds.)

18. Income of $14,000 was received by the Night Principal Trust Fund (see number 15). This amount was immediately transferred to the Night Operating Trust Fund and $12,600 was used to purchase library books.

REQUIRED: Prepare the journal entries necessary to record the above transactions and indicate the fund(s) or account group(s) used.

10

AUDITING AND FEDERAL GOVERNMENT ACCOUNTING AND REPORTING

LEARNING OBJECTIVES

After completion of this chapter, you should be able to:

Part I: Auditing

1. Define an audit and differentiate between a financial audit and a performance audit
2. Identify the major sources of authority that must be followed when performing an audit
3. Understand the concept of generally accepted auditing standards as issued by the American Institute of Certified Public Accountants (AICPA)
4. Explain how governmental audit standards relate to AICPA audit standards
5. Explain how a single audit compares with a governmental audit
6. Discuss the purpose of a single audit
7. Explain the different types of audit reports
8. Explain how reporting under the Single Audit Act is different from reporting for governmental auditing

Part II: Federal Government Accounting and Reporting

1. Explain the federal budgetary process
2. Discuss the federal Anti Deficiency Act

3. Describe six differences between accounts used by the federal government and those used by state and local governmental units
4. List the funds used by the federal government
5. Explain the function of the Federal Accounting Standards Advisory Board
6. Compare and contrast budgetary and proprietary accounting, as used by the federal government
7. Discuss commitment accounting
8. Prepare entries for the accounting cycle of a federal agency
9. Describe the financial statements used by federal agencies

PART I: AUDITING

WHAT IS AN AUDIT?

An audit is a review of activities or events to form a professional opinion as to whether those activities or events comply with a predetermined standard(s). Audits are commonly classified by the objective(s) involved. In general, these objectives are grouped into two broad categories: financial and related audits and performance audits. **Financial audits** and **financial related audits** are designed to determine if (1) the financial statements fairly present the financial position, results of operations, and cash flows of an entity, and (2) the entity has complied with all legal and regulatory requirements. **Performance audits** are designed to determine if (1) the goals of an entity are being achieved, (2) the management of an entity is operating the entity efficiently and effectively, or (3) the entity is complying with specific program laws and regulations. While financial audits are quite different from performance audits, an audit engagement may involve both types. Examples of these combined audits may include "contract audits," "grant audits," and audits of internal controls.

In this chapter, we will provide an overview of the audit process, concentrating on required standards and types of audit reports prepared.

SOURCES OF AUTHORITY FOR AUDITS

Financial audits must be performed according to generally accepted auditing standards (GAAS). These standards are published by the American Institute of Certified Public Accountants (AICPA) and provide auditors with specific guidance as to how to conduct financial audits. These standards apply to audits of commercial and governmental units.

In addition to GAAS, the U.S. General Accounting Office (GAO) has issued a publication entitled *Government Auditing Standards*. This publication, often referred to as the "yellow book," includes additional guidance for auditors when performing audits of governmental units. The combination of GAAS and the "yellow book" standards is generally referred to as "generally accepted government auditing standards" (GAGAS). This is typically the minimum level of standards to follow when auditing a governmental unit. If federal funds are involved, GAGAS is mandatory. In addition, some states mandate that GAGAS be followed, even if no federal funds are involved.

Depending on the amount of federal financial assistance received, additional regulations may also affect an audit. The one most commonly recognized is the Single Audit Act of 1984. Depending on the type of organization being audited, regulations published by the Office of Management and Budget (OMB) may also affect the audit. These would include OMB Circulars A-73, A-128, and A-133.

The AICPA also publishes audit guides in many areas, including governmental entities, colleges and universities, health-care providers, and other not-for-profit entities. These publications provide additional guidance for auditors.

GENERALLY ACCEPTED AUDITING STANDARDS (GAAS)

The AICPA, through its membership, has established standards for audits. These are included in *Codification of Statement on Auditing Standards* (see Table 10–1).

GENERALLY ACCEPTED GOVERNMENTAL AUDITING STANDARDS (GAGAS)

As noted previously, GAAS audits are often supplemented by the "yellow book" standards (GAGAS). GAGAS classifies the specific standards into the same three categories as noted in GAAS. The general standards and the field work standards are somewhat broadened by GAGAS. The biggest change, however, is found in the reporting standards. Under GAAS, the auditor issues one report which expresses an opinion on the fair presentation of the government's financial statements. Under GAGAS, two additional reports are also issued: one on the government's internal control structure and one on the government's compliance with laws and regulations having a material effect on the financial statements. Table 10–1 lists the auditing standards for conducting GAGAS audits under the 1994 "yellow book."

SINGLE AUDIT

One problem faced by governmental units in the past was the large number of audits to which they were subjected. It was not uncommon for a large governmental unit to have from twenty-five to fifty or more audits in a single year. Each

TABLE 10–1   Comparison of GAAS and GAGAS Standards

GAAS	GAGAS
GENERAL STANDARDS 1. The audit is to be performed by a person or persons having adequate technical training and proficiency as an auditor. 2. In all matters relating to the assignment, an independence in mental attitude is to be maintained by the auditor or auditors. 3. Due professional care is to be exercised in the performance of the audit and the preparation of the report.	GENERAL STANDARDS (FOR FINANCIAL AND PERFORMANCE AUDITS) 1. The staff assigned to conduct the audit should collectively possess adequate professional proficiency for the tasks required. 2. In all matters relating to the audit work, the audit organization and the individual auditors, whether government or public, should be free from personal and external impairments to independence, should be organizationally independent, and should maintain an independent attitude and appearance. 3. Due professional care should be used in conducting the audit and in preparing related reports. 4. Each audit organization conducting audits in accordance with these standards should have an appropriate internal quality control system in place and undergo an external quality control review.
STANDARDS OF FIELD WORK 1. The work is to be adequately planned and assistants, if any, are to be properly supervised. 2. A sufficient understanding of the internal control structure is to be obtained to plan the audit and to determine the nature, timing, and extent of the tests to be performed. 3. Sufficient competent evidential matter is to be obtained through inspection, observation, inquiries, and confirmations to afford a reasonable basis for an opinion regarding the financial statements under audit.	FIELD WORK STANDARDS (FOR FINANCIAL AUDITS) A. Planning *Required by the AICPA and GAGAS:* The work is to be properly planned, and auditors should consider materiality, among other matters, in determining the nature, timing, and extent of auditing procedures and in evaluating the results of those procedures. *Additional planning standard:* Auditors should follow up on known material findings and recommendations from previous audits. FIELD WORK STANDARDS (FOR PERFORMANCE AUDITS) 1. Work is to be adequately planned. 2. Staff are to be properly supervised. 3. When laws, regulations, and other compliance requirements are subject to audit objectives, auditors should design the audit to provide reasonable assurance about compliance with them. In all performance audits, auditors should be alert to situations or transactions that could be indicative of illegal acts or abuse.

(continued)

TABLE 10–1 Comparison of GAAS and GAGAS Standards (Continued)

GAAS	GAGAS
B. Irregularities, Illegal Acts, and Other Noncompliance *Required by the AICPA and GAGAS:* 1. Auditors should design the audit to provide reasonable assurance of detecting irregularities that are material to the financial statements. 2. Auditors should design the audit to provide reasonable assurance of detecting material misstatements resulting from direct and material illegal acts. 3. Auditors should be aware of the possibility that indirect illegal acts may have occurred. If specific information comes to the auditor's attention that provides evidence concerning the existence of possible illegal acts that could have a material indirect effect on the financial statements, the auditors should apply audit procedures specifically directed to ascertaining whether an illegal act has occurred. *Additional compliance standard for financial statement audits:* Auditors should design the audit to provide reasonable assurance of detecting material misstatements resulting from noncompliance with provisions of contracts or grant agreements that have a direct and material effect on the determination of financial statement amounts. If specific information comes to the auditor's attention that provides evidence concerning the existence of	4. Auditors should obtain an understanding of management controls that are relevant to the audit. When management controls are significant to audit objectives, auditors should obtain sufficient evidence to support their judgments about those controls. 5. Sufficient, competent, and relevant evidence is to be obtained to afford a reasonable basis for the auditor's findings and conclusions. A record of the auditor's work should be retained in the form of working papers. Working papers should contain sufficient information to enable an experienced auditor having no previous connection with the audit to ascertain from them the evidence that supports the auditor's significant conclusions and judgments.

possible noncompliance that could have a material effect on the financial statements, auditors should apply audit procedures specifically directed to ascertaining whether that noncompliance has occurred.

C. Internal Controls

Required by the AICPA and GAGAS:

Auditors should obtain a sufficient understanding of internal controls to plan the audit and determine the nature, timing, and extent of tests to be performed.

D. Working Papers

Required by the AICPA and GAGAS:

A record of the auditor's work should be retained in the form of working papers.

Additional working paper standard:

Working papers should contain sufficient information to enable an experienced auditor having no previous connection with the audit to ascertain from them the evidence that supports the auditor's significant conclusions and judgments.

REPORTING STANDARDS (FOR FINANCIAL AUDITS)

For financial statement audits, generally accepted government auditing standards (GAGAS) incorporate the AICPA's four generally accepted standards of reporting.

Additional reporting standards:

1. Auditors should communicate certain information related to the conduct and reporting of the audit to the audit committee or to the individuals with whom they have contracted for the audit.

STANDARDS OF REPORTING

1. The report shall state whether the financial statements are presented in accordance with generally accepted accounting principles.
2. The report shall identify those circumstances in which such principles have not been consistently observed in the current period in relation to the preceding period.
3. Informative disclosures in the financial statements are to be regarded as reasonably adequate unless otherwise stated in the report.

REPORTING STANDARDS (FOR PERFORMANCE AUDITS)

1. Auditors should prepare written audit reports communicating the results of each audit.
2. Auditors should appropriately issue the reports to make the information available for timely use by management, legislative officials, and other interested parties.
3. Report contents. Auditors should report
   a. The audit objectives and the audit scope and methodology.

(continued)

TABLE 10–1 Comparison of GAAS and GAGAS Standards (Continued)

GAAS	GAGAS
4. The report shall either contain an expression of opinion regarding the financial statements, taken as a whole, or an assertion to the effect that an opinion cannot be expressed. When an overall opinion cannot be expressed, the reasons therefore should be stated. In all cases where an auditor's name is associated with financial statements, the report should contain a clear-cut indication of the character of the auditor's work, if any, and the degree of responsibility the auditor is taking.[1]	2. Audit reports should state that the audit was made in accordance with generally accepted government auditing standards.
	3. The report on the financial statements should either (1) describe the scope of the auditor's testing of compliance with laws and regulations and internal controls and present the results of those tests or (2) refer to separate reports containing that information. In presenting the results of those tests, auditors should report irregularities, illegal acts, other material noncompliance, and reportable conditions in internal controls. In some circumstances, auditors should report irregularities and illegal acts directly to parties external to the audited entity.
	4. If certain information is prohibited from general disclosure, the audit report should state the nature of the information omitted and the requirement that makes the omission necessary.
	5. Written audit reports are to be submitted by the audit organization to the appropriate officials of the auditee and to the appropriate officials of the organizations requiring or arranging for the audits, including external funding organizations, unless legal restrictions prevent it. Copies of the reports should also be sent to other officials who have legal

b. Significant audit findings and, where applicable, auditor's conclusions.

c. Recommendations for actions to correct problem areas and to improve operations.

d. That the audit was made in accordance with generally accepted goverment auditing standards.

e. All significant instances of noncompliance and all significant instances of abuse that were found during or in connection with the audit. In some circumstances, auditors should report illegal acts directly to parties external to the audited entity.

f. The scope of their work on management controls and any significant weaknesses found during the audit.

g. The views of responsible officials of the audited program concerning auditors' findings, conclusions, and recommendations, as well as corrections planned.

h. Noteworthy accomplishments, particularly when management improvements in one area may be applicable elsewhere.

i. Significant issues needing further audit work to the auditors responsible for planning future audit work.

oversight authority or who may be responsible for acting on audit findings and recommendations and to others authorized to receive such reports. Unless restricted by law or regulation, copies should be made available for public inspection.

If certain information is prohibited from general disclosure, auditors should report the nature of the information omitted and the requirement that makes the omission necessary.

4. The report should be complete, accurate, objective, convincing, and as clear and concise as the subject permits.

5. Written audit reports are to be submitted by the audit organization to the appropriate officials of the auditee and to the appropriate officials of the organizations requiring or arranging for the audits, including external funding organizations, unless legal restrictions prevent it. Copies of the reports should also be sent to other officials who have legal oversight authority or who may be responsible for acting on audit findings and recommendations and to others authorized to receive such reports. Unless restricted by law or regulation, copies should be made available for public inspection.[2]

[1]AICPA, *Codification of Statements on Auditing Standards* (New York: AICPA), Section AU150. Copyright © 1993 by American Institute of Certified Public Accountants, Inc. Reprinted with permission.

[2]U.S. General Accounting Office, *Government Auditing Standards* (Washington, DC: GAO), June 1994, Chapters 3–7.

of these audits was conducted by a different federal or state audit agency or independent public accountant and was centered on one particular facet of the organization's operations—for example, revenue sharing, a research grant, or an entitlement program. The audits disrupted the operations of the governmental units and required a great deal of time and effort on the part of organizational personnel, not to mention the cost of the audits themselves.

To alleviate this problem, the U.S. Office of Management and Budget (OMB) proposed that "single audits" be performed on certain organizations. The premise of a **single audit** is that one carefully planned audit can perform the same function as many smaller audits, and can do so more efficiently and effectively. It can also greatly reduce the disruptions to the organization being audited. Essentially, a single audit is an expanded financial audit. However, it also includes certain elements of a compliance audit.

The authority for single audits comes from the Single Audit Act of 1984. In 1985, the OMB issued Circular A-128, *Audits of State and Local Governments*, to facilitate the implementation of the Single Audit Act. This document establishes specific audit requirements for state and local governmental units that receive financial assistance from the federal government and defines federal responsibilities for implementing and monitoring these requirements.

The requirements of the Single Audit Act and Circular A-128 apply to those state and local governmental organizations that *receive* federal financial assistance totaling $100,000 or more in any fiscal year. A governmental unit with federal financial assistance of $25,000 or more, but less than $100,000, in any fiscal year may elect to implement the requirements of the Single Audit Act in lieu of the specific compliance and financial audit requirements of the various programs for which they receive federal assistance. Governmental units receiving less than $25,000 in any fiscal year are exempt from the Single Audit Act and all other federal audit requirements. However, these organizations must maintain adequate accounting records and make them available to grantor federal agencies and the U.S. Comptroller General upon request.

Under the Single Audit Act, each governmental unit is assigned a **Cognizant Agency** by the OMB. This agency, which is usually the one providing the most federal funds to the governmental unit, represents the federal government in all matters pertaining to the audit. It is required, among other things, (1) to make certain that audits are performed in a timely manner and in accordance with the requirements of Circular A-128; (2) to coordinate, as far as is practicable, audits performed by or under contract to other federal agencies that are in addition to the single audit and to make certain that these audits build upon the single audit; (3) to make certain that the audit reports, plans for corrective action, and reports of illegal acts or irregularities are transmitted to the appropriate federal, state, and local officials; and (4) to make or obtain quality control reviews of the work of nonfederal audit organizations and, when appropriate, provide the results of these reviews to other organizations.

A single audit must include an audit of the governmental unit's general purpose financial statements (GPFS), additional tests of compliance with applica-

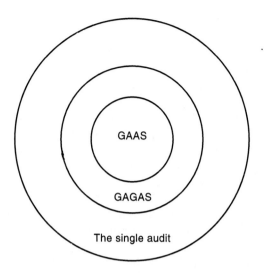

GAAS = Generally Accepted Auditing Standards
GAGAS = Generally Accepted Governmental Auditing Standards

EXHIBIT 10–1 Relationship among Generally Accepted Auditing
Standards, Generally Accepted Governmental Au-
diting Standards, and the Single Audit

ble legal requirements and reviews of the specific internal control systems of the various federal financial assistance programs. Each audit must be conducted in accordance with generally accepted *governmental* auditing standards, which are set forth in the U.S. General Accounting Office (GAO) publication *Government Auditing Standards*. As previously mentioned, these standards are based on the AICPA *Codification of Statements on Auditing Standards* for fieldwork and reporting. However, they establish additional requirements for compliance and internal control reviews and reports. Single audits may be performed by state or local governmental auditors or by public accountants who meet the independence and qualification standards set forth by the GAO.

In summary, auditing standards for governmental audits incorporate and broaden those used in commercial audits, and those used for a single audit incorporate and broaden those used in governmental audits. This relationship is reflected in Exhibit 10–1.

AUDIT REPORTS—REPORT ON FINANCIAL STATEMENTS

Auditors issue reports that express their conclusions as to how activities or events audited comply with the applicable predetermined standards. These reports are often referred to as the auditor's "opinion." As identified by the

AICPA, these opinions can be unqualified, qualified, or adverse, or the auditor may issue a disclaimer of opinion.

An **unqualified opinion** means that the financial statements comply with generally accepted accounting principles. This is the most common form of audit opinion. To avoid confusion, the AICPA has developed standard terminology for all audit opinions.

The typical audit report has three paragraphs. The first paragraph identifies the purpose of the audit and the responsibilities assumed by the auditor. The second paragraph, often referred to as the "scope paragraph," is used to identify the work done by the auditor. In this paragraph, the auditor indicates that the work was done in conformance with generally accepted auditing standards. The final paragraph is often referred to as the "opinion paragraph." In this part of the audit report, the auditor expresses an opinion as to whether or not the financial statements comply with GAAP. A typical unqualified audit opinion is illustrated in Exhibit 10–2.

A **qualified opinion** is issued when there is a material departure from generally accepted accounting principles or there is a limitation placed on the auditor's ability to perform generally accepted auditing procedures. The auditor's opinion paragraph will state that the financial statements are presented fairly except for the problem causing the limitation. An **adverse opinion** is issued when a material departure from generally accepted accounting principles is so great that the financial statements are not presented fairly. This means that there are material misstatements in the financial statements.

A **disclaimer of opinion** is issued by an auditor when there is a severe limitation(s) placed on the scope of the audit or the auditors lack independence. An

EXHIBIT 10–2   Auditor's Standard Report

INDEPENDENT AUDITOR'S REPORT

We have audited the accompanying balance sheet of X Company as of December 31, 19XX, and the related statements of income, retained earnings, and cash flows for the year then ended. These financial statements are the responsibility of the Company's management. Our responsibility is to express an opinion on these financial statements based on our audit.

We conducted our audit in accordance with generally accepted auditing standards. Those standards require that we plan and perform the audit to obtain reasonable assurance about whether the financial statements are free of material misstatement. An audit includes examining, on a test basis, evidence supporting the amounts and disclosures in the financial statements. An audit also includes assessing the accounting principles used and significant estimates made by management, as well as evaluating the overall financial statement presentation. We believe that our audit provides a reasonable basis for our opinion.

In our opinion, the financial statements referred to above present fairly, in all material respects, the financial position of X Company as of [at] December 31, 19XX, and the results of its operations and its cash flows for the year then ended in conformity with generally accepted accounting principles.

[*Signature*]

[*Date*]

Source: American Institute of CPAs, *Codification of Statements on Auditing Standards* (New York: AICPA), Section AU508.08. Copyright © 1993 by American Institute of Certified Public Accountants, Inc. Reprinted with permission.

EXHIBIT 10–3   Government Audit Report

 CITY OF BALTIMORE
KURT L. SCHMOKE, Mayor

DEPARTMENT OF AUDITS
ALLAN L. REYNOLDS, City Auditor
Room 321, City Hall
Baltimore, Maryland 21202

Deloitte & Touche

2 Hopkins Plaza
Baltimore, Maryland 21201-2983

Auditor's Report

December 7, 19X1

The Mayor, City Council, Comptroller and
Board of Estimates of the City of Baltimore, Maryland

We have audited the accompanying general purpose financial statements of the City of Baltimore, Maryland, as of and for the year ended June 30, 19X1, as listed in the table of contents. These financial statements are the responsibility of the City of Baltimore's management. Our responsibility is to express an opinion on these financial statements based on our audit.

We conducted our audit in accordance with generally accepted government auditing standards. Those standards require that we plan and perform the audit to obtain reasonable assurance about whether the financial statements are free of material misstatement. An audit includes examining, on a test basis, evidence supporting the amounts and disclosures in the financial statements. An audit also includes assessing the accounting principles used and significant estimates made by management, as well as evaluating the overall financial statement presentation. We believe that our audit provides a reasonable basis for our opinion.

In our opinion, the general purpose financial statements referred to above present fairly, in all material respects, the financial position of the City of Baltimore, Maryland at June 30, 19X1, and the results of its operations and cash flows of its proprietary and similar trust fund types for the year then ended, in conformity with generally accepted accounting principles.

As discussed in Note 3 to the financial statements, the City changed its method of recording depreciation in the Water and Waste Water Utility Enterprise Funds in 19X1.

Our audit was made for the purpose of forming an opinion on the general purpose financial statements taken as a whole. The combining and individual fund financial statements, as listed in the table of contents, are presented for purposes of additional analysis and are not a required part of the general purpose financial statements of the City of Baltimore, Maryland. Such information has been subjected to auditing procedures applied in our audit of the general purpose financial statements and, in our opinion, is fairly stated in all material respects in relation to general purpose financial statements taken as a whole.

The other data, listed under the "Statistical Section" in the table of contents, have not been audited by us and, accordingly, we express no opinion on such data.

Allan L. Reynolds
Allan L. Reynolds
City Auditor

Deloitte & Touche
Deloitte & Touche
Independent Certified
Public Accountants

Source: Adapted from a recent Comprehensive Annual Financial Report of the City of Baltimore, Maryland.

example of such a limitation is a situation in which an auditor cannot gather evidence because the client's records were destroyed by a hurricane.

In general, the same reporting language established by the AICPA for commercial audits is used for governmental audits. Since the scope of a governmental audit is much broader than that of a commercial audit, the auditor's report is much broader. This is evidenced by the audit report issued by Deloitte & Touche to the city of Baltimore, Maryland (see Exhibit 10–3).

SINGLE AUDIT REPORTS

In the section on audit reports, we discussed and illustrated a typical financial audit report for a governmental unit. As mentioned earlier, the Single Audit Act requires all governments that receive federal financial assistance of $100,000 or more in a fiscal year to have a single audit. A single audit must comply with AICPA reporting requirements, governmental auditing standards, and the Single Audit Act. As a result, the auditor is responsible for several reports:

1. A report on the financial statements as required by generally accepted auditing standards,
2. Reports on the internal control structure of the organization and the organization's compliance with applicable laws and regulations as required by governmental auditing standards (if fraud, waste, or abuse is found, an additional report is required), and
3. Reports on (a) the schedule of federal financial assistance received by the governmental unit, (b) the internal control structure relative to federal financial assistance programs, (c) compliance with general requirements (for example, a drug-free workplace and the Civil Rights Act), (d) compliance with applicable laws and regulations for each major program, and (e) compliance with applicable laws and regulations for each nonmajor program. If fraud, waste, or abuse is found, an additional report is required.

In a single audit, the auditor must include, with respect to the governmental unit's federal financial assistance programs, a supplementary schedule showing the total expenditures made for each program. As mentioned above, the Single Audit Act requires a report on the accuracy of the schedule of financial assistance *received* by the governmental unit. The auditor must make sure that all assistance is reported and that amounts received are appropriate.

The level of testing and reporting on internal controls and compliance depends on whether the program is a major or nonmajor program. The Single Audit Act defines **major federal programs** in terms of the total governmental unit's *expenditures* of all federal assisted programs. There is a sliding scale that is similar to the following:

- If total expenditures of federal funds are between $100,000 and $1,000,000, a major federal program is one that *spends* the larger of $300,000 or 3 percent of the total expenditures.

- If total expenditures of federal funds exceed $7 billion, a major federal program is one that *spends* more than $20 million.

Any federal program not meeting the definition of a major federal program is classified as a **nonmajor federal program**. Details of the additional testing and reporting requirements for major and nonmajor federal programs are beyond the scope of this text.

Single audit reports must be transmitted, within thirty days, to the appropriate federal officials and made available by the governmental unit for public inspection. If any material internal control weaknesses or incidents of noncompliance with applicable laws and regulations are found, the governmental unit must submit a plan of corrective action or a statement explaining why corrective action is not necessary.

Single audit reports contain many different individual reports. As a result, they are often ten or more pages in length. Due to this extreme length, a copy of a typical single audit report is not presented in this chapter. The relationship between the auditor's reports included in a commercial audit, a governmental audit, and a single audit is summarized in Exhibit 10–4.

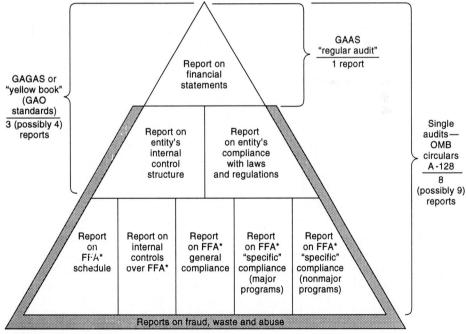

*Federal financial assistance

EXHIBIT 10–4 Comparison of Auditor's Reports
Source: Arthur Andersen & Co.

PART II: FEDERAL ACCOUNTING AND REPORTING

The federal government of the United States of America is a very large consumer of resources. With a budget of over one and one-half **trillion** dollars, it is the largest accounting entity in existence. Its activities affect literally everyone in the United States and almost everyone in the world. Therefore, it is important to understand the accounting system that has developed to control this monolith.

Like the accounting systems used by state and local governmental units, the federal accounting system is heavily influenced by both legal and economic considerations. It is based on a series of funds, and it uses budgetary accounting to control spending. It differs, however, in that:

1. The agency is considered the primary accounting unit, even though each agency is a small part of the entire U.S. government,
2. The accrual basis of accounting is used much of the time,
3. Fixed assets and inventories appear in the accounts of certain accounting/reporting units, and
4. The U.S. Treasury is used to receive and disburse cash, rather than a bank. Thus, no cash account is generally used.

In this section we will briefly cover the types of funds and procedures used by federal agencies to account for their resources. Before we begin this discussion, however, let us review the federal budgetary process and roles of various parties involved.

THE FEDERAL BUDGETARY PROCESS

The federal budgetary process begins about one and a half years before the beginning of a fiscal year (October 1). At this time overall policy issues are identified, budget projections are made, and preliminary program plans are presented to the President. The President reviews this information, along with data on projected revenues and economic conditions. On the basis of this review, he establishes general budgetary and fiscal policy guidelines for the fiscal year under discussion and for the four fiscal years that follow.

Using presidential guidelines, agencies prepare their budgetary requests. These requests are reviewed in detail by the departments of which the agencies are a part (e.g., the U.S. Forest Service is a part of the Department of Agriculture) and by the Office of Management and Budget (OMB).[1] After differences between OMB, the departments, and the agencies are resolved, revised agency budgets are presented to the President, who reviews them in light of the latest economic

[1]The OMB is an agency within the Executive Office of the President which has responsibility for the overall financial management of the federal government. It is ultimately responsible for preparing the executive budget and for apportioning appropriate resources to the various departments and agencies.

data and revenue estimates. Last-minute revisions are made, and the various agency budgets are combined into one document, which is presented to the Congress. The budgetary document represents the President's recommendations for new and existing programs, as well as his projections of receipts and expenditures.

Formal congressional review of the budget begins upon receipt of the budgetary document, usually the first Monday in February. Before passing **appropriations** for specific programs, the Congress must enact legislation which authorizes the programs and provides guidelines on funding levels. While many programs (such as Social Security) are authorized for several years or indefinitely, others (such as Space Exploration) require annual authorizations.

Requests for appropriations and for changes in revenue laws are first considered in the House of Representatives. The House Ways and Means Committee reviews proposed revenue measures and the House Appropriations Committee studies requests for appropriations. These committees then make their report to the entire House of Representatives, which acts on the revenue and appropriations bills. After the bills are approved, they are sent to the Senate, where the process is repeated. If the two houses of Congress cannot agree on the various fiscal measures, a conference committee (consisting of members of both houses) resolves the issues and submits a report to both houses for approval.

After approval by the Congress, the various revenue and appropriations measures are transmitted to the President in the form of **enrolled bills**. The President then approves or vetoes these bills. If appropriations bills are not passed by the beginning of the fiscal year, the Congress passes a **continuing resolution**. This resolution provides the authority for affected agencies to continue to spend at a maximum rate for a full year, until a specific date, or until their regular appropriations are approved. When the appropriations bill is signed by the President, **appropriations warrants** are sent to the various agencies by the Treasury. Each agency then revises its budget in accordance with the appropriations bill and, within thirty days, submits a request for apportionment to the OMB.

It should be noted that congressional appropriations are not based directly on expenditures. Rather, each agency is given the **authority to obligate** the government to ultimately make disbursements for expenditures, repayment of loans, and the like. A congressional appropriation is really nothing more than a spending **authority** or **limit** for that fiscal year. It does not mean that cash is immediately available for spending. Availability of cash is dependent upon many factors, such as inflows of tax revenues and the level of surplus funds from prior years. The relationship of budgeting authority to outlays is shown in Exhibit 10–5.

Sometimes the federal government engages in deficit spending. This happens when total expenditures are greater than total revenues of a period. In such instances the Treasury issues bonds (borrows money) to cover the deficit.

Most appropriations are for one year only. If they are not spent or obligated by the end of the fiscal year, they must be returned. In some cases, however, Congress makes multiyear or indefinite appropriations. Examples of this latter

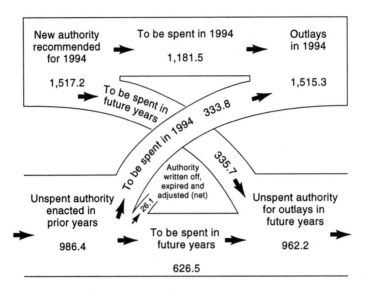

EXHIBIT 10–5   Relationship of Budget Authority to Outlays—1994
(in billions of dollars)

Source: Office of Management and Budget, *Budget of the United States Government* (Washington, DC: U.S. Government Printing Office, 1994), p. 98.

type of appropriation include those used to fund Social Security and to service public debt. The remainder of this chapter will be devoted to one-year appropriations.

When the OMB receives a **request for apportionment** from an agency, it **apportions** a part of the agency's appropriation to the department of which the agency is a part. This is done on a time period (usually quarterly) or activity basis. The purpose of the apportionment system is to help prevent agencies from obligating or spending more than their appropriations, to enable the Treasury to better match revenues and disbursements (cash management), and to restrict expenditures in areas in which the President believes that amounts appropriated by the Congress are excessive.

The last-mentioned use of the appropriation system, **presidential impounding**, has generated a great deal of controversy over the years. In 1974, Congress passed the **Impoundment Control Act of 1974**. This law provides that the President must report to the Congress any administrative action to postpone or eliminate spending authorized by law. **Deferrals**, which are temporary withholdings of authority to spend, cannot extend beyond the end of the fiscal year and may be overturned by **either** house of the Congress at any time. **Rescissions**, which are permanent cancellations of authority to spend, must be approved by the full Congress. If both houses of Congress do not approve, the withheld monies must be made available to the agency.

When a department receives its **apportionment** from OMB, the department head (or his or her representative) **allots** all or a part of the amount of the apportionment intended for each agency under the department's control. Each agency can only obligate (and spend) the allotted portion of its appropriation.

When an agency receives its allotment, it is free to spend up to that amount of money, within budgetary guidelines. Agency personnel, however, cannot spend more than the amount appropriated for (and allotted to) that agency without violating the **Anti Deficiency Act** (31 U.S.C. 1517 of the Revised Statutes). The main purposes of this act are to prevent the incurring of obligations, and making of disbursements, in excess of appropriations and to fix responsibility within each agency for the incurrence of obligations and expenditures. Agency personnel who violate this law are subject to both civil and criminal penalties.

Before an agency makes a disbursement, it generally "obligates" the monies. An **obligation** is similar to an encumbrance. It represents monies earmarked for a specific purpose. When the disbursement is made, the obligation is "reversed out," just like an encumbrance. Instead of writing a check, however, the agency sends a **disbursement schedule** to the Treasury. The Treasury then sends a check to the vendor. This process is illustrated in Exhibit 10–6.

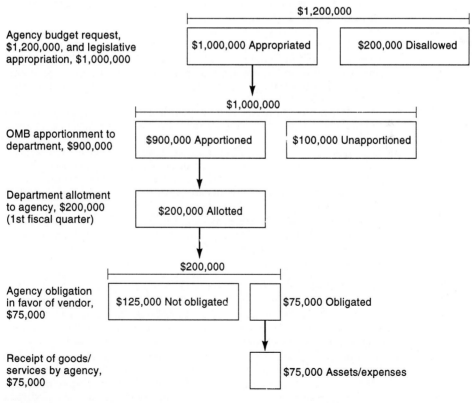

EXHIBIT 10–6 The Federal Accounting Cycle

FEDERAL VERSUS STATE AND LOCAL GOVERNMENTAL ACCOUNTING

Federal accounting is similar to state and local governmental accounting in that it uses a series of funds and budgetary accounts to control revenues and disbursements. Because of the size and varied objectives of the U.S. government, however, federal accounting is different in many ways:

1. **Use of Accrual Basis Accounting.** The federal government maintains its accounts on the **full accrual**, rather than on the modified accrual, basis. Under the full accrual basis of accounting, revenues are recognized (recorded) when earned. Expenditures are recognized when incurred. Under the modified accrual basis of accounting used by state and local governmental units, revenues are recognized when "measurable and available" while expenditures are recognized when incurred.

2. **Treatment of Inventories.** In federal accounting, inventories are treated in the same manner as they are in commercial accounting. When purchased, they are recorded in an asset account. When used, they are removed from the asset account and recorded in an expense account. This approach differs from the one often used by state and local governmental units. There, inventories are generally recorded in an expenditure account when purchased, regardless of when they will be used, and a "reserve for inventories" (an equity account) is used to report the amount of inventory on hand.

3. **The Accounting Entity.** In state and local governmental accounting, the central focus is upon the **entire** government unit. For example, the General Fund balance sheet illustrated in Chapter 2 is for the entire city of New Example, not just one department. While individual departments or other subunits of a governmental organization may issue separate operating statements, such statements are usually for internal use only.

   When accounting for federal agencies, however, separate accounting records are maintained and financial statements are issued for each agency and/or fund, as opposed to the entire U.S. government. This is because the federal government is so large that information on it, as a whole, has somewhat limited utility. For control and evaluative purposes, full sets of statements are necessary for each federal agency or entity within that agency. It should be remembered, however, that in most cases the agency statements are reporting on a **portion** of a particular fund of the U.S. government (e.g., the General Fund), not the entire fund.

4. **Treatment of Fund Balances.** Residual balances of funds used by state and local governmental units (assets minus liabilities or "net assets") are shown in the **Fund balance** accounts of those funds. They represent, among other things, the amount of monies available for expenditures. In federal accounting, activities of many different agencies can be recorded in a "common" fund. Since each agency is an accounting entity, it is necessary to use terms to identify the **portion** of each "common" fund which represents that agency's net assets. Terms used for this purpose are *Appropriated Capital, Capital Investment,* and *Cumulative Results of Operations*. It should be noted that, unlike those of governmental-type funds used by state and local governmental units, net assets of federal funds are not always liquid.

5. **Treatment of Cash.** Most funds used by state and local governmental units use a "Cash in Bank" account. Checks are drawn against this account to make disbursements, and the governmental unit has a "direct" relationship with the bank.

   Because of the size and nature of the federal government, individual agencies do not generally deal directly with banks. Rather, the Treasury acts as their banker.

At the beginning of a fiscal year, each agency is provided with an "account" with the Treasury for each appropriation. The size of this "account" is equal to the agency's appropriation plus any monies left over from previous periods that the agency has not been required to return. When an agency makes a disbursement, it sends a **disbursement schedule** to the Treasury. The Treasury writes a check for the amount of the schedule.

The account used by federal agencies to record their "claims" against the Treasury is "Fund balance with U.S. Treasury." When agencies receive monies from the Treasury, this account is debited. When the disbursements ordered by the agencies are made by the Treasury, this account is credited.

6. **Treatment of Fixed Assets.** In federal accounting, fixed (long-lived) assets appear on the balance sheets of many funds. They are capitalized and "written-off" (depreciated) over their useful lives, like assets of commercial enterprises. At the end of each period, adjusting entries are made to record (as expenses) amounts of depreciation taken during the period and to adjust accumulated depreciation (contra-asset) accounts. This treatment differs from the one provided these assets by the governmental-type funds used by state and local governmental units. There, long-lived assets are expensed when purchased and recorded in a General Fixed Assets Group of Accounts.

TYPES OF FUNDS USED IN FEDERAL ACCOUNTING

Two categories of funds are used in federal accounting: (1) funds used to account for monies derived from revenue-raising activities and (2) funds used to account for resources for which the federal government acts as a trustee or custodian. Funds used to account for monies derived from revenue-raising activities include:

1. **The General Fund.** This fund is used to account for receipts which are not earmarked for a specific purpose and "amounts appropriated by the Congress to be expended for the general support of the Government." As with state and local governmental units, there is **one** general fund for the entire federal government. However, within the federal government each appropriation is treated as a separate accounting entity, with its own "general fund" (containing a self-balancing set of accounts). These general funds are really subdivisions of **the** General Fund (of the federal government).

2. **Special Funds.** These funds are similar to special revenue funds used by state and local governmental units. They are used to account for receipts of monies from specific sources earmarked by law for special purposes, and the spending of these monies in accordance with specific legal provisions. They are not generally available on a continuing basis.

3. **Revolving Funds.** These funds are used to account for commercial-type operations of federal agencies, when revenues from such operations are significant and are available to the agencies without further congressional action. Revolving funds fall into two categories:
   a. **Public Enterprise Funds.** Funds used to account for revenues derived primarily from user charges received from nonfederal sources (e.g., admissions to national parks). They are very similar to Enterprise Funds used by state and local governmental units.

b.   **Intragovernmental Funds.** Funds used to account for revenues derived primarily from user charges received from other appropriations or funds. They are very similar to Internal Service Funds used by state and local governmental units.

4.   **Management Funds.** These funds are used to account for projects or agency operations which are charged to two or more appropriations (e.g., research activities financed by several agencies) and which do not involve a continuing cycle of appropriations. They consist primarily of "working fund" accounts (accounts used to record the receipt, and subsequent disbursement, of advance payments from other agencies or bureaus).

Funds used to account for resources for which the federal government acts as a trustee or custodian include:

1.   **Trust Funds.** These funds are used to account for receipts generated from trust agreements or statutes (e.g., Highway Trust Fund) and the spending of those receipts in carrying out specific purposes or programs, in accordance with the terms of the trust agreements or statutes. They are similar to Trust Funds used by state and local governmental units.

2.   **Deposit Funds.** These funds are used to account for monies collected, held in suspense, and later refunded or paid to another fund. They are also used to account for monies for which the federal government acts as a banker or agent for others. They are similar to Agency Funds used by state and local governmental units.

As with state and local governmental units, the majority of the activities of federal agencies are recorded in the General Fund. Therefore, the remainder of this chapter will be devoted to a discussion of procedures used by federal agencies to account, in this fund, for their activities.

SETTING FEDERAL ACCOUNTING STANDARDS

Federal accounting practices are primarily influenced by three oversight agencies—the Department of Treasury, the Office of Management and Budget, and the General Accounting Office (Comptroller General). In October 1990 the Secretary of the Treasury, the Director of OMB, and the Comptroller General established the Federal Accounting Standards Advisory Board (FASAB), a nine-member board whose purpose is to consider and recommend accounting principles for the Federal Government.

The FASAB considers financial and budgetary information needs of executive agencies, congressional oversight groups, and others who use federal financial information. After receiving input from interested parties, it develops accounting standards, which are initially published as "exposure drafts." The FASAB's sponsors then decide whether or not to adopt the recommended standards. If they do, the standards are published by the General Accounting Office and OMB and become effective. So far, one concept statement, *Objectives of Federal Financial Reporting*, and three standards have been adopted and published.

THE FEDERAL AGENCY ACCOUNTING CYCLE

Introduction

Accounting systems used by federal agencies must provide information for two purposes:

1. To help agency managers avoid overexpending or overobligating appropriations, actions which carry legal penalties, and
2. To account for assets entrusted to the care of agencies and for the equities in those assets—liabilities and capital.

As a result, federal agencies use a **two-track** accounting system. One track is a self-balancing set of **budgetary** accounts, which demonstrate budgetary compliance. The other track is a self-balancing set of **proprietary** accounts, which are used for financial management. Differences between budgetary-track and proprietary-track accounting, with respect to recognition of events which constitute transactions, are found in Exhibit 10–7. Notice the similarities between pro-

EXHIBIT 10–7 Summary of Key Differences between Budgetary and Proprietary Accounting in Recognition of Events Which Constitute Transactions

BUDGETARY ACCOUNTING	PROPRIETARY ACCOUNTING
Entries are made for commitment of funds in advance of preparing orders to procure goods and services.	Entries are not made for commitments.
Entries are made for obligation of funds at the time goods and services are ordered.	Entries are not made for obligations.
Entries are made to expend appropriations when goods and services chargeable to the appropriation are received, regardless of when they are used and regardless of when they are paid for.	Goods and services which will last more than a year and otherwise meet the criteria to qualify as assets are capitalized and expensed when consumed, regardless of what appropriation funded them and when they are paid for.
Entries are made only against an appropriation for transactions funded by the appropriation.	Goods and services consumed in the current period for which payment is to be made from one or more subsequent appropriations are recognized as expenses in the current period.
Entries are not made against an appropriation for transactions not funded by the appropriation.	Goods and services consumed in the current period, but paid for in prior periods, are expensed in the current period.

Source: U.S. General Accounting Office, *GAO Accounting Guide: Basic Topics Relating to Appropriations and Reimbursables* (Washington, DC: GAO, 1990), p. 3–2.

prietary accounting used by federal agencies and accounting used by commercial organizations. Key entries prepared by federal agencies are summarized in Exhibit 10–8 on page 487.

Illustrative Entries

Opening entries

The accounting cycle of a federal agency begins at the start of the fiscal year when the Congress makes (and the President approves) an **appropriation**. If the appropriation is $150,000, entries on the books of the agency are:

Budgetary entry	Other appropriations realized	150,000	
	Authority available for apportionment		150,000
	To record receipt of appropriation authority.		
Proprietary entry	Fund balance with Treasury	150,000	
	Appropriated capital		150,000
	To record receipt of appropriation warrant.		

The purpose of the first entry is to establish initial accountability by the agency for its appropriation. The debit to Other appropriations realized is made to distinguish the agency's basic operating appropriation from other special purpose appropriations it might have received. The second entry records the establishment of a "line of credit" with the Treasury. The account Fund balance with Treasury is the equivalent of a cash account while Appropriated capital represents the increase in the equity of the agency.

After Congress makes the appropriation, the Office of Management and Budget (OMB) **apportions** it to the department of which the agency is a part. As was mentioned earlier, OMB is an agency within the Executive Office of the President which has broad financial management powers. Among its responsibilities are the **apportionment** of appropriations among departments and the establishment of "reserves" in anticipation of cost savings, contingencies, and so on. Thus, the fact that an agency is appropriated a given amount of money by Congress does not always mean that the agency will have that amount to spend.

If all of the agency's appropriation is apportioned by OMB to the department of which the agency is a part, the entry on the books of the agency is:

Budgetary entry	Authority available for apportionment	150,000	
	Apportionment available for distribution		150,000
	To record the apportionment of monies by the Office of Management and Budget.		
Proprietary entry	None		

The amount of its apportionment that an agency can actually use is up to departmental management, which will **allot** a part of, or the entire, apportionment to the agency. Allotments are usually made each quarter. However, for

EXHIBIT 10–8   Summary of Key Entries Prepared by Federal Agencies

WHO ACTS?	WHAT ACTION?	BUDGETARY ENTRY	PROPRIETARY ENTRY

Congress	Appropriates	Other appropriations realized
		  Authority available for
		  apportionment
			Fund balance with Treasury
			  Appropriated capital

OMB	Apportions	Authority available for
		  apportionment
		  Apportionment available
		  for distribution
			None

Department	Allots	Apportionment available for
		  distribution
		  Allotments available for
		  commitment/obligation
			None

Agency	Commits	Allotments available for
		  commitment/obligation
		  Commitments available
		  for obligation
			None

Agency	Obligates	Commitments available for
		  obligation
		  Undelivered orders
			None

Agency	Receives services	Undelivered orders
		  Expended appropriations
			Operating/program expenses
			  Accounts payable
			
			Appropriated capital
			  Appropriated capital used

Agency	Receives goods
	  or equipment
		Undelivered orders
		  Expended appropriations
			Assets
			  Accounts payable
			
			Appropriated capital
			  Capital investment

Agency	Requests payment for
	  goods or equipment
		None	Accounts payable
			  Disbursements in transit

Agency	Uses goods	None	Operating/program expenses
			  Assets
			
			Capital investment
			  Appropriated capital used

Agency	Records depreciation	None	Operating/program expenses
			  Accumulated depreciation
			
			Capital investment
			  Appropriated capital used

simplicity, we will assume that the agency in this illustration receives its entire allotment at the beginning of the fiscal year. If departmental management allots $148,000 to the agency, the entry on the books of the agency is:

Budgetary entry

Apportionment available for distribution	148,000	
Allotments available for commitment/ obligation		148,000
To record allotment of monies to finance operations for entire year.		

Proprietary entry

None

The account Allotments available for commitment/obligation is very important. The balance of this account represents the amount of money available for the agency to carry out its operations. If the agency has not expended or obligated its apportionment and its allotments by the end of the fiscal year, it must return these monies to the Treasury. All of the above entries are made as of October 1, the first day of the fiscal year. This is done even if the appropriation bill has not been enacted by that date.

Operating entries

Once an agency receives notice of its allotment, it can begin (or continue) its fiscal operations. To enhance planning and fund control, many agencies use what is known as "commitment accounting." **Commitments** reserve budgetary authority from an allotment for the estimated amount of orders to be placed. They do not legally encumber the allotment. Rather, they formally disclose purchase requests before actual orders are placed. If requests are made by agency personnel to spend $100,000 of the agency's allotment on supplies and $12,000 on outside services, the entry to record the commitments is:

Budgetary entry

Allotments available for commitment/ obligation	112,000	
Commitments available for obligation		112,000
To record purchase requests placed for supplies and outside services.		

Proprietary entry

None

When a purchase order is issued or a commitment is made for salaries, an **obligation** is created. Obligations are the federal equivalent of encumbrances used by state and local governmental units. They charge the allotment with the most recent estimate of the cost of items ordered and release any related prior commitments. If the agency places formal purchase orders for supplies whose cost is expected to be $95,000, the entry is:

Budgetary entry

Commitments available for obligation	95,000	
Undelivered orders		95,000
To obligate funds for purchase of supplies.		

Proprietary entry

None

The debit in the budgetary entry represents the reduction of outstanding commitments. The credit represents the actual obligation and is similar to the Reserve for encumbrances account used by state and local governmental units.

When goods arrive and/or services are performed, the entries shown below are made. The budgetary entry removes the obligation in favor of the vendor. It also records the amount of the appropriation expended at this time. Assume that the actual cost of supplies ordered amounts to $94,000.

Budgetary entry	Undelivered orders	95,000	
	Expended appropriations		94,000
	Allotments available for commitment/ obligation		1,000
	To record expenditure of portion of allotment.		

Notice that since the actual cost of the supplies is less than the amount estimated, the difference is returned to Allotments available for commitment/obligation, from where it was first taken.

Proprietary entries	1.	Inventory of supplies	94,000	
		Accounts payable		94,000
		To record receipt of supplies.		
	2.	Appropriated capital	94,000	
		Capital investment		94,000
		To reclassify appropriated capital as capital investment.		

The first proprietary entry records the receipt of supplies and the resulting liability. It is similar to the entry that would be made by a commercial organization. Because the supplies are not consumed immediately, the agency records its equity in these items as "Capital investment" and, in the second proprietary entry, transfers an amount from Appropriated capital equal to the cost of the supplies. The effect of this entry is to change the nature of the government's equity from Appropriated capital, which provided the authority for the transaction, to Capital investment, which represents the government's equity in inventories and fixed assets.

In addition, when goods arrive and/or services are performed, a **disbursement schedule** is sent to the Treasury ordering it to pay the vendors. This does not reduce the agency's balance with the Treasury until checks are actually issued. As a result, the processing of payables is recorded in two steps. When the disbursement schedule is sent to the Treasury, the entry, assuming that the above purchase of supplies is the only transaction on the schedule, is:

Budgetary entry	None		
Proprietary entry	Accounts payable	94,000	
	Disbursements in transit		94,000
	To record request to Treasury for check(s).		

When the agency is notified by the Treasury that the check or check(s) requested have been issued, the entry on the agency's books is:

Budgetary entry	None		
Proprietary entry	Disbursements in transit	94,000	
	Fund balance with Treasury		94,000
	To record issuance of checks by the Treasury.		

If supplies costing $50,000 are used by the agency, their cost is recorded as an expense. This amount is also reclassified from Capital investment to Appropriated capital used, to show the financing source of the supplies. No budgetary entry is necessary since the expending of the appropriation has already been recorded.

Budgetary entry		None		
Proprietary entries	1.	Operating/program expenses-supplies	50,000	
		Inventory of supplies		50,000
		To record supplies used.		
	2.	Capital investment	50,000	
		Appropriated capital used		50,000
		To record financing source of supplies.		

Purchases of services are treated in the same manner as purchases of supplies except that, because they are used immediately upon receipt, a capital investment account is not used. Entries recording the commitment and obligation are similar to those shown for the purchase of supplies and when services (expected to cost $12,000) are received, the entries are:

Budgetary entry		Undelivered orders	12,000	
		Expended appropriations		12,000
		To record expenditure of portion of allotment.		
Proprietary entries	1.	Operating/program expenses—contractual services	12,000	
		Accounts payable		12,000
		To record receipt of contractual services.		
	2.	Appropriated capital	12,000	
		Appropriated capital used		12,000
		To record financing source of outside services.		

If a disbursement schedule is sent to the Treasury listing this expense, the entry is:

Budgetary entry	None		
Proprietary entry	Accounts payable	12,000	
	Disbursements in transit		12,000
	To record request to Treasury for check.		

Items like salaries, rent, and utilities are also recorded as expenses, just as they are in commercial organizations. However, entries recording the sources of financing and the expenditure of budgetary authority are also required. In many cases (as in this example) these items are not previously obligated. Assume that the agency incurs the following costs:

Rent	$ 6,000
Utilities	2,000
Miscellaneous	1,500
Salaries and benefits	22,000
Total	$31,500

The salaries will be paid immediately, while liabilities will be set up for the other costs. The entries to record these costs are:

Budgetary entry	Allotments available for commitment/ obligation	31,500	
	Expended appropriations		31,500
	To record expenditure of portion of allotment.		
Proprietary entries	Operating/program expenses—rent	6,000	
	Operating/program expenses—utilities	2,000	
	Operating/program expenses—miscellaneous	1,500	
	Operating/program expenses—salaries and benefits	22,000	
	Accounts payable		9,500
	Fund balance with Treasury		22,000
	To record certain operating expenses.		
	Appropriated capital	31,500	
	Appropriated capital used		31,500
	To record financing source of operating expenses.		

Agencies of the federal government record the cost of fixed assets as Invested capital. They also record depreciation on these assets. The entries to record the purchase of fixed assets are similar to those shown above to record the purchase of supplies.

Because depreciation is not chargeable against an appropriation, a budgetary entry is not necessary. However, proprietary entries are necessary to record the expense and increase in accumulated depreciation and to record the reduction of the book value of the assets. This reduction is recorded by means of a debit to Capital investment (an equity account) and a credit to Appropriated capital used, an account used to record financing sources. If depreciation of $8,000 is recorded, the entries are:

Budgetary entry	None		
Proprietary entries	Operating/program expenses—depreciation	8,000	
	Accumulated depreciation		8,000
	To record depreciation on fixed assets.		
	Capital investment	8,000	
	Appropriated capital used		8,000
	To reclassify capital investment as a financing source.		

If year-end entries are made to record accrued, but unpaid, salaries and benefits of $3,500 the entries are:

Budgetary entry	Allotments available for commitment/ obligation	3,500	
	Expended appropriations		3,500
	To record expenditure of portion of allotment.		
Proprietary entries	Operating/program expenses—salaries and benefits	3,500	
	Accrued funded payroll		3,500
	To record accrual of year-end payroll.		
	Appropriated capital	3,500	
	Appropriated capital used		3,500
	To record financing source of operating expenses.		

Closing entries

At the end of the year most appropriations lapse, unless they are classified as multiyear or no-year (permanent). This means that any monies that have not been spent or formally obligated by this time must be returned to the Treasury. These amounts cannot be carried forward to finance operations of the following year. Monies formally obligated by the end of the year, however, may be carried forward to meet given obligations. If these monies are not expended within five years, they must be returned to the Treasury.

After the transactions of the year are recorded and appropriate adjusting entries are prepared, budgetary entries are made to close accounts representing expired budget authority and Expended appropriations. Proprietary entries are made to close expense accounts and Appropriated capital used.

Budgetary entries	Apportionment available for distribution	2,000	
	Allotments available for commitment/ obligation	2,000	
	Commitments available for obligation	5,000	
	Other appropriations realized		9,000
	To close apportionment, allotment, and commitment accounts and to record expiration of budgetary authority.		
	Expended appropriations	141,000	
	Other appropriations realized		141,000
	To close expended appropriation account.		
Proprietary entries	Appropriated capital used	105,000	
	Operating/program expenses— supplies		50,000
	Operating/program expenses— contractual services		12,000
	Operating/program expenses— salaries and benefits		25,500
	Operating/program expenses— rent		6,000
	Operating/program expenses— utilities		2,000
	Operating/program expenses— miscellaneous		1,500
	Operating/program expenses— depreciation		8,000
	To close proprietary accounts.		

If the total of the balances in the expense accounts had differed from the balance in Appropriated capital used, the difference would have been taken to Net results of operations. This account would have been closed to Cumulative results of operations, an equity account. (It is possible that this account will be retitled "Future funding requirements" in the near future.)

FINANCIAL STATEMENTS USED BY FEDERAL AGENCIES

All federal agencies are required to prepare the following financial statements:

1. Balance sheet
2. Operating statement
3. Reconciliation of operating/program expenses to expended appropriations
4. Report on budget execution
5. Statement of cash flows

Some agencies also prepare a statement showing sources and uses of capital. The first four statements listed above are shown in Exhibits 10–9 through 10–12. The statement of cash flows and the capital statement are beyond the scope of this text. As far as possible, figures from the previous illustration have been used. However, on the balance sheet it has been necessary to assume certain figures since space considerations preclude the provision of beginning of period balances.

EXHIBIT 10–9   Balance Sheet of Federal Agency

Some Obscure Federal Agency
Balance Sheet
September 30, 19X1

Assets			
Fund balance with U.S. Treasury			$ 34,000
Inventory of supplies			44,000
Furniture		$65,000	
Less: Accumulated depreciation		(30,000)	35,000
Total assets			$113,000
Liabilities and Governmental Equity			
Liabilities:			
Disbursements in transit		$12,000	
Accounts payable		9,500	
Accrued funded payroll		3,500	
Total liabilities			$ 25,000
Equity of U.S. government:			
Appropriated capital		$ 9,000	
Capital investment		79,000	
Cumulative results of operations		-0-	
Total equity of U.S. government			88,000
Total liabilities and governmental equity			$113,000

EXHIBIT 10–10   Operating Statement of Federal Agency

Some Obscure Federal Agency
Operating Statement
For Fiscal Year Ended September 30, 19X1

Appropriated capital used		$105,000
Operating/program expenses:		
Salaries and benefits	$25,500	
Contractual services	12,000	
Supplies	50,000	
Rent	6,000	
Utilities	2,000	
Depreciation	8,000	
Miscellaneous	1,500	105,000
Net results of operations		-0-

EXHIBIT 10–11   **Reconciliation of Operating/Program Expenses to Expended Appropriations Statement of Federal Agency**

Some Obscure Federal Agency
Reconciliation of Operating/Program Expenses
to Expended Appropriations
For Fiscal Year Ended September 30, 19X1

Expended appropriations—FY19X1		$141,000
Operating/program expenses:		
Operating/program expenses	$105,000	
Add: Purchase of supplies	94,000	$199,000
Deduct: Supplies used	$ 50,000	
Depreciation	8,000	(58,000)
Total expended appropriations		$141,000

EXHIBIT 10–12   **Report on Budget Execution of Federal Agency**

Some Obscure Federal Agency
Report on Budget Execution
For Fiscal Year Ended September 30, 19X1

Budgetary authority:	
Appropriations realized	$150,000
Other budgetary authority	-0-
Total budgetary authority	$150,000
Status of budgetary resources:	
Obligations incurred	$141,000
Unobligated balances available	-0-
Unobligated balances not available	9,000
Total budgetary resources	$150,000
Relation of obligations to outlays and accrued expenses:	
Obligations incurred	$141,000
Unpaid obligations	(25,000)
Total outlays	126,000
Change in funded liabilities	25,000
Accrued expenses	$141,000

REVIEW QUESTIONS

Q10–1   What is an audit?

Q10–2   What is the difference between a financial audit and a performance audit?

Q10–3   List the major sources of authority for governmental audits.

Q10–4   What are the three categories of auditing standards issued by the AICPA?

Q10–5   How do governmental auditing standards differ from those issued by the AICPA?

Q10–6   What is the "yellow book"?

Q10–7   What is a single audit?

Q10–8   What is a cognizant agency?

Q10–9   What is an audit opinion?

Q10–10   List and define the types of audit opinions.

Q10–11   What reports must be prepared for a single audit?

Q10–12   What is a major federal program?

Q10–13   What is a nonmajor federal program?

Q10–14   How is depreciation handled in federal accounting? How does this treatment differ from that given to depreciation under state and local governmental accounting?

Q10–15   What is the significance and composition of "unexpended appropriations"?

Q10–16   What is the difference between an appropriation, an apportionment, and an allotment?

Q10–17   At the beginning of FY 19X1, Congress appropriated $2 million to the Bureau of Bird Watching. Can the director of this bureau immediately order $2 million worth of telescopes? If not, why not?

Q10–18   List the various types of funds used by federal agencies and the type of fund used by state and local governmental units that comes closest to matching each.

Q10–19   Briefly outline the budgetary process used by the federal government.

Q10–20   What is the Office of Management and Budget?

Q10–21   In federal government accounting, a commonly used term is *obligation*. What is an obligation and what is its equivalent in state and local governmental accounting?

Q10–22   List six differences between federal and municipal accounting.

Q10–23   What is the purpose of the Federal Accounting Standards Advisory Board?

Q10–24   What is "commitment accounting"?

Q10–25   What is the purpose of the "two-track" accounting system used by federal agencies?

CASES

C10–1 Sunview City receives and spends federal financial assistance from three programs as follows:

Program X	$10,000
Program Y	90,000
Program Z	20,000

The mayor of Sunview, John Bevel, believes that since the city does not receive at least $100,000 of federal financial assistance for any of the programs in which it participates, the city does not have a "major program" as defined by the Single Audit Act. The chief financial officer of the city, James Duhon, feels that Sunview meets the definition of a major program for Program Y. You have been hired as a consultant to solve the dispute. Write a report to the mayor identifying the "major" federal programs and justify your conclusion.

C10–2 You have been hired as a consultant to the mayor of Shade Tree. The mayor believes that a single audit is not worth the additional cost over a regular audit. Shade Tree receives and spends $190 million in federal assistance each year. Explain whether the city needs a single audit and discuss the advantages of a single audit to a city.

C10–3 Recently your manager expressed concern that there was a lack of planning and control in the placement of purchase orders by your agency. He felt that orders were placed on a "first come, first served basis" and when the allotment was used up there would be no money for the agency to continue operations vital to its mission. At an Association of Government Accountants meeting, a friend of yours employed by the National Finance Center mentioned that his agency uses commitment accounting to enhance planning and fund control. You became curious and called him for more information. Write a brief report explaining what commitment accounting is, what it does, how it works, and any negative factors that should be taken into consideration before implementing it.

EXERCISES

E10–1 (Multiple choice)
1. An audit designed to determine whether the goals of an entity are being achieved is called
    a. A financial audit
    b. A performance audit
    c. An opinion audit
    d. Either a financial audit or a performance audit

2. Grant audits usually are examples of a
    a. Financial audit
    b. Performance audit
    c. Opinion audit
    d. Combination of a and b
3. *Government Auditing Standards* is issued by
    a. The AICPA
    b. The GAO
    c. The OMB
    d. A joint effort of the AICPA, the GAO, and the OMB
4. Which of the following is *not* a general classification of auditing standards?
    a. General Standards
    b. Reporting Standards
    c. Opinion Standards
    d. Field Work Standards
5. Which of the following best describes governmental auditing standards as compared to commercial auditing standards?
    a. Governmental auditing standards are broader in scope than commercial auditing standards
    b. Commercial auditing standards are broader in scope than governmental auditing standards
    c. Governmental auditing standards are the same as commercial auditing standards
    d. There is no such concept as governmental auditing standards
6. Which of the following best describes governmental auditing as compared to a single audit?
    a. A governmental audit is broader in scope than a single audit
    b. A single audit is broader in scope than a governmental audit
    c. All governmental audits must be single audits
    d. The single audit concept applies only to commercial audits.
7. The yellow book contains
    a. A list of procedures to use when performing audits
    b. Generally accepted auditing standards
    c. Simple audit reports for different types of governmental units
    d. Generally accepted auditing standards for governmental audits
8. A single audit is required for a governmental unit when amounts received by the government from federal financial assistance exceeds
    a. $100,000
    b. $250,000
    c. $500,000
    d. $1,000,000

9. Specific guidance for conducting single audits is provided by
   a. OMB *Circular A-128*
   b. The yellow book
   c. NCGA *Statement 1*
   d. Both a and b

10. A qualified audit opinion is usually issued when
    a. There are no material deviations from reporting standards
    b. A limitation is placed on the auditor's ability to perform generally accepted auditing standards
    c. The information in the report is not presented fairly
    d. The auditor is not independent

E10–2 (Discussion related to a single audit)

The City of Jurassic receives federal financial assistance in excess of $10 million per year from several different federal agencies. As a result, it must have a single audit.

1. What is a single audit and how does it differ from a traditional audit?
2. Who is likely to be Jurassic's cognizant agency?
3. What reports must be provided by a single audit? When are they due?

E10–3 (Comparison of audits)

1. How does a traditional audit compare with a governmental audit?
2. How does a single audit compare with a governmental audit?

E10–4 (Audit opinions)

Identify the four major types of audit opinions and give an example of a situation that would require each to be used.

E10–5 (Audit reports)

Compare and contrast the types of audit reports required for a traditional audit, a governmental audit, and a single audit.

E10–6 (Major and nonmajor federal assistance programs)

Is it possible for a governmental unit to have both major and nonmajor federal assistance programs? Explain.

E10–7 (Matching)

Match the items in the right column below with those in the left column.

_____ 1.	Financial audit	a. Generally Accepted Auditing Standards
_____ 2.	AICPA	
_____ 3.	OMB	b. Audit opinion when the financial statements do not present the information fairly
_____ 4.	*Government Auditing Standards*	
_____ 5.	Unqualified opinion	c. Used when an auditor lacks independence
_____ 6.	Adverse opinion	d. A review to determine if the fi-

_____ 7. Cut-off level for a single
audit

_____ 8. GAGAS

_____ 9. GAAS

nancial statements present information fairly

e.   A review to determine if the
goals of an entity are being
achieved

f.   Yellow book

g.   American Institute of CPAs

h.   Office of Major Budgeting

i.   Audit opinion when the financial statements present the
information fairly

j.   Office of Management and
Budget

k.   Questioned costs

l.   Generally Accepted Governmental Auditing Standards

m. $250,000

n. $100,000

E10–8   (Reporting)

What should be included in the audit report of a governmental unit?

E10–9   (Multiple choice)

1.   Funds used by federal agencies to account for receipts of monies
from specific sources, earmarked by law for special purposes, are
   a.   Special Revenue Funds
   b.   Special funds
   c.   Revolving funds
   d.   Management funds

2.   Funds used to account for project or agency operations which are
charged to two or more appropriations and which do not involve a
continuing cycle of appropriations are
   a.   Special funds
   b.   Revolving funds
   c.   Internal Service Funds
   d.   Management funds

3.   Federal accounting standards are set by
   a.   The Congress
   b.   The Financial Accounting Standards Board (FASB)
   c.   The Federal Accounting Standards Advisory Board (FASAB)
   d.   The Governmental Accounting Standards Board (GASB)

4.   An unliquidated obligation represents
   a.   Monies that cannot be spent for any purpose
   b.   Monies that have already been spent
   c.   Monies that must be returned to the Treasury
   d.   Monies earmarked for a specific purpose

5. An apportionment of an appropriation to an agency is made by
   a. The Congress
   b. The Office of Management and Budget (OMB)
   c. The agency
   d. The department of which the agency is a part
6. Commitments
   a. Legally encumber an allotment
   b. Formally disclose purchase requests before actual orders are placed
   c. Represent the authority to spend money for a particular project
   d. Represent legally enforceable promises to specific vendors
7. The account used to show that an agency has requested payment by the Treasury to a certain vendor(s) is
   a. Fund balance with Treasury
   b. Accounts payable
   c. Disbursements in transit
   d. Processed invoices
8. Which of the following statements is *not* prepared by federal agencies?
   a. A balance sheet
   b. A statement of revenues, expenditures, and changes in fund balance
   c. An operating statement
   d. A report on budget execution

E10–10 (Matching)

Match the items in the right column below with those in the left column.

_____ 1.	An act of Congress which gives a department and/or agency authority to obligate the federal government to make disbursements for goods and services.	a. Rescission b. Obligation c. Disbursement schedule d. GASB e. Appropriation
_____ 2.	Document sent to the Treasury ordering it to pay vendors and/or employees	f. Revolving funds g. Apportionment h. FASAB
_____ 3.	Sets standards for federal government accounting	i. Allotment j. Management funds
_____ 4.	Funds used to account for commercial-type operations of federal agencies	k. Deferral l. Commitment
_____ 5.	Action by which OMB distributes amounts available for obligation to agencies	

_____ 6. Permanent cancelation of authority to spend

_____ 7. Reserves budgetary authority from an allotment for the estimated amount of orders to be placed

_____ 8. Federal equivalent of encumbrances used by state and local governmental units

_____ 9. Temporary withholding of authority to spend

E10–11 (Use of the budgetary accounts)

In federal accounting the most frequently used budgetary accounts are:

> Other appropriations realized
> Authority available for apportionment
> Apportionment available for distribution
> Allotments available for commitment/obligation
> Commitments available for obligation
> Undelivered orders
> Expended appropriations

REQUIRED: Determine which of the above account titles best describes each of the situations listed below:

1. Spending authority allotted, but not yet committed
2. Monies obligated, but not yet expended.
3. Spending authority apportioned, but not yet allotted, to an agency
4. The portion of an agency's appropriation that has been used
5. Spending authority appropriated, but not yet apportioned, by OMB
6. Spending authority reserved for the estimated amount of orders to be placed

E10–12 (Federal accounting cycle)

Easy Agency is a small, but politically powerful, agency within the Department of Whatever. The following transactions took place in October 19X1.

1. Easy Agency was notified that its FY 19X1 appropriation was $2,500,000.
2. OMB apportioned $600,000 to the Department of Whatever for the first quarter of the fiscal year.
3. The Department of Whatever's CEO allotted $200,000 to Easy Agency for its October operations.
4. Purchase orders placed during the month for materials and supplies were $150,000. (Easy Agency does not use commitment accounting.) The

materials and supplies arrived during the month, along with an invoice for $148,000.

5. Materials costing $100,000 and supplies costing $20,000 were used during the month. In addition, salaries amounting to $48,000 were paid on the last day of the month.

6. A disbursement schedule was sent to the Treasury ordering payment for the materials and supplies. One requesting payment of salaries had been sent earlier.

REQUIRED: Make appropriate journal entries to record the above transactions.

E10–13   (Monthly accounting cycle)

The Bureau of Canine Affairs was established, as a part of the Department of Wildlife, by an act of Congress and began operations on October 1. Below are the bureau's transactions for its first month of operations.

1. Congress passed and the President approved a $400,000 appropriation for the bureau.

2. The Office of Management and Budget apportioned $350,000 of the appropriation for use by the bureau.

3. The Secretary of Wildlife allotted $100,000 to the bureau for October's operations.

4. Purchase orders for equipment and supplies estimated to cost $70,000 were requested.

5. An order was placed with the Margaret Company for equipment expected to cost $25,000.

6. An order was placed with the Erica Company for supplies expected to cost $40,000.

7. The supplies ordered from the Erica Company were received, along with an invoice for $40,000.

8. A disbursement schedule was sent to the Treasury requesting payment of Erica's invoice.

9. The Treasury informed the bureau that the Erica Company invoice had been paid.

10. Employees of the agency were paid $30,000.

REQUIRED: Prepare journal entries to record the above transactions.

PROBLEMS

P10–1   (Accounting cycle for one month)

The Federal Commission on Incompetence in Government was formed on October 1, 19X1. This agency does *not* use commitment accounting. Among the transactions that took place that year were the following:

1. An appropriation of $6,500,000 was passed by the Congress and approved by the President. The monies are to be used for operating purposes.
2. The Office of Management and Budget notified the Department of Administration, of which the agency is a part, of the following schedule of apportionments:

First quarter	$2,000,000
Second quarter	2,000,000
Third quarter	1,500,000
Fourth quarter	1,000,000

3. The Department of Administration allotted $700,000 to the commission for its operations in October.
4. Purchase orders were placed in October for the following:

Materials	$150,000
Rent	50,000
Supplies	40,000

5. The payroll for the first two weeks of October amounted to $200,000. It was paid on October 15.
6. Invoices approved by the agency for payment were as follows:

XYZ Widget Co.—materials	$120,000
Scrooge Realty Co.—October rent	50,000
NOLA Office Supply—supplies	20,000
L & K Supply—supplies	10,000

The Treasury informed the commission that the invoices from XYZ Widget Co. and L & K Supply were paid in full and one half of the Scrooge Realty bill had been paid. Supplies and rent are expensed upon approval for payment. Materials are inventoried when purchased and expensed when used.

7. The payroll for the remainder of October was $200,000. It was paid on October 31.
8. Materials costing $85,000 were used during October.

REQUIRED:
1. Prepare appropriate journal entries for the transactions of October 19X1.
2. Prepare appropriate monthly closing entries. (Do not close out the budgetary accounts.)
3. Prepare a balance sheet for the commission as of October 31, 19X1.

4. Prepare an operating statement for the commission for the month of October 19X1.

P10–2 (Accounting cycle for one month)

The Star Gazing Agency was established by Congress to begin operations at the beginning of FY 19X1. Below are the agency's transactions during October, its first month of operations.

October 1 Congress passed and the President approved a $1,000,000 appropriation for this agency for FY 19X1.

October 1 Of the amounts appropriated, $950,000 was apportioned by OMB.

October 1 The Department of Outer Space allotted the Agency $100,000 to carry out its operations in October.

October 1 Purchase orders for materials and telescopes, estimated to cost $88,000, were requested.

October 4 Orders were placed for materials and telescopes estimated to cost $85,000.

October 10 The materials and telescopes ordered on October 4 were received, along with invoices for $88,000. The management of the agency accepted the materials and telescopes in spite of the higher price. An analysis of the invoices revealed that the cost of the telescopes was $18,000. The agency elected to expense the materials and telescopes in October, since it was expected that all of the materials would be used up and the telescopes would be worn out by the end of the month.

October 15 A disbursement schedule was sent to the Treasury, requesting that it pay invoices amounting to $60,000.

October 31 The Treasury informed the agency that it had paid invoices amounting to $55,000 to material and telescope vendors and that it had issued checks in the amount of $10,000 to cover salaries for October.

REQUIRED: 1. Prepare journal entries to record the events of October.
2. Post the journal entries prepared in number 1.
3. Prepare a preclosing trial balance.
4. Prepare appropriate closing entries. (*Hint*: Do not close out the budgetary accounts. This is done at the end of the year.)
5. Prepare a postclosing trial balance.
6. Prepare the following month-end statements:
   a. Balance sheet
   b. Operating statement
   c. Reconciliation of operating/program expenses to expended appropriations
   d. Report on budget execution

P10–3 (Closing entries and year-end financial statements)

The trial balance of the Science Research Agency for FY 19X1 is shown below:

	DEBITS	CREDITS
Budgetary accounts:		
Other appropriations realized	$3,868,000	
Authority available for apportionment		$ 150,000
Apportionment available for distribution		200,000
Allotments available for commitment/obligation		450,000
Commitments available for appropriation		182,000
Undelivered orders		25,000
Expended appropriations		2,861,000
	$3,868,000	$3,868,000
Proprietary accounts:		
Fund Balance with U.S. Treasury	$ 520,000	
Inventory of supplies	246,000	
Building and equipment	4,836,000	
Accumulated depreciation—building and equipment		$2,846,000
Accounts payable		133,000
Disbursements in transit		238,000
Due to other federal agencies		85,000
Appropriated capital		29,000
Capital investment		2,236,000
Cumulative results of operations		35,000
Appropriated capital used		3,482,000
Operating/program expenses—salaries	1,836,000	
Operating/program expenses—supplies	882,000	
Operating/program expenses—rent	122,000	
Operating/program expenses—depreciation	642,000	
	$9,084,000	$9,084,000

REQUIRED: 1. Prepare closing entries.
2. Prepare a year-end balance sheet.
3. Prepare an operating statement for FY 19X1.
4. Prepare a reconciliation of operating/program expenses to expended appropriations for FY 19X1. Assume that supplies purchased during the year amounted to $903,000.

P10–4 (Financial statements after initial month of operations)

The Bureau of Astrology was established October 1, 19X1. Its purpose is to provide astrological services to the general public. It is financed by an appropriation from Congress. Below are the transactions of the agency during October 19X1.

October 1   The agency received a certified copy of an appropriation warrant from the Department of Treasury for $900,000.

October 1   Of the amount available for apportionment, $850,000 was apportioned by the Office of Management and Budget.

October 1   Of the amount apportioned, $120,000 was allotted to the agency, by the Department of Outer Space, to finance its operations in October.

October 1   Purchase orders for materials and equipment estimated to cost $48,000 were requested.

October 3   Orders were placed for materials estimated to cost $30,000 and for equipment expected to cost $15,000.

October 15   All of the equipment ordered on October 3 was received, along with an invoice amounting to $14,800.

October 16   Some of the materials ordered on October 3 were received, along with an invoice for $22,000. The estimate of the cost of these materials used to obligate the monies on October 3 had been $22,500. A disbursement schedule for this invoice was sent to the Treasury.

October 27   The Treasury paid the vendor's invoice for the materials, $22,000.

October 31   Materials costing $18,000 were used by the agency during October.

October 31   Salaries for the month of October totaled $50,000.

              The agency's FICA contributions amounted to $2,000.

October 31   Depreciation of $1,200 was recorded by the agency.

REQUIRED:
1. Record the above transactions in general journal form.
2. Post the journal entries to the general ledger and compute the account balances.
3. Prepare a preclosing trial balance.
4. Prepare month-end closing entries. (*Hint*: Since this is month-end, you need not close the budgetary accounts.)
5. Prepare a postclosing trial balance.
6. Prepare the following financial statements:
   a. Balance sheet
   b. Operating statement
   c. Reconciliation of operating/program expenses to expended appropriations
   d. Report on budget execution

11

ACCOUNTING FOR COLLEGES AND UNIVERSITIES

LEARNING OBJECTIVES

After completion of this chapter, you should be able to:

1. Name four ways in which accounting for most colleges and universities differs from accounting for state and local governmental units
2. Explain the difference between private and governmental colleges and universities
3. List the sources of authority for accounting principles followed by colleges and universities
4. List the types of funds used by colleges and universities and discuss how each is used
5. Explain the difference between Restricted and Unrestricted Current Funds
6. Discuss the concept of formula funding
7. Distinguish between mandatory and nonmandatory transfers
8. Identify the financial statements used by governmental and by private colleges and universities
9. Prepare journal entries necessary to record the activities of colleges and universities

Preceding chapters of this text have focused on governmental units. Although such entities are very numerous, they represent only a portion of the not-for-profit organizations in existence. Other not-for-profit organizations are colleges and universities, hospitals, voluntary health and welfare organizations, and "other" not-for-profit organizations such as country clubs, labor unions, private schools, and religious organizations.[1] In this chapter we will discuss funds and accounting procedures used by colleges and universities. Since accounting systems used by private and parochial primary and secondary schools are more similar to systems used by colleges and universities than to ones used by governmental units, the material covered in this chapter is also applicable to those institutions.[2] The main focus of this chapter, however, is on colleges and universities.

Accounting methods and procedures used by colleges and universities are similar to those used by state and local governmental units in that both use fund accounting and, in many cases, budgetary and encumbrance accounts. The types of funds used, however, are different, with more emphasis being placed on recording revenue and fiduciary activities. In addition, account groups are not used to record fixed assets and long-term debt.

Colleges and universities are not as highly regulated by law as governmental units, so there is less need to use the accounting system as a means of ensuring legal compliance. As a result, accounting methods and procedures used by these institutions allow a greater degree of flexibility and adaptability to individual conditions than those used by governmental units. Finally, colleges and universities generally use the full accrual basis of accounting for all funds.

Colleges and universities can be classified as **private** or **governmental**. The distinction is based on their primary sources of financing. Private colleges and universities are financed by tuition and fees, private contributions, and contributions from sponsoring organizations like churches and benevolent societies. Governmental colleges and universities are financed by appropriations received from state and local governmental units, tuition and fees, and private contributions.

Until recently, there was little difference between the reporting requirements of private and governmental colleges and universities. However, since the issuance in 1994 of FASB *Statement of Financial Accounting Standards (SFAS) No. 117,* "Financial Statements of Not-for-Profit Organizations," this has changed. Although both types of institutions still tend to use the same fund structure and accounting procedures, reporting practices of each are now quite different. Financial statements produced by both types of institutions are covered in this chapter.

SOURCES OF AUTHORITY

The primary rule-making bodies for colleges and universities are the Financial Accounting Standards Board (FASB), which is responsible for private colleges and universities, and the Governmental Accounting Standards Board (GASB), which is responsible for governmental colleges and universities. The FASB has stated that the AICPA's industry audit guide, *Audits of Colleges and Universities,*

---

[1] A detailed listing of "other" not-for-profit organizations can be found in the AICPA's *Statement of Position (SOP) 78–10.* These organizations are discussed in Chapter 12.

[2] Funds and accounting procedures used by private schools are specifically covered by the AICPA's *Statement of Position (SOP) 78–10,* as amended.

and the AICPA's *Statement of Position (SOP) 74–8*, "Financial Accounting and Reporting by Colleges and Universities," contain "preferable accounting principles for purposes of justifying a change in accounting principles."[3]

The GASB has had little to say on the subject of colleges and universities. In 1991, however, it issued *Statement No. 15*, "Governmental College and University Accounting and Financial Reporting Models," in which it stated "that it considers both the AICPA College Guide model and the Governmental model to be acceptable for accounting and financial reporting by governmental colleges and universities."[4]

Colleges and universities following the "AICPA *College Guide* model" receive guidance from the AICPA's industry audit guide, *Audits of Colleges and Universities*.[5] This guide (referred to in this chapter as the *College Guide*) has recently been revised to include changes brought about by the issue of authoritative pronouncements since 1973, when the previous edition was published. Among these pronouncements are FASB *Statement of Financial Accounting Standards (SFAS) No. 93*, "Recognition of Depreciation by Not-for-Profit Organizations," and AICPA *Statement of Position (SOP) 74–8*, "Financial Accounting and Reporting by Colleges and Universities." Unfortunately there is no reference in this edition of the *College Guide* to *SFAS No. 117*.

Colleges and universities following the "governmental model" receive guidance from *National Council on Governmental Accounting (NCGA) Statement 1*, "Governmental Accounting and Financial Reporting Principles," "as modified by subsequent NCGA and GASB pronouncements."[6] They usually operate as governmental units or as departments or agencies of governmental units and often have taxing authority. Accounting and reporting practices of these institutions have already been covered in Chapters 2 through 9. Since most colleges and universities follow the AICPA *College Guide* model, the material presented in this chapter follows that model.

Another source of generally accepted accounting principles (GAAP) for colleges and universities is the *Financial Accounting and Reporting Manual for Higher Education* (FARM), published by the National Association of College and University Business Officers (NACUBO). This reference, which is in loose-leaf form and updated periodically, is used primarily by college and university administrators.

A third source of generally accepted accounting principles for colleges and universities is the *Higher Education Finance Manual*, published by the U.S. Department of Education. This publication provides information on accounting systems necessary to meet the requirements of the National Center for Educational Statistics, a federal agency that monitors activities of educational institutions. The

---

[3]Financial Accounting Standards Board, *Statement of Financial Accounting Standards No. 32*, "Specialized Accounting and Reporting Principles and Practices in AICPA Statements of Position and Guides on Accounting and Auditing Matters" (Norwalk, CT: FASB, 1979).

[4]Governmental Accounting Standards Board, *Statement No. 15*, "Governmental College and University Accounting and Financial Reporting Models" (Norwalk, CT: GASB, 1991).

[5]American Institute of Certified Public Accountants, *Audits of Colleges and Universities* (New York: AICPA, 1993).

[6]GASB, *Statement No. 15*.

AICPA *College Guide,* FARM, and the *Higher Education Finance Manual* were developed in a coordinated manner. As a result, they usually agree on what accounting methods and procedures should be used by colleges and universities.

FUNDS USED BY COLLEGES AND UNIVERSITIES

The following types of funds are ordinarily used by colleges and universities:

1. Current Funds
2. Loan Funds
3. Endowment and Similar Funds (Term Endowment and Quasi-Endowment)
4. Annuity and Life Income Funds
5. Agency Funds
6. Plant Funds

Current, Loan, Endowment, Term Endowment, and Plant Funds can be restricted or unrestricted. Annuity and Life Income Funds and Agency Funds *must* be restricted, while Quasi-Endowment Funds *must* remain unrestricted. To be classified as **restricted**, a fund must have restrictions placed on its use by persons or organizations *outside* the institution. Otherwise it must be classified as **unrestricted.** Restricted funds should be reported separately from unrestricted funds. Within each fund, restricted accounts should be reported separately from unrestricted accounts.

Current Funds

Current Funds are used to account for resources used to carry out general operations of the institution, operations "directly related" to the institution's primary objectives. These objectives usually consist of teaching, research, and public service. However, such auxiliary enterprises as residence halls, food services, and intercollegiate athletics are also considered to be directly related. The term *current* refers to the fact that these resources will be expended in a short period of time.

Current Funds serve many of the functions of the general funds used by governmental units. The scope of these funds, however, is wider, since many of the activities recorded in these funds (e.g., bookstores) are self-supporting. By contrast, similar activities are usually recorded in Enterprise Funds when conducted by governmental units.

Unrestricted current funds

As mentioned earlier, Current Funds can be unrestricted or restricted. The activities of **Unrestricted Current Funds** tend to be similar to those of General or Special Revenue Funds. Revenues of these funds are usually recorded by source. Among the more common sources of revenue are tuition and fees; federal, state, and local appropriations; gifts and grants; endowment income; sales and services of educational activities; and sales and services of auxiliary enterprises.

Another common (and important) source of revenues for many institutions, especially those operated by state governments, is "formula" funding. **Formula funding** was developed as a means of "depoliticalizing" the allocation of resources between the various educational institutions within a state. Under the formula, which is usually based on the cost of running a "typical" institution in a given region (e.g., the Southeast), a college or university is allowed a certain dollar amount for each type of student-credit-hour (SCH) earned by that institution.[7] For example, in Louisiana (as of this writing) the formula is as follows:

STUDENT'S ACADEMIC LEVEL	COST CATEGORY*	DOLLARS PER SCH
Doctoral	Higher cost	1028
Doctoral	Lower cost	929
Master's	Higher cost	396
Master's	Lower cost	264
Upper undergraduate	Higher cost	174
Upper undergraduate	Lower cost	127
Lower undergraduate	Higher cost	115
Lower undergraduate	Lower cost	84

*Since certain areas of study, such as science and engineering, require more resources than other areas, such as liberal arts and business, they are allowed more dollars under the formula.

Thus a public institution in Louisiana with the following enrollment (as of the tenth day of classes) receive $31,539,120 in formula funding:

STUDENTS' ACADEMIC LEVEL	COST CATEGORY	NO. OF STUDENTS	AVERAGE CREDIT HOURS PER STUDENT*	STUDENT CREDIT HOURS	DOLLARS PER SCH	DOLLARS FUNDED
Doctoral	Higher cost	40	12	480	$1,028	$ 493,440
Doctoral	Lower cost	60	12	720	929	668,880
Master's	Higher cost	1,200	12	14,400	396	5,702,400
Master's	Lower cost	800	12	9,600	264	2,534,400
Upper undergraduate	Higher cost	3,000	15	45,000	174	7,830,000
Upper undergraduate	Lower cost	1,000	15	15,000	127	1,905,000
Lower undergraduate	Higher cost	5,000	15	75,000	115	8,625,000
Lower undergraduate	Lower cost	3,000	15	45,000	84	3,780,000
Total formula funding						$31,539,120

*The number of hours taken by most students ranges from six hours for part-time students to eighteen hours for full-time students. It is assumed that the majority of students at this institution are full-time students.

[7]A student-credit-hour (SCH) is a measure of the number of students and the number of credit hours being taken at an institution. Its purpose is to provide a common denominator between part-time and full-time students. A student taking one three-credit-hour course is worth 3 SCHs. A student taking five three-credit-hour courses is worth 15 SCHs, and so on.

From the preceding discussion, it should be easy to see why certain institutions discourage dropping courses until after "enrollment day." It should also be obvious that "senior" institutions (those granting the largest number of advanced degrees) receive the lion's share of the available resources.

Expenditures of Unrestricted Current Funds should be classified by function. For internal operating purposes, they should also be classified by department and object (e.g., salaries). The major functional categories used by colleges and universities are (1) educational and general, (2) student aid, and (3) auxiliary enterprises. Functional subcategories include instruction, research, academic support, institutional support, operation and maintenance of plant, and scholarships, as well as those subcategories unique to the particular auxiliary enterprises operated by the institution.

Restricted current funds

Restricted Current Funds are used to account for financial resources available for operational purposes, but whose use is limited by external agencies and donors to specific activities, programs, departments, and so forth. They pose certain problems not encountered by unrestricted funds. First, they cannot be designated as restricted by the governing board or operating management of the institution. If these parties could make such a designation, they would also have the power to "unrestrict" the fund. Thus the fund would not be a true restricted fund. Restricted Current Funds are used only to reflect limitations placed on the use of certain resources by parties *outside* the organization.

Transactions recorded in Restricted Current Funds consist largely of the receipt of cash (or other assets), the making of expenditures, and the earning of revenues. Revenues of Restricted Current Funds of **governmental** colleges and universities are not considered to be "earned" until they have been expended in the manner set forth by the donor or the party placing the restriction. When these monies are first received, they are reported as additions to fund balance. They are recognized as revenues when the required expenditures are made. Thus, total revenues reported by these funds will equal total expenditures. Any amounts not spent on refunds to grantors will be reported as "Other transfers and additions." As with other funds, revenue and expenditure accounts are closed at the end of the period.

Revenues of Restricted Current Funds of **private** colleges and universities were originally treated in the same manner as those of governmental colleges and universities. In 1994, however, the FASB issued *Statement of Financial Accounting Standards (SFAS) No. 116*, "Accounting for Contributions Received and Contributions Made." Under this statement, not-for-profit organizations subject to FASB guidance must recognize contributions received "as revenues or gains *in the period received* (emphasis added) and as assets, decreases of liabilities, or expenses depending on the form of benefits received."[8] Thus contributions re-

---

[8]Financial Accounting Standards Board, *Statement of Financial Accounting Standards No. 116*, "Accounting for Contributions Received and Contributions Made" (Norwalk, CT: FASB, 1994).

ceived by private colleges and universities are recorded as revenues at the time of receipt, not when the required expenditures are made.

Interfund transfers

Transfers from Current (Restricted and Unrestricted) Funds to other types of funds of a college or university can be mandatory or nonmandatory. **Mandatory transfers** are transfers "arising out of (1) binding legal agreements related to the financing of educational plant, such as amounts for debt, retirement, interest, and required provisions for renewals and replacements of plant, not financed from other sources; and (2) grant agreements with agencies of the federal government, donors, and other organizations to match gifts and grants to loan and other funds."[9] They may be made from either Restricted or Unrestricted Current Funds. **Nonmandatory transfers** are transfers made to other fund groups "at the discretion of the governing board to serve a variety of objectives, such as additions to loan funds, additions to quasi-endowment funds, general or specific plant additions, voluntary renewals and replacements of plant, and prepayments on debt principal."[10] Transfers from Current Funds to other funds are recorded and reported separately from expenditures of those funds.

Account classifications

Asset and liability accounts used by Current Funds are usually current in nature, just like the ones used by the General Funds of municipalities. Because of the use of accrual accounting, however, these funds include prepaid expenses and deferred charges (expenses paid, but applicable to future periods) among their assets and deferred credits (monies collected in advance) among their liabilities. Current Funds can also show long-term debt among their liabilities, as long as the debt is not related to fixed asset acquisitions. Such cases, however, are rare.

Fund balances are segregated into two categories: allocated and unallocated. The **allocated fund balance** shows the portion of the fund balance that represents the institution's equity in its auxiliary enterprises, its hospitals, and so forth, and the portion reserved for outstanding encumbrances. In addition, any other allocations established by the operating management or the governing board of the institution or by external parties should be disclosed. The **unallocated fund balance** is a residual figure, representing the fund's "free" balance.

Recording transactions

Transactions recorded in the Unrestricted Current Fund of a college or university consist primarily of revenues, expenditures, and transfers to other funds. Since these transactions are recorded on the (full) accrual basis, inventoriable items such as supplies are recorded as assets when purchased and as expendi-

---

[9]National Association of College and University Business Officers, *Financial Accounting and Reporting Manual for Higher Education* (Washington, DC: NACUBO, 1990), para. 340.
   [10]Ibid.

tures when used. Illustrated below are sample transactions for typical Unrestricted Current Fund transactions:

1. Revenues of $1 million are received from tuition and fees. Of this amount, $900,000 is received in cash and $100,000 is still to be received:

Cash	900,000	
Accounts receivable	100,000	
Revenues—educational and general		1,000,000

To record revenues from tuition and fees.

Note: If it is expected that not all the receivables will be collected, it is appropriate to set up an allowance for uncollectible accounts. This is done by means of a debit to an expenditure account and a credit to an allowance account for the amount expected to remain uncollected.

2. Tuition scholarships worth $30,000 are awarded to deserving students.

Expenditures—educational and general	30,000	
Revenues—educational and general		30,000

To record the revenues and corresponding expenditures relating to tuition scholarships.

Note: Even though no resources are actually received or expended, it is customary to show the tuition that would have been received as a revenue, offset by a corresponding expenditure representing the "cost" of the scholarship.

3. Revenues from auxiliary enterprises amount to $150,000.

Cash	150,000	
Revenues—auxiliary enterprises		150,000

To record the revenues from the various auxiliary enterprises.

4. Materials and supplies purchased during the year amount to $300,000. Invoices amounting to $50,000 are outstanding at year-end.

Inventory—materials and supplies	300,000	
Cash		250,000
Accounts payable		50,000

To record the purchase of materials and supplies.

5. Materials and supplies used during the year amount to $220,000. Of this amount, $180,000 is used for educational activities and $40,000 is used by the auxiliary enterprises.

Expenditures—educational and general	180,000	
Expenditures—auxiliary enterprises	40,000	
Inventory—materials and supplies		220,000

To record the cost of materials and supplies used during the year.

6. Wages, salaries, and other operating expenses (such as utilities and insurance) amount to $810,000. Of this amount, $760,000 is chargeable to educational and general operations and $50,000 is chargeable to auxiliary enterprises.

Expenditures—educational and general	760,000	
Expenditures—auxiliary enterprises	50,000	
Cash		810,000

To record the wages, salaries, and other operating expenditures incurred during the year.

7. Grants-in-aid to students total $50,000.

Expenditures—student aid	50,000	
Cash		50,000

To record grants-in-aid awarded to students during the year.

8. In accordance with the loan agreement, a transfer of $50,000 is made to the Fund for Retirement of Indebtedness to pay interest and principal currently due on the mortgage on the new security building (see p. 524).

Mandatory transfers to the Fund for		
Retirement of Indebtedness	50,000	
Cash		50,000

To record the payment on the mortgage carried on the new security building.

9. A "voluntary" transfer of $10,000 is made to the Unexpended Plant Fund for the purchase of library books.

Nonmandatory transfers to the Unexpended		
Plant Fund	10,000	
Cash		10,000

To record the cost of library books financed by the Unrestricted Current Fund.

10. A grant of $10,000 is received from the Kezar Foundation to be used in the general operations of the university.

Cash	10,000	
Revenues—gifts and grants		10,000

To record receipt of a general operating grant from the Kezar Foundation.

11. The revenue, expenditure, and transfer accounts are closed out at year-end.

Revenues—educational and general	1,030,000	
Revenues—auxiliary enterprises	150,000	
Revenues—gifts and grants	10,000	
Expenditures—educational and general		970,000
Expenditures—auxiliary enterprises		90,000
Expenditures—student aid		50,000
Mandatory transfers to the Fund for Retirement of Indebtedness		50,000
Nonmandatory transfers to the Unexpected Plant Fund		10,000
Fund balance—unallocated		20,000

To close out revenue, expenditure, and
transfer accounts.

As we mentioned earlier, monies received by the Restricted Current Funds of governmental colleges and universities are not considered "earned" until they have been expended in the manner stipulated by the donor or the party placing the restriction. When these monies are first received, they are recorded as additions to fund balance. They are recognized as revenues when the required expenditures are made. To illustrate, assume the following:

1. A donation of $100,000 is made to a *governmental* university. Of this amount, $60,000 is to be spent for library operations and $40,000 is to be used for special payments to faculty who write textbooks:

Cash	100,000	
Fund balance—library operations		60,000
Fund balance—special faculty salary supplements		40,000

To record receipt of cash designated for
library operations and for special payments
to faculty who write textbooks.

2. When expenditures of Restricted Current Funds, which are required by donors or parties placing the restrictions, are made, expenditure accounts are debited and Cash and/or payable accounts are credited. In this case, $50,000 is spent on library operations, and $30,000 is spent for faculty salary supplements:

Expenditures—library operations	50,000	
Expenditures—special faculty salary supplements	30,000	
Cash		80,000

To record expenditures for library operations and special faculty salary supplements.

3. Revenues of Restricted Current Funds are recognized to the extent that expenditures have taken place for the designated purposes. In this example, revenues of the period will equal amounts expended in entry number 2.

Fund balance—library operations	50,000	
Fund balance—special faculty salary supplements	30,000	
Revenues—restricted gifts		80,000
To recognize revenues of period.		

4. At the end of the fiscal year, revenue and expenditure accounts of the Restricted Current Funds are closed out as follows:

Revenues—restricted gifts	80,000	
Expenditures—library operations		50,000
Expenditures—special faculty salary supplements		30,000
To close out revenue and expenditure accounts.		

If the donation in the above example had been made to a *private* university, it would have been considered "earned" when received. A revenue would have been recorded at that time, and expenditures would have been recorded when incurred. The entries would have been as follows:

1.
Cash	100,000	
Revenues—restricted gifts		100,000
To record receipt of cash designated for library operations and for special payments to faculty who write textbooks.		

2.
Expenditures—library operations	50,000	
Expenditures—special faculty salary supplements	30,000	
Cash		80,000
To record expenditures for library operations and special faculty salary supplements.		

3. No entry

4.
Revenues—restricted gifts	100,000	
Expenditures—library operations		50,000
Expenditures—special faculty salary supplements		30,000
Fund balance		20,000
To close out revenue and expenditure accounts.		

Loan Funds

Loan Funds are used to account for monies that will be lent to students, faculty, and other personnel of the college or university. The monies are received from governmental units, foundations, and individual donors, as well as the borrowers (which is why Loan Funds are called "revolving" funds). Interest received from borrowers and income from temporary investments is usually used to "cover" operating expenses and bad debts, as well as additional loans. As with commercial accounting, an allowance for uncollectible accounts should be established.

Endowment and Similar Funds

Endowment and Similar Funds are funds whose principal is nonexpendable and is invested in order to produce income. **Endowment Funds** are funds for which donors or other external parties have stipulated that principal must be maintained intact and invested in order to produce income which may, depending on the terms of the donation, be expended or added to the principal of the fund.

The designation "similar funds" is given to Term Endowment and Quasi-Endowment Funds. **Term Endowment Funds** are similar to Endowment Funds. However, all or a part of the principal of these funds may be expended after a given period of time or when a specific event occurs.

Quasi-Endowment Funds are funds that the governing board of the institution, rather than an external party, has decided to set aside. Principal and income of these funds may be utilized at the discretion of the governing board. As a result, they are unrestricted.

Generally speaking, income earned on the principal (dividends, interest, rents, etc.) of Endowment and Similar Funds is used for institutional purposes. Capital gains are usually reinvested and treated as additional principal on which income will be earned.

Investment income of Endowment and Similar Funds is reported as either restricted or unrestricted. If reported as restricted, it should be treated as an "addition" to either the appropriate unexpended endowment income account in the Restricted Current Fund or to the fund balances of Loan, Endowment, or Plant Funds, depending on the terms of the restrictions. If reported as unrestricted, it should be treated as an addition to Unrestricted Current Fund revenues.

Assets of Endowment and Similar Funds consist primarily of cash and investments. They may also include accounts receivable, prepaid items, and amounts due from other fund groups. Investments can consist of stocks and bonds, as well as real estate, patents, copyrights, royalties, and participations in oil-drilling ventures. Liabilities of these funds consist primarily of amounts due to other fund groups. There can, however, be claims or other forms of indebtedness against the assets representing investments (e.g., mortgages).

Fund balances of Endowment and Similar Funds are increased by means of gifts, bequests, income, and capital gains required by the gift instrument to be added to the principal of the funds, and transfers to Quasi-Endowment Funds from other fund groups. Fund balances of these funds are reduced by withdrawals and transfers to other fund groups and by losses on investment transactions.

Annuity and Life Income Funds

The Annuity and Life Income Funds group is made up of two subgroups: Annuity Funds and Life Income Funds. **Annuity Funds** are used to account for resources given to the institution with the stipulation that a *specified dollar amount* be paid to the donor or to other parties for a particular period of time. At the end of that period, the principal of the fund is transferred to the fund category specified in the agreement or, in the absence of any mention of this point in the agreement, to the Unrestricted Current Fund. **Life Income Funds** are used to account for resources given to the institution with the stipulation that *all income earned* by these resources be paid to the donor or other parties for a specified period of time, usually the lifetime of the person receiving the income.

Assets of Annuity and Life Income Funds include cash, securities, and other types of investments. They may be handled separately or they may be pooled with assets of other funds. If they are pooled, detailed records that specifically identify the annuity, life income, and other (e.g., endowment) portions of the pool and the income attributable to each, and ensure that the various regulatory provisions are being followed, must be maintained.

Liabilities of Annuity and Life Income Funds include claims against any assets held by the funds (e.g., a mortgage against rental property), annuity or life income payments currently due, and amounts due to other fund groups. In addition, Annuity Funds must show, as a liability, the present value of future annuity payments. This amount is determined by actuarial calculations, which are periodically updated.

Increases in fund balances of Annuity and Life Income Funds are caused by new gifts and income from (and gains on) investments. Gifts made to Annuity Funds must be offset by a liability equal to the actuarial value of future payments to the donors.

Decreases in fund balances of Annuity and Life Income Funds are caused by transfers to other fund groups, upon termination of the annuity or life income agreements, and losses on investments. In addition, changes must periodically be made to Annuity Funds when adjustments are made to their liability and fund balance accounts to reflect changes in the life expectancies of their recipients and in their anticipated return on investments.

Upon termination of an annuity or life income agreement, the principal of the fund is transferred to the fund group specified in the agreement or, in the absence of such a stipulation, to the Unrestricted Current Fund. Its nature must be clearly identified so that it will not appear that a new gift has been received. If few in number and small in amount, Annuity Funds may be recorded in the Endowment and Similar Funds group.

Agency Funds

Agency Funds are used to account for resources that the institution holds as custodian or fiscal agent for students, faculty, members of the staff, and various institution-related organizations. These funds are similar to the Agency Funds used by governmental units.

Assets of Agency Funds include cash, receivables, temporary investments, and amounts due from other fund groups. Liabilities of Agency Funds include accounts payable, amounts due to other fund groups, and the balances of persons or organizations for which the institution is acting as custodian, fiscal agent, or depository. Since assets must always equal liabilities, there are no fund balances in this fund group.

Plant Funds

The **Plant Funds** group is used to record transactions related to the acquisition, replacement, existence, and financing of long-lived assets, including those of auxiliary enterprises. It consists of four self-balancing subgroups:

1. **Unexpended Plant Funds.** This subgroup is used to account for resources used to acquire long-lived plant assets, as well as liabilities associated with such acquisitions.
2. **Funds for Renewals and Replacements.** This subgroup is used to account for resources that will finance the renewal or replacement (as opposed to the acquisition) of long-lived plant assets.
3. **Funds for Retirement of Indebtedness.** This subgroup is used to account for resources set aside to pay interest charges on and to retire long-term debt associated with plant assets. Funds for Retirement of Indebtedness are similar to Debt Service Funds used by governmental units.
4. **Investment in Plant.** This subgroup is used to account for the cost (or fair market value at time of donation) of long-lived plant assets (other than those of Endowment and Similar Funds) and the sources from which the assets are funded, including any associated liabilities.

Assets of Unexpended Plant Funds, Funds for Renewals and Replacements, and Funds for Retirement of Indebtedness are derived from the following sources:

1. Funds from external agencies
2. Student fees and assessments from debt service or other plant purposes, which create an obligation equivalent to an externally imposed restriction and which are not subject to the discretionary right of the governing board to use for other purposes
3. Transfers, both mandatory and nonmandatory, from other fund groups
4. Borrowings from external sources for plant purposes
5. Borrowings by advances from other fund groups
6. Income and net gains from investments in the unrestricted and restricted elements of each of the subgroups.[11]

These assets consist of cash, investments, amounts due from other fund groups, accounts and notes receivable, and deposits with others. In addition, Unexpended Plant Funds and Funds for Retirement of Indebtedness are often used to record construction in progress.

Liabilities of Unexpended Plant Funds and Funds for Renewals and Replacements usually consist of accounts, notes, mortgages, and bonds payable, as well as amounts due to other fund groups. Liabilities of Funds for Retirement of

[11]Ibid., para. 381.

Indebtedness usually consist of amounts due to fiscal agents, other debt service charges, and amounts due to other fund groups.

Fund balances of Unexpended Plant Funds, Funds for Renewals and Replacements, and Funds for Retirement of Indebtedness represent unexpended resources of these subgroups. They should be maintained so that unexpended resources originating from board-designated, unrestricted monies are distinguished from unexpended resources originating from monies whose use is restricted by legal provisions or by external parties. This can be accomplished by maintaining separate project accounts for each type of fund and separate accounts for each debt.

Additions to the fund balances of all three subgroups are the same as the sources of assets listed above, except for borrowings. Deductions from the fund balances of Unexpended Plant Funds and Funds for Renewals and Replacements include expenditures for new plant or for renewals and replacements of plant, losses on investments, return of unrestricted monies back to Unrestricted Current Funds, and other appropriate charges, such as certain fund-raising expenses.

Deductions from the fund balances of Funds for Retirement of Indebtedness include expenditures for interest and repayment of principal, trustees' expenses, and fees and losses on investments. Encumbrances in any of the Plant Funds that are outstanding as of the reporting date should be reported by means of a note to the financial statements or as allocations of the fund balances.

The primary purpose of the Investment in Plant subgroup is to maintain a listing of fixed assets used by the institution and of any construction in progress that is not listed in the Unexpended Plant Funds or the Funds for Renewals and Replacements subgroup. Liabilities associated with these assets are also recorded in the Investment in Plant subgroup. The assets of this subgroup usually include land, buildings, fixtures, equipment, and library books, as well as construction in progress.

Sources of assets of the Investment in Plant subgroup include the following:

1. Capitalized completion costs of projects transferred from the Unexpended Plant Funds and Funds for Renewals and Replacements subgroups
2. Capitalized costs of construction in progress transferred from the Unexpended Plant Funds and the Funds for Renewals and Replacements subgroups at the reporting date, unless held in those subgroups until completion of the project
3. Donations (at fair market value on date of gift) of plant assets
4. The cost of long-lived assets financed by expenditures of Current and other funds, except for Endowment and Similar Funds[12]

Liabilities of the Investment in Plant subgroup can include amounts owed on accounts, notes, leaseholds, bonds, and mortgages, as well as amounts due to other fund groups, which are associated with the renewal, replacement, or acquisition of fixed (plant) assets.

The fund balance of this subgroup is called Net Investment in Plant. It rep-

[12]Ibid., para. 385.

resents the carrying value of assets over liabilities and is increased by means of the acquisition of plant assets, less their associated liabilities, and through the retirement of debt incurred to acquire, renew, or replace those assets. The fund balance is decreased when the disposition of plant assets takes place and when depreciation is recorded.

Recording transactions in Plant Funds is relatively easy. It differs from recording transactions in Current Funds in that no revenues or expenses are recorded. Only changes in assets, liabilities, and fund balance are recorded. Even depreciation, an expense in most other organizations, is treated as a direct reduction of Net Investment in Plant.

To illustrate, assume that a transfer of $100,000 is received from a Quasi-Endowment Fund to finance a new security building and that a mortgage of $500,000 is taken out to provide the remainder of the monies necessary to complete this project. Entries in the Unexpended Plant Fund are:

Cash	100,000	
Fund balance		100,000
To record transfer from Quasi-Endowment Fund, to be used to build new security building.		
Cash	500,000	
Mortgage payable		500,000
To record receipt of cash from a mortgage on new security building.		

The entry in the Quasi-Endowment Fund is:

Income from investments	100,000	
Cash		100,000
To record payment of quasi-endowment income to Unexpended Plant Fund.		

If the building is one-half complete at the end of the year (and the costs are as budgeted), the entry in the Unexpended Plant Fund is:

Construction in progress	300,000	
Cash		300,000
To record cost of construction completed to date on new security building.		

If library books are purchased for $10,000 and this purchase is recorded as an expense, the entry in the Unexpended Plant Fund is:

Fund balance	10,000	
Cash		10,000
To record purchase of library books.		

When the previously mentioned building is completed and transferred to the Investment in Plant subgroup, the entry in the Unexpended Plant Fund is:

Mortgage payable	500,000	
Fund balance	100,000	
Construction in progress		300,000
Cash		300,000

To record completion of security building and transfer of this building (and accompanying mortgage) to Investment in Plant subgroup.

The entry in the Investment in Plant subgroup is:

Building	600,000	
Mortgage payable		500,000
Net investment in plant		100,000

To record transfer of completed security building to Investment in Plant subgroup.

If depreciation amounting to $15,000 is taken on the building, the following entry is made in the Investment in Plant subgroup:

Net investment in plant	15,000	
Accumulated depreciation		15,000

To record depreciation on security building for the year.

When a piece of equipment is retired or a building is sold or demolished, the following entry is made in the Investment in Plant subgroup:

Net investment in plant	2,000	
Equipment		2,000

To record sale of motor vehicle used by campus security.

Entries in the Funds for Retirement of Indebtedness consist largely of those used to record the receipt of monies to service debt and to record the actual payments made for interest and repayment of principal.

For example, assume that $50,000 is received from the Unrestricted Current Fund for the payment of interest and principal on the mortgage on the security building, which is recorded in the Investment in Plant subgroup. Entries in the Fund for Retirement of Indebtedness to record the receipt of the monies and the payment of interest ($10,000) and principal on the mortgage are:

1.	Cash	50,000	
	Fund balance		50,000

To record receipt of monies to
pay interest and principal currently due on mortgage on security building.

2.	Fund balance	50,000	
	Cash		50,000

To record payment of interest
($10,000) and principal
($40,000) currently due on
mortgage on security building.

The entry in the Investment on Plant subgroup is:

Mortgage payable	40,000	
Net investment in plant		40,000

To record payment of a portion
of mortgage on security building
by Fund for Retirement of Indebtedness.

ACCOUNTING PROBLEMS OF COLLEGES AND UNIVERSITIES

Accounts of colleges and universities are usually maintained on the (full) accrual
basis—that is, revenues are recognized (reported) when earned and expenditures
are recognized when materials or services are used. As with municipalities, expenditures of colleges and universities include operating expenses (except for depreciation, which will be covered later) and the acquisition cost of capital assets,
such as laboratory equipment, library books, and computers. Expenses applicable
to the current period but not recorded on that date should be accrued, while those
applicable to future periods should be deferred (recognized in a future period).

One problem that is unique to educational institutions occurs when an academic term encompasses parts of two fiscal years (e.g., the summer terms at
some institutions run from early June through early August; the fiscal years of
many of these institutions, however, end on June 30). When this happens, all revenues and expenditures of the academic term in question should be reported in
the fiscal year in which the program is "predominately conducted."

Like municipalities, colleges and universities often use encumbrance accounting in order to maintain control over expenditures and to prevent over-
spending. The methods of handling encumbrances used by colleges and universities are often the same as those used by governmental units (see Chapter 5),
although simpler methods are permissible. For example, many small institutions
use informal memorandum records. However, any method is acceptable as long
as it involves proper control, provides useful information, and is flexible and cost
effective.

Colleges and universities should use budgetary accounting. The procedures and accounts used under such systems are similar to those found in municipal accounting. The account titles, however, are somewhat different. For example, the following entry is prepared after the governing body approves the budget:

Estimated (or unrealized) revenues	XXXXXX	
Estimated expenditures (or budget allocations for expenditures)		XXXXXX
Unallocated budget balance		XXXXXX
To record approval of budget by governing body.		

Any revisions to the budget are recorded by appropriate debits and credits to the accounts shown above. At the end of the fiscal year, the budgetary accounts are reversed out, just as they are in municipal accounting.

As with other organizations, sound cash management is critical to the survival of colleges and universities. When these organizations have excess cash (e.g., at the beginning of a semester or after receiving a sizable donation), they usually invest it in interest-bearing securities.

Colleges and universities often find it advantageous to pool the investments of various funds. In addition to permitting administrative economies, the use of an investment pool makes possible a broad variety of investments. Such diversification provides a greater degree of safety and stability of revenue than is possible with a series of smaller, unrelated investments. When assets are placed in a pool, however, the identity of each fund must be maintained. This is accomplished through the use of individual accounts for the principal of each fund participating in the pool.

When investments are received as gifts, they are usually reported at their fair market (or appraised) value at the date of the gift. Alternatively, investments may be reported at their current market value, as long as this basis is used for all of the institution's investments. If this latter method is used, unrealized gains and losses should be reported in the same manner that realized gains and losses are reported under the cost basis. Any differences between the carrying value and the fair market or appraised value should be shown by the "selling" fund as realized (already incurred) gains or losses.

Depreciation

As with governmental-type funds used by municipalities, depreciation is not reported as an operating expense by colleges and universities. The reasoning behind this policy is that users should not, through the tuition and fees they pay, be required to finance the recovery of an investment in plant and equipment, which is usually acquired by means of gifts and governmental appropriations. When capital asset acquisitions are financed from Current Funds, they are reported as expenditures of those funds in the year of acquisition.

To provide more information to statement users, however, many institutions report an allowance for depreciation on their balance sheets and a provision for depreciation in the "investment in plant" subgroups of their Plant Fund groups. They also record depreciation on fixed assets held as investments by their Endowment and Similar Funds groups, in order to maintain the distinction between income from and principal of these investments—a treatment similar to that given to Nonexpendable Trust Funds used by governmental units.

Recently, the Financial Accounting Standards Board (FASB) issued *Statement of Financial Accounting Standards (SFAS) No. 93*, "Recognition of Depreciation by Not-for-Profit Organizations," which requires most not-for-profit organizations, including colleges and universities, to recognize depreciation on most long-lived, tangible assets. The reasoning behind this requirement is that these assets eventually wear out and organizations need to know at what rate this is occurring. This reasoning assumes, of course, that depreciation is a true measure of wear and tear, an assumption not universally shared by accountants.

Many college and university officials and officials of governmental organizations do not believe depreciation should be reported, for the reasons stated at the beginning of this section. As a result, the Governmental Accounting Standards Board (GASB) has suggested that governmental entities—such as colleges and universities and other organizations with counterparts in the private sector—ignore *SFAS No. 93* and wait until it issues its own statements on issues that relate to depreciation. Therefore, reporting of depreciation is optional for governmental colleges and universities. For illustrative purposes, however, we will assume that depreciation is recorded by all colleges and universities.

Auxiliary Enterprises

Auxiliary enterprises are self-sustaining activities of colleges and universities that provide goods and services to students, faculty, staff, and, in some cases, to the general public. Examples include intercollegiate athletics, residence halls, and bookstores. Auxiliary enterprises often operate at a profit. Earnings from these activities are used to support other activities (such as "minor" sports) and to service debt used to construct facilities like recreation centers and student centers.

Accounting for auxiliary enterprises of colleges and universities differs from that of proprietary activities of governmental units. Whereas revenues and expenses, as well as assets and liabilities, of the latter are recorded in a separate fund, revenues and expenditures of auxiliary enterprises of colleges and universities are recorded in the Current Funds, as are short-term assets and liabilities. Fixed assets and long-term debt of these enterprises are recorded in the Plant Funds.

Institutions Operated by Religious Groups

It is quite common for a religious group to operate an educational institution. When this happens, records of the educational institution should be segregated from those of the religious group, and the educational institution should be treated as a separate entity. When services are contributed by members of the religious group, they should be recorded in the accounts and on the financial statements at fair market value. These amounts can be determined by relating them to the compensation (including fringe benefits) provided to lay personnel performing similar duties. The value of the services performed by members of the religious groups should be recorded as both a gift revenue and an expenditure. Any living costs, personal allowances, and so forth, that are unique to this relationship and are not provided to lay personnel should be deducted from the gift revenue.

FINANCIAL STATEMENTS OF COLLEGES AND UNIVERSITIES

Originally, both governmental and private colleges and universities prepared the same financial statements. In 1994, the FASB issued *Statement of Financial Accounting Standards (SFAS) No. 117*, "Financial Statements of Not-for-Profit Organizations." The purpose of this statement was to encourage uniform financial reporting among not-for-profit organizations. Before the issuance of *SFAS No. 117*, colleges and universities, not-for-profit hospitals, voluntary health and welfare organizations, and other not-for-profit organizations produced different external financial statements. It was felt that if these organizations followed guidance offered in this statement, the comparability, relevance, and understandability of financial statements issued by these organizations would be enhanced.

Since private colleges and universities receive guidance from the FASB, they are now required to use the new reporting formats. Governmental colleges and universities, however, receive guidance from the GASB which has, as of this writing, been silent on the subject of reporting although it does have a project on its agenda to reconsider reporting models acceptable for colleges and universities. Because they are not required to follow *SFAS No. 117*, it appears that governmental colleges and universities will continue to use the "traditional" (or NACUBO) reporting model. As only financial statements are discussed in *SFAS No. 117*, it is assumed that the fund structure previously discussed will continue to be used by both private and governmental colleges and universities. In this section, the traditional reporting format is presented, followed by the format suggested by *SFAS No. 117*.

Governmental Colleges and Universities

Three basic financial statements are generally used by governmental colleges and universities: a balance sheet; a statement of changes in fund balances; and a statement of current funds revenues, expenditures, and other changes.

An example of a **balance sheet** is shown in Table 11–1. Notice that all funds and fund groups used by the Governmental University are presented on the same report in a **"pancake" format.**[13] This format, which is the one most com-

---

[13]A columnar format, with a column for each major fund, is also acceptable.

TABLE 11-1

Governmental University
Balance Sheet
June 30, 19X1
With Comparative Figures at June 30, 19X0

Assets	CURRENT YEAR	PRIOR YEAR	Liabilities and Fund Balances	CURRENT YEAR	PRIOR YEAR
Current Funds			*Current Funds*		
Unrestricted:			Unrestricted:		
Cash	$ 210,000	$ 110,000	Accounts payable	$ 125,000	$ 100,000
Investments	450,000	360,000	Accrued liabilities	20,000	15,000
Accounts receivable, less allowance of $18,000 both years	228,000	175,000	Students' deposits	30,000	35,000
			Due to other funds	158,000	120,000
Inventories, at lower of cost (first-in, first-out basis) or market	90,000	80,000	Deferred credits	30,000	20,000
			Fund balance	643,000	455,000
Prepaid expenses and deferred charges	28,000	20,000	Total unrestricted	1,006,000	745,000
Total unrestricted	1,006,000	745,000			
Restricted:			Restricted:		
Cash	145,000	101,000	Accounts payable	14,000	5,000
Investments	175,000	165,000	Fund balances	446,000	421,000
Accounts receivable, less allowance of $8,000 both years	68,000	160,000			
Unbilled charges	72,000	—			
Total restricted	460,000	426,000	Total restricted	460,000	426,000
Total current funds	1,466,000	1,171,000	Total current funds	1,466,000	1,171,000
Loan Funds			*Loan Funds*		
Cash	30,000	20,000	Fund balances:		
Investments	100,000	100,000	U.S. government grants refundable	50,000	33,000
Loans to students, faculty, and staff less allowance of $10,000 current year and $9,000 prior year	550,000	382,000	University funds		
			Restricted	483,000	369,000
Due from restricted funds	3,000	—	Unrestricted	150,000	100,000
Total loan funds	683,000	502,000	Total loan funds	683,000	502,000

(continued)

TABLE 11–1 (Continued)

Assets

	CURRENT YEAR	PRIOR YEAR
Endowment and Similar Funds		
Cash	100,000	101,000
Investments	13,900,000	11,800,000
Total endowment and similar funds	14,000,000	11,901,000
Annuity and Life Income Funds		
Annuity funds:		
Cash	55,000	45,000
Investments	3,260,000	3,010,000
Total annuity funds	3,315,000	3,055,000
Life income funds:		
Cash	15,000	15,000
Investments	2,045,000	1,740,000
Total life income funds	2,060,000	1,755,000
Total annuity and life income funds	5,375,000	4,810,000
Plant Funds		
Unexpended:		
Cash	275,000	410,000
Investments	1,285,000	1,590,000
Due from unrestricted current funds	150,000	120,000
Total unexpended	1,710,000	2,120,000

Liabilities and Fund Balances

	CURRENT YEAR	PRIOR YEAR
Endowment and Similar Funds		
Fund balances:		
Endowment	7,800,000	6,740,000
Term endowment	3,840,000	3,420,000
Quasi-endowment—unrestricted	1,000,000	800,000
Quasi-endowment—restricted	1,360,000	941,000
Total endowment and similar funds	14,000,000	11,901,000
Annuity and Life Income Funds		
Annuity funds:		
Annuities payable	2,150,000	2,300,000
Fund balances	1,165,000	755,000
Total annuity funds	3,315,000	3,055,000
Life income funds:		
Income payable	5,000	5,000
Fund balances	2,055,000	1,750,000
Total life income funds	2,060,000	1,755,000
Total annuity and life income funds	5,375,000	4,810,000
Plant Funds		
Unexpended:		
Accounts payable	10,000	—
Notes payable	100,000	—
Bonds payable	400,000	—
Fund balances		
Restricted	1,000,000	1,860,000
Unrestricted	200,000	260,000
Total unexpended	1,710,000	2,120,000

Plant Funds and Agency Funds — Assets

Renewals and replacements:		
Cash	5,000	4,000
Investments	150,000	286,000
Deposits with trustees	100,000	90,000
Due from unrestricted current funds	5,000	—
Total renewals and replacements	260,000	380,000
Retirement of indebtedness:		
Cash	50,000	40,000
Deposits with trustees	250,000	253,000
Total retirement of indebtedness	300,000	293,000
Investment in plant:		
Land	500,000	500,000
Improvements other than buildings (net of accumulated depreciation of $77,500 and $52,500)	975,000	1,110,000
Buildings (net of accumulated depreciation of $15,300,000 and $13,300,000)	24,000,000	24,060,000
Equipment (net of accumulated depreciation of $7,450,000 and $6,450,000)	14,000,000	14,200,000
Library books	100,000	80,000
Total investment in plant	39,575,000	39,950,000
Total plant funds	41,845,000	42,743,000
Agency Funds		
Cash	50,000	70,000
Investments	60,000	20,000
Total agency funds	110,000	90,000

Plant Funds and Agency Funds — Liabilities and Fund Balances

Renewals and replacements:		
Fund balances		
Restricted	25,000	180,000
Unrestricted	235,000	200,000
Total renewals and replacements	260,000	380,000
Retirement of indebtedness:		
Fund balances		
Restricted	185,000	125,000
Unrestricted	115,000	168,000
Total retirement of indebtedness	300,000	293,000
Investment in plant:		
Notes payable	790,000	810,000
Bonds payable	2,200,000	2,400,000
Mortgages payable	400,000	200,000
Net investment in plant	36,185,000	36,540,000
Total investment in plant	39,575,000	39,950,000
Total plant funds	41,845,000	42,743,000
Agency Funds		
Deposits held in custody for others	110,000	90,000
Total agency funds	110,000	90,000

Accompanying Summary of Significant Accounting Policies and Notes to Financial Statements not included.

Source: Adapted from *Financial Accounting and Reporting Manual for Higher Education*, para. 606, by permission of the National Association of College and University Business officers.

TABLE 11–2

Governmental University
Statement of Changes in Fund Balances
Year Ended June 30, 19X1

	Current Funds UNRESTRICTED	Current Funds RESTRICTED	LOAN FUNDS	ENDOWMENT AND SIMILAR FUNDS	ANNUITY AND LIFE INCOME FUNDS	Plant Funds UNEXPENDED	Plant Funds RENEWALS AND REPLACEMENTS	Plant Funds RETIREMENT OF INDEBTEDNESS	Plant Funds INVESTMENT IN PLANT
Revenues and Other Additions									
Unrestricted current fund revenues	$7,540,000								
Expired term endowment—restricted						50,000			
State appropriations—restricted						50,000			
Federal grants and contracts—restricted		500,000							
Private gifts, grants and contracts—restricted		370,000	100,000	1,500,000	800,000	115,000		65,000	15,000
Investment income—restricted		224,000	12,000	10,000		5,000	5,000	5,000	
Realized gains on investments—unrestricted				109,000					
Realized gains on investments—restricted			4,000	50,000		10,000	5,000	5,000	
Interest on loans receivable			7,000						
U.S. government advances			18,000						
Expended for plant facilities (including $100,000 charged to current funds expenditures)									2,550,000
Retirement of indebtedness									220,000
Accrued interest on sale of bonds									
Matured annuity and life income restricted to endowment				10,000				3,000	
Total revenues and other additions	7,540,000	1,094,000	141,000	1,679,000	800,000	230,000	10,000	78,000	2,785,000
Expenditures and Other Deductions									
Educational and general expenditures	4,400,000	1,014,000							

Auxiliary enterprises expenditures	1,830,000								
Indirect costs recovered		35,000							
Refunded to grantors		20,000	10,000						
Loan cancellations and write-offs			1,000						
Administrative and collection costs			1,000					1,000	
Adjustments of actuarial liability for annuities payable					75,000				
Expended for plant facilities (including noncapitalized expeditures of $50,000)						1,200,000	300,000	220,000	
Retirement of indebtedness								190,000	
Interest of indebtedness									115,000
Disposal of plant facilities									3,025,000
Provision for depreciation									
Expired term endowments ($40,000 unrestricted, $50,000 restricted to plant)				90,000					
Matured annuity and life income funds restricted to endowment					10,000				
Total expenditures and other deductions	6,230,000	1,069,000	12,000	90,000	85,000	1,200,000	300,000	411,000	3,140,000
Transfers Among Funds—Additions (Deductions)									
Mandatory:	(340,000)							340,000	
Principle and interest	(170,000)						170,000		
Renewals and replacements	(2,000)		2,000						
Loan fund matching grant	(650,000)		50,000	550,000		50,000			
Unrestricted gifts allocated									
Portion of unrestricted quasi-endowment funds investment gains appropriated	40,000			(40,000)					
Total transfers	(1,122,000)		52,000	510,000		50,000	170,000	340,000	
Net increase/(decrease) for the year	188,000	25,000	181,000	2,099,000	715,000	(920,000)	(120,000)	7,000	(355,000)
Fund balance at beginning of year	455,000	421,000	502,000	11,901,000	2,505,000	2,120,000	380,000	293,000	36,540,000
Fund balance at end of year	643,000	446,000	683,000	14,000,000	3,220,000	1,200,000	260,000	300,000	36,185,000

Accompanying Summary of Significant Accounting Polices and Notes fo Financial Statements not included.

Source: Adapted from *Financial Accounting and Reporting Manual for Higher Education*, para. 611, by permission of the National Association of College and University Business Officers.

monly used, has the advantage of saving space. In addition, it enables the user to see the "big picture" at one glance. This, of course, is the same reason used to justify the use of combined financial statements by municipalities. Unlike the accounts shown in the combined balance sheets of municipalities, however, the accounts of the various funds shown in the balance sheet of a college or university are not totaled, even in memorandum form.

To provide adequate disclosure, activities of all separately incorporated, but related, units or self-supporting auxiliary enterprises for which the institution is responsible (e.g., university presses, research organizations, agricultural units, etc.) should be (1) included in the basic financial statements of the institution or (2) presented in separate financial statements cross-referenced to the basic financial statements of the institution. At the very minimum, they should be adequately disclosed in the notes to the financial statements.

The second statement, the **statement of changes in fund balances,** informs users of activities that caused the balances of each fund to change. It shows all additions to, deductions from, and transfers between the various funds. All funds used by the institution are shown on this statement except for one type: Agency Funds. Agency Funds used by colleges and universities, like the ones used in municipal accounting, have no fund balances. Their assets must always equal their liabilities. Therefore they would be out of place on a statement of changes in fund balances. An example of a statement of changes in fund balances is shown in Table 11–2. While this information is generally presented in columnar fashion in a single statement, separate statements are permissible for each fund group. As was true of the balance sheet, the columns of the statement of changes in fund balances should not be cross-footed (added), as the totals are likely to be misleading.

The **statement of current funds revenues, expenditures, and other changes** is one that is unique to governmental colleges and universities. It reports on activities of the **Current Funds.** It presents the revenues, by source, and the expenditures, by function, of the Current Funds. It also presents all the other changes that take place within these funds. While similar in form and content to an income or operating statement, it does not purport to show net income or results of operations of the Current Funds. Rather, its purpose is to inform the reader of details of sources and uses of Current Funds and to allow the institution to report the total of Restricted and Unrestricted Current Funds expended for each functional category.

The net changes in fund balances represented on the statement of current funds revenues, expenditures, and other changes should be the same as the changes in Current Funds shown on the statement of changes in fund balances. An example of a statement of current funds revenues, expenditures, and other changes is shown in Table 11–3. Notice that only activities of Current Funds are reported on this statement. This is because these funds are the only **operational-type** funds used by colleges and universities. The other funds used by these institutions are generally fiduciary in nature or are used to record activities included

TABLE 11-3

Governmental University
Statement of Current Funds Revenues, Expenditures, and Other Changes
Year Ended June 30, 19X1

| | Current Year | | | PRIOR |
	UNRESTRICTED	RESTRICTED	TOTAL	YEAR TOTAL
Revenues				
Tuition and fees	$2,600,000		$2,600,000	$2,300,000
Federal appropriations	500,000		500,000	500,000
State appropriations	700,000		700,000	700,000
Local appropriations	100,000		100,000	100,000
Federal grants and contracts	20,000	$ 375,000	395, 000	350,000
State grants and contracts	10,000	25,000	35,000	200,000
Local grants and contracts	5,000	25,000	30,000	45,000
Private gifts, grants, and contracts	850,000	380,000	1,230,000	1,190,000
Endowment income	325,000	209,000	534,000	500,000
Sales and services of educational activities	190,000		190,000	195,000
Sales and services of auxiliary enterprises	2,200,000		2,200,000	2,100,000
Expired term endowment	40,000		40,000	
Other sources (if any)				
Total current revenues	7,540,000	1,014,000	8,554,000	8,180,000
Expenditures and mandatory Transfers				
Educational and general:				
Instruction	2,960,000	489,000	3,449,000	3,300,000
Research	100,000	400,000	500,000	650,000
Public service	130,000	25,000	155,000	175,000
Academic support	250,000		250,000	225,000
Student services	200,000		200,000	195,000
Institutional support	450,000		450,000	445,000
Operation and maintenance of plant	220,000		220,000	200,000
Scholarships and fellowships	90,000	100,000	190,000	180,000
Educational and general expenditures	4,400,000	1,014,000	5,414,000	5,370,000
Mandatory transfers for:				
Principal and interest	90,000		90,000	50,000
Renewals and replacements	100,000		100,000	80,000
Loan fund matching grant	2,000		2,000	
Total educational and general	4,592,000	1,014,000	5,606,000	5,500,000

(continued)

TABLE 11–3 (Continued)

| | Current Year | | | PRIOR |
	UNRESTRICTED	RESTRICTED	TOTAL	YEAR TOTAL
Auxiliary enterprises:				
Expenditures	1,830,000		1,830,000	1, 730,000
Mandatory transfers for:				
Principal and interest	250,000		250,000	250,000
Renewals and				
replacements	70,000		70,000	70,000
Total auxiliary				
enterprises	2,150,000		2,150,000	2,050,000
Total expenditures				
and mandatory				
transfers	6,742,000	1,014,000	7,756,000	7,550,000
Other Transfers and				
Additions/(Deductions)				
Excess of restricted				
receipts over transfers				
to revenues		45,000	45,000	40,000
Refunded to grantors		(20,000)	(20,000)	
Unrestricted gifts				
allocated to other funds	(650,000)		(650,000)	(510,000)
Portion of quasi-				
endowment gains				
appropriated	40,000		40,000	
Net increase in fund				
balances	$ 188,000	$ 25,000	$ 213,000	$ 160,000

Accompanying Summary of Significant Accounting Polices and Notes to Financial Statements not included.

Source: Adapted from *Financial Accounting and Reporting Manual for Higher Education,* para. 621, by permission of the National Association of College and University Business Officers.

in the purchase, financing, and disposition of plant assets and endowment and loan-type activities of the institutions.

Private Colleges and Universities

Under *SFAS No. 117,* financial statements prepared by not-for-profit organizations "shall include a statement of financial position as of the end of the reporting period, a statement of activities and a statement of cash flows for the reporting period, and accompanying notes to financial statements."[14] A statement of financial position is similar to a balance sheet while a statement of activities is comparable to an operating statement. Financial statements must be for the entire entity and net assets, revenues and expenses, and gains and losses of the reporting institution must be separately reported, on the statement of financial position and

[14]FASB *Statement No. 117,* para. 6.

the statement of activities, by type of restriction—permanently restricted, temporarily restricted, and unrestricted. *SFAS No. 117* describes reporting formats, but it does not state how the elements of each statement should be valued.

The main focus of statements prepared under *SFAS No. 117* is the institution as a whole. Instead of a fund-by-fund report, *SFAS No. 117* uses a homogenous group concept. That is, financial statement elements are aggregated into similar groups. Examples of these groups include cash and cash equivalents, accounts receivable, marketable securities, and land, buildings, and equipment. Assets with donor-imposed restrictions must be reported separately from unrestricted assets of a similar nature.

An example of a **Statement of Financial Position** is shown in Table 11–4. Notice first that the balances in each fund have been combined (or aggregated) and that all assets and all liabilities are shown together, in a manner similar to balance sheets produced by commercial enterprises. This gives a better picture of the institution as a whole and makes the statement easier to read, especially to readers who are only familiar with financial statements of commercial organizations.

Notice also that the term *net assets* is used to describe the equity of the institution and that net assets are divided into unrestricted, temporarily restricted, and permanently restricted components. Notes B and C (not illustrated) would provide specific information on the nature of the restrictions as to programs, length of restrictions, and assets restricted. Note A, of course, would discuss required accounting policy disclosures.

Notice finally that assets and liabilities are listed on the basis of their relative liquidity. Thus, cash and contributions receivable that are restricted by their donors to the acquisition of buildings and equipment are reported as Assets restricted to investment in plant and equipment rather than simply as Cash or Contributions receivable, and are shown just above Property, plant, and equipment. In addition, cash and cash equivalents of Endowment Funds, which are currently awaiting reinvestment in long-term investments, are shown as Long-term investments.

The **statement of activities** is the basic operating statement of a private college or university. Its primary purpose is "to provide relevant information about (a) the effects of transactions and other events and circumstances that change the amount and nature of net assets, (b) the relationships of those transactions and other events and circumstances to each other, and (c) how the organization's resources are used in providing various programs and services."[15] Like the statement of financial position, this statement should focus on the institution as a whole, and the change in net assets shown should articulate to the net assets reported in the other statements.

A statement of activities is illustrated in Table 11–5. Notice that revenues and gains are reported as increases in net assets while expenses and losses are

---

[15]Ibid., para. 17.

TABLE 11–4

Private University
Statements of Financial Position
June 30, 19X1 and 19X0

	19X1	19X0
Assets		
Cash and cash equivalents	$ 600,000	$ 360,000
Tuition and interest receivable		
Less: allowance of $20,000 in both years	240,000	265,000
Inventories and prepaid expenses	80,000	100,000
Contributions receivable	100,000	75, 000
Short-term investments	75,000	105,000
Assets restricted to investment in plant and equipment	125,000	150, 000
Property, plant, and equipment (net)	56,000,000	58,000,000
Long-term investments	1,500,000	1,200,000
Total assets	$58,720,000	$60,255,000
Liabilities and Net Assets		
Liabilities:		
Accounts payable	$ 850,000	$ 600,000
Accrued liabilities	150,000	200,000
Advances from federal government	1,000,000	800,000
Deposits held for others	200,000	300,000
Annuities payable	1,500,000	1,200,000
Notes payable	750,000	500,000
Bonds payable	3,000,000	6,500,000
Total liabilities	7,450,000	10,100,000
Net assets:		
Unrestricted	27,650,000	26,985,000
Temporarily restricted (Note B)	8,250,000	8,750,000
Permanently restricted (Note C)	15,370,000	14,420,000
Total net assets	51,270,000	50,155,000
Total liabilities and net assets	$58,720,000	$60,255,000

Accompanying Summary of Significant Accounting Policies and Notes to Financial Statements not included.

treated as decreases in net assets. Notice also that net assets are shown by type of restriction and increases and decreases are netted at the bottom of the statement and added to the total net assets at the beginning of the year, to determine net assets at the end of the year.

Several different formats are permissible for the statement of activities. The format shown in Table 11–5 is in a columnar format, with a column for each type of restriction and a total column. The advantage of this format is that it makes possible the presentation of aggregated information about contributions and investment income for the entity as a whole, and it shows the effect of expirations of donor restrictions.

The **statement of cash flows** provides relevant information about cash re-

TABLE 11–5

Private University
Statement of Activities
Year Ended June 30, 19X1

	UNRESTRICTED	TEMPORARILY RESTRICTED	PERMANENTLY RESTRICTED	TOTAL
Operating Revenues, Gains, and Other Support				
Tuition and fees	$ 6,200,000			$ 6,200,000
Federal grants	350,000			350,000
Contributions	800,000	$ 50,000	$ 290,000	1,140,000
Auxiliary enterprises	500,000			500,000
Income from endowment	2,000,000			2,000,000
Realized gains on long-term investments	50,000	75,000	60,000	185,000
Net assets released from restrictions (Note D):				
Meeting of program restrictions	60,000	(60,000)		
Expiration of time restrictions	25,000	(25,000)		
Total operating revenues and gains	9,985,000	40,000	350,000	10,375,000
Operating Expenses				
Educational and general:				
Instruction	4,100,000			4,100,000
Research support	1,600,000			1,600,000
Academic support	2,400,000			2,400,000
Institutional support	1,400,000			1,400,000
Maintenance and operation of plant	1,250,000			1,250,000
Total educational and general	10,750,000			10,750,000
Auxiliary enterprises	385,000			385,000
Payment on annuity and Life Income Funds	45,000			45,000
Total operating expenses	11,180,000			11,180,000
Excess operating revenues and gains over operating expenses	(1,195,000)	40,000	350,000	(805,000)
Nonoperating Items				
Private gifts and grants	1,750,000	75,000		1,825,000
Income on investments	95,000			95,000
Reclassified net assets		(600,000)	600,000	
Matured Life Income Funds	15,000	(15,000)		
Changes in net assets due to nonoperating items	1,860,000	(540,000)	600,000	1,920,000
Changes in total net assets	665,000	(500,000)	950,000	1,115,000
Net assets at beginning of year	26,985,000	8,750,000	14,420,000	50,155,000
Net assets at end of year	$27,650,000	$8,250,000	$15,370,000	$51,270,000

Accompanying Summary of Significant Accounting Policies and Notes to Financial Statements not included.

TABLE 11–6

Private University
Statement of Cash Flows
Year Ended June 30, 19X1

Cash Flows from Operating Activities	
Increase in net assets	$1,115,000
Adjustments to reconcile change in net assets to net cash provided by operating activities:	
Depreciation	2,000,000
Decrease in tuition and interest receivable	25,000
Decrease in inventories	20,000
Increase in pledges receivable	(25,000)
Decrease in short-term investments	30,000
Increase in accounts payable	250,000
Decrease in accrued liabilities	(50,000)
Increase in advances from federal government	200,000
Decrease in deposits held for others	(100,000)
Increase in annuities payable	300,000
Capital gains used	(50,000)
Net cash provided by operating activities	3,715,000
Cash Flows from Investing Activities	
Proceeds from sale of investments	785,000
Purchase of investments	(900,000)
Net cash used for investing activities	(115,000)
Cash Flows from Financing Activities	
Decrease in restricted assets	25,000
Increase in notes payable	250,000
Decrease in bonds payable	(3,500,000)
Capital gains restricted for reinvestment	(135,000)
Net cash used for financing activities	(3,360,000)
Net increase in cash and cash equivalents	240,000
Cash and cash equivalents at beginning of year	360,000
Cash and cash equivalents at end of year	$ 600,000

Accompanying Summary of Significant Accounting Policies and Notes to Financial Statements not included.

ceipts and cash payments of an institution during the period. *SFAS No. 117* permits the use of the direct and the indirect method. A statement using the direct method is presented in Table 11–6. Notice the tie-in to the cash and cash equivalents shown on the statement of financial position.

REVIEW QUESTIONS

Q11–1   Name four ways in which accounting for colleges and universities is different from accounting for state and local governmental units.

Q11–2   List the types of funds used by colleges and universities and describe the purpose of each.

Q11–3   What determines whether a fund is restricted or unrestricted?

Q11–4   Why are the Current Funds the only funds used by colleges and universities to record expenses?

Q11–5   When should contributions to Restricted Current Funds be recognized as revenues?

Q11–6   Why is depreciation on fixed assets not shown by the Current Operating Funds? Why is it shown among the fixed assets of the Endowment Funds?

Q11–7   How should the services performed by religious personnel of church-related schools be valued?

Q11–8   What is the difference between *restricted* and *unrestricted* assets?

Q11–9   How does the budgetary accounting used by colleges and universities differ from that used by state and local governmental units?

Q11–10   What is the most authoritative source of information on the accounting methods and procedures that should be used by colleges and universities?

Q11–11   Describe the controversy surrounding depreciation for colleges and universities. Do you think these institutions should be required to depreciate their fixed assets? Why?

Q11–12   List the financial statements that must be prepared by (1) governmental colleges and universities and (2) private colleges and universities.

Q11–13   The Dhogg Foundation made a donation of $50,000 to Khatt University, to be used to equip a psychology laboratory. The money is expected to be spent the following year. How should this donation be recorded if Khatt University is a public university? A private university?

EXERCISES

E11–1   (Unrestricted Current Funds)
During the year, the following transactions were recorded in the Unrestricted Current Fund of Shorthorn University:
1. Revenues from tuition and fees amounted to $1.5 million, all of which had been collected by year-end.
2. Revenues of the auxiliary enterprises amounted to $500,000 cash.
3. Materials and supplies used during the year amounted to $700,000, of which $400,000 was chargeable to educational activities and $300,000 was chargeable to the auxiliary enterprises.
4. Salaries and wages amounted to $1 million. Of this amount, $800,000 was chargeable to educational activities and $200,000 was chargeable to auxiliary activities.
5. A transfer of $100,000 was made to the Fund for the Retirement of

Indebtedness to pay part of the principal and interest due on certain outstanding mortgages.

REQUIRED: 1. Prepare journal entries to record the above transactions in the Unrestricted Current Fund.
            2. Prepare the journal entry or entries necessary to close out the revenue, expenditure, and transfer accounts at year-end.

E11–2 (Loan Funds)

In 19X1, the J. Urbington Banks Foundation donated $300,000 to Friendly State University to be used exclusively for student loans. During the year, loans amounting to $200,000 were made. The remaining monies in the fund were invested and, at the end of the year, $10,000 in interest (cash) had been received. In addition, $50,000 was repaid by the students, along with $3,000 in interest. At the end of the year, the Student Loan Fund issued a check for $1,000 to the Unrestricted Current Fund to cover certain administrative costs of processing loans.

REQUIRED: Prepare the appropriate journal entries in the Student Loan Fund necessary to record the above transactions.

E11–3 (Plant Funds)

In 19X1, Sunshine State University received a donation of $5 million to be used to build a new library. During the year, construction of the library was started; by the end of the year, it was one-third complete. Costs incurred up to this point amounted to $2 million, all paid in cash. In September 19X2, the library was completed. The actual cost of the structure was $4.8 million. The remainder of the donation was transferred to the Unrestricted Current Fund. Depreciation on the library in 19X2 amounted to $30,000.

REQUIRED: Prepare the journal entries in the Plant Funds and in the Unrestricted Current Fund necessary to record the above events. How would your entries differ if Sunshine had been a private university?

E11–4 (Multiple choice)

1. Which of the following should be used in accounting for not-for-profit colleges and universities?
    a. Fund accounting and accrual accounting
    b. Fund accounting but *not* accrual accounting
    c. Accrual accounting but *not* fund accounting
    d. Neither accrual accounting nor fund accounting
2. Which of the following receipts is properly recorded in a university's Restricted Current Fund?
    a. Tuition
    b. Student laboratory fees

    c. Housing fees

    d. Research grants

3. In the Loan Fund of a college or university, each of the following types of loans would be found except

    a. Student

    b. Staff

    c. Building

    d. Faculty

4. Which of the following is utilized for current expenditures by a not-for-profit university?

	UNRESTRICTED CURRENT FUND	RESTRICTED CURRENT FUND
a.	No	No
b.	No	Yes
c.	Yes	No
d.	Yes	Yes

5. For the summer session of 19X1, Cajun University assessed its students $1,700,000 (net of refunds), covering tuition and fees for educational and general purposes. However, only $1,500,000 was expected to be realized because scholarships totaling $150,000 were granted to students, and tuition remissions of $50,000 were allowed to faculty members' children attending Cajun. What amount should Cajun include in its Unrestricted Current Fund as revenues from student tuition and fees?

    a. $1,500,000

    b. $1,550,000

    c. $1,650,000

    d. $1,700,000

(AICPA adapted)

6. On January 2, 19X1, John Reynolds established a $500,000 trust, the income from which is to be paid to Mansfield University for general operating purposes. The Wyndham National Bank was appointed by Reynolds as trustee of the fund. What journal entry is required on Mansfield's books?

		DEBITS	CREDITS
a.	Memorandum entry only		
b.	Cash	$500,000	
	Endowment Fund balance		$500,000
c.	Nonexpendable Endowment Fund	$500,000	
	Endowment Fund balance		$500,000
d.	Expendable Funds	$500,000	
	Endowment Fund balance		$500,000

(AICPA adapted)

7. Beehive College is sponsored by a religious group. Volunteers from this religious group regularly contribute their services to Beehive and are paid nominal amounts to cover their commuting costs. During 19X1, the total amount paid to these volunteers aggregated $12,000. The gross value of services performed by them, determined by reference to lay-equivalent salaries, amounted to $300,000. What amount should Beehive record as expenditures in 19X1 for these volunteers' services?
    a. $312,000
    b. $300,000
    c. $12,000
    d. $-0-

    (AICPA adapted)

8. Tuition waivers for which there is no intention of collection from students should be classified by a not-for-profit university as

	REVENUE	EXPENDITURES
a.	No	No
b.	No	Yes
c.	Yes	Yes
d.	Yes	No

    (AICPA adapted)

9. The following expenditures were among those incurred by Alum University during 19X1:

Administrative data processing	$ 50,000
Scholarships and fellowships	100,000
Operation and maintenance of physical plant	200,000

    The amount to be included in the functional classification "Institutional support" expenditures account is
    a. $50,000
    b. $150,000
    c. $250,000
    d. $350,000

    (AICPA adapted)

10. The following receipts were among those recorded by Glen Mills State College during 19X1:

Unrestricted gifts	$500,000
Restricted Current Funds (expended for current operating purposes)	200,000
Restricted Current Funds (not yet expended)	100,000

The amount that should be included in Current Funds revenues is
a. $800,000
b. $700,000
c. $600,000
d. $500,000

E11–5 (Plant renovations)

The board of trustees of Bayou College approved plans to renovate the library. The following transactions relate to this project:

1. To help finance the project, a mortgage of $1 million was secured.
2. A transfer of $200,000 was made from the Restricted Current Fund to cover the remaining costs of the project.
3. The project was completed, before the end of the year, at a total cost of $1.1 million. Upon completion, the project was transferred to the Investment in Plant Fund, along with the accompanying mortgage.
4. The unspent monies were transferred to the Unrestricted Current Fund.
5. Before the close of the year, $75,000 was transferred from an Endowment Fund to assist in the repayment of the mortgage and in the payment of interest on that debt.
6. The current installment of the mortgage, $50,000, was paid before the close of the year.

REQUIRED: Prepare the journal entries necessary to record the above transactions in the appropriate Plant Funds. In the margin of each entry, state which fund is being used to record that particular transaction.

PROBLEMS

P11–1 (Current Funds)

In 19X1 the legislature of the state of Texiana granted a charter to Southeast Texiana State College along with the right to use a sizable piece of land "in perpetuity." During the year, the following transactions took place:

1. Unrestricted revenues received were as follows:

Student tuition and fees	$2,800,000
Unrestricted gifts and grants	500,000
Governmental appropriations	1,000,000
Revenues from auxiliary enterprises	300,000
Other revenues	200,000
	$4,800,000

2. The Association of Anonymous Used Car Dealers contributed $100,000 to the college, with the stipulation that these monies be used to equip a laboratory to study consumer behavior.

3. Of the student tuition and fees assessed, $2,750,000 was collected. It was estimated that $30,000 would never be collected.
4. Materials costing $1 million were purchased on account and placed in inventory during the year.
5. Expenditures recorded in the Unrestricted Current Fund were:

Educational		
Materials	$ 200,000	
Salaries	1,500,000	
Other expenses	200,000	$1,900,000
Administrative and Student Services		
Materials	100,000	
Salaries	200,000	
Other	50,000	350,000
Library		
Books	500,000	
Materials	100,000	
Salaries	70,000	
Other	30,000	700,000
Plant Operations		
Rental of temporary buildings	200,000	
Wages and salaries	100,000	
Materials	400,000	
Other	100,000	800,000
Auxiliary Enterprises		
Wages and salaries	50,000	
Operating supplies	30,000	
Other	20,000	100,000
Total unrestricted expenditures		$3,850,000

6. During the year, $900,000 was paid to the vendors who supplied materials.
7. A mandatory transfer of $500,000 was made to the Plant Fund to start construction of a classroom building.
8. Grants of $50,000 and $30,000 were awarded to Dr. Hal Lynch and Dr. Jan Martinek, respectively, to assist with their research into causes of buyer resistance. Both awards were used up by the end of the year.
9. At the end of the year, a transfer of $47,000 was received from the Endowment Fund. The original donor of these monies requested they be used for faculty travel.

REQUIRED: 1. Prepare journal entries to record the above transactions in the appropriate Current Fund.
            2. Prepare a balance sheet, a statement of changes in fund balances, and

a statement of current funds revenues, expenditures, and other changes.

P11–2   (Loan, Endowment, and Annuity Funds)

During its first year of operations, Southeast Texiana State College had the following transactions, which should be recorded in its Loan Funds, Endowment and Similar Funds, and/or its Annuity and Life Income Funds.

1. Dr. Phyllis Copeland donated $100,000 to the college to be used for student loans. Of this amount, $50,000 was invested in preferred stock.

2. The descendants of a former student donated $500,000 to the college to establish an Endowment Fund. The earnings of the fund were to be used for faculty travel. The money was invested in government securities, purchased at par value.

3. Securities worth $100,000 were donated to the Endowment Fund by the Wolf Mann family.

4. The Moriarity family donated $200,000 to the college to be used to set up an Annuity Fund. These monies were promptly invested. Any earnings on these monies, up to $10,000, were to be sent to Mr. S. Holmes at the end of each year. Any excess earnings were to be transferred to the Unrestricted Current Fund.

5. During the year, loans amounting to $45,000 were made to needy students. All loans were expected to be repaid.

6. During the year, the Endowment Fund earned $50,000 of interest on its investments. Of this amount, $45,000 was received in cash. The remaining amount will be received shortly after the end of the fiscal year.

7. While testing a used car, one student had an unfortunate accident. His loan, amounting to $2,000, was written off as uncollectible.

8. Some securities were sold by the Endowment Fund at a profit of $2,000. This amount was transferred to a Restricted Current Fund, along with the $45,000 of interest received in number 6.

9. Earnings on investments of the Annuity Fund amounted to $15,000. Of this amount, all of which had been received in cash by year-end, $10,000 was paid to Mr. S. Holmes and $5,000 was transferred to the Unrestricted Current Fund.

10. During the year, student loans amounting to $10,000 were repaid, along with accrued interest of $500. As of the end of the year, interest accrued on loans still outstanding was $2,000. This amount will be collected when the loans are repaid. In addition, on the last day of the fiscal year, the college received a check for $3,000, representing the annual dividend on the preferred stock.

REQUIRED: 1. Prepare journal entries to record the transactions listed above. Indicate which fund or funds are affected by each transaction.
2. Prepare a balance sheet and a statement of changes in fund balances for the Loan Fund, the Endowment and Similar Funds, and the Annuity Fund.

✗ P11–3 (Plant Funds)

During the fiscal year 19X1, the following activities took place on the campus of Southeast Texiana State College; a new institution located somewhere in Texiana.

1. The citizens of Texiana donated $200,000 to the college, to be used for a classroom building and a laboratory building.
2. A mortgage of $3 million was taken out on the classroom building.
3. Construction of the classroom building was completed during the year at a cost of $3.5 million. The building and its accompanying mortgage were transferred to the appropriate subgroup.
4. Dr. Frank N. Burger donated $500,000 to the college, to be used to pay the interest on and principal of the mortgage. The money was immediately invested in government securities.
5. At the end of the year, the laboratory building was one-half complete. Costs incurred to date were $100,000.
6. A gift of $100,000 was presented to the Plant Fund by Melissa Parker. Ms. Parker expressly stated that the monies should be used for the purchase of equipment. Her wish was immediately carried out by means of an $80,000 purchase of classroom equipment.
7. Government securities, purchased for $200,000 with part of Dr. Frank N. Burger's donation, were sold for $220,000. In addition, interest of $40,000 was earned and collected on these *and* the unsold securities. The entire amount was paid to the First National Bank of Monroe, the holder of the mortgage. Of this amount, $60,000 was for interest and $200,000 was for the repayment of principal.
8. An uninsured piece of laboratory equipment, costing $1,000 and financed by the Plant Fund, was destroyed.
9. Depreciation on the classroom building amounted to $250,000 in 19X1.

REQUIRED: 1. Prepare ~~appropriate~~ journal entries to record the above transactions.
2. ~~Prepare a combined balance sheet and a statement of changes in fund balances for the Plant Funds, as of the end of the fiscal year.~~

In the appropriate sub groups.

P11–4 (Problem from Uniform Certified Public Accountant Examination on journal entries for Current Funds)

A partial balance sheet of Rapapo State University, as of the end of its fiscal year ended July 31, 19X1, is presented on the next page:

RAPAPO STATE UNIVERSITY
CURRENT FUNDS BALANCE SHEET
JULY 31, 19X1

Assets	
Unrestricted:	$200,000
Cash	
Accounts receivable—tuition and fees, less allowance	
for doubtful accounts of $15,000	360,000
Prepaid expenses	40,000
Total unrestricted	600,000
Restricted:	
Cash	10,000
Investments	210,000
Total restricted	220,000
Total current funds	$820,000
Liabilities and Fund Balances	
Unrestricted:	
Accounts payable	$100,000
Due to other funds	40,000
Deferred revenue—tuition	
and fees	25,000
Fund balance	435,000
Total unrestricted	600,000
Restricted:	
Accounts payable	5,000
Fund balance	215,000
Total restricted	220,000
Total current funds	$820,000

The following information pertains to the year ended July 31, 19X1:

1. Cash collected from students' tuition totaled $3,000,000. Of this amount, $362,000 represented accounts receivable outstanding at July 31, 19X0; $2,500,000 was for current-year tuition; and $138,000 was for tuition applicable to the semester beginning in August 19X1.

2. Deferred revenue at July 31, 19X0, was earned during the year ended July 31, 19X1.

3. Accounts receivable at July 31, 19X0, which were not collected during the year ended July 31, 19X1, were determined to be uncollectible and were written off against the allowance account. At July 31, 19X1, the allowance account was estimated at $10,000.

4. During the year, an unrestricted appropriation of $60,000 was

made by the state. This state appropriation was to be paid to Rapapo sometime in August 19X1.

5. During the year, unrestricted cash gifts of $80,000 were received from alumni. Rapapo's board of trustees allocated $30,000 of these gifts to the student loan fund.

6. During the year, investments costing $25,000 were sold for $31,000. Restricted fund investments were purchased at a cost of $40,000. Investment income of $18,000 was earned and collected during the year.

7. Unrestricted general expenses of $2,500,000 were recorded in the voucher system. At July 31, 19X1, the unrestricted accounts payable balance was $75,000.

8. The restricted accounts payable balance at July 31, 19X0, was paid.

9. The $40,000, due to other funds at July 31, 19X0, was paid to the Plant Fund as required.

10. One-quarter of the prepaid expenses at July 31, 19X0, expired during the current year and pertained to general educational expenses. There was no addition to prepaid expenses during the year.

REQUIRED: 1. Prepare journal entries in summary form to record the foregoing transactions for the year ended July 31, 19X1. Number each entry to correspond with the number indicated in the description of its respective transaction. Your answer sheet should be organized as follows:

| ENTRY | | Current Funds | | | |
| | | Unrestricted | | Restricted | |
NO.	ACCOUNTS	DEBIT	CREDIT	DEBIT	CREDIT

2. Prepare a statement of changes in fund balances for the year ended July 31, 19X1.

P11–5 (Financial statements of a private university)

Shown on p. 551 is a trial balance of Tulola University, a private institution.

During the year, the following adjustments were made to net assets:

1. Reclassified net assets of $200,000 from temporarily restricted to permanently restricted.

2. Released net assets of $50,000 from a temporary restriction because of the expiration of a time restriction.

REQUIRED: Prepare a statement of financial position and a statement of activities for Tulola University for 19X1.

Tulola University
Trial Balance
June 30, 19X1

	DEBITS	CREDITS
Cash and cash equivalents	$ 1,150,000	
Tuition and other accounts receivable	360,000	
Allowance for uncollectible accounts		$ 10,000
Inventories	50,000	
Assets restricted to investment in plant and equipment	440,000	
Property, plant and equipment (net)	17,500,000	
Long-term investments	9,800,000	
Accounts payable		$ 685,000
Advances from federal government		150,000
Annuities payable		580,000
Notes payable		1, 875,000
Bonds payable		12,000,000
Net assets (beginning):		
Unrestricted		8,100,000
Temporarily restricted		1,500,000
Permanently restricted		2,700,000
Tuition and fees		2,500,000
Federal grants		1,750,000
Auxiliary enterprise revenue		3,400,000
Income from endowments		200,000
Contributions:		
Unrestricted		100,000
Temporarily restricted		250,000
Permanently restricted		500,000
Private gifts:		
Unrestricted		250,000
Temporarily restricted		50,000
Income on investments—all unrestricted		500,000
Operating expenses:		
Instruction	2,800,000	
Research support	500,000	
Academic support	1,100,000	
Maintenance and operation of plant	900,000	
Auxiliary enterprises	2,500,000	
	$37,100,000	$37,100,000

12

ACCOUNTING FOR VOLUNTARY HEALTH AND WELFARE ORGANIZATIONS AND OTHER NOT-FOR-PROFIT ORGANIZATIONS

LEARNING OBJECTIVES

After completion of this chapter, you should be able to:

1. Distinguish between a voluntary health and welfare organization and an "other" not-for-profit organization
2. Identify the types of organizations included in the 78–10 category
3. List at least ten types of 78–10 organizations
4. Identify the sources of authority for accounting procedures used by voluntary health and welfare organizations and 78–10 organizations
5. List the funds used by voluntary health and welfare organizations and by 78–10 organizations
6. Name and discuss the financial statements used by voluntary health and welfare organizations and 78–10 organizations
7. Discuss the treatment of depreciation by voluntary health and welfare organizations and 78–10 organizations
8. Explain how grants and payments to affiliated organizations are handled
9. Prepare journal entries necessary to record the activities of a voluntary health and welfare organization and a 78–10 organization
10. Prepare financial statements for a voluntary health and welfare organization and a 78–10 organization

Voluntary health and welfare organizations (VHWOs) are nongovernmental organizations that receive voluntary contributions from the general public that are used for health, welfare, or community services. These organizations, which are also known as human service organizations, are operated on a not-for-profit basis and are exempt from many taxes.[1] Examples of VHWOs include the American Cancer Society, the Boy Scouts of America, the National Urban League, and the Young Women's Christian Association of the U.S.A. Accounting principles specifically related to these organizations are prescribed in *Audits of Voluntary Health and Welfare Organizations,* which is published by the American Institute of Certified Public Accounts.[2]

Other not-for-profit organizations (ONPOs) are those not-for-profit organizations which, until 1978, were not covered by existing audit guides. They include the following:

- Cemetary organizations
- Civic organizations
- Fraternal organizations
- Labor unions
- Libraries
- Museums
- Other cultural institutions
- Performing arts organizations
- Political parties
- Private and community foundations
- Private elementary and secondary schools
- Professional associations
- Public broadcasting stations
- Religious organizations
- Research and scientific organizations
- Social and country clubs
- Trade associations
- Zoological and botanical societies[3]

In 1978, the Accounting Standards Division of the American Institute of Certified Public Accountants (AICPA) issued *Statement of Position 78–10,* titled "Accounting Principles and Reporting Practices for Certain Nonprofit Organizations" (SOP 78–10). The purpose of this statement was to " . . . recommend financial accounting principles and reporting practices for nonprofit organizations not covered by exist-

[1]AICPA, *Audits of Voluntary Health and Welfare Organizations* (New York: AICPA, 1974), p. v.

[2]Other sources that are based on the audit guide and provide more detailed coverage are *Accounting & Financial Reporting: A Guide for United Ways and Not-for-Profit Human Service Organizations* published by the United Way of America; and *Standards of Accounting and Financial Reporting for Voluntary Health and Welfare Organizations* published by the National Health Council.

[3]AICPA, *Audits of Certain Nonprofit Organizations* (New York: AICPA, 1981), pp. 1–2. The *Audit Guide* indicates that this listing is not intended to be all-inclusive.

ing guides. . . . "[4] In 1981, the AICPA issued an audit and accounting guide, *Audits of Certain Nonprofit Organizations*. Together these two publications form the basis of those generally accepted accounting principles that are unique to not-for-profit organizations and for which there was previously no specific audit guide. These organizations are collectively referred to as **78–10 organizations** as well as ONPOs.

It should be noted that the Financial Accounting Standards Board has the final authority for determining accounting procedures used by the organizations discussed in this chapter. The audit guides for voluntary health and welfare organizations and "other" nonprofit organizations, and SOP 78–10 have been formally adopted by the FASB. Since then, FASB *Statement No. 116*, "Accounting for Contributions Received and Contributions Made," and FASB *Statement No. 117*, "Financial Statements of Not-for-Profit Organizations," have been issued, which modify the treatment of contributions received by and external financial reporting requirements of voluntary health and welfare organizations and 78–10 organizations.

FUNDS USED

Fund accounting is followed by voluntary health and welfare organizations and 78–10 organizations[5] because they normally have resources whose use is restricted as well as resources whose use is unrestricted. The funds generally used are the following:

1. **Current Unrestricted Fund** (or its equivalent). Included in this fund are unrestricted resources that are available for the general operations of the organization. The distinction between *restricted* and *unrestricted* is the same as that used for colleges and universities and hospitals; that is, restricted resources are those whose use is limited by outside third parties. Therefore, resources restricted in use by the governing board of an organization are included in the organization's Current Unrestricted Fund. Since land, buildings, and equipment are usually accounted for in a separate fund, the Current Unrestricted Fund is generally used to account for current assets that can be used in the operations of the organization at the discretion of its management.
2. **Current Restricted Funds** (or their equivalents). Included in these funds are resources available for use in the operations of an organization, as specified by a donor, a grantor, and so forth. Typical sources of these resources are restricted gifts and grants, restricted endowment income, and so on.
3. **Land, Building, and Equipment Fund** (or its equivalent). This fund is used to account for land, buildings, and equipment currently in use in the operations of the organization, together with any associated depreciation and long-term debt. In addition, it is used to account for resources whose use is restricted to the acquisition of land, buildings, or equipment.

While the funds identified above are generally used by all NFPOs, some of these organizations need "special" funds to allow for the unique characteristics

---

[4]AICPA, *Statements of Position of the Accounting Standards Division as of January 1, 1980* (New York: AICPA), para. 10,250.002.

[5]To simplify future references to voluntary health and welfare organizations and 78–10 organizations, they will collectively be referred to as "not-for-profit organizations" (NFPOs). Not-for-profit colleges and universities and hospitals are discussed in other chapters.

of their operating environment. Examples of such funds are Endowment Funds, Custodian (Agency) Funds, Loan Funds, Annuity Funds, and Strike Funds. Since these funds either are discussed in other chapters or have self-explanatory titles, we will not discuss them here.

FINANCIAL STATEMENTS

Due to the intangible nature of many of the services offered by NFPOs, it is practically impossible to place a monetary value on them. Thus it is impossible to prepare financial statements that can measure the results of operations in the same sense as those used for business enterprises. The basic functions of the financial reporting process for NFPOs are therefore limited to (1) providing information on how the resources of the organization were obtained and used during the period, (2) presenting the resources available for future use at the end of the period, and (3) reporting on the organization's ability to continue to supply services in the future.

The financial statements of NFPOs are prepared for four general types of users of financial information: (1) the management group of the organization (e.g., directors and other individuals who are responsible for carrying out day-to-day operations of the organization); (2) government officials who have oversight responsibility for such organizations; (3) individuals who contribute resources to the organization; and (4) constituents of the organization.[6]

To provide financial information to this diverse group, three basic financial statements are prepared by not-for-profit organizations. These are (1) a statement of financial position, (2) a statement of activities, and (3) a statement of cash flows.[7] In addition, voluntary health and welfare organizations prepare a statement of functional expenses, a statement that reports expenses by functional classifications and by natural classifications.[8]

Statement of Financial Position

A statement of financial position provides important information about the assets, liabilities, and net assets of the organization and their relationship to each other. This information, when used with information on other financial statements and related disclosures, helps interested parties to assess the organization's ability to continue operations and its liquidity, financial flexibility, ability to meet obligations, and future financing needs.[9] It focuses on *the organization as a whole*, as opposed to individual funds, and reports *total* assets, liabilities, and net assets. Notice that the term *net assets* is now used rather than the term *fund balance*, which was used in previous chapters.

[6]An in-depth discussion of these objectives and users is included in *Statement of Financial Accounting Concepts No. 4*, "Objectives of Financial Reporting by Nonbusiness Organizations" (Norwalk, CT: FASB, 1980).

[7]*FASB Statement No. 117*, "Financial Statements of Not-for-Profit Organizations" (Norwalk, CT: FASB, 1994), para. 6.

[8]Ibid., para. 2.

[9]Ibid., para. 9.

It appears that most not-for-profit organizations are continuing to use their existing fund structures to record transactions, for purposes of control and convenience. They then aggregate amounts in these funds that possess similar characteristics (e.g., cash and cash equivalents, marketable securities, and other investment assets held for long-term purposes, etc.) when they prepare financial statements. When aggregating assets, they do not classify ones with donor-imposed restrictions with ones that are unrestricted and currently available.

Under FASB *Statement No. 117*, net assets must be reported as permanently restricted, temporarily restricted, and unrestricted, depending on the existence and nature of **donor-imposed** restrictions. The existence and nature of these restrictions must be reported on the face of the statement of financial position or in the notes to the financial statements or both. **Permanently restricted net assets** are ones "resulting:

(a) from contributions and other inflows of assets whose use by the organization is limited by donor-imposed stipulations that neither expire by passage of time nor can be fulfilled or otherwise removed by actions of the organization,
(b) from other enhancements and diminishments subject to the same kinds of stipulations, and
(c) from reclassifications from (or to) other classes of net assets as a consequence of donor-imposed stipulations."[10]

Temporarily restricted net assets are net assets "resulting:

(a) from contributions and other inflows of assets whose use by the organization is limited by donor-imposed stipulations that either expire by passage of time or can be fulfilled and removed by actions of the organization pursuant to those stipulations,
(b) from other asset enhancements and diminishments subject to the same kinds of stipulations, and
(c) from reclassifications to (or from) other classes of net assets as a consequence of donor-imposed stipulations, their expiration by passage of time, or their fulfillment and removal by actions of the organization pursuant to those stipulations."[11]

Unrestricted net assets are ones that are neither permanently nor temporarily restricted. The only limits on their use are ones resulting from the nature of the organization and the environment in which it operates and contractual agreements with creditors, suppliers, and others entered into in the ordinary course of business. Information about such limits should be disclosed in the notes to the financial statements.

The statement of financial position of a typical not-for-profit organization is shown in Table 12–1. FASB *Statement No. 117* does not specify or preclude any one format. As a result, both vertical and horizontal formats are permitted, as are single and multicolumn and single and multipage formats. Notice that assets are presented in order of liquidity, while liabilities are presented in approximate order of expiration. The refundable advance shown on this statement refers to a

[10]Ibid., para. 168.
[11]Ibid.

TABLE 12–1

Not-for-Profit Organization
Statements of Financial Position
June 30, 19X1 and 19X0
(Expressed in Thousands)

	19X1	19X0
Assets		
Cash and cash equivalents	$ 75	$ 460
Accounts and interest receivable	2,130	1,670
Inventories and prepaid expenses	610	1,000
Contributions receivable	3,025	2,700
Short-term investments	1,400	1,000
Assets restricted to investment in land, buildings, and equipment	5,210	4,560
Land, buildings, and equipment	61,700	63,590
Long-term investments	218,070	203,500
Total assets	$292,220	$278,480
Liabilities and Net Assets		
Liabilities:		
Accounts payable	$ 2,570	$ 1,050
Refundable advance		650
Grants payable	875	1,300
Notes payable		1,140
Annuity obligations	1,685	1,700
Long-term debt	5,500	6,500
Total liabilities	10,630	12,340
Net assets:		
Unrestricted	115,228	103,670
Temporarily restricted (Note B)	24,342	25,470
Permanently restricted (Note C)	142,020	137,000
Total net assets	281,590	266,140
Total liabilities and net assets	$292,220	$278,480

Accompanying notes to financial statements not included.

Source: Adapted from *FASB Statement No. 117*, "Financial Statements of Not-for-Profit Organizations" (Norwalk, CT: FASB, 1994), para. 156.

donor's conditional promise to give, whose conditions have not been met. Net assets are presented by type and are disclosed in detail in the notes to the financial statements (not included in Table 12–1).

Statement of Activities

A statement of activities provides information "about

(a) the effects of transactions and other events and circumstances that change the amount and nature of net assets,

(b)   the relationships of those transactions and other events and circumstances to each other, and

(c)   how the organization's resources are used in providing various programs or services."[12]

Like the statement of financial position, it focuses on the organization *as a whole* and reports the change in net assets, by level of restriction, for the period. These changes should articulate with the changes in net assets in the statement of financial position.

A statement of activities can be prepared in a single column or a multi-column format. The latter is preferred because it enables the reader to observe, at a glance, the effects of revenues, gains, other support, expenses, and losses on each category of net assets. It also enables the reader to observe, at a glance, the effect on net assets of changes in levels of restrictions. A statement of activities prepared in a multicolumn format is shown in Table 12–2.

Expenses incurred by not-for-profit organizations must be reported on the statement of activities or in the notes to the financial statements "by their functional classification such as major classes of program services and supporting activities."[13] When functional classifications are used, individual expenses are reported by function or program. Thus, such items as salaries and supplies used by each program are reported as expenses of those activities. Functional classifications are required because they enable the reader to determine the cost of various programs offered by the organization. The organization's programs should also be described in the notes to the financial statements.

For financial reporting purposes, a **program** is considered to be an activity that is directly related to the purpose(s) for which the organization was established. While most organizations are involved in many programs, it is possible that an organization may have only one such activity.

Expenses identified as **management and general** are those associated with the overall direction and management of the organization, in addition to those associated with record-keeping, the annual report, and so forth. **Fund raising and other supporting services** expenses are ones associated with the solicitation of money, materials, and the like, for which the individual or organization making the contribution receives no direct economic benefit. They include such items as printing, personnel, the cost of maintaining a mailing list, and the cost of any gifts that are sent to prospective contributors.

Statement of Functional Expenses

Voluntary health and welfare organizations are required to prepare a statement of functional expenses. This statement identifies each program and support service, and the amount of each expense, on an object (by type) basis. It is prepared in a matrix format. A statement of functional expenses is shown in Table 12–3.

---

[12]Ibid., para. 17.
[13]FASB *Statement No. 117*, para. 26.

TABLE 12–2

Not-for-Profit Organization
Statement of Activities
Year Ended June 30, 19X1
(in thousands)

	UNRESTRICTED	TEMPORARILY RESTRICTED	PERMANENTLY RESTRICTED	TOTAL
Revenues, Gains, and Other Support				
Contributions	$ 8,640	$ 8,110	$ 280	$ 17,030
Fees	5,400			5,400
Income on long-term investments (Note E)	5,600	2,580	120	8,300
Other investment income (Note E)	850			850
Net unrealized and realized gains on long-term investments (Note E)	8,228	2,952	4,620	15,800
Other	150			150
Net assets released from restrictions (Note D):				
Satisfaction of program restrictions	11,990	(11,990)		
Satisfaction of equipment acquisition restrictions	1,500	(1,500)		
Expiration of time restrictions	1,250	(1,250)		
Total revenues, gains, and other support	43,608	(1,098)	5,020	47,530
Expenses and Losses				
Program A	13,100			13,100
Program B	8,540			8,540
Program C	5,760			5,760
Management and general	2,420			2,420
Fund raising	2,150			2,150
Total expenses (Note F)	31,970			31,970
Fire loss	80			80
Actuarial loss on annuity obligations		30		30
Total expenses and losses	32,050	30		32,080
Change in net assets	11,558	(1,128)	5,020	15,450
Net assets at beginning of year	103,670	25,470	137,000	266,140
Net assets at end of year	$115,228	$24,342	$142,020	$281,590

Accompanying notes to financial statements not included.

Source: Adapted from FASB *Statement No. 117*, "Financial Statements of Not-for-Profit Organizations" (Norwalk, CT: FASB, 1994), para. 159.

TABLE 12–3

Voluntary Health and Welfare Service
Statement of Functional Expenses
Year Ended December 31, 19X2
(With Comparative Totals for 19X1)

	Program Services					Supporting Services			Total Expenses	
	RESEARCH	PUBLIC HEALTH EDUCATION	PROFES-SIONAL EDUCATION AND TRAINING	COMMUNITY SERVICES	TOTAL	MANAGE-MENT AND GENERAL	FUND RAISING	TOTAL	19X2	19X1
Salaries	$ 45,000	$291,000	$251,000	$269,000	$ 856,000	$331,000	$368,000	$ 699,000	$1,555,000	$1,433,000
Employee health and retirement benefits	4,000	14,000	14,000	14,000	46,000	22,000	15,000	37,000	83,000	75,000
Payroll taxes, etc.	2,000	16,000	13,000	14,000	45,000	18,000	18,000	36,000	81,000	75,000
Total salaries and related expenses	51,000	321,000	278,000	297,000	947,000	371,000	401,000	772,000	1,719,000	1,583,000
Professional fees and contract service payments	1,000	10,000	3,000	8,000	22,000	26,000	8,000	34,000	56,000	53,000
Supplies	2,000	13,000	13,000	13,000	41,000	18,000	17,000	35,000	76,000	71,000
Telephone and telegraph	2,000	13,000	10,000	11,000	36,000	15,000	23,000	38,000	74,000	68,000
Postage and shipping	2,000	17,000	13,000	9,000	41,000	13,000	30,000	43,000	84,000	80,000
Occupancy	5,000	26,000	22,000	25,000	78,000	30,000	27,000	57,000	135,000	126,000
Rental of equipment	1,000	24,000	14,000	4,000	43,000	3,000	16,000	19,000	62,000	58,000
Local transportation	3,000	22,000	20,000	22,000	67,000	23,000	30,000	53,000	120,000	113,000
Conferences, conventions, meetings	8,000	19,000	71,000	20,000	118,000	38,000	13,000	51,000	169,000	156,000
Printing and publications	4,000	56,000	43,000	11,000	114,000	14,000	64,000	78,000	192,000	184,000
Awards and grants	1,332,000	14,000	119,000	144,000	1,609,000	—	—	—	1,609,000	1,448,000
Miscellaneous	1,000	4,000	6,000	4,000	15,000	16,000	21,000	37,000	52,000	64,000
Total expenses before depreciation	1,412,000	539,000	612,000	568,000	3,131,000	567,000	650,000	1,217,000	4,348,000	4,004,000
Depreciation of buildings and equipment	2,000	5,000	6,000	10,000	23,000	7,000	4,000	11,000	34,000	32,000
Total expenses	$1,414,000	$544,000	$618,000	$578,000	$3,154,000	$574,000	$654,000	$1,228,000	$4,382,000	$4,036,000

Accompanying notes to financial statements not included.
Source: AICPA, *Audits of Voluntary Health and Welfare Organizations* (New York: AICPA, 1974), pp. 44–45.

Notice the use of a column for each program service and supporting service and a line for each type of expense. Notice also that depreciation is shown as a line item, whereas it is "buried" in the statement of activities. Although they are not required to prepare a statement of functional expenses, many 78–10 organizations elect to do so because of the usefulness of this statement to managers and others concerned with specific costs incurred by these organizations.

Statement of Cash Flows

A statement of cash flows provides the user of the financial statements with information on cash receipts and cash payments of the organization during the same period as the statement of activities. The statement is organized so that the effect of operating, investing and financing, activities on cash flows are clearly shown. Due to its complexity, it is not discussed in this chapter. However, such a statement is shown in Table 12–4.

SPECIAL PROBLEMS

Contributions

Generally speaking, contributions must be reported as revenues or gains in the period they are received. They must be reported as assets, decreases of liabilities, or expenses, depending on their nature. They must also be reported as either restricted support or unrestricted support.

Contributions can be received without donor-imposed restrictions or with permanent or temporary donor-imposed restrictions. Unrestricted contributions should be reported on the statement of activities as unrestricted revenues or gains (unrestricted support), which increase unrestricted net assets. Contributions accompanied by donor-imposed restrictions should be reported as restricted support, although they may be reported as unrestricted support if the restrictions are met in the same reporting period and the organization reports consistently from period to period. These contributions will increase permanently restricted or temporarily restricted net assets.

Receipts of pledges (unconditional promises to give) whose payments are due in future periods must be reported as restricted support "unless explicit donor stipulations or circumstances surrounding the receipt of a promise make clear that the donor intended it to be used to support activities of the current period."[14] When reporting pledges, the following must be disclosed:

a. Amounts of promises receivable within one year, from one to five years, and in more than five years, and
b. The allowance for uncollectible pledges.[15]

---

[14]FASB *Statement No. 116,* para. 15.
[15]Ibid., para. 24.

TABLE 12–4

Not-for-Profit Organization
Statement of Cash Flows
Year Ended June 30, 19X1
(in thousands)

Cash flows from operating activities:	
Change in net assets	$15,450
Adjustments to reconcile change in net assets to net cash used by	
operating activities:	
Depreciation	3,200
Fire loss	80
Actuarial loss on annuity obligations	30
Increase in accounts and interest receivable	(460)
Decrease in inventories and prepaid expenses	390
Increase in contributions receivable	(325)
Increase in accounts payable	1,520
Decrease in refundable advance	(650)
Decrease in grants payable	(425)
Contributions restricted for long-term investment	(2,740)
Interest and dividends restricted for long-term investment	(300)
Net unrealized and realized gains on long-term investment	(15,800)
Net cash used by operating activities	(30)
Cash flows from investing activities:	
Insurance proceeds from fire loss on building	250
Purchase of equipment	(1,500)
Proceeds from sale of investments	76,100
Purchase of investments	(74,900)
Net cash used by investing activities	(50)
Cash flows from financing activities:	
Proceeds from contributions restricted for:	
Investment in endowment	200
Investment in term endowment	70
Investment in plant	1,210
Investment subject to annuity agreements	200
	1,680
Other financing activities:	
Interest and dividends restricted for reinvestment	300
Payments of annuity obligations	(145)
Payments on notes payable	(1,140)
Payments on long-term debt	(1,000)
	(1,985)
Net cash used by financing activities	(305)
Net decrease in cash and cash equivalents	(385)
Cash and cash equivalents at beginning of year	460
Cash and cash equivalents at end of year	$ 75

Accompanying notes to financial statements not included.

Source: Adapted from *FASB Statement No. 117*, "Financial Statements of Not-for-Profit Organizations" (Norwalk, CT: FASB, 1994), para. 160.

Subscription and Membership Income

For many 78–10 organizations, subscription and membership income are the primary basis of support for their operating activities. In general, these items are recognized as revenue in the period or periods in which they can be used to pay for services rendered by the organization. For example, membership dues that are collected in September of each year, but apply to calendar-year memberships, are recognized as revenue during the period in which the individual receives membership privileges—in this case the calendar year.

Items such as nonrefundable initiation fees and life membership fees can cause some measurement problems. Like membership dues, the key factor for revenue recognition lies in the period over which these fees pay for services rendered by the organization. Thus, these items should be recognized as revenue on a basis that reflects the services available to the members during this period of time. If, in fact, the items are not related to services rendered but are actually contributions, they should be recognized as revenue in the period or periods in which the organization is entitled to them.

Donated Materials, Facilities, and Services

If donated materials and facilities of a significant amount are used by an organization, a **contribution** should be recorded, along with an **offsetting expense,** based on the fair market value of the items contributed. If, however, the items contributed are merely passed through the organization to individuals receiving services of the organization, they should not be recorded as contributions.

When the same logic is applied to donated services, the situation is somewhat different. If the value of the services is significant, they should be recorded "if the services received

(a) create or enhance nonfinancial assets, or
(b) require specialized skills, are provided by individuals possessing those skills, and would typically need to be purchased if not provided by donation."[16]

When these conditions are met, a contribution should be recorded for the value of the services donated, along with an offsetting expense. In addition, the organization must describe "the programs or activities for which those services were used, including the nature and extent of contributed services received for the period and the amount recognized as revenues for the period."[17] If possible, the fair value of contributed services received, but not recognized as contributions, should be disclosed.

[16]Ibid., para. 9.
[17]Ibid., para. 10.

Grants and Payments to Affiliated Organizations

Not-for-profit organizations making grants to other organizations or individuals should report the expense and decrease in assets or increase in liabilities in the period in which the recipient is entitled to receive the grant. In those instances in which a grant may be revoked in future years, at the discretion of the grantor institution, the unpaid amount should be recorded only when the grant is renewed. However, if only routine performance is required, the entire amount of the grant should be expensed in the initial period.

Payments to an affiliated state or national organization by a local organization should be reported on the statement of activities as an expense or a deduction from revenues, depending on the arrangement (contract) between the two organizations.

Items Contributed to Collections

Generally speaking, donated items like works of art, historical artifacts and rare books are "recognized as revenues or gains if collections are capitalized and shall not be recognized as revenues or gains if collections are not capitalized."[18] (When a collection is capitalized, it is treated as an asset on which depreciation is recorded.) If an organization chooses to capitalize its collection, it can do so retroactively or prospectively. It must, however, follow a consistent policy. It cannot capitalize selected collections or items within a collection.

Many accountants feel that the treatment of all contributed items as revenues is misleading. For example, a museum in dire financial straits might receive a painting valued at $1 million, which it plans to display. Potential donors, noting the million-dollar revenue and corresponding increase in net assets, are likely to conclude that the museum does not need their support.

In response to this problem, the FASB has stated that an organization has the option of not capitalizing "works of art, historical treasures, and similar assets if the donated items are added to collections that meet *all* of the following conditions:

    a. Are held for public exhibition, education, or research in furtherance of public service rather than financial gain,

    b. Are protected, kept unencumbered, cared for, and preserved, and

    c. Are subject to an organizational policy that requires the proceeds from sales of collection items to be used to acquire other items for collections."[19]

Requirements a and b are usually easy to meet. Requirement c, however, creates problems if an organization needs to raise money for other purposes, especially since a consistent capitalization policy must be followed.

[18]Ibid., para. 13.
[19]Ibid., para. 11.

If an organization does not capitalize its collections, it must report the following information "on the face of its statement of activities, separately from revenues, expenses, gains, and losses:

a. Costs of collection items purchased as a decrease in the appropriate class of net assets
b. Proceeds from sale of collection items as an increase in the appropriate class of net assets
c. Proceeds from insurance recoveries of lost or destroyed collection items as an increase in the appropriate class of net assets."[20]

It must also describe its collections, "including their relative significance, and its accounting and stewardship policies for collections."[21] If items in the collection are deaccessed (removed from the collection) during the period, the organization must also "(a) describe the items given away, damaged, destroyed, lost, or otherwise deaccessed during the period or (b) disclose their fair value."[22] In addition, these disclosures must be referred to in a line item shown on the face of the statement of financial position.

Depreciation

Voluntary health and welfare organizations and 78–10 organizations must report depreciation on all long-lived, exhaustible tangible assets—except for certain works of art and historical treasures "whose economic benefit or service potential is used up so slowly that their estimated useful lives are extraordinarily long."[23] These organizations do not need to depreciate inexhaustible long-lived assets, such as gem collections in museums. They must, however, catalog and control such assets. They must also disclose information on long-lived assets and depreciation methods used, in the notes to their financial statements.

Conditional Promises to Give

Conditional promises to give are based on "the occurrence of a specified future and uncertain event to bind the promisor."[24] They are recognized "when the conditions on which they depend are substantially met, that is, when the conditional promise becomes unconditional."[25] A receipt of assets with a conditional promise to contribute is accounted for as a refundable advance until such time as the conditions have been "substantially" met. If assets are received with ambiguous donor stipulations, the gift should be presumed to be a conditional promise.

[20]Ibid., para. 26.
[21]Ibid., para. 27.
[22]Ibid.
[23]FASB, *Statement of Financial Accounting Standards No. 93*, "Recognition of Depreciation by Not-for-Profit Organizations" (Norwalk, CT: FASB, 1987), para. 6.
[24]FASB *Statement No. 116*, para. 22.
[25]Ibid.

When conditional promises to give are received, the following must be disclosed:

a. The total amount promised, and
b. A description and the amount for each group of promises having similar characteristics, such as promises conditioned upon the establishment of new programs, completion of facilities and raising of matching gifts by a specified date.[26]

Investment Activities

Investment income and gains and losses incurred when disposing of investments should be reported on the statement of activities "as increase or decreases in unrestricted net assets unless their use is temporarily or permanently restricted by explicit donor stipulations or by law."[27] For example, a donor may stipulate that investment income be used to support a particular project. In this case, the investment income would be reported as an increase in temporarily restricted net assets.

In some instances the investment income and gains and losses from investment activities must be added to the principal, in accordance with the terms of the endowment. Such items should be reported as increases in permanently restricted net assets.

ILLUSTRATIVE TRANSACTIONS OF NOT-FOR-PROFIT ORGANIZATIONS

Assume that the Society for the Rehabilitation of Addled Professors of Accounting (SRAPA), a voluntary health and welfare organization, is formed at the beginning of 19X1. It receives its support from the public-at-large, as well as through the United Way. SRAPA owns a building and various pieces of equipment, which are used to carry out its services—counseling and education programs. It uses the following funds:

1. Current Unrestricted Fund
2. Current Restricted Fund
3. Land, Buildings, and Equipment Fund

The transactions for each fund, for 19X1, are as follows:

Current Unrestricted Fund

1. Unrestricted pledges of $130,000, which apply to the current period, are made by various people. Of this amount, $15,000 is not expected to be collectible.

[26]Ibid., para. 25.
[27]FASB *Statement No. 117*, para. 22.

Contributions receivable	130,000	
Allowance for uncollectible contributions		15,000
Support—contributions		115,000

To record pledges received and estimated un-collectibles

2. **Contributions receivable of $110,000 are collected, and contributions of $12,000 are written off.**

Cash	110,000	
Allowance for uncollectible contributions	12,000	
Contributions receivable		122,000

To record collection and write-off of certain pledges.

3. **Of the above amount, $20,000 is invested in government securities for use as management sees fit.**

| Investments | 20,000 | |
| Cash | | 20,000 |

To record purchase of government securities.

4. **The society's allocation from the United Way amounts to $65,000. From this amount a share of the United Way's fund-raising costs—$5,000—is deducted.**

Cash	60,000	
United Way fund-raising costs	5,000	
Received from United Way		65,000

To record 19X1 allocation from United Way.

5. **A fund-raising book sale is held. The event raises $12,000. Out of this amount, however, $3,000 of related direct costs are incurred and paid.**

| Cash | 12,000 | |
| Support—special events | | 12,000 |

To record support from book sale.

| Expenditures—fund raising | 3,000 | |
| Cash | | 3,000 |

To record direct costs of book sale.

6. **Investment income of $2,000 is earned during the year. Of this amount, $1,500 is received by year-end.**

Cash	1,500	
Accrued interest receivable	500	
Revenue—investment income		2,000

To record 19X1 investment income.

7. **Membership dues of $2,500 are collected during the year.**

| Cash | 2,500 | |
| Revenues—membership dues | | 2,500 |

To record receipt of membership dues.

8. Services donated to the society are as follows:
   a. A psychologist provides counseling to a number of accounting professors at no cost. The services are valued at $3,000.
   b. An attorney performs certain legal work for free. The services are valued at $600.

Expenses—counseling services	3,000	
Expenses—administration	600	
Support—donated services		3,600

To record receipt of donated services.

9. Supplies, with a market value of $800, are donated to the society by a local accounting firm. They are used in the general operation of the organization.

| Expenses—administration | 800 | |
| Support—donated supplies | | 800 |

To record receipt of donated supplies.

10. Salaries and wages incurred during the year (including fringe benefits) are allocated as follows:

Administration	$25,000
Counseling services	60,000
Education	50,000
Fund raising	5,000

By year-end all salaries, wages, and fringe benefits have been paid.

Expenses—administration	25,000	
Expenses—counseling services	60,000	
Expenses—education	50,000	
Expenses—fund raising	5,000	
Cash		140,000

To record salaries, wages, and fringe benefits for 19X1.

11. Other expenses are allocated as follows:

Contractual services:		
Counseling services	$10,000	
Education	5,000	$15,000
Supplies (all education)		10,000
Miscellaneous expenses:		
Administration	$5,000	
Counseling services	2,000	
Education	3,000	
Fund raising	1,000	11,000
Total		$36,000

Of this amount, all but $4,000 has been paid by year-end.

Expenses—administration	5,000	
Expenses—counseling services	12,000	
Expenses—education	18,000	
Expenses—fund raising	1,000	
Accounts payable		4,000
Cash		32,000

To record expenses incurred in 19X1 and payment of vouchers.

12. The closing entry for 19X1 is:

Support—contributions	115,000	
Support—special events	12,000	
Support—donated services	3,600	
Support—donated materials	800	
Revenues—investment income	2,000	
Revenues—membership dues	2,500	
Received from United Way	65,000	
Expenses—administration		31,400
Expenses—counseling services		75,000
Expenses—education		68,000
Expenses—fund raising		9,000
United Way fund-raising costs		5,000
Fund balance—unrestricted		12,500

To close revenue, support, expense, and fund-raising cost accounts.

Current Restricted Fund

1. Pledges of $20,000 and cash gifts of $10,000 are received, with the stipulation that they be used only for special educational programs over the next five years. Twenty percent of the pledges are estimated to be uncollectible.

Cash	10,000	
Contributions receivable	20,000	
Allowance for uncollectible contributions		4,000
Support—contributions		26,000

To record restricted gifts and pledges

2. Restricted-purpose pledges of $15,000 are collected and another $2,000 are written off.

Cash	15,000	
Allowance for uncollected contributions	2,000	
Contributions receivable		17,000

To record collection and write-off of restricted pledges.

3. Special educational expenses of $21,000 are paid by this fund in 19X1.

Expenses—special education	21,000	
Cash		21,000

To record expenses of special education program.

4. The closing entry is:

Support—contributions	26,000	
Expenses—special education		21,000
Fund balance—restricted		5,000

To close support and expense accounts.

Land, Building, and Equipment Fund

1. The society received a grant of $250,000 from the Kezar Foundation, to be used for the purchase of a building and equipment.

Cash	250,000	
Support—contributions		250,000

To record contribution for purchase of building and equipment.

2. An investment of $100,000 is made in government securities.

Investments	100,000	
Cash		100,000

To record investment in government securities.

3. Equipment costing $50,000 is purchased, using the resources donated by the Kezar Foundation.

Equipment	50,000	
Cash		50,000

To record purchase of equipment with monies restricted for that purpose

4. A building is purchased for $400,000. A down payment of $80,000 is made and a mortgage is taken out for the remainder.

Building	400,000	
Mortgage payable		320,000
Cash		80,000

To record purchase of building with restricted monies and mortgage.

5. Interest of $8,000 is received on the investment in government securities.

Cash	8,000	
Revenue—investment income		8,000

To record earnings on investments.

6. Payments of $10,000 are made on the mortgage during the year. Of this amount, $8,000 is for interest.

Mortgage payable	2,000	
Expenses—interest	8,000	
Cash		10,000
To record payments on mortgage.		

7. Depreciation for the year amounts to $20,000 on the building and $10,000 on the equipment. It is allocated as follows:

Administration	$3,000
Counseling services	10,000
Educational services	16,000
Fund raising	1,000

Depreciation expense—administration	3,000	
Depreciation expense—counseling services	10,000	
Depreciation expense—educational services	16,000	
Depreciation expense—fund raising	1,000	
Accumulated depreciation—building		20,000
Accumulated depreciation—equipment		10,000
To record depreciation on buildings and equipment for 19X1.		

8. The closing entry is as follows:

Contributions	250,000	
Revenue—investment income	8,000	
Expenses—interest		8,000
Depreciation expense—administration		3,000
Depreciation expense—counseling services		10,000
Depreciation expense—educational services		16,000
Depreciation expense—fund raising		1,000
Fund balance—unexpended		220,000
To close contributions, revenue, and expense accounts.		

The fund balance of the Land, Building, and Equipment Fund is generally separated into "unexpended" and "expended" portions. The **unexpended portion** equals the total of the balances in the Cash, Investment, and, in some cases, the net amount in the Contributions receivable accounts. The **expended portion** equals the net book value of the fixed assets (original cost less accumulated depreciation), less the amounts outstanding on any associated mortgages. At the end of each reporting period, it is necessary to adjust the unexpended fund balance to reflect the expended portion. The adjustment at the end of 19X1 is $102,000 ($50,000 + $400,000 − $320,000 + $2,000 − $30,000 = $102,000). The entry to make this adjustment is:

| Fund balance—unexpended | 102,000 | |
| Fund balance—expended | | 102,000 |

To adjust fund balance—expended to reflect
the change in net investment in fixed assets.

If the organization in the above illustration had been a 78–10 organization, certain fund titles would have been different. The Current Unrestricted Fund and the Current Restricted Fund would have been called the Operating Fund—Unrestricted and the Operating Fund—Restricted, respectively. The Land, Buildings, and Equipment Fund would most likely have been called the Plant Fund. Except for the different fund names, the entries shown for the Current Unrestricted Fund would have been similar for both types of organizations.

REVIEW QUESTIONS

Q12–1   What is the difference between a *voluntary health and welfare organization* and an *"other" not-for-profit organization?*

Q12–2   Identify several organizations that would be classified in the "voluntary health and welfare" category.

Q12–3   What is the purpose of *SOP 78–10?*

Q12–4   What body has the final authority for determining the accounting procedures used by voluntary health and welfare organizations and 78–10 organizations?

Q12–5   Identify and briefly describe the funds generally used by voluntary health and welfare organizations and by 78–10 organizations.

Q12–6   Which three basic financial statements are used by voluntary health and welfare organizations?

Q12–7   Comment on the following statement: 78–10 organizations must prepare the same financial statements as voluntary health and welfare organizations.

Q12–8   How are uncollected pledges reported in the financial statements of voluntary health and welfare organizations?

Q12–9   What is *deferred revenue?*

Q12–10 What is the *functional basis* for reporting expenses?

Q12–11 How do *program expenses* differ from *supporting expenses?*

Q12–12 What is the purpose of the statement of functional expenses for a voluntary health and welfare organization?

EXERCISES

E12–1   (Funds used by voluntary health and welfare organizations)
Using the coding system below, indicate which fund or funds would be used to record each of the transactions described.

CUF—Current Unrestricted Fund
CRF—Current Restricted Fund
LBEF—Land, Building, and Equipment Fund
EF—Endowment Fund

1. The organization received unrestricted contributions of $400,000. Of this amount, $390,000 is expected to be collected.
2. Jane Public gave the organization securities with a market value of $1.2 million. The gift provided that the principal must be maintained intact; however, the income could be spent for any purpose that had the governing board's approval.
3. Unrestricted contributions that were designated for use in the following year were received. These contributions totaled $50,000.
4. Salaries of employees involved in rendering services to the public totaled $75,000.

E12–2 (Recording journal entries for voluntary health and welfare organizations)

Prepare the journal entries necessary to record the data given in Exercise 12–1. In addition, indicate which fund is used for each entry.

E12–3 (Multiple choice)

1. Why do voluntary health and welfare organizations record depreciation of fixed assets?
   a. Fixed assets are more likely to be material in amount in a voluntary health and welfare organization than in other not-for-profit organizations
   b. Voluntary health and welfare organizations purchase their fixed assets, and therefore have a historical cost basis from which to determine amounts to be depreciated
   c. A fixed asset used by a voluntary health and welfare organization has alternative uses in private industry, and this opportunity cost should be reflected in the organization's financial statements
   d. Contributors look for the most efficient use of funds; and since depreciation represents a cost of employing fixed assets, it is appropriate that a voluntary health and welfare organization reflect it as a cost of providing services

(AICPA)

2. Which of the following funds of a voluntary health and welfare organization does not have a counterpart fund in governmental accounting?
   a. The Current Unrestricted Fund
   b. The Land, Building, and Equipment Fund
   c. A Custodian Fund
   d. An Endowment Fund

(AICPA adapted)

3. Which of the following financial statements is required for a voluntary health and welfare organization, but not for a 78–10 organization?
   a. Statement of financial position
   b. Statement of activities
   c. Statement of functional expenses
   d. Statement of cash flows

4. Endowment income that is restricted in use to finance the operations of a voluntary health and welfare organization should be recorded in
   a. The Current Unrestricted Fund
   b. A Current Restricted Fund
   c. An Endowment Fund
   d. An Annuity Fund

5. A mortgage on the land and buildings owned by a voluntary health and welfare organization should be reported in
   a. The Current Unrestricted Fund
   b. A Current Restricted Fund
   c. The Land, Building, and Equipment Fund
   d. A Loan Fund

6. Which of the following funds may have one or more items of public support or revenue?
   a. The Current Unrestricted Fund
   b. The Land, Building, and Equipment Fund
   c. An Endowment Fund
   d. All of the above could have one or more items of public support or revenue

7. The Prevent Cancer Organization incurred several expenses during 19X1. Which of the following would *not* be classified as program support?
   a. Instruction for cancer prevention to the general public
   b. Pamphlets mailed to the general public regarding the "danger signals of cancer"
   c. Postage announcing the 19X1 Kickoff Dinner
   d. Salaries of personnel who perform cancer research

8. Aviary Haven, a voluntary health and welfare organization funded by contributions from the general public, received unrestricted pledges of $500,000 during 19X1. It was estimated that 12 percent of these pledges would be uncollectible. By the end of 19X1, $400,000 of the pledges had been collected; and it was expected that $40,000 more would be collected in 19X2, with the balance of $60,000 to be written off as uncollectible. Donors did not specify any periods during which the donations were to be used. What amount should Aviary include under public support in 19X1 for net contributions?
   a. $500,000
   b. $452,000

c. $440,000
d. $400,000

(AICPA adapted)

9. The following expenditures were among those incurred by a non-profit botanical society during 19X1:

Printing of annual report	$10,000
Unsolicited merchandise sent to encourage contributions	20,000

What amount should be classified as fund-raising costs in the society's statement of activities?

a. $0
b. $10,000
c. $20,000
d. $30,000

(AICPA adapted)

E12–4   (Statement of activities for a country club)
The following information was taken from the records of the Land's End Country Club. All account balances are as of the end of the accounting year, June 30, 19X1.

Cash	$ 12,000
Dues	631,000
Locker room rentals to members	20,000
Expenses associated with the golf course	255,000
Expenses associated with the tennis courts	105,000
Initiation fees	78,000
Prepaid expenses	8,000
Administration expenses	65,000
Fees: Golf course	87,000
Swimming pool	44,000
Tennis courts	12,000
Expenses associated with the swimming pool	31,000
Land, buildings, and equipment	800,987
Investments	56,000
19X1 assessments against members for capital improvements	200,000
Net assets—6/30/x0	97,000

REQUIRED: Prepare a statement of activities for the Land's End Country Club.

E12–5   (Financial statement reporting of plant-type assets of not-for-profit organizations)
When discussing not-for-profit organizations with several of your colleagues, you discovered that one friend feels that plant-type assets should be recorded in a separate fund while another feels that they should be reported as part of the Unrestricted Current Fund. Which position is correct? Why?

E12–6 (Journal entries for a not-for-profit organization)

The Society to Save Humankind from Its Ills, a voluntary health and welfare organization, was founded in 19X1. This organization conducts two types of programs: education and testing. During 19X1, the following events took place:

1. Pledges amounting to $200,000 were received. Of this amount, $50,000 was restricted for the use of a special research program. All of the restricted pledges and $140,000 of the unrestricted pledges are expected to be collected.

2. Les Miller made a $1,000 cash contribution, to be used as the directors of the society see fit. However, Mr. Miller stipulated that it not be used until 19X2.

3. The restricted pledges were all collected. With respect to the unrestricted pledges, $120,000 was collected and $5,000 was written off.

4. The society received a $10,000 allocation from the United Fund. Of this amount, $2,000 was deducted for fund-raising costs.

5. The society invested $10,000 of unrestricted funds in government securities. Earnings on these resources amounted to $500 in 19X1.

6. During the year, $40,000 of restricted funds is spent on research projects.

7. A grant of $500,000 was made to the society by the Allen Company. The grant was to be used to purchase equipment and for a down payment on a building. Cash donations of $10,000, for the purpose of debt service (paying interest and principal on the mortgage), were also received.

8. Equipment was purchased for $75,000, using resources donated by the Allen Company.

9. A down payment of $400,000 was made on a building costing $1,000,000. A 20-year mortgage was taken out for the remainder.

10. The following services were donated to the society, all of which should be recorded:
    a. Free accounting work by a local accounting firm—$500
    b. Free tests by a national testing laboratory—$1,000
    c. The services, at no cost, of several teachers from a local junior college. They conducted physical fitness and wellness programs—$2,000

    In addition, the accounting firm donated supplies worth $200.

11. Salaries, wages, and other operating expenses for 19X1 amounted to $135,000. They were paid with unrestricted monies and were allocated as follows:

Administration	$20,000
Education	90,000
Testing	15,000
Fund raising	10,000

12. Interest of $8,000 was paid on the mortgage during the year.
13. Depreciation amounted to $50,000 on the building and $10,000 on the equipment. It was allocated as follows:

	BUILDING	EQUIPMENT
Administration	$10,000	—
Education	20,000	$3,000
Testing	20,000	7,000

14. Revenues from membership dues amounted to $18,000 in 19X1.

REQUIRED: Prepare journal entries for the transactions listed above, by fund, including the appropriate closing entries.

PROBLEMS

P12–1 (Preparation of financial statements for a not-for-profit organization)
You have recently been hired by the Society for the Elimination of Apathy. This organization does research into the causes of apathy. The accounting records were maintained according to GAAP during the year; however, due to a computer malfunction, the accounts have become jumbled. You should prepare in good form for the society for 19X1:

1. A statement of financial position
2. A statement of activities, and
3. A statement of functional expenses.

DEBITS	
Cash—unrestricted	$1,000,000
Investments of restricted funds	500,000
Management and general expenses—unrestricted	400,000
—depreciation	10,000
Investment of unrestricted funds	500,000
Land, buildings, and equipment at cost	4,000,000
Research expenses—unrestricted	3,000,000
—restricted	200,000
—depreciation	70,000
Community services expenses—unrestricted	800,000
—restricted	10,000
Fund-raising expenses—unrestricted	150,000
—restricted	1,000
Pledges receivable—unrestricted	400,000
Cash—land, building, and equipment	10,000
Cash—restricted	8,000
Investment—land, building, and equipment	500,000
Other receivables—unrestricted	5,000

Detailed expenses:

	RESEARCH	COMMUNITY SERVICES	MANAGEMENT	FUND RAISING
Salaries and payroll taxes	$2,000,000	$500,000	$300,000	$30,000
Professional fees	535,000	100,000	60,000	20,000
Supplies	650,000	10,000	1,000	3,000
Postage	7,000	100,000	1,000	40,000
Printing	3,000	60,000	23,000	55,000
Miscellaneous	5,000	40,000	15,000	3,000
Depreciation	70,000	—	10,000	—

CREDITS

Mortgage payable—land, building, and equipment	$1,000,000
Fund balance—restricted—research grants	508,000
Accounts payable—unrestricted	300,000
Contributions—unrestricted	4,800,000
—restricted	200,000
—land, building, and equipment*	99,000
Research grants payable—unrestricted	1,000,000
Fund balance—unrestricted—designated for new equipment (12/31/X1)	500,000
—undesignated (12/31/X1)	105,000
Investment income—undesignated	45,000
—restricted	49,000
—land, building, and equipment	48,000
Gain on sale of investments—unrestricted	5,000
Fund balance—land, building, and equipment—expended	1,500,000
unexpended—restricted	510,000
Accumulated depreciation	1,500,000
Miscellaneous revenue—undesignated	3,000
—restricted	2,000
—land, building, and equipment	1,000

*Report as 19X1 revenue.

Note:

1. Equipment costing $20,000 was acquired during the year by using unrestricted funds.
2. The beginning fund balances were:

Unrestricted	$ 122,000
Restricted	468,000
Land, building, and equipment	1,922,000

P12–2   (Journal entries for a voluntary health and welfare organization)
Following are some of the transactions for the EI (Eye Institute) during 19X1.

1. Pledges were received as follows:

Unrestricted	$3,000,000
Restricted to research	1,000,000

2. During the year, 90 percent of all pledges were collected.
3. Amounts received from the United Fund totaled $1.5 million.
4. The EI paid $20,000 to the United Fund as its share of the fund-raising costs for 19X1.
5. Salaries for 19X1 totaled $500,000, and the related payroll costs were $100,000. The entire amount was paid in cash.
6. An additional parcel of land and a small building were acquired, using assets segregated for that purpose. The land was appraised for $75,000 and the building was appraised for $160,000. The institute paid $23,500 down and financed the remainder of the appraised value with a mortgage.
7. Depreciation for the year was $246,000.
8. The following general operating costs were paid:

Professional management fees	$ 75,000
Professional fees for research	500,000
Supplies	5,000
Printing	15,000
Utilities	100,000
Miscellaneous	15,000

9. Restricted resources were used as follows:

Research salaries	$300,000
Payroll cost	30,000
Supplies	20,000
Postage	150,000

10. Unrestricted contributions received in 19X1, but designated for use in 19X2, totaled $35,000.
11. Equipment that cost $3,000 was acquired with unrestricted funds.
12. At the end of the year, management estimates that all the pledges outstanding in the Current Restricted and the Land, Building, and Equipment Funds will be collected; however, $10,000 of the pledges in the Current Unrestricted Fund will probably not be collected.
13. At the end of the year, supplies that cost $500 were still on hand (see number 8).
14. Interest paid on the mortgage on the land and building was $20,000.

15. The distribution of expenses into functional categories in the Current Unrestricted Fund was as follows:*

Fund raising	$ 12,000
Management and general	88,500
Research	850,000
Public service	359,000
	$1,309,500

16. The distribution of expenses into functional categories in the Current Restricted Fund was as follows:*

Research	$305,000
Public service	55,000
Fund raising	140,000
	$500,000

17. The distribution of depreciation and the interest on the mortgage was as follows:*

Management and general	$22,000
Fund raising	6,000
Research	215,000
Community service	23,000
	$266,000

*Assume journal entries are made for the distribution.

REQUIRED: Prepare the journal entries necessary to record the above data; also indicate the fund used for each entry.

P12-3 Financial statements for a religious organization

Avalon Church Federation uses three funds to account for its activities: an Operating Fund, which is unrestricted; a Loan Fund which is temporarily restricted; and a Plant Fund which is permanently restricted. Because of the satisfaction of certain program restrictions during the year, $10,000 was transferred from the Loan Fund to the Operating Fund. The following data were taken from the accounting records of the federation on December 31, 19X1.

Cash—operating	$ 130,000
—loan	18,000
—plant	8,000
Land, building, and equipment—plant (net)	1,250,000
Fund balance (12/31/X0)—Operating Fund	299,000
—Loan Fund	378,000
—Plant Fund	999,000
Accounts payable—operating	75,000
—plant	40,000
Support and revenue—contributions	
—unrestricted	975,000
—plant	140,000

Expenses—general and administrative	
—unrestricted	180,000
—plant	20,000
Expenses—fund raising	
—unrestricted	5,000
—plant	2,000
Prepaid expenses—operating	20,000
Accounts receivable (net)—operating	16,000
Loans receivable—loans	390,000
Support and revenue—fees for services	
—unrestricted	50,000
Support and revenue—investment income	
—plant	51,000
Support and revenue—interest on loans	
—loan	40,000
Contributions receivable (net)	
—unrestricted	218,000
—plant	307,000
Mortgage payable—plant	1,000,000
Investments—plant	540,000
Expenses—pastoral	
—unrestricted	500,000
—plant	78,000
Expenses—education	
—unrestricted	300,000
—plant	5,000
Expenses—cemeteries	
—unrestricted	40,000
—plant	20,000

REQUIRED: Prepare a statement of financial position and a statement of activities for Avalon Church Federation for FY 19X1.

P12–4 (Problem from Uniform Certified Public Accountant Examination comparing treatment of certain transactions by governmental units and voluntary health and welfare organizations)

Listed below are four independent transactions or events that relate to a local government and to a voluntary health and welfare organization:

1. $25,000 was disbursed from the General Fund (or its equivalent) for the cash purchase of new equipment.
2. An unrestricted cash gift of $100,000 was received from a donor.
3. Listed common stocks with a total carrying value of $50,000, exclusive of any allowance, were sold by an Endowment Fund for $55,000, before any dividends were earned on these stocks. There are no restrictions on the gain.
4. $1,000,000 face amount of general obligation bonds payable were sold at par, with the proceeds required to be used solely for construction of a new building. This building was completed at a total cost of $1,000,000, and the total amount of bond issue proceeds was disbursed in connection therewith.

REQUIRED: a.   For each of the above-listed transactions or events, prepare journal entries, without explanations, specifying the affected funds and account groups, and showing how these transactions or events should be recorded by a local government whose debt is serviced by general tax revenues.

b.   For each of the above-listed transactions or events, prepare journal entries, without explanations, specifying the affected funds, and showing how these transactions or events should be recorded by a voluntary health and welfare organization that maintains a separate Plant Fund.

(AICPA)

P12–5   (Prepartion of financial statements for a voluntary health and welfare organization)

Following are the adjusted Current Funds trial balances of the Community Association for Handicapped Children, a voluntary health and welfare organization, at June 20, 19X1. Assume that items listed as "restricted" are temporarily restricted.

Community Association for Handicapped Children
Adjusted Current Funds Trial Balances
June 30, 19X1

	Unrestricted		Restricted	
	DEBIT	CREDIT	DEBIT	CREDIT
Cash	$ 40,000		$ 9,000	
Bequest receivable			5,000	
Pledges receivable	12,000			
Accrued interest receivable	1,000			
Investments (at cost, which equals market)	100,000			
Accounts payable and accrued expenses		$ 50,000		$ 1,000
Deferred revenue		2,000		
Allowance for uncollectible pledges		3,000		
Fund balances, July 1, 19X0:				
Designated		12,000		
Undesignated		26,000		
Restricted				3,000
Transfers of endowment fund income		20,000		
Contributions		300,000		15,000
Membership dues		25,000		
Program service fees		30,000		
Investment income		10,000		
Deaf children's program	120,000			
Blind children's program	150,000			
Management and general services	45,000		4,000	
Fund-raising services	8,000		1,000	
Provision for uncollectible pledges	2,000			
	$478,000	$478,000	$19,000	$19,000

REQUIRED: a.   Prepare a statement of activities for the year ended June 30, 19X1.

b.   Prepare a statement of financial position as of June 30, 19X1.

(AICPA adapted)

...cepted accounting principles for

...ces accounted for in the General Funds
restricted and unrestricted resources
4   ...r funds included in the Donor-Restricted Funds for

5.   ...are financial statements for a hospital
6.   ...repare the journal entries normally used in the General Funds to record the operating activities of hospitals
7.   Prepare the journal entries normally used in the Donor-Restricted Funds to record the use of restricted assets
8.   Define a "DRG"
9.   Explain the concept of the DRG reimbursement system used by Medicare
10. Contrast the DRG reimbursement system used by Medicare with the traditional cost-reimbursed system used by Blue Cross

Part II: Privately owned hospitals

11. Explain how contributions are recorded and reported
12. Prepare financial statements

For many years hospital accounting existed in almost a vacuum. Recently, however, a tremendous amount of attention has been directed toward the operating activities of these institutions and all the other organizations offering health care. This interest has resulted from the growth of **third-party health-care insurers** and rising costs. The third parties involved in financing the cost of health care are the federal and state governments and private insurance companies. The public programs that receive the most attention are Medicare and Medicaid. Medicare is primarily financed by the federal government through the Social Security program; Medicaid is a welfare-type program financed by both the federal and state governments.

Concern over rising health-care cost and limited accessibility has brought the concept of national health-care insurance to the forefront. As a result, hospitals, doctors, pharmaceutical companies, and others in the health-care industry have come under attack from the media and the country's legislative bodies. Steps are currently being taken at both the federal and state levels to revise our health-care delivery systems. Thus some of the third-party insurers are playing a larger role in this industry than ever before.

The interest of these third-party insurers, together with rising costs, has caused great emphasis to be placed on the accounting and reporting systems of hospitals and related health-care institutions. Health-care accounting is important because health-care insurers base their payments to an institution on allowable costs, some form of fixed rate reimbursement, or a combination of both. Thus the measurement and control of costs are critical. (The subject of reimbursement is examined later in this chapter.)

There is no separate set of generally accepted principles applicable only to hospitals. Instead, these institutions follow the same general rules and procedures for external reporting as other organizations. The division of authority between the GASB and the FASB that is discussed in Chapter 1 is relevant to these institutions. Hospitals that operate for a profit and voluntary not-for-profit hospitals are under the domain of the FASB, while government hospitals are under the domain of the GASB. Since this text is based on accounting for governmental units, we will follow the practices as outlined by the GASB. We have also included some of the recommendations included in *Audits of Providers of Health Care Services*[1] (Health Care Audit Guide). The American Hospital Association and the Healthcare Financial Management Association have also been active in developing accounting and reporting for hospitals.

Following these rules, governmental hospitals should be accounted for in an Enterprise Fund, and, as such, should follow a capital maintenance measurement focus and the full accrual basis of accounting. Although accounting rules followed by business organizations form the basis for hospital GAAP, in those

---

[1]American Institute of Certified Public Accountants, *Audits of Providers of Health Care Services* (New York: AICPA, 1993). Included in this publication are Statements of Position issued by the AICPA as of May 1, 1993. At the time of this writing, the AICPA's Health Care Committee is working on a revision of the Health Care Audit Guide. An overview of some of the changes is included in the "Concluding Note" at the end of this chapter.

situations in which a particular accounting principle is not applicable to hospital operations it should be ignored. The provisions of GASB *Statement No. 20*, as discussed in the section on Internal Service Funds, also apply to accounting for hospitals.

Part I of this chapter covers accounting and reporting for hospitals that are under the Governmental Accounting Standards Board (GASB). Hospitals that are under the Financial Accounting Standards Board (FASB) are discussed in Part II.

Part I: Government Owned Hospitals

SECTION I—AN OVERVIEW OF HOSPITAL ACCOUNTING

Funds used by hospitals are categorized into two groups: General Funds and Donor-Restricted Funds. **General Funds** are used to account for day-to-day operations of a hospital and its nonrestricted resources. **Donor-Restricted Funds** are used to account for resources that must be used in compliance with the terms of an agreement, like a gift or grant. Notice that a restricted fund is used only when there is an *external* limitation placed on the use of the resources and the resources are not related to a bond agreement or third-party reimbursement.

General Funds

Balance sheet

As previously mentioned, General Funds are used to account for all assets and liabilities not included in the Donor-Restricted Funds. These assets and liabilities include operating resources, assets whose use is limited, assets and liabilities in agency funds, and plant resources. **Operating resources** are assets and liabilities associated with the normal daily operations of a hospital. Thus we find that current assets used in operations are reported in this group. These assets include items such as cash, receivable, inventories, and prepaid expenses. In addition, the current liabilities associated with daily operations are also included in this group. These include items such as accounts payable, notes payable, and accrued expenses.

Table 13–1 is an example of a typical balance sheet for a hospital. (A format similar to Table 13–4 is used by some hospitals.) Notice that the statement is divided into the two major groups of funds described above: General Funds and Donor-Restricted Funds. Operating resources include current assets, current liabilities, deferred third-party reimbursement, and estimated malpractice liabilities.

Assets whose use is limited are resources that are (1) set aside by the governing board for a specific purpose, (2) proceeds of debt issues and hospital funds on deposit with a trustee that have limited use, and (3) other resources whose use is limited by an agreement between the hospital and an outside party who is not the donor or grantor. Carefully study the types of assets in this cate-

TABLE 13-1   Balance Sheet—Hospital

Sample Hospital
Balance Sheets
December 31, 19X7 and 19X6

	19X7	19X6		19X7	19X6
Assets			*Liabilities and Fund Balances*		
General Funds			Current liabilities:		
Current assets:			Current installments of long-term debt		
Cash and cash equivalents	$ 3,103,000	$ 4,525,000	(note 7)	$ 970,000	$ 1,200,000
Assets whose use is limited—required for			Current portion of capital lease obliga		
current liabilities (notes 5, 7, and 8)	970,000	1,300,000	tions (note 7)	500,000	550,000
Patient accounts receivable, net of			Accounts payable	2,217,000	2,085,000
estimated uncollectibles of $2,500,000			Accrued expenses	3,396,000	3,225,000
in 19X7 and $2,400,000 in 19X6	15,100,000	14,194,000	Estimated third-party payor settle-		
Estimated third-party payor settlements—			ments—Medicaid (note 2)	2,143,000	1,942,000
Medicare (note 3)	441,000	600,000	Deferred third-party reimbursement	200,000	210,000
			Advances from third-party payors	122,000	632,000
			Current portion of estimated malprac-		
Supplies, at lower of cost (first-in,			tice costs (note 8)	600,000	500,000
first-out) or market	1,163,000	938,000	Retainage and construction accounts		
Other current assets	321,000	403,000	payable	955,000	772,000
Due from donor-restricted funds, net	—	500,000	Due to donor-restricted funds	300,000	—
Total current assets	21,098,000	22,460,000	Total current liabilities	11,403,000	11,116,000
Assets whose use is limited (notes 5, 7,					
and 8):			Deferred third-party reimbursement	746,000	984,000
By board for capital improvements	11,000,000	10,000,000			
By agreement with third-party payors			Estimated malpractice costs, net of cur-		
for funded depreciation	9,234,000	6,151,000	rent portion (note 8)	3,207,000	2,182,000
Under malpractice funding arrangement—			Long-term debt, excluding current install-		
held by trustee	3,007,000	2,682,000	ments (note 7)	22,644,000	23,614,000
Under indenture agreement—held by					
trustee	11,708,000	11,008,000	Capital lease obligations, excluding cur-		
Total assets whose use is limited	34,949,000	29,841,000	rent portion (note 7)	500,000	400,000
Less assets whose use is limited and that			Fund balance	69,310,000	64,567,000
are required for current liabilities	970,000	1,300,000			
Noncurrent assets whose use is limited	33,979,000	28,541,000			
Property and equipment, net (notes 6 and 7)	51,038,000	50,492,000			
Other assets:					
Prepaid pension cost (note 12)	85,000	35,000			
Deferred financing costs	693,000	759,000			
Investment in affiliated company (note 4)	917,000	576,000	Commitments and contingent liabilities		
			(notes 3, 6, 8, 12, and 16)	—	—
Total other assets	1,695,000	1,370,000		$107,810,000	$102,863,000
	$107,810,000	$102,863,000			
Donor-Restricted Funds			Accounts payable	$ 205,000	$ 72,000
Specific-purpose funds			Deferred grant revenue	92,000	—
Cash	$ 378,000	$ 378,000	Due to general funds	—	255,000
Investments, at cost that approximates			Fund balance	1,422,000	1,041,000
market	728,000	455,000		$ 1,719,000	$ 1,368,000
Grants receivable	613,000	535,000			
	$ 1,719,000	$ 1,368,000			
Plant replacement and expansion funds			Due to general funds	$ —	$ 345,000
Cash	$ 24,000	$ 321,000	Fund balance	558,000	521,000
Investments, at cost that approximates					
market	252,000	165,000			
Pledges receivable, net of estimated					
uncollectibles of $60,000 in 19X7 and					
$120,000 in 19X6	132,000	380,000			
Due from general funds	150,000	—		$ 558,000	$ 866,000
	$ 558,000	$ 866,000			
Endowment funds			Fund balance	$ 5,259,000	$ 6,073,000
Cash	$ 1,253,000	$ 653,000			
Investments, net of $175,000 valuation					
allowance in 19X7, market value					
$3,798,000 in 19X7 and $5,013,000 in					
19X6 (note 9)	3,856,000	5,320,000			
Due from general funds	150,000	100,000		$ 5,259,000	$ 6,073,000
	$ 5,259,000	$ 6,073,000			

See accompanying notes to financial statements.

Source: American Institute of Certified Public Accountants, *Audits of Providers of Health Care Services*, May 1993, Appendix A. Copyright © 1993 by American Institute of Certified Public Accountants, Inc. Reprinted with permission.

gory. Notice in Table 13–1 that in 19X7 there were $970,000 of current liabilities that were to be paid from these assets and that the remainder were noncurrent assets whose use is limited. Details of the specific types of assets included in each category (e.g., cash, securities, etc.) are identified in note 5.

Agency Funds are resources a hospital holds that belong to other persons, such as patients and doctors. These are similar to the Agency Funds used by governmental units. There are no separate assets identified as Agency Funds in Table 13–1.

Plant resources are property, plant, and equipment used by a hospital in its general operations and any related liabilities. In general, the General Funds category is used to account for all assets and liabilities not included in Donor-Restricted Funds. In Table 13–1, property, plant, and equipment, net of accumulated depreciation, total $51,038,000 on December 31, 19X7. Long-term debt associated with property, plant, and equipment is reported in the $22,644,000 and in the capital lease liability. Details of specific assets and accumulated depreciation are reported in note 6.

The net assets of the General Funds, $69,310,000, is reported as *Fund balance*. Notice that this amount increased by almost $5 million from 19X6 to 19X7.

Operating statement

The operating statement of a hospital is the statement of revenues and expenses of General Funds (see Table 13–2). In general, the full accrual basis of accounting is used. Therefore, we are measuring expenses and not expenditures, and depreciation is included in the measurement of income. Review Table 13–2. Notice that *patient service revenue* is the main sources of revenue for the operations of the hospital. *Net patient service revenue* is the excess of the gross billings for services less provisions for charity care, contractual adjustments with third parties, and other similar items the hospital does not expect to collect. These adjustments do *not* include a provision for uncollectible accounts. The "other similar items" will be examined later in this chapter. Included in this category, however, are charges for patient room and board, use of an operating room or a recovery room, and other professional services such as laboratory fees.

Other revenue is generated by normal day-to-day activities, other than patient care, that are related to the organization's central operations. It includes revenue from student tuition, parking fees, and gift shop revenues. In addition, it includes gifts, grants, and endowment income restricted by donors to finance charity care.

Operating expenses are expenses incurred in the day-to-day operations of a hospital. These include nursing, general and administrative services, interest and depreciation. The classifications used in Table 13–2 are common for hospital operating statements.

Nonoperating gains (losses) are peripheral or incidental gains and losses related to hospital operations. These include unrestricted gifts, donated services, gains and losses on investment transactions, and income from investments whose use is limited by the board.

The final figure on the operating statement is labeled *Revenues and gains*

TABLE 13–2   Statements of Revenue and Expenses of General Funds—Hospital

Sample Hospital
Statements of Revenue and Expenses of General Funds
Years Ended December 31, 19X7 and 19X6

	19X7	19X6
Net patient service revenue (notes 3 and 7)	$92,656,000	$88,942,000
Other revenue	6,010,000	5,380,000
Total revenue	98,666,000	94,322,000
Expenses (notes 7, 8, 12, and 16):		
Professional care of patients	53,016,000	48,342,000
Dietary services	4,407,000	4,087,000
General services	10,888,000	9,973,000
Administrative services	11,075,000	10,145,000
Employee health and welfare	10,000,000	9,335,000
Medical malpractice costs	1,125,000	200,000
Depreciation and amortization	4,782,000	4,280,000
Interest	1,752,000	1,825,000
Provision for bad debts	1,010,000	1,103,000
Total expenses	98,055,000	89,290,000
Income from operations	611,000	5,032,000
Nonoperating gains (losses):		
Unrestricted gifts and bequests (note 11)	822,000	926,000
Loss on investment in affiliated company (note 4)	(37,000)	(16,000)
Income on investments of endowment funds	750,000	650,000
Income on investments whose use is limited:		
By board for capital improvements	1,120,000	1,050,000
By agreements with third-party payors for funded depreciation	850,000	675,000
Under indenture agreement	100,000	90,000
Other investment income	284,000	226,000
Nonoperating gains, net	3,889,000	3,601,000
Revenue and gains in excess of expenses and losses	$ 4,500,000	$ 8,633,000

See accompanying notes to financial statements.

Source: American Institute of Certified Public Accountants, *Audits of Providers of Health Care Services,* New York, May 1993, Appendix A. Copyright © 1993 by American Institute of Certified Public Accountants, Inc. Reprinted with permission.

in excess of expenses and losses. This is the "net income" of a hospital. It is important to note that revenues (and expenses) and gains (and losses) associated with Donor-Restricted Funds are not included in the operating statement for a hospital. These items are reported on the statement of changes in fund balances.

Statement of changes in fund balances

The statement of changes in fund balances for the General Funds is a summary reconciliation of the beginning and ending fund balances of the included funds. Table 13–3 is a typical statement reporting the changes in fund balances.

TABLE 13–3   Statements of Changes in Fund Balances—Hospital

Sample Hospital
Statements of Changes in Fund Balances
Years Ended December 31, 19X7 and 19X6

	19X7				19X6			
		Donor-Restricted Funds				Donor-Restricted Funds		
	GENERAL FUNDS	SPECIFIC-PURPOSE FUNDS	PLANT REPLACEMENT AND EXPANSION FUNDS	ENDOWMENT FUNDS	GENERAL FUNDS	SPECIFIC-PURPOSE FUNDS	PLANT REPLACEMENT AND EXPANSION FUNDS	ENDOWMENT FUNDS
Balances at beginning of year	$64,567,000	$1,041,000	$521,000	$6,073,000	$56,679,000	$ 933,000	$501,000	$5,973,000
Additions:								
Revenues and gains in excess of expenses and losses	4,500,000	—	—	—	8,633,000	—	—	—
Gifts, grants, and bequests (notes 10 and 11)	—	869,000	220,000	—	—	558,000	290,000	—
Investment income	—	62,000	20,000	—	—	50,000	15,000	—
Net realized gain on sale of investments	—	—	100,000	—	—	—	20,000	100,000
Transfer to finance property and equipment additions	243,000	—	(243,000)	—	255,000	—	(255,000)	—
	4,743,000	931,000	97,000	—	8,888,000	608,000	70,000	100,000
Deductions:								
Provision for uncollectible pledges	—	—	(60,000)	—	—	—	(50,000)	—
Capital contribution to Sample Health System (note 11)	—	—	—	—	(1,000,000)	—	—	—
Net realized loss on sale of investments	—	—	—	(639,000)	—	—	—	—
Unrealized loss on marketable equity securities (note 9)	—	—	—	(175,000)	—	—	—	—
Transfer to other revenue	—	(550,000)	—	—	—	(500,000)	—	—
	—	(550,000)	(60,000)	(814,000)	(1,000,000)	(500,000)	(50,000)	—
Balance at end of year	$69,310,000	$1,422,000	$558,000	$5,259,000	$64,567,000	$1,041,000	$521,000	$6,073,000

See accompanying notes to financial statements.

Source: American Institute of Certified Public Accountants, *Audits of Providers of Health Care Services*, New York, May 1993, Appendix A. Copyright © 1993 by American Institute of Certified Public Accountants, Inc. Reprinted with permission.

Notice that for the General Funds the statement includes the bottom line of the operating statement, Revenue and gains in excess of expenses and losses, and transfers to or from other funds. Since detailed revenues, expenses, gains, and losses are identified on the operating statement of the General Funds, there is no need to repeat them on the statement of changes in fund balances. Notice, however, how much more detail is reported for the Donor-Restricted Funds. We will explain why this is done later in this chapter.

Statement of cash flows for general funds

The GASB requires a statement of cash flows for all government owned hospitals. Since government owned hospitals are reported as Enterprise Funds and we have not emphasized the preparation of cash flow statements, we will not provide a cash flow statement for a government owned hospital. A cash flow statement for an Enterprise Fund is contained in Chapter 7. Since we did not illustrate a cash flow statement for a nongovernmental unit, we have included one for a privately owned hospital in Part II of this chapter. The major differences between the FASB and the GASB version are that the GASB requires

1. A four-level classification of cash flows: (a) operations, (b) noncapital financing, (c) capital financing, and (d) investing
2. Restricted and unrestricted cash flows to be included on the statement
3. Cash flows from assets whose use is limited to be included on the statement

Donor-Restricted Funds

Donor-Restricted Funds are used to account for resources available to a hospital that have limitations placed on their use by donors or grantors. These generally include Endowment Funds, Plant Replacement and Expansion Funds, and Specific Purpose Funds. The Health Care Audit Guide provides for two major subgroups of Donor-Restricted Funds: temporarily restricted funds and permanently restricted funds. **Temporarily restricted funds** are those funds whose restrictions on use are not permanent. They include Term Endowment Funds, Plant Replacement and Expansion Funds, Specific Purpose Funds, and Other Donor-Restricted Funds (primarily Annuity Funds and Life Income Funds). **Permanently restricted funds** are those that have timeless restrictions on their use, such as Endowment Funds.

Temporarily restricted funds

Term Endowment Funds are used when resources are donated to a hospital and the terms of the agreement require that the principal be maintained for a specific period of time or until other restrictions have been satisfied. After the term restriction(s) has been satisfied, the principal can be used as the hospital desires or as prescribed in the endowment contract. Thus a Term Endowment Fund is similar to a Nonexpendable Trust Fund in governmental accounting. The financial reporting of the fund's income depends on whether it is restricted or unrestricted. If the income is restricted, it is usually reported in a Specific Purpose Fund, Plant Replacement and Expansion Fund, or as other operating revenue in the General Funds. If it is unrestricted, the income should be reported in the General Funds as nonoperating gains. In either case, it is not reported as revenue in the Term Endowment Fund.

Plant Replacement and Expansion Funds are used to accumulate resources contributed by outsiders that can only be used to replace existing plant assets or to expand the existing plant. When the expenditures are made to acquire the assets, the necessary resources are transferred to the General Funds.

Specific Purpose Funds consist of resources that are donor- or grantor-restricted for specific operating purposes. For example, if an individual donates funds to a hospital for cancer research, these funds are recorded in a Specific Purpose Fund. As the research expenses are incurred, they are recorded in the General Funds. Periodically an amount equal to the research is transferred from the Specific Purpose Fund to the General Funds to "cover" the expenses. This transfer is generally recorded as other revenue in the General Funds and a reduction of fund balance in the Specific Purpose Fund.

Other Donor-Restricted Funds consist of resources that are donor or grantor restricted like Student Loan Funds, Annuity Funds, and Life Income Funds. **Student Loan Funds** are resources whose use is limited to making loans to medical students. These resources from donors or grantors are loaned to students who must repay them, usually with interest. The interest is used to "cover" operating expenses and bad debts, as well as to make additional loans. If a portion of the loans can be "forgiven," these funds are temporarily restricted funds. If the entire loan must be repaid, these funds should be classified as permanently restricted funds.

Annuity Funds are donor or grantor resources that require a *specific dollar amount* to be paid to the donor or other party for a specified period of time. This dollar amount is usually in the form of income. Such a situation occurs when a donor gives resources to a hospital, but some form of periodic income payments must be made to a specific party in the form of income to that party. Thus a donor can give a principal amount to a hospital and reserve a guaranteed income for a particular period of time. After the time elapses or a specific event occurs, the principal is available to the hospital to be used for a restricted or unrestricted purpose.

Life Income Funds are donor resources that require *all of the income* earned by these resources to be paid to the donor or other party for a specified period of time. This period of time is usually the lifetime of the person receiving the income. Life Income Funds are similar to Annuity Funds. The difference is that Annuity Funds require a specific amount to be paid to another party each year, while Life Income Funds require the entire amount of the earnings of the fund to be paid to another party each year. After a specified period of time, the *principal* of both funds is available to the hospital to be used for a restricted or unrestricted purpose.

Permanently restricted funds

Permanently restricted funds are donor-provided resources whose principal must be maintained and whose income is usually available for a hospital to use for either an unrestricted or a restricted purpose. These types of funds are called **Endowment Funds**. Accounting procedures for these funds are similar to those followed by Nonexpendable Trust Funds used by governmental units. Financial reporting of the fund's income depends on whether it is restricted or unrestricted. If the income is restricted, it is usually reported in a Specific Purpose Fund, Plant Replacement and Expansion Fund, or as other operating revenue in the General Funds. If it is unrestricted, the income should be reported in the General Funds as nonoperating gains. In either case, it is not reported as revenue in the Term Endowment Fund.

Donated funds maintained in a separate trust

In some instances, a donor may create a legal trust that is independent of the hospital. When this happens, the hospital does not have control over the resources of the trust because the trust is administered by a third party. Income from such a trust is usually given to the hospital. Since the hospital does not have control over the principal of the trust, these resources are not reported on the hospital's balance sheet. The hospital is required, however, to disclose information about these funds in the notes to the financial statements. If the principal of the fund reverts to the hospital after some time or specified event, the hospital may report these assets on its financial statements.

Financial Statements for Donor-Restricted Funds

Balance sheet

Refer again to Table 13–1, the balance sheet of Sample Hospital. Notice that assets of the Donor-Restricted Funds usually consist of cash, investments, and receivables. Due to the nature of the limitations on the use of these assets, they are usually invested until the hospital has incurred expenses or purchased assets that comply with the donor's restrictions. The equity side of the balance sheet usually consists of amounts due to other funds and the fund balance.

Operating statement

Operating statements are *not* prepared for the Donor-Restricted Funds. Instead a statement of changes in fund balances, such as that in Table 13–3, is presented. Notice that a summary of the changes in the balance of the General Funds also is included. The most important feature of this statement, however, is that the changes in the donor- or grantor-restricted funds are *never* reported as income or loss but rather as changes in fund balance. An operating statement is only prepared for the daily operations of the hospital accounted for in the General Funds.

To provide the information necessary to prepare the statement of changes in fund balances, the source of each change is needed. Therefore we will identify these items as Fund balance, followed by an identification of the event that caused fund balance to change. For example, earnings from investments would be credited to Fund balance—investment income. Remember that these items are *not* considered to be revenues.

Statement of cash flows

When discussing financial reporting for governmental units, we indicated that whenever the full accrual basis of accounting is used and a balance sheet and an income statement are presented, a statement of cash flows also should be provided. The same rules apply to hospital reporting. As previously mentioned, a detailed discussion of the cash flow statement is beyond the scope of this text.

Now that you have an understanding of the funds and the financial statements involved in hospital accounting, we will discuss the operating transactions generally incurred by these funds.

SECTION II—ACCOUNTING PROCEDURES FOR THE GENERAL FUNDS

The General Funds include the overall operations of a hospital, assets whose use is limited, Agency Funds, and plant resources. Since Agency Funds are discussed in Chapter 8, they are not included here. The major source of operating revenue for a hospital is from nursing services and other professional services. These items are recorded at the *gross* (established) rate. To illustrate, assume that the regular charges for these services are $1,700,000. To record this information, the following entry is made:[2]

Patient accounts receivable	1,700,000	
Patient service revenues		1,700,000
To record gross patient service revenue.		

Although we use one account for each type of revenue, remember that this is a *control* account and it is used in the same manner as a control account in governmental accounting. Subsidiary records are used to accumulate the revenues for the unit to which the patient was admitted or whose services were used; for example, room and board, general nursing services, surgery, pediatrics, obstetrics, radiology, and EKG. Total patient service revenue is reported on the operating statement net of provisions for charity care, contractual rate adjustments with

[2]Assume that the hospital used in this illustration has been in operation for several years.

third parties, and other similar items that the hospital does not expect to collect. This amount, however, is not reduced by a provision for uncollectible accounts.

In the health-care industry, it is common for third parties to pay for medical costs. These third parties usually place limits on the amount that they will reimburse the hospital. Whether the reimbursement is based on allowable costs or some form of a fixed rate, the amount "allowed" by the third-party payer is often less than the established rates. The difference between these two amounts is referred to as a *contractual adjustment*. Usually the hospital will not collect these amounts. In such instances the uncollectible amounts are written off. If the hospital can bill the difference between the amount charged and the amount reimbursed by third-party payers from the patients, these amounts are not included in the contractual adjustments. Instead they are billed to the patients. (The subject of reimbursement is examined later in this chapter.)

Other types of adjustments to gross patient revenues are made for charity work and "discounts" granted to the clergy, volunteers, and employees. In these cases the adjustments represent the amount of the established billing rates that the hospital will not collect. The only difference lies in the reason they will not be collected.

The deduction for bad debts is an estimate of the uncollectible accounts. This estimate is usually made by the allowance method. Since the allowance method for accounting for bad debts has already been discussed in relation to governmental accounting, it will not be reexamined here.

If the hospital encounters contractual adjustments of $90,000 and charity services of $50,000, and its management estimates uncollectible accounts to be $65,000, the following entry is made:

Provision for contractual adjustments	90,000	
Provision for charity services	50,000	
Uncollectible accounts expense	65,000	
Allowance for contractual adjustments		5,000
Allowance for uncollectible accounts		65,000
Patient accounts receivable		135,000
To record deductions from patient revenues.		

Since we are using entries that summarize a hospital's activities over a full year, it is important to remember that some of the revenue deductions are realized during the year, but others will not be realized until some time in the future. For example, some contractual adjustments have been determined during the year and can be applied directly against the patient's account, whereas in other cases the amount must be estimated. In the above journal entry, it was assumed that $85,000 of contractual adjustments were realized during the year and that an amount of only $5,000 had to be estimated at the end of the year.

In case of charity services, however, a hospital should classify a patient as a "charity patient" as soon as possible. Therefore the entire amount of the provision for charity services ($50,000) is deducted directly from Patient accounts receivable. Like the realized contractual adjustments, these amounts are known and the specific receivables to which they apply are also known. The net result of these two situations is a credit to Patient accounts receivable for $135,000 ($85,000 for contractual adjustments plus $50,000 for charity services).

In addition, you will recall from previous discussions that the uncollectible account allowance is used because it is not known which patients will turn out to be "bad debts." As a result, the entire amount of the estimated bad debts must be debited to the *Uncollectible accounts expense* and credited to the *Allowance for uncollectible accounts*. Thus each element in the above entry must be carefully analyzed.

During the year, collections of $1,400,000 of receivables are recorded as follows:

Cash	1,400,000	
Patient accounts receivable		1,400,000
To record collection of receivables.		

The expenses related to the general operation of a hospital consist of nursing and other professional services, general services, fiscal services, and administrative services. The entry used to record some of these is (amounts assumed):

Professional care of patients expense	750,000	
Dietary services expense	50,000	
General services expense	200,000	
Administrative services expense	145,000	
Interest expense	155,000	
Cash		1,100,000
Accounts payable, salaries payable, etc.		200,000
To record certain operating expenses.		

For simplicity, we have combined the recording and payment of expenses in the above entry, and we have combined several liability items. Since we are dealing with summary journal entries that cover an entire year, this will have no effect on the results of our illustrations.

During the year, the acquisition and use of inventory items is recorded as follows (amounts assumed):

Inventories	150,000	
Accounts payable		150,000
To record purchase of inventory.		
Professional care of patients expense	70,000	
Dietary services expense	50,000	
Administrative services expense	20,000	
Inventories		140,000
To record use of inventory.		

Since full accrual accounting is used for hospitals, items of property, plant, and equipment are recorded as assets when acquired and are depreciated over their useful lives. The entry to record this expense is as follows (amounts assumed):

Depreciation expense	200,000	
Accumulated depreciation—plant and equipment		200,000
To record depreciation for the year.		

Revenues received from parking fees, the cafeteria, and so forth, are recorded as follows (amounts assumed):

Cash	245,000	
Other receivables	5,000	
Other revenues		250,000
To record other revenues.		

Individuals such as nurses and doctors will occasionally donate their services to a hospital. This situation is prevalent in those hospitals operated by religious groups. Donated services are recorded as expenses at their fair value and offsetting credits are made to a nonoperating gain account. If $10,000 of such services is received during the year, the following entry is made:

Professional care of patents expense	10,000	
Nonoperating gains—donated services		10,000
To record the value of donated professional services.		

Requirements for recording donated services are very stringent. In general, a hospital must control the employment and duties of the donors, the services must be of significant value, and a reasonable basis for valuation of the services must be determined.[3] Donated services are not normally recorded for government-owned hospitals.

Receipt of a $100,000 unrestricted cash donation is recorded as follows:

Cash	100,000	
Nonoperating gains—cash donations		100,000
To record receipt of unrestricted cash donations.		

Other types of contributions (donations) are often received by hospitals. Supplies and commodities (such as medicines or materials) donated to a hospital and donations to cover the cost of charity services are recorded as other revenues.

---

[3]The FASB has issued a statement regarding the accounting procedures for contributions. At the time of this writing, the GASB has not endorsed this new statement. The provisions of the new statement are discussed in Part II of this chapter.

The General Funds often borrow and repay loans. If a hospital repays $15,000 of short-term loans, pays $3,000 in interest, and accrues $1,000 of additional interest, the following entry is made:

Notes payable	15,000	
Interest expense	4,000	
Cash		18,000
Interest payable		1,000

To record payment made on the principal of notes outstanding and the interest expense for the year.

As previously mentioned, segregation of funds by the managing board does *not* create a restricted fund. Segregated funds are treated as unrestricted (assets whose use is limited) because the board has the authority to change any previous actions. In our example we will assume that the managing board of the hospital has a fund that is used to provide resources for modernizing plant and equipment. During the year, the board transfers an additional $5,000 to the fund and investments made by the fund earn $3,000, of which $2,000 is received in cash. The entries to record these events are:

Cash—board-designated for plant and equipment	5,000	
Cash		5,000

To record board designation of resources for plant and equipment replacement.

Undesignated fund balance	5,000	
Fund balance designated for plant and equipment		5,000

To record an action of the board to designate resources for the acquisition of plant and equipment

Cash—board-designated for plant and equipment	2,000	
Interest receivable—board-designated investments	1,000	
Nonoperating gains—investment revenue		3,000

To record income from board-designated investments.

Undesignated fund balance	3,000	
Fund balance designated for plant and equipment		3,000

To record designation of fund balance for income on board- designated investments.

During the year, the hospital issues $5 million of twenty-year bonds to provide funds for the acquisition of new X-ray equipment. These resources are deposited directly with the First National Bank, as prescribed in the bond indenture. (Thus they are classified as assets whose use is limited.) The following entry should be made when the bonds are issued:

Cash—acquisition of equipment	5,000,000	
Bonds payable		5,000,000
To record the issuance of bonds and the deposit of the proceeds.		

Later in the year, the hospital uses some of the bond proceeds to acquire new equipment for its operating rooms. The following entry is necessary to record the acquisision:

Equipment	1,060,000	
Cash—acquisition of equipment		1,060,000
To record the purchase of operating room equipment.		

During the year, a hospital incurs several interfund transactions. To conserve space and provide an adequate explanation of these events, we will defer their discussion until a later section of this chapter. Since these and other entries will be recorded in the General Funds, closing entries will also be discussed in a later section of this chapter.

SECTION III—ACCOUNTING PROCEDURES FOR DONOR-RESTRICTED FUNDS

Hospital accounting uses the classification **Donor-Restricted Funds** to identify funds that have resources whose use is limited by external third-party donors or grantors. These funds are grouped as Temporarily Restricted Funds and Permanently Restricted Funds. Specific types of funds included in these groups are:

Temporarily restricted funds

1. Specific Purpose Funds
2. Plant Replacement and Expansion Funds
3. Term Endowment Funds
4. Other Donor-Restricted Funds
   a. Student Loan Funds
   b. Annuity Funds
   c. Life Income Funds

Permanently restricted funds

1.   Endowment Funds

We will limit our discussion of accounting procedures for Donor-Restricted Funds to Specific Purpose Funds, Plant Replacement and Expansion Funds, and Endowment Funds because these are the restricted funds most used by hospitals.

Specific Purpose Funds

Specific Purpose Funds consist of resources that are donor restricted for specific operating purposes. To illustrate, assume that a hospital receives a $500,000 grant from the K & A Drug Company that is intended to provide funds for research into methods of providing care and counseling for individuals who have become addicted to drugs. The entry to record the receipt of the grant is:

Cash	500,000	
Fund balance—K & A		500,000
To record receipt of research grant.		

If the managing board immediately invests $460,000 of the grant in marketable securities, the following entry is made:

Marketable securities	460,000	
Cash		460,000
To record the investment of grant proceeds.		

Expenses associated with the research program are recorded in the General Funds, and an appropriate amount of cash is transferred from the Specific Purpose Fund to the General Funds to "cover" the expenses. If the hospital pays $25,000 for the research program's expenses, the following entries are made:

Entries in the books of the General Funds

Research expenses	25,000	
Cash		25,000
To record research expenses.		
Due from K & A Fund	25,000	
Other revenue		25,000
To record amount due from K & A Fund.		
Cash	25,000	
Due from K & A Fund		25,000
To record receipt of cash from K & A Fund.		

Transfer to General Funds	25,000	
Due to General Funds		25,000
To record transfer to General Funds.		
Due to General Funds	25,000	
Cash		25,000
To record payment of cash to General Funds.		

Note that in the above entries the expense is recorded in the books of the General Funds and is offset by the other revenue. The effect of these transactions on the Specific Purpose Fund is reported in the statement of changes in fund balance.

If we assume that the income from the investment activity of the Specific Purpose Fund has the same restriction as the original grant, the following entry is made to record it (amounts assumed):

Cash	45,000	
Interest receivable	3,000	
Fund balance—investment income		48,000
To record investment income for the year.		

If the investment is not restricted, it is recorded in the same way as a nonoperating gain.

Plant Replacement and Expansion Funds

Plant Replacement and Expansion Funds are used to accumulate resources contributed by third-party donors or grantors that can only be used to replace existing plant assets or to expand existing plant. Since plant items are part of the General Funds, acquisition of these assets results in a transfer from the Plant Replacement and Expansion Fund to the General Funds. Assume that Mrs. John T. Kyeth donates $100,000 cash to a hospital and that this money must be used to replace existing assets. The receipt of this donation is recorded in the Plant Replacement and Expansion Fund as follows:

Cash	100,000	
Fund balance—Kyeth		100,000
To record gift from Mrs. Kyeth.		

The acquisition of equipment using the Kyeth gift is recorded as follows (amount assumed):

Entry in the books of the Plant Replacement and Expansion Fund	Transfer to General Funds Cash To record acquisition of equipment from the Kyeth Fund.	80,000	80,000

Entry in the books of the General Funds	Equipment
	   Transfer from Plant Replacement
	     and Expansion Fund
	To record acquisition of equipment from restricted funds.
		80,000	80,000

If resources of the fund are invested in marketable securities, recording investment income is determined by the restrictions, if any, placed on that income. The same restrictions that apply to the gift or grant usually apply to any income earned by investing the resources. Therefore, the investment income is recorded in the Plant Replacement and Expansion Fund as follows (amounts assumed):

Cash	1,500	
Interest receivable	500	
Fund balance—Kyeth—investment income		2,000
To record investment income.		

If there are no restrictions on the use of the investment income, it is recorded in the General Funds as a nonoperating gain.

Endowment Funds (Temporary and Permanent)

Endowment Funds are used when a donor gives a hospital a principal sum that must be maintained intact. The income from the investment of the assets can be either restricted or unrestricted in use. To illustrate, assume that an individual, Paige Boosie, gives a hospital marketable securities with a fair market value of $500,000. The receipt of the gift is recorded as follows:

Marketable securities	500,000	
Fund balance—Boosie Endowment		500,000
To record the receipt of Boosie Endowment Fund securities.		

If use of the income from the endowment is *restricted*—for example, to finance the cost of cancer research—it is recorded as an increase in fund balance in a Specific Purpose Fund. If this income totals $30,000 during the year and $25,000 of that amount is received in cash, the following entries are made:

Entry in the	Cash	25,000	
books of the	Interest receivable	5,000	
Endowment	Due to Specific Purpose Fund		30,000
Fund	To record investment income due to a Specific Purpose Fund.		
Entry in the	Due from Endowment Fund	30,000	
books of the	Fund balance—investment income		30,000
Specific Pur-	To record investment income from the Boosie		
pose Fund	Endowment Fund.		

Remember that revenues and expenses are *not* reported in the restricted funds. Instead, these items are classified as increases or decreases in fund balance. Therefore the above credit to Fund balance—investment income is a credit to the Fund balance account. The investment income designation is used in order to identify the source of the change in fund balance (see Table 13–3).

Use of the resources by the Specific Purpose Fund is similar to the accounting for the K & A grant illustrated earlier.

If the income is *not restricted* in its use, it is recorded as a nonoperating gain in the General Funds as follows:

Entry in the	Cash	25,000	
books of the	Interest receivable	5,000	
Endowment	Due to General Funds		30,000
Fund	To record investment income due to the General Funds.		
Entry in the	Due from Endowment Fund	30,000	
books of the	Nonoperating gains—investment revenue		30,000
General	To record unrestricted endowment revenue.		
Funds			

Note that under both of the assumptions the original recording of the assets earned was in the Endowment Fund and a "due to" account was used. The purpose of this sequence is to provide information for controlling the use of income from Endowment Funds.

SECTION IV—THE CLOSING PROCESS

The closing process for hospitals is similar to that used by other institutions. All the temporary accounts that were used during the period must be closed and their balances transferred to the Fund balance account for each fund.

In several of the preceding illustrations, we presented alternative solutions to situations involving the use of income in the restricted funds. To illustrate closing entries, we assume that:

1. The earnings of the Boosie Endowment Fund are not restricted—that is, they are recorded as nonoperating gains in the General Funds.

2. The $48,000 of investment earnings in the K & A Specific Purpose Fund and the $2,000 of investment earnings in the Kyeth Plant Replacement and Expansion Fund are restricted—that is, they remain in each fund.

Given these assumptions, the following closing entries are appropriate:

Entries in	Patient service revenue	1,700,000	
the books of	Other revenues	275,000	
the General	Nonoperating gains—donated services	10,000	
Funds	Nonoperating gains—cash donations	100,000	
	Nonoperating gains—investment revenue	33,000	
	Provision for contractual adjustments		90,000
	Provision for charity services		50,000
	Uncollectible accounts expense		65,000
	Professional care of patients		830,000
	Dietary services expense		100,000
	General services expense		200,000
	Adminstrative services expense		165,000
	Interest expense		159,000
	Depreciation expense		200,000
	Research expense		25,000
	Fund balance		234,000
	To close the revenue and expense accounts into fund balance.		
	Transfer from Plant Replacement and Expansion Fund	80,000	
	Fund balance		80,000
	To close the transfer accounts into fund balance.		
Entry in the	Fund balance—investment income	2,000	
books of the	Fund balance	78,000	
Plant Re-	Transfer to General Funds		80,000
placement	To close the temporary accounts into fund balance.		
and Expan-			
sion Fund			
Entry in the	Fund balance—investment income	48,000	
books of the	Transfer to General Funds		25,000
Specific Pur-	Funds balance—K & A grant		23,000
pose Fund	To close the temporary accounts into fund balance.		

Note that the only funds that have revenue and expense accounts are the General Funds. All the other hospital funds reflect the changes resulting from equity-type transactions by using Fund balance accounts. A review of Tables 13–2 and 13–3 will indicate how these items are reported in the financial statements.

SECTION V—REIMBURSEMENT PROGRAMS

One of the unique features of the health-care industry is the role played by third-party insurers. Health-care insurance programs have been established by the federal and state governments and by private insurance companies. The most popular programs are Medicare, Medicaid, and Blue Cross/Blue Shield. **Medicare** is a federal program that generally provides medical insurance for individuals who (1) qualify for Social Security and have attained age sixty-five, (2) are permanently disabled, or (3) elect coverage of physician's services at age sixty-five and agree to pay insurance premiums for this coverage. **Medicaid** is a program that is funded by both the federal and the various state governments and provides medical insurance for individuals who cannot afford to pay for health-care services. **Blue Cross/Blue Shield** is one of the largest insurance companies that furnish prepaid health insurance.

Prospective Medicare Plan

The Tax Equity and Fiscal Responsibility Act (TEFRA) required the Department of Health and Human Services to develop a **prospective reimbursement plan** for Medicare cases to replace the previously used cost-reimbursement plan. The problems with the cost-reimbursement plan were directly related to the *cost-based* nature of the reimbursement procedures. These problems can be summarized as follows:

1. There was little incentive for a hospital to be run efficiently, since reimbursement was generally based on costs incurred.
2. The same services may be reimbursed at different amounts for different hospitals.
3. The reimbursement process has created an excessively burdensome reporting process.[4]

The prospective reimbursement plan stipulates that payments to hospitals are based on the type of treatments provided the patient. For this purpose, types of illnesses and treatments have been categorized into **Diagnosis-Related Groups (DRGs)**. The actual amount reimbursed depends on the payment amount determined in advance by the government for each DRG. While there may be some differences in reimbursement amount in different areas of the country, each hospital in a given geographic area receives the same amount for each DRG, depending on its classification as urban or rural. Thus an uncomplicated appendectomy results in the same reimbursement to all hospitals in a given urban or rural area. This was *not* the case under the previously used cost-reimbursed system.

TEFRA also provided for separate consideration for several types of hospitals, such as pediatric and psychiatric hospitals. This initial exemption results

---

[4]"Executive Summary of 'The Report to Congress on Hospital Prospective Payment for Medicare,'" *Healthcare Financial Management*, 37, No. 3 (March 1983), 67–68.

from the fact that DRGs have not yet been developed for these institutions. Therefore the cost-based reimbursement system is still used in certain instances.

Efficient hospitals benefit from the prospective reimbursement plan because they are allowed to retain any reimbursement in excess of their cost. Inefficient hospitals, however, have to absorb any costs in excess of the reimbursement.

Efficiently operated hospitals benefit from this plan because they receive a reimbursement amount based upon the *average* cost of the DRG in the census division (region) in which they are located. Therefore this plan has several operating strategy implications for hospital management. Among these are:

1. Careful review of the staffing mix of the hospital
2. More efficient budgetary control through the use of a cost accounting system
3. Increased control over the use of supplies
4. Careful review of underutilized capital equipment
5. Establishment and monitoring of patient discharge planning systems, with the intent of minimizing the patient's stay in the hospital
6. More efficient policies relative to standard admission procedures, tests, and so on
7. Improved internal review of existing procedures[5]

Other Reimbursement Plans

Reimbursement under Medicaid usually follows the rules established for Medicare because of the federal matching funds provision of the Medicaid program and because Medicaid reimbursement generally is limited to the amount that would have been paid under Medicare for like services. Thus many states have adopted the new Medicare prospective reimbursement plan for Medicaid cases.

Private health-care insurance programs are not directly related to either Medicare or Medicaid. Therefore, changes in either of these systems will not necessarily produce changes in the reimbursement methods followed by companies such as Blue Cross. Blue Cross reimburses hospitals based on the terms of the contract in force in the state in which the hospital is located. These reimbursement plans generally vary from a cost-plus basis to reimbursement based on the charges made by the hospital for the services performed. A hospital that participates in the Blue Cross program usually agrees not to bill the patients for amounts in excess of the types of charges *covered* by Blue Cross. Examples of *noncovered* charges, which may be billed to the patients, include the difference between the charges for a private room and those for a semiprivate room and television rentals. Other examples of third-party payers include systems such as preferred-provider organizations and health-maintenance organizations. While these have accounting implications, a discussion of their effects is beyond the scope of this text.

[5]American Hospital Association, "Medicare Prospective Pricing: Legislative Summary and Management Implication," *Medicare Payment: Cost-Per-Case Management, Special Report 3*, April 1983, p. 6. Reprinted with permission of the American Hospital Association, copyright 1983.

Universal Health Care

At the time of the writing of this text, the U.S. Congress and President Clinton are debating the specific provisions of a universal health-care bill. This legislation is designed to assure everyone in the Untied States access to reasonably priced health-care insurance. Since the debate is in its early stages, it is impossible to predict the form of the final bill. However, the universal health-care bill may cause many changes in our health-care delivery system, and possibly, in accounting and reporting the financial data for that system.

Part II: Privately Owned Hospitals

AN OVERVIEW OF ACCOUNTING AND FINANCIAL REPORTING CHANGES

In 1993, the FASB issued *Statement No. 116*, "Accounting for Contributions Received and Contributions Made," and *Statement No. 117*, "Financial Statements of Not-for-Profit Organizations." These statements directly affect accounting and reporting for privately owned not-for-profit hospitals. Key features of these statements are summarized in this section.

Contributions

Statement No. 116 provides guidance for accounting and reporting of contributions. A key term used in this statement is **unconditional promise to give**. This commitment to give resources is contingent only on passage of time or on demand by the recipient. In general, contributions pledged and those actually received should be recorded as revenues (or gains) by the recipient *in the period received* and as expenses by the donor. Contributions should be valued at fair market value. If property is involved, its value should usually be measured by either quoted market prices or independent appraisals.

In some situations, a promise to give is contingent on some future event, for example, the death of the donor. This is a **conditional promise to give**. These gifts are not recognized as revenue until the conditions of the gift are substantially met. They must, however, be disclosed in the notes to the financial statements.

The asset side of contributions received and promises to give is recorded by the classifications of the assets: unrestricted assets, temporarily restricted assets, and permanently restricted assets. These categories are defined in Part I of this chapter.

At times unconditional promises to give are received in the current period, but the resources will not be received until a future period. These should be reported as temporarily restricted net assets. An exception to this is an instance in which the donor specifically states that the donation is intended to support current activities. In this type of situation, the donation should be reported as an unrestricted asset. Expirations of temporary restrictions on assets should be recognized in the period expenses are incurred for the restricted purpose.

Contributions of long-lived assets (fixed assets) are reported as a part of restricted net assets if the donors place restrictions on the length of time such assets can be used or the accounting policies of the institution limits use of the assets. If a gift or grant is received for the acquisision of fixed assets, it should be recognized in the period the assets are acquired.

Service contributions should not be recognized unless at least one of two conditions exist. The first is that nonfinancial assets are created or improved. The second is that specifically qualified individuals provide services that would have had to have been purchased if they had not been donated.

Financial Reporting

Statement No. 117 provides guidance for financial reporting for not-for-profit organizations. Three financial statements are required:

- Statement of financial position,
- Statement of activities, and
- Statement of cash flows.

Net assets and revenues and expenses (gains and losses) must be classified on these statements by type of restriction—permanently restricted, temporarily restricted, or unrestricted. *Statement No. 117* describes the format for reporting the various financial statement elements, but it does not include discussion of how these elements should be valued.

The main focus of financial statements is the organization as a whole. This concept is borrowed from the combined governmental statements; however, the reporting requirements differ. Instead of a fund-by-fund report, *Statement No. 117* uses a homogeneous group concept. That is, financial statement elements are aggregated into similar groups. Examples of these groups are cash and cash equivalents; accounts receivable; marketable securities; and land, buildings, and equipment. Any assets that have donor-imposed restrictions must be reported separately from unrestricted assets of a similar nature.

While *Statement No. 117* applies to all not-for-profit organizations that come under the FASB, governmental health-care units may continue to follow the accounting procedures illustrated in Part I of this chapter.

Statement of financial position (balance sheet)

A statement of financial position (balance sheet) prepared under the requirements of *Statement No. 117* is presented in Table 13–4. Compare this with the balance sheet illustrated in Table 13–1. Notice that the overall format of the statements is different. In Table 13–1 the focus of attention is on the particular fund type: General Funds, Specific Purpose Funds, and the like. In Table 13–4, however, the emphasis is on the homogenous grouping of all assets and liabilities, and only the "Net assets" (the equivalent of fund balance) are segregated by

TABLE 13-4 Statements of Financial Position—Health-Care Unit

Private Hospital
Statements of Financial Position
December 31, 19X1 and 19X0

	19X1	19X0
Assets		
Cash and cash equivalents	$ 75,000	$ 460,000
Patient accounts and notes receivable	2,130,000	1,670,000
Inventories and prepaid expenses	610,000	1,000,000
Contributions receivable	3,025,000	2,700,000
Short-term investments	1,400,000	1,000,000
Restricted assets in Specific Purpose Funds	1,210,000	1,200,000
Restricted assets in Plant Replacement and Expansion Funds	1,900,000	1,760,000
Restricted assets in Endowment Funds	2,100,000	1,600,000
Long-term investments	218,070,000	203,500,000
Land, buildings, and equipment	61,700,000	63,590,000
Total assets	$292,220,000	$278,480,000
Liabilities and Net Assets		
Liabilities:		
Accounts payable	$ 2,000,000	$ 1,000,000
Refundable advance	-0-	650,000
Accrued expenses payable	570,000	50,000
Estimated malpractice costs	875,000	1,300,000
Notes payable	-0-	1,140,000
Annuity obligations	1,685,000	1,700,000
Long-term debt	5,500,000	6,500,000
Total liabilities	10,630,000	12,340,000
Net assets:		
Unrestricted	115,228,000	103,670,000
Temporarily restricted	24,342,000	25,470,000
Permanently restricted	142,020,000	137,000,000
Total net assets	281,590,000	266,140,000
Total liabilities and net assets	$292,220,000	$278,480,000

Accompanying Summary of Significant Accounting Policies and Notes to Financial Statements not included.

Source: Adapted from Financial Accounting Standards Board *Statement No. 117*, "Financial Statements of Not-for-Profit Organizations" (Norwalk, CT: FASB, 1994); and AICPA, *Audits of Providers of Health Care Services* (New York: AICPA, 1993). Copyright © 1993 by American Institute of Certified Public Accountants, Inc. Reprinted with permission.

type of restriction. A key feature of the *Statement No. 117* balance sheet is that all due to and due from accounts are eliminated against each other.

To maintain a proper accounting of the restrictions placed on the use of each asset held, many health-care units will keep the same accounting records described in Part I of this chapter and use a work sheet (usually called a crossover work sheet) to combine the information in each fund. This work sheet is similar to the combined and combining financial statements illustrated in

Chapter 9. A key difference is that two columns are used for eliminations. These are used to eliminate the due to and due from accounts. A partial work sheet is illustrated in Table 13–5.

Statement of activities

The other financial statements required by *Statement No. 117* are illustrated in Tables 13–6 and 13–7. The statement of activities illustrated in Table 13–6 follows one of several possible formats, but this one seems to best fit the operations of a hospital. Notice that this statement combines the information presented in Tables 13–2 and 13–3. The net assets that are temporarily restricted and permanently restricted are reported by fund category (Specific Purpose Funds, Term Endowment Funds, etc.), usually in the notes to the financial statements. This detail may also be presented on the face of the financial statements.

Statement of cash flows

A cash flow statement is included for illustrative purposes. Detailed discussion of this statement is beyond the scope of this text.

Concluding Note

At the time of this writing, the AICPA's Health Care Committee is working on a revision of the Health Care Audit Guide. This new audit guide is due to be released as an exposure draft in late 1994. The Committee has tentatively decided that the basic financial statements should be similar to those in *Statement No. 117*. Specifically, the Committee plans to recommend the following statements:

1. Balance sheet (similar to that in Table 13–4, except it will have a classified format—current assets, current liabilities, etc.)
2. Statement of operations (similar to that presented in Table 13–2 for unrestricted net assets)
3. Statement of changes in net assets (similar to that in Table 13–3 for *all* changes in net assets grouped into three categories: unrestricted, temporarily restricted, and permanently restricted, rather than by fund type)
4. Statement of cash flows (similar to Table 13–7)

TABLE 13–5   Partial Work Sheet to Combine Fund Accounts

	GENERAL FUNDS	SPECIFIC PURPOSE FUNDS	ENDOWMENT FUNDS	Eliminations		TOTAL
				DEBITS	CREDITS	
Cash and cash equivalents	$10,000	$12,000				$22,000
Patient accounts receivable	8,000	—				8,000
Supplies	5,000	2,000	$1,000			8,000

TABLE 13–6   Statement of Activities—Health-Care Unit

Private Hospital
Statement of Activities
Year Ended December 31, 19X1

	UNRESTRICTED	TEMPORARILY RESTRICTED	PERMANENTLY RESTRICTED	TOTAL
Revenues, Gains, and Other Support				
Net patient service revenue	$ 12,840,000			$ 12,840,000
Contributions	1,200,000	8,110,000	280,000	9,590,000
Income from long-term investments	5,600,000	2,580,000	120,000	8,300,000
Other investment income	850,000			850,000
Net realized and unrealized gains on long-term investments	8,228,000	2,952,000	4,620,000	15,800,000
Other	150,000			150,000
Net assets released from restrictions:				
Satisfaction of program restrictions	11,990,000	(11,990,000)		
Satisfaction of equipment acquisition restrictions	1,500,000	(1,500,000)		
Expiration of time restrictions	1,250,000	(1,250,000)		
Total revenues, gains, and other support	43,608,000	(1,098,000)	5,020,000	47,530,000
Expenses and Losses				
Professional care of patients	13,795,000			13,795,000
Dietary services	1, 786,000			1,786,000
General services	3,680,000			3,680,000
Administrative services	3,746,000			3,746,000
Employee health and welfare	3,998,000			3,998,000
Medical malpractice costs	502,000			502,000
Depreciation and amortization	3,200,000			3,200,000
Interest	870,000			870,000
Provision for bad debts	193,000			193,000
Fund raising	200,000			200,000
Total expenses	31,970,000			31,970,000
Fire loss	80,000			80,000
Actuarial loss on annuity obligations		30,000		30,000
Total expenses and losses	32,050,000	30,000		32,080,000
Change in net assets	11,558,000	(1,128,000)	5,020,000	15,450,000
Net assets at beginning of year	103,670,000	25,470,000	137,000,000	266,140,000
Net assets at end of year	$115,228,000	$24,342,000	$142,020,000	$281,590,000

Accompanying Summary of Significant Accounting Policies and Notes to Financial Statements not included.

Source: Adapted from Financial Accounting Standards Board *Statement No. 117*, "Financial Statements of Not-for-Profit Organizations" (Norwalk, CT: FASB, 1994); and AICPA, *Audits of Providers of Health Care Services* (New York: AICPA, 1993). Copyright © 1993 by American Institute of Certified Public Accountants, Inc. Reprinted with permission.

TABLE 13–7 Statement of Cash Flows—Health-Care Unit

Private Hospital
Statement of Cash Flows
Year Ended December 31, 19X1

Cash flows from operating activities:		
Change in net assets	$15,450,000	
Adjustments to reconcile changes in net assets to cash flows from operating activities:		
Depreciation	3,200,000	
Fire loss	80,000	
Actuarial loss on annuity obligations	30,000	
Increase in patient accounts and notes receivable	(460,000)	
Decrease in inventories and prepaid expenses	390,000	
Increase in contributions receivable	(325,000)	
Increase in accounts payable	1,000,000	
Increase in accrued expenses	520,000	
Decrease in refundable advance	(650,000)	
Decrease in estimated malpractice costs	(425,000)	
Contributions restricted for long-term investment	(2,740,000)	
Interest and dividends restricted for long-term investment	(300,000)	
Net unrealized and realized gains on long-term investments	(15,800,000)	
Cash used for operating activities		$ (30,000)
Cash flows from investing activities:		
Insurance proceeds from fire loss on building	250,000	
Purchase of equipment	(1,500,000)	
Proceeds from sale of investments	76,100,000	
Purchase of investments	(74,900,000)	
Cash used for investing activities		(50,000)
Cash flows from financing activities:		
Proceeds from contributions restricted for:		
Investment in endowment	200,000	
Investment in term endowment	70,000	
Investment in plant	1,210,000	
Investment subject to annuity agreements	200,000	
	1,680,000	
Other financing activities:		
Interest and dividends restricted for reinvestment	300,000	
Payments of annuity obligations	(145,000)	
Payments on notes payable	(1,140,000)	
Payments on long-term debt	(1,000,000)	
	(1,985,000)	
Cash used by financing activities		(305,000)
Net decrease in cash and cash equivalents		(385,000)
Cash and cash equivalents at beginning of year		460,000
Cash and cash equivalents at end of year		$ 75,000
Supplemental data:		
Noncash investing and financing activities:		
Gifts of equipment	$ 140,000	
Gift of paid-up life insurnce, cash surrender value	80,000	
Interest paid	382,000	

Accompanying Summary of Significant Accounting Policies and Notes to Financial Statements not included.

Source: Adapted from Financial Accounting Standards Board *Statement No. 117*, "Financial Statements of Not-for-Profit Organizations" (Norwalk, CT: FASB, 1994); and AICPA, *Audits of Providers of Health Care Services*, (New York: AICPA, 1993). Copyright © 1993 by American Institute of Certified Public Accountants, Inc. Reprinted with permission.

These proposed statements are similar to those in *Statement No. 117*. The principal difference between them and those illustrated in this chapter for *Statement No. 117* is the separation of activities into two separate statements. While we did not illustrate this format, it is a possible option under *Statement No. 117*.

Since this information is not available in its final form at the time of this writing, we included statements from the "current" audit guide for comparison purposes. We feel that the accounting procedures illustrated in this chapter will continue to be used to segregate restricted resources for the reasons previously mentioned, and the crossover work sheet mentioned in this section likely will be used by hospitals to prepare their financial statements. At time of this writing, the GASB has not issued a new statement regarding the reporting format for government owned hospitals.

REVIEW QUESTIONS

PART I

Section I

Q13–1   Which major publications deal specifically with the application of generally accepted accounting principles for hospitals?

Q13–2   Does GAAP for government owned hospitals follow commercial GAAP?

Q13–3   Distinguish between General Funds and Donor-Restricted Funds.

Q13–4   What activities are accounted for in the General Funds?

Q13–5   What are assets whose use is limited?

Q13–6   What is the difference between *operating resources* and *board-designated resources*?

Q13–7   How do *nonoperating gains (losses)* differ from *revenues and expenses* in the General Funds?

Q13–8   How is the income of restricted funds reported in hospital financial statements? Does this differ from General Funds income?

Q13–9   What is the difference between *restricted funds* and *General Funds*?

Q13–10 What is the difference between *Endowment Funds* and *Specific Purpose Funds*?

Q13–11 How do *Annuity Funds* differ from *Life Income Funds*?

Q13–12 Is a cash flow statement required for hospitals?

Section II

Q13–13 Hospital charges are recorded at the gross or established rate. How does the accounting system allow for a situation where an insurance company pays only a portion of the established rate?

Q13–14 How are donated services recorded?

Q13–15 How are resources segregated by the managing board?

Section III

Q13–16 Where are expenditures funded by Specific Purpose Funds reported?

Q13–17 How are assets purchased by a Plant Replacement and Expansion Fund reported in hospital financial statements?

Q13–18 How is income from Endowment Funds reported?

Section IV

Q13–19 Is it necessary to have a separate closing entry (or entries) for each fund?

Q13–20 What types of accounts are closed each period?

Q13–21 Are closing entries for hospitals different from those used for other fund accounting systems?

PART II

Q13–22 Distinguish between an unconditional promise to give and a conditional promise to give.

Q13–23 When should service contributions be recorded?

Q13–24 How does the balance sheet required by FASB *Statement No. 117* differ from the traditional hospital balance sheet?

Q13–25 How does the activities statement required by FASB *Statement No. 117* differ from the traditional hospital operating statement?

CASES

PART I

C13–1 Rodney deFine, the chief administrative officer of the First Street Hospital, is having an argument with Jane Bronson, the hospital's controller. Mr. deFine has recently received a gift of $100,000 from a wealthy benefactor. He wants to put money into a board-designated fund because if that is done, the board can do whatever it wants with the money. Ms. Bronson, however, feels that the hospital should talk with the donor to determine if there are any particular uses he wishes for his donation. Mr. deFine is concerned that if the donor wishes to use the money in a manner that does not meet the hospital's immediate needs, the hospital may have to turn away some patients because of a lack of facilities.

How would you handle this dilemma?

C13–2 Several young doctors have banded together to start a small outpatient-type hospital in a poor neighborhood in their spare time. This hospital is part of a large system of hospitals owned by the state. Since each of the doctors received his or her education free from the state in the form of scholarships, each feels a responsibility to help the citizens. These doctors plan to work at the hospital without pay. The chief administrative officer, Ms. Sara Stone, does not believe that the value of the donated services should appear in the financial statements of the hospital. The controller, Mr. Lucien LeDoux, feels that the conditions under which the services were donated require that they be recorded. Ms. Stone feels that if the revenue associated with the services is recorded it will look like the hospital has a great deal more revenue than it actually has, which may cause it a problem when seeking donations and grants. In addition, because of its simplistic operations, the doctors will look like they are taking large amounts out of the operating funds of the hospital in the form of salaries. On this latter point, the doctors are adamant; they do not want the value of their services recorded.

How would you respond to this situation?

C13–3 The chief administrative officer of the East Jeff Hospital, Ms. Vera Thomas, is attempting to find resources to add a new wing to the hospital. For the past several years, many patients have had to be turned away because of a lack of space. The hospital has a large endowment, but all earnings from these funds are restricted to various operating purposes; for example, providing continuing education for nurses and maintaining the parking lot. Ms. Thomas has approached you and asked if a recently received gift from T. W. Wealthy could be used to begin expansion. Mr. Wealthy donated $1 million to the hospital, but it was in his deceased wife's name. Ms. Wealthy recently died from cancer, and Mr. Wealthy established a cancer research fund in her name.

How would you respond to Ms. Thomas?

C13–4 Ms. Kathy Joewalski, the controller of the Green Lawn Hospital, is working with Ms. Rose Gloro to plan the hospital's first development fund campaign. Ms. Gloro wants the drive to be successful, and she would like to have as few limitations on the use of the monies raised as possible. Ms. Joewalski, however, feels that the hospital must ask the donors if they want to limit their use of these funds because of the accounting and reporting restrictions with which she must comply. Ms. Gloro is the wife of the chief administrative officer (CAO), Mr. Josef Gloro, and he and the managing board would like the money as free from restrictions as possible, even if it means overlooking restrictions placed on some donations. Mr. Gloro realizes that large donations are easily traced and the donor may wish to be informed of how his or her money was used, but smaller donations could easily be intermixed and the same explanation of use could be given to several of these types of donors. Besides, Mr. Gloro indicated that during his seven-year tenure as the hospital's CAO, not one small donor asked how his or her money was used. After all, he states, "If the gifts are used to further the hospital's operations, doesn't the entire community benefit?"

How would you react to this situation?

EXERCISES

PART I

Section I

E13–1   (Fill-in-the-blanks—general terminology)

1. The AICPA publishes the _____ as a source of information on hospital accounting.
2. There (is or is not) _____ a separate set of generally accepted accounting principles for hospitals.
3. Operating resources and board-designated resources are subdivisions of the _____ .
4. Endowment Funds, Plant Replacement and Expansion Funds, and Specific Purpose Funds are included in the _____ .
5. The daily operations of a hospital are accounted for in the _____ Funds.
6. Parking fees, cafeteria revenues, and pharmacy revenues are reported on the _____ as _____ .
7. Hospitals use the _____ basis of accounting.

E13–2   (Multiple choice—use of funds)

The Brite-Hope Hospital uses the following types of funds:

    a. General Funds
    b. Endowment Funds
    c. Plant Replacement and Expansion Funds
    d. Specific Purpose Funds

Using the letters given above, identify which fund or funds would be used to account for the following events:

1. The operations of the cafeteria.
2. A gift received from an individual for medical research (at this time consider only the receipt of the gift).
3. Income is earned on investments of money donated by the Manybucks Corporation (the original gift and all income earned must be used to provide up-to-date equipment for the hospital).
4. The hospital received $1 million in securities from an individual. The principal of the gift must be maintained intact. (Consider only the receipt of the gift).

5. The managing board of the hospital decided to start a fund for cancer research. It transferred $30,000 into the fund. Which fund would be used to record the receipt of the money?
6. The payment of salaries to the nursing staff.
7. Depreciation if recorded on the equipment in use.
8. The purchase of additional hospital equipment.

E13–3 (Identification of financial statements for hospital funds)

The following codes are available for some of the various types of financial statements issued by hospitals:

> BS—Balance Sheet
> SRE—Statement of Revenues and Expenses
> SFB—Statement of Changes in Fund Balance

Using these codes, identify which statement or statements would be prepared for each of the following funds:

1. General Funds _____
2. Endowment Funds _____
3. Plant Replacement and Expansion Funds _____
4. Specific Purpose Funds _____

E13–4 (Matching)

Match the items on the right with those on the left by placing the letter of the best match in the space provided.

_____ 1. General Funds		a. All income is required to be paid to the donor or other designated party for a period of time
_____ 2. Donor-Restricted Funds		
_____ 3. Patient service revenue		
_____ 4. Statement of changes in fund balances		b. Resources whose use is limited by a third-party donor or guarantor
_____ 5. Life Income Funds		c. Requires payments of specific amounts to be made to the donor or other party for a particular period of time
_____ 6. Nonoperating gains and losses		
_____ 7. Assets whose use is limited		
_____ 8. Annuity Fund		d. Reported as part of the General Funds
_____ 9. Balance sheet		e. Used to report investment income of Specific Purpose Funds
_____ 10. Statement of revenue and expenses		f. Peripheral or incidental gains or losses of a hospital
		g. Prepared for the General Funds
		h. Prepared for all funds
		i. Main source of revenue for a hospital
		j. Used to account for the day-to-day operations of a hospital

Section II

E13–5 (General Funds transactions)

The following transactions were incurred by the Numb Hospital during January 19X3:

1. The hospital billed its patients for $250,000.
2. Nurses and doctors employed by the hospital were paid their salaries, $100,000.
3. The chief administrative officer was paid her salary of $10,000.
4. The hospital paid its utility bill, $5,000.
5. Depreciation on the equipment was $34,000.
6. Doctors donated services valued at $3,000.
7. The board transferred $1,000 into a special management fund for contingencies.
8. An unrestricted donation of $4,000 was received.

REQUIRED: Record the above entries in the General Funds of the Numb Hospital.

E13–6 (General Funds transactions)

The managing board of the H Memorial Hospital established an Emergency Fund in order to provide for emergency repairs to hospital assets. During 19X1, $12,000 was used to repair the electrical system of the emergency rooms. Prepare the journal entry or entries necessary to record the use of the $12,000 of Emergency Fund assets. If more than one fund is involved, identify the funds used.

E13–7 (Recognition of depreciation for governmental units, colleges and universities, and hospitals)

Compare and contrast the method or methods of accounting recognition of depreciation for governmental units, colleges and universities, and hospitals.

E13–8 (Accounting for uncollectible patient accounts)

The Metro County Hospital could not collect the amount billed to a patient. The patient declared bankruptcy and had no assets with which to pay his debts. Assuming the patient owed the hospital $3,000, prepare the entry or entries necessary to record the uncollectible account if the hospital uses the "allowance method." After preparing the necessary entry or entries, indicate what effect the write-off will have on the balance sheet.

Section III

E13–9 (Use of funds)

The following transactions relate to the Tableaux Hospital. Indicate which fund or funds would be used to record the data.

1. Collected $2,345 from a patient.
2. Received a $100,000 grant from Toosuups Drug Company for a study of the effects of morphine on female patients.
3. Received unrestricted gifts of $50,000.
4. Purchased equipment for $125,000 by using resources previously accumulated in the Plant Replacement and Expansion Fund.
5. Research expenses totaling $12,000 were incurred in studying the effects of morphine on female patients.
6. The board decided to begin a fund for nursing education. Initially $10,000 of general hospital resources was transferred to the fund.
7. Marketable securities with a fair value of $15,000 were donated by WFJ, Inc. in order to help the hospital acquire new equipment.
8. The securities in number 7 produced income of $5,000. Assume that the investment income is restricted in the same way as the original gift.

E13–10 (Transactions involving restricted and **General Fund**s)

Using the same information given in Exercise 13–9, prepare the journal entries that would be used to record the data. Identify each type of fund used.

E13–11 (Description of the receipt and use of a gift)

A wealthy individual gave $500,000 to the City Hospital for the construction of a new surgery wing. *Explain* how the gift would be recorded and how the use of the funds would affect the financial statements of the hospital. Do not use journal entries.

E13–12 (Journal entries for the receipt and use of a gift)

Using the same information given in Exercise 13–11, prepare the journal entries that would be used to record the data. In addition, identify the fund or funds in which the entries would be recorded.

Section IV

E13–13 (Explanation of the closing process)

Explain the dual purpose of closing entries and relate the procedure to the financial statement reporting of fund balance.

E13–14 (Closing entries from data created by students)

Make up a trial balance for each type of fund that hospitals generally use. Use your imagination and knowledge regarding the type of transactions incurred by each type of fund. After you have completed the trial balances, prepare the necessary closing entries for each fund. As a practical suggestion, limit the number of temporary accounts in each trial balance to four or five.

E13–15 (Closing entries)

Prepare the closing entry (entries) necessary using the information from Exercise 13–5.

Section V

E13–16 (Discussion of the prospective Medicare reimbursement plan and federal expenditures)

Explain how the prospective reimbursement system for Medicare should help reduce federal expenditures for health care.

E13–17 (Explanation of the Medicare prospective reimbursement plan)

Assume that you have been hired as a consultant for the Faith Memorial Hospital. Your first task is to explain the Medicare prospective reimbursement plan to the controller. Outline the points you would make in your presentation.

PART II

E13–18 (Contributions)

Discuss how each of the following would affect the financial statements of Hope Hospital.
1. T. J. Goodfellow made the Medical Foundation the beneficiary of his life insurance. The policy had a face value of $1 million.
2. Two dozen students from the Martin Fortier High School donated their services to Hope Hospital. They worked in the afternoons after school. These students performed general tasks in the hospital.

E13–19 (Financial statements)

Using the following codes, indicate which statement would be used to report each item for a private hospital.

> BS—balance sheet (statement of financial position)
> SA—statement of activities
> CF—cash flow statement

_____ 1. Land, buildings, and equipment
_____ 2. Contributions
_____ 3. General services expense
_____ 4. Cash used to purchase equipment
_____ 5. Contributions receivable
_____ 6. Temporarily restricted net assets
_____ 7. Refundable advance
_____ 8. Restricted assets in Specific Purpose Funds
_____ 9. Estimated liability for malpractice costs
_____ 10. Fund-raising costs

PROBLEMS

PART I

Section I

P13–1 (Use of funds in hospital accounting)
Six different types of funds are generally used in hospital accounting. Identify at least three types of transactions that would require the use of each fund.

P13–2 (Analysis of the operations of a hospital)
You have been hired as a consultant to the managing board of Sample Hospital. Review the information presented in the statement of revenues and expenses contained in Table 13–2 and comment on the operations of the hospital.

P13–3 (Preparation of a balance sheet)
The following information is selected from the accounts of Serene Hospital:

General Funds
Cash and cash equivalents	$ 1,553
Assets whose use is limited—current	546
Accounts payable	600
Accrued expenses	1,614
Property, plant, and equipment (net)	25,519
Patient accounts receivable (net of estimated uncollectibles of $1,200)	6,922
Assets whose use is limited—noncurrent	14,270
Other current assets	202
Other assets	100
Current portion of long-term debt	250
Long-term debt	11,807
Due from other funds	175

Donor-Restricted Funds
Specific Purpose Funds:
Cash and cash equivalents	100
Accounts payable	36
Due to General Funds	125
Grants receivable	250

Plant Replacement and Expansion Funds:
Cash	160
Investments	85
Due to General Funds	50

Endowment Funds:
Cash	25
Investments	500

REQUIRED: Prepare a balance sheet for Serene Hospital as of December 31, 19X1.

P13–4 (Preparation of a statement of revenues and expenses)

The following selected information was taken from the books and records of Ward Street Hospital as of and for the year ended June 30, 19X1:

1. Patient service revenue totaled $16,000,000 with allowances amounting to $3,400,000. Other operating revenue aggregated $346,000 and included $160,000 from Specific Purpose Funds. Revenue of $6,000,000, recognized under cost-reimbursement agreements, is subject to audit and retroactive adjustment by third-party payers. Estimated retroactive adjustments under these agreements have been included in allowances.

2. Unrestricted gifts and bequests of $410,000 were received.

3. Unrestricted income from endowment funds totaled $160,000. Income from assets whose use is limited by the board totaled $82,000.

4. Operating expenses totaled $13,370,000 and included $500,000 for depreciation computed on the straight-line basis. However, accelerated depreciation is used to determine reimbursable costs under certain third-party reimbursement agreements. Net cost reimbursement revenue amounting to $220,000, resulting from the difference in depreciation methods, was deferred to future years.

5. Also included in operating expenses are pension costs of $100,000, in connection with a noncontributory pension plan covering substantially all of Ward Street Hospital's employees. Accrued pension costs are funded currently. Prior service cost is being amortized over a period of 20 years. The actuarially computed value of vested and nonvested benefits at year-end amounted to $3,000,000 and $350,000 respectively. The assumed rate of return used in determining the actuarial present value of accumulated plan benefits was 8 percent. The plan's net assets available for benefits at year-end was $3,050,000.

6. Gifts and bequests are recorded at fair market values when received.

7. Patient service revenue is accounted for at established rates on the accrual basis.

REQUIRED:
1. Prepare a formal statement of revenues and expenses for Ward Street Hospital for the year ended June 30, 19X1.

2. Draft the appropriated disclosures in separate notes accompanying the statement of revenues and expenses, referencing each note to its respective item in the statement

(AICPA adapted)

P13–5 (Matching)

Match items on the right with those on the left by placing the letter of the best match in the space provided.

_____ 1. Used to account for day-to-day operations of a hospital

_____ 2. Annuity Funds

_____ 3. Used to account for resources that must be used in compliance with the terms of an agreement, like a gift or grant

_____ 4. Resources set aside for a specific purpose by a hospital's governing board

_____ 5. Revenues from Specific Purpose Funds

_____ 6. Used to account for resources donated to a hospital for which the principal must be maintained intact

_____ 7. Specific Purpose Funds

_____ 8. AICPA audit guide for hospitals

_____ 9. Statement of revenue and expenses of General Funds

_____ 10. Donor resources that require all of the income earned by those resources to be paid to the donor or other party for a specified period of time

a. Donor-Restricted Funds
b. Prepared only for the General Funds
c. Endowment Fund
d. *Audits of Providers of Health Care Services*
e. Used to account for resources that are donor restricted for a particular operating purpose
f. General Funds
g. Assets whose use is limited
h. Reported on a statement of changes in fund balances
i. Donor resources that require a specific amount to be paid to the donor or other party for a particular period of time
j. Life Income Funds

Section II

P13–6 (Multiple Choice)

1. Under Cura Hospital's established rate structure, patient service revenues of $9,000,000 would have been earned for the year ended December 31, 19X0. However, only $6,750,000 was expected to be collected because of charity allowances of $1,500,000 and discounts of $750,000 to third-party payors. For the year ended December 31, 19X0, what amount should Cura record as net patient service revenue?
   a. $6,750,000
   b. $7,500,000
   c. $8,250,000
   d. $9,000,000

2. In June 19X1, Park Hospital purchased medicines from Jove Pharmaceutical Co. at a cost of $2,000. However, Jove notified Park that the invoice was being canceled and that the medicines were

being donated to Park. Park should record this donation of medicines as

  a. A memorandum entry only
  b. Other revenue of $2,000
  c. A $2,000 credit to operating expenses
  d. A $2,000 credit to nonoperating gains and losses

3. Cedar Hospital has a marketable equity securities portfolio that is appropriately included in the noncurrent assets in the General Funds. The portfolio has an aggregate cost of $300,000. It had an aggregate fair market value of $250,000 at the end of 19X2 and $290,000 at the end of 19X1. If the portfolio was properly reported in the balance sheet at the end of 19X1, the reported value of the securities at the end of 19X2 should be

  a. $0
  b. $360,000
  c. $250,000
  d. $290,000

4. Ross Hospital's accounting records disclosed the following information:

Net resources invested in plant assets	$10,000,000
Assets whose use is limited	2,000,000

What amount should be included as part of General Funds?

  a. $12,000,000
  b. $10,000,000
  c. $2,000,000
  d. $0

5. Cura Hospital's property, plant, and equipment, net of depreciation, amounted to $10,000,000 with related mortgage liabilities of $1,000,000. What amount should be included in the donor-restricted funds?

  a. $0
  b. $1,000,000
  c. $9,000,000
  d. $10,000,000

6. Proceeds from sale of cafeteria meals and guest trays to visitors operated by a hospital would normally be included in

  a. Net patient service revenue
  b. Nonoperating revenue
  c. Other revenue
  d. Nonoperating gains and losses

7. Which of the following normally would be included in Other Revenue of a hospital?

	REVENUE FROM EDUCATIONAL PROGRAMS	UNRESTRICTED GIFTS
a.	Yes	No
b.	Yes	Yes
c.	No	Yes
d.	No	No

The following information relates to the next three questions:

Metro General is a municipally owned and operated hospital and a component unit of Metro City. The council acts as the hospital's governing board. In 19X1, the hospital received $7,000 in unrestricted gifts and $4,000 in unrestricted bequests. The hospital has $800,000 in long-term debt and $1,200,000 in fixed assets.

The hospital has transferred certain resources to a hospital guild. Substantially all of the guild's resources are held for the benefit of the hospital. The hospital controls the guild through contracts that provide it with the authority to direct the guild's activities, management, and policies. The hospital has also assigned certain of its functions to a hospital auxiliary, which operates primarily for the benefit of the hospital. The hospital does *not* have control over the auxiliary. The financial statements of the guild and the auxiliary are *not* consolidated with the hospital's financial statements. The guild and the auxiliary have total assets of $20,000 and $30,000, respectively.

Before the hospital's financial statements were combined with those of the city, the city's statements included data on one Special Revenue Fund and one Enterprise Fund. The city's statements showed $100,000 in Enterprise Fund long-term debt; $500,000 in Enterprise Funds fixed assets; $1,000,000 in general long-term debt; and $6,000,000 in general fixed assets.

8. The hospital's fixed assets should be reported in the city's combined balance sheet as
   a. Hospital fixed assets of $1,200,000 in a separate "discrete presentation" hospital column
   b. Special Revenue Fund–type fixed assets of $1,200,000 in the General Fixed Assets Account Group column
   c. Part of $1,700,000 Enterprise Fund-type fixed assets in the Enterprise Fund–type column
   d. Part of $7,200,000 general fixed assets in the General Fixed Assets Account Group

9. The hospital's long-term debt should be reported in the city's combined balance sheet as
   a. Part of $900,000 Enterprise Fund–type long-term debt in the Enterprise Fund–type column
   b. An $800,000 contra amount against fixed assets

    c. Part of the $1,800,000 General Long-Term Debt Account Group

    d. A separate "discrete presentation" of $800,000 in the hospital column

10. What account or accounts should be credited for the $7,000 of unrestricted gifts and the $4,000 of unrestricted bequests?

a.	Other revenue	$11,000
b.	Nonoperating gains and losses	11,000
c.	Other revenue	7,000
	Nonoperating gains and losses	4,000
d.	Nonoperating gains and losses	7,000
	Other revenue	4,000

                                                            (AICPA adapted)

P13–7 (Journal entries and financial statements—General Funds)

City Hospital was established in 19X1. This nonprofit hospital began operations in January of that year. The following transactions occurred during the year:

1. In order to supply cash to begin operations, long-term revenue bonds were issued. The proceeds were $1,800,000. The bonds were issued for their face value.

2. The physical assets of the hospital were purchased for $1,500,000 cash. The appraised value of the land, building, and equipment was $300,000, $700,000 and $500,000 respectively.

3. Patients were billed a total of $3 million. The entire amount was for nursing services.

4. Inventory was purchased for $8,000 cash.

5. Patients were billed separately for professional services other than nursing care. The amount of the billing was $100,000.

6. The managing board decided to set up a fund for the replacement of the used equipment it had purchased in number 2. An initial contribution of $20,000 was made to the fund.

7. The entire amount transferred to the fund in number 6 was invested in marketable securities.

8. Inventories were used as follows:

Nursing care	$6,000
Dietary services	1,000

9. Patient receivables of $2,500,000 were collected.

10. Additional equipment was acquired, using general resources, $1,400.

11. Securities purchased by the board-designated resources were sold for $8,300. The original cost was $7,800. The difference represents investment revenue.

12. Operating expenses of the hospital were $1,750,000. Included in this amount were outstanding debts at the end of the year, $34,000;

the remainder were paid during the year. The expenses should be charged as follows:

Nursing care	$1,100,000
Dietary services	200,000
General services	150,000
Administrative services	300,000

13. Interest on the bonds for the year was $175,000. Of this amount, $87,500 was paid in cash.
14. The board-designated resources were used to pay $8,300 for new equipment.
15. Depreciation was recorded as follows: building $70,000; equipment, $51,000.

REQUIRED:
1. Prepare all the journal entries necessary to record the above transactions and identify the fund or funds involved.
2. Prepare a statement of revenues and expenses for the General Funds for 19X1.
3. Prepare a statement of changes in fund balance for the General Funds for 19X1.
4. Prepare a balance sheet for the General Funds at December 31, 19X1.

P13-8   (Journal entries and financial statements—General Funds)
Following is a trial balance for the Metro General Hospital:

Metro General Hospital
General Funds
Trial Balance
December 31, 19X1

Cash	$ 6,000	
Patient accounts receivable	20,000	
Allowance for uncollectible receivables		$ 3,000
Inventories	5,000	
Land	300,000	
Building	1,000,000	
Accumulated depreciation—building		34,000
Equipment	1,500,000	
Accumulated depreciation—equipment		55,000
Accounts payable		8,000
Bonds payable		2,000,000
Undesignated fund balance		731,000
	$2,831,000	$2,831,000

During 19X2, the following transactions took place:
1. Patients were billed for $1.5 million. Of this amount, $1.2 million was nursing services revenue and the remainder was other professional services revenue.

2. Inventories of $56,000 were purchased on credit.
3. Operating expenses were incurred as follows:

Nursing services expense	$375,000
Other profession service expense	265,000
General services expense	200,000
Administrative services expense	90,000

Assume that all the expenses were incurred on credit.

4. The board decided to establish a fund whose income would be used for the continuing education of nurses. An initial amount of $5,000 was used to establish the fund.
5. The full amount transferred in number 4 was invested in marketable securities.
6. Collections of patient receivables totaled $1,200,000. In addition, $3,000 of patient receivables was written off as uncollectible.
7. Payments of accounts payable totaled $900,000.
8. The use of inventories was recorded as follows:

Nursing services	$30,000
General services	20,000

9. The provision for estimated uncollectible accounts for the year was $2,000.
10. Income from board-designated investments was $300. The entire amount was collected in cash. Assume that the cash remained in the General Funds.
11. Depreciation was recorded as follows: building, $10,000; equipment, $12,000.
12. Interest of $100,000 was paid in cash.

REQUIRED:
1. Prepare all the journal entries necessary to record the above transactions and identify the fund or funds involved.
2. Prepare a statement of revenue and expenses for the General Funds for 19X2.
3. Prepare a statement of changes in fund balance for the General Funds for 19X2.
4. Prepare a balance sheet for the General Funds at December 31, 19X2.

Section III

P13–9 (Multiple choice)
1. On March 1, 19X0, Allan Rowe established a $100,000 Endowment Fund, the income from which is to be paid to Elm Hospital for general operating purposes. Elm does not control the fund's principal. Rowe appointed West National Bank as trustee of this fund. What

journal entry is required by Elm to record the establishment of the endowment?

   a. Cash   100,000

        Nonexpendable endowment fund   100,000

   b. Cash   100,000

        Endowment fund balance   100,000

   c. Nonexpendable endowment fund   100,000

        Endowment fund balance   100,000

   d. Memorandum entry only

2. In 19X1, Pyle Hospital received a $250,00 pure Endowment Fund grant. Also in 19X1, Pyle's governing board designated, for special uses, $300,000 which had originated from unrestricted gifts. What amount of these resources should be accounted for as part of the General Funds?

   a. $0

   b. $250,000

   c. $300,000

   d. $550,000

3. Revenue of a hospital from grants specified by the donor for research would normally be included in

   a. Nonoperating revenue

   b. Other revenue

   c. Net patient service revenue

   d. Nonoperating gains and losses

4. Revenue from educational programs of a hospital normally would be included in

   a. Nonoperating revenue

   b. Net patient service revenue

   c. Nonoperating gains and losses

   d. Other revenue

The following information relates to the next three questions:

Lori Hospital has a fiscal year ending on May 31. In March 19X1, a $300,000 unrestricted bequest and a $500,000 pure endowment grant were received. In April 19X1, a bank notified Lori that the bank received $10,000 to be held in permanent trust by the bank. Lori is to receive the income from this donation.

5. Lori should record the $300,000 unrestricted bequest as

   a. Nonoperating gains and losses

   b. Other revenue

   c. A direct credit to the Fund balance account

   d. A credit to operating expenses

6. The $500,000 pure Endowment Grant

   a. May be expended by the governing board only to the extent of the principal since the income from this fund must be accumulated

b. Should be reported as nonoperating revenue when the full amount of principal is expended

c. Should be recorded as a memorandum entry only

d. Should be accounted for as donor-restricted funds upon receipt

7. The $10,000 donation being held by the bank in permanent trust should be

a. Recorded in Lori's restricted endowment fund

b. Recorded by Lori as nonoperating revenue

c. Recorded by Lori as other operating revenue

d. Disclosed in notes to Lori's financial statements

8. Hospital financial resources are required by a bond indenture to be used to finance construction of a new pediatrics facility. In which of the following hospital funds should these resources be reported?

a. Agency

b. Trust

c. General

d. Endowment

9. In addition to the statement of changes in fund balance, which of the following financial statements should government-owned hospitals prepare?

a. Balance sheet and income statement

b. Balance sheet, income statement, and statement of changes in financial position

c. Balance sheet, statement of revenues and expenses, and statement of cash flows

d. Statement of funds, statement of revenues and expenses, and statement of cash flows

10. Land valued at $400,000 and subject to a $150,000 mortgage was donated to Beaty Hospital without restriction as to use. Which of the following entries should Beaty make to record this donation?

a.	Land	400,000	
	Mortgage payable		150,000
	Endowment fund balance		250,000
b.	Land	400,000	
	Debt fund balance		150,000
	Contributions		250,000
c.	Land	400,000	
	Debt fund balance		150,000
	Endowment fund balance		250,000
d.	Land	400,000	
	Mortgage payable		150,000
	Unrestricted fund balance		250,000

(AICPA adapted)

P13–10   (Journal entries and financial statements for restricted funds)

The West Street Hospital had the following transactions during 19X1.

1. A gift of $100,000 was received from Warso Stores. The terms of the gift specified that the principal amount must be maintained intact permanently. The income could be spent for any purpose that would help the hospital. The total amount of the gift was immediately invested in marketable securities.

2. First Construction Company gave the hospital a grant of $500,000 for cancer research. The proceeds from the grant were invested in marketable securities.

3. Paigekat Company donated $200,000 to the hospital for the construction of a building addition that would be devoted to dealing with mental patients.

4. Architectural fees for the building addition for the mental unit were paid in cash, $30,000. The remainder of the Paigekat gift was invested in marketable securities.

5. During the year, the hospital began a fund-raising drive for the mental unit. Pledges totaling $200,000 and cash donations totaling $30,000 were received. (*Hint*: Record the pledges as receivables.)

6. Investment income of $30,000 was received in cash on the First Construction Company Fund investments. In addition, $20,000 of investments matured. The hospital paid face value upon purchasing these securities. Assume that the investment income is restricted in the same way as the original grant.

7. Cancer research costs of $45,000 were incurred and paid by the General Funds. The First Construction Company Fund reimbursed the General Funds for these expenditures.

8. Income of $8,000 was earned by the Warso Stores Fund investments. Of this amount, $7,000 was received in cash.

9. Collections of pledges during the year totaled $80,000.

10. The General Funds paid $20,000 for part of the cost of the construction of the mental unit.

REQUIRED:

1. Prepare all the journal entries necessary to record the above transactions in the restricted funds of the West Street Hospital and identify each fund used. If an entry would not be recorded in a restricted fund, write "No entry" next to the transaction number.

2. Prepare a statement of changes in fund balances for the restricted funds for 19X1.

3. Prepare a balance sheet for each restricted fund as of December 31, 19X1.

P13–11   (Journal entries and selected financial statements for hospitals)

Following is a trial balance for the Darwin Memorial Hospital:

Darwin Memorial Hospital
General Funds
Trial Balance
July 1, 19X2

Cash	$ 12,000	
Patient accounts receivable	40,000	
Allowance for uncollectible patient accounts		$ 4,000
Land	600,000	
Buildings	2,500,000	
Accumulated depreciation—building		650,000
Equipment	2,000,000	
Accumulated depreciation—equipment		400,000
Accounts payable		15,000
Notes payable		100,000
Bonds payable		2,000,000
Fund balance		1,983,000
	$5,152,000	$5,152,000

During the 19X2–X3 fiscal year, the following selected transactions took place:

1. Patients were billed a total of $2 million. Of this amount, $1.3 million was for nursing services and the remainder was for other professional services.
2. Several patient accounts were classified as uncollectible and written off. These accounts totaled $2,000.
3. The MVT Corporation gave the hospital a grant for research into the use of a verbally operated microscope. The grant was for $500,000. The entire amount was immediately invested in marketable securities.
4. Operating expenses were incurred as follows:

Nursing services	$550,000
Other professional services	300,000
General services	300,000
Administrative services	175,000
Dietary services	100,000

Assume that all expenses were incurred on credit.
5. Patient receivables of $2,010,000 were collected.
6. Accounts payable of $1,400,000 were paid.
7. Several individuals in the community contributed a total of $1 million for the expansion of the burn unit of the hospital. This money was invested in marketable securities until the plans for the unit were completed. The fund was titled the Burn Unit Fund.
8. Interest expense on the outstanding debt was $210,000. Of this amount, $105,000 was paid in cash.

9.   The managing board decided to establish a fund for the development of its professional staff. The amount transferred from general hospital resources was $25,000. The new fund was called the Professional Improvement Fund.

10. The construction and planning costs incurred on the new burn unit totaled $200,000. This amount was paid from the Burn Unit Fund Cash account. To make these payments, investments that originally cost $190,000 were sold for $205,000. In addition, $10,000 cash income was received on the investments. Assume that the income from the investments has the same restrictions as the original donation.

11. During the year, the hospital received $25,000 cash income from the investment of the MVT grant money. Assume that the investment income is restricted in the same way as the original grant.

12. Research costs associated with the MVT grant were $20,000. These costs were paid with cash generated by the investment of the original grant.

13. Jane Dooe gave the hospital $15,000, which must be maintained intact. The income from the gift can be used in any way the managing board feels is helpful to the hospital. The money was immediately invested in marketable securities.

14. Investments in the Jane Dooe Fund earned $2,000 during the year. Of this amount $1,900 was received in cash.

REQUIRED: 1.   Prepare all the journal entries necessary to record the above transactions and identify the fund or funds involved.

2.   Prepare a statement of changes in fund balance for each of the restricted funds for the fiscal year 19X2–X3.

3.   Prepare a balance sheet for each of the restricted funds at June 30, 19X3.

Section IV

P13–12   (Closing entries—General Funds)
Using the data given in Problem 13–8, prepare the closing entry or entries necessary for the General Funds.

P13–13   (Closing entries—General Funds)
Using the data given in Problem 13–7, prepare the closing entry or entries necessary for the General Funds.

P13–14   (Closing entries—restricted funds)
Using the data given in Problem 13–10, prepare the closing entry or entries necessary for the restricted funds.

P13–15   (Closing entries—all hospital funds)
Using the data given in Problem 13–11, prepare the closing entry or entries necessary for all the funds used by the hospital.

Section V

P13–16 (Analysis of the effects of the Medicare prospective reimbursement plan)

Contact a hospital administrator in your area and discuss the changes that the prospective Medicare reimbursement plan caused in his or her hospital operations. Did the overall results benefit the hospital?

P13–17 (Analysis of a DRG schedule)

Contact the Medicare office in your region and obtain a DRG reimbursement schedule. Discuss this schedule with a local hospital administrator. Identify those areas that are not realistic for his or her hospital.

P13–18 (Multiple choice)

1. Third-party insurers can be grouped as
   a. Private insurance companies
   b. Insurance provided by the federal and state governments
   c. Both a and b
   d. None of the above

2. A prospective reimbursement plan for hospital costs
   a. Reimburses hospitals based on the costs they incur
   b. Reimburses hospitals based on the type of treatments provided a patient.
   c. Either a or b
   d. Both a and b

3. A "DRG" is
   a. A new drug recently developed through hospital research
   b. A shortened form of the word *diagnosis*
   c. A diagnosis related group
   d. A diagnosis related to gathering information

4. Which of the following is a problem with a cost-reimbursed system?
   a. There is little incentive for a hospital to be run efficiently because reimbursement is based on costs incurred
   b. The same services may be reimbursed at different amounts for different hospitals
   c. The reimbursement process has created an excessively burdensome reporting process
   d. All of the above

5. Which of the following is a possible operating strategy for a hospital receiving DRG reimbursements?
   a. Careful review of the staffing mix of the hospital
   b. Increased control over the use of supplies
   c. More efficient budgetary control through the use of a cost accounting system
   d. All of the above

6. Medicare is
   a. A federal program that provides medical insurance to individuals
   b. A state program that provides medical insurance to individuals
   c. A private insurance program that provided medical insurance to individuals
   d. None of the above
7. Medicaid is
   a. A federal program that provides medical insurance to individuals
   b. A state program that provides medical insurance to individuals
   c. A private insurance program that provides medical insurance to individuals
   d. None of the above
8. Universal health care is
   a. A federal program that will work exactly like Medicare
   b. A proposed federal program that will provide reasonably priced insurance to all individuals in the United States
   c. A program for diagnosing disease
   d. None of the above
9. *Audits of Providers of Health Care Services* is
   a. The audit guide for hospitals
   b. A book providing all of the generally accepted accounting principles for hospitals
   c. A book of all GASB accounting principles for hospitals
   d. A textbook for college classes

PART II

P13–19 (Preparation of a statement of financial position using FASB *Statement No. 117*)

Using the information presented below, prepare a statement of financial position for General Hospital for the year ended June 30, 19X1.

Cash and cash equivalents	$ 137,500
Accrued expenses payable	585,000
Accounts payable	1,000,000
Interest expense	500,000
Short-term investments	700,000
Restricted assets in Specific Purpose Funds	1,005,000
Annuity obligations	902,500
Long-term investments	105,035,000
Net patient service revenue	7,100,000

Inventories and prepaid expenses	305,000
Long-term debt	3,020,000
Actuarial loss on annuity obligations	56,000
Patient notes and accounts receivable	965,000
Restricted asses in Endowment Funds	2,050,000
Estimated malpractice costs liability	137,500
Administrative services expenses	1,789,000
Contributions receivable	1,912,500
Restricted assets in Plant Replacement and Expansion Funds	950,000
Land, buildings, and equipment	29,850,000
Contribution revenue	578,000
Net assets: Unrestricted	56,614,000
Temporarily restricted	15,671,000

P13–20 (Preparation of a statement of activities using FASB *Statement No. 117*) Using the information presented below, prepare a statement of activities for Memorial Hospital for the year ended June 30, 19X1.

	UNRESTRICTED	TEMPORARILY RESTRICTED	PERMANENTLY RESTRICTED
Professional care of patients expense	$ 6,987,500		
Contributions receivable	456,000		
Dietary services expenses	895,500		
Other revenues	25,000		
Cash purchases of equipment	50,000		
Depreciation and amortization	1,600,000		
Net assets released from restrictions	7,370,000	$(7,370,000)	
Medical malpractice costs	251,000		
Net assets at beginning of year	47,421,000	9,711,000	$75,600,000
Income from long-term investments	2,800,000	1,290,000	60,000
Fund-raising expenses	140,000		
Net realized and unrealized gains on long-term investments	4,114,000	1,476,000	2,310,000
Payments on notes payable	66,000		
Liability for refundable advances	78,000		
Provision for bad debts	96,500		
Interest expense	435,000		
Other investment income	425,000		
Patient accounts and notes receivable	3,230,000		
Contributions	550,000	4,055,000	140,000
Administrative services	3,872,000		
Net patient service revenue	7,000,000		
General services expense	1,840,000		

14

FUNDAMENTALS OF BOOKKEEPING

LEARNING OBJECTIVES

After completion of this chapter, you should be able to:

1. Define and distinguish between assets, liabilities, and capital
2. Explain the logic of the accounting equation
3. Explain the relationship between revenues and capital
4. Explain the relationship between expenses and capital
5. State the rules of debit and credit for assets, liabilities, capital, revenues, and expenses
6. Prepare an income statement, a statement of changes in owner's capital, and a balance sheet
7. Record transactions in a general journal
8. Post transactions from a general journal to a general ledger
9. Prepare adjusting and closing journal entries
10. Identify and explain the steps in the accounting cycle

SECTION I—WORK SHEET ANALYSIS OF TRANSACTIONS

All organizations, whether they are designated as profit-oriented (business type) or non-profit-oriented (nonbusiness type), must keep records that reflect the acquisition and use of their resources. These resources, commonly called **assets,** represent items of value that are either owned or controlled by the organization. Common examples of assets are cash, buildings, and equipment. The operations of an organization are centered on use of these resources for the purpose for which the organization was established.

These operations usually result in incurrence of economic obligations called **liabilities.** An example of a typical liability is a note payable to a bank. Whenever a business borrows money, the owner or the manager usually signs a note specifying the interest rate, repayment schedule, and so forth. Another example of a liability is a debt that is owed to another organization for supplies or services that were received.

Every organization must have some type of equity interest. This equity interest represents the source of the assets to the organization. Assets are provided by two major equity sources: liabilities and capital. **Liabilities** are assets provided by creditors. **Capital** is the assets provided by the owner(s).

While this textbook covers materials relevant to nonbusiness organizations, it is often easier to understand the basic accounting model by using a profit-oriented business as an illustrating tool. Therefore, this chapter will deviate from the nonbusiness organization model in order to develop the basic recording and classifying system.

The Accounting Equation

The relationship between the three elements defined above can be expressed in an equation form. This equation is generally referred to as the **accounting equation** and is written

Assets = Liabilities + Capital

This equation states that the assets (resources) of an organization are equal to the sources of those assets: liabilities and capital. Since the statement is in the form of an equation, it *must always be in balance.* Therefore, the dollar value of the assets must always equal the dollar value of liabilities plus the dollar value of capital.

Recording Business Transactions

An organization encounters many different types of events in the course of its day-to-day operations. The basic accounting records are concerned only with economic events that cause a change in one or more of the elements included in the accounting equation: assets, liabilities, and capital. Therefore, when considering whether to record an event in the accounting records, it must first be determined if any of these elements have changed.

To establish an understanding of the items defined above, consider the operations of a computer education service that was started on January 2, 19X1, by Kyle Thomas. Mr. Thomas intends to operate his business by providing computer education classes for individuals who have purchased personal computers. Mr. Thomas will also provide these services to individuals who desire to learn more about computers.

On January 2, Mr. Thomas deposited $10,000 of his personal cash into a bank account. This cash will be used exclusively by the business. Remember, the entity concept requires that the operations of an organization be kept separate from the owner's personal financial records. Therefore, we will consider only those transactions that affect the assets, liabilities, and capital of the business. This deposit causes an increase in the asset Cash. It also causes a corresponding increase in capital. This transaction is reflected in the accounting equation, as shown in Table 14–1.

Two important observations about the transaction in Table 14–1 should be made:

1. The dollar amount of the items, included in the transaction *must* balance in terms of the equation. That is, the net change in the assets must equal the net change in the liabilities plus (minus) the net change in capital.
2. The equation itself must balance after the transaction has been recorded.

On January 3, Mr. Thomas purchased ten computers. The computers cost $30,000. He made a down payment of $3,000 and financed the remainder through the French Quarter Bank. Recording this transaction will cause the accounting equation to expand, as shown in Table 14–2.

Several observations should be made regarding this purchase:

1. The assets of the business increased by $27,000: Cash decreased by $3,000 and computers increased by $30,000.
2. The business now owes the bank $27,000. Thus a liability exists that must be reflected in the system.

TABLE 14–1

		ASSETS	=	LIABILITIES	+	CAPITAL
		Cash				K. Thomas, Capital
Owner invests cash in the business	+	$10,000 $10,000	= =	-0-	+ +	$10,000 $10,000

TABLE 14–2

		ASSETS			=	LIABILITIES	+	CAPITAL
		Cash		Computers		Notes Payable to Bank		K. Thomas, Capital
Previous balances		$10,000			=			$10,000
The firm purchased computers	−	$ 3,000 $ 7,000	+ +	$30,000 $30,000	= =	+$27,000 $27,000	+	$10,000

3. The computers are recorded at their full cost, $30,000, even though Mr. Thomas borrowed $27,000 in order to purchase them.

In summary, the business now has assets totaling $37,000—that is, $27,000 contributed by creditors (the bank) and $10,000 contributed by the owner. Notice that the acquisition of the computers did not affect the owner's capital, since he did not contribute any additional assets to the business as a result of this transaction.

A simple method of analyzing a transaction in terms of its effect on the accounting equation is to ask four questions:

1. Did any asset or assets increase or decrease?
2. Did any liability or liabilities increase or decrease?
3. Did the capital increase or decrease?
4. Does the transaction have a balanced effect on the equation?

For example, consider the acquisition of the computers:

1. The asset Cash decreased by $3,000 and the asset Computers increased by $30,000.
2. The liability Notes payable to bank increased by $27,000.
3. There was no change in capital.
4. The transaction increased assets by $27,000 and had a similar effect on total liabilities and capital. Therefore, the accounting equation is still in balance.

While this type of analysis may seem cumbersome, it will be a great help when more complex transactions are encountered.

In order to have an office for the operation of the business, Mr. Thomas rented office space from the Mardi Gras Realty Company for $2,000 per month. Since the rental contract required payments at the beginning of each month, he immediately wrote a check for $2,000. Applying the four-step analysis, the transaction has the following effects on the accounting equation:

1. The asset Cash decreased by $2,000. Since the business now has "control" over the use of office space for the month of January, another asset has been acquired. This type of asset is usually called **Prepaid rent,** and it increased by $2,000. No other assets have changed as a result of this transaction.
2. Since the business does not owe any more or any less as a result of this transaction, no liabilities have changed.
3. Since the net effect of this transaction has been a decrease in one asset and an increase in another, the owner's share of the total assets did not change. Therefore, there is no change in capital.
4. The transaction had a balanced effect on the accounting equation. The decrease in one asset was offset by an increase in another asset. Liabilities and capital were not affected by this transaction.

The result of the above analysis on the accounting equation is shown in Table 14–3. Notice that the total of the assets ($37,000) is equal to the total of the liabilities plus the capital ($37,000).

TABLE 14–3

	ASSETS			=	LIABILITIES	+	CAPITAL
	Cash	Computers	Prepaid Rent		Notes Payable to Bank		K. Thomas, Capital
Previous balances	$7,000	+ $30,000		=	$27,000	+	$10,000
The firm paid the rent for the month	− $2,000		+ $2,000	=			
	$5,000	+ $30,000	+ $2,000	=	$27,000	+	$10,000

At the end of January, Mr. Thomas sent bills to his students. Assume that the amount due him for services performed in January was $5,000. Applying the four-step analysis it can be determined that

1. Sending out of the bills is a formal recognition that Mr. Thomas's customers owe him $5,000 for services he rendered. As a result, he has a claim against each of them. These claims are assets because they give him the right to collect the amounts due. The title usually given to these assets is **Accounts receivable.** No other assets changed as a result of this transaction.

2. Since the business does not owe any more or any less as a result of this transaction, no liabilities have changed.

3. The result of the above analysis (steps 1 and 2) reflects an increase in assets of $5,000. Since each transaction must always have a balancing effect on the equation, and there were no changes in liabilities, there must have been an increase in capital of $5,000 (see discussion below).

4. The transaction had a balanced effect on the accounting equation: assets increased by $5,000, and liabilities + capital increased by $5,000.

The results of the above analysis on the accounting equation are shown in Table 14–4. Notice that the total of the assets ($42,000) is equal to the total of the liabilities plus the capital ($42,000).

In the above approach, we "backed into" the effect that assets generated through the profit-oriented operations of the business have on capital. The same

TABLE 14–4

	ASSETS				=	LIABILITIES	+	CAPITAL
	Cash	Computers	Prepaid Rent	Accounts Receivable		Notes Payable to Bank		K. Thomas, Capital
Previous balances	$5,000	+ $30,000	+ $2,000		=	$27,000	+	$10,000
The firm billed customers				+ $5,000	=		+	$ 5,000
	$5,000	+ $30,000	+ $2,000	+ $5,000	=	$27,000	+	$15,000

results can be achieved by a direct analysis. A general rule can be made regarding this type of transaction.

Assets generated through the profit-oriented activities of a business always increase the owner's capital.

Therefore, whenever a business increases its assets by carrying out the activities for which it was established, the owner's capital will always increase. This increase in capital is referred to as **revenue.**

Next, assume that Mr. Thomas received a $300 utility bill for the month. Since the due date on the bill is February 10, it will not be paid until next month. The four-step analysis results in the following effects on the accounting equation:

1. Since the business does not have title to or control over any items of value that it did not have before this transaction, there are no changes in assets.
2. The business now owes money to an additional creditor. The receipt of the bill is a formal recognition of this fact. It necessitates recording a liability of $300. The title normally given to this account is **Accounts payable.**
3. The result of the above analysis (steps 1 and 2) reflects an increase in liabilities with no corresponding increase in assets. Since each transaction must have a balanced effect on the equation, there must have been a decrease in capital of $300 (see discussion below).
4. The transaction had a balanced effect on the accounting equation: Assets did not change, and the net effect on liabilities + capital was zero ($300 − $300).

The result of the above analysis on the accounting equation is shown in Table 14–5. Notice that the total of the assets ($42,000) is equal to the total of the liabilities plus the capital ($42,000).

In the above approach, we backed into the effect that liabilities incurred in the profit-oriented operations of the business have on capital. The same results can be achieved by a direct analysis. A general rule can be made regarding this type of transaction.

Assets used in or liabilities incurred through the profit-oriented activities of a business always reduce the owner's capital.

TABLE 14–5

	ASSETS				=	LIABILITIES		+	CAPITAL
	Cash	Computers	Prepaid Rent	Accounts Receivable		Notes Payable to Bank	Accounts Payable		K. Thomas, Capital
Previous balances	$5,000 +	$30,000 +	$2,000 +	$5,000	=	$27,000		+	$15,000
The firm received a bill for utilities					=		+ $300	−	$ 300
	$5,000 +	$30,000 +	$2,000 +	$5,000	=	$27,000 +	$300	+	$14,700

This decrease in capital is referred to as an **expense.**

Although numerous other types of transactions could be illustrated for the operations of a business, those selected above should be sufficient to enable you to understand the process used for determining the effect of each transaction on the accounting equation.

SECTION I REVIEW EXERCISE

The following exercise should be completed by using the approach previously described. After completing a work sheet, compare it with the solution that follows so that you can determine how well you understand the concepts involved.

In this exercise, assume that Ms. Paige Keith is an independent tour guide who works for several large tour companies. Her income is determined by the number of individuals on each tour she hosts. To start the business, Ms. Keith incurred the following transactions:

19X1

June

1   Ms. Keith placed $5,000 cash into a bank account to be used in the operations of her business, Kaki Tours.

2   Ms. Keith signed a contract with Tel-Ans, a telephone-answering service. The service cost $50 per month, payable at the beginning of each month. Ms. Keith paid Tel-Ans $50.

4   Ms. Keith paid Print Faster $55 for stationery and the various forms she needed.

5   Ms. Keith purchased office equipment for $250. She paid $25 down and will pay the remainder in 30 days.

7   Ms. Keith purchased additional office supplies costing $125. She paid cash for these supplies.

10   Ms. Keith billed several tour companies for tours she conducted during the month. The total billing was $300.

15   Ms. Keith received $250 from companies she billed earlier that month.

18   Ms. Keith hired an assistant and agreed to pay him 25 percent of her revenue from the tours that he helped to organize.

20   Ms. Keith deposited $130 in her bank account. This amount was collected from various walking tours she conducted.

25   Ms. Keith shared an office with someone and she paid $75 for her share of the June rent (including utilities).

30   Ms. Keith billed several tour companies for a total of $400 for tours she conducted during the month.

SOLUTION TO SECTION I REVIEW EXERCISE

The solution is found in Table 14–6.

TABLE 14–6

		ASSETS				=	LIABILITIES	+	CAPITAL
	Cash	Accounts Receivable	Prepaid Services	Office Supplies	Office Equipment		Accounts Payable		P. Keith, Capital
19X1									
June 1	+$5,000								+$5,000
2	–$ 50		+$50						
4	–$ 55			+$ 55					
5	–$ 25				+$250		+$225		
7	–$ 125			+$125					
10		+$300							+$ 300
15	+$ 250	–$250							
18	No transaction—no assets, liabilities, or capital have changed. Nothing is owed to the assistant until he completes some work.								
20	+$ 130								+$ 130
25	–$ 75								–$ 75
30		+$400							+$ 400
	$5,050	$450	$50	$180	$250		$225		$5,755

Total Assets* = $5,980   Total liabilities + Capital* = $5,980

*Cumulative totals after each transaction were omitted in order to conserve space.

SECTION II—USE OF ACCOUNTS: DEBIT AND CREDIT ANALYSIS

Use of Accounts

The analysis in Section I of this chapter will supply the data necessary to reflect the acquisition, use, and disposal of the resources of any small organization. However, as the organization expands, the use of a work sheet to analyze transactions becomes too cumbersome. Consider, for example, the size of the work sheet that would be necessary to record the transactions encountered by General Motors or Shell Oil. Companies of this size will encounter thousands of transactions and have many different kinds of assets, liabilities, and so forth. Therefore, a more efficient system of analysis has been developed. This system is based on the accounting equation, as was the work sheet. However, it utilizes a different form of analysis.

Rather than use columns on a work sheet, an **account** is used to accumulate the increases and decreases in assets, liabilities, and capital. Since it is much easier to accumulate changes if like items are grouped, the increases are accumulated on one side of the account and the decreases on the other. Arbitrarily, the increases (+) in assets have been accumulated on the left and the decreases (–) on the right. As a result, it is much easier and faster to calculate the balance in an account at any point in time. This produces the following situation:

ASSETS
+ | –

Since the system is based on the accounting equation, the following relationship develops:

$$\underset{+\ |\ -}{\underline{\text{ASSETS}}} = \underset{|}{\underline{\text{LIABILITIES}}} + \underset{|}{\underline{\text{CAPITAL}}}$$

When the account form is transferred to the right side of the equation and is used to accumulate changes in liabilities and capital, the signs must change. The increases are accumulated on the right side and the decreases on the left side. This maintains the mathematical integrity of the transaction analysis and of the system:

$$\underset{+\ |\ -}{\underline{\text{ASSETS}}} = \underset{-\ |\ +}{\underline{\text{LIABILITIES}}} + \underset{-\ |\ +}{\underline{\text{CAPITAL}}}$$

Debit and Credit Analysis

In accounting terminology the left side of an account is referred to as the **debit side** and the right side is referred to as the **credit side.** Note that the terms *debit* and *credit* refer *only to position.* Without any association with a particular account, these terms *do not* mean plus or minus. Once a particular type of account has been considered, however, the terms do refer to plus or minus. For example, when assets are considered (see the illustration above), increases are accumulated on the left, or debit, side, while decreases are accumulated on the right, or credit, side. Liabilities and capital, however, are increased or decreased in the opposite manner: Debits represent decreases, while credits represent increases. These rules are summarized in Table 14–7.

To complete the system, revenues and expenses must be analyzed in terms of their debit/credit effect. At the end of each period, it is important that management study the relative size of the individual revenues and expenses incurred in operating an organization. In the previous illustrations, revenues and expenses were recorded as direct increases or decreases in capital. To make such an analysis easier, however, we will begin to accumulate the changes in each revenue and expense in a separate account. This will avoid the rather cumbersome task of sorting out the revenues and expenses after they have been combined in the capital account.

The debit/credit analysis of revenues and expenses is based on the relationship of each to capital. Remember that revenues and expenses were defined as directly affecting the capital of a firm. Since revenues cause capital to increase,

TABLE 14–7

TYPE OF ACCOUNT	INCREASES	DECREASES
Assets	Debits	Credits
Liabilities	Credits	Debits
Capital	Credits	Debits

they are recorded as credits. Any reductions of revenues are recorded as debits. This is shown in the following illustration:

REVENUES

Debits	Credits
−	+

Note the *direct* relationship with capital. Capital is increased with credits. Since revenues increase capital, *revenues* are increased with *credits*. Capital is decreased with debits. Since decreases in revenue are decreases in capital, revenues are decreased with debits.

Expenses follow the same logic. The analysis, however, is a bit more complex. **Expenses** have been defined as those decreases in capital associated with the profit-oriented activities of the business. Therefore, as expenses increase, the amount of capital decreases. A decrease in capital is recorded as a debit (see Table 14–7). Continuing with this logic, then, an increase in an expense must be recorded with a debit. This procedure reflects the decrease in capital that is taking place.

This analysis can be extended to include a decrease in an expense, which results in a credit to the expense account and reflects the increase in capital that is taking place. This is shown in the following illustration:

EXPENSES

Debits	Credits
+	−

Table 14–8 summarizes the debit/credit rules for the types of transactions covered so far. Owner withdrawals will be considered in a later section of this chapter.

Notice that this system is based on the mathematical integrity of the accounting equation. As a result, the equality mentioned in Section I still exists—that is, the accounting equation must be balanced after the result of each transaction has been recorded. In terms of debit and credit, this equality can be stated as follows:

The total number of dollars of debits for any transaction must EQUAL the total number of dollars of credits.

This is an important rule to remember because it affects the integrity of the entire accounting system.

TABLE 14–8

TYPE OF ACCOUNT	INCREASES	DECREASES
Assets	Debits	Credits
Liabilities	Credits	Debits
Capital	Credits	Debits
Revenues	Credits	Debits
Expenses	Debits	Credits

Transaction Analysis Using Debit and Credit

The effects of a transaction can now be measured in terms of debits and credits that reflect increases or decreases in the accounts. Following are several examples taken from the Review Exercise in Section I.[1]

TRANSACTION		ANALYSIS	
June 1	Ms. Keith invested $5,000 cash into a bank account to be used in the operations of her business, Kaki Tours.	*Debit:*	Cash, $5,000—to reflect the increase in this asset.
		Credit:	P. Keith, Capital, $5,000—to reflect the increase in capital.
June 2	Ms. Keith signed a contract with Tel-Ans, a telephone-answering service. The service cost $50 per month, payable at the beginning of each month. Ms. Keith paid Tel-Ans $50.	*Debit:*	Prepaid services, $50—to reflect the increase in this asset.
		Credit:	Cash, $50—to reflect the decrease in this asset.
June 4	Ms. Keith paid Print Faster $55 for stationery and the various forms she needed.	*Debit:*	Office supplies, $55—to reflect the increase in this asset.
		Credit:	Cash, $55—to reflect the decrease in this asset.
June 5	Ms. Keith purchased office equipment for $250. She paid $25 down and will pay the remainder in 30 days.	*Debit:*	Office equipment, $250—to reflect the increase in this asset.
		Credit:	Cash, $25—to reflect the decrease in this asset.
		Credit:	Accounts payable, $225—to reflect the increase in this liability.

SECTION II REVIEW EXERCISE

Using the information presented below, prepare an analysis of the remaining transactions of Ms. Keith's tour business similar to that presented above. Compare your results with the solution that follows.

TRANSACTION

June 7 Ms. Keith purchased additional office supplies costing $125. She paid cash for these supplies.

June 10 Ms. Keith billed several tour companies for tours she conducted during the month. The total billing was $300.

June 15 Ms. Keith received $250 from companies she billed earlier that month.

June 18 Ms. Keith hired an assistant and agreed to pay him 25 percent of her revenue from the tours that he helped to organize.

June 20 Ms. Keith deposited $130 in her bank account. This amount was collected from various walking tours she conducted.

June 25 Ms. Keith shared an office with someone and she paid $75 for her share of the June rent (including utilities).

---

[1]The effects of the transactions on the individual accounts are summarized in Table 14–9.

June 30   Ms. Keith billed several tour companies for a total of $400 for tours she conducted during the month.

SOLUTION TO SECTION II REVIEW EXERCISE

June 7   *Debit:* Office supplies, $125—to reflect the increase in this asset.
          Credit: Cash, $125—to reflect the decrease in this asset.
June 10   *Debit:* Accounts receivable, $300—to reflect the increase in this asset.
          Credit: Tour revenue, $300—to reflect the increase in capital from profit-oriented activities.
June 15   *Debit:* Cash, $250—to reflect the increase in this asset.
          Credit: Accounts receivable, $250—to reflect the decrease in this asset.
June 18   No transaction: no assets, liabilities, or capital have changed. Nothing is owed to the assistant until he completes some work.
June 20   *Debit:* Cash, $130—to reflect the increase in this asset.
          Credit: Tour revenue, $130—to reflect the increase in capital from profit-oriented activities.
June 25   *Debit:* Office rent expense, $75—to reflect the decrease in capital from profit-oriented activities.
          Credit: Cash, $75—to reflect the decrease in this asset.
June 30   *Debit:* Accounts receivable, $400—to reflect the increase in this asset.
          Credit: Tour revenue, $400—to reflect the increase in capital from profit-oriented activities.

The results of the above transactions in the accounts are summarized in Table 14–9.

TABLE 14–9

CASH		ACCOUNTS RECEIVABLE		PREPAID SERVICES		OFFICE SUPPLIES	
5,000	50	300	250	50		55	
250	55	400				125	
130	25	700	250			180	
	125	450					
	75						
5,380	330						
5,050							

OFFICE EQUIPMENT		ACCOUNTS PAYABLE		P. KEITH, CAPITAL		TOUR REVENUE	
250			225		5,000		300
							130
							400
							830

OFFICE RENT EXPENSE	
75	

COMPLETION OF SECTION II REVIEW EXERCISE

Table 14–9 reflects each transaction in the Review Exercise in Section I. In order to keep the exercise short, however, several transactions were omitted. These items will now be analyzed:

1. The assistant was not paid for the services he performed. Since this amount is owed at the end of the month, the amount earned must be recorded. This entry will record the liability owed and the effect on capital of the services performed by the assistant. Assuming this amount is $40, the following entry is necessary:

Debit: Salary expense, $40—to reflect the decrease in capital from profit-oriented activities.
Credit: Salary payable, $40—to reflect the increase in liabilities.

2. By the end of June, the services performed by Tel-Ans for the month were "used up" and no longer had any value. The following entry, therefore, is necessary:

Debit: Telephone-answering expense, $50—to reflect the decrease in capital from profit-oriented activities.
Credit: Prepaid services, $50—to reflect the decrease in this asset.

Note: To save time, most companies record entries such as the payment for answering services directly in an expense account. This eliminates the need for a second entry like the one described above. If this procedure had been followed here, the June 2 entry would have required a debit to Telephone-answering expense and a credit to Cash for $50. Notice that the effect of these two procedures on the accounting equation is the same: Assets decrease and Capital decreases.

3. Office supplies totaling $180 were purchased in June. During the month some of these supplies were used. Assuming the cost of the supplies used was $30, the following entry is necessary:

Debit: Office supplies expense, $30—to reflect the decrease in capital from profit-oriented activities.
Credit: Office supplies, $30—to reflect the decrease in this asset.

4. The final item that must be considered is office equipment. Whenever a business purchases an asset, it is really buying a "bundle of services." As these services are used up, an expense is recorded. (This process is explained in the preceding entry for the asset Office

supplies.) Using the services of an asset such as Office equipment is generally referred to as **depreciation.** Since this is the using up of an asset in the profit-oriented activities of the business, it is recognized as an expense. The following entry is, therefore, necessary (assume the amount is $5):

Debit: Depreciation expense—office equipment, $5—to record the decrease in capital from profit-oriented activities.

Credit: Accumulated depreciation—office equipment, $5—to reflect the decrease in the asset. Accumulated depreciation is credited instead of the asset itself because it is important to maintain the original cost in a separate account. The Accumulated depreciation account is treated as a negative, or contra, asset— the effect is the same as crediting the Office equipment account directly (see Table 14–13).

After these transactions have been entered into the system, the accounts will appear as shown in Table 14–10.

TABLE 14–10

CASH		ACCOUNTS RECEIVABLE		PREPAID SERVICES		OFFICE SUPPLIES	
5,000	50	300	250	50	50	55	30
250	55	400		-0-		125	
130	25	700	250			180	30
	125	450				150	
	75						
5,380	330						
5,050							

OFFICE EQUIPMENT		ACCUMULATED DEPRECIA-TION—		ACCOUNTS PAYABLE	
250			5		225

SALARY PAYABLE		P. KEITH, CAPITAL		TOUR REVENUE		OFFICE RENT EXPENSE	
	40		5,000		300	75	
					130		
					400		
					830		

SALARY EXPENSE		TELEPHONE-ANSWERING EXPENSE		OFFICE SUPPLIES EXPENSE		DEPRECIATION EXPENSE— OFFICE EQUIPMENT	
40		50		30		5	

SECTION III—FINANCIAL STATEMENTS

The purpose of accounting is to provide information to decision makers. Such information helps reduce the uncertainty that exists relative to the future. Data presented in the form used in Table 14–10 are not as helpful as data that are grouped into meaningful statements. The statements commonly used are (1) an activity (income) statement, (2) a statement of changes in owner's capital, (3) a balance sheet, and (4) a statement of cash flows.

An activity statement compares the revenues earned with the expenses incurred in earning those revenues, and it reports the resulting net income or net loss. For a profit-oriented organization, this statement is called an **income statement.** An income statement for Ms. Keith's business—Kaki Tours—is shown in Table 14–11.

The **statement of changes in owner's capital** provides a reconciliation of the beginning and ending owner's capital balance. Items that increase owner's capital include the investments by the owner and net income for the period. Items that decrease the balance are owner's withdrawals and net losses. Owner's withdrawals are covered later in this chapter. A statement of changes in owner's capital is shown in Table 14–12.

The final statement that will be illustrated is the **balance sheet.** This statement reflects the balances of the asset, liability, and capital accounts at the end of the period (see Table 14–13).

An understanding of the accounting system requires an understanding of the relationship between the financial statements. Notice how the net income for the period is taken from the income statement and is used to determine the ending balance in the owner's capital account. Notice also how the ending balance in the owner's capital account is used to balance the balance sheet.

A **statement of cash flows** should also be prepared for a business, but a discussion of its preparation is beyond the scope of this text.

TABLE 14–11

KAKI TOURS
INCOME STATEMENT
FOR THE MONTH ENDED JUNE 30, 19X1

Revenue		
Tour revenue		$830
Expenses		
Office rent expense	$75	
Salary expense	40	
Telephone-answering expense	50	
Office supplies expense	30	
Depreciation expense—office equipment	5	200
Net Income		$630

TABLE 14–12

KAKI TOURS
STATEMENT OF CHANGES IN OWNER'S CAPITAL
FOR THE MONTH ENDED JUNE 30, 19X1

P. Keith, Capital, June 1, 19X1	$ -0-
Investment during June	5,000
Income for June	630
P. Keith, Capital, June 30, 19X1	$5,630

TABLE 14–13

KAKI TOURS
BALANCE SHEET
JUNE 30, 19X1

Assets		
Cash		$5,050
Accounts receivable		450
Office supplies		150
Office equipment	$250	
Less: Accumulated depreciation	5	245
Total assets		$5,895 ←
Liabilities and Capital		
Liabilities:		
Accounts payable		$ 225
Salary payable		40
Total liabilities		$ 265
Capital:		
P. Keith, Capital		5,630
Total liabilities and capital		$5,895 ←

Assets =
Liabilities +
Capital

SECTION III REVIEW EXERCISE

Using the information presented below, prepare an income statement, a statement of changes in owner's capital, and a balance sheet for the Star Company. Compare your statements with the solution that follows. Assume that the business was started on August 1, 19X1, and that account balances given are as of August 31, 19X1.

	Balance	
	DEBIT	**CREDIT**
Cash	$20,000	
Accounts receivable	8,000	
Office supplies	4,000	
Delivery equipment	20,000	
Accumulated depreciation—delivery equipment		$ 400
Accounts payable		4,000
Notes payable to bank		19,600
Interest payable		1,000
F. T. Tillis, Capital		18,000
Service revenue		16,000
Oil and gas expense	4,000	
Salaries expense	1,500	
Interest expense	600	
Depreciation expense—delivery equipment	400	
Miscellaneous expenses	500	
	$59,000	$59,000

SOLUTION TO SECTION III REVIEW EXERCISE

STAR COMPANY
INCOME STATEMENT
FOR THE MONTH ENDED AUGUST 31, 19X1

Revenue		
Service revenue		$16,000
Expenses		
Oil and gas expense	$4,000	
Salaries expense	1,500	
Interest expense	600	
Depreciation expense—delivery equipment	400	
Miscellaneous expenses	500	7,000
Net Income		$ 9,000

STAR COMPANY
STATEMENT OF CHANGES IN OWNER'S CAPITAL
FOR THE MONTH ENDED AUGUST 31, 19X1

F. T. Tillis, Capital, August 1, 19X1	$ -0-
Investment during August	18,000
Income for August	9,000
F. T. Tillis, Capital, August 31, 19X1	$27,000

STAR COMPANY
BALANCE SHEET
AUGUST 31, 19X1

Assets		
Cash		$20,000
Accounts receivable		8,000
Office supplies		4,000
Delivery equipment	$20,000	
Less: Accumulated depreciation—delivery equipment	400	19,600
Total assets		$51,600
Liabilities and Capital		
Liabilities:		
Accounts payable		$4,000
Notes payable to bank		19,600
Interest payable		1,000
Total liabilities		$24,600
Capital:		
F. T. Tillis, Capital		27,000
Total liabilities and capital		$51,600

SECTION IV—JOURNALS AND LEDGERS

The analysis in Section II provides sufficient data to prepare financial statements for any organization. It does, however, have two major shortcomings: (1) there is no system that cross-references the various data to the basic transactions, and (2) there is no formal recording format. These shortcomings are alleviated through the use of journals and ledgers.

The Journal

The **journal** is a book in which every transaction that affects the accounting equation is recorded in *chronological* order. Thus the journal is often referred to as the "book of original entry." As such, it is a permanent record of all the transactions of a business. The form used is shown in Exhibit 14–1.

Continuing the example used in Sections I and II, let us reconsider the first transaction illustrated. The following steps are used when entering information in the journal (follow each step by referring to the journal entry in Exhibit 14–1):

1. The year is written at the top of each page in the Date column.
2. The month of the transaction is entered. As additional transactions are entered, the month is usually not rewritten unless the same journal page is used for more than one month.
3. The third item of information is the date of the transaction. Since this helps separate

GENERAL JOURNAL

Page 1

Date 19X1	Description	P.R.	Debit	Credit
Aug. 1	Cash	101	5000 —	
	P. Keith, Capital	301		5000 —
	Owner invested $5,000 in the business.			

EXHIBIT 14–1

transactions, the date for each transaction is usually entered—even if it is the same as that of the preceding transaction.

4.   The debit account is entered next to the left-hand margin in the Description column. If there is more than one debit account in a transaction, all the debit items must be entered before any credit items are entered.

5.   Each debit amount is entered in the Debit money column.

6.   The credit account or accounts are entered and are *slightly indented* to the right.

7.   The respective credit amount or amounts are placed in the Credit money column.

8.   The final part of the entry is the explanation. Here a brief description of the transaction is entered. This helps to explain the event that has been recorded. It can be useful when attempting to analyze the events that caused a particular account to change.

The journal shown in Exhibit 14–1 is referred to as a **general journal.** Although other types of journals exist, a description of their use is beyond the scope of this text. The column titled P.R. (Posting Reference) will be explained later.

A line is usually skipped between journal entries in order to help separate the entries and to make the information included in the journal easier to read.

The Ledger and Posting

Changes in the accounting equation are accumulated in the journal by transaction. To provide more information to decision makers, these data must be summarized in useful categories. This is done in the **ledger.** Thus the ledger is a book with a separate page used to accumulate transaction data for *each account.* The traditional two-column ledger account is shown in Exhibit 14–2.

Recording information in the ledger is referred to as **posting.** Posting is the process of transferring information from the journal to the ledger. The following steps are used when posting a debit entry to the ledger (follow each step by referring to the ledger in Exhibit 14–2):

1.   The year is entered as the first item in the Date column on the debit side of the account. As in the journal, it is entered only once.

2.   The next item of information is the month. It is placed beneath the year and is entered only once unless the same ledger page is used for more than one month.

GENERAL LEDGER

Cash   Account No. 101

Date 19X1	Item	P.R.	Debit	Date	Item	P.R.	Credit
June 1		1	5000 –				

P. Keith, Capital   Account No. 301

Date	Item	P.R.	Debit	Date 19X1	Item	P.R.	Credit
				June 1		1	5000 –

EXHIBIT 14–2

3. The date of the transaction is the next piece of information placed in the ledger.
4. The amount of the transaction is then entered in the Debit money column.
5. Finally, the P.R. (Posting Reference) column is used to enter the page number where the transaction is recorded in the journal.
6. The account number (for Cash it is 101) is entered in the *journal* in the P.R. column (see Exhibit 14–1). Thus the cross-referencing system has been completed. The journal entry can be traced to the ledger, and the ledger entry can be traced back to the original transaction in the journal.

The above steps have followed the posting of a debit to the Cash account. The process is the same for each credit entry except that the recording is made on the credit side of the account. (See Exhibit 14–2 for the P. Keith, Capital, account, and follow the steps previously listed.)

The ledger referred to in Exhibit 14–2 is a **general ledger.** Although other types of ledgers exist, a description of their use is beyond the scope of this chapter.

SECTION IV REVIEW EXERCISE

Record the entries for Kaki Tours, following the format in Exhibit 14–1; post the entries to the appropriate accounts, following the format in Exhibit 14–2. (The entries are described in Section III of this chapter. Don't forget the four entries used to "complete the exercise.") After performing these steps, compare your answer with the solution provided on pp. 656–659. You should begin by recording the first transaction—the deposit by Ms. Keith—in the journal.

SOLUTION TO SECTION IV REVIEW EXERCISE

GENERAL JOURNAL

Page 1

Date 19X1		Description	Ref.	Dr.	Cr.
June	1	Cash	101	5000 —	
		P. Keith, Capital	301		5000 —
		Owner invested $5,000 in the business.			
	2	Prepaid services	102	50 —	
		Cash	101		50 —
		Paid Tel-Ans for telephone answering services.			
	4	Office supplies	104	55 —	
		Cash	101		55 —
		Purchased stationery from Print Faster.			
	5	Office equipment	107	250 —	
		Cash	101		25 —
		Accounts payable	201		225 —
		Purchased office equipment.			
	7	Office supplies	104	125 —	
		Cash	101		125 —
		Purchased office supplies.			
	10	Accounts receivable	103	300 —	
		Tour revenue	401		300 —
		Billed tour companies for tours conducted.			
	15	Cash	101	250 —	
		Accounts receivable	103		250 —
		Collected accounts receivable.			
	20	Cash	101	130 —	
		Tour revenue	401		130 —
		Collected cash for tours conducted.			
	25	Office rent expense	501	75 —	
		Cash	101		75 —
		Paid rent on office.			
	30	Accounts receivable	103	400 —	
		Tour revenue	401		400 —
		Billed tour companies for tours conducted.			

GENERAL JOURNAL

Page 2

Date 19X1	Description	Ref.	Dr.	Cr.
June 30	Salary expense	502	40 –	
	Salary payable	202		40 –
	Recorded unpaid salary of assistant.			
30	Telephone answering expense	503	50–	
	Prepaid services	102		50 –
	Recorded telephone answering services used.			
30	Office supplies expense	504	30 –	
	Office supplies	104		30 –
	Recorded office supplies used.			
30	Depreciation expense – office equipment	505	5–	
	Accumulated depreciation – office equipment	108		5–
	Recorded depreciation for June.			

GENERAL LEDGER

Cash   101

Date 19X1	Item	P.R.	Debit	Date 19X1	Item	P.R.	Credit
June 1		1	5000 –	June 2		1	50 –
15		1	250 –	4		1	55 –
20		1	130 –	5		1	25 –
	(5,050)		5380 –	7		1	125 –
				25		1	75 –
							330 –

Prepaid services   102

Date 19X1	Item	P.R.	Debit	Date 19X1	Item	P.R.	Credit
June 2	(∅)	1	50 –	June 30		2	50 –

Accounts receivable   103

Date 19X1	Item	P.R.	Debit	Date 19X1	Item	P.R.	Credit
June 10		1	300 –	June 15		1	250 –
30		1	400 –				
	(450)		700 –				

Office supplies   104

Date 19X1	Item	P.R.	Debit	Date 19X1	Item	P.R.	Credit
June 4		1	55 –	June 30		2	30 –
7	(150)	1	125 –				
			180 –				

Office equipment   107

Date 19X1	Item	P.R.	Debit	Date	Item	P.R.	Credit
June 5		1	250 –				

Accumulated depreciation — office equipment   108

Date	Item	P.R.	Debit	Date 19X1	Item	P.R.	Credit
				June 30		2	5 –

Accounts payable   201

Date	Item	P.R.	Debit	Date 19X1	Item	P.R.	Credit
				June 5		1	225 –

Salary payable   202

Date	Item	P.R.	Debit	Date 19X1	Item	P.R.	Credit
				June 30		2	10 –

P. Keith, Capital   301

Date	Item	P.R.	Debit	Date 19X1	Item	P.R.	Credit
				June 1		1	5000 –

Tour revenue   401

Date	Item	P.R.	Debit	Date 19X1	Item	P.R.	Credit
				June 10		1	300 –
				20		1	130 –
				30	(830)	1	400 –
							830 –

Office rent expense   501

Date 19X1	Item	P.R.	Debit	Date	Item	P.R.	Credit
June 25		1	75 –				

Salary expense   502

Date 19X1	Item	P.R.	Debit	Date	Item	P.R.	Credit
June 30		2	40 –				

Telephone–answering expense   503

Date 19X1	Item	P.R.	Debit	Date	Item	P.R.	Credit
June 30		2	50 –				

Office supplies expense   504

Date 19X1	Item	P.R.	Debit	Date	Item	P.R.	Credit
June 30		2	30 –				

Depreciation expense — office equipment   505

Date 19X1	Item	P.R.	Debit	Date	Item	P.R.	Credit
June 30		2	5 –				

SECTION V—COMPLETION OF THE BOOKKEEPING PROCESS

The Trial Balance

In previous illustrations the financial statements were prepared directly from information recorded in the accounts. To help locate errors that may have been made in the recording or posting process, a **trial balance** is usually prepared. The trial balance is a columnar listing of each account, together with its balance. If both the debit and credit columns are equal, the system is in balance (see Table 14–14).

There can be errors within the system even if the debit and credit columns in the trial balance are equal. Examples of such errors include: (1) entries that are not recorded, (2) amounts debited (credited) to incorrect accounts, and (3) complete entries recorded for incorrect amounts.

The financial statements are usually prepared directly from trial balance data. In some systems, a formal adjusting process must be completed before the statements can be prepared. Such a process is discussed below.

Adjusting Entries

Adjusting entries are designed to bring the financial records up-to-date before the statements are prepared. In many instances the books are not maintained on a current basis in order to save time during the period. A prominent example in the Kaki Tours illustration is depreciation. Remember that depreciation was

TABLE 14–14

KAKI TOURS
TRIAL BALANCE
AUGUST 31, 19X1

	DEBITS	CREDITS
Cash	$5,050	
Accounts receivable	450	
Office supplies	150	
Office equipment	250	
Accumulated depreciation—office equipment		$ 5
Accounts payable		225
Salary payable		40
P. Keith, Capital		5,000
Tour revenue		830
Office rent expense	75	
Salary expense	40	
Telephone-answering expense	50	
Office supplies expense	30	
Depreciation expense—office equipment	5	
	$6,100	$6,100

recorded in order to give recognition to the fact that the services of the asset (Office equipment) were being "used up."

Logic would indicate that the "using up" process is a gradual one that does not suddenly occur at the end of the period. If the books were to be maintained on a current basis, an entry for depreciation would frequently have to be made. Since financial statements are prepared only periodically, however, it is not necessary to have the books up-to-date until it is time to prepare the statements. Therefore, adjusting entries are made at the end of each period before the financial statements are prepared.

In addition to depreciation in our illustration, another item that must be adjusted is Prepaid services. Although the services were used each day, it was not necessary to record the using up of the asset until the end of the period. (An exploration of all the types of adjustments is beyond the scope of this text; however, the reader should be alert to the need for these entries.)

Closing the Books

In this chapter the accounting equation was originally used to account for the acquisition and use of the resources of an organization. Table 14–1, which explained how transactions affect the equation, contained only three types of accounts: assets, liabilities, and capital. These are generally referred to as the **permanent** or **real accounts.** They are labeled **permanent** because they are carried from one period to another. Thus the ending balance of Cash of one period will be the beginning balance of Cash for the next period.

As the illustrations in this chapter became more complex, the changes in capital resulting from operations of the business were accumulated in separate accounts called revenues and expenses. The purpose of these accounts was to identify the particular operating items causing capital to change. Thus these accounts became the source of the data that were presented on the activity (income) statement. These data were used to help decision makers evaluate the effectiveness of the use of the resources available to management.

Once such an evaluation has been made for the current period, however, the data lose their importance. The generation of revenue and the incurrence of expenses are relative to a certain period of time. It serves little purpose to know that a business that has been in operation for one hundred years has accumulated $500 million in revenue. Information on revenues and expenses is useful only for evaluating the operations of an organization on a period-by-period basis. As a result, revenue and expense accounts are generally referred to as **temporary** or **nominal accounts.**

If temporary (revenue and expense) accounts are to be used to generate information relative to certain periods, they must be closed out (reduced to a zero balance) at the end of each period; and the balances in those accounts must be transferred to capital. The ledger in Table 14–10 shows a balance in the P. Keith, Capital, account, of $5,000, the initial contribution by Ms. Keith. Analysis of the balance sheet in Table 14–13, however, indicates a capital balance of $5,630. The reason for the difference between these two figures is that the former, the one found in the ledger, does not include the income for the period. Since the effects of operations have already been recorded in the asset and liability accounts,[2] they must also be reflected in the capital account so that the balance sheet will balance.

In summary, the trial balance figure for capital does not include the effect of operating the business. Therefore, it must be updated. In addition, the revenue and expense accounts must be reduced to zero in order to begin accumulating data for the next period. The process of achieving these goals is referred to as **closing the books.** The closing entry for Kaki Tours at June 30, 19X1, is shown in Exhibit 14–3.

The purpose of the closing process is to zero out the balances of the temporary accounts and transfer the net income for the period to the capital account. The steps involved in this process are as follows:

1. Debit each revenue account for the credit balance currently in the account.
2. Credit each expense account for the debit balance currently in the account.
3. Debit or credit the capital account for the amount needed to balance the journal entry—make the debits equal the credits. This is the amount of the net income or loss.

After posting these entries to the accounts, the general ledger will look like the one shown in Exhibit 14–4. (Notice that the balance in each account that has more than one entry has been circled.)

Notice also that the revenue and expense accounts are the only accounts that have had their balances reduced to zero. The assets, the liabilities, and the capital accounts all have balances that will be carried into the next period as the

GENERAL JOURNAL

3

Date 19X1		Description	Ref.	Dr.	Cr.
June	30	Tour revenue	401	830 –	
		Office rent expense	501		75 –
		Salary expense	502		40 –
		Telephone-answering expense	503		50 –
		Office supplies expense	504		30 –
		Depreciation expense—office equipment	505		5 –
		P. Keith, Capital	301		630 –
		Record closing the revenue and expense accounts and transfer the net income to capital.			

EXHIBIT 14–3

[2]Revenues and expenses were defined earlier in this chapter in terms of their effect on assets and liabilities.

GENERAL LEDGER

Cash   101

Date 19X1	Item	P.R.	Debit	Date 19X1	Item	P.R.	Credit
June 1		1	5000 —	June 2		1	50 —
15		1	250 —	4		1	55 —
30		1	130 —	5		1	25 —
	(5,050)		5380 —	7		1	125 —
				25		1	75 —
							330 —
	Not Closed						

Prepaid services   102

Date 19X1	Item	P.R.	Debit	Date 19X1	Item	P.R.	Credit
June 2	(∅)	1	50 —	June 30		2	50 —
	Not Closed						

Accounts receivable   103

Date 19X1	Item	P.R.	Debit	Date 19X1	Item	P.R.	Credit
June 10		1	300 —	June 15		1	250 —
30	(450)	1	400 —				
			700 —				
	Not Closed						

Office supplies   104

Date 19X1	Item	P.R.	Debit	Date 19X1	Item	P.R.	Credit
June 4		1	55 —	June 30		2	30 —
7	(150)	1	125 —				
			180 —				
	Not Closed						

Office equipment   107

Date 19X1	Item	P.R.	Debit	Date	Item	P.R.	Credit
June 5		1	250 —				
	Not Closed						

EXHIBIT 14–4

Accumulated depreciation — office equipment   108

Date	Item	P.R.	Debit	Date 19X1	Item	P.R.	Credit
				June 30		2	5 —

Not Closed

Accounts payable   201

Date	Item	P.R.	Debit	Date 19X1	Item	P.R.	Credit
				June 5		1	225 —

Not Closed

Salary payable   202

Date	Item	P.R.	Debit	Date 19X1	Item	P.R.	Credit
				June 30		2	40 —

Not Closed

P. Keith, Capital   301

Date	Item	P.R.	Debit	Date 19X1	Item	P.R.	Credit
				June 1		1	5000 —
				30		3	630 —
							5630

Not Closed

Tour revenue   401

Date 19X1	Item	P.R.	Debit	Date 19X1	Item	P.R.	Credit
June 30		3	830 —	June 10		1	300 —
				20		1	130 —
				30	(830)	1	400 —
			830 —				830 —

Office rent expense   501

Date 19X1	Item	P.R.	Debit	Date 19X1	Item	P.R.	Credit
June 25		1	75 —	June 30		3	75 —

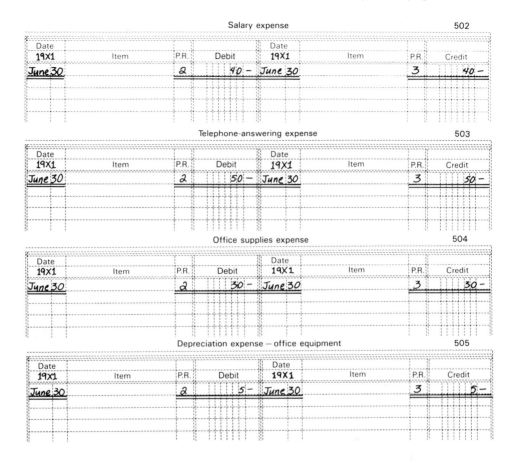

beginning balances in those accounts. The zero balance in Prepaid services is due to the simplicity of the example, not the closing process.

Withdrawals by the Owner

At this point it is important to discuss another type of transaction that can be recorded in the system. Withdrawals by the owner are not treated as an expense of the operations of a business. Therefore, had Ms. Keith taken money or other assets from the business, the entry would have required a reduction of assets (credit) and a debit to an account called P. Keith, Withdrawals. This latter account would have been closed at the end of the period into Ms. Keith's capital. That is, the withdrawals account would have been credited and the capital account debited. This sequence of entries was omitted from the basic example because it has no counterpart in a nonbusiness system.

The Accounting Cycle

The process described in this chapter is normally referred to as the **accounting cycle.** It can be summarized in the following six steps:

1. Record entries in the journal.
2. Post the entries to the ledger.
3. Prepare a trial balance.
4. Adjust the accounts as necessary.
5. Prepare the financial statements.
6. Close the temporary accounts.

This cycle is repeated every accounting period. In specific cases it may be expanded or contracted to fit the particular circumstances facing the organization.

SECTION V REVIEW EXERCISE

Using the information in Table 14–15, prepare the necessary closing entry in the general journal at December 31, 19X1, and fill in the blanks that follow. Compare your results with the solution provided.

After posting the closing entry, indicate the balance of each of the accounts listed below:

Cash $_____

Accounts payable $ _____

Amy Norris, Capital $_____

Service revenue $ _____

Rent expense $ _____

What was the net income for the period?_____

TABLE 14–15

ACCOUNT	BALANCE
Cash	$12,000
Accounts receivable	15,000
Prepaid rent	1,000
Office equipment	30,000
Accumulated depreciation—office equipment	14,000
Accounts payable	5,000
Notes payable to bank	10,000
Amy Norris, Capital	25,000
Service revenue	40,000
Depreciation expense—equipment	7,000
Rent expense	15,000
Salary expense	14,000

SOLUTION TO SECTION V REVIEW EXERCISE

GENERAL JOURNAL   Page 5

Date 19X1	Description	P.R.	Debit	Credit
Dec. 31	Service revenue		40000 —	
	Depreciation expense--equipment			7000 —
	Rent expense			15000 —
	Salary expense			14000 —
	Amy Norris, Capital			4000 —
	To record the closing of the revenue and expense accounts and transfer the net income to capital.			

Cash $12,000
Accounts payable $5,000
Amy Norris, Capital $29,000 ($25,000 + $4,000)
Service revenue $-0- (closed)
Rent expense $-0- (closed)

The income for the period was $4,000 (the amount closed into capital).

REVIEW QUESTIONS

Section I

Q14–1   Define the following terms:
   a.   Assets
   b.   Liabilities
   c.   Capital
   d.   Revenue
   e.   Expense

Q14–2   Write the accounting equation.

Q14–3   Must the accounting equation always balance? Why?

Section II

Q14–4   Identify the rules of debit and credit with respect to assets, liabilities, capital, revenues, and expenses.

Q14–5   A student of basic accounting made the following statement: "For each account debited, there must be another account credited for the same amount." Do you agree? Why or why not?

Q14–6   Why do credits increase the capital account?

Section III

Q14–7   What are the three basic financial statements illustrated in the text?

Q14–8   Describe the interrelationship between the three statements in Q14–7.

Q14–9   Why is it important to put the appropriate date or time period on a financial statement?

Section IV

Q14–10 What is a journal and how is it used in the accounting process?

Q14–11 What is a ledger and how is it used in the accounting process?

Q14–12 How are journals and ledgers interrelated in an accounting system?

Section V

Q14–13 What is the purpose of adjusting entries?

Q14–14 Which accounts are closed at the end of an accounting period? Why are these accounts closed?

Q14–15 If the columns of a trial balance total to the same amount, the information included in the accounts must be correct. Do you agree or disagree? Why?

EXERCISES

Section I

E14–1   (Preparing transactions)
        For each of the following categories, compose a transaction that will cause that category to increase and one that will cause it to decrease:
        a.   Assets
        b.   Liabilities
        c.   Capital
        d.   Revenues
        e.   Expenses

E14–2   (Associating changes with specific accounts)
        For each of the following transactions of the Kit-Kat Company, identify the accounts that would be increased and those that would be decreased:
        a.   The owner invested $25,000 in the business.
        b.   Rent for the month was paid to Jiffy Realty Company, $500.
        c.   A secretary was hired at a monthly salary of $550.
        d.   Customers were billed for services rendered, $700.
        e.   The utilities bill for the month was paid, $234.

E14–3   (Calculating the change in capital from balance sheet data)

The beginning and ending balances in certain account categories of the Release Company are listed below:

ACCOUNT CATEGORIES	BEGINNING BALANCES	ENDING BALANCES
Assets	$306,000	$307,000
Liabilities	$107,000	$110,000

Based upon this information, what was the change in capital for the period?

Section II

E14–4   (Using debits and credits)

Identify the account(s) that would be debited and/or credited as a result of the following transactions:
a.   The owner invested $10,000 in the business.
b.   Supplies were purchased for cash, $800.
c.   Service revenue of $1,000 was received in cash.
d.   Customers were billed for services rendered, $500.
e.   Employees were paid their salaries totaling $800.
f.   Collections of accounts receivable totaled $300.
g.   Rent for the month was paid, $350.
h.   Salaries owed employees at the end of the month totaled $100.
i.   Supplies costing $300 were used.

E14–5   (Associating debits and credits with account categories)

Each of the account categories listed in Exercise 14–1 is increased with either a debit or credit. Indicate which is used to record an increase in each type of account and identify the usual balance in that account category.

E14–6   (Using debits and credits)

William T. Fudd III acts as a rental agent for several large apartment houses. Mr. Fudd's income is determined by a commission on the number of apartments he rents. During the month of January, Mr. Fudd incurred the following transactions. Identify the debits and credits to record each event.

19X1
January   2   Mr. Fudd placed $20,000 cash into a bank account to be used in the operation of his business, Apartment Locators.
2   Mr. Fudd hired a secretary and agreed to pay her $700 per month.
4   Mr. Fudd borrowed $10,000 from the Security Bank, signing a note for that amount.
5   Mr. Fudd purchased, for cash, office equipment that cost $3,000.

10   Mr. Fudd paid the rent for the month, $300.

14   Mr. Fudd received a check from one apartment complex owner for $3,000. This amount was his commission for renting apartments during the first two weeks of January.

17   Mr. Fudd paid his secretary half of the agreed-upon salary.

30   Mr. Fudd earned an additional $3,000 of commissions. He has not received these amounts; therefore, he sent bills to the owners.

31   Mr. Fudd collected $500 from one of the owners billed on January 30.

31   Mr. Fudd made a payment on his loan. The total payment was $1,200, of which $200 was interest. The remainder was a reduction of the amount of the loan.

Section III

E14–7   (Computation of balance sheet amounts)

Based upon the following information, compute total assets, total liabilities, and total capital; in addition, determine whether or not all of the accounts are listed. (*Note:* This is the first month of operations of the business.)

Cash	$22,000
Accounts receivable	12,000
Accounts payable	15,000
Equipment	50,000
Rent expense	11,000
Service revenue	74,000
Notes payable	17,000
Accumulated depreciation	25,000
Depreciation expense	12,500
Office supplies	3,000
Office supplies expense	8,000
Salaries payable	4,000

E14–8   (Relating accounts and financial statements)

Identify the financial statement on which each of the following items would appear:
a.   Bonds payable
b.   Rent revenue
c.   Owner's capital, beginning balance
d.   Cash
e.   Equipment
f.   Supplies expense
g.   Depreciation expense
h.   Service revenue
i.   Accounts receivable
j.   Accounts payable
k.   Owner's capital, ending balance

l. Rent expense
m. Accumulated depreciation
n. Net income
o. Salaries payable
p. Land
q. Supplies on hand

E14–9 (Fill-in-the-blanks—definitions)

Match the items in the right column below with those in the left column.

_____ 1. Statement of changes in owner's capital
_____ 2. Income statement
_____ 3. Net income
_____ 4. Additional investment by the owner
_____ 5. Ending balance in owner's capital
_____ 6. Balance sheet

a. A financial statement that presents the revenues and expenses of a business
b. A financial statement that presents a reconciliation of the beginning and ending owner's capital
c. An increase in owner's capital
d. A financial statement that presents the assets, liabilities, and owner's capital of a business
e. Can be found on a balance sheet and a statement of changes in owner's capital
f. An excess of revenues over expenses

Section IV

E14–10 (Recording transactions in a general journal)

Record the following transactions in general journal form for the Control Company, a private investigation service:

19X1
January

2 Susan Bigger invested $10,000 in the business.
2 Ms. Bigger paid the rent on office space for January, $500.
4 Ms. Bigger purchased office supplies on credit for $200.
5 Ms. Bigger billed customers for $5,000 for services performed.
10 Ms. Bigger acquired an automobile for use in the business. The cost was $4,500. She paid $1,000 as a down payment and signed a note for the remainder.
15 Customers paid Ms. Bigger $3,500 on their accounts.
20 Ms. Bigger billed customers for $2,000.
25 Ms. Bigger acquired the services of Answer Company, a telephone-answering service. She paid $10 for their services for the remainder of the month.
31 Depreciation of $100 was recorded on the automobile.
31 Office supplies used during the month totaled $100.

31   The utilities bills arrived in the mail; they totaled $800. Ms. Bigger will pay them in February.

31   The cost of gasoline and oil for the automobile for the month was $134. Ms. Bigger paid the service station that amount.

E14–11   (Posting to a general ledger)

Post the transactions in Exercise 14–10 to general ledger accounts.

E14–12   (Recording transactions in a general journal)

Using the data in Exercise 14–6, record the transactions in general journal form.

Section V

E14–13   (Preparing a trial balance)

Using the following information, prepare a trial balance for the Forfeit Company at June 30, 19X1.

Accumulated depreciation—equipment	$4,000
Taxes payable	200
Equipment	24,000
Cash	20,000
Utilities expense	1,000
Depreciation expense—equipment	600
Notes payable	24,000
Salaries expense	20,000
R. Key, Capital	15,800
Office supplies	2,000
Service revenue	32,000
Rent expense	8,600
Accounts payable	1,600
Office supplies expense	1,400

E14–14   (Preparing closing entries and determining the ending balance in capital)

Prepare the appropriate closing entry based on the information in Exercise 14–13 and determine the ending balance in R. Key, Capital.

E14–15   (Preparing a trial balance)

Prepare a trial balance based upon the information in Exercises 14–10 and 14–11.

PROBLEMS

Section I

P14–1   (Analyzing transactions on a work sheet)

The following transactions relate to the Escape Travel Agency for March 19X1:

1   Mary Ann Ferrit invested $36,000 in a travel agency.

2   Mary Ann paid $700 rent on office space for the month.

3   Mary Ann purchased office equipment for $5,200, paying $200 as a down payment and signing a thirty-day note for the remainder.

4   Printers, Inc., sold $1,000 of office supplies to Mary Ann. She will pay this amount in thirty days.

6   Mary Ann hired Lauralee as a secretary and agreed to pay her $450 per month.

10 The *Times* sent the agency a bill for $400 for advertising for the month. This amount was paid immediately.

15 Sales of tickets and tours for the first half of the month totaled $30,000. This amount was received in cash.

18 Mary Ann wrote checks totaling $22,000 to several airlines and national tour services for tickets.

20 Mary Ann sent out bills to clients totaling $15,000.

28 Clients paid $12,000 on their open accounts.

30 The utilities bills were received and paid. They totaled $800.

30 The agency received bills from various airlines and national tour services for $14,000. These will be paid in April.

30 The rent for April was paid.

31 Office supplies on hand at the end of the month totaled $500.

31 Lauralee was paid her monthly salary.

31 Mary Ann wrote a check for $280 for the March 31 payment on the office equipment. Included in this amount was $50 for interest.

REQUIRED: Analyze the above transactions on a work sheet similar to that illustrated in the text. You will need columns for Cash, Accounts receivable, Prepaid rent, Prepaid advertising, Office supplies, Office equipment, Accounts payable, Notes payable, and Mary Ann Ferrit, Capital.

P14–2   (Analyzing transactions on a work sheet)

The following transactions relate to Rosie's Auto Repair Shop. Record each on a work sheet similar to the one illustrated in the text.

19X1
September 1   Rose Gloro invested $10,000 in the business.

1   Ms. Gloro rented space adjacent to a large automobile parts store. The lease specified a monthly rental of $800. This amount was paid for September.

2   Ms. Gloro contracted with the Auto Parts Place to supply her with automobile parts at discount prices on credit. She will pay for them at the end of each month.

3   Ms. Gloro purchased a complete tool kit from the Auto Parts Place. The tools cost a total of $5,000. The entire amount was paid immediately. For simplicity, assume all of the tools are treated as a single asset for accounting purposes.

3   Ms. Gloro paid $400 in deposits for various utilities. Each of the de-

posits will be returned after five years or the closing of her business, whichever occurs first. These deposits included electricity, telephone, and water.

3   Ms. Gloro paid Pink-Pages $50 for an ad in the September issue of its monthly telephone directory.

4   Ms. Gloro charged customers $350 to repair their cars. The entire amount was collected in cash. While doing the repair work, she purchased parts costing $45.

9   Ms. Gloro purchased office supplies costing $130, cash.

12   Repairs for the week totaled $2,560; the entire amount was collected in cash. The cost of parts was $435.

15   Ms. Gloro paid her employees $500.

16   Ms. Gloro purchased office furniture for $200. She paid $50 down and will pay the remainder during the next thirty days.

18   Ms. Gloro "ran a special" on tune-ups. She advertised the special price in the *Daily News*. The cost of the ad, $100, was paid in cash.

19   Repairs for the week totaled $3,500. The cost of the parts was $1,000. A total of $2,500 was collected in cash; the remainder will be collected in the future.

30   Utility bills totaling $500 were received. Rose will pay these next month.

30   Ms. Gloro paid her employees $2,000.

30   Ms. Gloro recorded repairs for the last eleven days of the month. These totaled $4,500. The parts cost $2,000. She collected $4,000 from her customers; the remainder will be collected in the future.

30   Rose collected $500 from her customers on their accounts.

30   Rose paid the parts store the amount owed.

30   Office supplies costing $45 were used during the month.

REQUIRED: Analyze the above transactions on a work sheet similar to that illustrated in the text. You will need columns for Cash, Accounts receivable, Prepaid rent, Prepaid advertising, Office supplies, Office furniture, Tools, Utility deposits, Accounts payable, and Rose Gloro, Capital.

P14–3   (Analyzing transactions on a work sheet using inventory)
The following transactions related to the Trade-Mart Discount Store for November 19X1:

1   Sherman Shasha contributed $100,000 to a start a new business, the Trade-Mart Discount Store.

1   Sherman purchased land for $10,000 and a small building for $50,000. He paid $5,000 down and signed a mortgage for the remainder.

2   Sherman purchased $40,000 of goods to be sold in the store. He paid $10,000 down and put the rest on a charge account that is due at the end of the month. The merchandise was purchased from Regional Sales, Inc. (*Hint:* Use an asset account—Inventory.)

3   Equipment costing $2,000 was acquired; $400 was paid in cash and the remainder is due in sixty days.

4   Office supplies costing $500 were acquired for cash.

4   The business made utility deposits totaling $1,000. These amounts will be used to pay the final utility bill and the remainder will be returned.

5   Sherman contacted the local newspaper and purchased an advertisement. The cost of the ad was $450. The newspaper will send a bill for that amount.

7   Sales for the first week of operations totaled $25,000. Of this amount, $5,000 was cash and $20,000 was credit card sales. The VICCA credit card company charges the retailer a 2 percent fee for the use of the card. VICCA will pay the business twice a month for the sales using their card. The fee charged to the retailer is paid at the end of each month. (*Hint:* The credit card fee should be recorded as a separate expense.)

8   The bill for the newspaper ad arrived. Sherman decided to pay it later in the month.

15   Employees were paid their salaries, $5,000.

15   Sherman collected the amount due from VICCA.

18   Sales totaling $45,000 were recorded: $7,000 were cash sales; the remainder were VICCA card sales.

20   The newspaper bill was paid.

23   Sales totaling $25,000 were recorded: $4,000 were cash sales; the remainder were VICCA card sales.

24   Additional inventory was acquired from Regional Sales Company. The total amount was $50,000. Sherman paid $15,000 down, with the remainder due at the end of the month.

30   Sales totaling $30,000 were recorded; all were VICCA card sales.

30   Sherman paid Regional Sales the amount owed to that company.

30   Employee salaries of $7,000 were paid.

30   The utilities bills were received and paid. The total amount was $2,500.

30   A bill was received from the Ace Delivery Service for $800. Sherman had signed a contract with Ace to deliver certain merchandise sold by the store. The bill will be paid next month.

30   Sherman collected the amount due from VICCA.

30   The first payment on the building mortgage was made. The total amount was $1,000, of which $600 was interest.

30   At the end of the month there was $4,000 of inventory in the store.

30   Sherman paid VICCA the amount owed.

30   Office supplies used during the month totaled $400.

REQUIRED: Analyze the above transactions on a work sheet similar to that illustrated in the text. You will need columns for Cash, Accounts receivable, Inventory, Office supplies, Prepaid advertising, Land, Building, Equipment, Utility deposits, Accounts payable, Mortgage payable, and Sherman Shasha, Capital.

Section II

P14–4   (Debit and credit analysis of transactions)

Using the information given in Problem 14–1, indicate which account(s) would be debited and which account(s) would be credited for each transaction.

P14–5   (Debit and credit analysis of transactions)

Using the information given in Problem 14–2, indicate which account(s) would be debited and which account(s) would be credited for each transaction.

P14–6   (Debit and credit analysis of transactions)

Using the information given in Problem 14–3, indicate which account(s) would be debited and which account(s) would be credited for each transaction. (*Note:* The cost of inventory sold should be debited to "Cost of goods sold" when it is sold.)

Section III

P14–7   (Preparation of financial statements)

The following information was taken from the financial records of the Clear Company. The balances listed are as of the end of the accounting year, December 31, 19X1, the first year of operations.

	Balance	
	DEBIT	CREDIT
Cash	$10,000	
Accounts receivable	4,000	
Office supplies	2,000	
Delivery equipment	10,000	
Accumulated depreciation—delivery equipment		$ 200
Notes payable to bank		9,800
Interest payable		500
Accounts payable		2,000
W. T. Foxx, Capital		9,000
Delivery revenue		8,000
Expenses of operating delivery trucks	2,000	
Salary expense	1,000	
Interest expense	300	
Depreciation expense—delivery equipment	200	
	$29,500	$29,500

REQUIRED: Prepare the following financial statements:
1. Income statement
2. Statement of changes in owner's capital
3. Balance sheet

P14–8   (Matching accounts and financial statements)
Following are several financial statement classifications and accounts:

Revenue	R
Expense	E
Asset	A
Liability	L
Owner's capital (balance sheet)	C
Statement of changes in owner's capital	SC

Caution: Some items may appear in more than one statement classification.

Example: __A__ Cash
_____ 1. Notes payable
_____ 2. Additional investment by owner
_____ 3. Automobile
_____ 4. Depreciation expense—automobile
_____ 5. Prepaid rent
_____ 6. Utilities expense
_____ 7. Consulting revenue
_____ 8. Accounts payable
_____ 9. Ending balance in owner's capital
_____ 10. Office supplies
_____ 11. Accumulated depreciation—automobile
_____ 12. Salaries payable
_____ 13. Office supplies expense
_____ 14. Service revenue
_____ 15. Interest expense
_____ 16. Accounts receivable
_____ 17. Loans made to other companies
_____ 18. Deposit made with utility company. This amount will be repaid to the company for which we are keeping the records in five years.
_____ 19. Cash held in a separate bank account from that mentioned above. This money will be used to buy a building in a few years.

REQUIRED: Identify the proper financial statement classification for each account by placing the appropriate key letter in the space provided.

P14–9   (Preparation of financial statements)
Following are the balances in the accounts of the V. Sera Company as of the year ended December 31, 19X2, unless otherwise noted:

Notes payable	$18,000
Cash	24,000
Consulting revenue	74,000
V. Sera, Capital (4/30/X2)	20,000
Office supplies expense	22,000
Accounts receivable	16,000
Rent expense	30,000
Office supplies	6,000
Service revenue	20,000
Accounts payable	2,000
Salary expense	2,000
Gasoline and oil expense	6,000
Prepaid rent (for 19X3)	6,000
Interest expense	2,000
Automobile	24,000
Depreciation expense—automobile	4,000
Accumulated depreciation—automobile	8,000

Note: The owner made an additional investment of $10,000 in the business on April 15, 19X2. This amount is included in the capital balance above.

REQUIRED: Prepare the following financial statements:
1. Income statement
2. Statement of changes in owner's capital
3. Balance sheet

P14–10   (Preparation of financial statements)

Following are the balances in the accounts of the Compost Company as of the year ended December 31, 19X2, unless otherwise noted:

Accounts payable	$1,000
Service revenue	15,000
Cash	22,000
Salary expense	5,000
Prepaid rent (for 19X3)	1,000
F. Willow, Capital (1/1/X2)	29,000
Utilities expense	4,000
Office equipment	20,000
Commission revenue	10,000
Rent expense	8,000
Depreciation expense—office equipment	1,000
Accumulated depreciation—office equipment	3,000

Note: The owner made an additional investment of $3,000 in the business on May 4, 19X2. This amount is not included in the capital balance above.

REQUIRED: Prepare the following financial statements:
1. Income statement
2. Statement of changes in owner's capital
3. Balance sheet

Section IV

P14–11 (Recording and posting transactions)

Use the information given in Problem 14–1. In addition, assume that the depreciation on the office equipment is $100.

REQUIRED: 1.   Record the transactions in general journal form.
2.   Post the transactions to the appropriate general ledger accounts.

P14–12 (Recording and posting transactions)

Use the information given in Problem 14–2. In addition, assume that the depreciation on the tools is $150 and the depreciation on the office equipment is $5.

REQUIRED: 1.   Record the transactions in general journal form.
2.   Post the transactions to the appropriate general ledger accounts.

P14–13 (Recording and posting transactions)

Use the information given in Problem 14–3. In addition, assume that the depreciation on the building is $500 and the depreciation on the equipment is $5.

REQUIRED: 1.   Record the transactions in general journal form.
2.   Post the transactions to the appropriate general ledger accounts.

Section V

P14–14   (Preparing a trial balance and a closing entry)

REQUIRED: Based on the answers you obtained in Problem 14–11:
1.   Prepare a trial balance.
2.   Prepare a closing entry.
3.   Post the closing entry to the general ledger accounts.

P14–15   (Preparing a closing entry)

REQUIRED: Based on the answers you obtained in Problem 14–12:
1.   Prepare a trial balance.
2.   Prepare the closing entry.

P14–16   Preparing a trial balance and a closing entry)

REQUIRED: Based on the answers you obtained in Problem 14–13:
1.   Prepare a trial balance.
2.   Prepare the closing entry.
3.   Post the closing entry to the general ledger accounts.

INDEX